McGRAW-HILL MATHEMATICS

Douglas H. Clements

Kenneth W. Jones

Lois Gordon Moseley

Linda Schulman

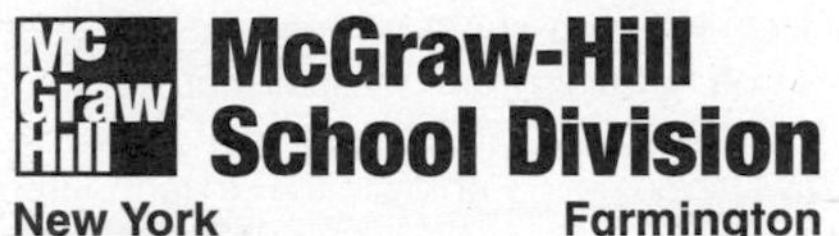
McGraw-Hill School Division

New York Farmington

PROGRAM AUTHORS

Dr. Douglas H. Clements

Kenneth W. Jones

Lois Gordon Moseley

Dr. Linda Schulman

CONTRIBUTING AUTHORS

Dr. Liana Forest

Christine A. Fernsler

Dr. Kathleen Kelly-Benjamin

Maria R. Marolda

Dr. Richard H. Moyer

Dr. Walter G. Secada

CONSULTANTS

Multicultural and Educational Consultants

Rim An

Sue Cantrell

Mordessa Corbin

Dr. Carlos Diaz

Carl Downing

Linda Ferreira

Judythe M. Hazel

Roger Larson

Josie Robles

Veronica Rogers

Telkia Rutherford

Sharon Searcy

Elizabeth Sinor

Michael Wallpe

Claudia Zaslavsky

COVER PHOTOGRAPHY Jade Albert for MMSD.

PHOTOGRAPHY All photographs are by the McGraw-Hill School Division (MMSD), David Mager for MMSD, Ken Lax for MMSD and Scott Harvey for MMSD except as noted below.
Table of Contents • Bruce Plotkin/Liaison International: iii b. • Tony Arruzo/The Image Works: iv m. • Amanda Merullo/Stock Boston, Inc.: v m. • Charles Thatcher/Tony Stone Images: vi m. • Doug David: vi b. • Chris Luneski/Image Cascade: vii t. • HMS Images/The Image Bank: vii m. • Peter Beck/The Stock Market: viii b. • Terry Vine/Tony Stone Images: ix t. • Darryl Torckler/Tony Stone Images: ix m. • Henley & Savage/The Stock Market: ix b. • Richard Gross/The Stock Market: x m. • **Chapter 1** • Tom McCarthy/The Stock Market: 1 t. • Henley & Savage/The Stock Market: 1 b. • Brent Petersen/The Stock Market: 3 • Brent Petersen/The Stock Market: 17 • Doug David: 32 b. • Eric Wheater: 40 b.r. • **Chapter 2** • Tom McCarthy/The Stock Market: 43 • Lawrence Migdale/Stock Boston, Inc.: 44 • Brooklyn Museum of Art: 50 b.l. • Tony Arruza/The Image Works: 55 t. • Nancy Simmerman/Tony Stone Images: 66 • Bruce Plotkin/Liaison International: 73 t. • **Chapter 3** • John Stuart/The Image Bank: 77 • Tom Tracey/The Stock Market: 89 t.r. • Jeff Greenberg/Photo Researchers: 97 • **Chapter 4** • Porter Gifford/Gamma Liaison: 123 • George Kleiman/Photo Researchers: 138 t.r. • **Chapter 5** • Doug David for MMSD: 153 t.r.i. • Doug David for MMSD: 154 • Amanda Merullo/Stock Boston: 158 • John M. Roberts/The Stock Market: 159 • Stephanie Hollyman/Liaison International: 169 • Russkinne/Comstock: 178 • **Chapter 6** • Steve Niedorf/The Image Bank: 183 • Charles Thatcher/Tony Stone Images: 193 t. • Charlie Westerman/Liaison International: 193 b. • D. Young-Wolff/PhotoEdit: 200 • Maxwell Mackenzie/Uniphoto: 206 • **Chapter 7** • HMS Images/The Image Bank: 231 • Monica Stevenson for MMSD: 235 b.i. • Chris Luneski/Image Cascade: 243 t.r. • Don Smetzer/Tony Stone Images: 244 • Superstock, Inc.: 250 b.r. • **Chapter 8** • Vedros & Associates/Liaison International: 269 t.r. • Doug David for MMSD: 270 • Mark Segal/Tony Stone Images: 272 t.r. • Tom Tracy/The Stock Market: 274 • Doug David for MMSD: 280 b.i. • Doug David for MMSD: 294 b.r. • **Chapter 9** • Uniphoto: 297 • Index Stock: 301 t. • Frank Moscati/The Stock Market: 302 b.r. • Richard Hutchings/PhotoEdit: 302 t.l. • Steve Dunwell/The Image Bank: 302 t.r. • David Young-Wolff/Tony Stone Images: 302 b.l. • Comstock: 302 m.l. • Bob Daemmrich/Uniphoto: 302 m.r. • Tom McCarthy/PhotoEdit: 308 t.l. • Daemmrich/The Image Works: 308 t.r. • Myrleen Ferguson MR/PhotoEdit: 308 m.l. • Jim Pickerell/The Image Works: 308 m.r. • Tony Freeman/PhotoEdit: 308 b.l. • David Young Wolff/Tony Stone Images: 308 b.r. • Doug David: 310 b. • Vivian Holbrooke/The Stock Market: 321 b.r. • Brad Martin/The Image Bank: 322 t.r. • **Chapter 10** • Stephen Dalton/Photo Researchers: 333 • Peter Beck/The Stock Market: 334 t. • Lawrence Migdale: 334 b. • David Forbert/Superstock, Inc.: 341 • Kelvin Altken/Peter Arnold, Inc.: 345 • Darryl Torckler/Tony Stone Images: 357 t. • Kevin & Cat Sweeney/Tony Stone Images: 357 b. • Terry Vine/Tony Stone Images: 364 • Michael Lustbader/Photo Researchers: 372 m.r. • **Chapter 11** • Henley & Savage/The Stock Market: 375 • Michael L. Peck & Dolores R. Fernandez: 391 t. • Renee Lynn/Photo Researchers: 394 b.m.i. • **Chapter 12** • Robert E. Daemmrich/Tony Stone Images: 409 • Superstock, Inc.: 415 • Richard Gross/The Stock Market: 425 • Joe Sohm/Chromosohm/Photo Researchers: 426 • David Young-Wolff/PhotoEdit: 437

ILLUSTRATION Winky Adam; 213, 216, 248, 250 • Jo Lynn Alcorn: 383, 386 • Bill Basso; 85, 86, 119, 120 • Shirley Beckes; 23, 24 • Menny Borovski; 27, 28, 36, 37, 89, 115, 117, 123, 124, 132, 234, 235, 236, 238, 239, 245, 246, 250, 252, 256, 257, 296, 298, 301, 302, 317, 318, 319, 320, 324, 325 • Ken Bowser; 83, 84, 302, 312, 337 • Lizi Boyd: 219, 277, 294, 388, 389, 402, 403 • Hal Brooks; 91, 92 • Roger Chandler: 345, 346, 353, 368 • Genevieve Claire: 356, 363, 364, 397, 398 • Margaret Cusack; 184, 188, 232 • Nancy Davis: 270, 276 • Betsy Day: 206, 214, 223 • Daniel Del Valle; 106, 109, 133, 134, 243, 314, 327 • Denise & Fernando: 180 • Eldon Doty: 178, 181 • Gloria Elliott: 142, 145, 146, 159, 160, 169 • Arthur Friedman; 326 • Doreen Gay-Kassel; 7, 9 , 156, 165, 335, 336, 338, 341, 357, 376, 380, 382 • Michael Grejniec; 112, 113, 114, 137, 148, 157, 174, 175, 176, 177, 189, 190 • Shari Halpern: 149, 151, 162, 163, 194, 203, 204, 205, 221 • Tom Leonard: 358 • Franklin Hammond; 88 • Oki Han: 164 • Eileen Hine: 165 • Rita Lascaro; 144, 199, 228, 291, 292, 390, 396, 303, 304 • Jim Maltese; 47, 48, 53, 72 • Claude Martinot; 5, 6, 19, 20, 410, 422, 430, 433, 437, 439, 444• Hatley Mason; 121, 135, 136, 138, 234, 241 • Bonnie Matthews; 242 • Daphne McCormack; 131 • Hima Pamoedjo; 33, 39, 54, 73, 79, 80, 130 • Brenda Pepper; 87, 93, 94, 101, 102, 103, 127, 128, 129, 139 • Lisa Pomerantz; 15, 35, 38, 350, 351, 354, 406 • Mary Power; 62, 64, 315, 316, 324, 325, 359, 365, 370, 371 • Ellen Rixford; 31, 32 • Audrey Schorr; 45, 46, 95 • Fred Schrier; 259 • Jackie Snider: 171, 172, 265, 267, 289 • Terri Starrett; 16 • Matt Straub; 21, 22, 39, 97, 98, 273, 274, 275, 281, 287, 288, 412, 414, 416, 418, 436, 445 • Peggy Tagel; 2, 3, 42, 43, 182, 183, 230, 231, 262, 263, 296, 297, 305, 306, 332, 333, 374, 375, 408, 409 • Mike Takagi; 13 • Don Tate; 44, 55, 67, 68, 70, 71, 107, 108, 239, 240, 241, 434, 448 • Terry Taylor: 195, 196, 199, 200, 207, 209, 221, 222, 225, 228, 417, 423, 435 • George Ulrich; 299, 300, 311, 330 • Sally Jo Vitsky; 4, 81, 122, 285, 286, 290, 419, 420, 424 • Matt Wawiorka; 11, 25, 41 • Nina Wallace: 404, 405.

McGraw-Hill School Division

A Division of The McGraw-Hill Companies

McGraw-Hill School Division
1221 Avenue of the Americas
New York, New York 10020

Printed in the United States of America
ISBN 0-02-109430-6 / 1
2 3 4 5 6 7 8 9 043/073 02 01 00 99 98 97

Contents

1 Rhino Country

2 Getting Around

3 Food for 10

4 Folktales and Rhymes

5 Number Fun

6 One Big Family

7 High-Flying Kites

8 Our Store

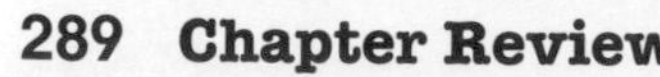

9 Fun and Games

10 Under the Water

11 Dinosaurs and Me

12 Music

Welcome to your new math book!

This year you will learn about many ways to use math in your world.

How many children in all?

How much does it cost?

How long is a foot?

At Home

Dear Family,

We are beginning the first chapter in our mathematics book. During the next few weeks we are going to learn about numbers and patterns and solving problems.

My class will also be talking about rhinos and other wild animals. Please help me complete this interview.

Your child,

____
Signature

Interview

Did you ever see a rhino? ____________________

Where did you see it? (Check as many as you want.)

❑ Zoo ❑ Safari park ❑ Television or movie

❑ Other ________________________

What do you remember most about the rhino?

❑ How big it was ❑ Its horns

❑ Other ____________________

____

Rhino Country

Numbers to 10

Listen to the story *Rhino Country.*

Tell what you know about rhinos.

Name

What Do You Know?

Match.

Talk

How many [rhino] ?

How many [bird] ?

Portfolio

Name

Working Together

You need .

Make a group.

Put some here.

Draw your  group.

Draw a group with more.

Try These!

Count. Draw a group with more.

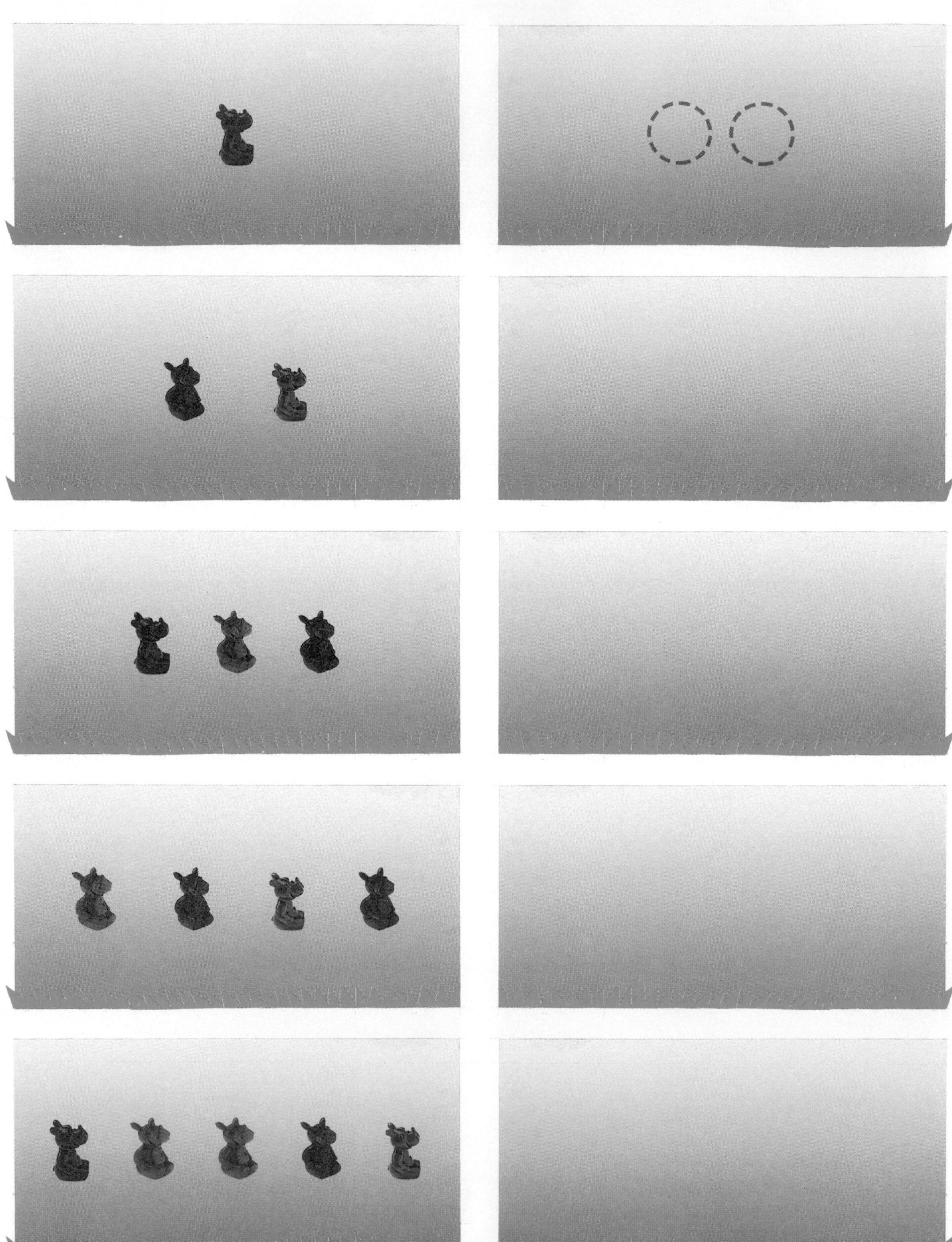

At Home You may want to ask your child to tell about drawing groups with *more* objects.

Name

One, Two, Three

Show how many.	Draw.	Write.
horns		2
tails		
toes		
ears		

Try These!

Count. Draw. Write.

3

Talk about patterns you see.

At Home

Ask your child to count things found at home.

Name

Four and Five

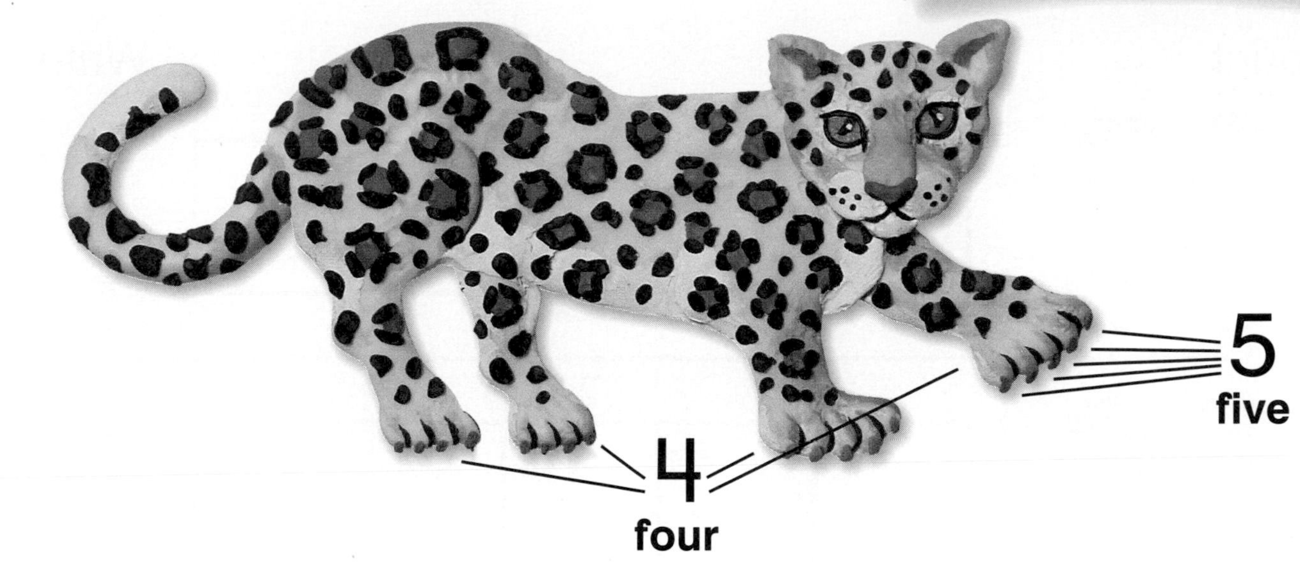

Show.

Draw.

Write.

5

Try These!

Count. Draw. Write.

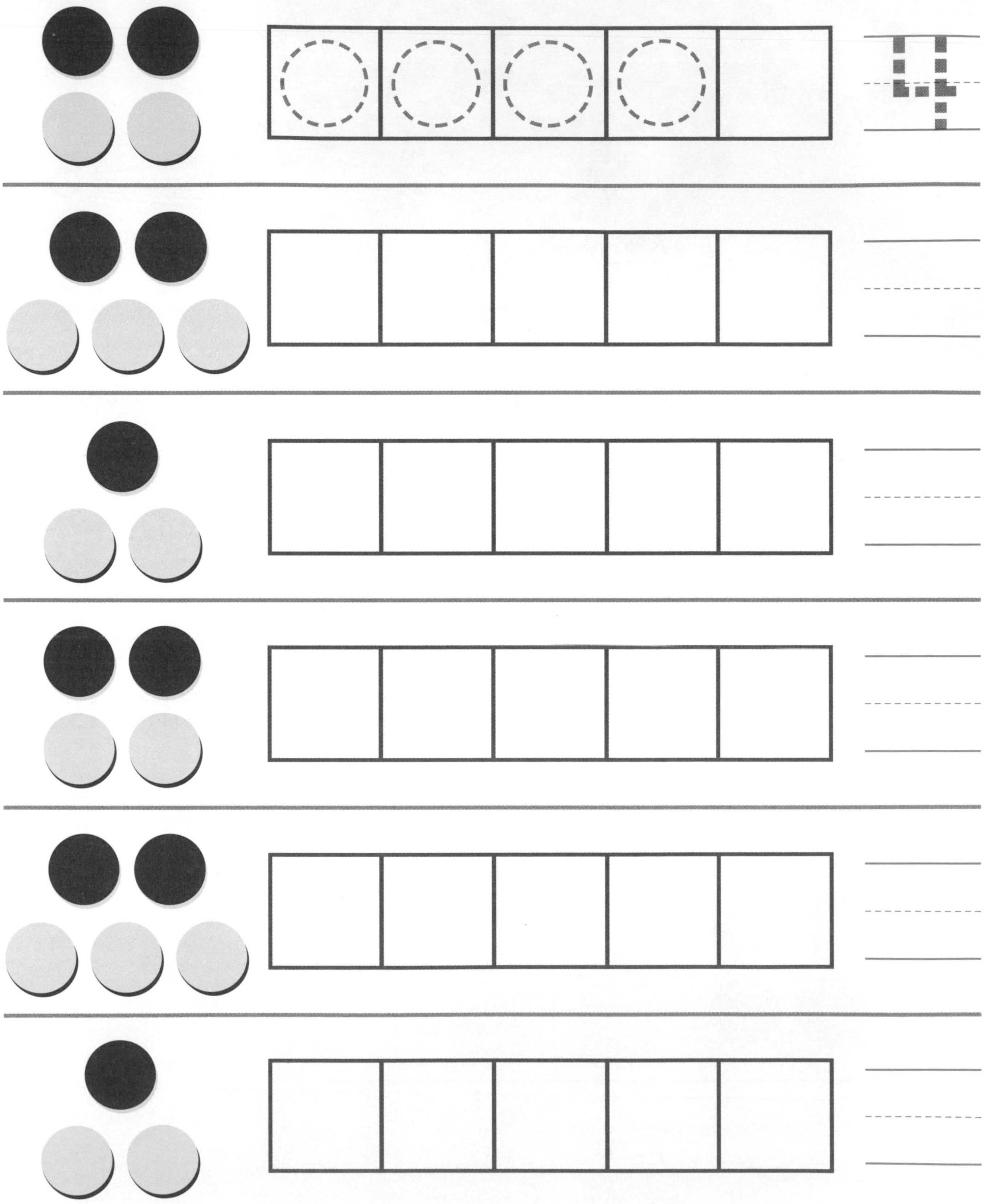

4

Draw a picture to show your favorite number.

At Home

Encourage your child to count objects and tell you how many.

Name

Where's the Rhino?

Color.

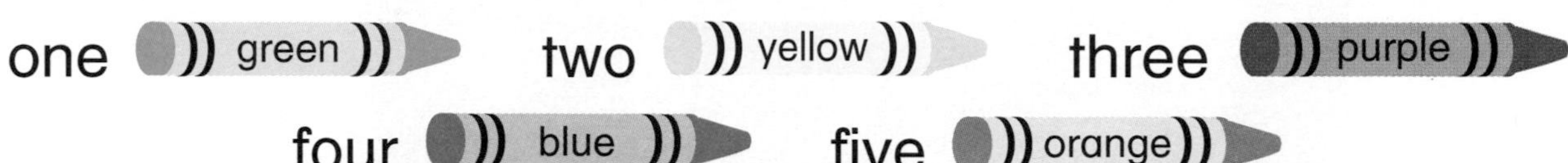

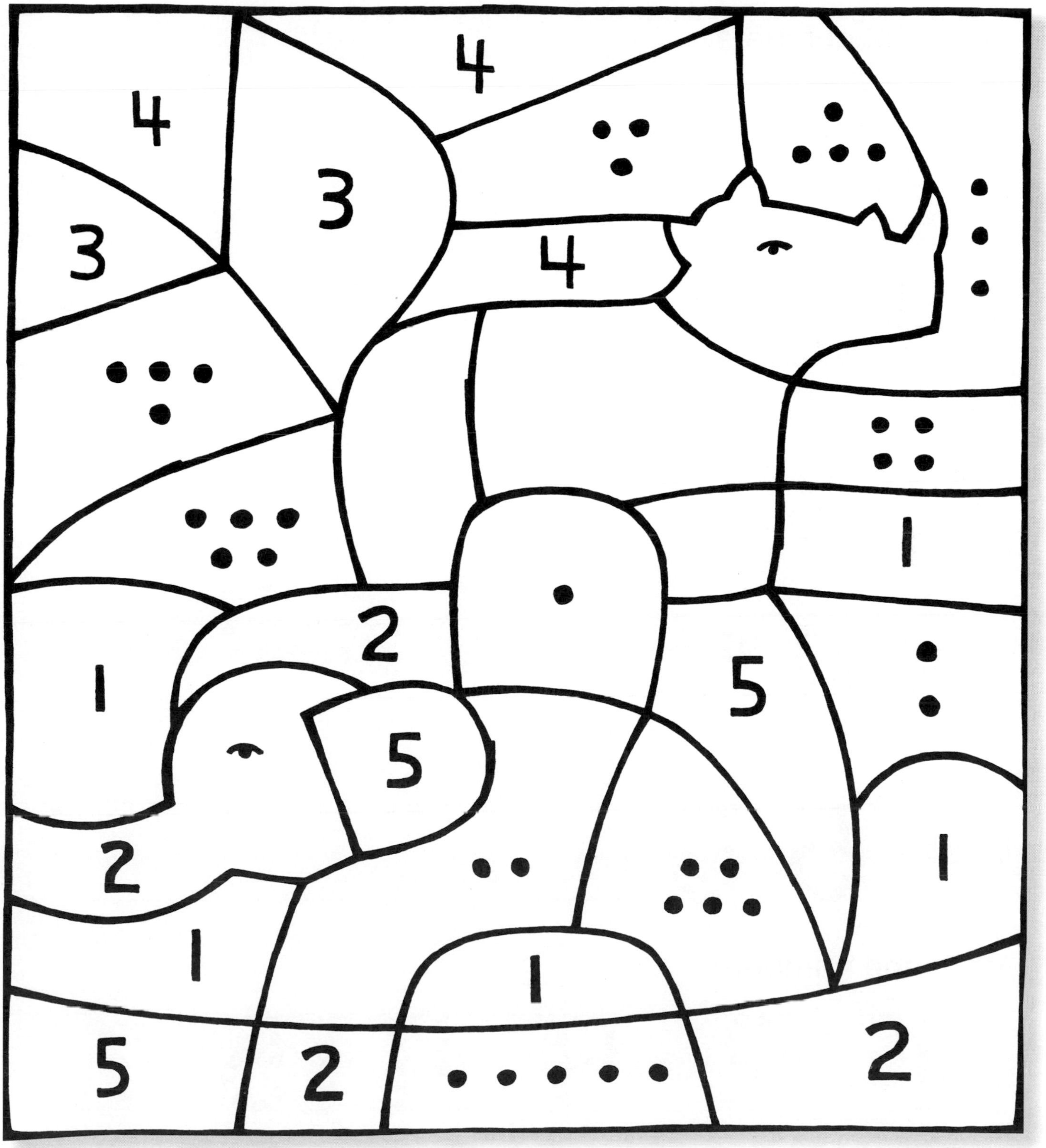

4
4
3
3
4
2
1
5
1
5
2
1
1
1
5
2
2

Write the numbers.

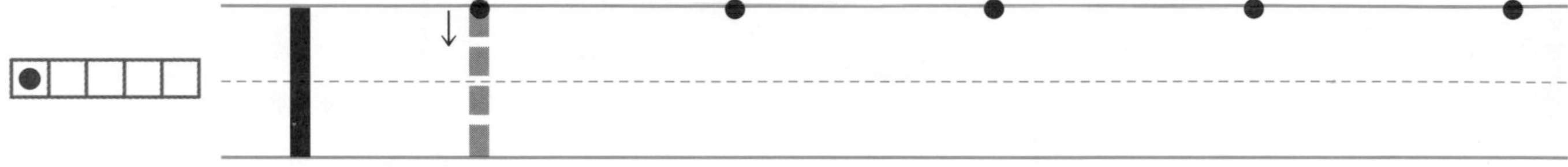

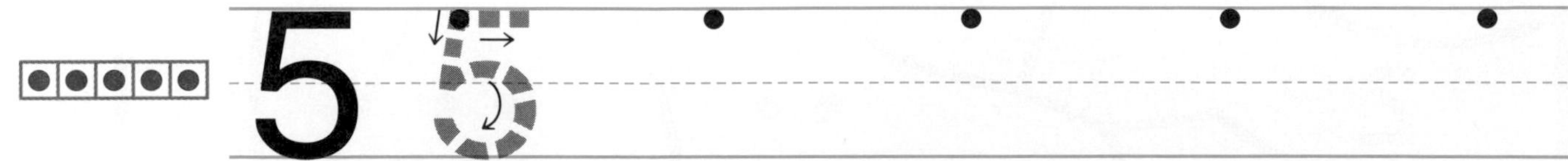

Write the numbers.

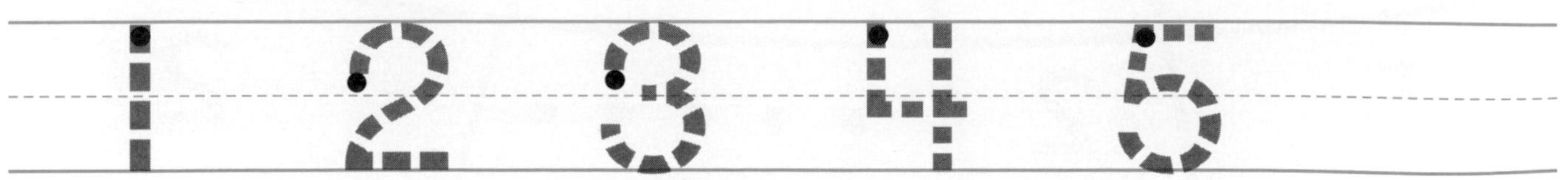

Name

Zero

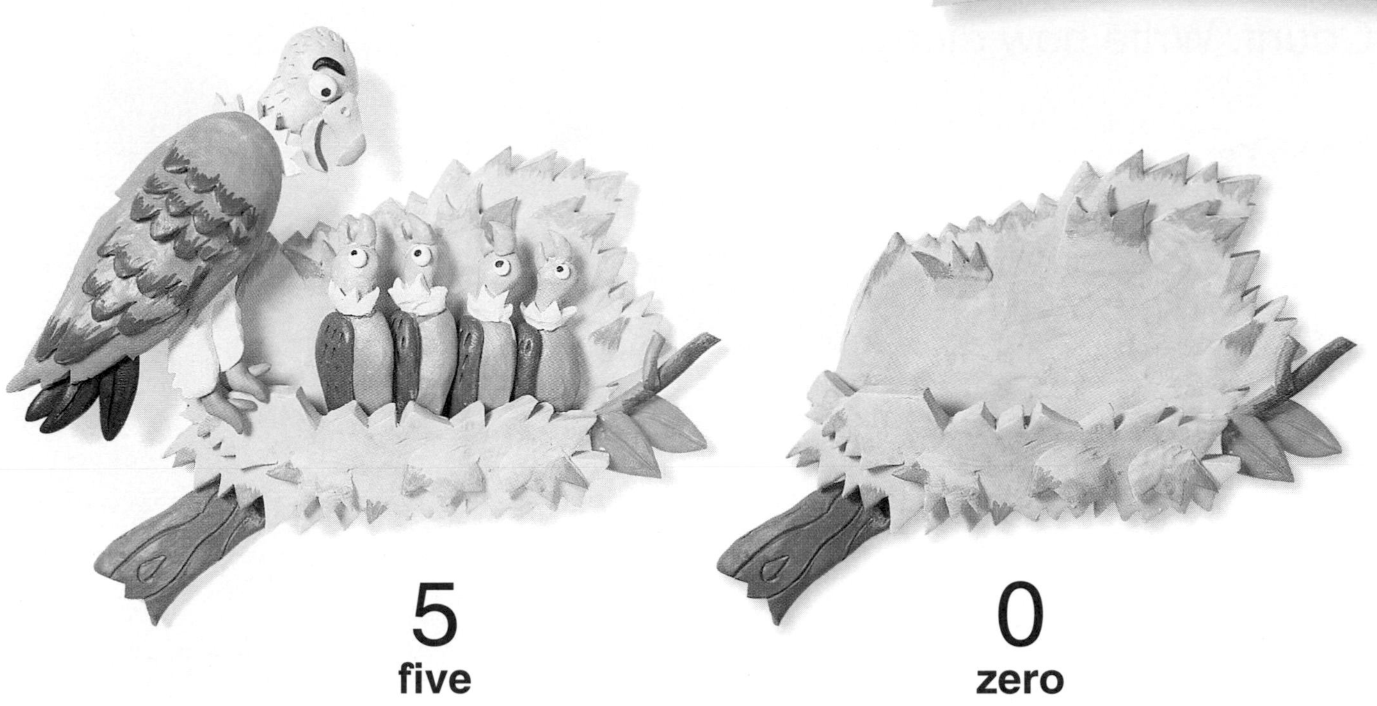

Write how many.

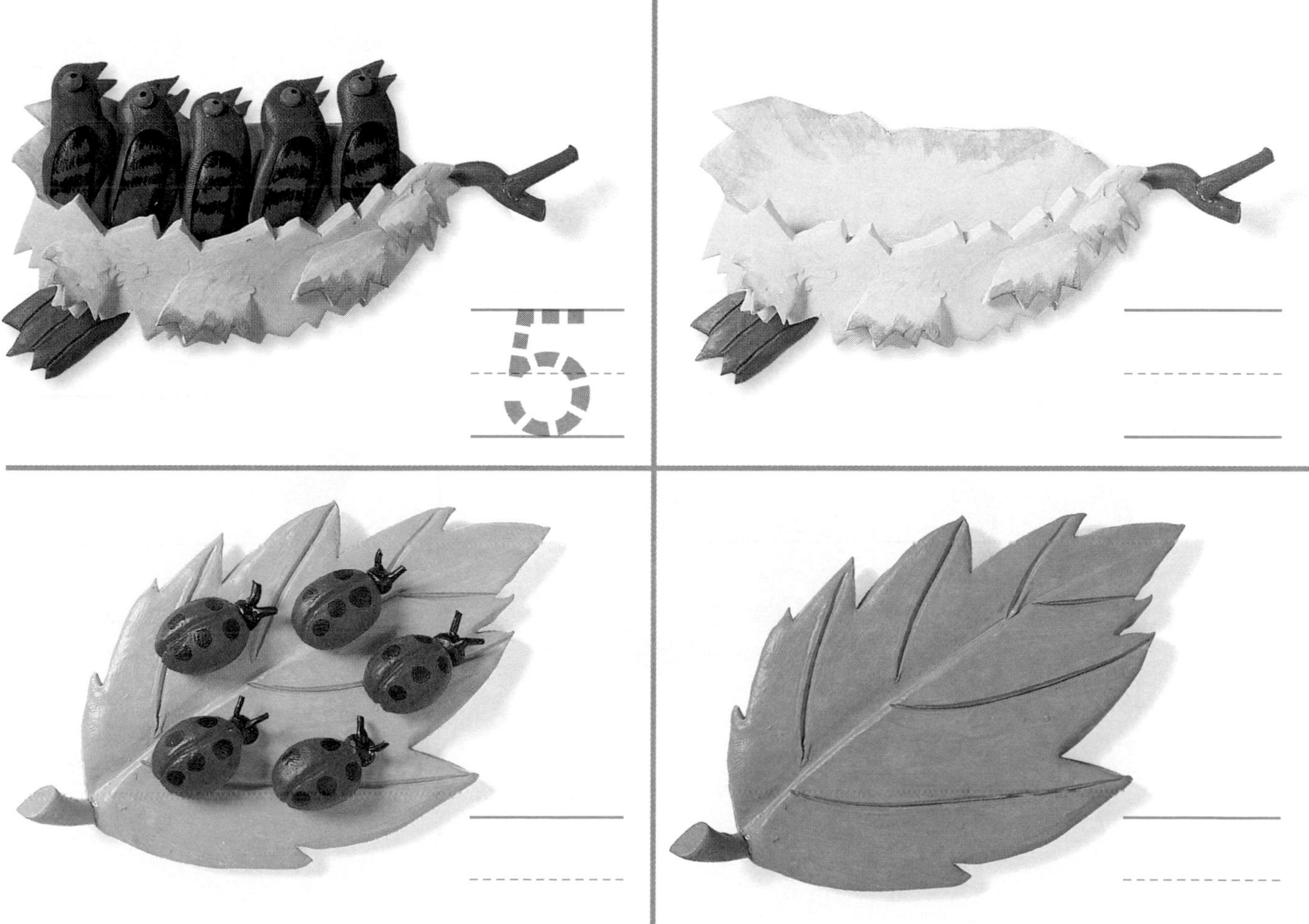

Count. Write how many.

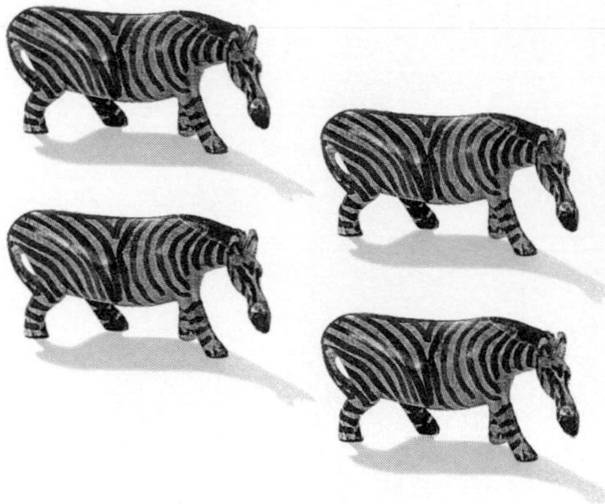

4

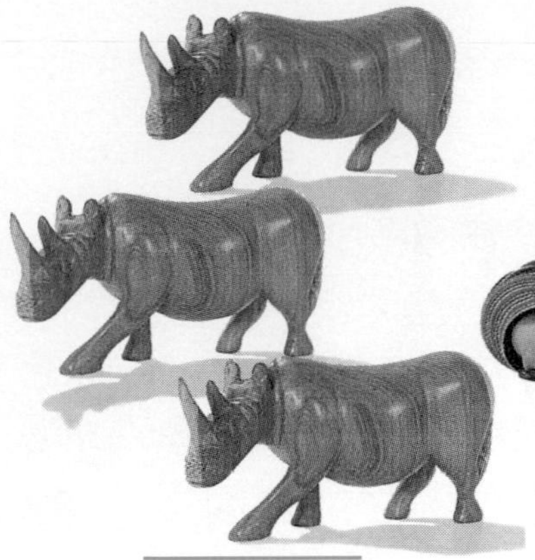

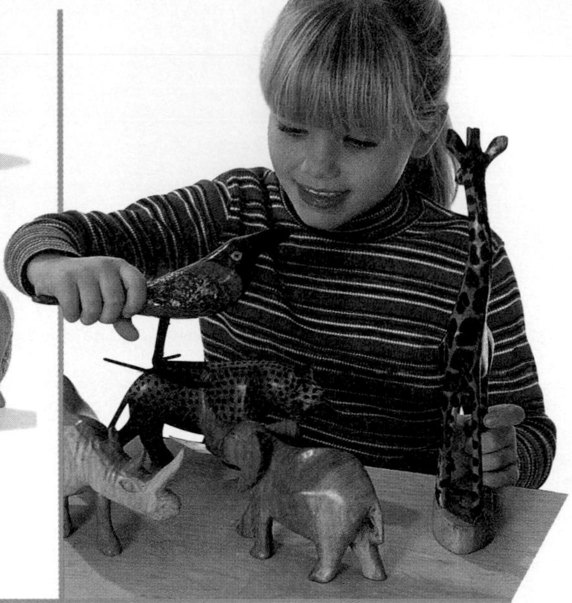

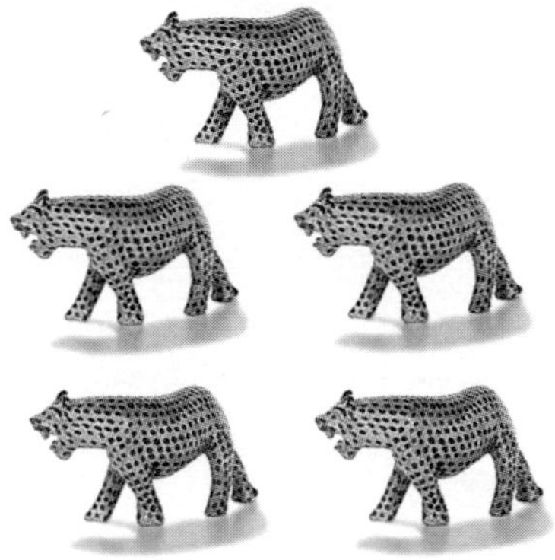

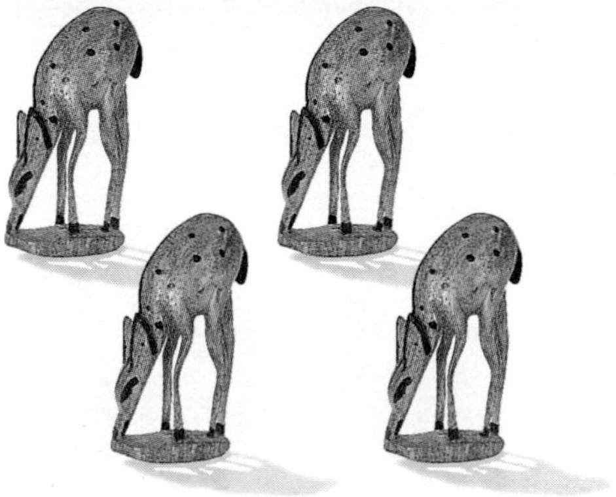

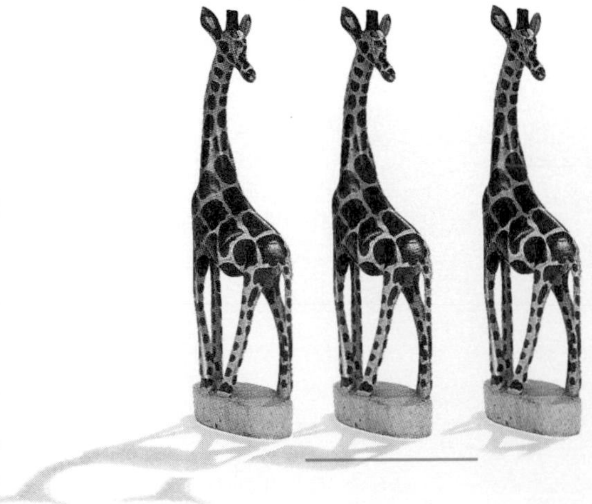

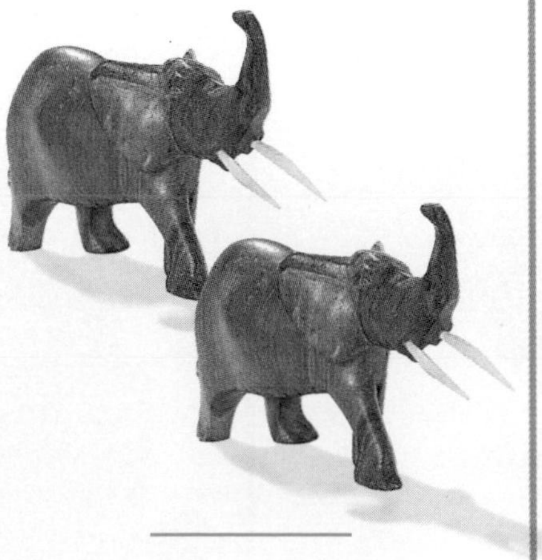

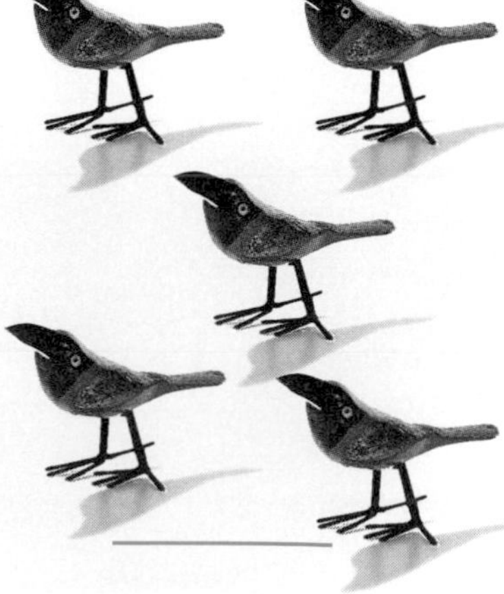

You may want to ask your child to show you sets of 0 to 5 objects.

Name

Midchapter Review

Draw. Write.

2

5

3

4

Do your best!

Write how many.

Show 5 in many different ways.

Extra Practice

Game!

Animal Walk

You need a and a .

Take turns.

- Spin and move.
- 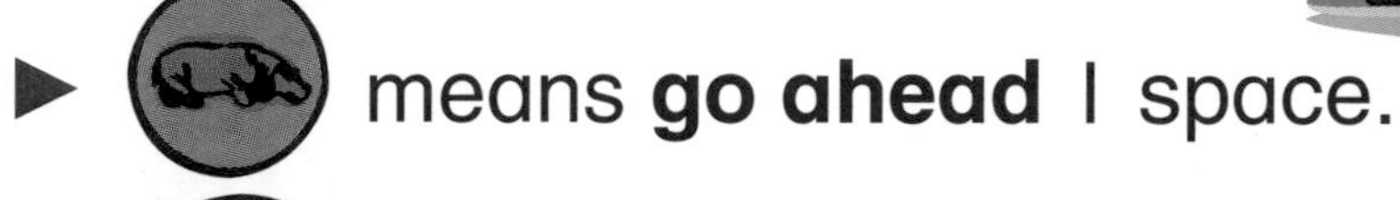 means **go ahead** 1 space.
- means **go back** 2 spaces.
- Play until you reach **End.**

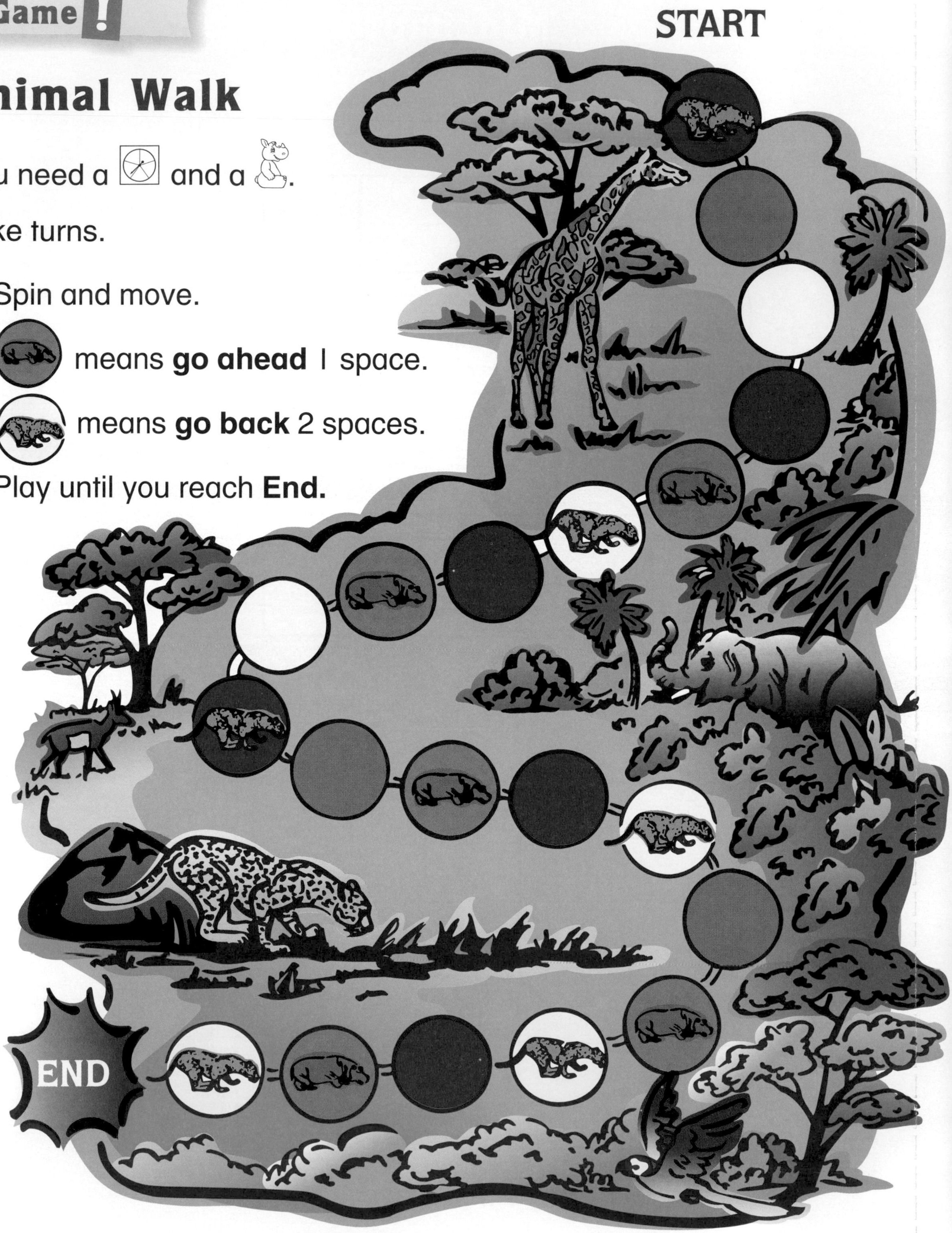

START

END

Real-Life Investigation
Applying Counting

Name

Counting on Ourselves

Count the parts of a rhino.

Working Together

- ▶ Find things that show 0, 1, 2, 3, 4, 5 on your partner.
- ▶ Draw what you find.
- ▶ Write the numbers.

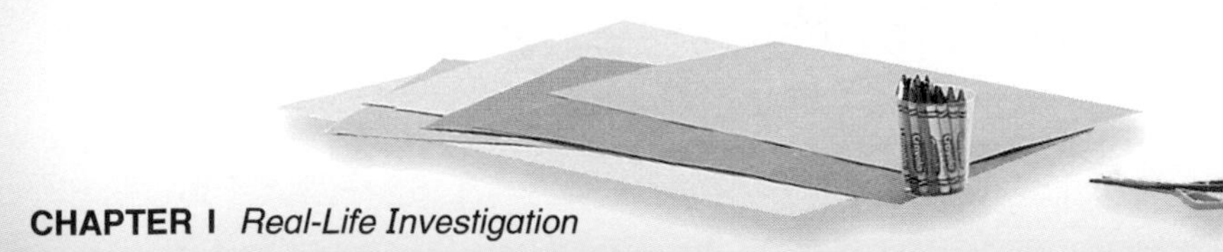

Decision Making

Make a class picture for 0, 1, 2, 3, 4, 5. Decide how to show what each group counted.

Write a report.

1. Tell about the class picture.
2. What can you tell about the numbers?

More to Investigate

PREDICT What else can you count in your classroom?

EXPLORE Find things that show other numbers.

FIND How would your class picture change?

Name

Explore Activity

Numbers to 10

Working Together

You need .

Make a group.

Put some here.

Draw your  group.

Draw a group with fewer.

Try These!

Count. Draw a group with fewer.

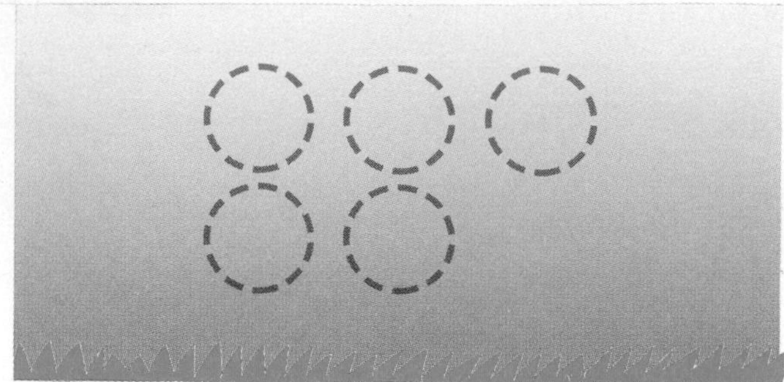

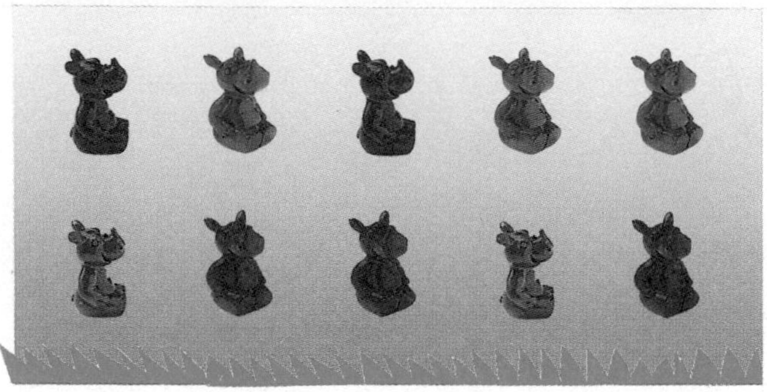

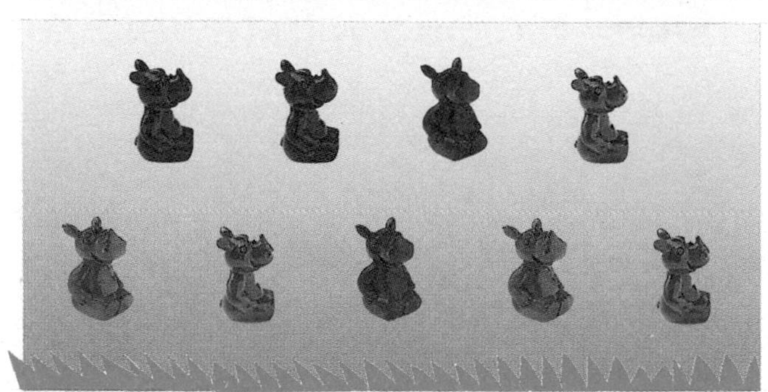

More to Explore

Estimation

Do not count.

Look.
Ring the group with fewer.

You may want to ask your child to tell about drawing sets with *fewer* objects.

Name

Six, Seven, Eight

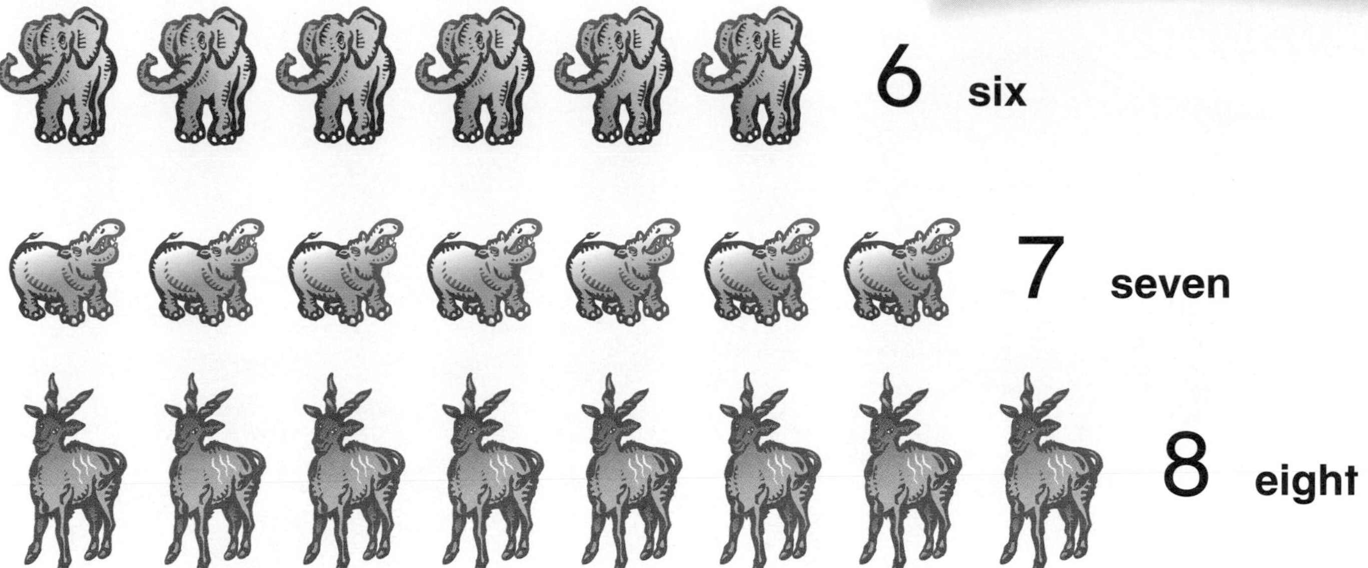

Count. Draw. Write.

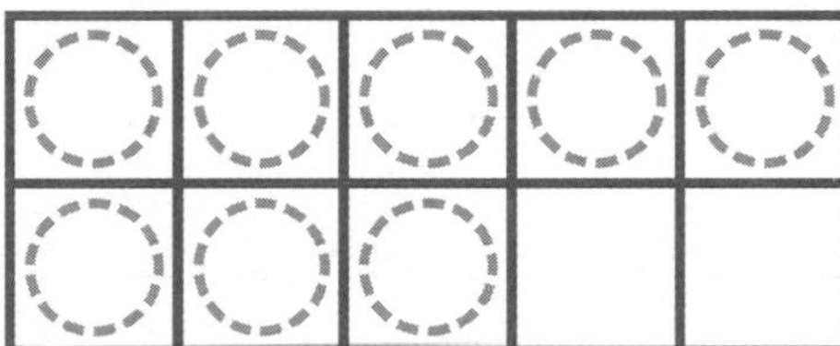
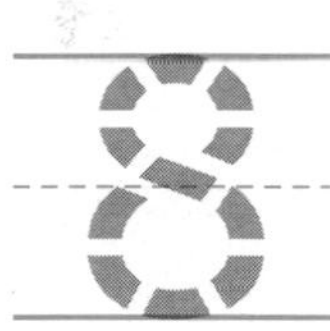

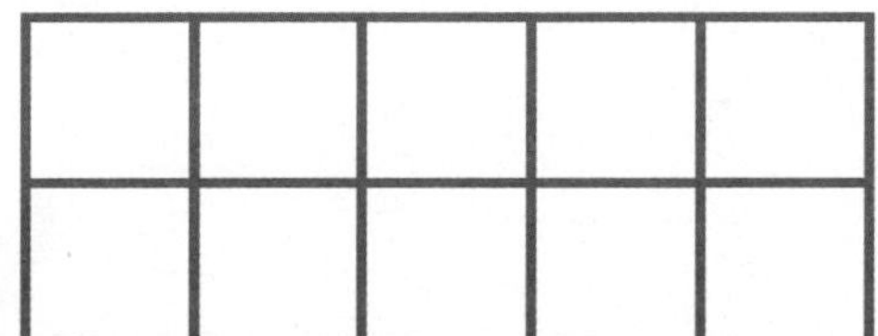

Try These!

Write how many.

At Home

Encourage your child to tell you a story about the picture.

Name

Nine and Ten

9 nine

10 ten

Count. Draw. Write.

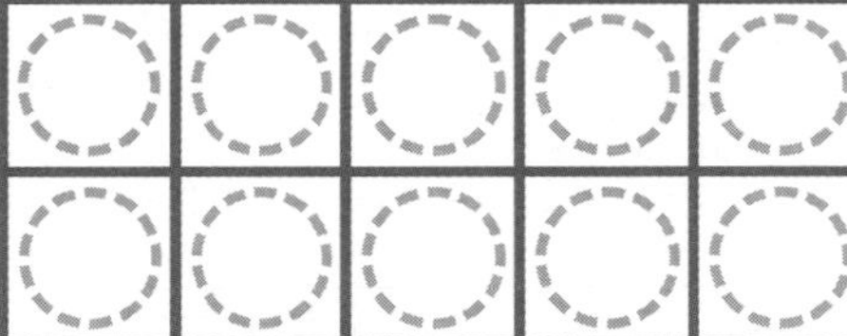

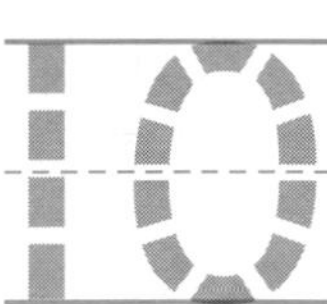

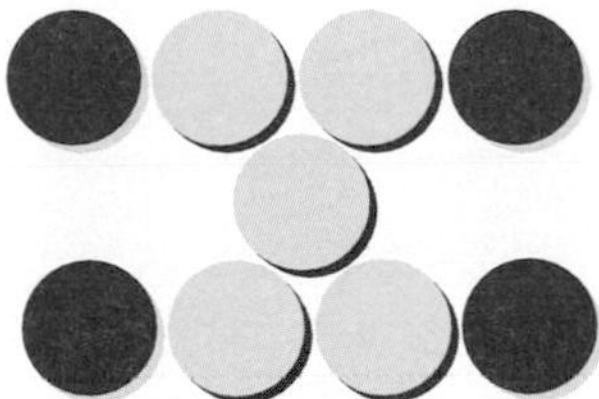

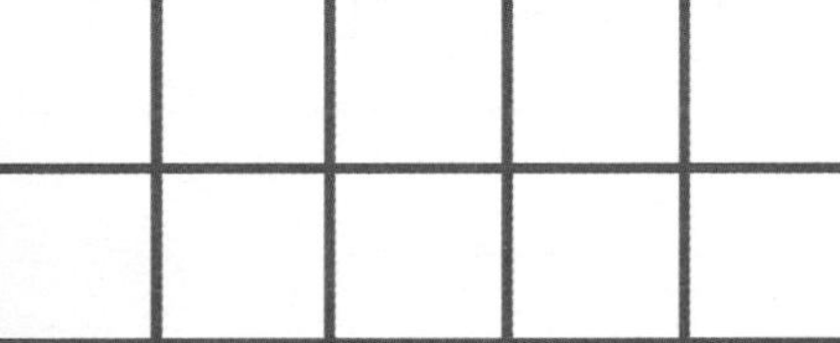

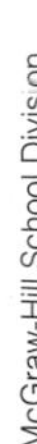

Try These!

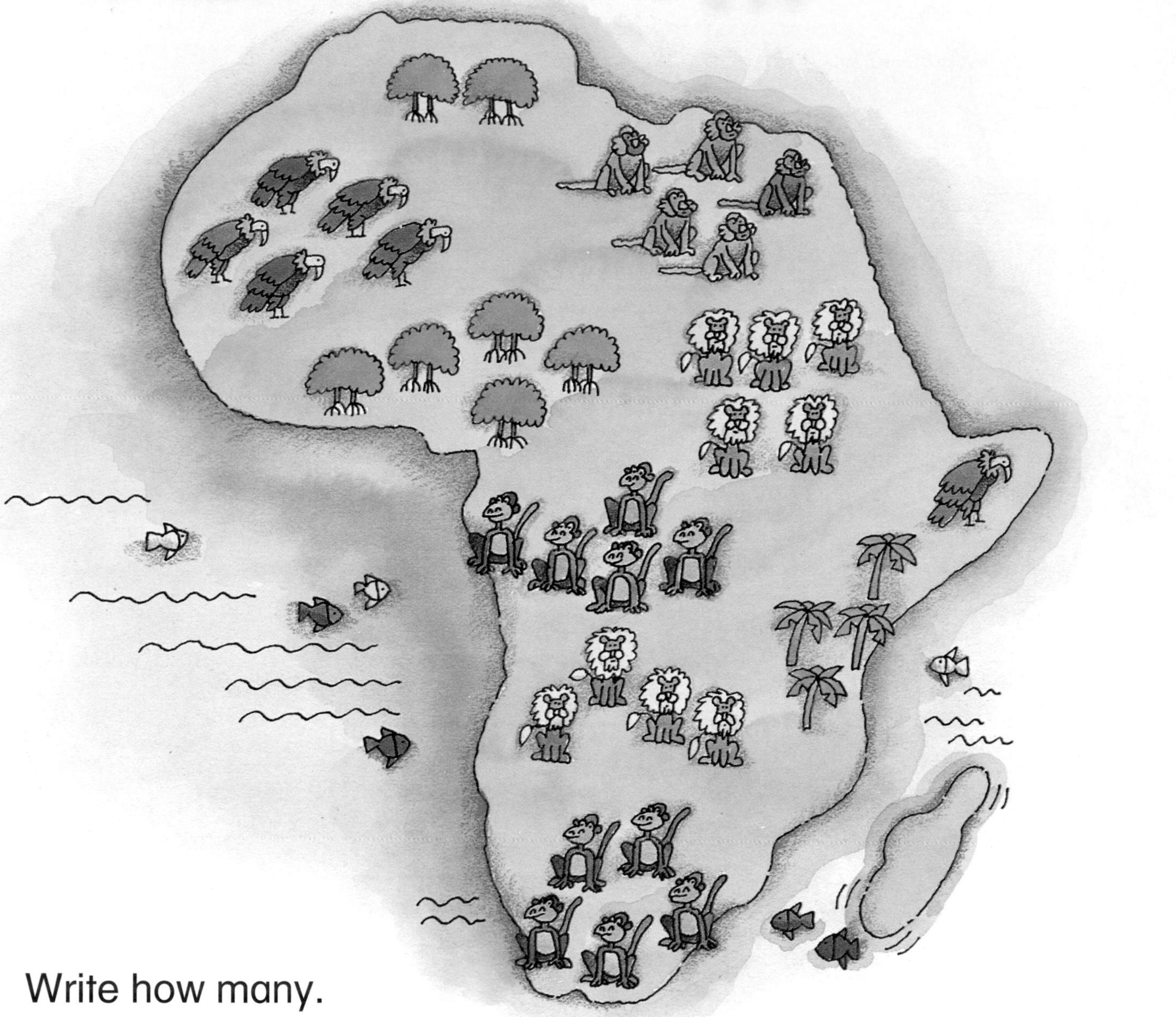

Write how many.

9

At Home Have your child show you how to count the monkeys.

Name

Extra Practice

Game !

Climb to the Top

You need 10 ◐ and a spinner.

Take turns.

- Spin.
- Put a ◐ on the dots for the number.
- Play until you cover all the spaces.

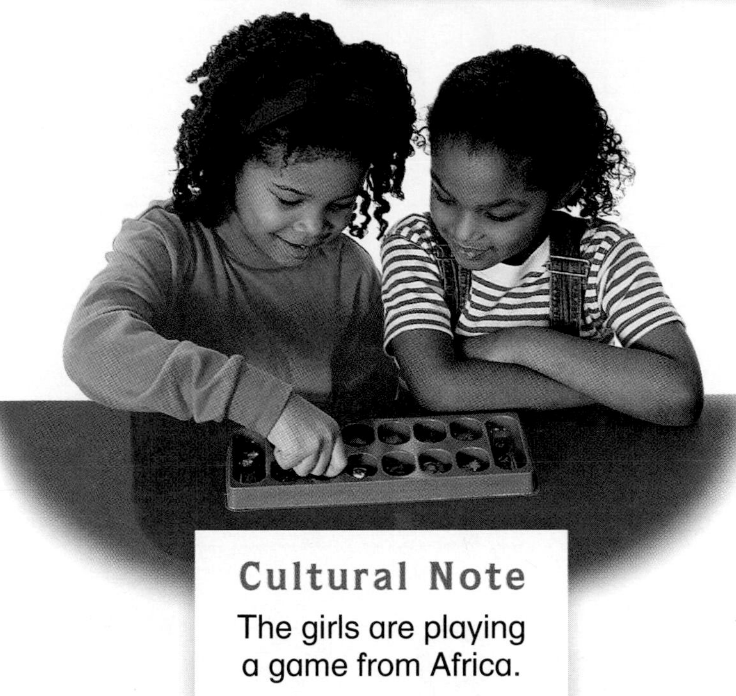

Cultural Note

The girls are playing a game from Africa.

Write.

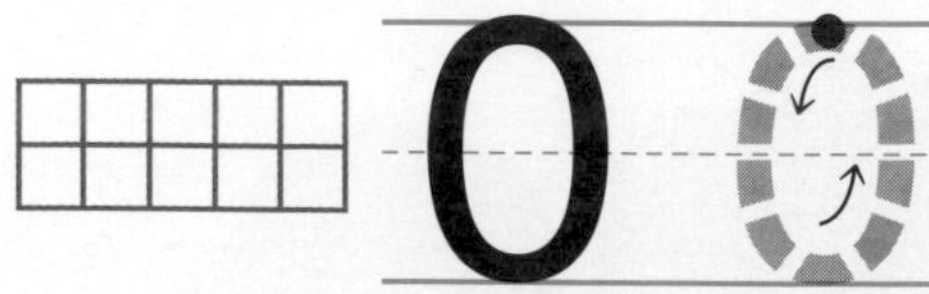

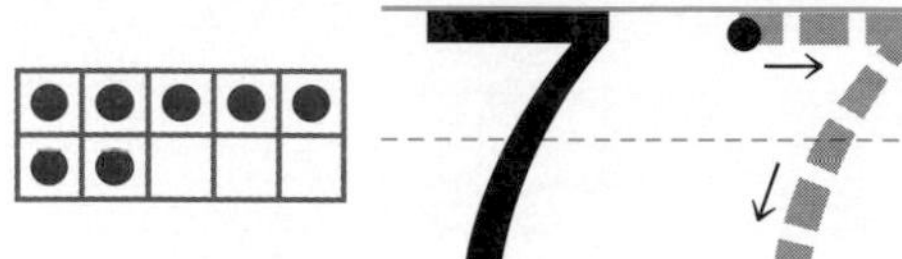

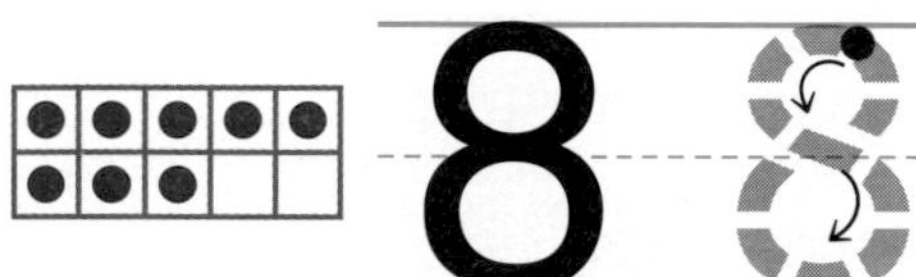

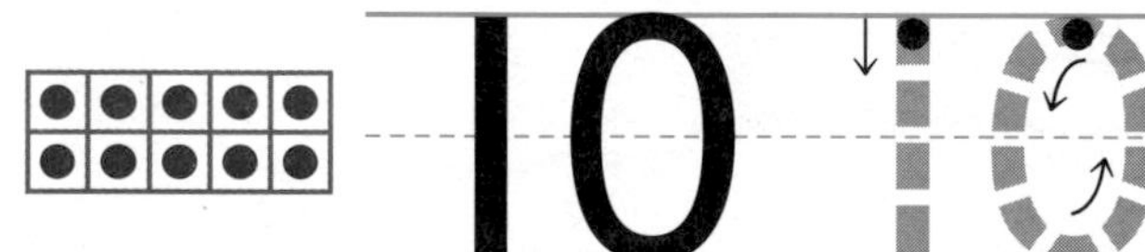

Do your best.

Write the numbers.

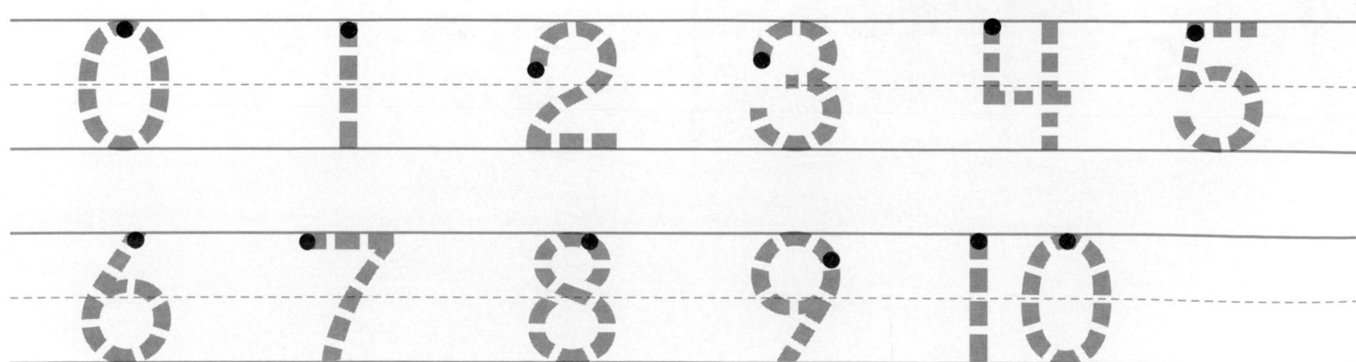

Name

Use a Pattern

You need 10 .

Listen to the problem.

Use to copy the pattern.
Color.

Dembe's beads

____ ____

Cora's beads

____ ____

Grandma's beads

____ ____

Try These!

Listen to the problem.

Kim's beads

Len's beads

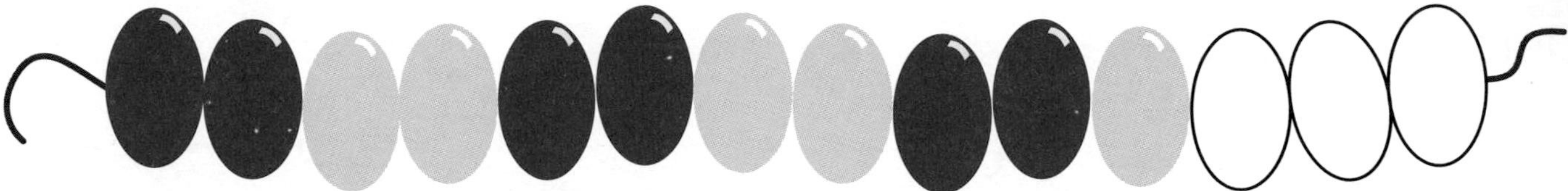

Jan's beads

Your beads

Your partner's beads

Have your child make a pattern and then tell about it.

Name ____________________

Order Numbers

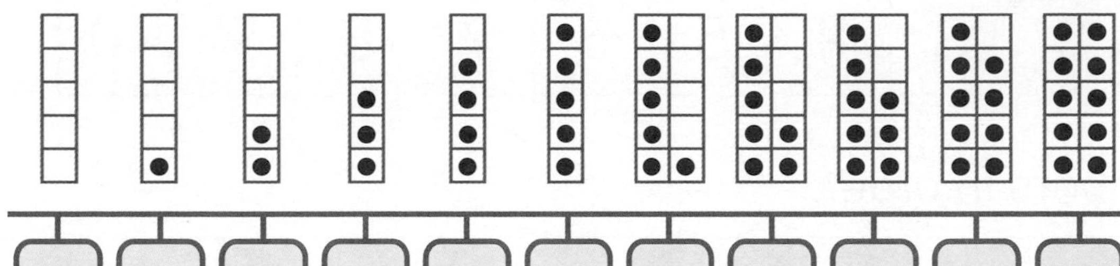

Write the missing number.

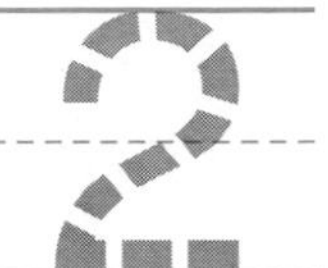

0 1 2 3 4 ☐ 6 7 8 9 10 ______

0 1 2 3 4 5 6 7 8 ☐ 10 ______

0	1	2	3	4	5	6	7	8	9	10

Write the numbers in order.

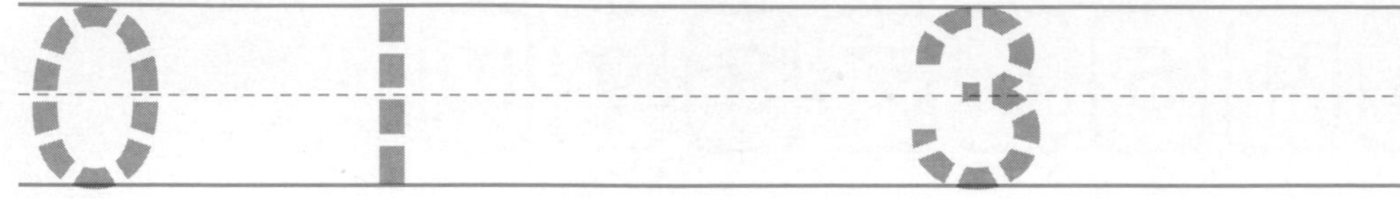

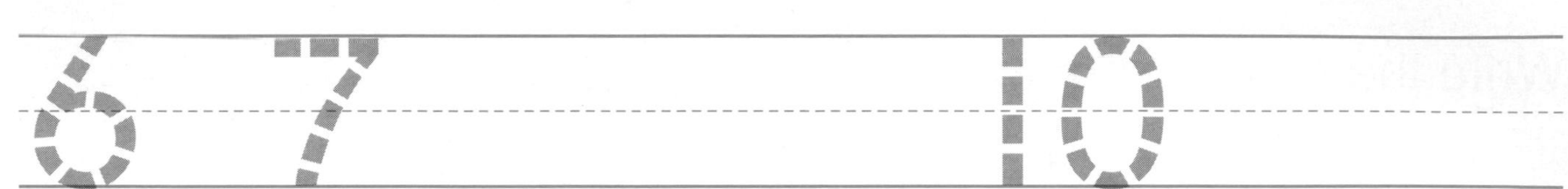

Count backward and write the numbers.

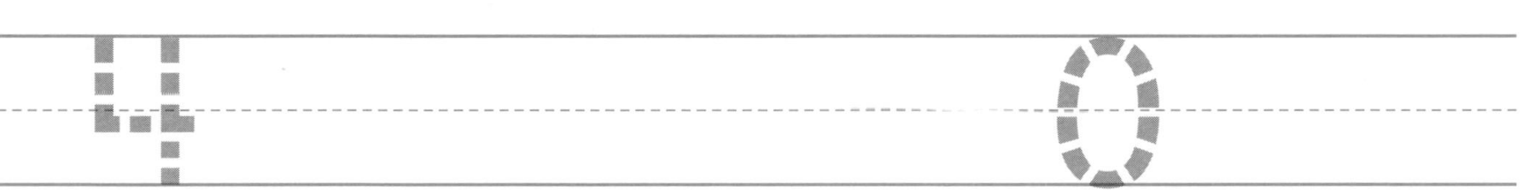

Mixed Review

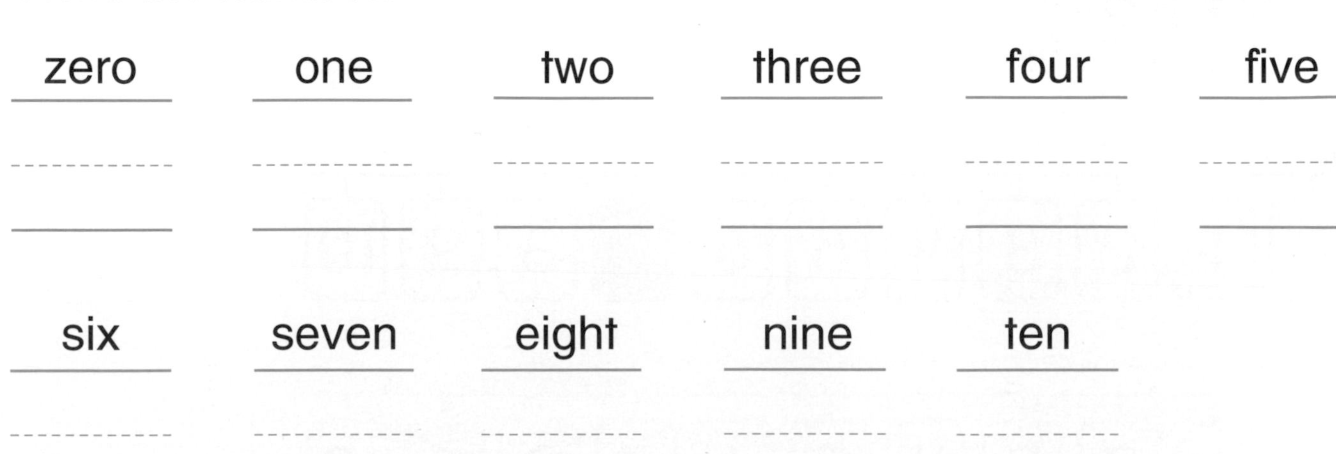

Write the number.

zero one two three four five

six seven eight nine ten

At Home

Encourage your child to count things at home, outside, and in pictures.

Name

I penny
I¢
I cent

2 pennies
2¢
2 cents

Working Together

You need (penny).

- You show some (penny).
- Your partner shows some (penny).
- Draw all the (penny).
- Write how many cents.

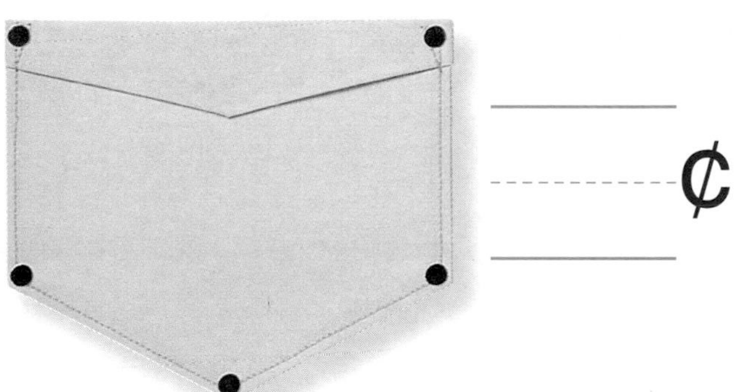

¢

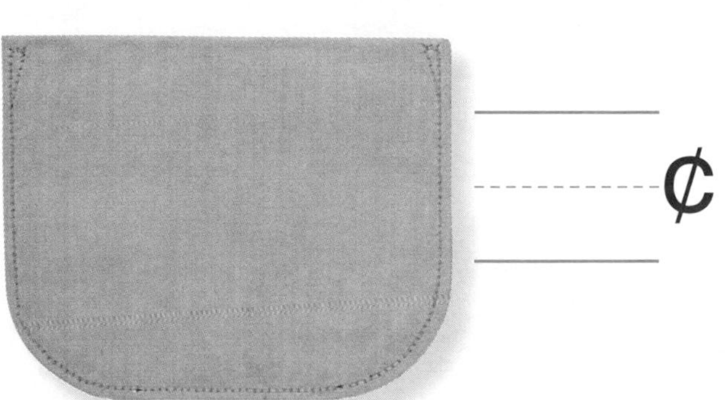

¢

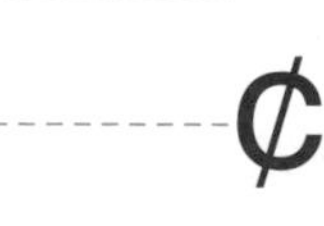

Try These!

Write how many cents.

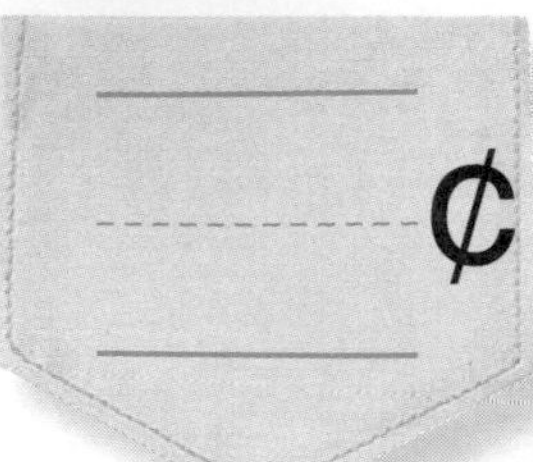

Cultural Connection

More Pennies

Singapore

¢

Bermuda

¢

At Home Hold out from 1 to 10 pennies. Ask your child to count how many cents you have in your hand.

Name

Number Patterns

Listen to the problem.

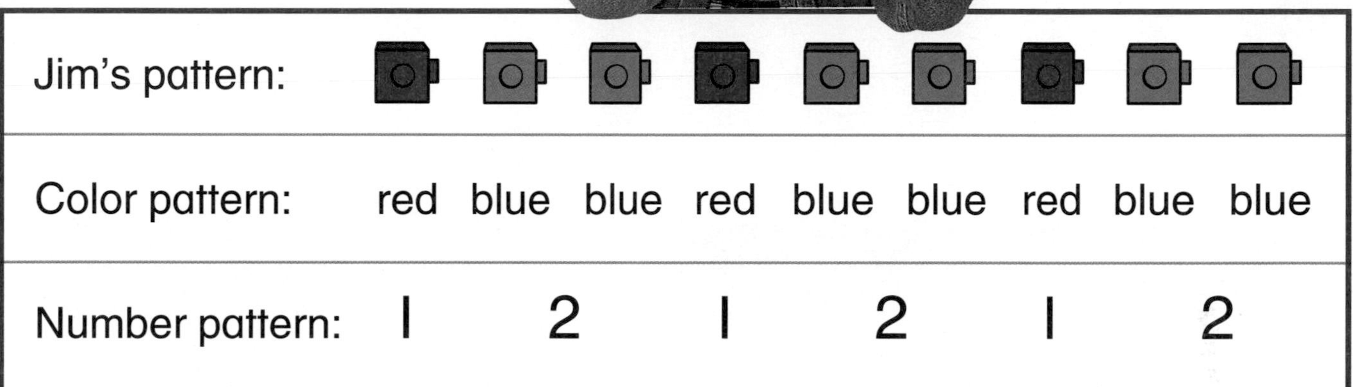

Jim's pattern:									
Color pattern:	red	blue	blue	red	blue	blue	red	blue	blue
Number pattern:	1	2		1	2		1	2	

The pattern is 1 red 2 blue.

Use numbers to show the pattern.

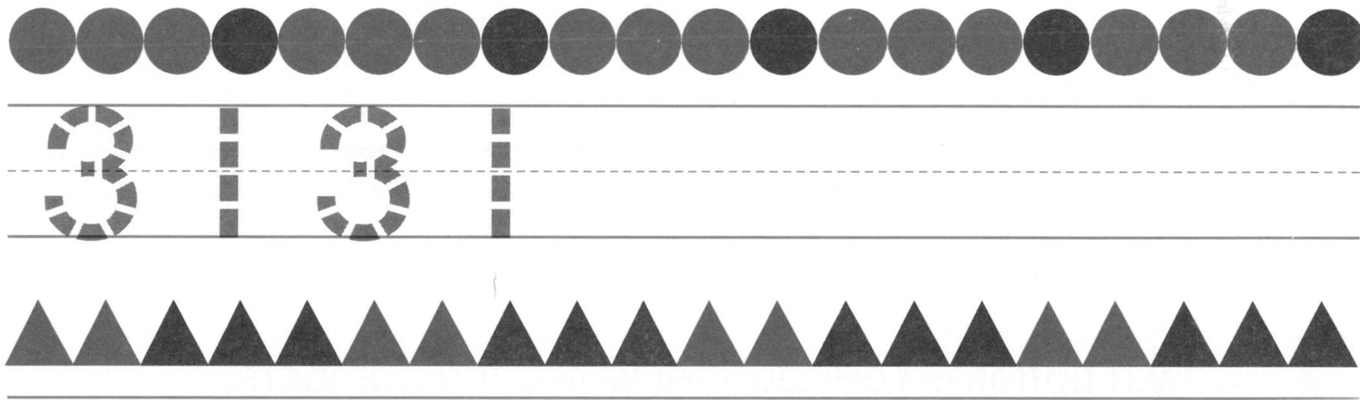

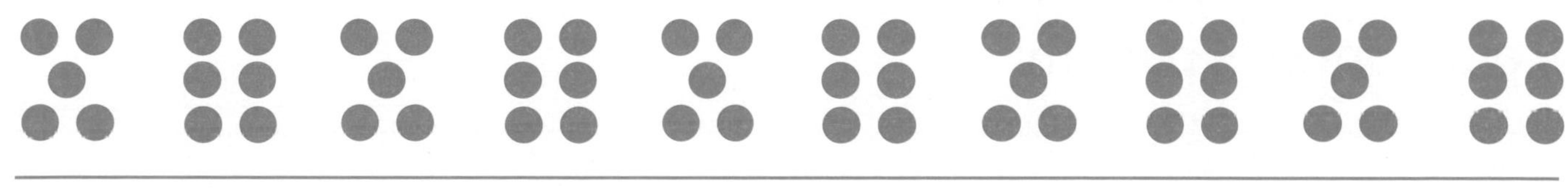

Try These!

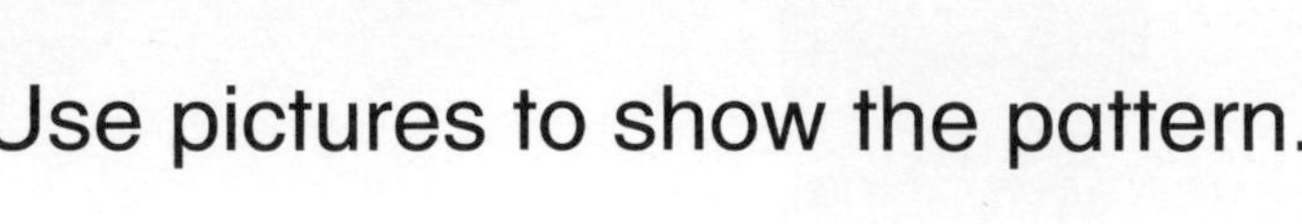
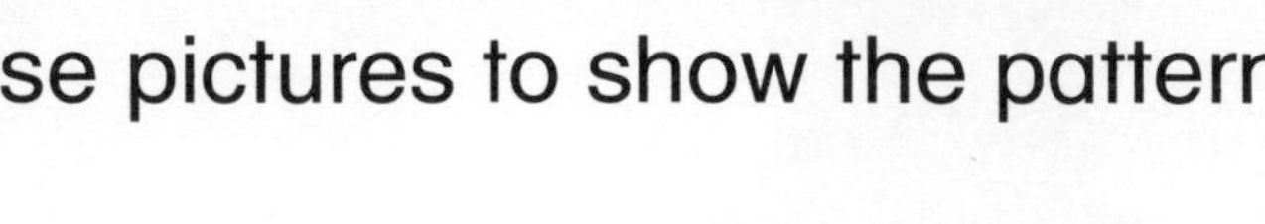

Listen to the problem.

Use pictures to show the pattern.

4 2 4 2 4 2

Write and Share

Jessie drew this pattern.

Use numbers to show Jessie's pattern.

Draw a pattern. Your partner writes the numbers.

Your partner's pattern:

At Home: Ask your child to show his or her pattern with numbers.

Name

Chapter Review

Write how many.

1 

2 

3

4 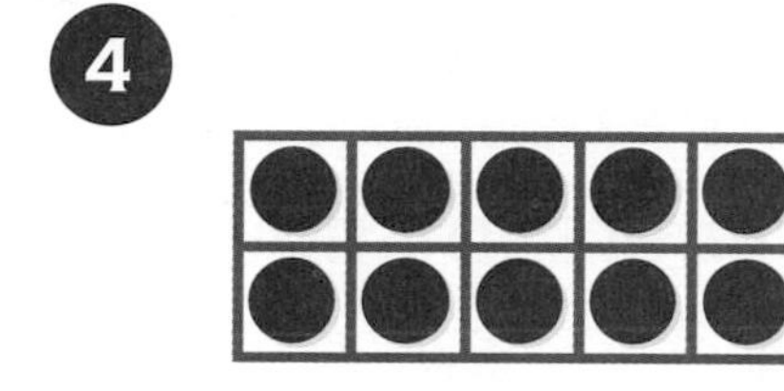

Write how many cents.

5 

¢

6 

¢

7 Write the numbers in order.

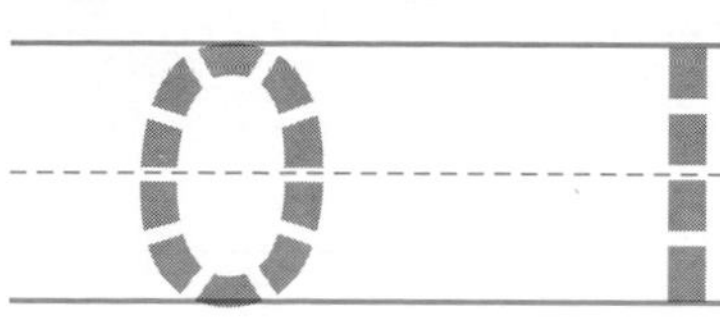

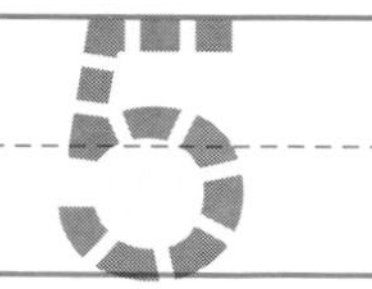

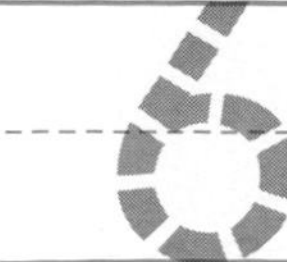

Listen to the problems.

8 Grandma's beads

9 Jan's beads

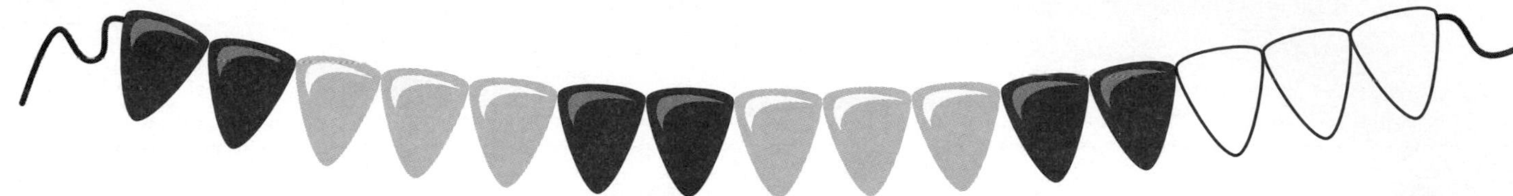

10 Use numbers to show the pattern.

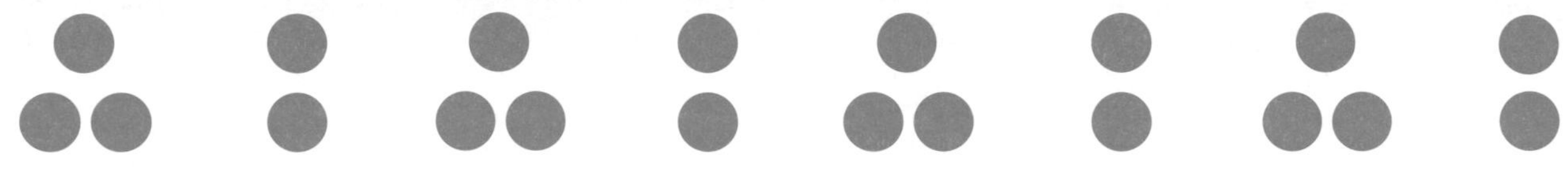

What Do You Think?

Which is the fastest to count?

☑ Check one.

☐  ☐  ☐ 

Why? ______________________________

Show what you know about patterns.
Draw. Write.

Name

Chapter Test

Write how many.

  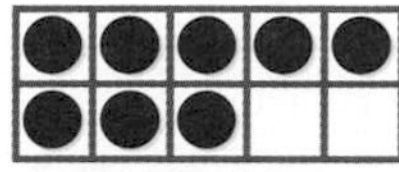 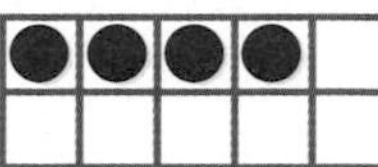

Write how many cents.

   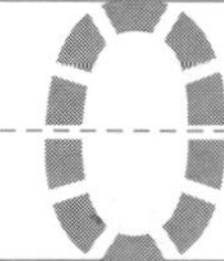 ¢

   ¢

  ¢

Write the numbers in order.

7 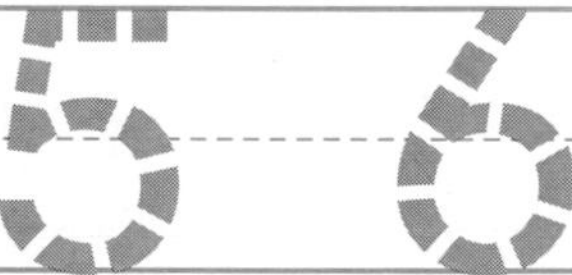 5 6 10

8 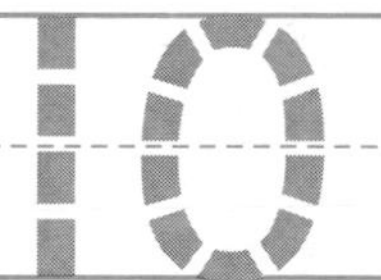 0 2 5

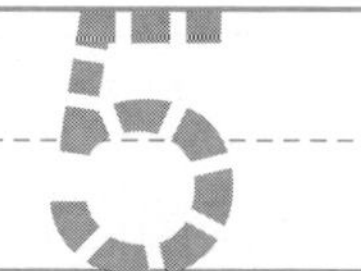

 Listen to the problem.

9 Jeff's beads

10  Vicky's beads 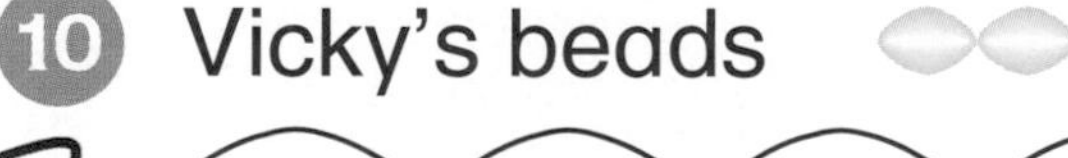

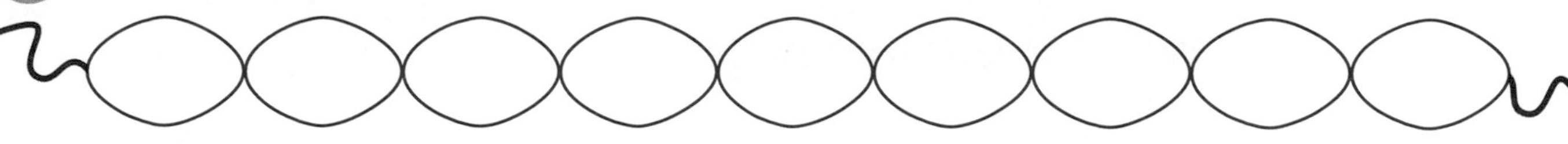

Performance Assessment

What Did You Learn?

Listen to the problem.

How many  ? ______

How many  ? ______

How many  ? ______

How many  ? ______

You may want to put this page in your portfolio.

Name ______________________________

Tally Marks

Ask 10 friends.
Use tally marks to show how many.

| = 1 vote
~~||||~~ = 5 votes

Which animal do you like the best?	

Write how many.

 ______   ______  ______

Curriculum Connection

Social Studies

Kamba Counting

The Kamba people have a way to show numbers with their fingers.

1	2	3	4	5
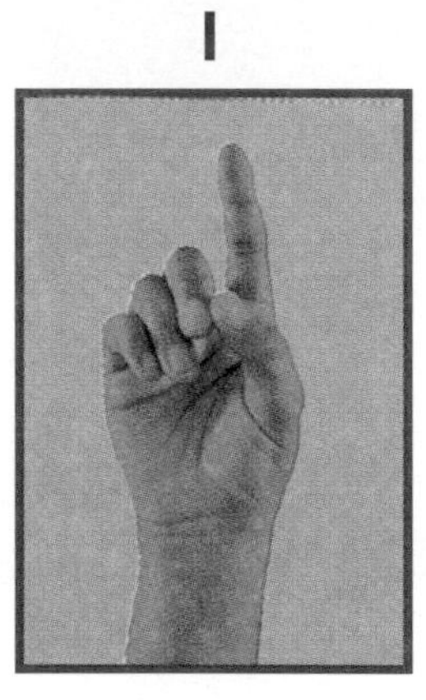	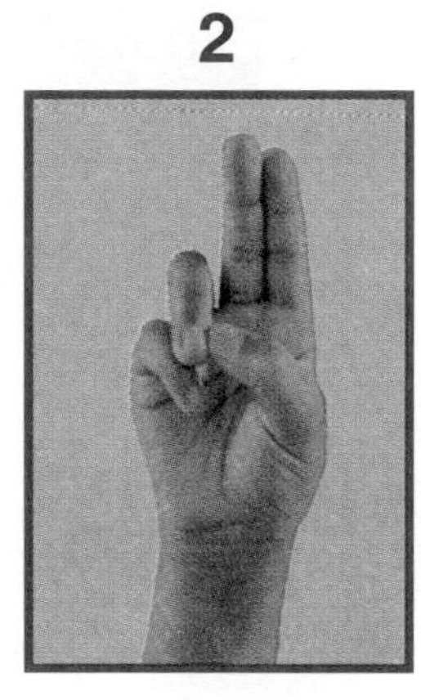	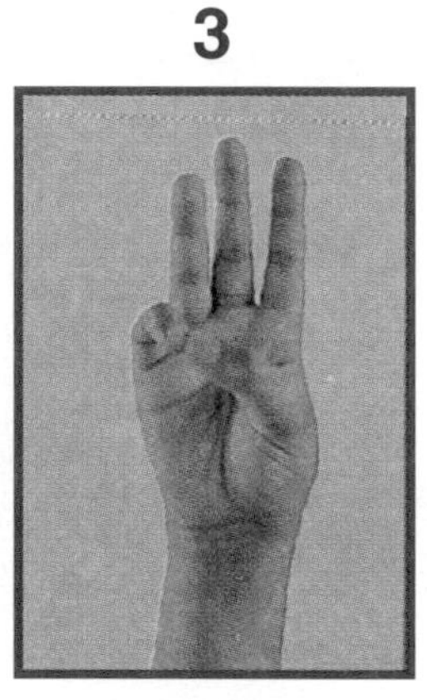	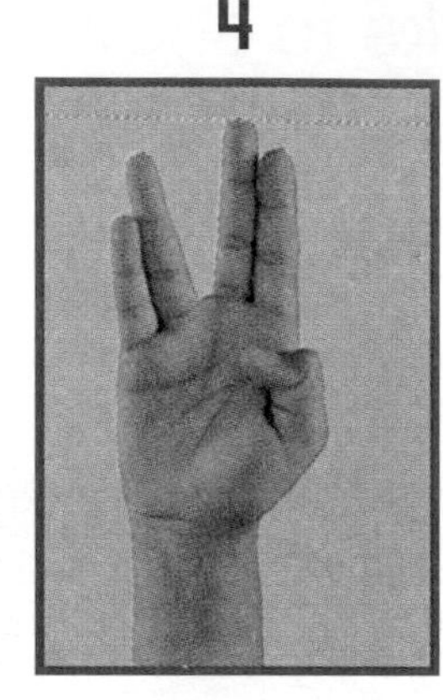	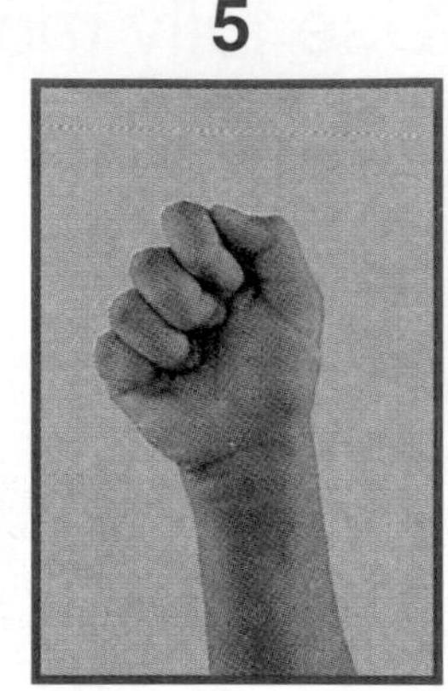
6	7	8	9	10
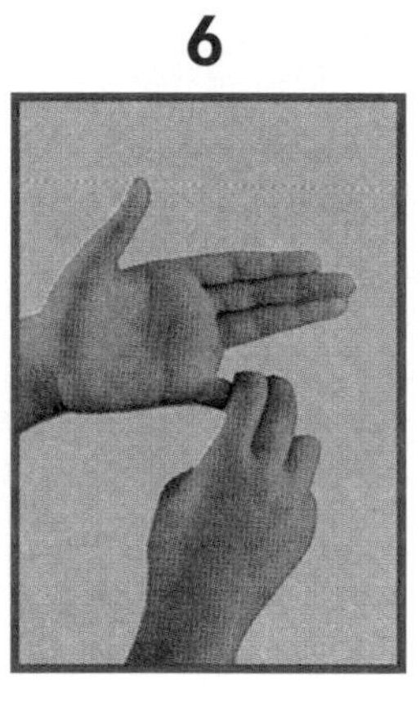	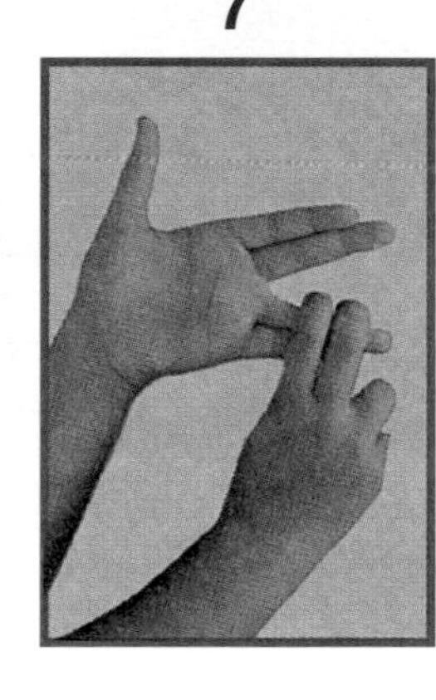	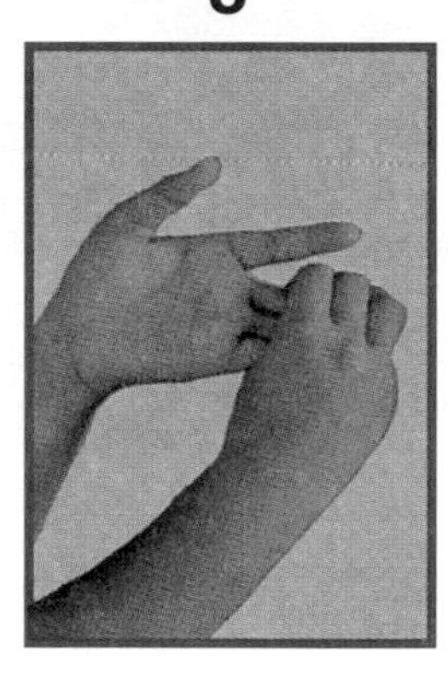	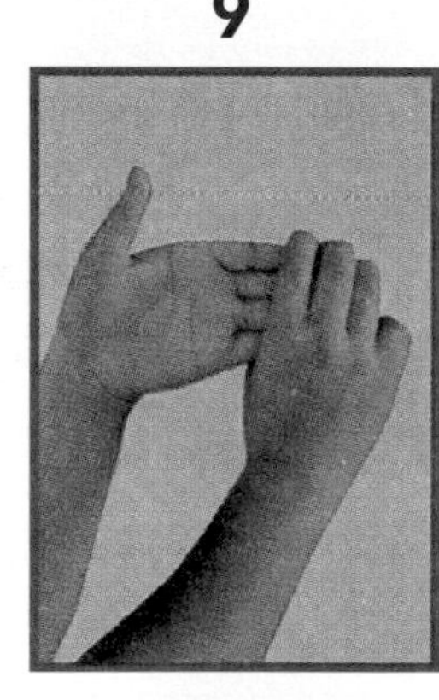	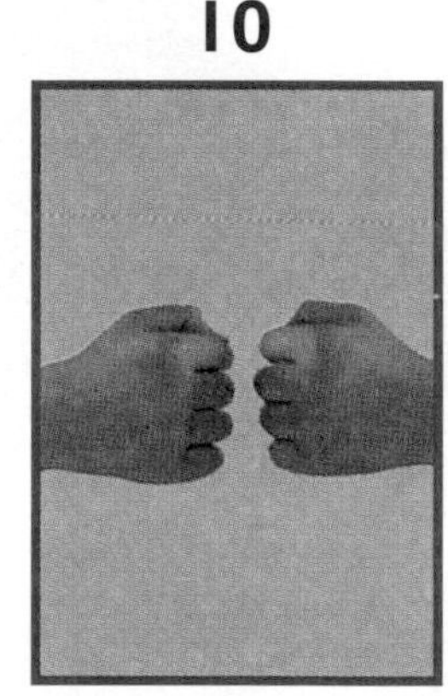

Show 6 with your fingers.
Show 6 the Kamba way.
Why do both ways use two hands?

- Think of a number.
  Make it the Kamba way.
- Show your friend.
  Let your friend say the number.

Name

The Dotted Giraffe!

PLAYERS 2

MATERIALS 10 pennies

DIRECTIONS Say a number from 1 to 10. Put a penny on the space that shows that number of dots. Play until you cover all the spaces.

Play this game with your child to practice counting from 1 to 10.

Dear Family,

We are beginning a new chapter in our mathematics book. We will be learning about parts of numbers.

Total	Part	Part
5	3	2

Five can be 3 and 2, or 4 and 1, or just 5.

We will also be talking about transportation and all the ways we can get around. Please help me complete this interview.

Your child,

____
Signature

Interview

Which are your favorite ways to get around?
(You may check more than one.)

- ❑ Car
- ❑ Bus
- ❑ Train
- ❑ Plane
- ❑ Bicycle
- ❑ Truck
- ❑ Other ______________________

If you won a free trip, where would you go?

____

Getting Around

Exploring Part-Part-Whole

CHAPTER 2

Listen to the story *Bus Stops.*

Do you ride a bus? Tell about where it stops.

Name

What Do You Know?

1. 

How many ? ____

How many ? ____

2. 

How many ? ____

How many ? ____

Draw some in a wagon.

Write how many .

Write how many .

Name ______________________

Working Together

You need 10 cubes, 10 cubes, a red crayon, and a blue crayon.

Listen to your teacher.

Color.

1. Your train

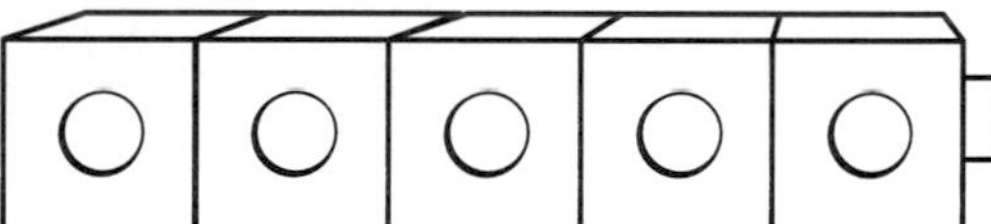

Your partner's train

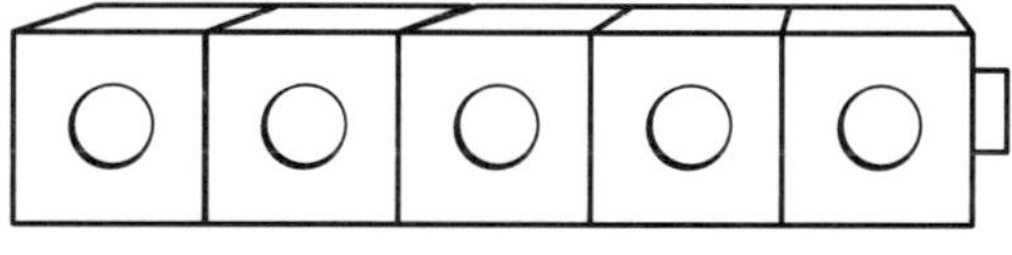

2. Your train

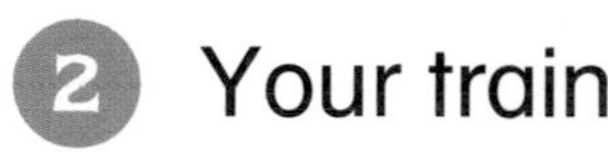

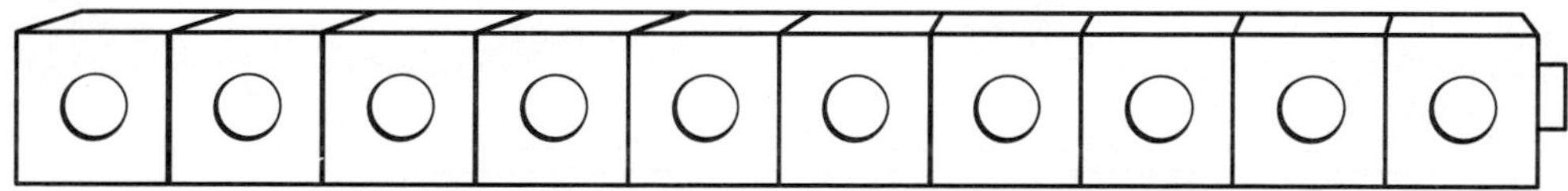

Your partner's train

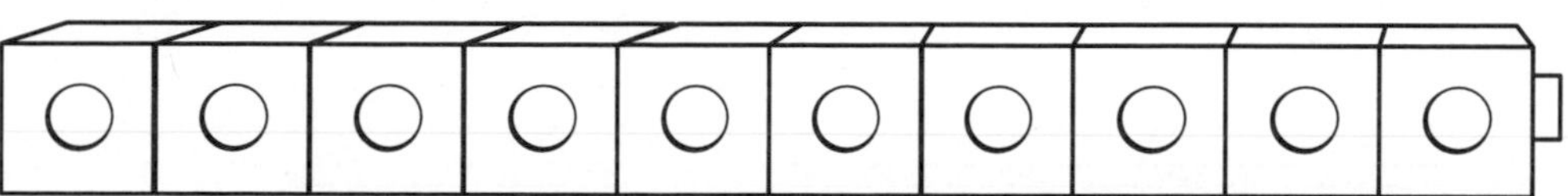

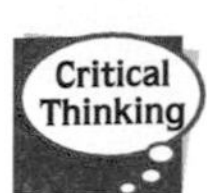

How are the trains for 10 the same?
How are the trains for 10 different?

Try These!

Make trains with ◘ and ◘. Color.

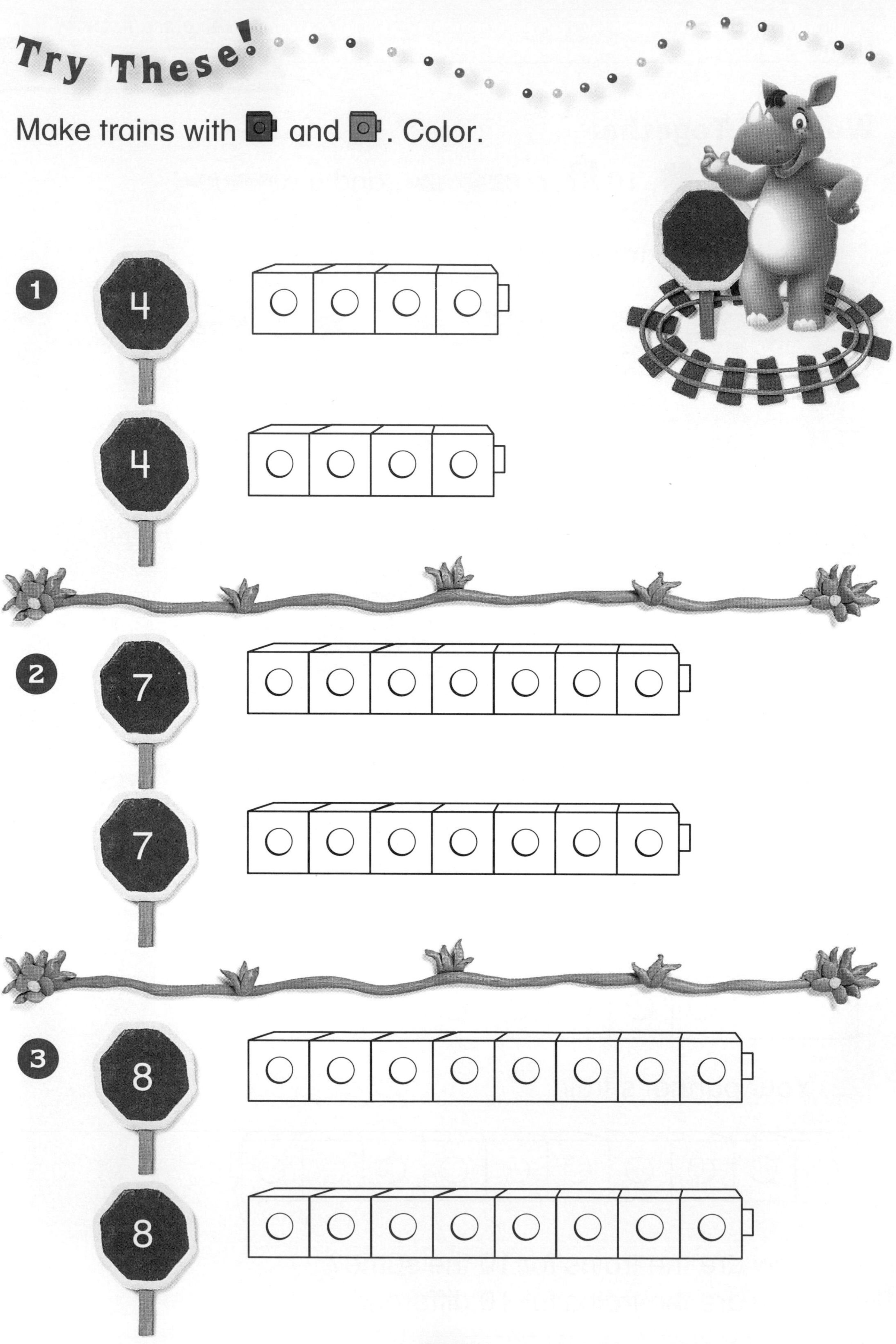

At Home Ask your child to tell you how many red cubes and blue cubes are in each train.

Name

Make Cube Trains

You need 10 ■, 10 ■, a red crayon, and a blue crayon.

Make a train for the total.

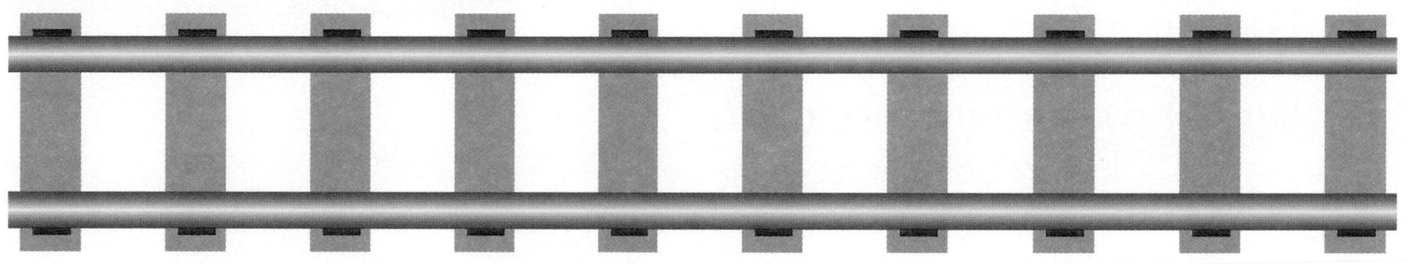

Draw. Write how many ■ and ■.

Total | Parts

1

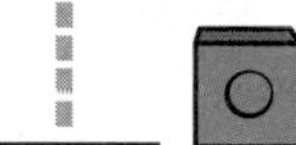
2 ■ 1 ■

2

___ ■ ___ ■

3

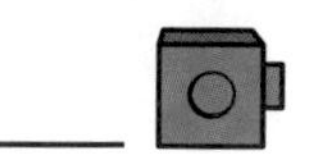
___ ■ ___ ■

Does everyone have the same train for 6? Why or why not?

Try These!

- Write a total.
- Make the train with ■ and ■.
- Draw it.
- Write how many ■ and ■.

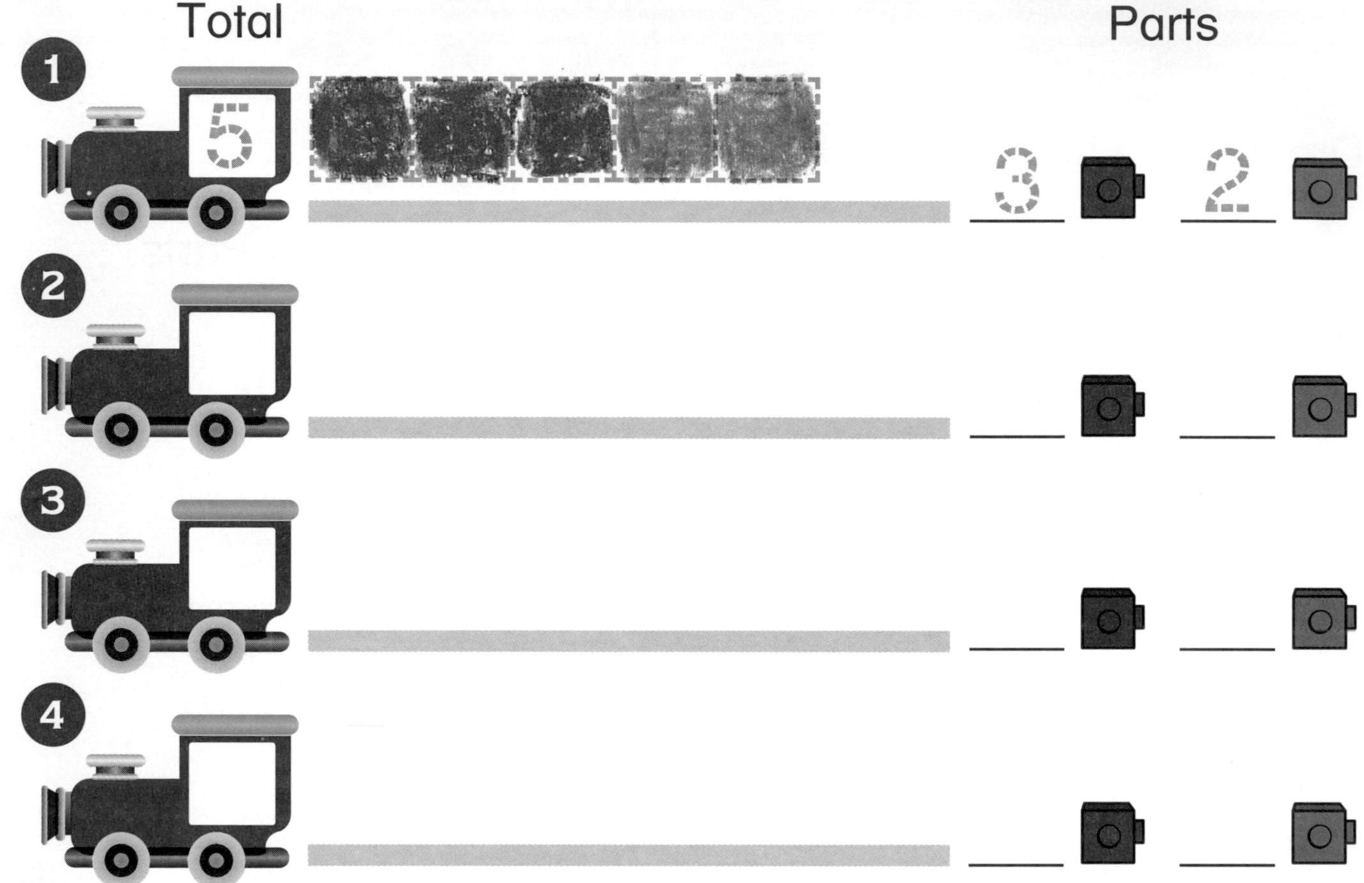

Talk to your partner about your trains.

Mixed Review

5 Use numbers to show the pattern.

  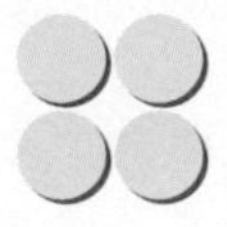     

4 3 ___ ___ ___ ___ ___ ___

Your child made trains from connecting cubes. Ask your child to tell about them.

Name

Parts and Totals

You need 10 cubes, 10 cubes, a red crayon, and a blue crayon.

Make different trains for 4.
Color. Write the parts and total.

Parts Total

1 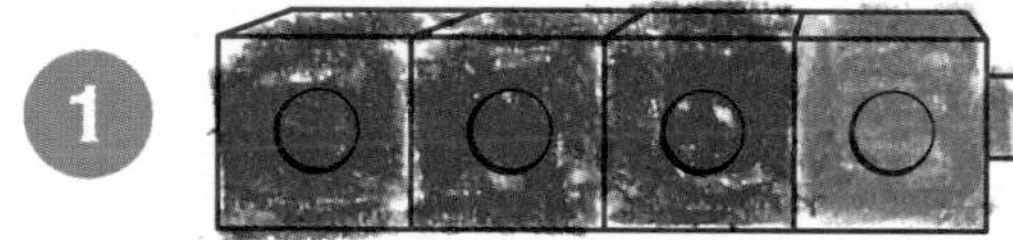     

3 1 4

2 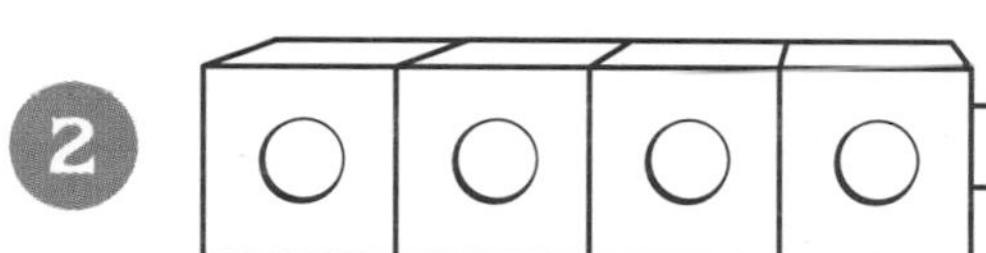  

 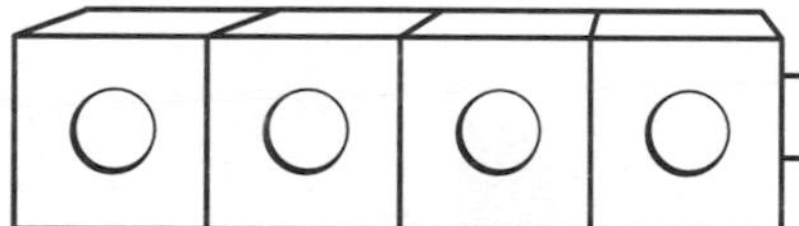  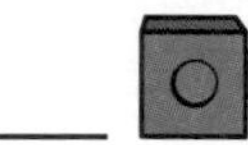

 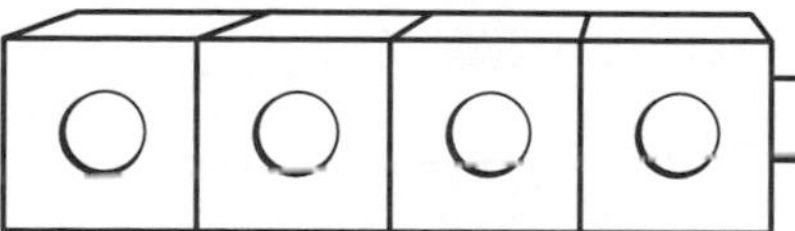  

 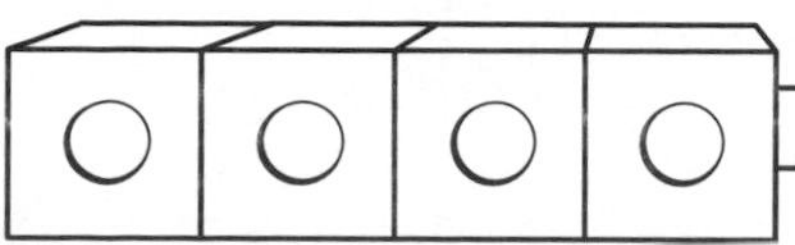  

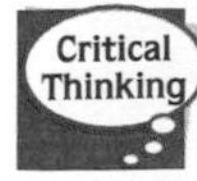

Critical Thinking: Do you think there are more or fewer trains for 7 than 4? Why?

Try These!

Make different trains for 3 with .
Color. Write the parts and total.

		Parts			Total
 1	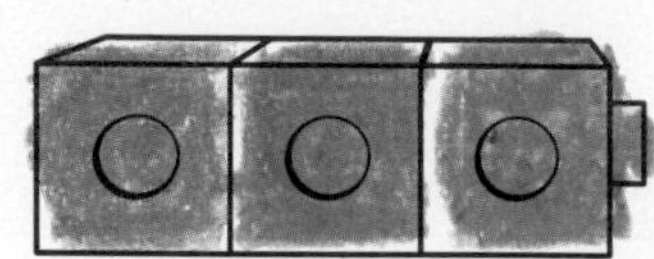	0 	3  		3 
 2	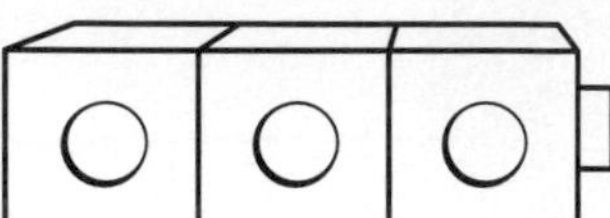	___ 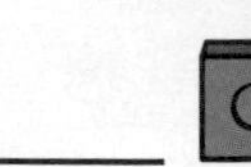	___		___ 
3	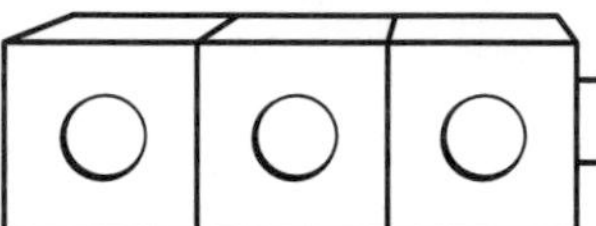	___ 	___		___
4	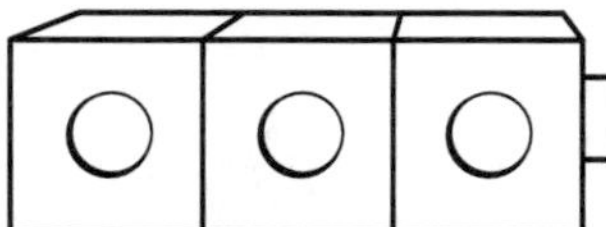	___ 	___ 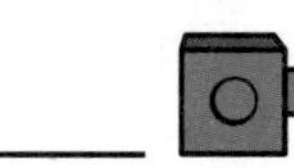		___ 

Cultural Connection

Native American Patterns

This blanket was made by Native American weavers.

How many ▪? ____

How many ▪? ____

How many ▪? ____

Total ____

Have your child tell you how to make trains for 3.

Name ___

Act It Out

Problem-Solving Strategy

Read | Plan | Solve | Look Back

Listen: Listen to the problem.

1

3 girls 2 boys 5 children

2 At the 

____ children ____ sitting ____ standing

3 At the 

____ blue trains ____ red trains ____ trains

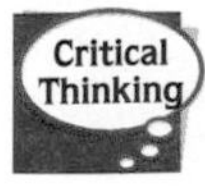

How can you solve problem 1 using cubes?

Try These!

1. At the BUS STOP

____ grown-ups ____ children ____ people

2. At the BIKE ROUTE

____ red bicycles ____ blue bicycles ____ bicycles

3. At the PICNIC AREA

____ children ____ boys ____ girls

4. At the [traffic light sign]

____ vans ____ green van ____ red vans

More to Explore Problem Solving

Make up a problem.

At Home Have your child tell you about the school bus picture above.

Name

Midchapter Review

Draw a train.
Write how many ◼ and ◻.

Total Parts

1  ____ ◼ ____ ◻

2  ____ ◼ ____ ◻

Color different trains for 7.
Write the parts and total.

Parts Total

3 ____ ◼ ____ ◻ ____

4 ____ ◼ ____ ◻ ____

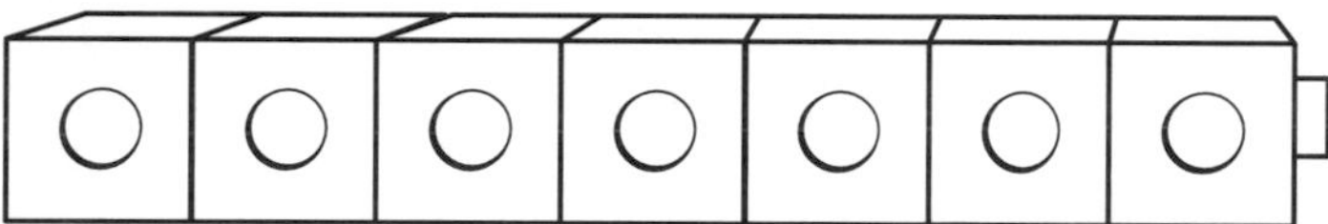

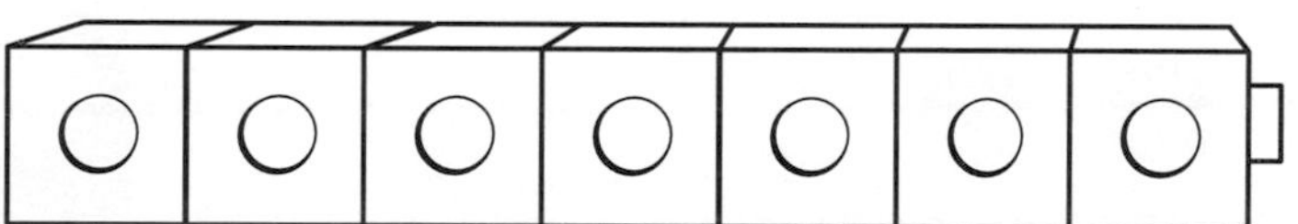

5 Listen to the problem.

At the 

____ boys ____ girls ____ children

Show as many different trains for 6 as you can.

Extra Practice

Game!

Shake and Spill

You need 10 counters and a cup.

- Take turns.
- Put 10 counters in the cup.
- Shake and spill.
- Cross out the row that shows your parts.

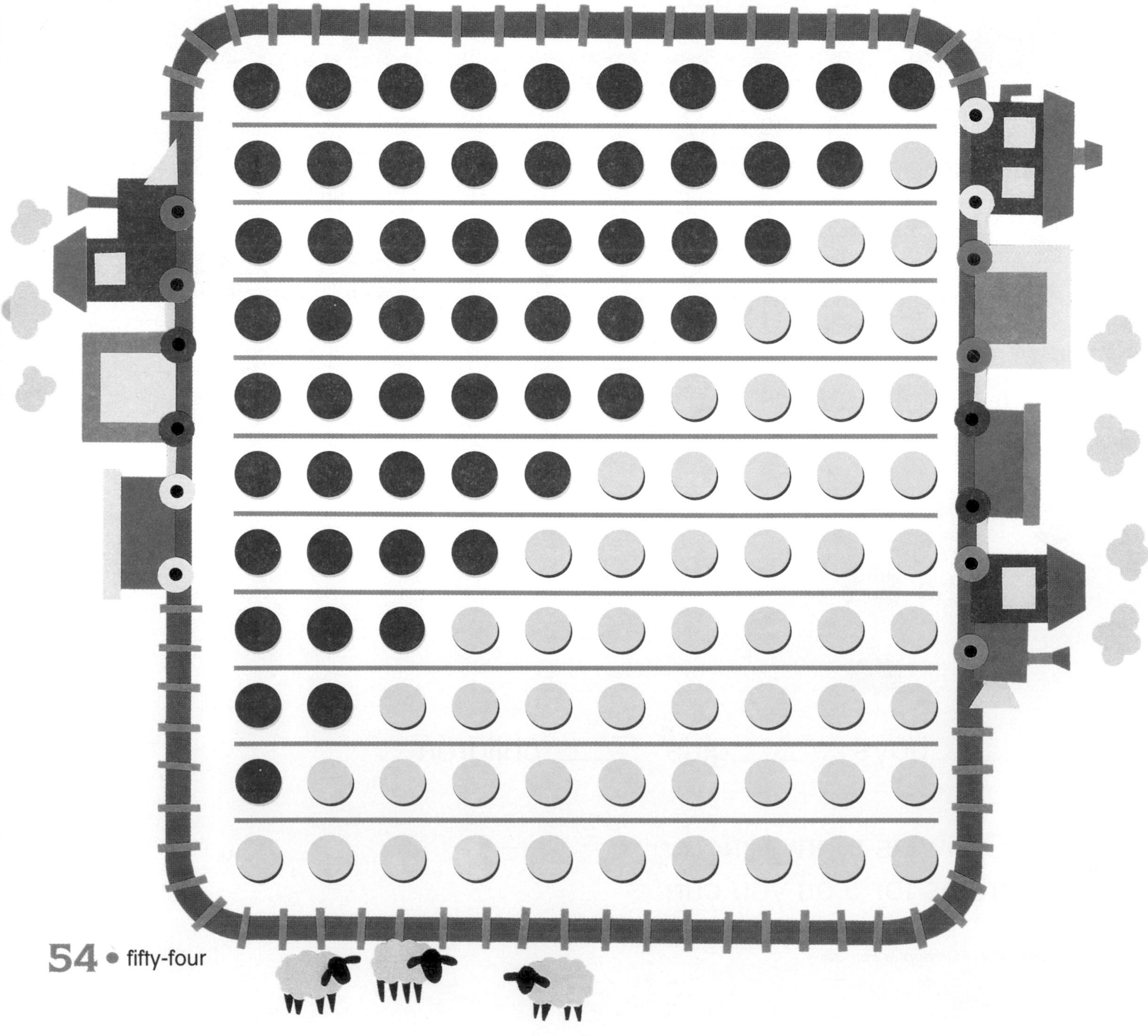

Real-Life Investigation

Applying Counting

Name

Neighborhood Traffic

What is traffic? Does it go by your school?

Working Together

Take a survey.

Decide what to count.

Cultural Note

One way people get around in Haiti is on buses called *tap-taps.*

Show how many your group counted.

Decision Making

Decide how to show what you learned about traffic.
You could make a class graph.

Write a report.

1. Show how you counted and recorded.
2. Tell what the class graph shows.

More to Investigate

PREDICT What if you counted at a different time.
What would the numbers show?

EXPLORE Choose a different time.
Take a survey.
Make a new class graph.

FIND How are the graphs the same?
How are the graphs different?

Name ____________________

More Parts and Totals

You need 10 counters

and a 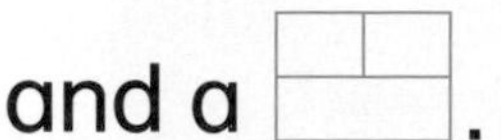.

► Show the parts.

► Write the total.

1
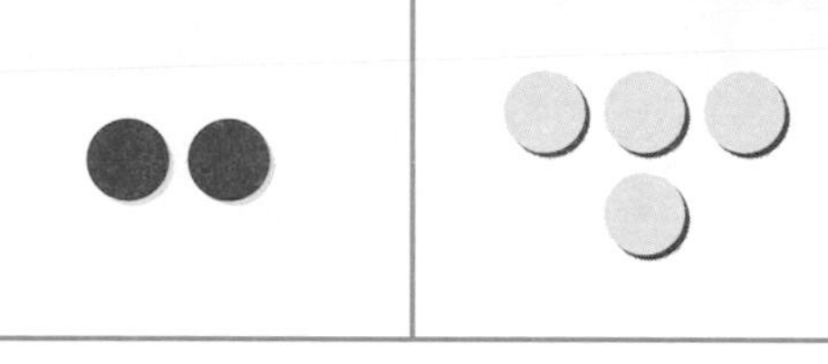

Total: 6

2
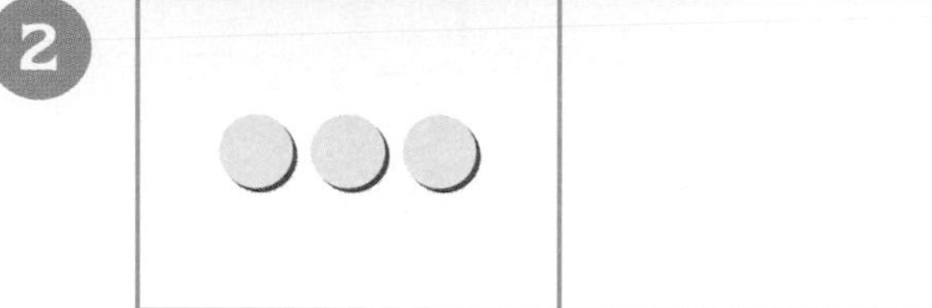

Total: ____

3
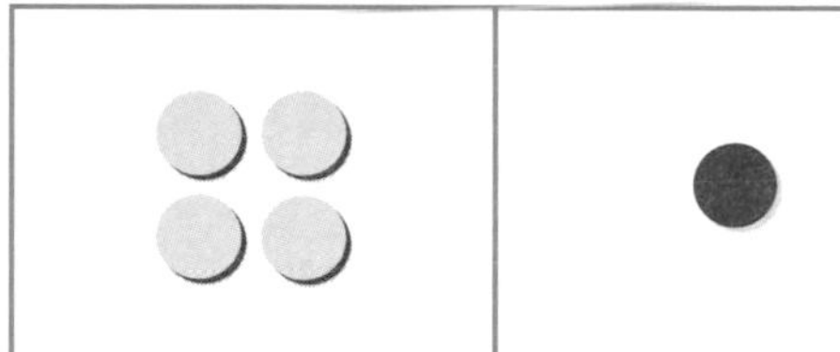

Total: ____

4
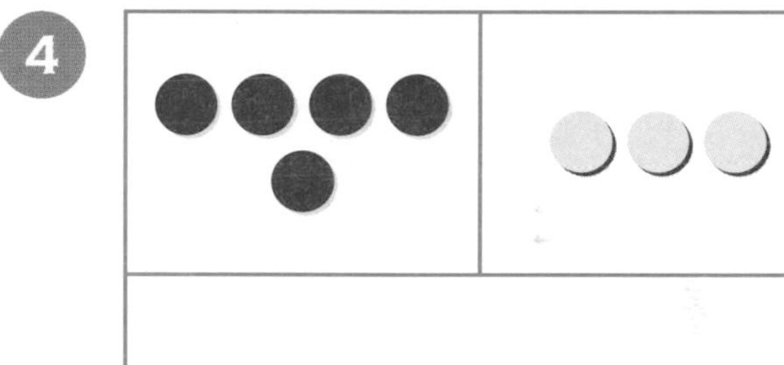

Total: ____

5
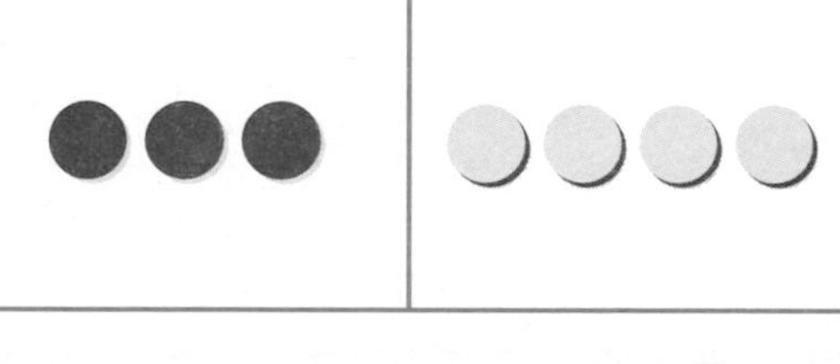

Total: ____

6
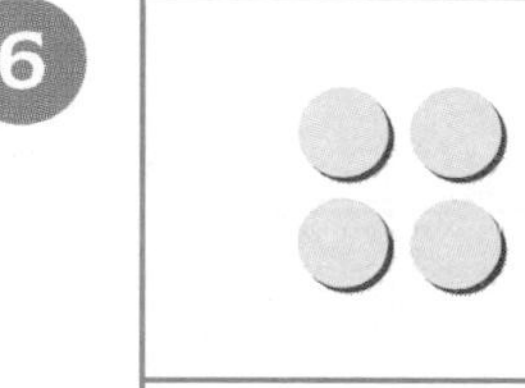

Total: ____

Suppose you move a red counter to a yellow part. Does the total change? Why?

Try These!

How many cars in all?
Find the total.

Total: 5

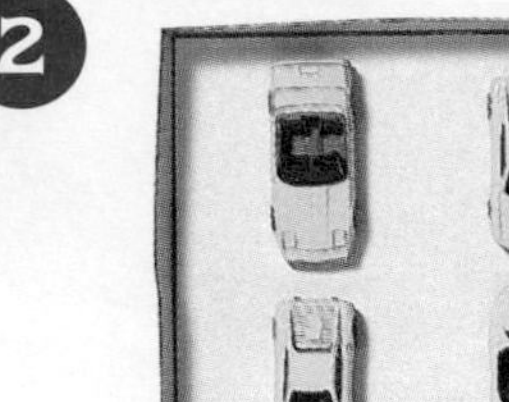 

Total: ____

Total: ____

 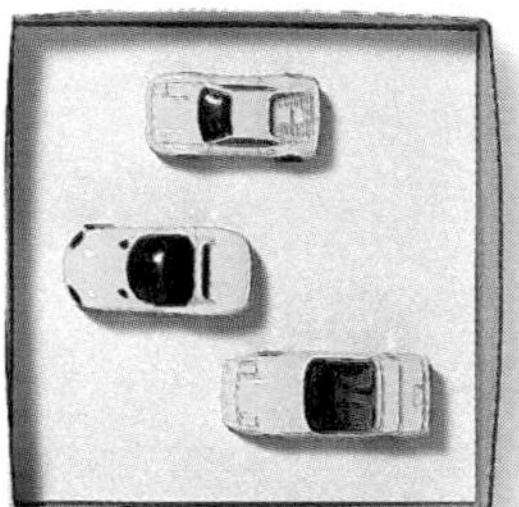

Total: ____

 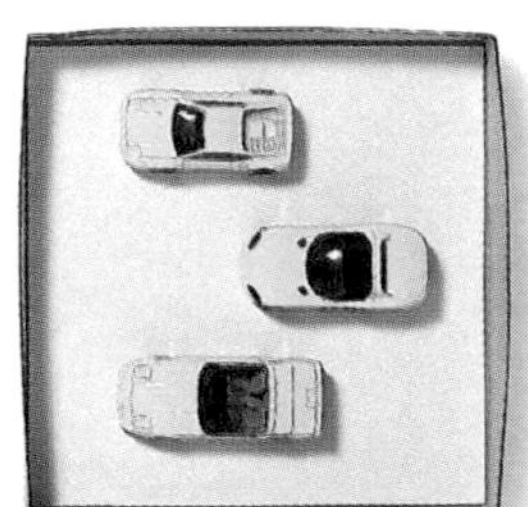

Total: ____

Total: ____

Total: ____

Total: ____

Ask your child to explain how to find the total number of cars in the pairs of boxes.

Name

You need 10  and a 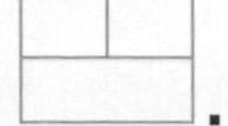.

Find the total.

1

2	5
7	

2

1	4

3

2	2

4

6	4

5

2	4

6

3	1

7

0	1

8

5	3

9

7	1

Critical Thinking How can you show 8 another way?

Try These!

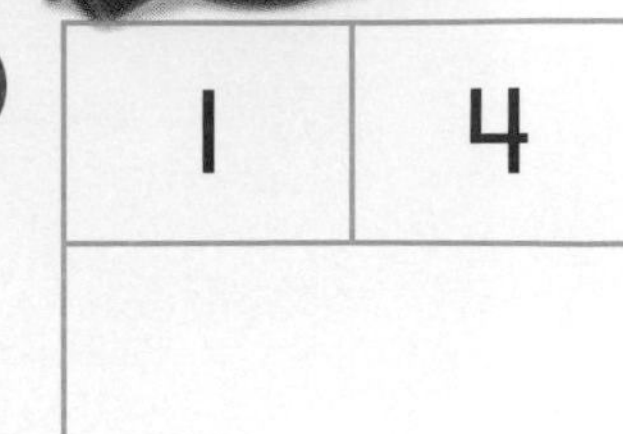

Find the total.

1

2	2
4	

2

0	2

3

1	4

4

2	1

5

5	2

6

4	5

Mixed Review

Write how many.

7

____

8

____

9

____

10

____

At Home

Put 3 things in your left hand. Put 2 things in your right hand. Ask your child to find the total.

Name

Working Together

You need 10 .

- Take turns.
- You show one part.
- Your partner shows the missing part.
- Write.

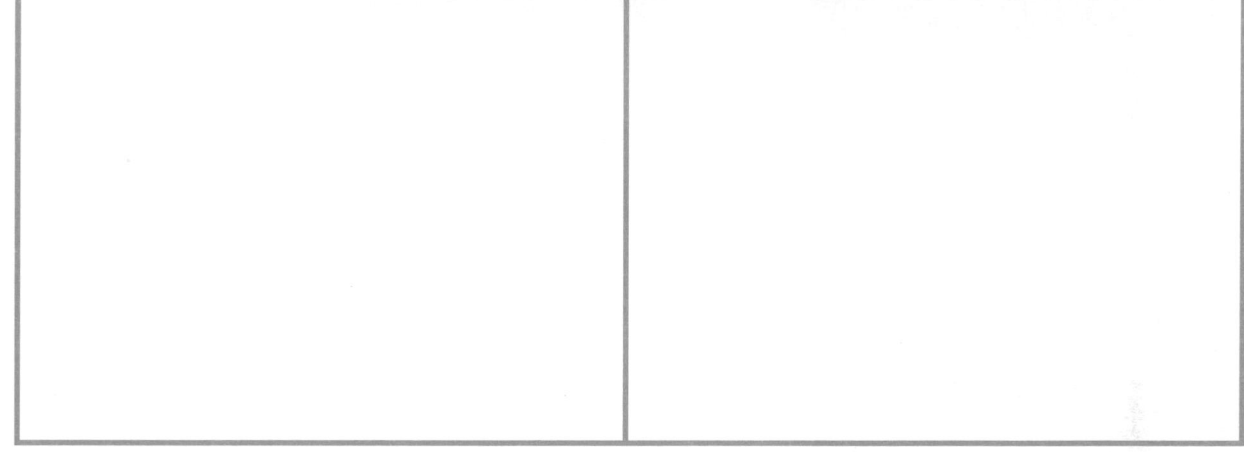

1 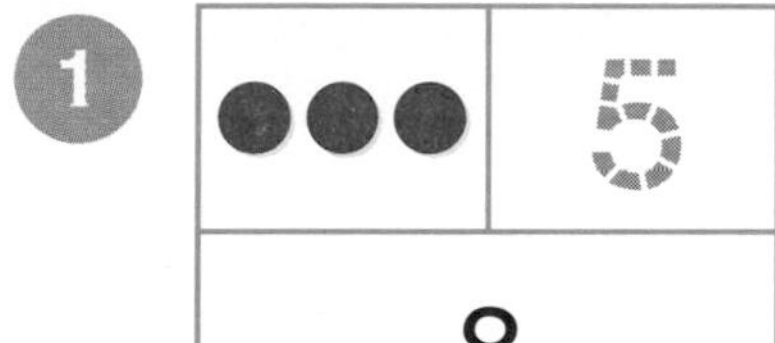

2 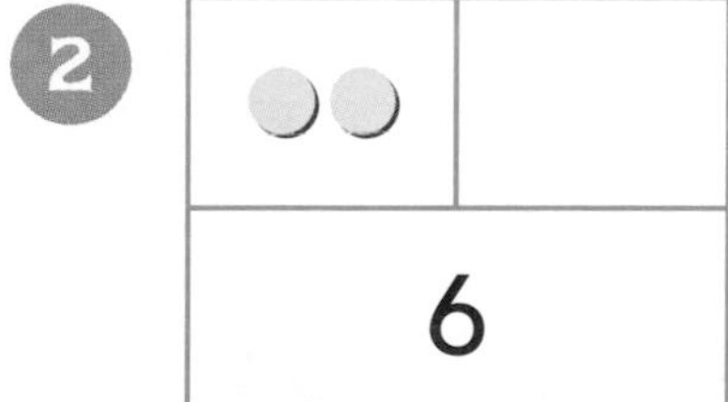

3 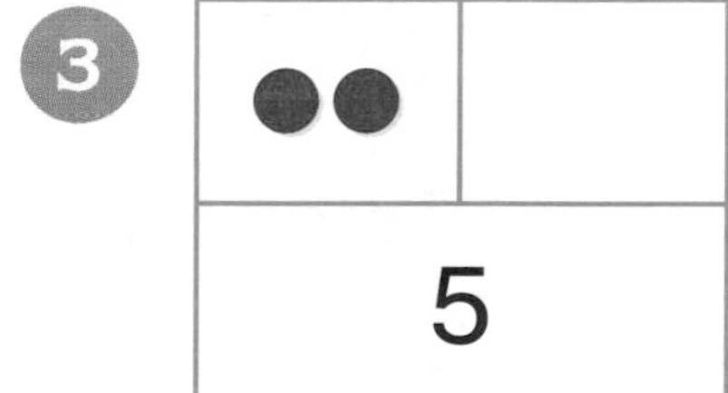

4 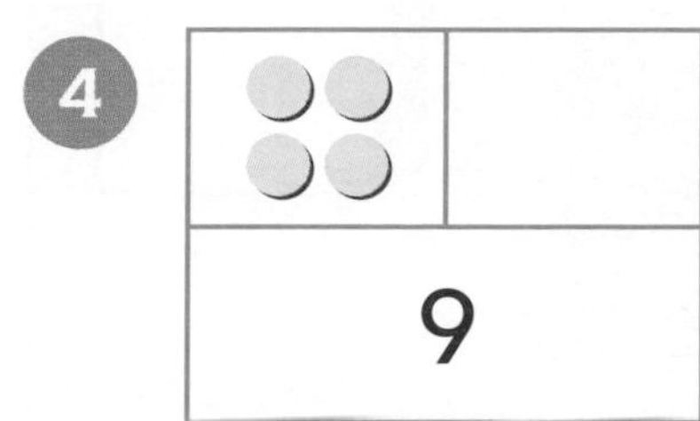

5 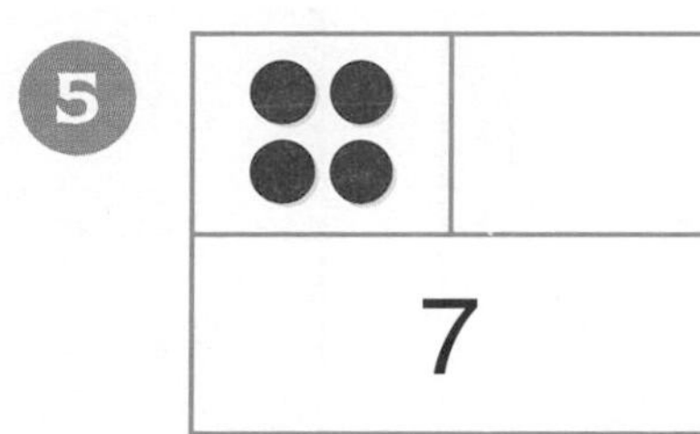

6 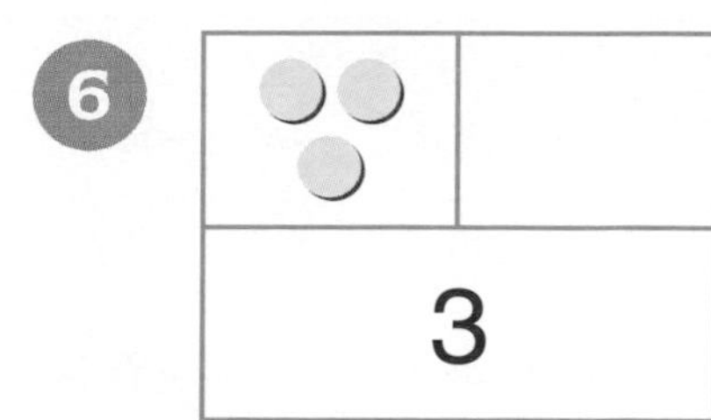

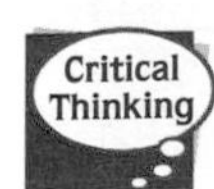

When can two parts be the same number?

Try These!

Use counters if you want to.

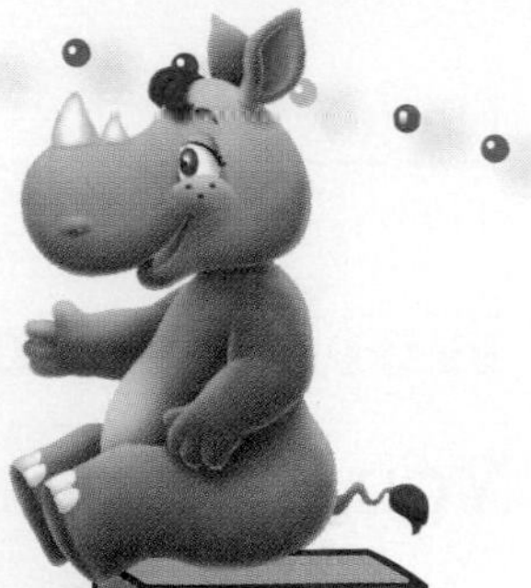

How many trucks are in the box?

1. 2
Total: 7 trucks

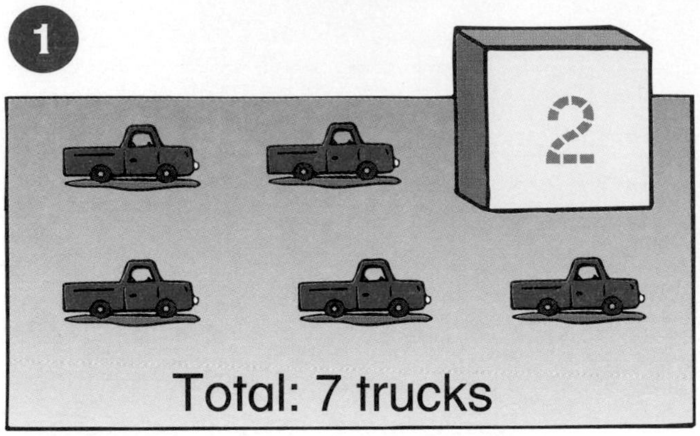

2. Total: 4 trucks

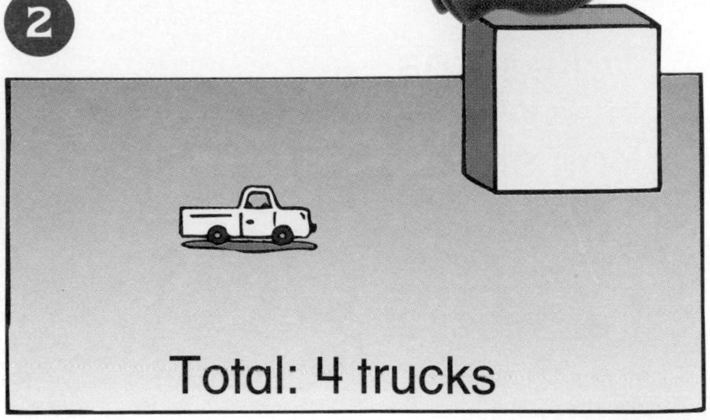

3. Total: 8 trucks

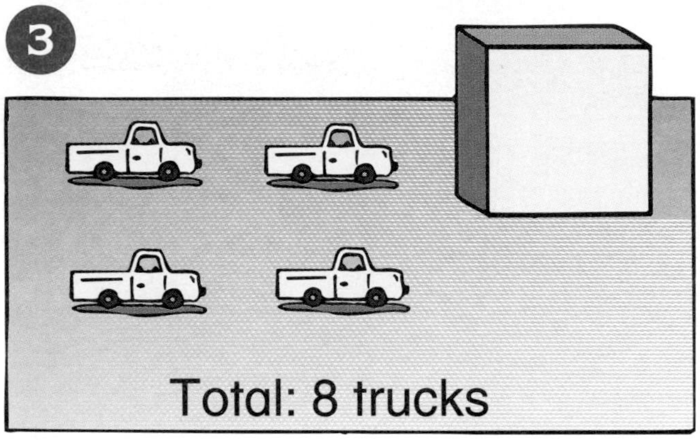

4. Total: 6 trucks

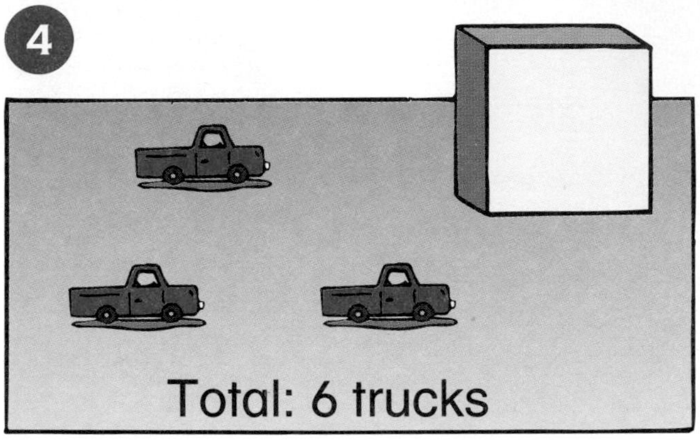

5. Total: 5 trucks

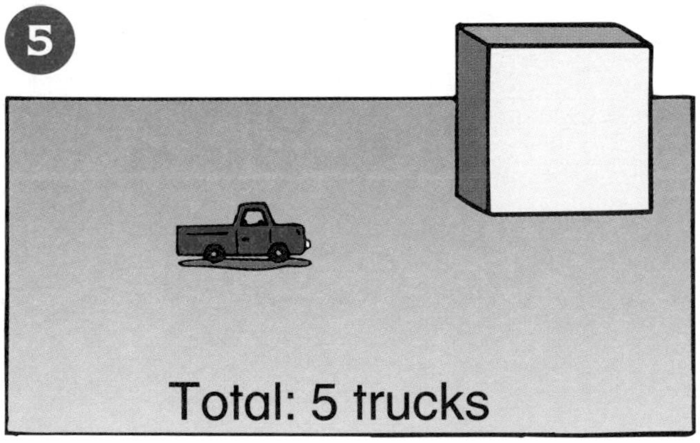

6. Total: 9 trucks

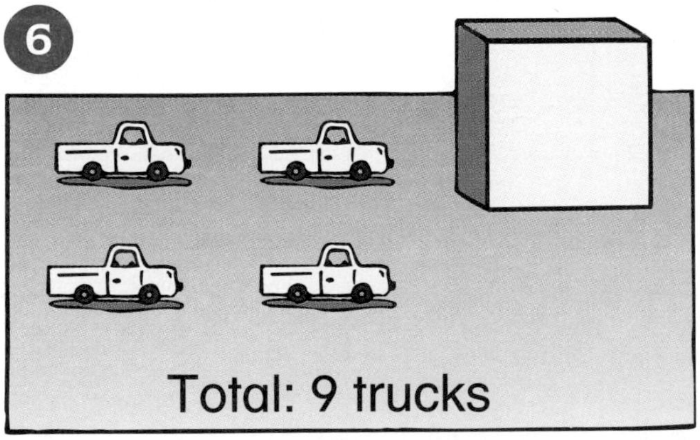

7. Total: 10 trucks

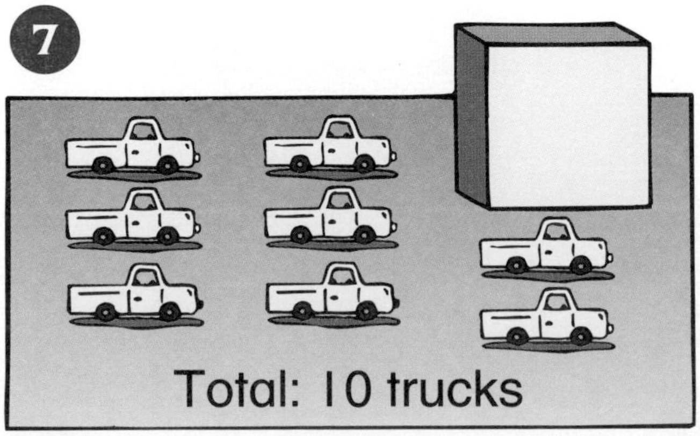

8. Total: 7 trucks

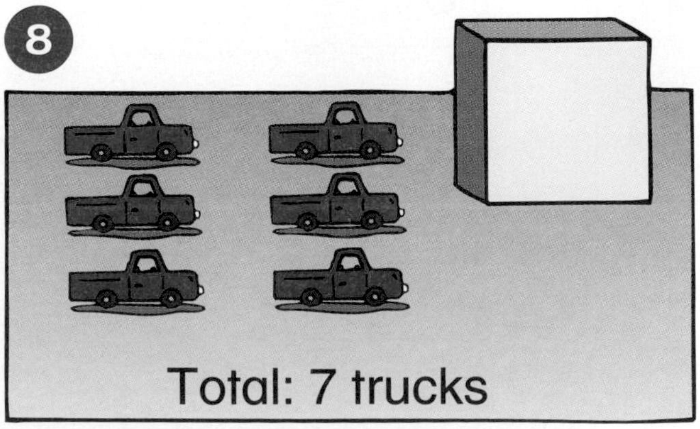

Tell a partner about the trucks in the boxes.

Show your child 8 pennies. Hide some with your hand. Ask your child how many are hidden.

Name

Find the Missing Part

You need 10 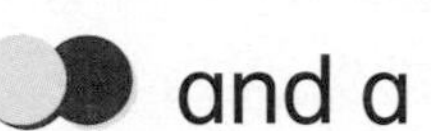 and a .

- Show the total.
- Show the part.
- Find the missing part.
- Write.

1.

2	4
6	

2.

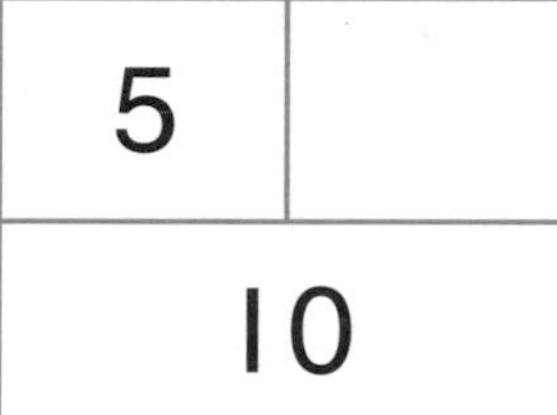

5	
10	

3.

1	
7	

4.

6	
8	

5.

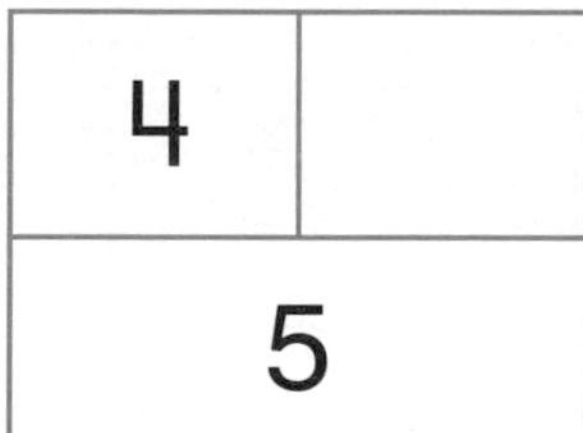

4	
5	

6.

0	
4	

7.

5	
9	

8.

2	
7	

9.

1	
3	

Is the missing part more or less than the total? Why?

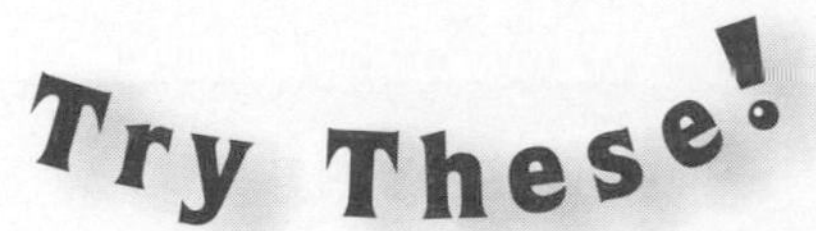

Find the missing part.

2

3	
10	

3

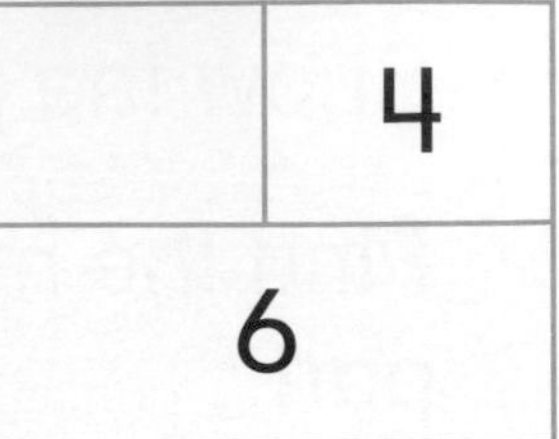

4

2	
2	

5

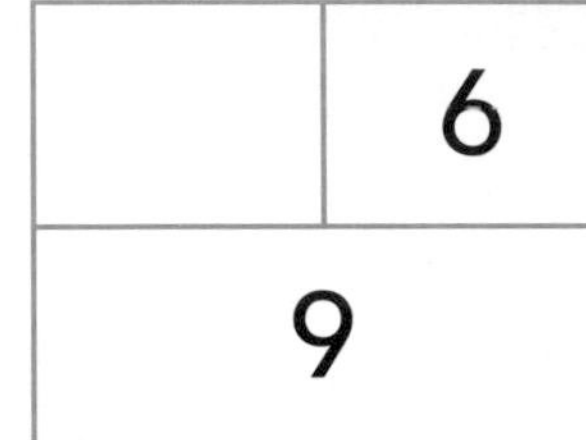

6

	4
8	

More to Explore Logical Reasoning

Ring the correct box.

The box has 2 cars.

It has more trucks than cars.

The box has 3 boats.

It has more boats than planes.

Ask your child to tell you a math story about one of the animal pictures.

Name

Guess and Count

You need paper and 10 .

Listen to the rules.

Winner: the player with the most ✔

Total	Part	Guess	✔

Total	Part	Guess	✔

Total	Part	Guess	✔

Total	Part	Guess	✔

Total	Part	Guess	✔

Total	Part	Guess	✔

Total	Part	Guess	✔

Total	Part	Guess	✔

Find the total.

1 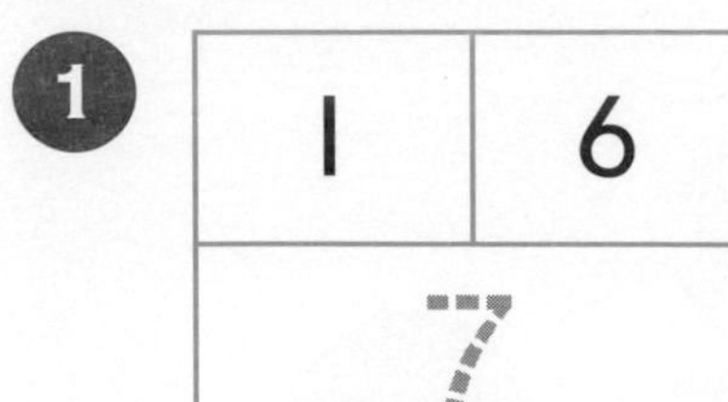

2		3	
8	0	3	2

4		5		6	
4	5	5	5	2	1

Find the missing part.

7		8		9	
3	4	5		0	
7		8		4	

10		11		12	
2			3	3	
9		10		6	

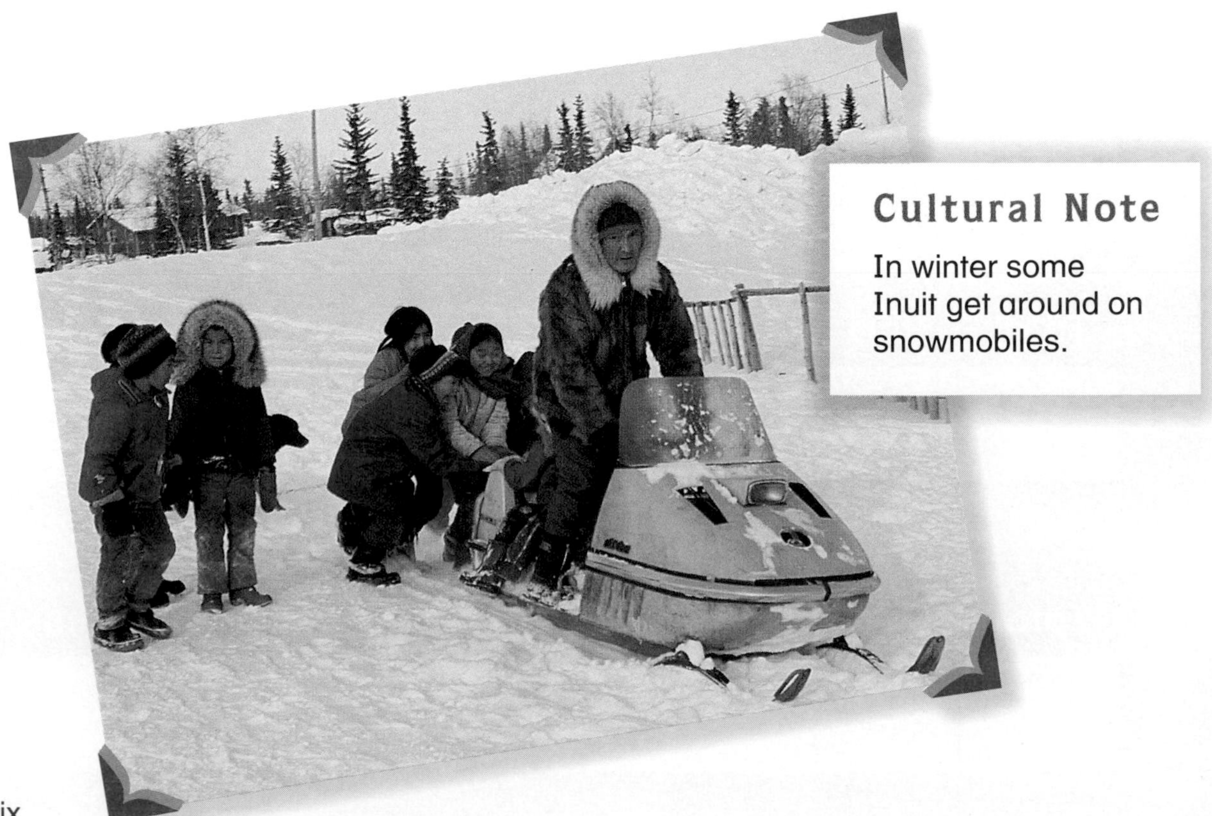

Cultural Note

In winter some Inuit get around on snowmobiles.

Name ______________________

Problem Solvers at Work

Read
Plan
Solve
Look Back

What Is the Question?

 Listen to the problem.

How many green cars?

 What does the problem tell you?

 cars  blue cars

What do you need to find?

____ green cars

2

How many children?

 What does the problem tell you?

____ girls ____ boys

What do you need to find?

____ children

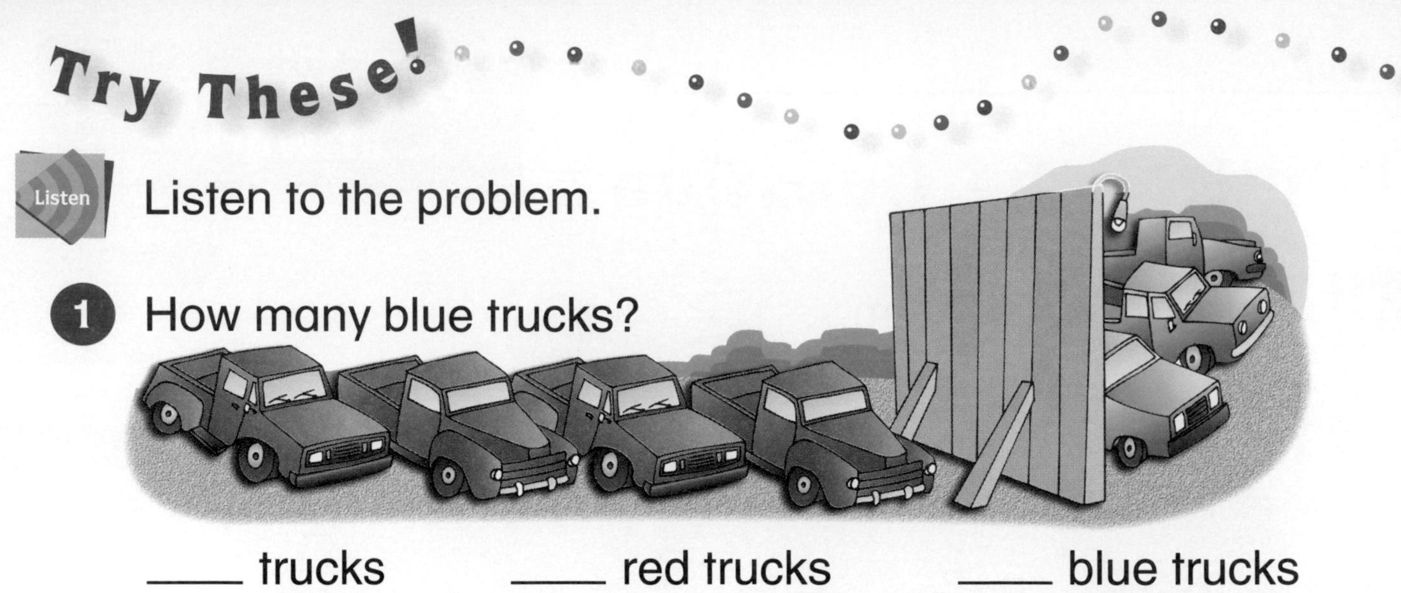

Listen to the problem.

1 How many blue trucks?

____ trucks ____ red trucks ____ blue trucks

Kara said there were 7 blue trucks.
What did she do wrong?

Gericol Goodman
Elephant's Fork School
Suffolk, Virginia

2 Solve Gericol's problem. ____ hearts

3 Draw a picture. Write a question.

Your partner's answer to your question: ____________________

Your answer to your question: ____________________

At Home: We are learning to solve oral problems. Have your child make up problems for the pictures and questions on this page.

Name

Chapter Review

Color different trains for 6.
Write the parts and total.

Parts Total

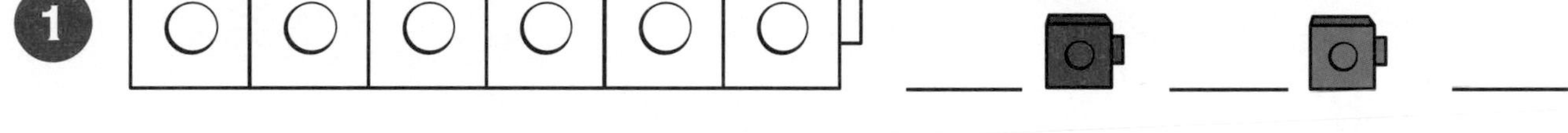

1 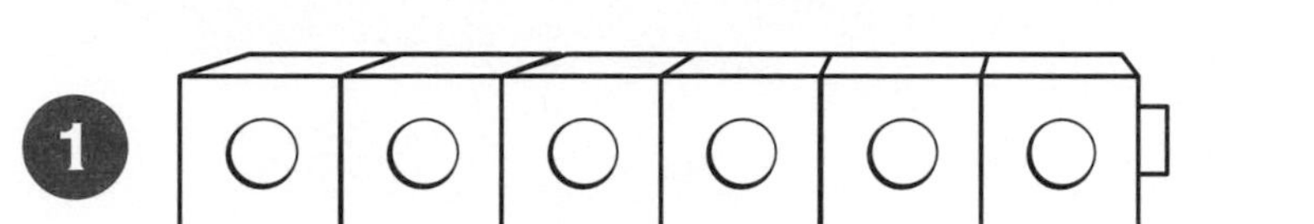 ___ ___ ___

2 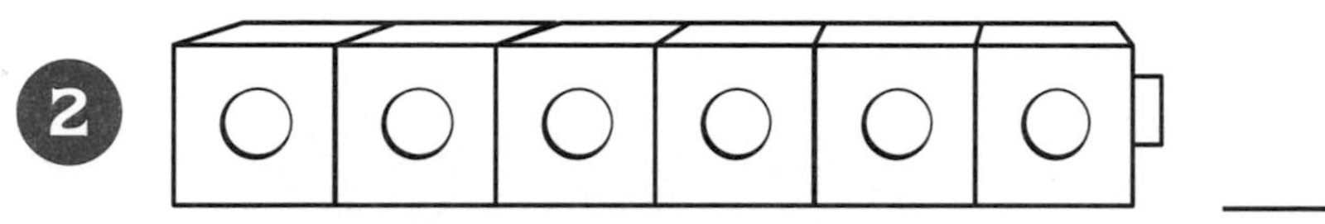 ___  ___  ___

Find the total.

3 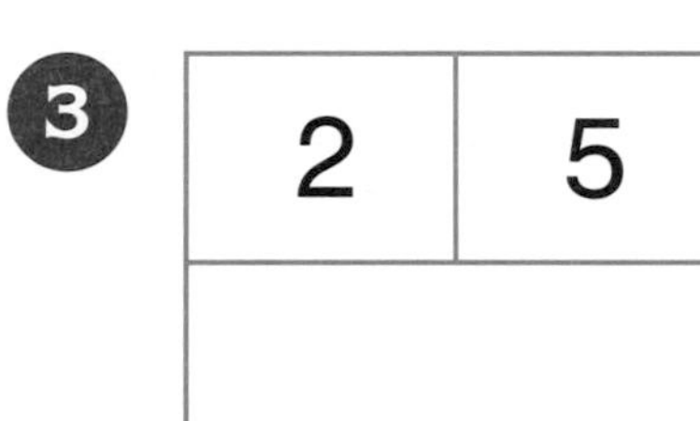

4 

5

5	3

6

4	2

Find the missing part.

7 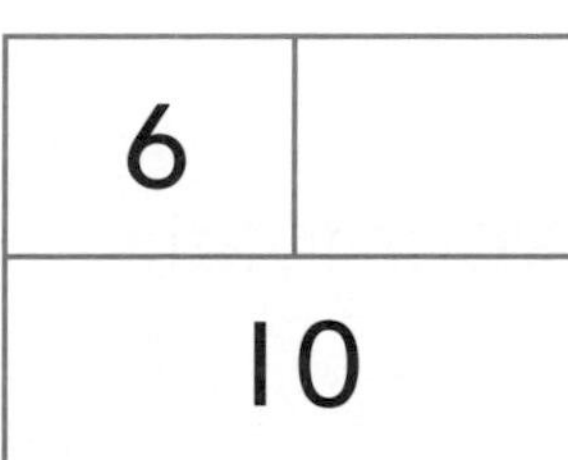

8

2	
8	

Listen to the problem.

9

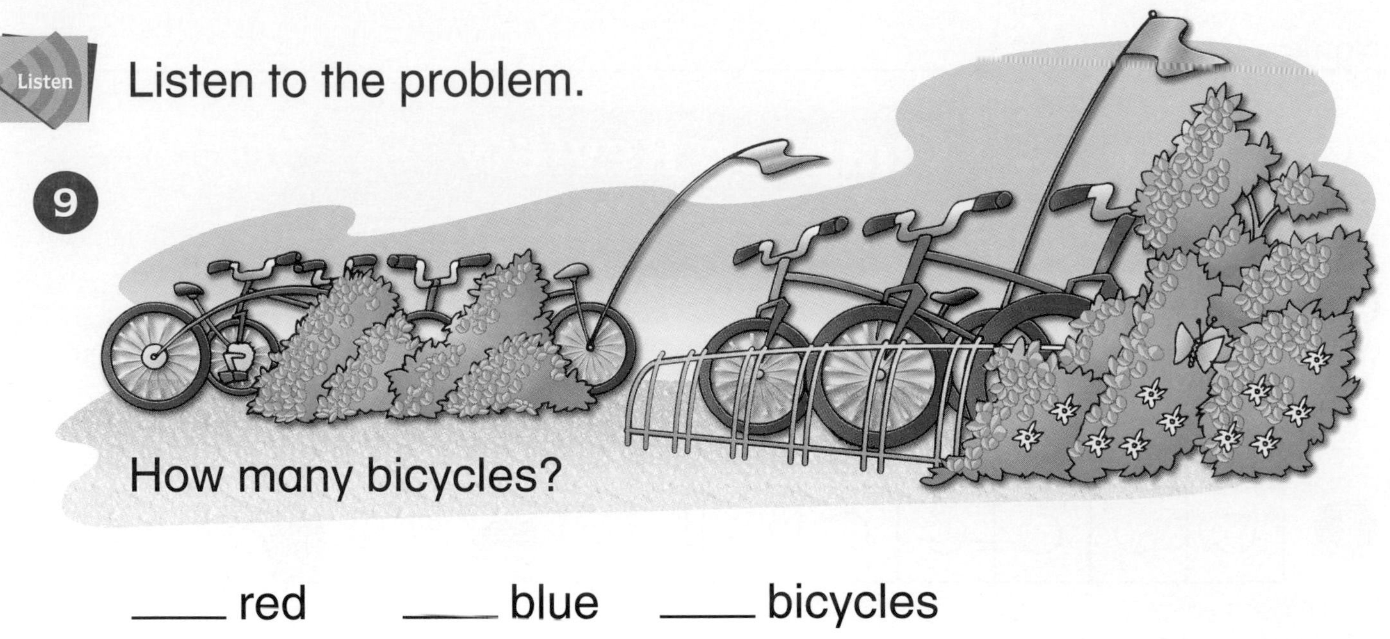

How many bicycles?

____ red ____ blue ____ bicycles

10

How many animals? ____

What Do You Think?

What do you think about finding parts and totals?
☑ Check one.

☐ Easy ☐ A little hard ☐ Hard

Why? ______________________________

Choose a total.
Show how you find parts for your total.

Name

Chapter Test

Color different trains for 5.
Write the parts and total.

Parts | Total

1 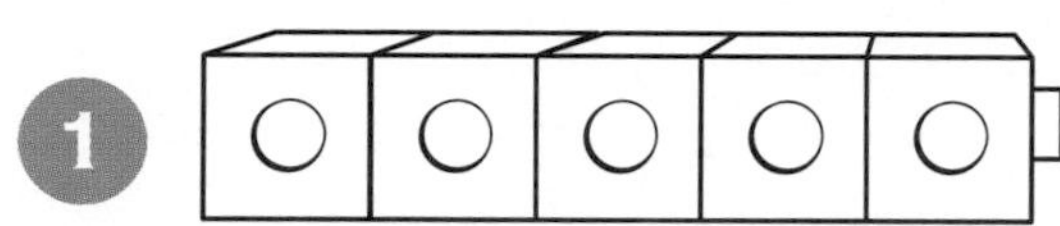 ____ ____ ____

2 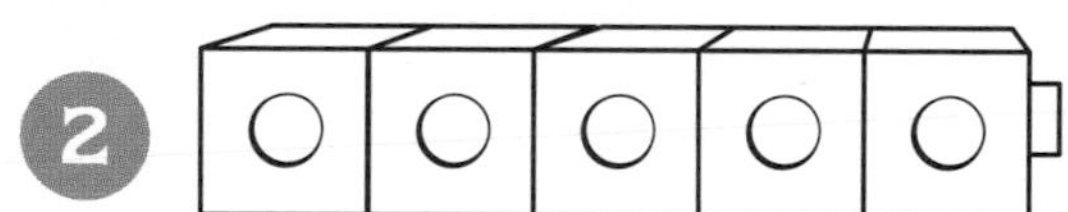 ____ ____ ____

Find the total or missing part.

3 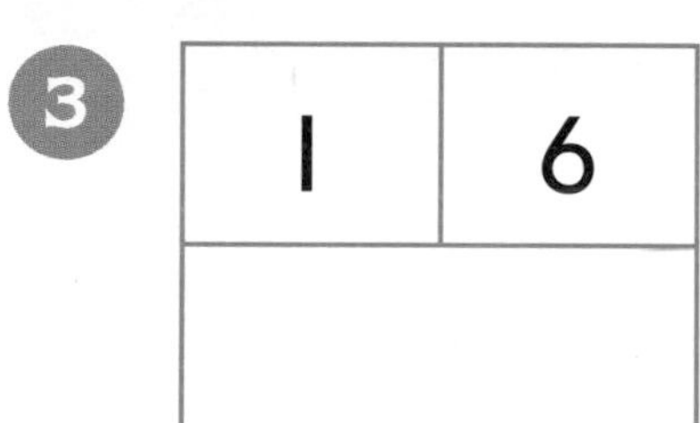

1	6

4 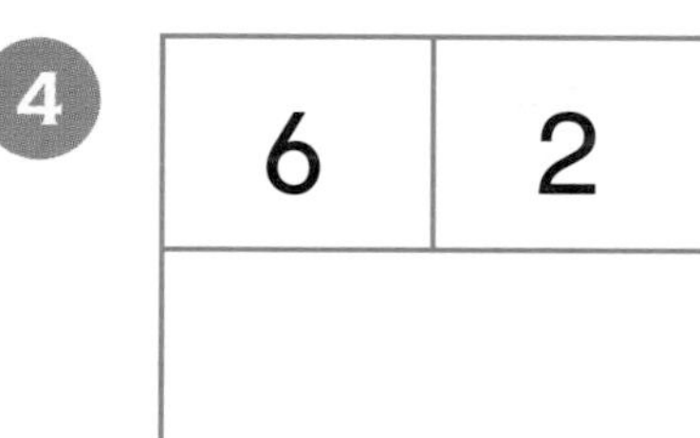

6	2

5 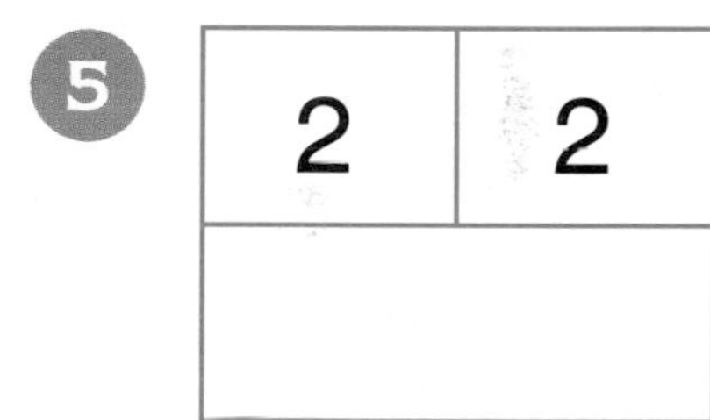

2	2

6 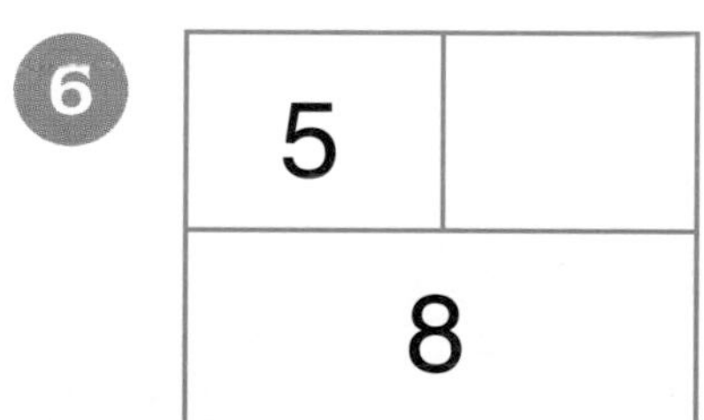

5	
8	

7 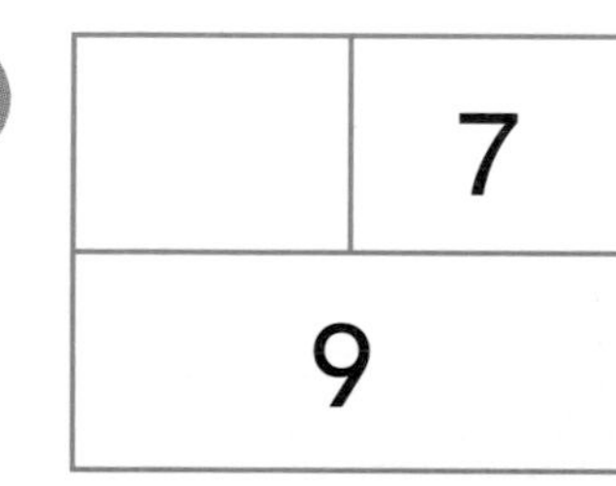

	7
9	

8 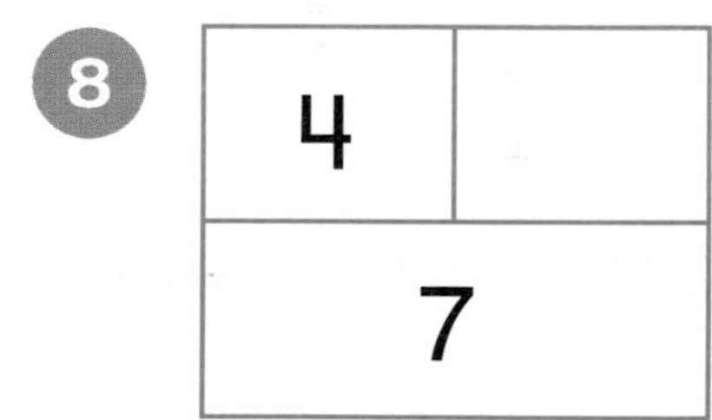

4	
7	

Listen to the problems.

9 

____ boys ____ girls ____ children

10 

____ red boats ____ blue boats ____ boats

What Did You Learn?

Listen to the problem.

Show trains for 7.
Write how many in each part.

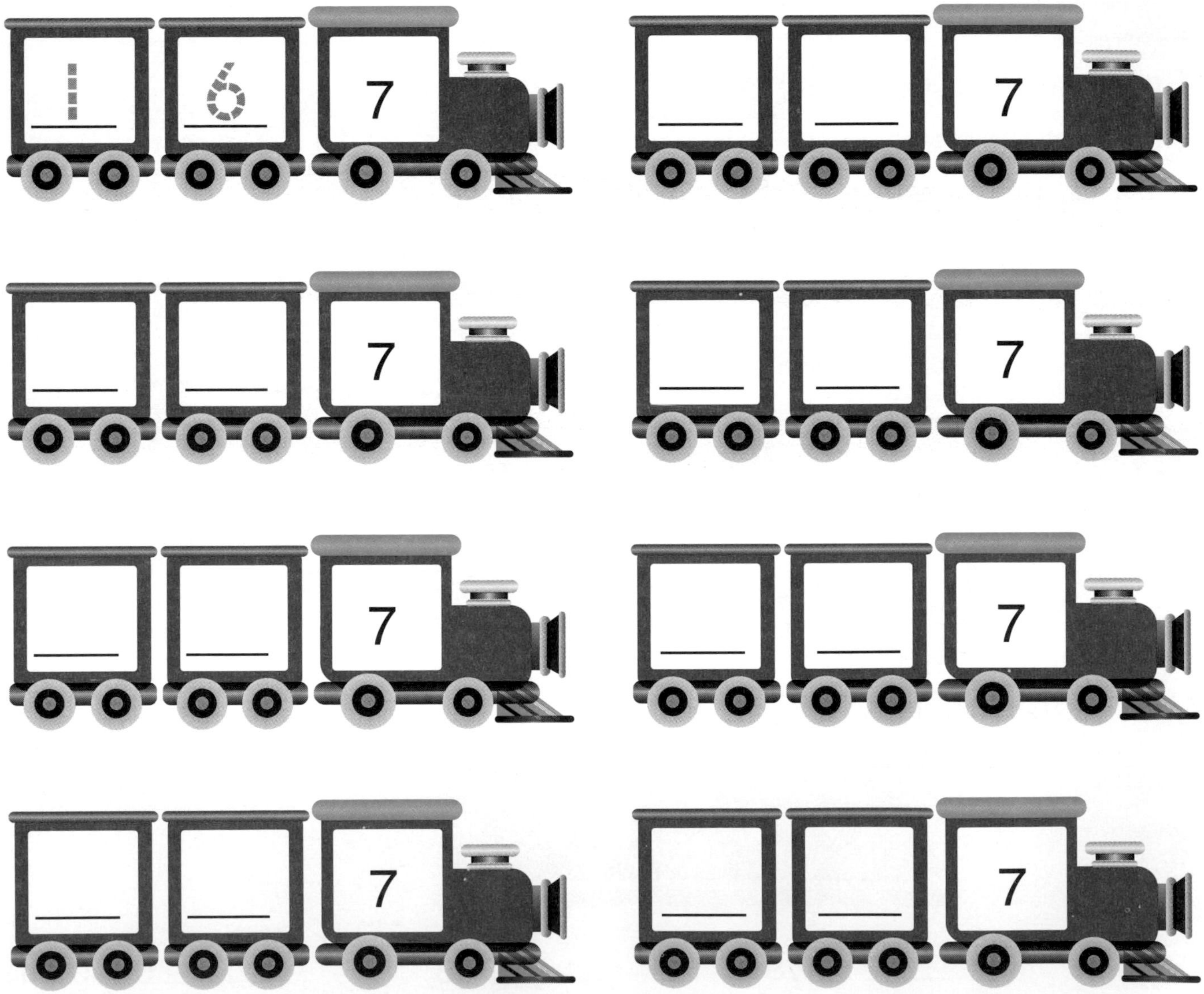

1 ___ 6 ___ 7

___ ___ 7

___ ___ 7

___ ___ 7

___ ___ 7

___ ___ 7

___ ___ 7

___ ___ 7

You may want to put this page in your portfolio.

Math Connection

Functions

Name ______________________________

Complete a Table

Draw. Complete the table.

Write how many.

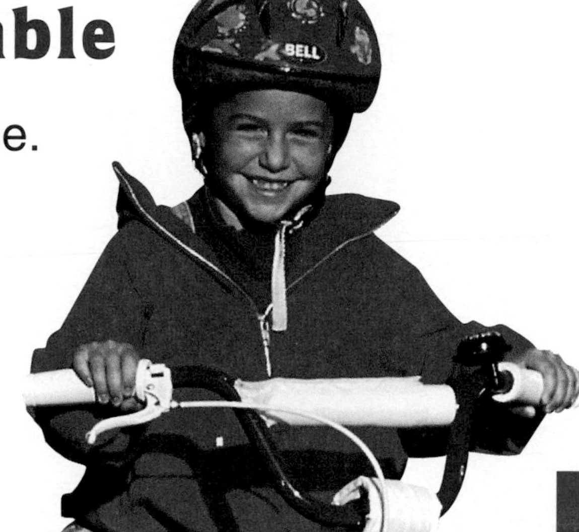

	Bikes	Wheels
	1	2

Make a Pattern

You know how to make patterns.

Tell what shape comes next.

How many △? ____ How many □? ____

How many shapes in all? ____

At the Computer

1. Use stamps. Make a pattern.
2. Record the parts. Record the total.
3. Make another pattern.

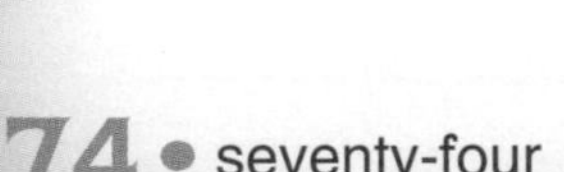

Home Connection

Chapter 2 Wrap-Up

Name ______________________________

Wheel Count

Where we counted: ______________________________

Number of wheels: ________________

Number of vehicles: ________________

We counted more ________________ than ________________.

Take your child to a spot where there are bicycles or cars. Try a parking lot, driveway, garage, or other place. Have your child count the number of vehicles and the number of wheels and tell whether he or she counted more wheels or vehicles.

Dear Family,

We are starting a new chapter in our mathematics book. We are going to learn about adding numbers. This is like parts and totals, but we will use pictures and numbers to show addition.

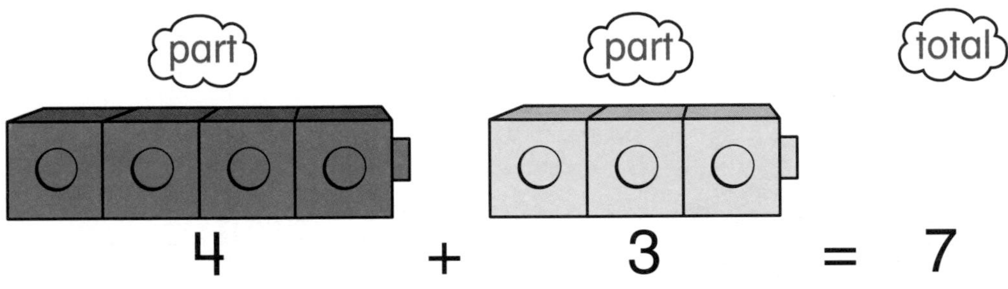

We will also be talking about favorite foods and shopping for groceries. Please help me complete this interview.

Your child,

____
Signature

Interview

Where do you like to shop for food?
(You may check more than one.)

- ❑ Supermarket
- ❑ Farmer's market
- ❑ Neighborhood store
- ❑ Food club
- ❑ Other ______________________

What is your favorite food? ______________________

Food for 10
Beginning to Add

Listen to the story *Feast for 10.*

Tell what you know about shopping for food.

Name

What Do You Know?

You need 10 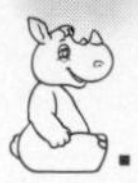 .

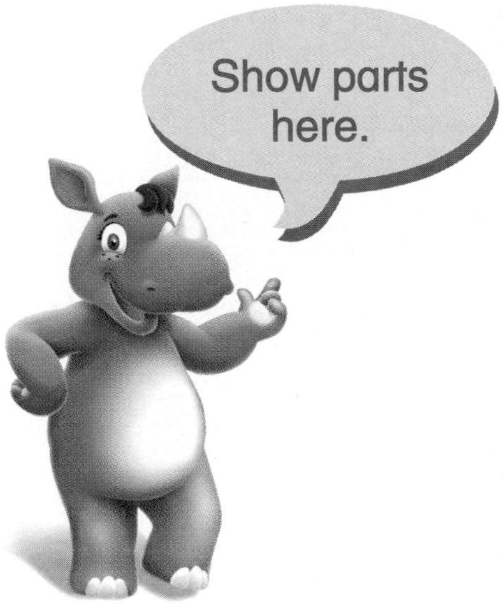

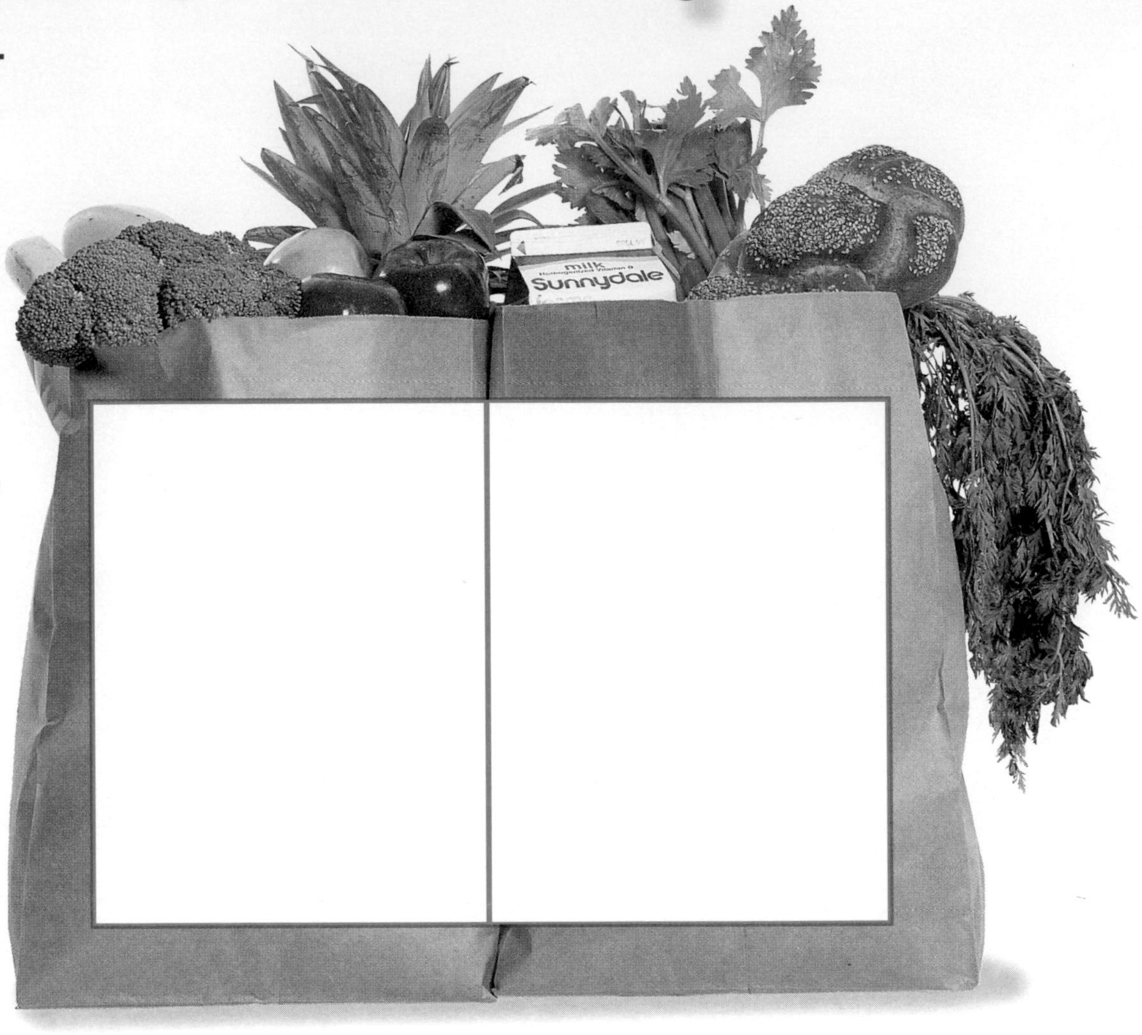

Write the total.

3	2

5	1

4	6

2

7	2

3	4

3	5

Show parts for your favorite number.

Name

Working Together

You need 10 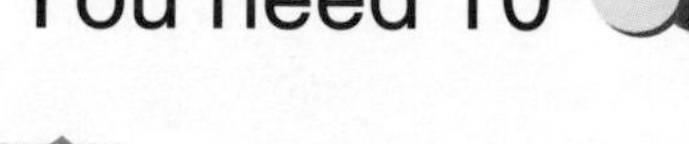.

Listen to the story.

Show the parts. Draw.

Write the total.

	Part	Part	Total
1	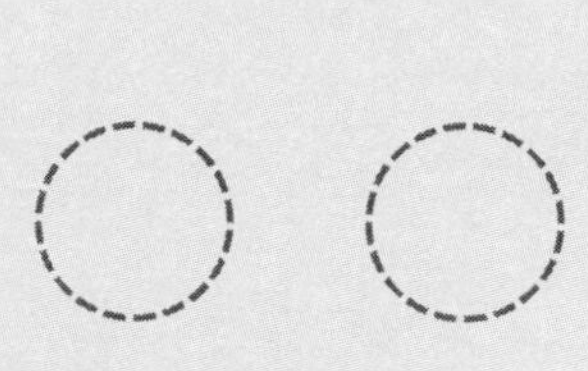 2	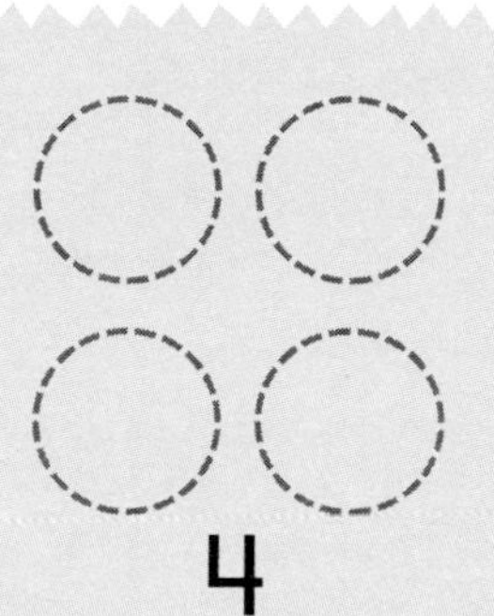 4	6 
2	3 	1 	___ 
3	5	4	___ 

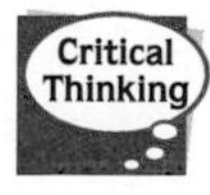

Why do you get the same totals as your partner?

Try These!

Take turns.

You tell a story about parts.
Your partner draws the parts
and writes the total.

	Part	Part	Total
1	○ 1	○ ○ ○ 3	4
2	3	2	___
3	2	5	___
4	5	5	___

Draw and write to show parts and a total.

At Home: Ask your child to tell you a story about exercise 1 above.

Name

You need 10 .

Draw. Add.

1. 1 + 2 = 3

2. 2 + 2 = ____

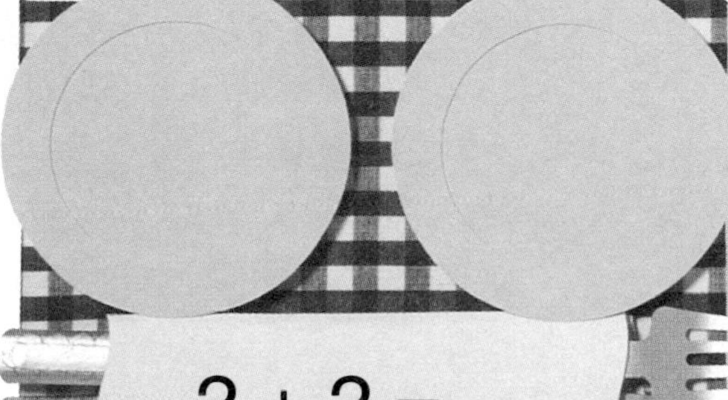

3. 3 + 2 = ____

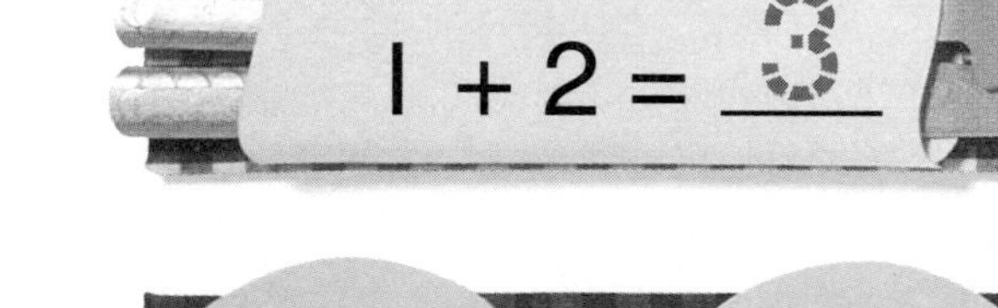

4. 4 + 1 = ____

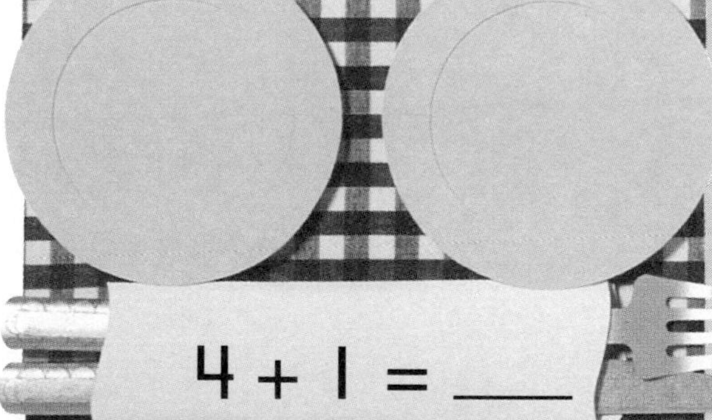

5. 3 + 3 = ____

6. 5 + 2 = ____

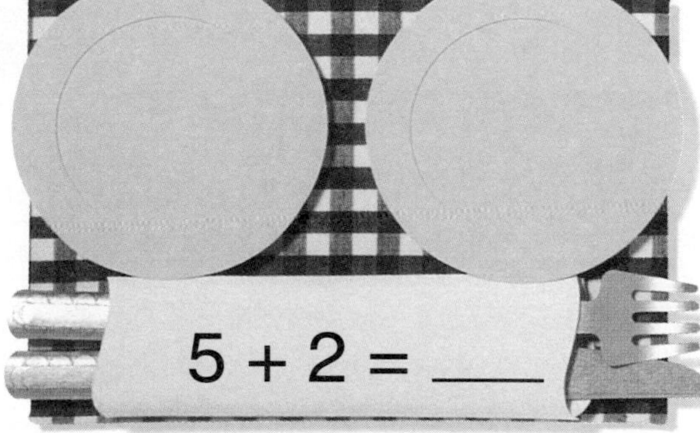

Try These!

Add.

1 + 3 = 4

3 + 4 = ___

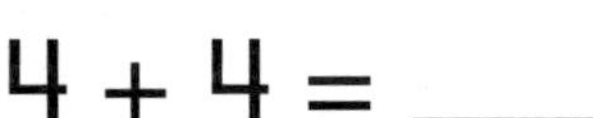

4 + 4 = ___

1 + 5 = ___

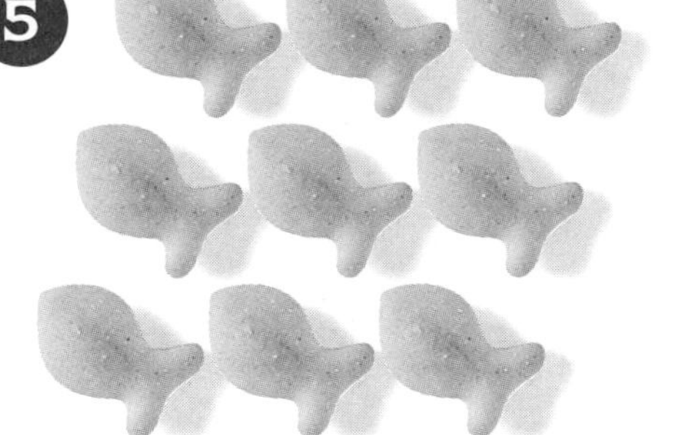

9 + 1 = ___

3 + 3 = ___

Mixed Review

Write the numbers in order.

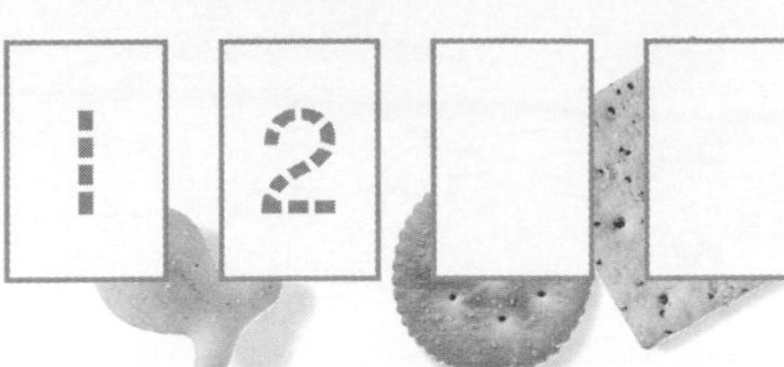

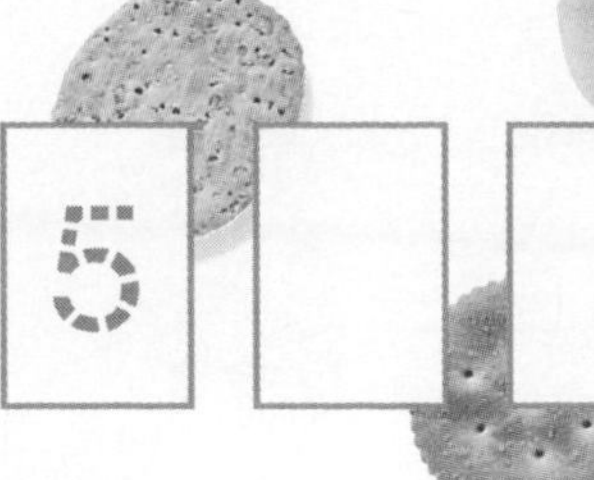

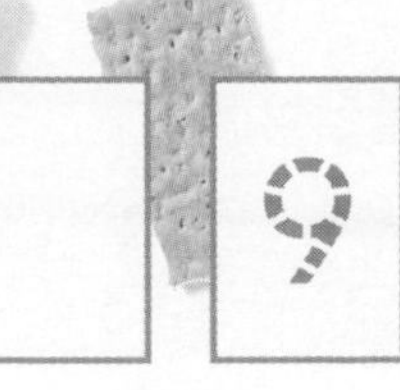

1	2			5				9	

At Home: Your child has begun to add. Have your child tell you about the addition exercises on this page.

Name ____________________

More Addition Sentences

addition sentence 2 + 1 = 3

sum

Write the addition sentence.

1.

3 + 1 = 4

2.

1 + 1 = 2

3.

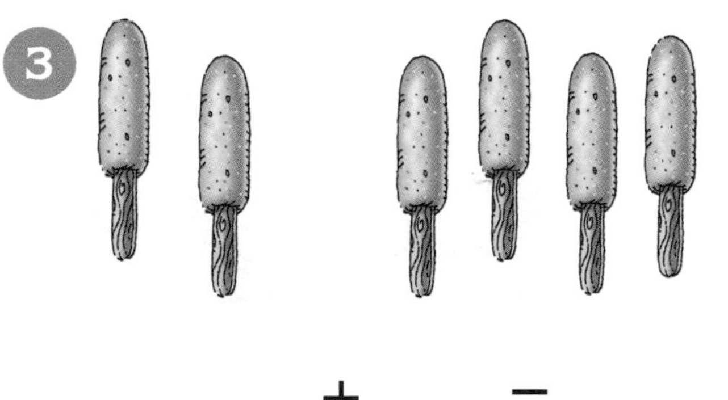

___ + ___ = ___

4.

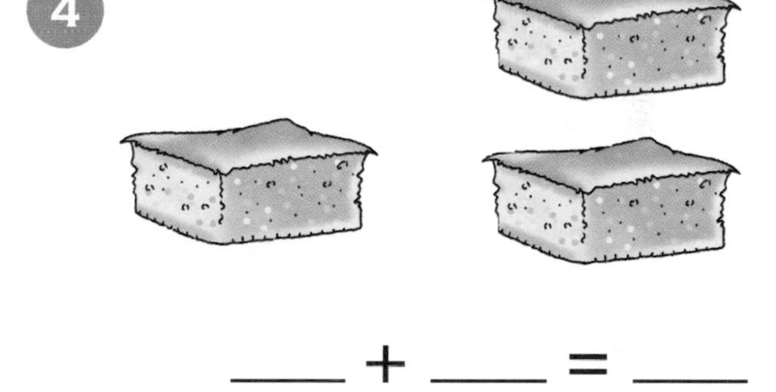

___ + ___ = ___

5.

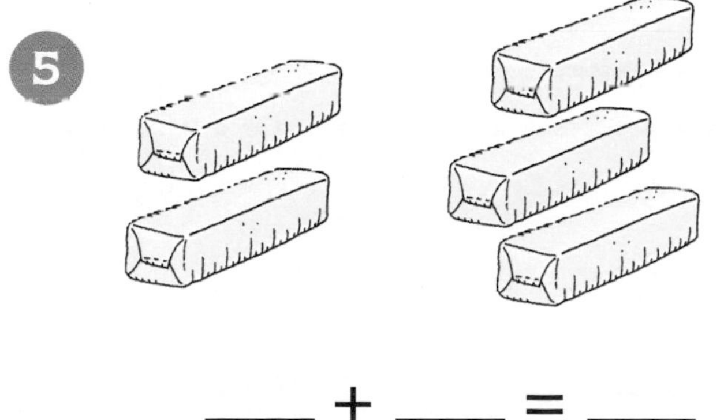

___ + ___ = ___

6.

___ + ___ = ___

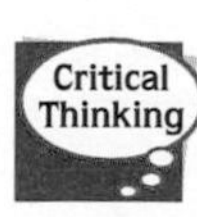

What is an addition story you can tell about 3 + 1?

Try These!

Write the addition sentence.

1

4 + 5 = 9

2

___ + ___ = ___

3
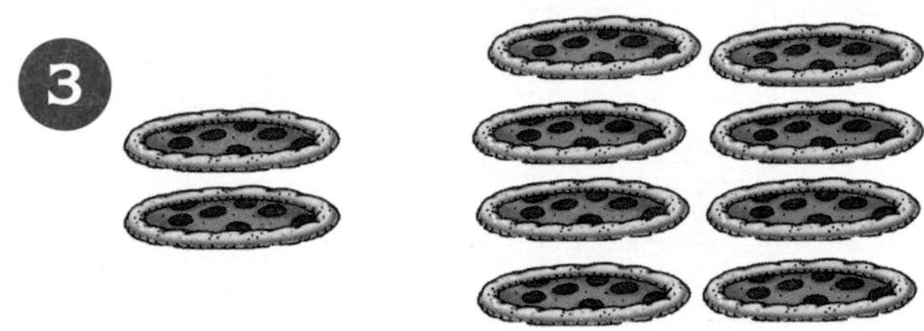

___ + ___ = ___

4
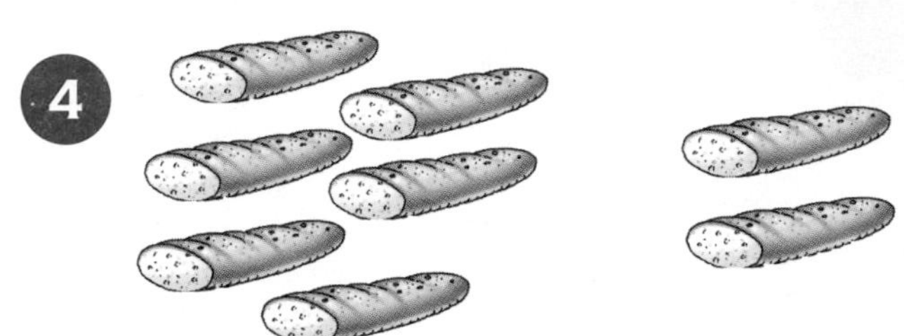

___ + ___ = ___

5
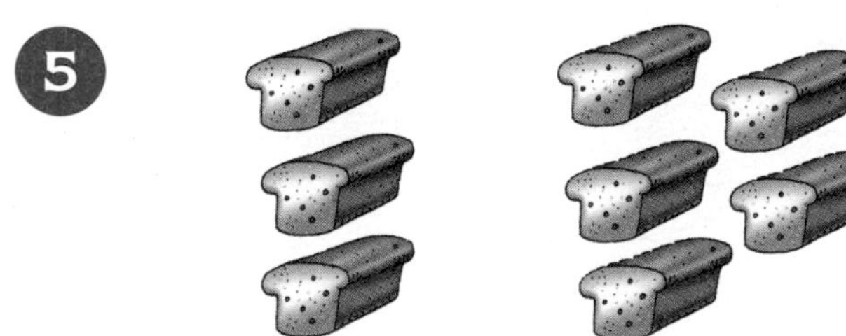

___ + ___ = ___

6

___ + ___ = ___

More to Explore Patterns

Look for a pattern. Complete.

0 + 0 = ___　　1 + 0 = ___　　2 + 0 = ___

3 + 0 = ___　　4 + 0 = ___　　5 + 0 = ___

At Home We are learning to write addition sentences. Have your child tell you about the exercises on this page.

Name ______

Write an Addition Sentence

You need 10 .

Listen to the problem.

Find how many in all.

1. At the store 5 in all

3 + 2 = 5

Tell how you found the answer.

2. At the party ___ in all

___ + ___ = ___

3. At school ___ in all

___ + ___ = ___

Try These!

Make up a problem for the picture.
Find how many in all.

___ in all

___ + ___ = ___

2

___ in all

___ + ___ = ___

3

___ in all

___ + ___ = ___

More to Explore — Spatial Sense

Find how many 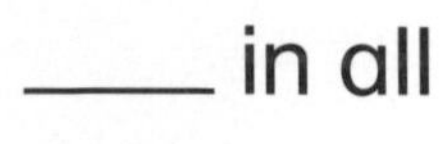 in all.

___ in all

___ + ___ = ___

Ask your child to tell you a story about one of these pictures.

Name

Midchapter Review

Find how many in all.

1. At the party ____ in all

____ + ____ = ____

Add.

2.  

3 + 3 = ____

3.  

1 + 5 = ____

4.   

6 + 2 = ____

5.  

5 + 4 = ____

Write the addition sentence.

6.  

____ + ____ = ____

7.   

____ + ____ = ____

8.  

____ + ____ = ____

9. 

____ + ____ = ____

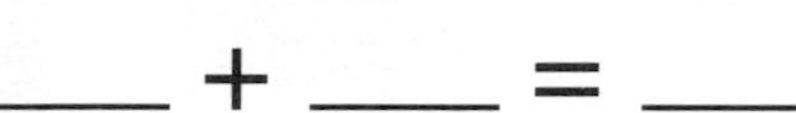

10. What does 2 + 1 = 3 mean?

____

Draw a picture that shows addition.

Extra Practice

Game!

I Show, You Find

You need 2 [rhino counter] and 10 [cube].

Listen

Listen to the rules.

Take turns.

- ► You put [rhino counter] on 2 numbers.
- ► Your partner adds.
- ► Score 1 point if the sum is correct.

Play until you get 10 points.

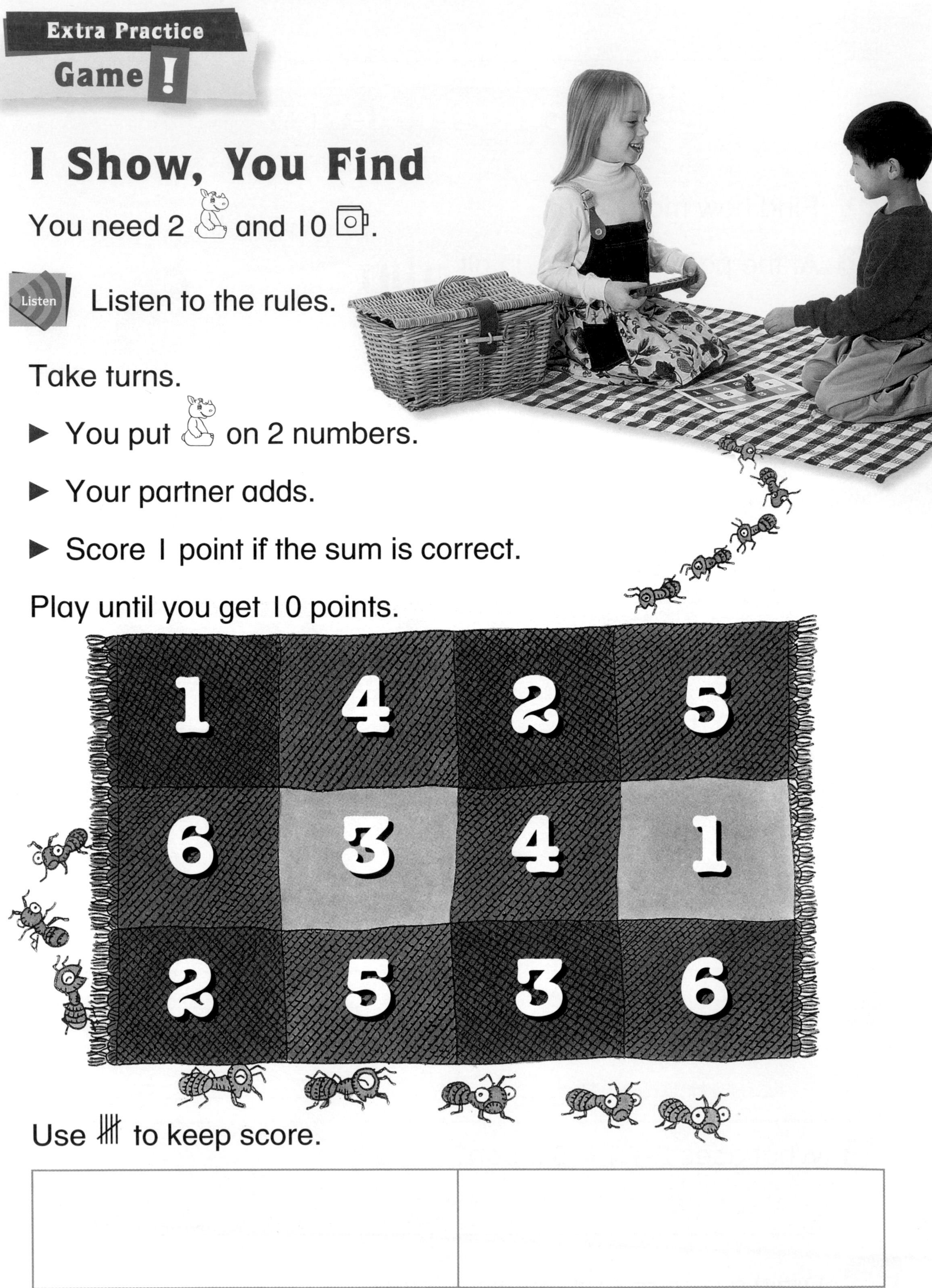

Use |||| to keep score.

Name ______________________

Ice Cream Time

Make an ice cream cone.

Working Together

You need 1 ●, 1 ●, 1 ○, and a crayon.

- Find different ways to stack the ●, ●, and ○.
- Color to show each way.

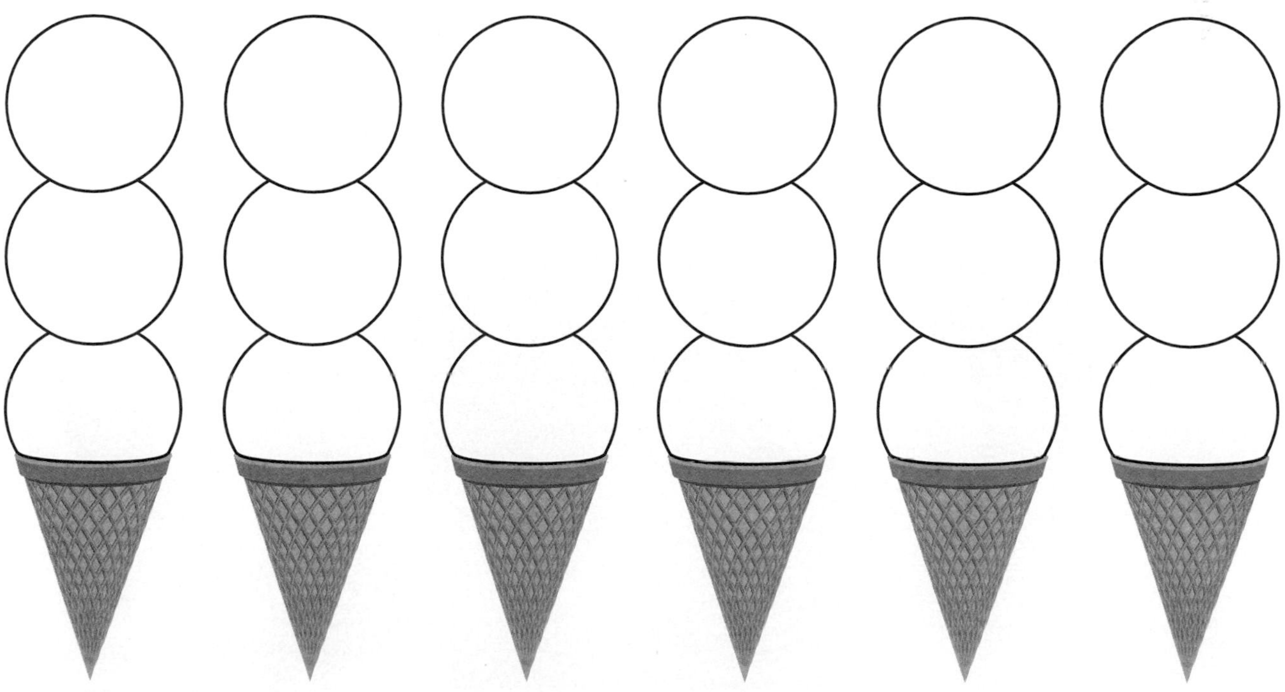

How many ways to stack? ____

Decision Making

1. Choose your own 3 colors.
   Find different ways to stack the ice cream.

Write a report.

2. Tell how many ways you found to stack each time.

3. How do you know you found all the ways to stack?

More to Investigate

PREDICT What if you have a ●, ●, ▼, and ▽.
How many ways to stack?

EXPLORE Try it.
Color to show each way.

FIND Did you find all the ways?
How do you know?

Name ____________________

Addition Fact Pairs

You need 10 .

Show 🪙 here.

Find how many cents in all.

1. 2¢ + 4¢ = 6 ¢ 4¢ + 2¢ = 6 ¢

Why is the sum the same?

2. 5¢ + 0¢ = ___¢ 0¢ + 5¢ = ___¢

3. 3¢ + 4¢ = ___¢ 4¢ + 3¢ = ___¢

4. 1¢ + 2¢ = ___¢ 2¢ + 1¢ = ___¢

5. 0¢ + 3¢ = ___¢ 3¢ + 0¢ = ___¢

6. 2¢ + 5¢ = ___¢ 5¢ + 2¢ = ___¢

7. 9¢ + 0¢ = ___¢ 0¢ + 9¢ = ___¢

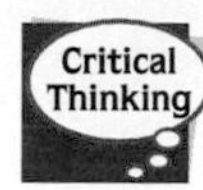

What happens when you add 0?

Try These!

Use pennies if you want to.

1  

1¢ + 4¢ = 5¢

 2 4¢ + 5¢ = ___¢

5¢ + 4¢ = ___¢

 3 2¢ + 0¢ = ___¢

0¢ + 2¢ = ___¢

 4 6¢ + 1¢ = ___¢

1¢ + 6¢ = ___¢

5 3¢ + 2¢ = ___¢

2¢ + 3¢ = ___¢

 6 0¢ + 4¢ = ___¢

4¢ + 0¢ = ___¢

7 5¢ + 2¢ = ___¢

2¢ + 5¢ = ___¢

 8 2¢ + 2¢ = ___¢ 0¢ + 0¢ = ___¢

 9 4¢ + 4¢ = ___¢ 3¢ + 3¢ = ___¢

10 5¢ + 5¢ = ___¢ 1¢ + 1¢ = ___¢

Show how you add (penny).

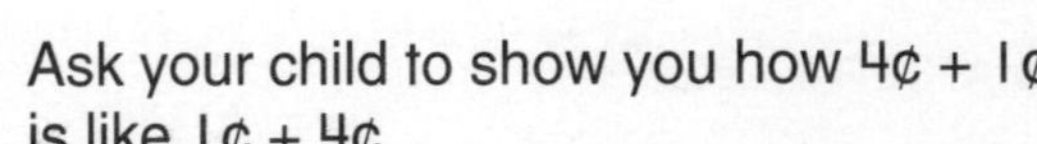

Ask your child to show you how 4¢ + 1¢ is like 1¢ + 4¢.

Name ____________________

Counting On

You can **count on** to add.
Start at 4. Count on 2.

4 + 2 = 6

Do you have to count the 4 eggs first? Why?

Count on to add.

3 + 1 = 4

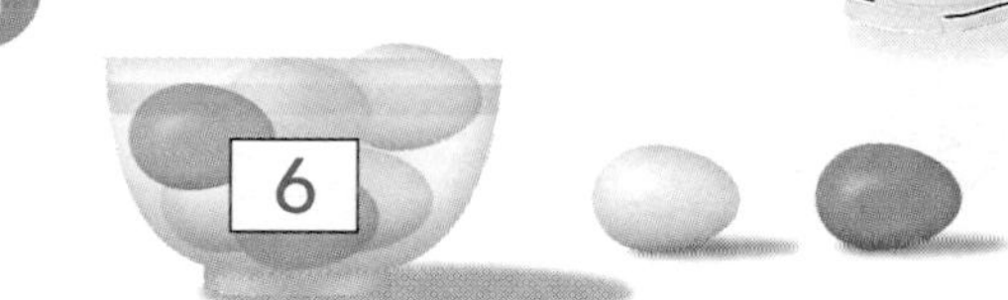

6 + 2 = ___

5 + 3 = ___

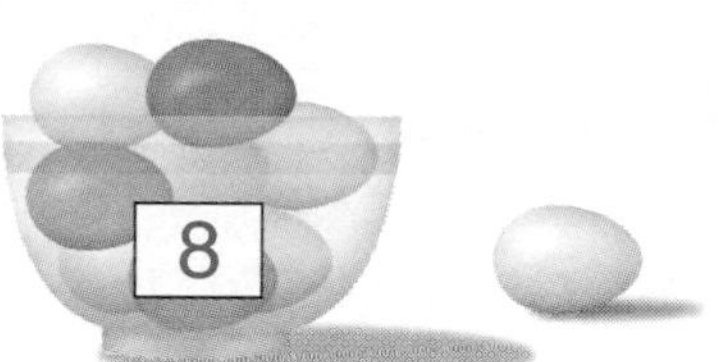

8 + 1 = ___

5 + 1 = ___

3 + 3 = ___

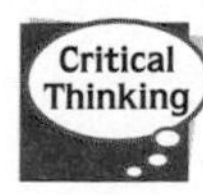

Why can you count on to add?

Try These!

Count on to add.

1 

$6 + 1 = $ 7

2 

$4 + 3 = $ ___

3	5 + 2 = ___	3 + 1 = ___	2 + 3 = ___
4	6 + 3 = ___	2 + 2 = ___	7 + 1 = ___
5	8 + 2 = ___	9 + 1 = ___	4 + 2 = ___
6	3 + 3 = ___	5 + 3 = ___	2 + 0 = ___
7	8 + 1 = ___	6 + 2 = ___	7 + 3 = ___

Mixed Review

Write parts for the total.

8 

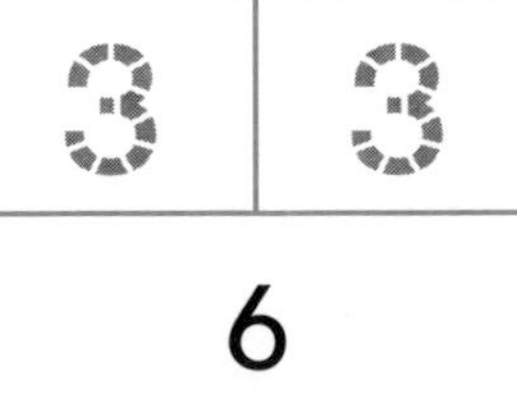

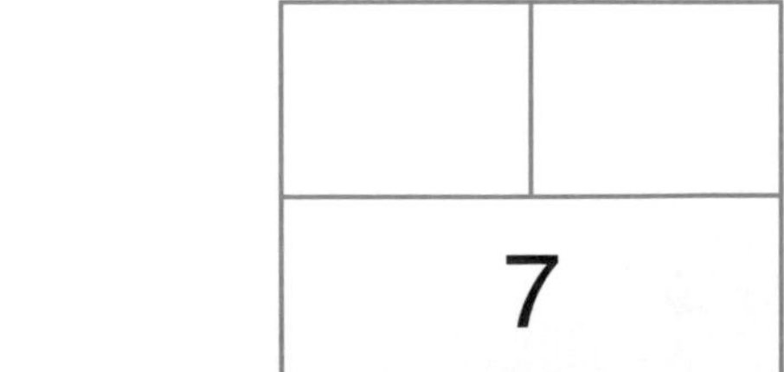

9 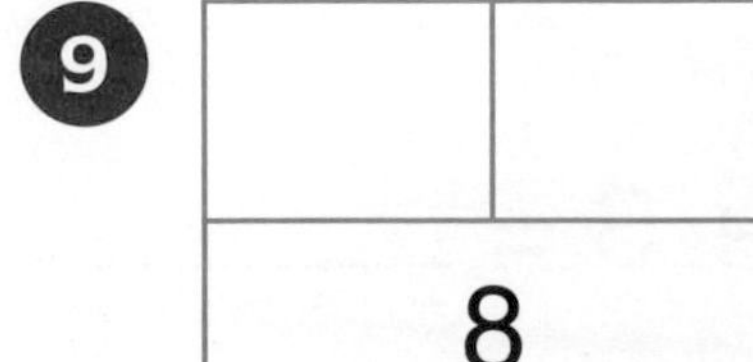

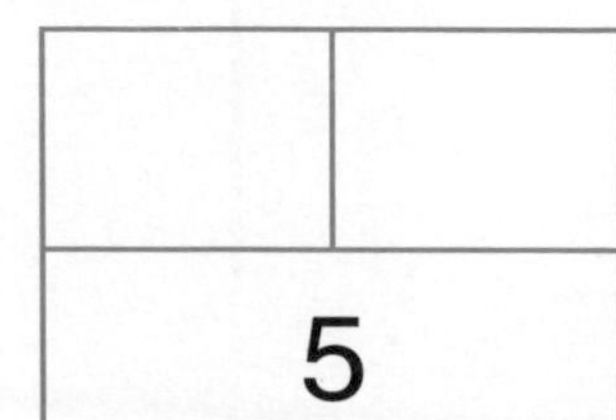

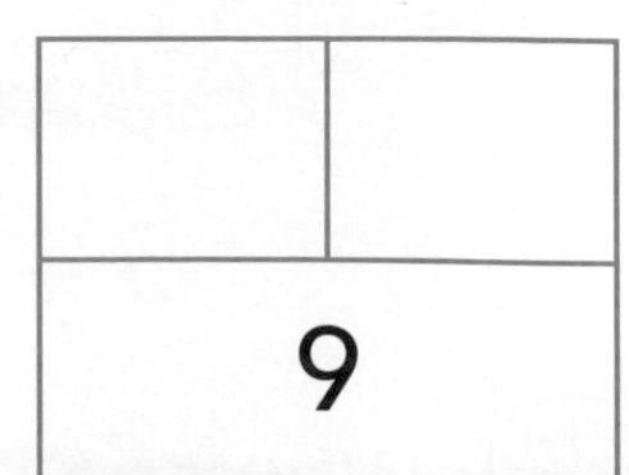

At Home: Ask your child to tell you about counting on to add.

Name

More Counting On

Start at 6. Count on 3.

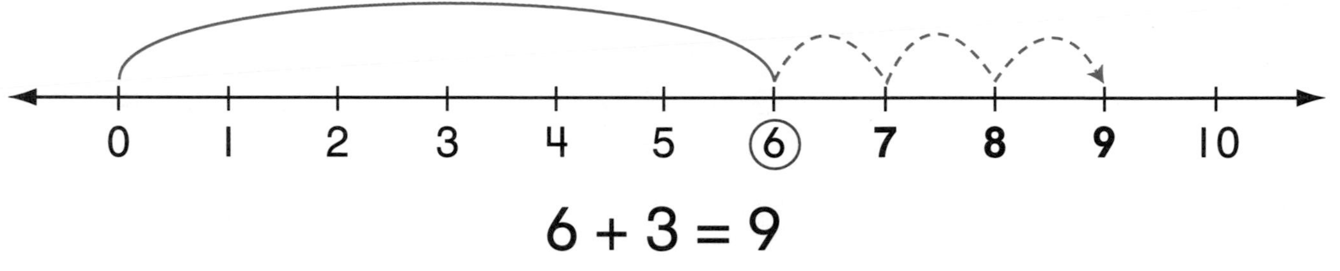

6 + 3 = 9

Count on to add.

1

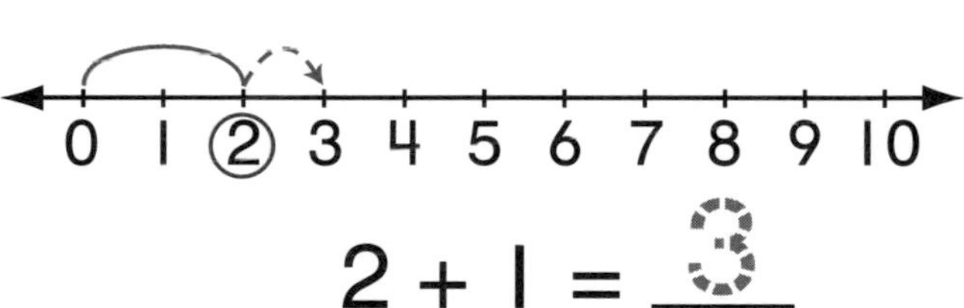

2 + 1 = 3

2

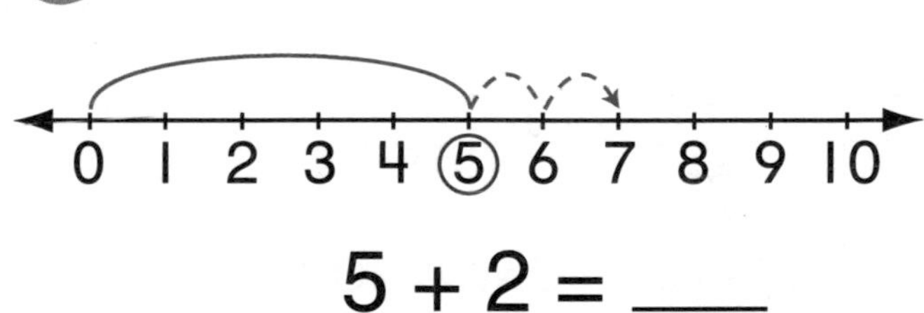

5 + 2 = ____

3

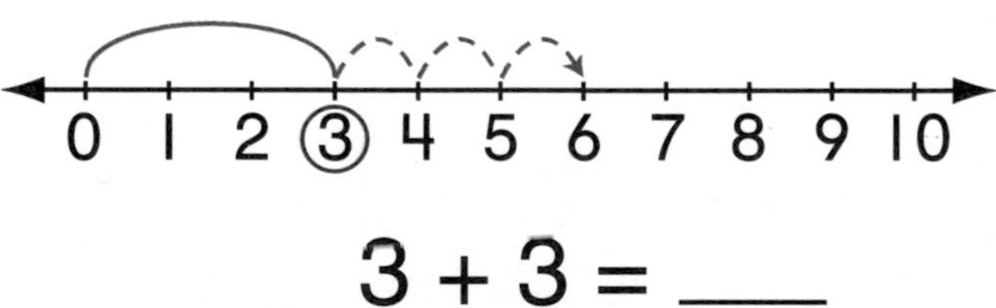

3 + 3 = ____

4

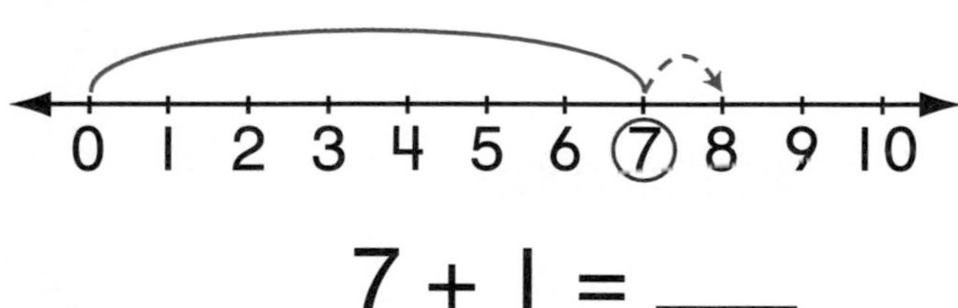

7 + 1 = ____

5

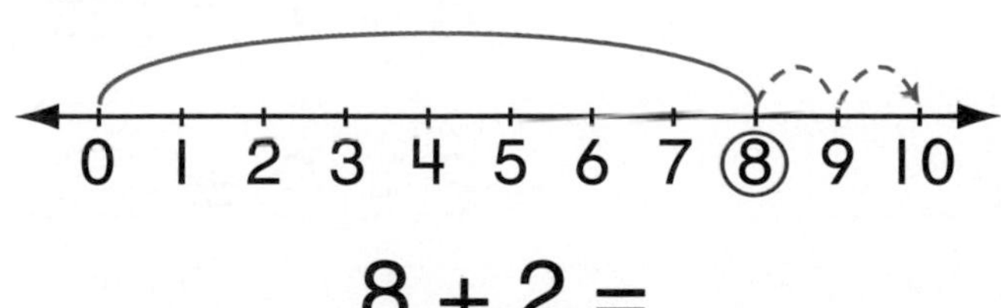

8 + 2 = ____

6

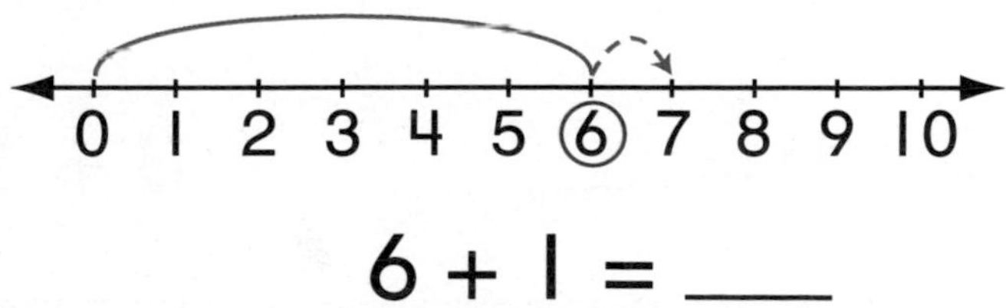

6 + 1 = ____

Try These!

Add.

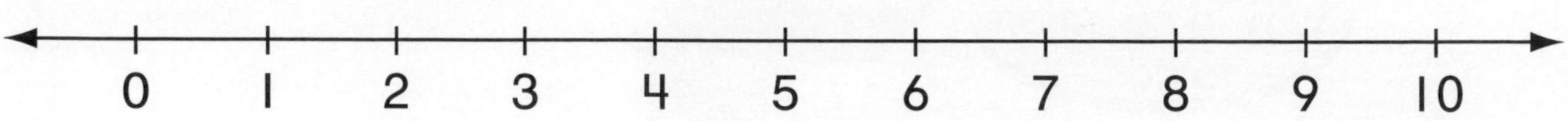

1	7 + 1 = 8	5 + 2 = ___	4 + 1 = ___
2	6 + 2 = ___	4 + 3 = ___	1 + 1 = ___
3	2 + 1 = ___	8 + 1 = ___	7 + 2 = ___
4	3 + 2 = ___	7 + 3 = ___	4 + 0 = ___
5	5 + 3 = ___	9 + 1 = ___	6 + 1 = ___

Cultural Connection

The Ancient Inca

This is an old way to count.

Add on the rope.

3 + 2 = ___	5 + 1 = ___	6 + 3 = ___
5 + 2 = ___	7 + 2 = ___	8 + 1 = ___
3 + 0 = ___	3 + 1 = ___	8 + 2 = ___

At Home

Ask your child to show you how to count on to add on the number line.

Name

Supermarket Race

You need 2 and a .

Take turns.

- Roll the .
- Move that many spaces.
- Next turn. Add.
- Move that many spaces.

Winner: first player to get to **Checkout**

Start

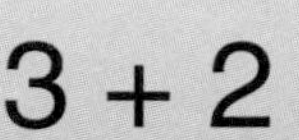

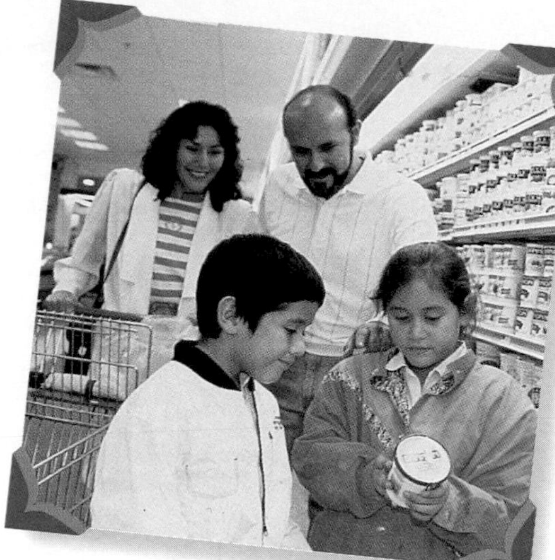

3 + 2

6 + 2

5 + 1 | 3 + 1 | 7 + 2 | 2 + 2

1 + 1

1 + 0 | 4 + 2 | 5 + 0 | 3 + 3 | 4 + 1 | 1 + 2 | 4 + 3

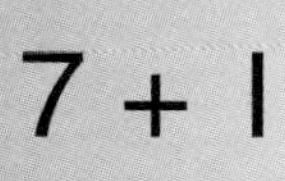

7 + 1

2 + 3 | 5 + 3 | 2 + 1 | 5 + 2 | 2 + 0 | 6 + 3 | 6 + 1

Checkout

Add.

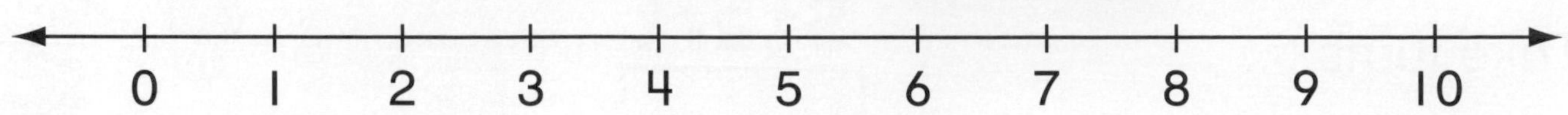

1	4 + 3 = 7	1 + 0 = ___	4 + 1 = ___
2	6 + 2 = ___	8 + 1 = ___	2 + 2 = ___
3	1 + 1 = ___	5 + 1 = ___	1 + 3 = ___
4	6 + 3 = ___	3 + 2 = ___	5 + 3 = ___
5	4 + 2 = ___	8 + 2 = ___	6 + 1 = ___
6	7 + 1 = ___	2 + 0 = ___	2 + 1 = ___
7	1 + 2 = ___	9 + 1 = ___	5 + 2 = ___
8	3 + 0 = ___	3 + 1 = ___	2 + 3 = ___

Find how many in all.

9

___ in all

___ + ___ = ___

10

___ in all

___ + ___ = ___

Name ___

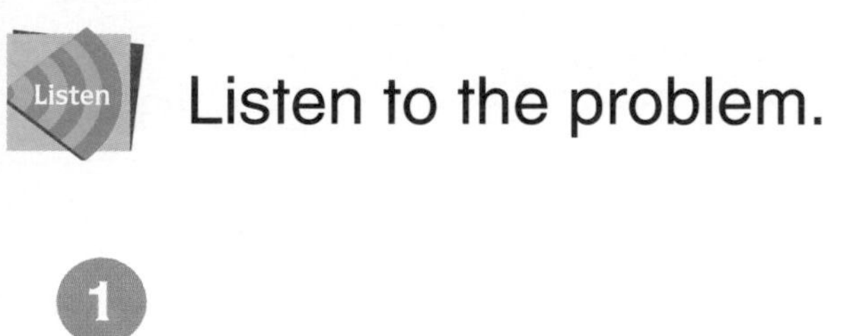

Listen to the problem.

1

What do you need to find?
Can you add to find the answer?

Write how many.
Ring which is more. ___ ___

2 At the store

___ in all

___

3 In school

___ ___

Try These!

1 How many in all?

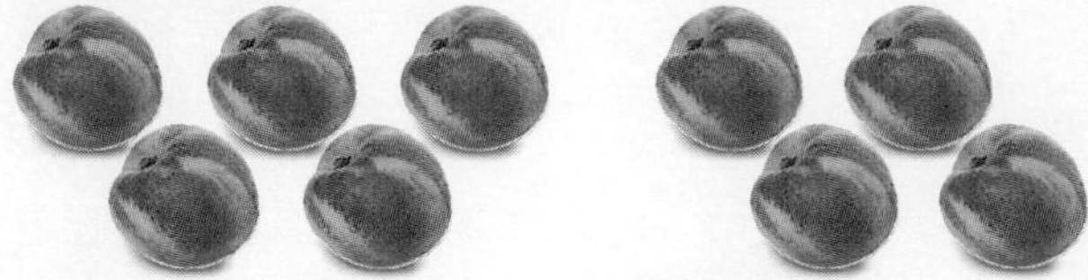

____ in all

____

2 Show what comes next.

____ ____ ____

3 Solve Diane's problem. ______________________

Talk How did you solve Diane's problem?

4 Write Write a problem.
Have a partner solve it.

Your partner's answer: ______________________

At Home Ask your child to tell you about the problem he or she wrote.

Name

Chapter Review

Write the addition sentence.

1

___ + ___ = ___

2

___ + ___ = ___

Add.

3

5 + 3 = ___

4

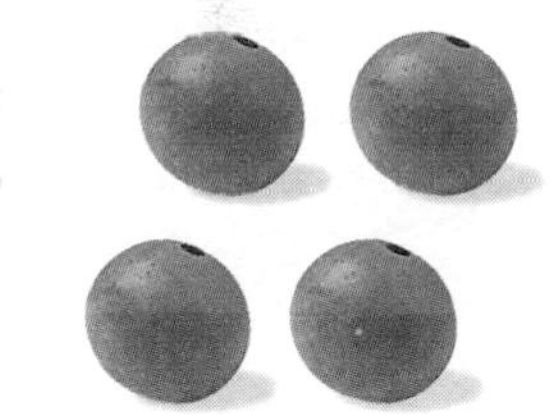

6 + 4 = ___

5. 3 + 1 = ___

6. 3 + 3 = ___

7. 6 + 3 = ___

8. 4 + 0 = ___

9. 2 + 2 = ___

10. 5 + 1 = ___

11. 3 + 2 = ___

12. 1 + 1 = ___

13. 6 + 1 = ___

14. 2 + 1 = ___

15. 5¢ + 2¢ = ___¢

16. 8¢ + 2¢ = ___¢

Find how many in all.

17

____ in all

____ + ____ = ____

18

____ in all

____ + ____ = ____

19

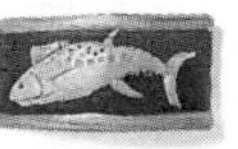

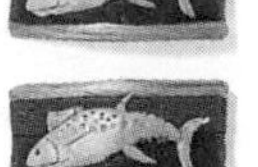

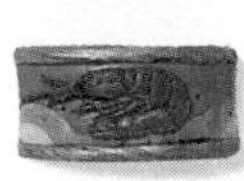

____ in all

____ + ____ = ____

---

20 Show what comes next.

____ ____ ____ ____

What Do You Think?

How do you add 7 + 2?

☑ Check one.

☐ With  ☐ With 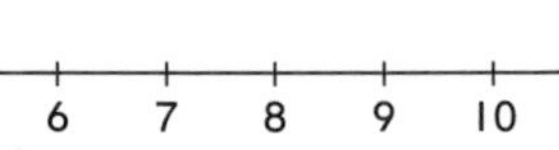

☐ In my head

Why? ______________________________

Draw an addition picture.
Write the addition sentence.

Name ____________________

Chapter Test

Write the addition sentence.

1  

___ + ___ = ___

2  

___ + ___ = ___

Add.

3  

4 + 5 = ___

4  

3 + 4 = ___

5 8 + 0 = ___

6 7 + 3 = ___

7 4¢ + 2¢ = ___¢

8 6¢ + 3¢ = ___¢

Find how many in all.

9     

___ in all

___ + ___ = ___

10    

___ in all

___ + ___ = ___

Performance Assessment

What Did You Learn?

You and your partner need a [spinner], 10 [counters], and a [number line].

- Spin.
- Write the number.
- Add.

3 + ___ = ___

4 + ___ = ___

2 + ___ = ___

6 + ___ = ___

7 + ___ = ___

5 + ___ = ___

Tell how you added.

You may want to put this page in your portfolio.

Name ______________________

Addition Tables

Complete the table. Use counting.

+	0	1	2	3	4	5	6	7	8	9
0	0	1	2	3		5	6	7	8	9
1	1	2	3	4	5		7	8	9	10
2	2	3	4	5	6	7		9	10	
3	3		5	6	7	8	9	10		
4	4	5	6	7	8	9	10			
5	5		7	8	9	10				
6	6	7	8		10					
7		8	9	10						
8	8		10							
9	9									

Use the table to add.

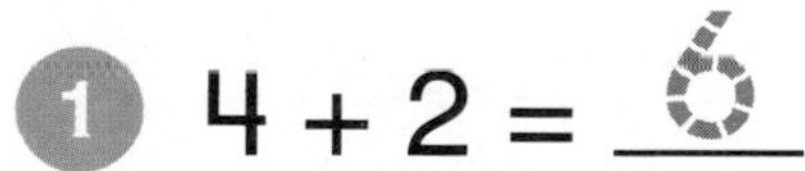

1. 4 + 2 = 6   5 + 3 = ___   2 + 2 = ___

2. 7 + 3 = ___   6 + 2 = ___   4 + 3 = ___

Curriculum Connection

Language Arts

Dot Stories

What number stories can you tell about the pictures below?

You need 10 dots.

- Draw a picture using some dots.
- Tell a number story about your dot picture.
- Trade pictures with a partner.
- Tell another number story.

Name

Cumulative Review

Choose the letter of the correct answer.

1 Find the missing part.

3	?
5	

ⓐ 2
ⓑ 3
ⓒ 4
ⓓ 5

2 Add.

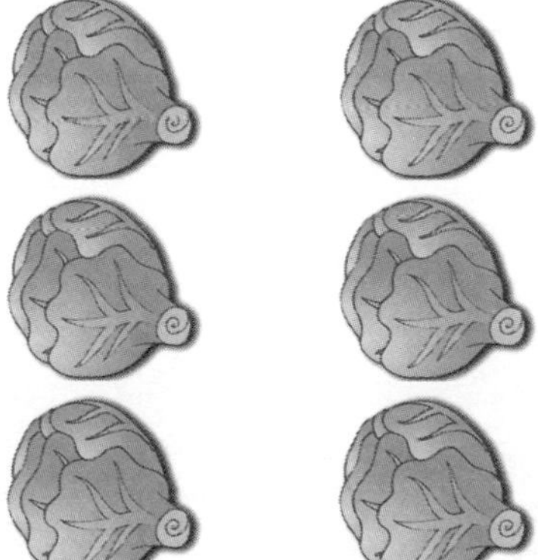

3 + 3 = ?

ⓐ 3
ⓑ 5
ⓒ 6
ⓓ 7

3 How many cents?

ⓐ 3
ⓑ 4
ⓒ 5
ⓓ 6

4 Find the total.

3	6
?	

ⓐ 3
ⓑ 7
ⓒ 8
ⓓ 9

5 Add.

5 + 4 = ?

ⓐ 8
ⓑ 9
ⓒ 10
ⓓ not here

6 How many?

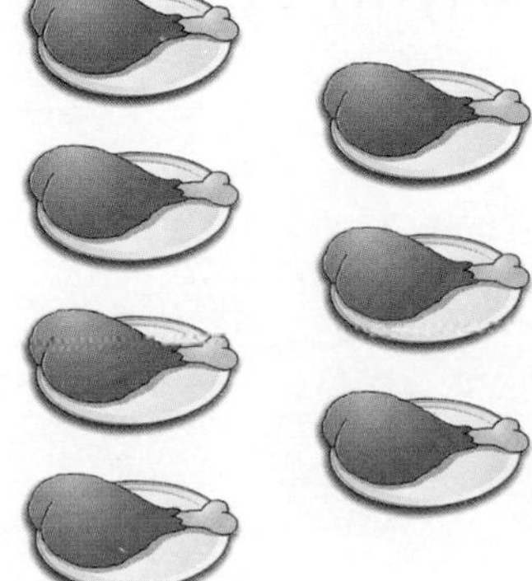

ⓐ 5
ⓑ 6
ⓒ 7
ⓓ 8

7 How many animals?

- ⓐ 3
- ⓑ 4
- ⓒ 5
- ⓓ 6

---

8 How many children?

- ⓐ 1
- ⓑ 2
- ⓒ 3
- ⓓ 4

---

9 How many in all?

- ⓐ 3
- ⓑ 4
- ⓒ 5
- ⓓ 6

---

10 How many in all?

- ⓐ 3
- ⓑ 4
- ⓒ 7
- ⓓ 8

Name ________________________________

Food Totals

3 + 4 = 7

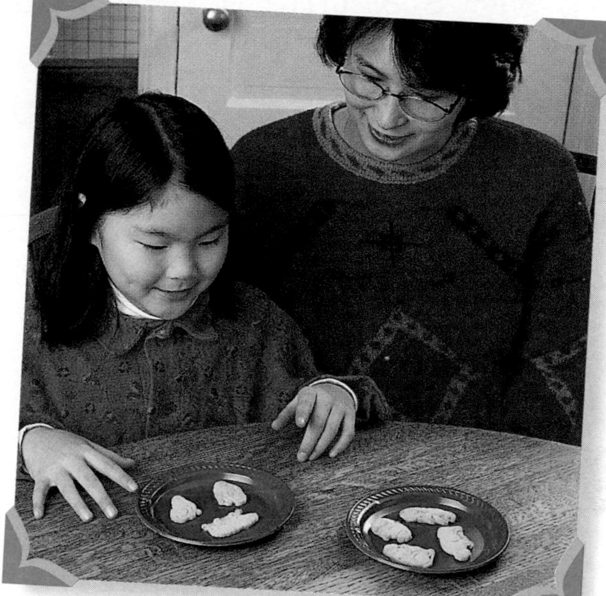

Draw. Write the addition.

___ + ___ = ___

___ + ___ = ___

___ + ___ = ___

___ + ___ = ___

___ + ___ = ___

Choose food items such as crackers, raisins, or dried macaroni to help your child practice addition. Use 2 plates to show 2 groups of a food item for a total of no more than 10. Your child draws to show the 2 groups, adds, and then writes the addition sentence.

Dear Family,

We are starting a new chapter in our mathematics book. We are going to learn to subtract. We will use pictures and numbers to show subtraction.

$$6 - 2 = 4$$

We will also be talking about folktales and favorite stories. Please help me complete this interview.

Your child,

____
Signature

Interview

What kind of stories do you like?
(You may check more than one.)

- ❑ Folktales
- ❑ True stories
- ❑ Mysteries
- ❑ Nursery rhymes
- ❑ Other _______________________

Did you have a favorite story when you were a child? _______________________

What was it? _______________________

____

Folktales and Rhymes
Beginning to Subtract

CHAPTER 4

Listen to the tale *The Great Ball Game.*

Tell about other tales you know.

Name

What Do You Know?

You need 10 .

Find the missing part.

1

5	
7	

4	
5	

4	
8	

2

	6
10	

	2
6	

	1
4	

Show how you find the missing part.

Name ________________

Subtraction Stories

Working Together

You need 10 .

Listen to the story.

- Show the total.
- Draw the parts.
- Write the number for the part that is left.

	Total	Part	Part
1	5	2	3
2	6	2	___
3	8	3	___

Critical Thinking: How can you check that the part you write is correct?

Try These!

Take turns.

- ► You show the total.
- ► Your partner takes part away and draws it.
- ► You draw and write the part that is left.

	Total	Part	Part
1	3	2	___
2	7	3	___
3	5	4	___
4	6	1	___

Have your child tell you a story about exercise 1 above.

Name ____________________

Subtraction Sentences

You need 10 .
Subtract.

MOTHER'S CUPBOARD

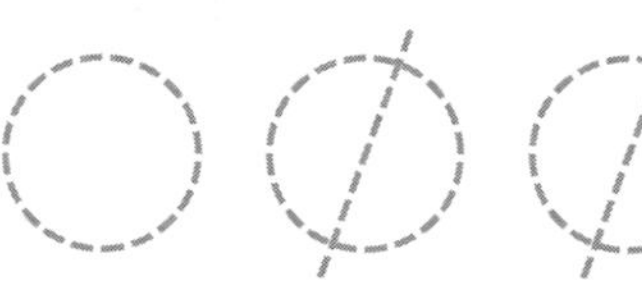

Draw. Subtract.

1. $6 - 3 = \underline{3}$

2. $8 - 5 =$ ___

3. $9 - 4 =$ ___

4. $4 - 2 =$ ___

5. $5 - 3 =$ ___

6. $3 - 1 =$ ___

Try These!

Find what is left in Mother Hubbard's cupboard.

1 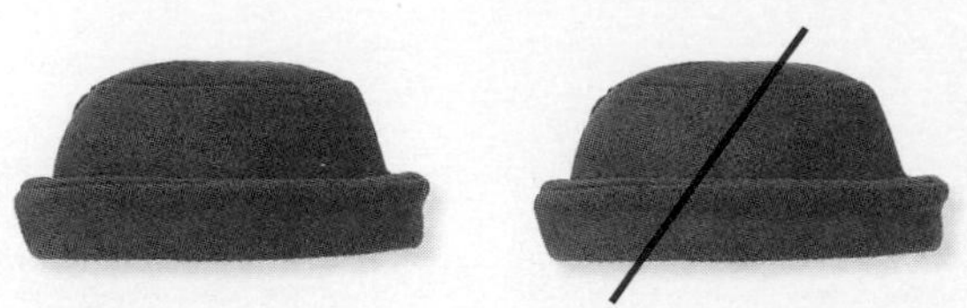

2 − 1 = 1

2 

4 − 3 = ___

3 

6 − 2 = ___

4 

7 − 5 = ___

5 

8 − 4 = ___

6 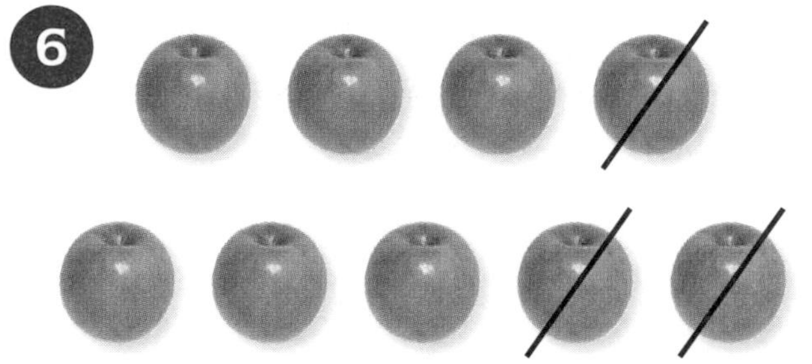

9 − 3 = ___

Mixed Review

Add.

7 5 + 1 = ___ 7 + 3 = ___ 6 + 2 = ___

8 3 + 3 = ___ 8 + 2 = ___ 7 + 1 = ___

Your child has begun to subtract. Have your child tell you about the subtraction exercises on this page.

Name

More Subtraction Sentences

MOTHER'S CUPBOARD

subtraction sentence 8 − 2 = 6

Write the subtraction sentence.

1
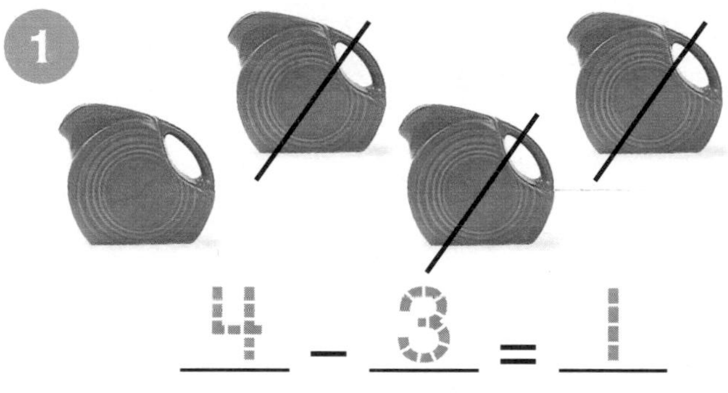

4 − 3 = 1

2

___ − ___ = ___

3
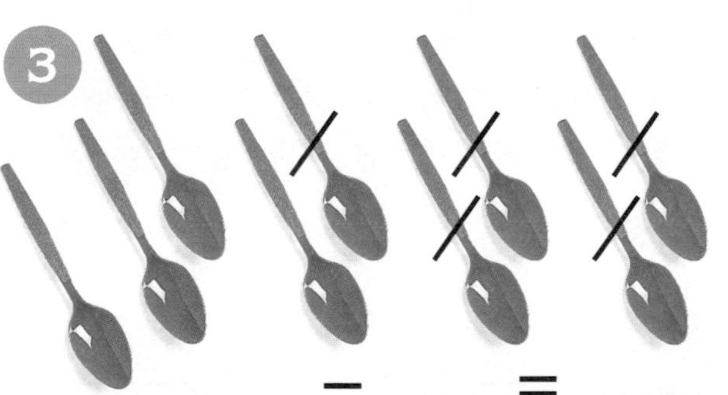

___ − ___ = ___

4
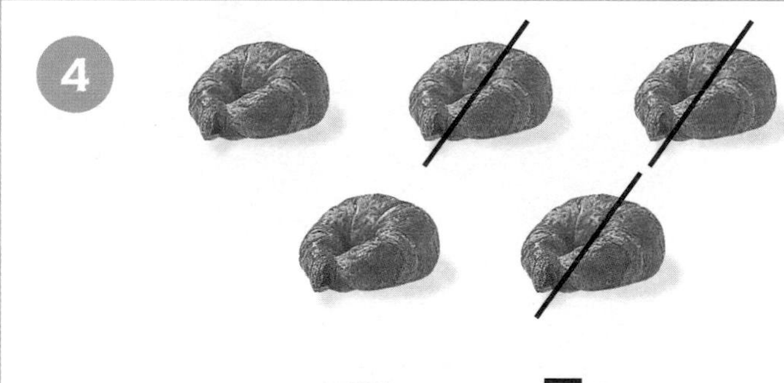

___ − ___ = ___

5

___ − ___ = ___

6
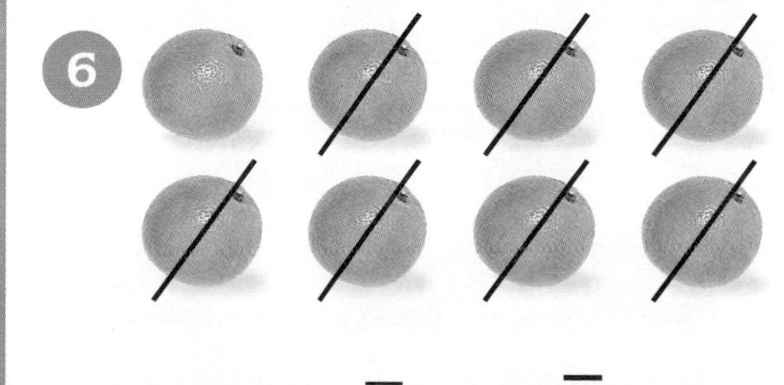

___ − ___ = ___

Try These!

Write the subtraction sentence.

1 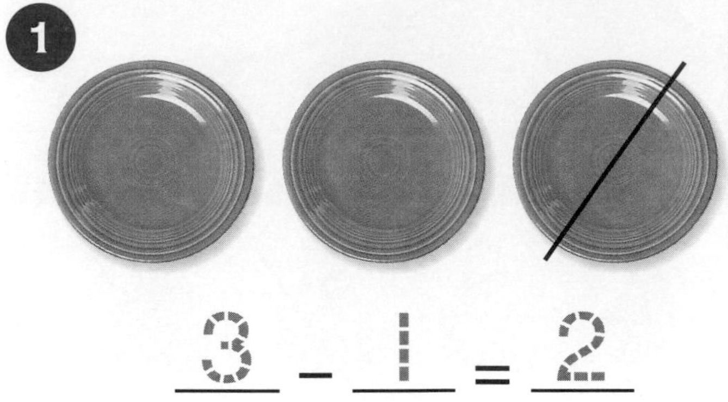

3 – 1 = 2

2 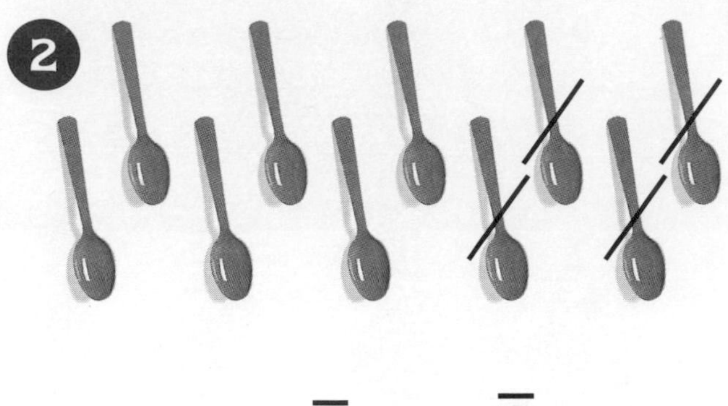

___ – ___ = ___

3 

___ – ___ = ___

4 

___ – ___ = ___

5 

___ – ___ = ___

6 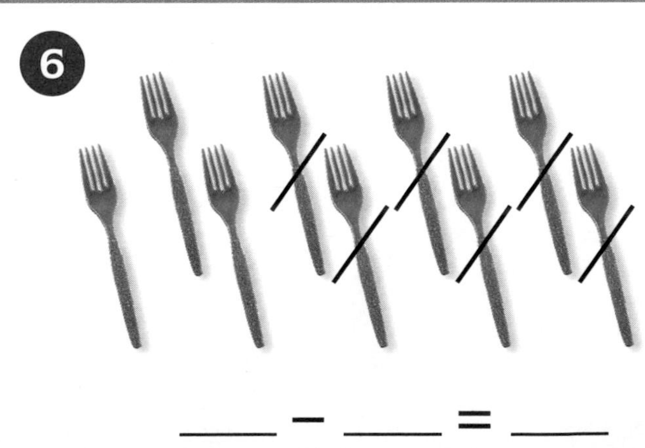

___ – ___ = ___

7 

___ – ___ = ___

8 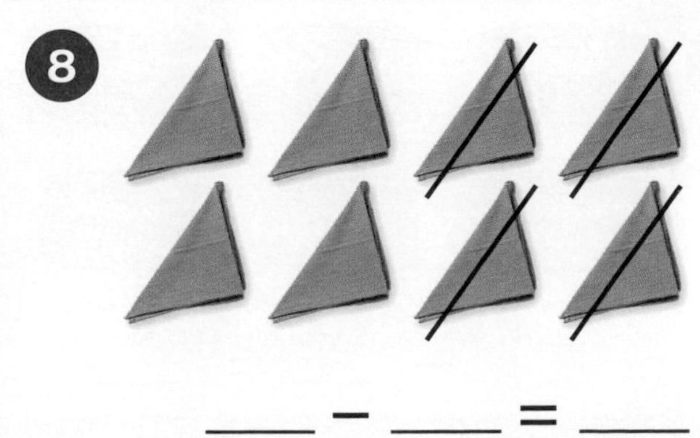

___ – ___ = ___

We are learning to write subtraction sentences. Have your child tell you about the exercises on this page.

Name ____________

Write a Subtraction Sentence

You need 10 .

Listen to the problem.

1. At the river 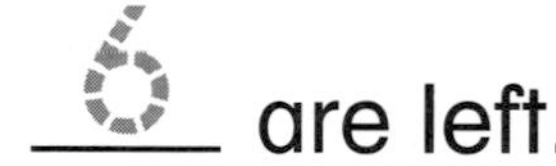 6 are left.

9 – 3 = 6

Tell how you found the answer.

2. At the waterfall ____ are left.

____ – ____ = ____

3. At the game ____ are left.

____ – ____ = ____

Make up a different problem about 10 rhinos.

Try These!

Make up a problem for the picture.
Find how many are left.

1  

2 are left.

4 – 2 = 2

---

2  

____ are left.

____ – ____ = ____

---

3  

____ are left.

____ – ____ = ____

More to Explore

Number Sense

There are 5 sheep.
How many are hiding? ____

There are 10 goats.
How many are hiding? ____

At Home
Ask your child to tell you a subtraction story about the ballplayers in problem 3.

Name ______

Midchapter Review

Find how many are left.

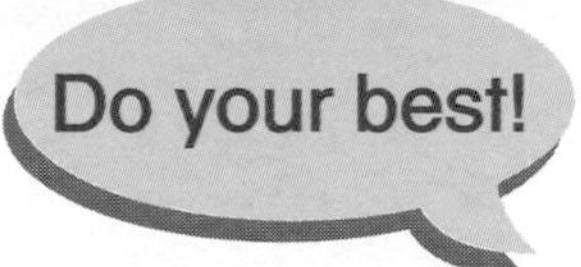

1. At the game ____ are left.

____ – ____ = ____

Subtract.

2.     

6 – 3 = ____

3.  

8 – 5 = ____

4.     

9 – 4 = ____

5.     

4 – 2 = ____

Write the subtraction sentence.

6.     

____ – ____ = ____

7.     

____ – ____ = ____

8.     

____ – ____ = ____

9.    

____ – ____ = ____

10. What does 7 – 3 = 4 mean?

______

Draw a picture that shows subtraction.

Extra Practice

Game!

Collect Them All

You need a .

Take turns.

- Roll the .
- Write the number you roll to show a difference.
- Fill the page.

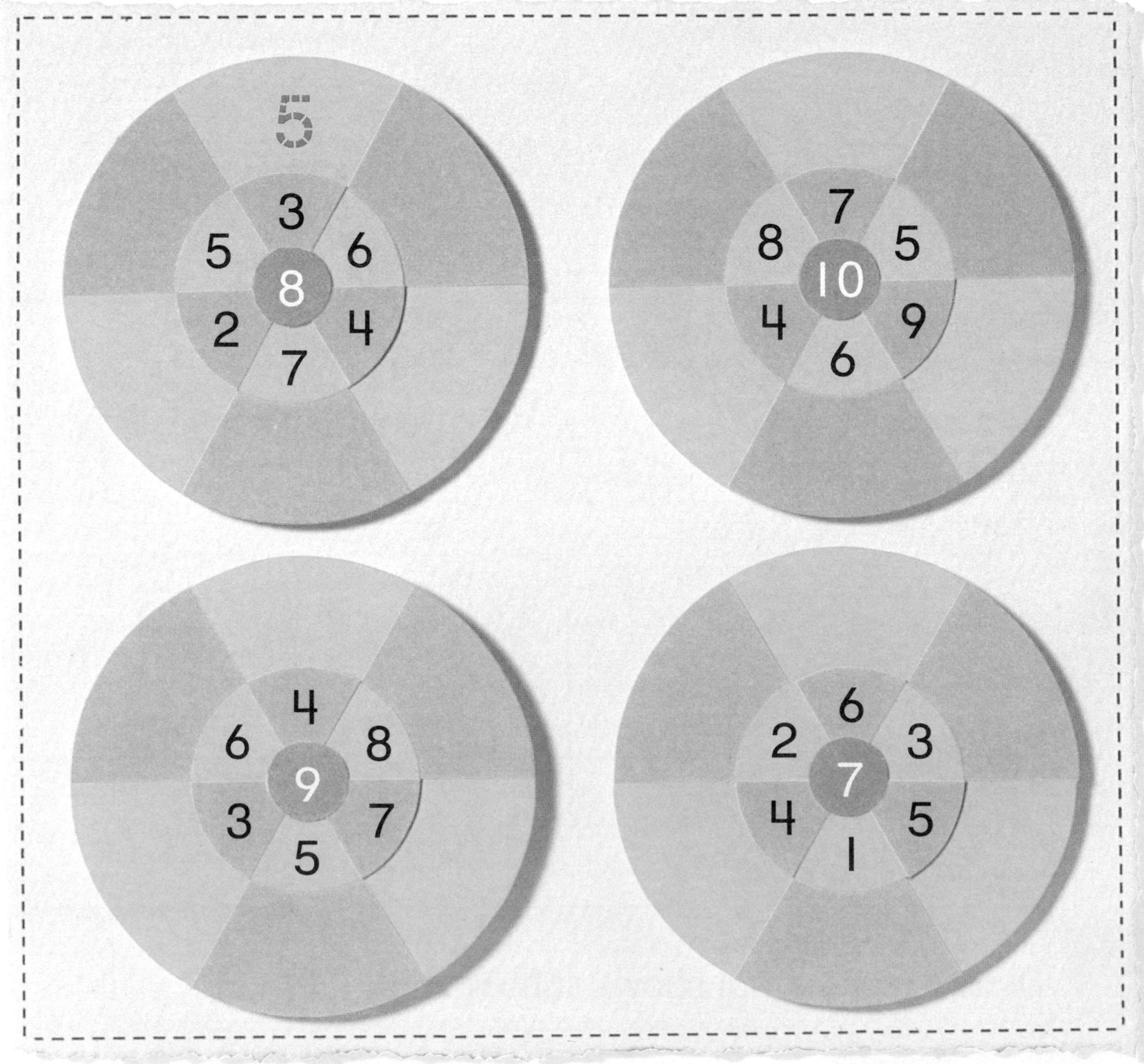

8: 3, 6, 4, 7, 2, 5 — 5

10: 7, 5, 9, 6, 4, 8

9: 4, 8, 7, 5, 3, 6

7: 6, 3, 5, 1, 4, 2

Name ______________________________

Books and More Books

Listen to *The Great Ball Game.*

What kind of book is *The Great Ball Game*? What kinds of books do you have in your classroom library?

Cultural Note

Ball games have been played by Native Americans for centuries.

Working Together

- Sort some books from the classroom library.
- Decide how you want to sort the books.

How many different kinds of books do you have?

Show how you sorted.

Decision Making

Choose another way to sort the books.

Show how you sorted.

1. How many kinds of books do you have now?

____

2. Do you have more or fewer kinds of books?

____

Write a report.

3. Show what you found.

4. Tell how you sorted the books each time.

More to Investigate

PREDICT What kinds of book do your classmates like best?

EXPLORE Take a survey.

FIND What kind of book is the most popular book on your survey?

Name

Subtraction Fact Pairs

Find how many cents are left.

1. 4¢ – 3¢ = 1 ¢
2. 4¢ – 1¢ = 3 ¢

How are the parts different?

3. 

5¢ – 0¢ = ___¢

4. 

5¢ – 5¢ = ___¢

5. 

7¢ – 2¢ = ___¢

6. 

7¢ – 5¢ = ___¢

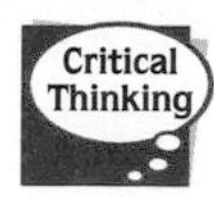

What happens when you subtract 0¢?

Try These!

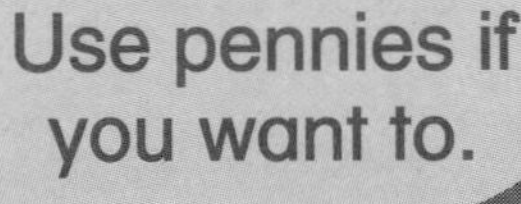

Subtract.

1. 5¢ – 4¢ = 1 ¢

2. 7¢ – 2¢ = ___¢
   7¢ – 5¢ = ___¢
3. 3¢ – 0¢ = ___¢
   3¢ – 3¢ = ___¢
4. 9¢ – 8¢ = ___¢
   9¢ – 1¢ = ___¢
5. 6¢ – 2¢ = ___¢
   6¢ – 4¢ = ___¢
6. 8¢ – 8¢ = ___¢
   8¢ – 0¢ = ___¢
7. 10¢ – 9¢ = ___¢
   10¢ – 1¢ = ___¢

Mixed Review

Count backward.

8. 7, 6, 5, 4
9. 9, ___, ___, ___
10. 5, ___, ___, ___
11. 6, ___, ___, ___
12. 3, ___, ___, ___
13. 8, ___, ___, ___

At Home: Ask your child to show you how to subtract zero pennies.

Name

Counting Back

You can **count back** to subtract.
Start at 7. Count back 2.

7 − 2 = 5

How do you know how many beans are left in the bag?

Count back to subtract.

1 

3 − 1 = 2

2 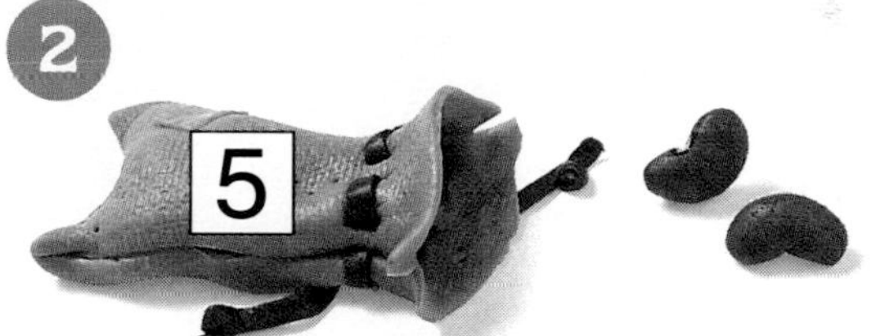

5 − 2 = ___

3 

4 − 3 = ___

4 

9 − 1 = ___

5 

8 − 3 = ___

6 

6 − 2 = ___

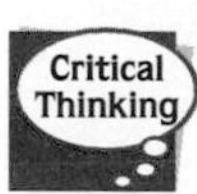

How does counting back help you subtract?

Try These!

Count back to subtract.

1 

2 − 1 = 1

2 

5 − 3 = ___

3. 6 − 1 = ___ 7 − 2 = ___ 10 − 2 = ___
4. 8 − 2 = ___ 4 − 1 = ___ 9 − 2 = ___
5. 10 − 3 = ___ 3 − 2 = ___ 5 − 1 = ___
6. 9 − 1 = ___ 7 − 3 = ___ 8 − 3 = ___
7. 5 − 2 = ___ 10 − 2 = ___ 6 − 3 = ___

More to Explore Patterns

Look for a pattern. Complete.

9 − 1 = ___ 5 − 1 = ___

8 − 1 = ___ 4 − 1 = ___

7 − 1 = ___ 3 − 1 = ___

6 − 1 = ___ 2 − 1 = ___

At Home: Ask your child to tell you about counting back to subtract.

Name

More Counting Back

Here is another way to count back to subtract.

Start at 9. Count back 3.

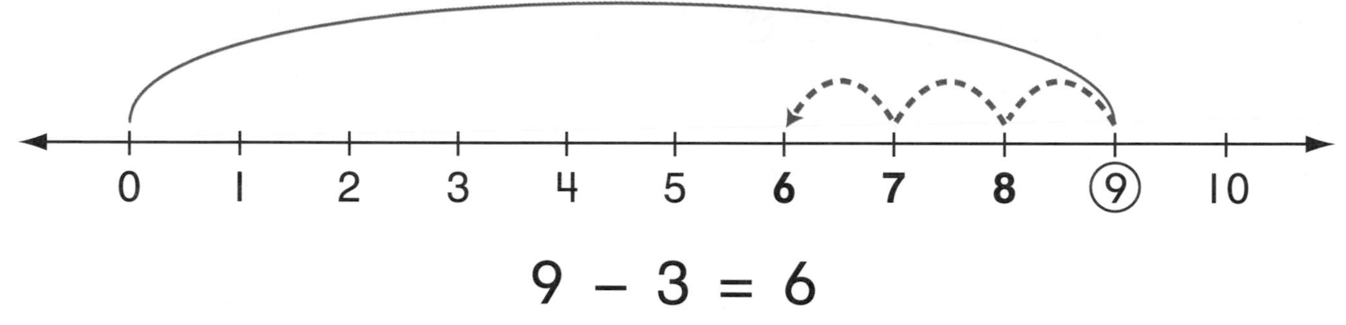

9 − 3 = 6

Count back to subtract.

1

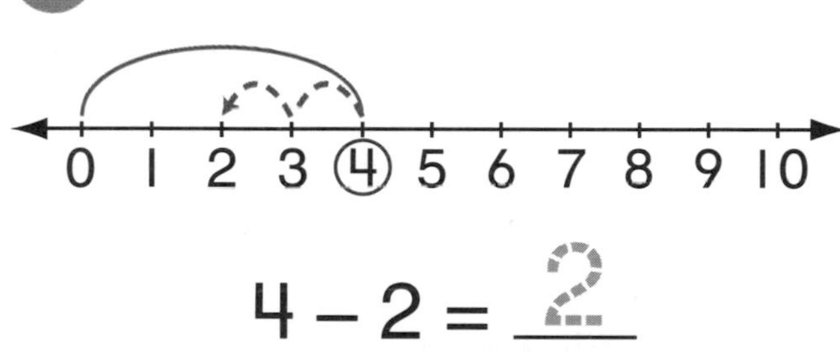

4 − 2 = 2

2

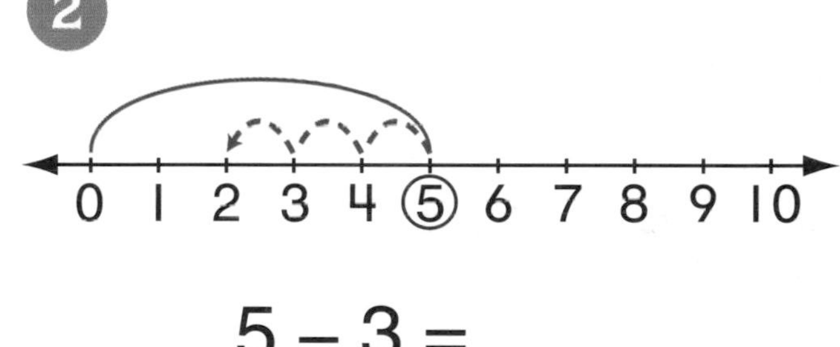

5 − 3 = ___

3

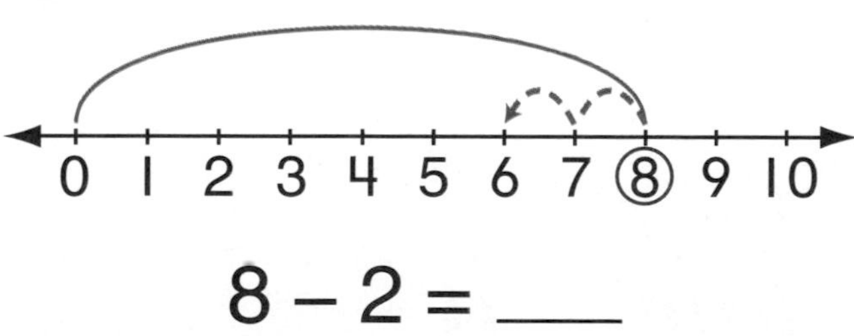

8 − 2 = ___

4

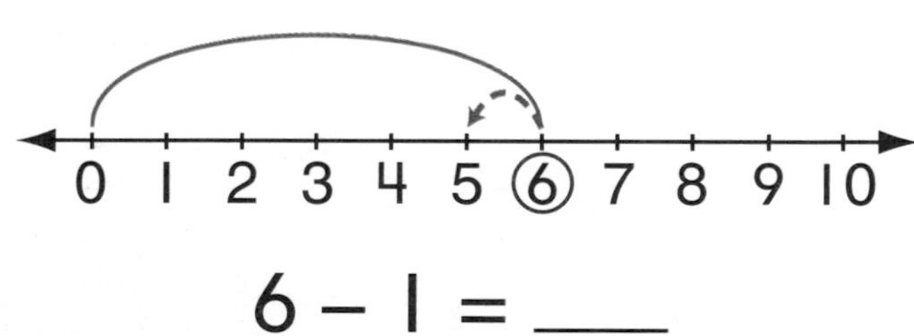

6 − 1 = ___

5

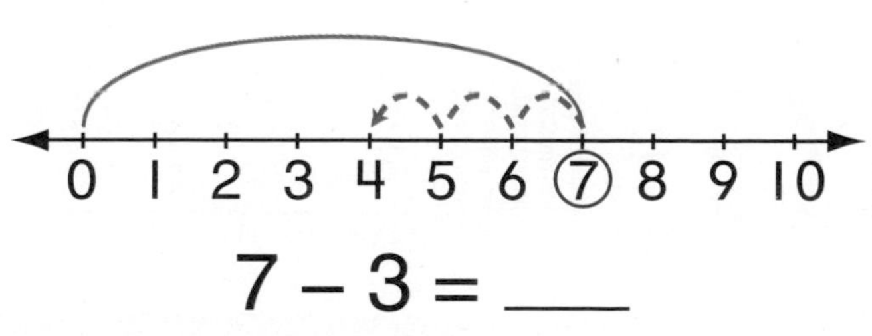

7 − 3 = ___

6

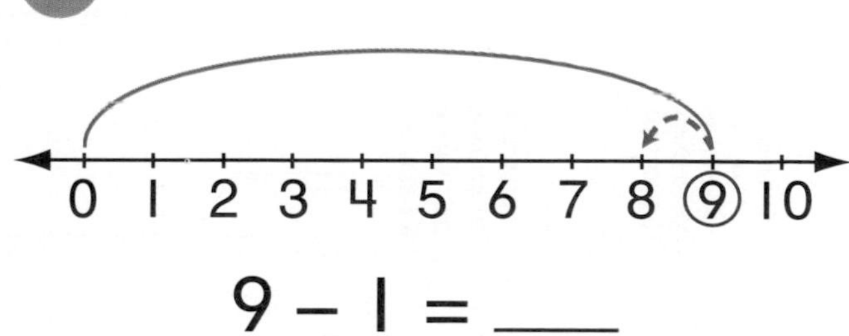

9 − 1 = ___

Try These!

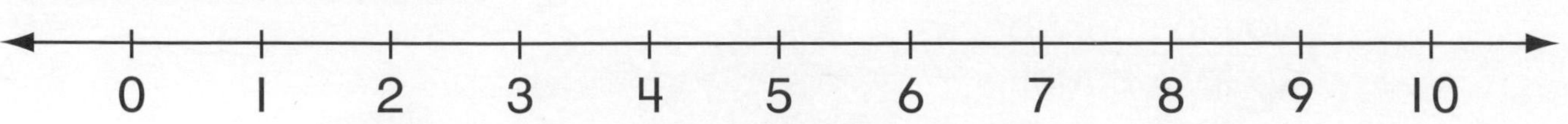

0 1 2 3 4 5 6 7 8 9 10

1. 10 – 1 = 9 4 – 3 = ___ 2 – 2 = ___
2. 6 – 3 = ___ 8 – 1 = ___ 7 – 2 = ___
3. 5 – 1 = ___ 3 – 3 = ___ 9 – 3 = ___
4. 8 – 2 = ___ 10 – 3 = ___ 2 – 1 = ___
5. 3 – 1 = ___ 4 – 2 = ___ 6 – 2 = ___

Cultural Connection

Egyptian Numbers

These numbers were used a long time ago.

| = 1 ∩ = 10

You can subtract with Egyptian numbers.

(10) ∩ – (1) | = (9) |||||||||

(6) |||||| – (2) || = (4) ___

||||| – |||| = ___

∩ – |||||| = ___

At Home

Ask your child to show you how to count back to subtract on a number line.

Name

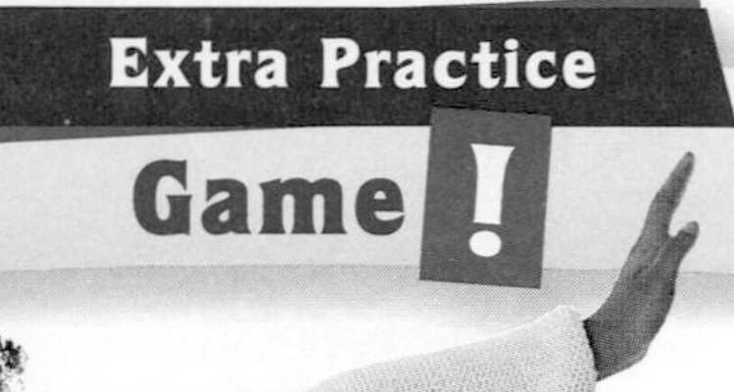

Flying South

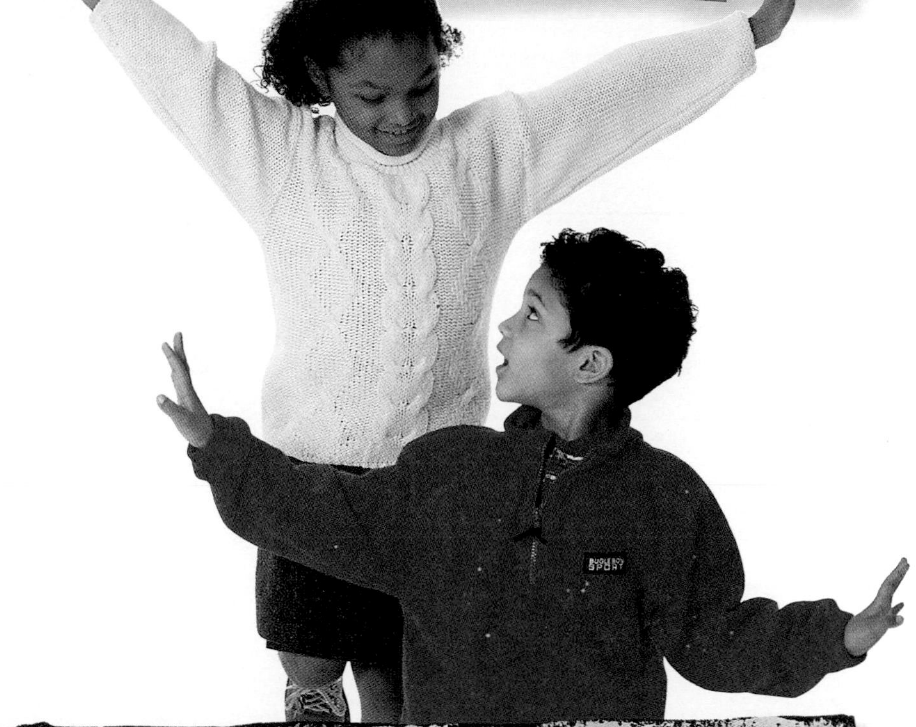

You need 2 and a .

- Put your on 10.
- Take turns. Spin.
- Subtract. Move your to the difference.

The first player to get to **South** wins.

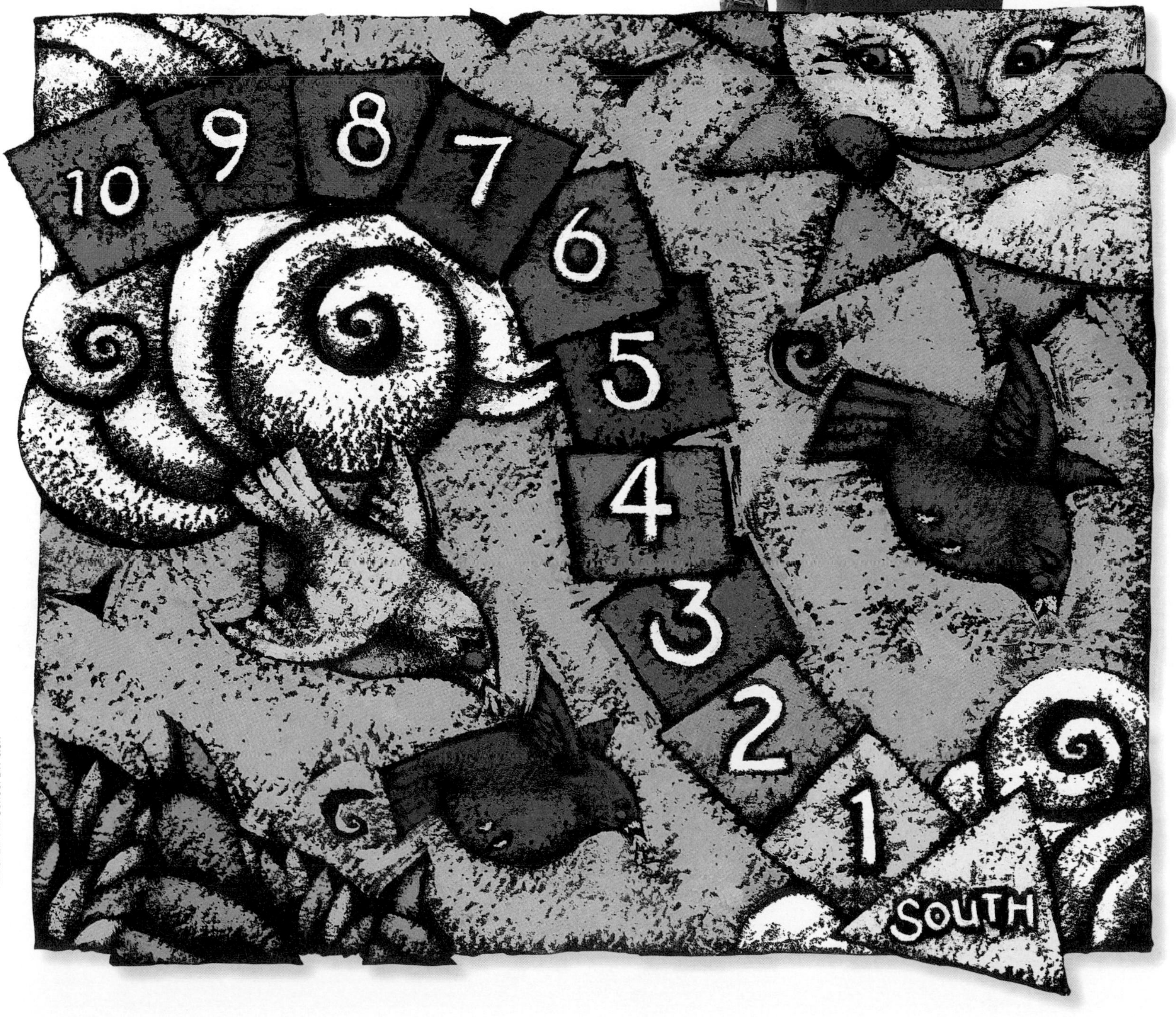

10 9 8 7 6 5 4 3 2 1 SOUTH

Subtract.

0 1 2 3 4 5 6 7 8 9 10

1. 8 − 2 = 6   2 − 1 = ___   5 − 0 = ___
2. 9 − 3 = ___   7 − 2 = ___   6 − 2 = ___
3. 10 − 2 = ___   1 − 1 = ___   3 − 2 = ___
4. 4 − 2 = ___   10 − 3 = ___   9 − 0 = ___
5. 8 − 1 = ___   7 − 1 = ___   5 − 2 = ___
6. 6 − 3 = ___   2 − 0 = ___   8 − 3 = ___
7. 4 − 1 = ___   9 − 2 = ___   8 − 0 = ___
8. 7 − 3 = ___   10 − 1 = ___   9 − 1 = ___

Find out how many are left.

9. 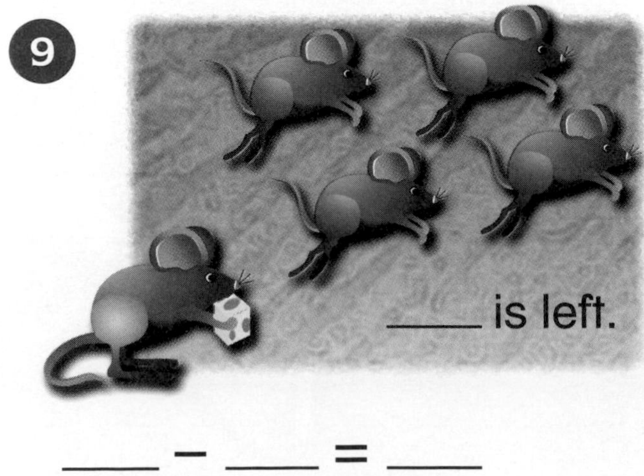

___ is left.

___ − ___ = ___

10. 

___ are left.

___ − ___ = ___

Name ____________________

Can You Subtract to Solve?

Listen to the problem.

What do you need to find?
Can you subtract to find the answer?

Animals  

____ − ____ = ____

2 How many are left?

____ left

____

3 How many in all?

____ in all

____

When do you subtract to solve a problem?

Try These!

Listen to the problem.

1 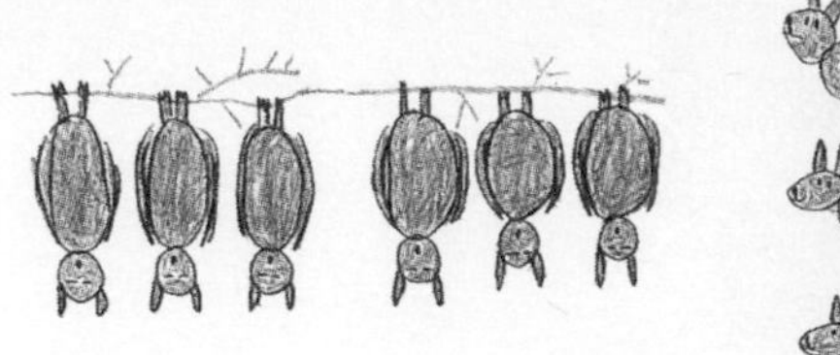

____ in all

____

2 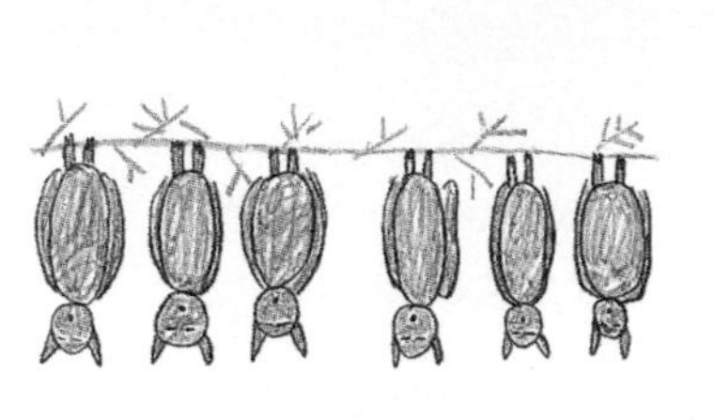 

____ are left.

____

Write and Share

STUDENT TO STUDENT

Jamal wrote this problem.

Jamal McKenzie
Snowden School
Memphis,
Tennessee

How many birds are left?

3 Solve Jamal's problem. ________________

How did you solve Jamal's problem?

4 Write a problem.
Have a partner solve it.

Your partner's answer: ________________

Ask your child to tell you about the problem he or she wrote.

Name

Chapter Review

Write the subtraction sentence.

1. 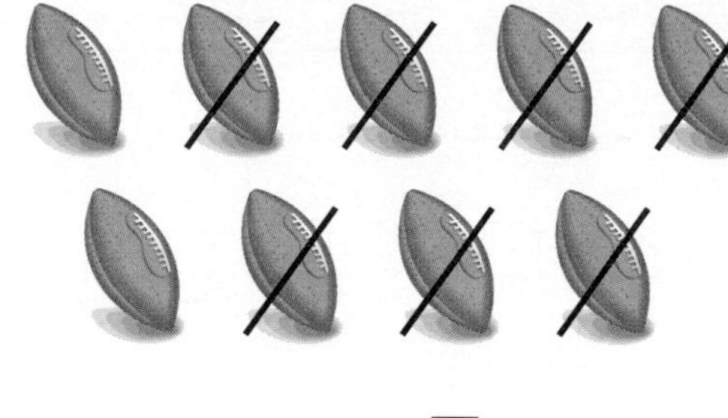

___ − ___ = ___

2.

___ − ___ = ___

Subtract.

3. 

7 − 4 = ___

4. 

8 − 6 = ___

5. 6 − 1 = ___

6. 3 − 2 = ___

7. 5 − 5 = ___

8. 9 − 1 = ___

9. 9 − 3 = ___

10. 8 − 3 = ___

11. 4 − 2 = ___

12. 6 − 2 = ___

13. 7 − 3 = ___

14. 5 − 0 = ___

15. 2¢ − 2¢ = ___¢

16. 4¢ − 1¢ = ___¢

Listen to the problem.

17

____ are left.

____ – ____ = ____

18

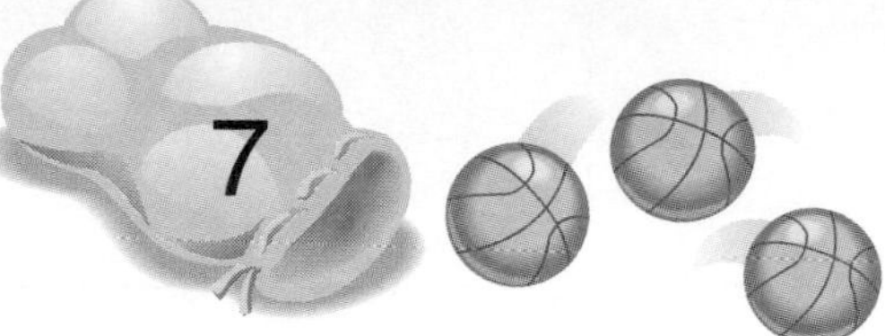

____ are left.

____ – ____ = ____

19

____ are left.

____ – ____ = ____

20

____ in all

____ + ____ = ____

What Do You Think?

How do you subtract 7 – 2?

☑ Check one.

☐ With  ☐ With 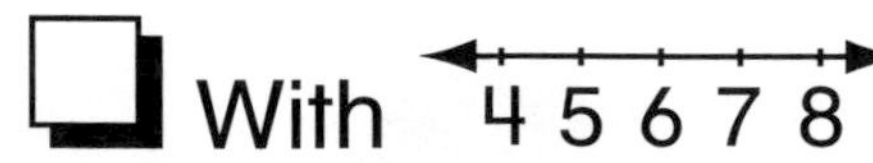

☐ In my head

Why? ______________________________

Draw a subtraction picture.
Write the subtraction sentence.

Name

Chapter Test

Write the subtraction sentence.

1 

___ − ___ = ___

2

___ − ___ = ___

Subtract.

3 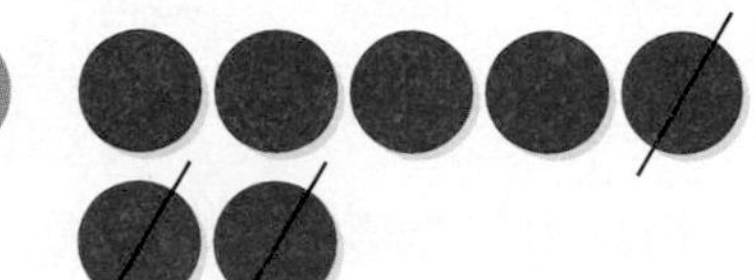

7 − 3 = ___

4 

9 − 5 = ___

5 5 − 0 = ___

6 8 − 3 = ___

7 5¢ − 5¢ = ___¢

8 6¢ − 1¢ = ___¢

Find how many are left.

9   

___ are left.

___ − ___ = ___

10 

___ are left.

___ − ___ = ___

Performance Assessment

What Did You Learn?

You need 10 ◐.

Make up a subtraction problem for each picture.

Write a subtraction sentence for each problem.

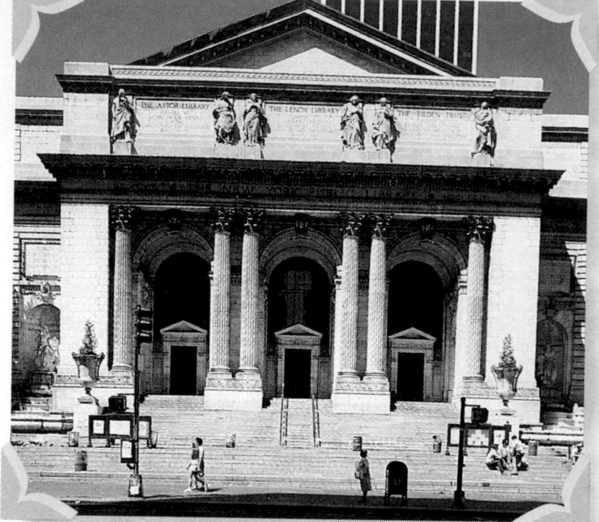

1 

____

2 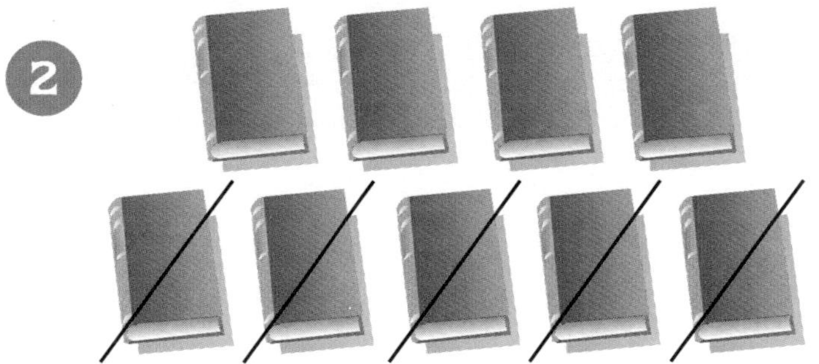

____

3 

____

You may want to put this page in your portfolio.

Math Connection
Algebra

Name ______________________________

Missing Addend

Find how many beans are hidden.

1 5 in all

2 + 3 = 5

2 4 in all

3 + 1 = 4

3 7 in all

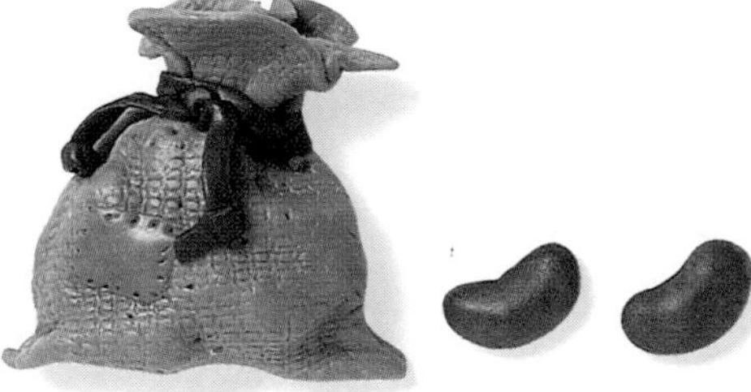

___ + 2 = 7

4 6 in all

___ + 4 = 6

5 3 in all

___ + 2 = 3

6 8 in all

___ + 7 = 8

Technology Connection

Computer

Subtract Pennies

How does using counters help you subtract?

You have 8 pennies.
You spend 5 pennies.
How many pennies are left?

____ pennies

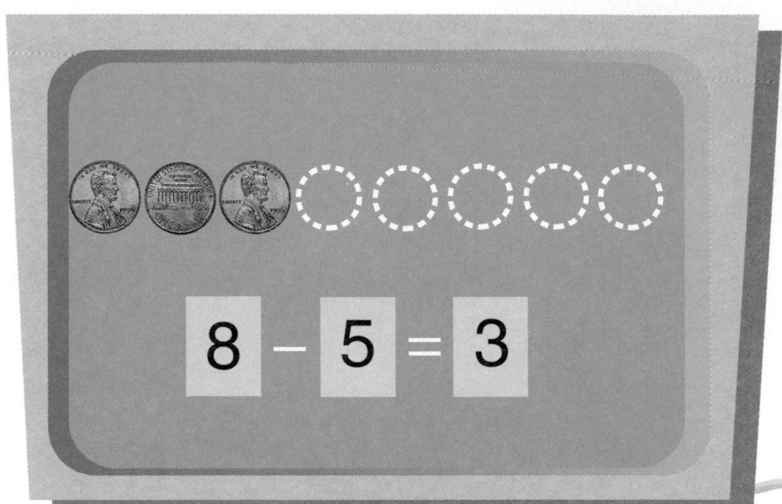

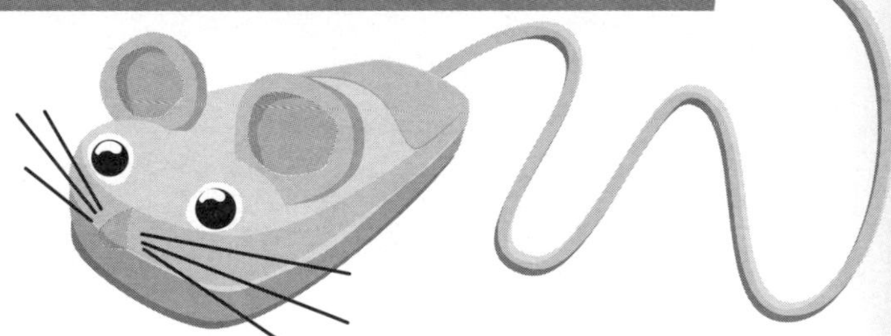

At the Computer

Use penny models to solve.

1. You have 6 pennies
   You spend 2 pennies.
   How many pennies are left? ____ pennies

2. You spend 3 pennies.
   You have 5 pennies left.
   How many pennies did you start with? ____ pennies

3. Write a problem.
   Show how to solve it with penny models.

Name

Penny Subtraction

PLAYERS 2

MATERIALS 10 pennies, 2 colors of crayons

DIRECTIONS One player shows some of the pennies and tells an amount to subtract. The other player subtracts and colors to show how many cents are left.

Play until all the boxes are colored.

4¢	9¢	5¢
1¢	8¢	6¢
3¢	2¢	7¢

At Home: Play this game with your child. Your child can count the pennies before you say the amount to subtract. Vary the starting amount. Your child uses the pennies to subtract.

At Home

Dear Family,

We are beginning a new chapter in mathematics. We will be learning more about addition and subtraction.

$$\begin{array}{r} 4 \\ +\,3 \\ \hline 7 \end{array} \qquad \begin{array}{r} 7 \\ -\,3 \\ \hline 4 \end{array}$$

We will also be talking about the circus and ways to have fun with numbers. Please help me complete this interview.

Your child,

____
Signature

Interview

What kind of circus acts do you like?
(You may check more than one.)

❑ Animals ❑ Trapeze artists

❑ Acrobats ❑ Clowns

❑ Other _______________

What is the most fun at a circus?

____

Number Fun
Adding and Subtracting to 10

Listen to the story *Number One Number Fun.*

Talk about how you have fun with numbers.

Name

What Do You Know?

5¢ 2¢ 6¢ 4¢ 3¢

Mike has 9¢ to buy balloons.
He buys a balloon and a balloon.

1 How much money does Mike spend? ____¢

5¢ + 2¢ = ____¢

2 How much money does Mike have left? ____¢

Write the subtraction sentence. ________________

You have 9¢.
Show which balloon you would buy.
Write the addition sentence.

Name ____________________

Another Way to Add

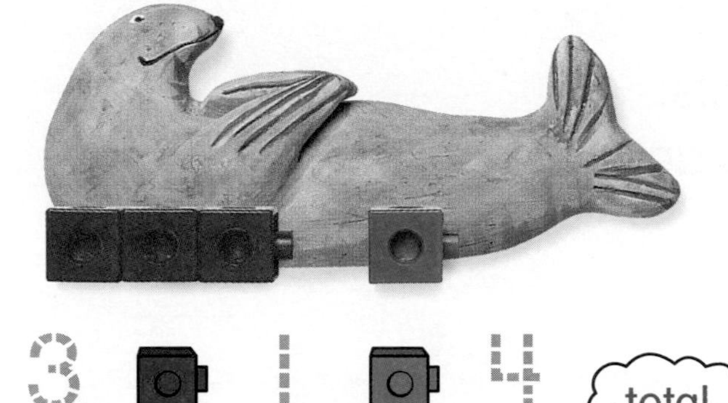

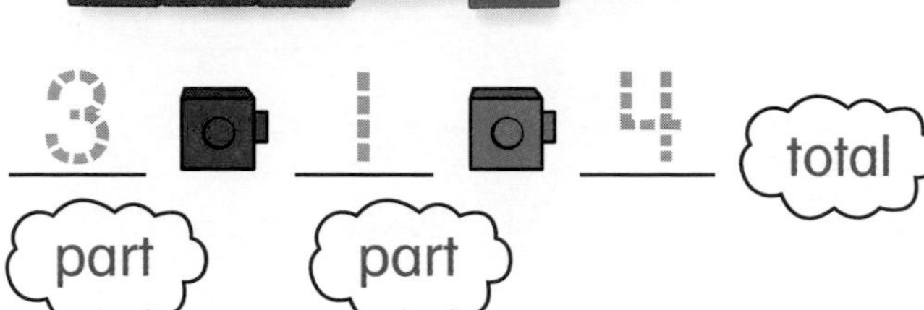

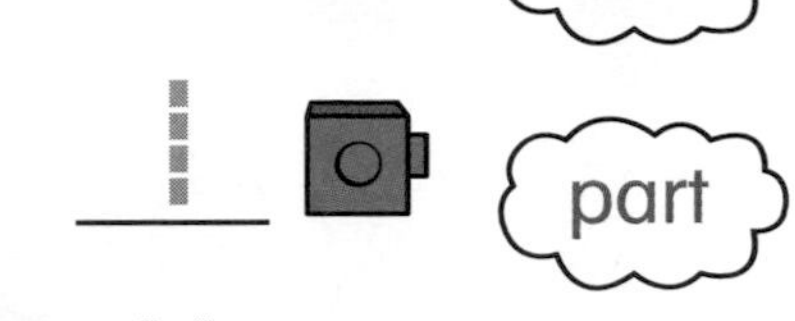

3 part

1 part

4 total

Tell a story about red parts and blue parts.

Working Together

You need 5 and 5 .

Take turns.

- You show a red part.
- Your partner shows a blue part.
- Write numbers for the parts and the totals.

1

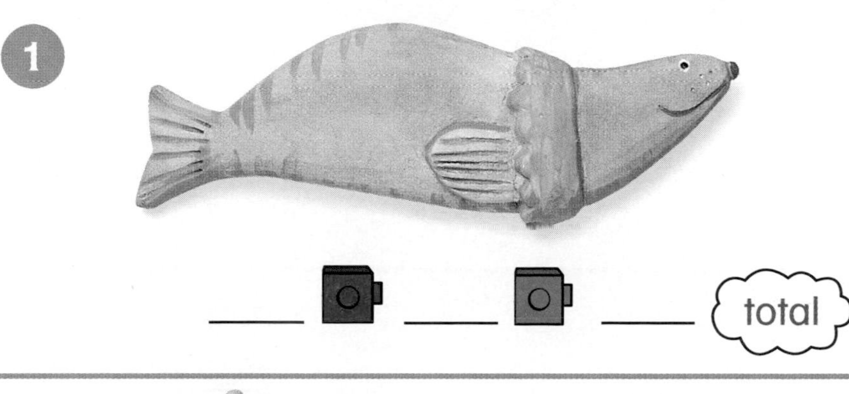

____ ____ ____ total

2

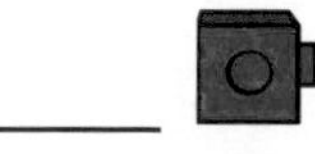

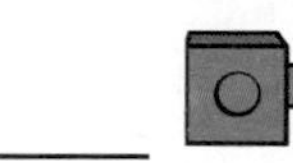

____ ____ ____ total

Try These!

Tell a story about the animals.
Write numbers for the parts and the totals.

1

2

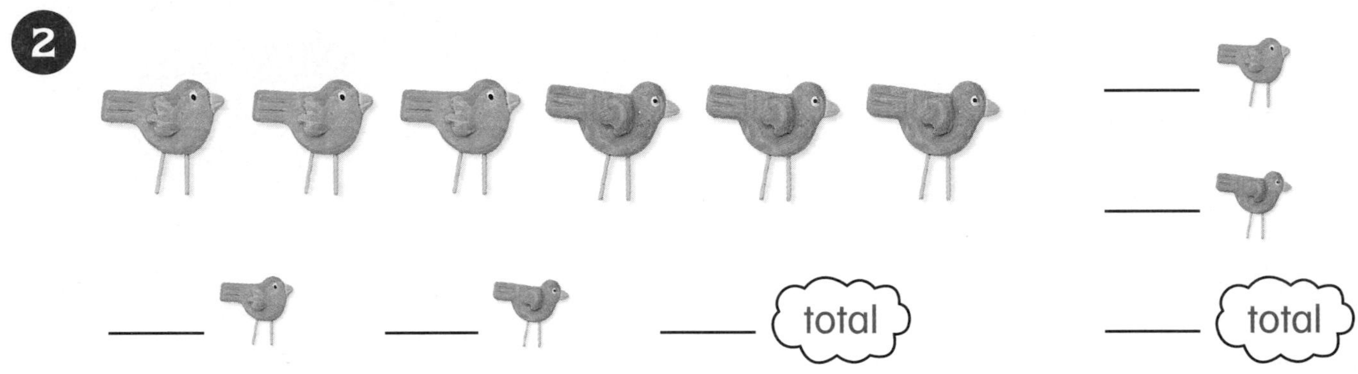

3

4

We explored parts and totals going across and going down. Ask your child to tell you a story about one of the pictures.

Name

Vertical Addition

4 + 2 = 6

sum

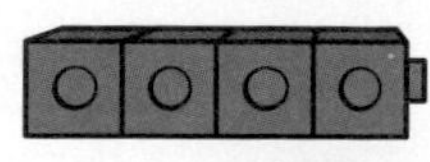

  4
+ 2
  6

sum

You need 9 and 9 .

- Show parts with .
- Color to show the parts.
- Find the sum.

1. 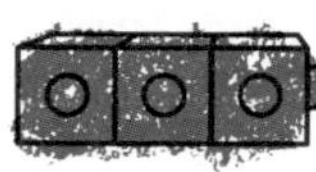

  3
+ 0
  3

2. 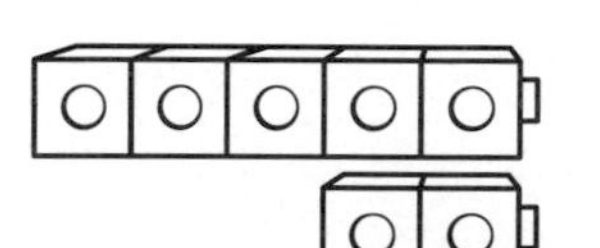

  1
+ 4

3. 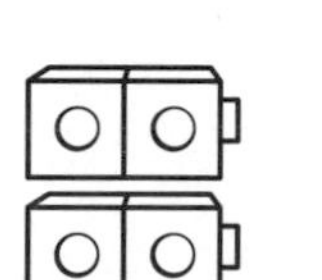

  2
+ 2

4.

  5
+ 2

5. 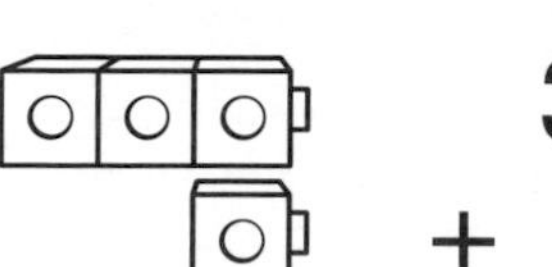

  3
+ 1

6.

  3
+ 4

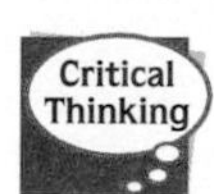

How could you use to show addition?

Try These!

Add.

1.

$$\begin{array}{r} 4 \\ +\ 3 \\ \hline 7 \end{array}$$

2.

$$\begin{array}{r} 5 \\ +\ 2 \\ \hline \end{array}$$

3.

$$\begin{array}{r} 8 \\ +\ 2 \\ \hline \end{array}$$

4.

$$\begin{array}{r} 6 \\ +\ 3 \\ \hline \end{array}$$

5.

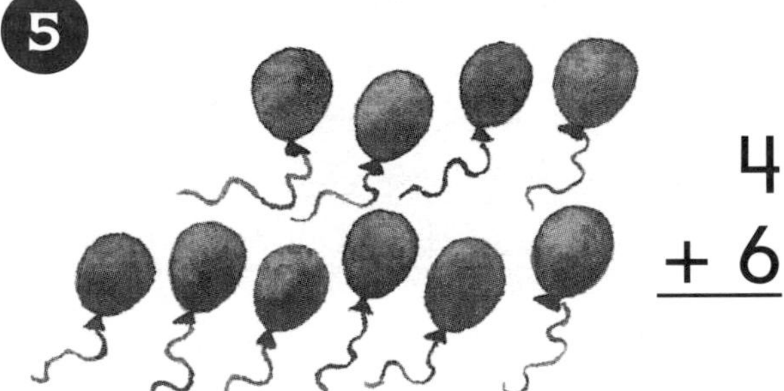

$$\begin{array}{r} 4 \\ +\ 6 \\ \hline \end{array}$$

6.

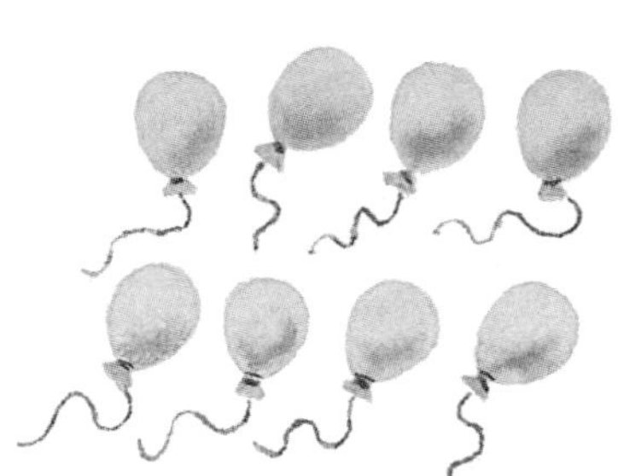

$$\begin{array}{r} 4 \\ +\ 4 \\ \hline \end{array}$$

Mixed Review

7. $5 - 1 =$ ____ $5 - 2 =$ ____ $5 - 3 =$ ____

8. $6 - 1 =$ ____ $6 - 2 =$ ____ $6 - 3 =$ ____

We learned another way to show addition. Ask your child to explain the 4 + 2 example on page 147.

Name

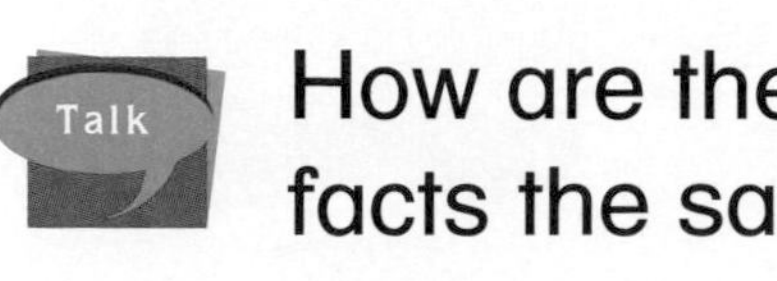

How are these facts the same?

Draw the other part. Add.

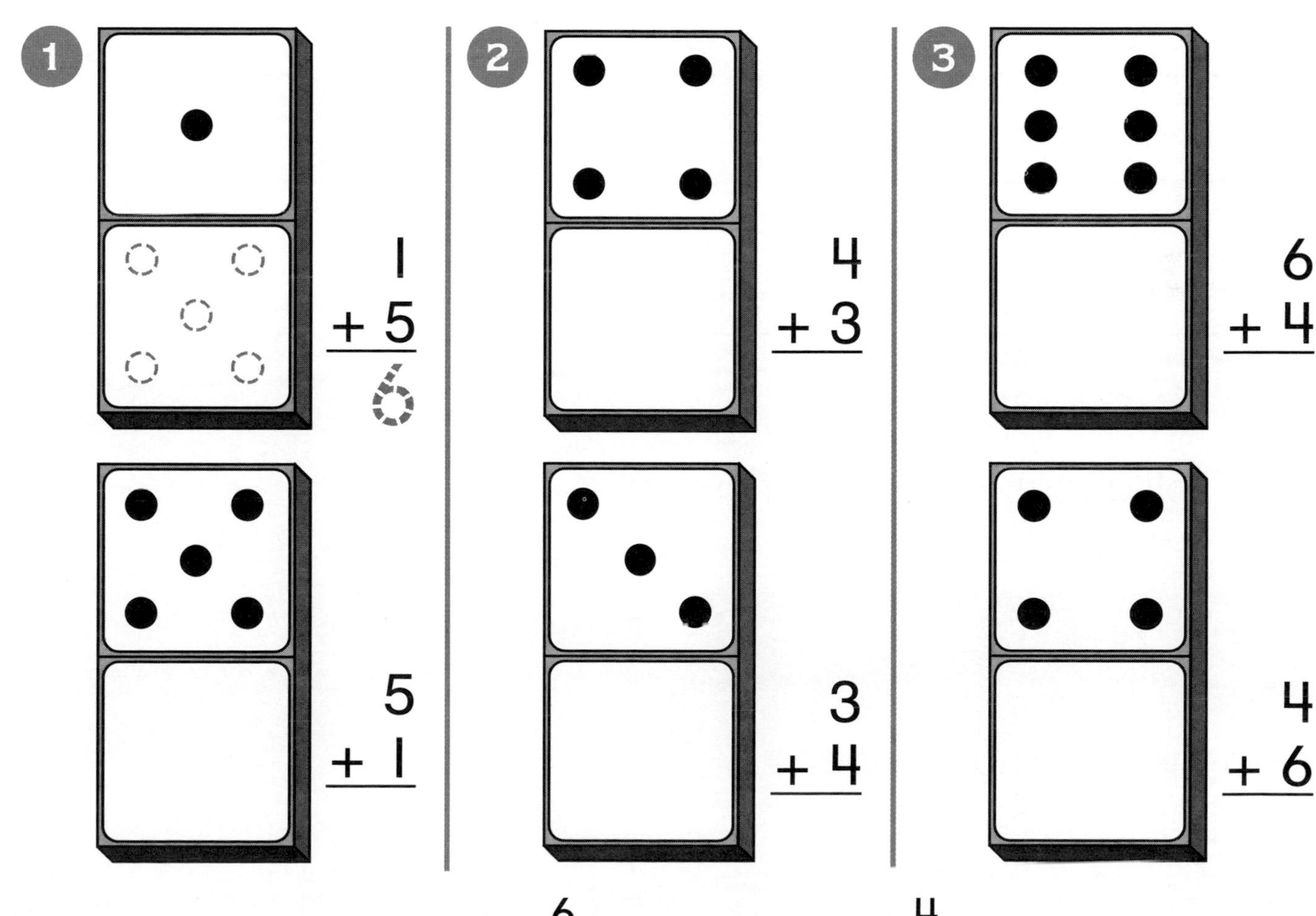

Critical Thinking

Why is the sum for $\begin{array}{r}6\\+4\\\hline\end{array}$ the same as $\begin{array}{r}4\\+6\\\hline\end{array}$?

Try These!

Add.

1. $\begin{array}{r} 3 \\ +\,3 \\ \hline 6 \end{array}$

2. 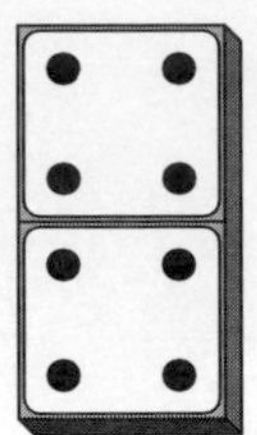 $\begin{array}{r} 4 \\ +\,4 \\ \hline \end{array}$

3. $\begin{array}{r} 5 \\ +\,5 \\ \hline \end{array}$

4. $\begin{array}{r} 7 \\ +\,2 \\ \hline \end{array}$ $\begin{array}{r} 2 \\ +\,7 \\ \hline \end{array}$ $\begin{array}{r} 1 \\ +\,6 \\ \hline \end{array}$ $\begin{array}{r} 6 \\ +\,1 \\ \hline \end{array}$ $\begin{array}{r} 9 \\ +\,0 \\ \hline \end{array}$ $\begin{array}{r} 0 \\ +\,9 \\ \hline \end{array}$

5. $\begin{array}{r} 5 \\ +\,3 \\ \hline \end{array}$ $\begin{array}{r} 3 \\ +\,5 \\ \hline \end{array}$ $\begin{array}{r} 4 \\ +\,2 \\ \hline \end{array}$ $\begin{array}{r} 2 \\ +\,4 \\ \hline \end{array}$ $\begin{array}{r} 3 \\ +\,7 \\ \hline \end{array}$ $\begin{array}{r} 7 \\ +\,3 \\ \hline \end{array}$

6. $\begin{array}{r} 2 \\ +\,8 \\ \hline \end{array}$ $\begin{array}{r} 8 \\ +\,2 \\ \hline \end{array}$ $\begin{array}{r} 6 \\ +\,3 \\ \hline \end{array}$ $\begin{array}{r} 3 \\ +\,6 \\ \hline \end{array}$ $\begin{array}{r} 8 \\ +\,1 \\ \hline \end{array}$ $\begin{array}{r} 1 \\ +\,8 \\ \hline \end{array}$

Tell about each pair of sums.

More to Explore Algebra Sense

Find the missing number.

$\begin{array}{r} 5 \\ +\,\boxed{2} \\ \hline 7 \end{array}$ $\begin{array}{r} 2 \\ +\,\square \\ \hline 7 \end{array}$ $\begin{array}{r} 1 \\ +\,\square \\ \hline 8 \end{array}$ $\begin{array}{r} 7 \\ +\,\square \\ \hline 8 \end{array}$ $\begin{array}{r} 2 \\ +\,\square \\ \hline 4 \end{array}$

At Home: We learned about related addition facts. Ask your child to tell you how the pairs of execises are the same.

Name ____________________

Extra Practice Activity!

Rhino Riddle

Add.

r	v	a	e	r
1 + 0 = 1	4 + 6 =	1 + 1 =	6 + 3 =	7 + 1 =

i	g	b	y	c
3 + 2 =	3 + 1 =	2 + 4 =	4 + 3 =	1 + 2 =

Match sums to answer the riddle.

How does a rhino go to the circus?

In a ___ ___ ___ ___
(10) (9) (8) (7)

___ ___ ___   ___ ___ r!
(6) (5) (4)   (3) (2) (1)

Add.

1 $\begin{array}{r}4\\+6\\\hline 10\end{array}$ $\begin{array}{r}5\\+2\\\hline\end{array}$ $\begin{array}{r}3\\+3\\\hline\end{array}$ $\begin{array}{r}7\\+2\\\hline\end{array}$ $\begin{array}{r}4\\+4\\\hline\end{array}$ $\begin{array}{r}9\\+1\\\hline\end{array}$

2 $\begin{array}{r}3\\+7\\\hline\end{array}$ $\begin{array}{r}5\\+4\\\hline\end{array}$ $\begin{array}{r}2\\+2\\\hline\end{array}$ $\begin{array}{r}4\\+1\\\hline\end{array}$ $\begin{array}{r}9\\+0\\\hline\end{array}$ $\begin{array}{r}1\\+6\\\hline\end{array}$

3 $\begin{array}{r}5\\+3\\\hline\end{array}$ $\begin{array}{r}3\\+1\\\hline\end{array}$ $\begin{array}{r}7\\+0\\\hline\end{array}$ $\begin{array}{r}6\\+4\\\hline\end{array}$ $\begin{array}{r}5\\+5\\\hline\end{array}$ $\begin{array}{r}6\\+0\\\hline\end{array}$

4 $\begin{array}{r}8\\+1\\\hline\end{array}$ $\begin{array}{r}6\\+2\\\hline\end{array}$ $\begin{array}{r}0\\+8\\\hline\end{array}$ $\begin{array}{r}5\\+1\\\hline\end{array}$ $\begin{array}{r}0\\+5\\\hline\end{array}$ $\begin{array}{r}4\\+5\\\hline\end{array}$

Draw lines to match.

5 $\begin{array}{r}8\\+2\\\hline\end{array}$ $\begin{array}{r}1\\+7\\\hline\end{array}$ $\begin{array}{r}6\\+3\\\hline\end{array}$

10 9 8

$\begin{array}{r}7\\+1\\\hline\end{array}$ $\begin{array}{r}3\\+6\\\hline\end{array}$ $\begin{array}{r}2\\+8\\\hline\end{array}$

6 

$\begin{array}{r}2\\+4\\\hline\end{array}$ $\begin{array}{r}2\\+3\\\hline\end{array}$ $\begin{array}{r}3\\+4\\\hline\end{array}$

7 6 5

$\begin{array}{r}4\\+2\\\hline\end{array}$ $\begin{array}{r}4\\+3\\\hline\end{array}$ $\begin{array}{r}3\\+2\\\hline\end{array}$

Name

Add Money

Find how much money Kim needs.

$$\begin{array}{r} 3¢ \\ +\ 5¢ \\ \hline 8¢ \end{array}$$

You need 10 (penny).
Add to find how much money.

1 

$$\begin{array}{r} 6¢ \\ +\ 1¢ \\ \hline ¢ \end{array}$$

2 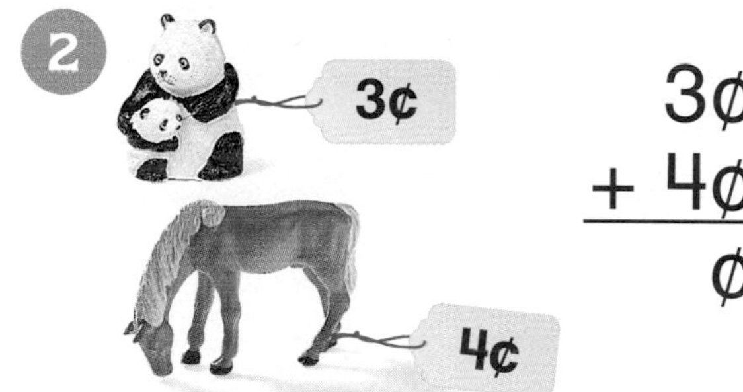

$$\begin{array}{r} 3¢ \\ +\ 4¢ \\ \hline ¢ \end{array}$$

3 

$$\begin{array}{r} 8¢ \\ +\ 2¢ \\ \hline ¢ \end{array}$$

4 (5¢) (4¢)

$$\begin{array}{r} 5¢ \\ +\ 4¢ \\ \hline ¢ \end{array}$$

5 

$$\begin{array}{r} 7¢ \\ +\ 3¢ \\ \hline ¢ \end{array}$$

6 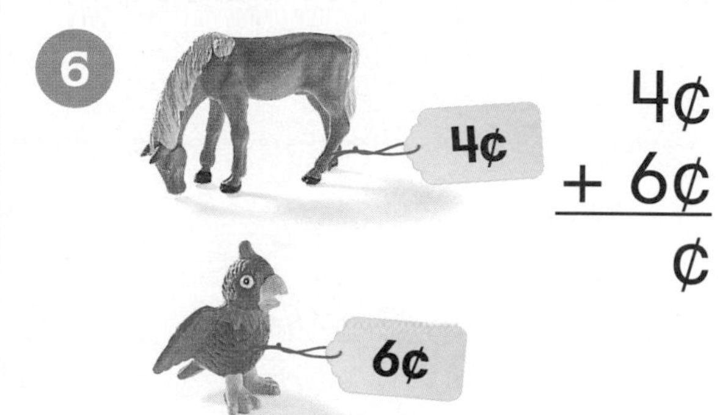

$$\begin{array}{r} 4¢ \\ +\ 6¢ \\ \hline ¢ \end{array}$$

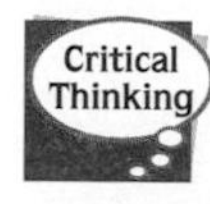

Which of the toys could you buy for 6¢?

Try These!

Use pennies if you want to.

Add.

1 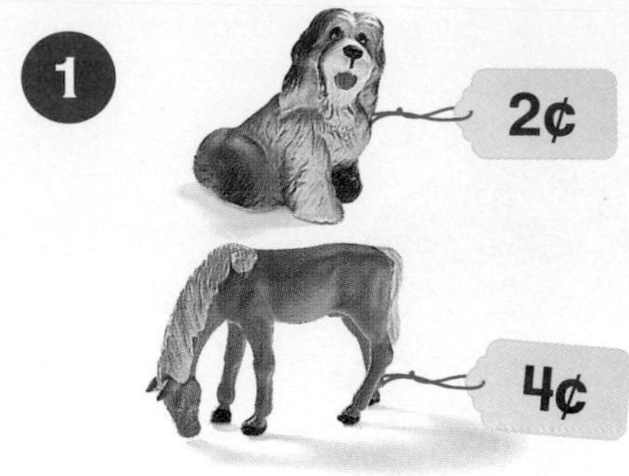

$$\begin{array}{r} 2¢ \\ +\ 4¢ \\ \hline 6¢ \end{array}$$

2 

$$\begin{array}{r} 5¢ \\ +\ 1¢ \\ \hline ¢ \end{array}$$

3 

$$\begin{array}{r} 9¢ \\ +\ 1¢ \\ \hline ¢ \end{array}$$

4 

$$\begin{array}{r} 3¢ \\ +\ 6¢ \\ \hline ¢ \end{array}$$

5

1¢	7¢	2¢	4¢	1¢	3¢
+ 3¢	+ 2¢	+ 5¢	+ 4¢	+ 8¢	+ 3¢
¢	¢	¢	¢	¢	¢

6

5¢	4¢	3¢	9¢	6¢	8¢
+ 4¢	+ 3¢	+ 5¢	+ 1¢	+ 2¢	+ 2¢
¢	¢	¢	¢	¢	¢

7

3¢	5¢	4¢	8¢	4¢	5¢
+ 7¢	+ 5¢	+ 4¢	+ 1¢	+ 6¢	+ 3¢
¢	¢	¢	¢	¢	¢

Draw and write about adding money.

At Home: Show your child 2 pennies in one hand and 4 pennies in the other. Ask how much money you have in both hands.

Name

Midchapter Review

Do your best!

Add.

1. 4 + 3 = ___

2. 6 + 4 = ___

3. 3 + 5 = ___

4. 1 + 8 = ___

5. 5 + 5 = ___

6. 8 + 2 = ___

7. 1 + 9 = ___

8. 3 + 6 = ___

9. 3 + 7 = ___

10. 2 + 4 = ___

11. 5 + 4 = ___

12. 3 + 3 = ___

13. 4 + 6 = ___

14. 4¢ + 4¢ = ___¢

15. 2¢ + 5¢ = ___¢

16. 4¢ + 1¢ = ___¢

17. 7¢ + 2¢ = ___¢

18. 2¢ + 3¢ = ___¢

19. 4¢ + 5¢ = ___¢

20. Why are 3 + 1 and $\begin{array}{r}3\\+\,1\\\hline\end{array}$ the same?

___

Journal

Write or draw about ways to add.

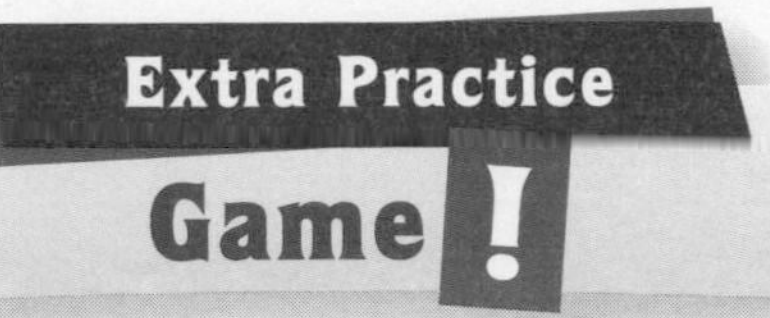

Cover the Circus Wagon

You need 2 and 9 .

Take turns.

- ▶ Roll the 2 .
- ▶ Add. Put a on the sum.
- ▶ Get 3 in a row.

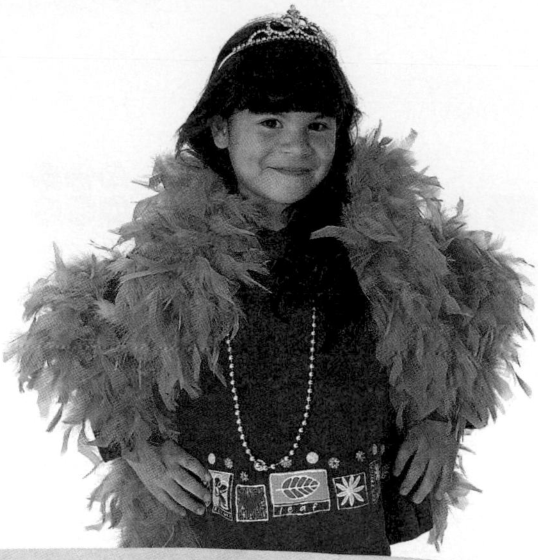

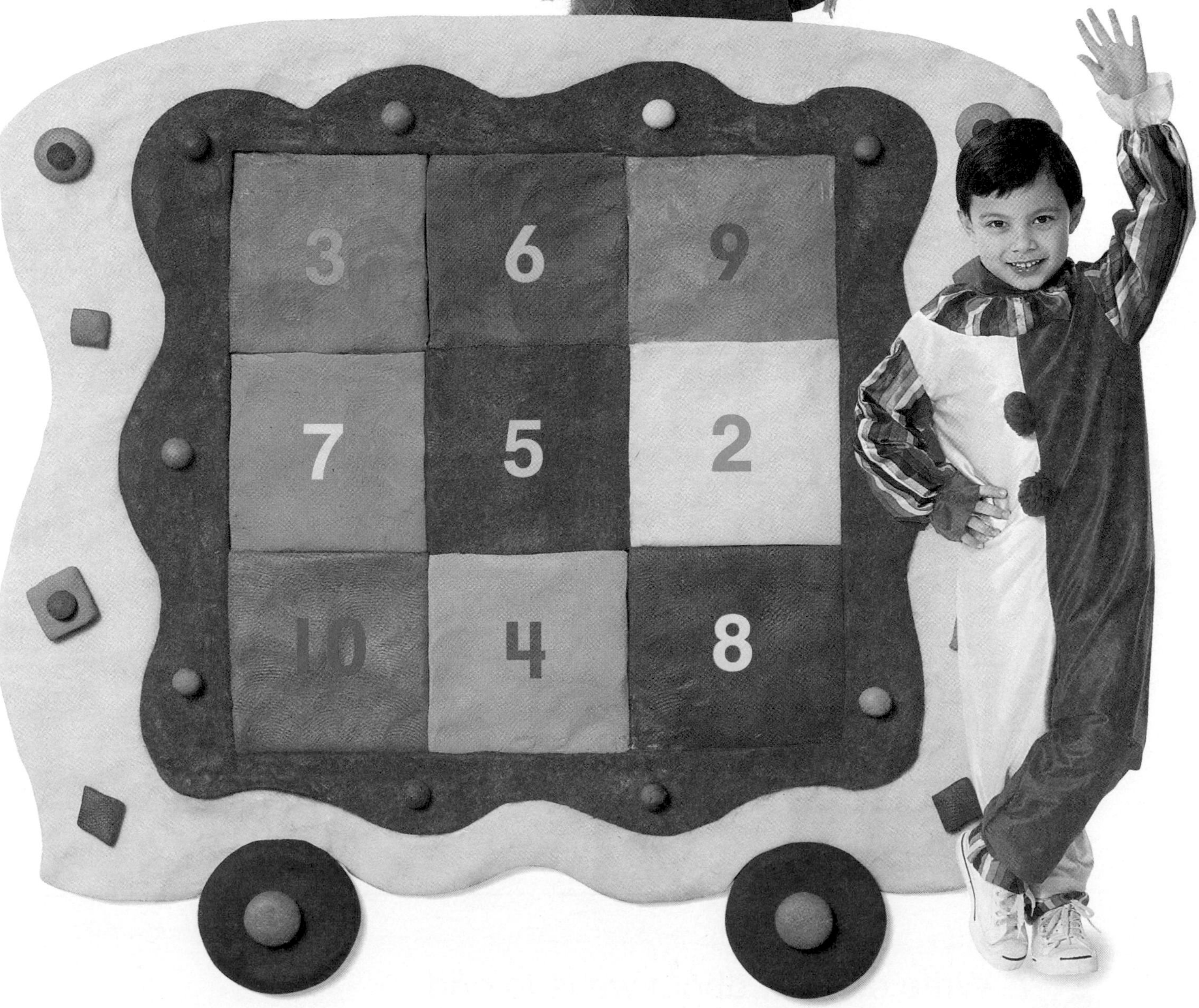

3	6	9
7	5	2
10	4	8

Real-Life Investigation

Applying Addition

Name

Circus Fun

Listen to *Number One Number Fun*.

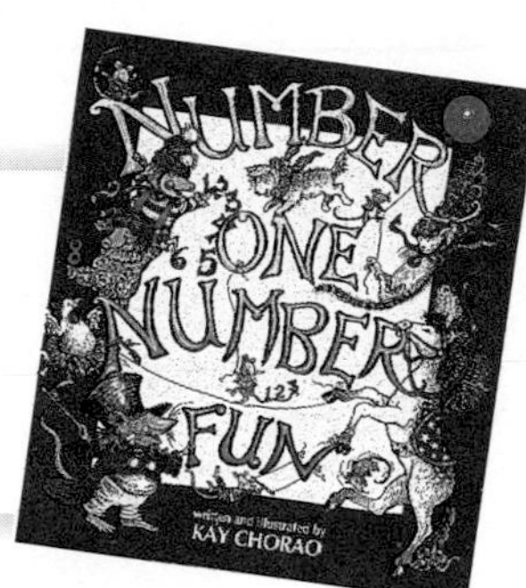

Take a survey. Ask this question:

“Would you be brave enough to swing on a trapeze?”

Make a class graph.

1. How many children said *yes*? ______

2. How many children said *no*? ______

3. Did more children say *yes* or *no*? ______

   How many more? ______

Decision Making

1. Write a question to ask.
   Take another survey.

   ____

   ____

2. Make a class graph.

Write a report.

3. Tell what you found out.
4. Use numbers to show what you learned.

Cultural Note
In Russia, the Moscow Circus School teaches children math and trains them to perform.

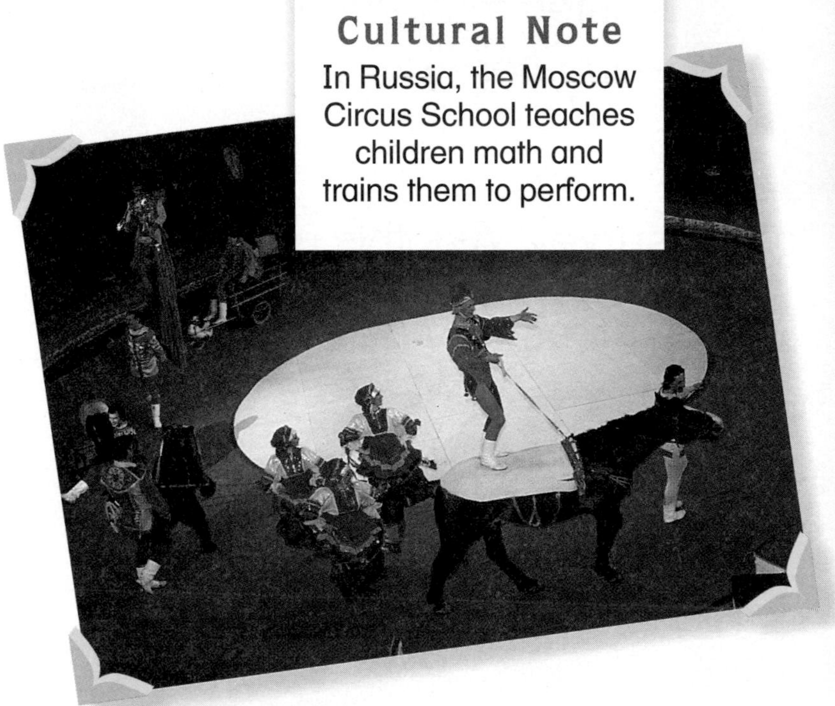

More to Investigate

PREDICT What if you ask another class. Will you get the same numbers?

EXPLORE Try it. Then make another graph.

FIND Compare the two graphs. How are they alike? How are they different?

Name

Explore Activity

Another Way to Subtract

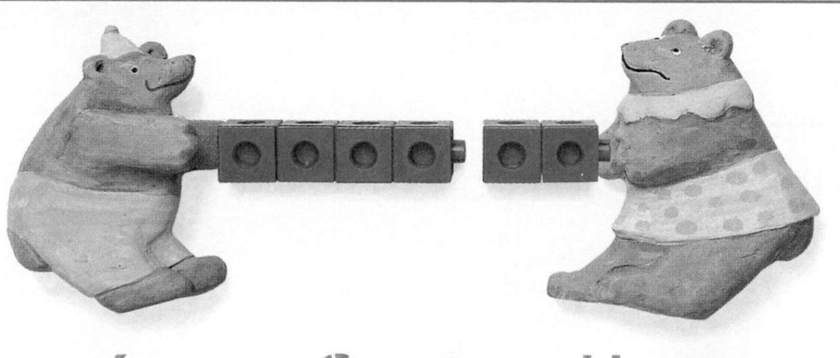

Tell a story about taking away 2 cubes.

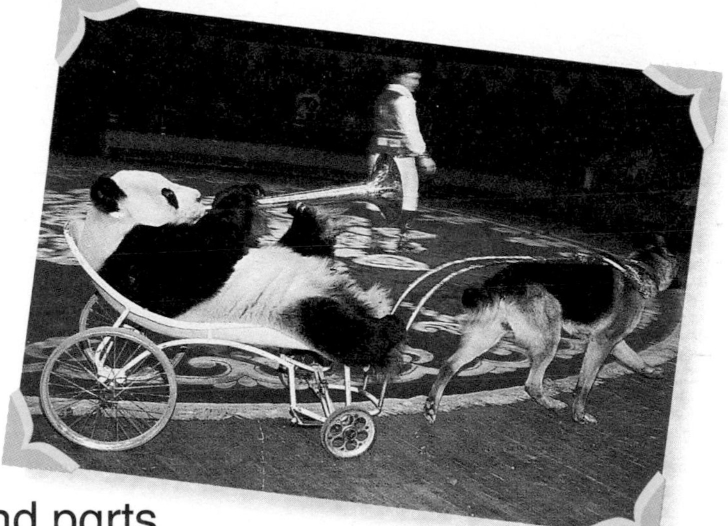

Working Together

You need 10 [cube].

Take turns.

- You make a train.
- Your partner snaps off a part.
- Write numbers for the totals and parts.

1

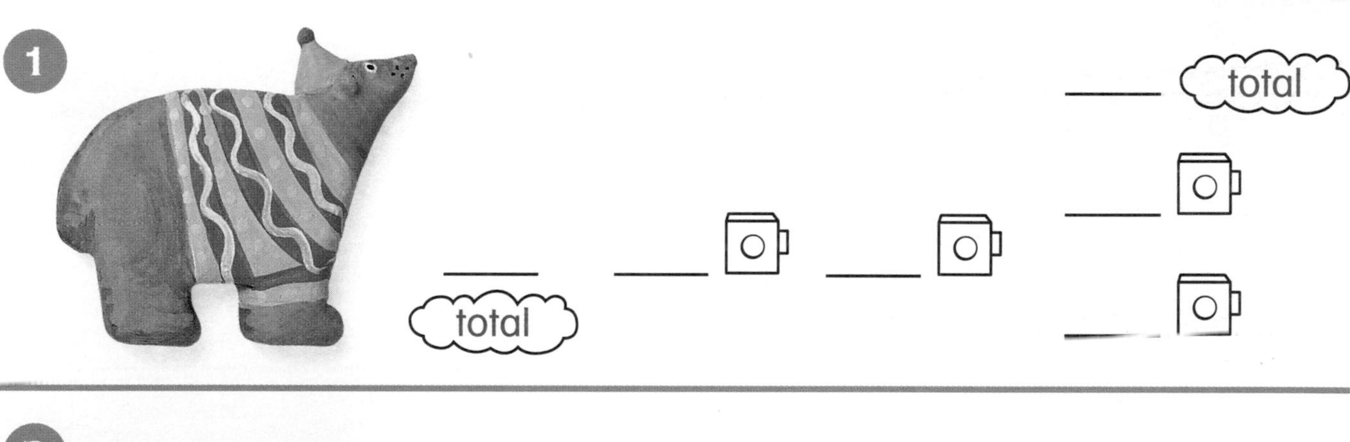

2

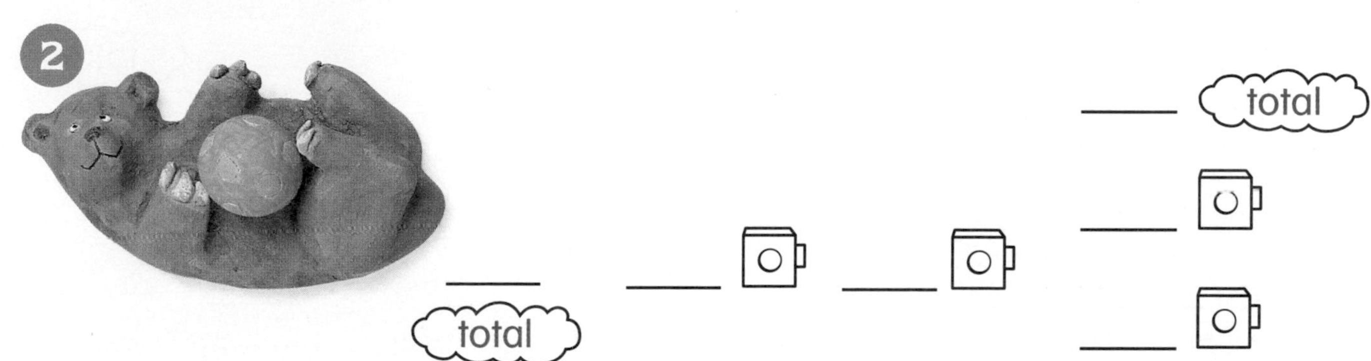

Try These!

Talk

Tell a story about the animals.
Write numbers for the totals and parts.

1

2

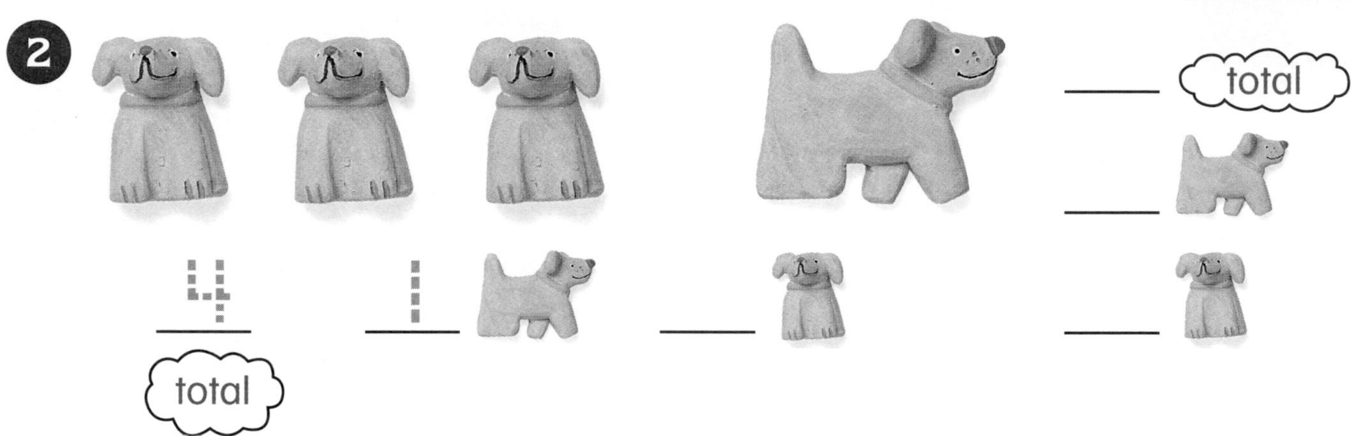

3

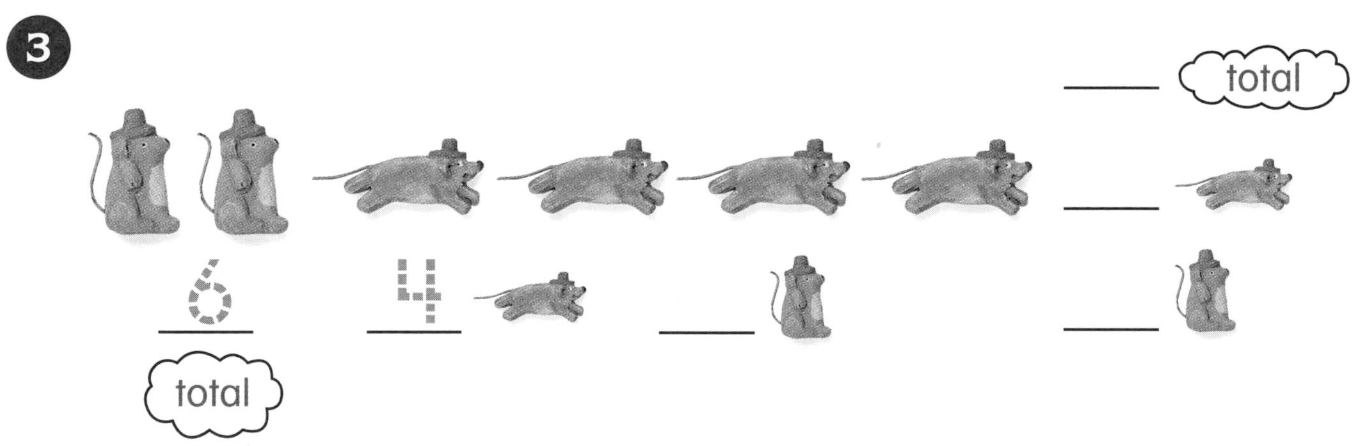

4

We explored totals and parts going across and down.
Ask your child to tell you a story about one of the pictures.

Name

Vertical Subtraction

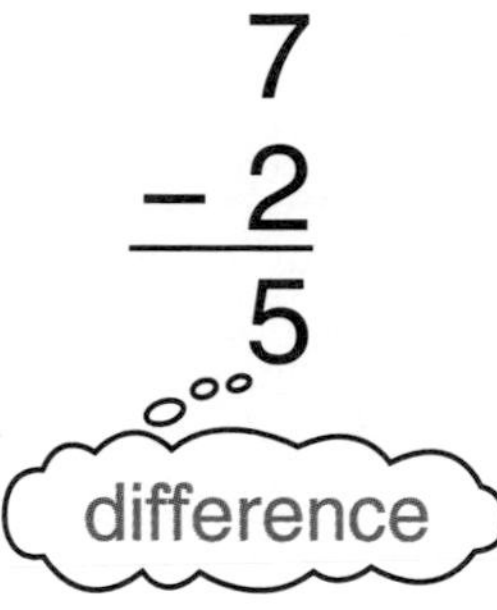

$7 - 2 = 5$

difference

$$\begin{array}{r} 7 \\ -\ 2 \\ \hline 5 \end{array}$$

difference

You need 10 .

- Show the total. Take away part.
- Cross out that part.
- Find the difference.

1 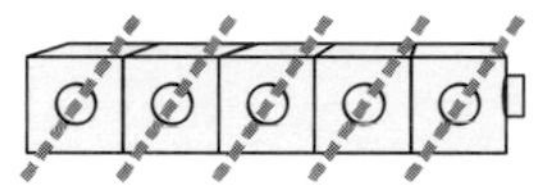

$$\begin{array}{r} 5 \\ -\ 5 \\ \hline 0 \end{array}$$

2

$$\begin{array}{r} 4 \\ -\ 3 \\ \hline \end{array}$$

3 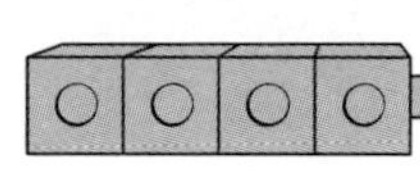

$$\begin{array}{r} 4 \\ -\ 2 \\ \hline \end{array}$$

4

$$\begin{array}{r} 3 \\ -\ 3 \\ \hline \end{array}$$

5 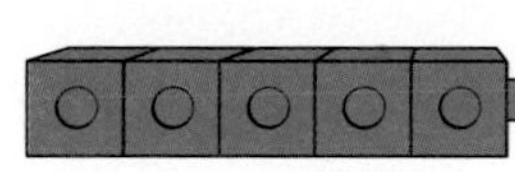

$$\begin{array}{r} 5 \\ -\ 2 \\ \hline \end{array}$$

6 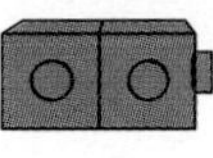

$$\begin{array}{r} 2 \\ -\ 0 \\ \hline \end{array}$$

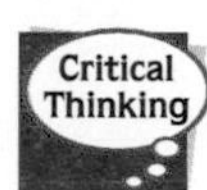

What if there are 6 red and 2 blue cubes. What subtraction could you show?

Subtract.

1 $\begin{array}{r} 10 \\ -\ 2 \\ \hline 8 \end{array}$

2 $\begin{array}{r} 6 \\ -\ 3 \\ \hline \end{array}$

3 $\begin{array}{r} 9 \\ -\ 3 \\ \hline \end{array}$

4 $\begin{array}{r} 8 \\ -\ 2 \\ \hline \end{array}$

5 $\begin{array}{r} 6 \\ -\ 4 \\ \hline \end{array}$

6 $\begin{array}{r} 9 \\ -\ 5 \\ \hline \end{array}$

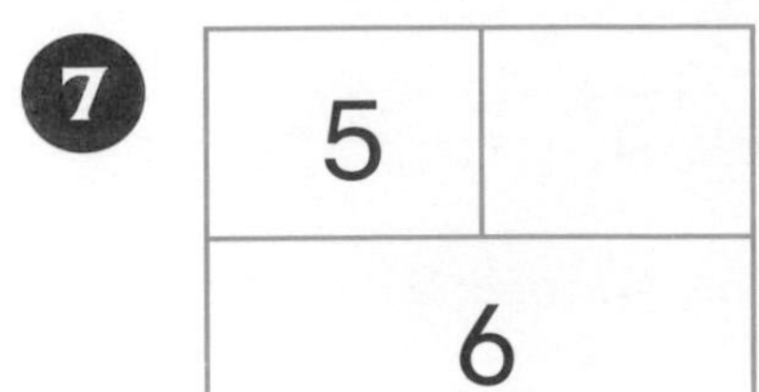

Find the missing part.

7

5	
6	

	5
7	

4	
8	

	3
9	

At Home
We learned another way to show subtraction.
Ask your child to explain the 7 – 2 example on 161.

Name

Related Subtraction Facts

How are these facts different?

Draw the missing part. Subtract.

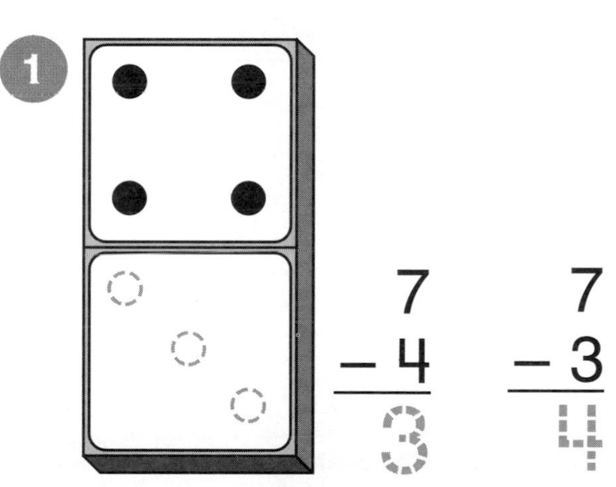

1.
$$\begin{array}{r} 7 \\ -\ 4 \\ \hline 3 \end{array} \qquad \begin{array}{r} 7 \\ -\ 3 \\ \hline 4 \end{array}$$

2.
$$\begin{array}{r} 6 \\ -\ 1 \\ \hline \end{array} \qquad \begin{array}{r} 6 \\ -\ 5 \\ \hline \end{array}$$

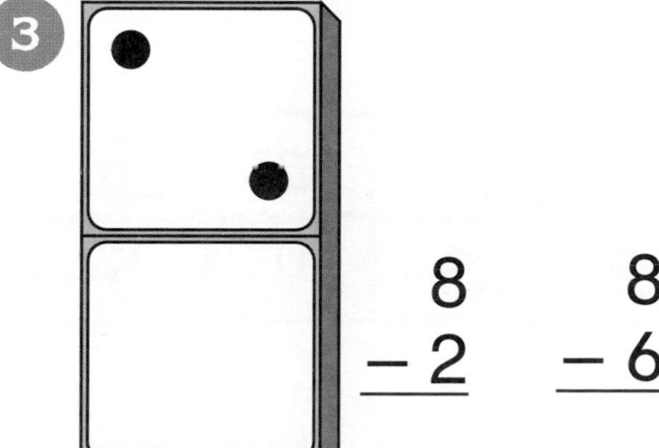

3.
$$\begin{array}{r} 8 \\ -\ 2 \\ \hline \end{array} \qquad \begin{array}{r} 8 \\ -\ 6 \\ \hline \end{array}$$

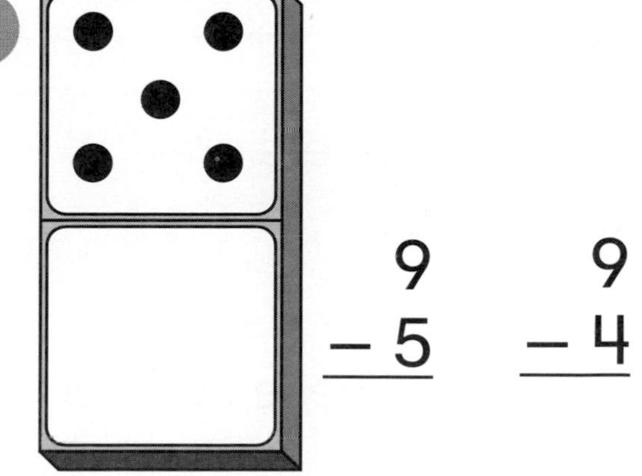

4.
$$\begin{array}{r} 9 \\ -\ 5 \\ \hline \end{array} \qquad \begin{array}{r} 9 \\ -\ 4 \\ \hline \end{array}$$

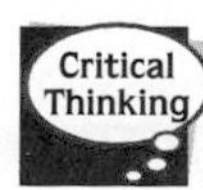

How could you show this subtraction with crossing out?

Try These!

Subtract.

1
  6
− 3
  3

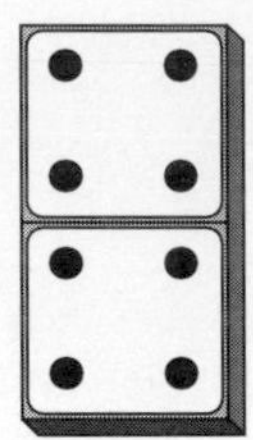

2
  8
− 4

3
  10
− 5

4

7	7	9	9	8	8
− 2	− 5	− 2	− 7	− 5	− 3

5

6	6	10	10	7	7
− 4	− 2	− 7	− 3	− 1	− 6

6

9	9	10	10	9	9
− 9	− 0	− 2	− 8	− 1	− 8

Cultural Connection

Chinese Numbers

Chinese numbers are like pictures.

一	二	三	四	五
1	2	3	4	5

Write the Chinese number that is 1 less.

___ 三 ___ 五 ___ 二

At Home: We learned about related subtraction facts. Ask your child to tell you how the pairs of facts are alike.

Name

Number Fun House

Subtract. Color to match differences.

1 or 2 — blue	5 — purple	7 — yellow
3 or 4 — green	6 — orange	8 — red

$8 - 0 = 8$	$9 - 2$	$9 - 1$	$10 - 3$	$10 - 2$	$7 - 0$
$7 - 3$	$8 - 2$	$10 - 6$	$9 - 5$	$10 - 4$	$8 - 4$
$8 - 5$	$9 - 3$	$9 - 8$	$7 - 2$	$7 - 1$	$6 - 2$
$9 - 6$	$5 - 3$	$8 - 3$	$8 - 6$	$5 - 0$	$10 - 7$
$9 - 4$	$4 - 3$	$8 - 1$	$6 - 1$	$6 - 5$	
$10 - 9$					$10 - 5$

Subtract.

1

10	6	9	7	9
− 9	− 6	− 8	− 6	− 0
1				

2

8	10	6	8	5	9
− 8	− 5	− 1	− 6	− 5	− 2

3

9	5	7	10	6	8
− 4	− 2	− 5	− 8	− 4	− 1

4

7	10	6	8	9	7
− 4	− 7	− 3	− 7	− 6	− 0

Match related facts. Subtract.

9	10	10
− 3	− 4	− 1
6		

10	9	10
− 9	− 6	− 6
	3	

9	9	10
− 5	− 2	− 7

9	10	9
− 7	− 3	− 4

Name ____________________

Subtract Money

Find how much money Josh has left.

$$\begin{array}{r} 10¢ \\ -\ 5¢ \\ \hline 5¢ \end{array}$$

You need 10 ¢.
Subtract to find how much money is left.

1 

$$\begin{array}{r} 10¢ \\ -\ 7¢ \\ \hline ¢ \end{array}$$

2 

$$\begin{array}{r} 9¢ \\ -\ 5¢ \\ \hline ¢ \end{array}$$

3 

$$\begin{array}{r} 10¢ \\ -\ 6¢ \\ \hline ¢ \end{array}$$

4 

$$\begin{array}{r} 7¢ \\ -\ 7¢ \\ \hline ¢ \end{array}$$

5 

$$\begin{array}{r} 8¢ \\ -\ 5¢ \\ \hline ¢ \end{array}$$

6 

$$\begin{array}{r} 7¢ \\ -\ 4¢ \\ \hline ¢ \end{array}$$

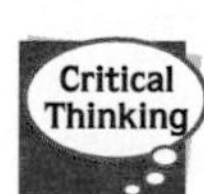

You have 5¢. How much more money do you need to buy duck food?

Try These!

Use pennies if you want to.

Subtract.

1 

  9¢
− 6¢
  3¢

  7¢
− 1¢
   ¢

 10¢
− 4¢
   ¢

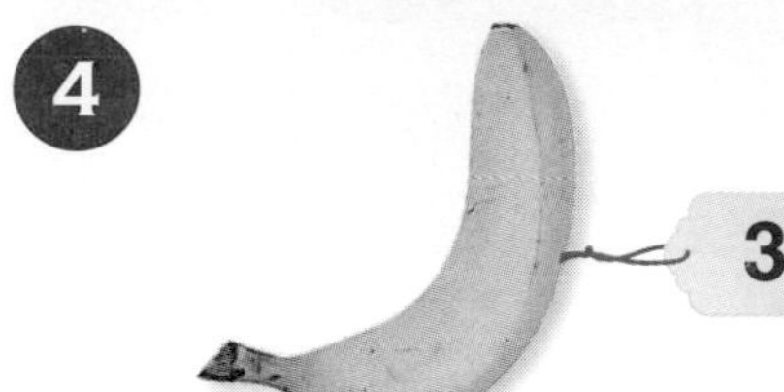

  8¢
− 3¢
   ¢

5

10¢	9¢	7¢	8¢	9¢	6¢
− 7¢	− 5¢	− 3¢	− 6¢	− 2¢	− 5¢
¢	¢	¢	¢	¢	¢

6

8¢	10¢	4¢	9¢	5¢	7¢
− 2¢	− 5¢	− 1¢	− 9¢	− 2¢	− 6¢
¢	¢	¢	¢	¢	¢

7

4¢	10¢	5¢	9¢	6¢	8¢
− 4¢	− 8¢	− 1¢	− 8¢	− 3¢	− 5¢
¢	¢	¢	¢	¢	¢

More to Explore Patterns

Complete.

9	8	7	6	☐	☐	☐
− 3	− 3	− 3	− 3	− 3	− 3	− 3
6						

At Home: Show your child 10 pennies. Ask how many you would have left if you spent 6¢.

Name

Addition and Subtraction

$$\begin{array}{r} 5 \\ +\ 3 \\ \hline 8 \end{array} \qquad \begin{array}{r} 8 \\ -\ 3 \\ \hline 5 \end{array}$$

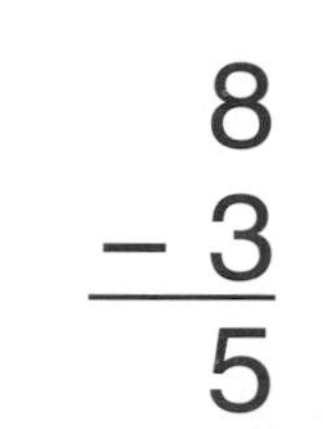

Tell a story about the picture.

You need 9 and 9 .

Show some and show some .
Draw them.
Write the addition and subtraction.

1 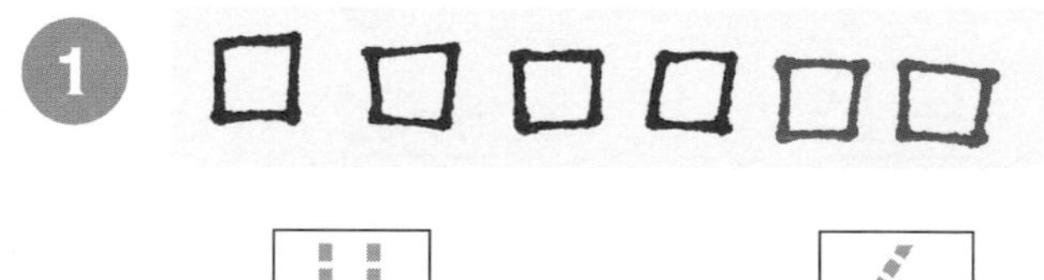

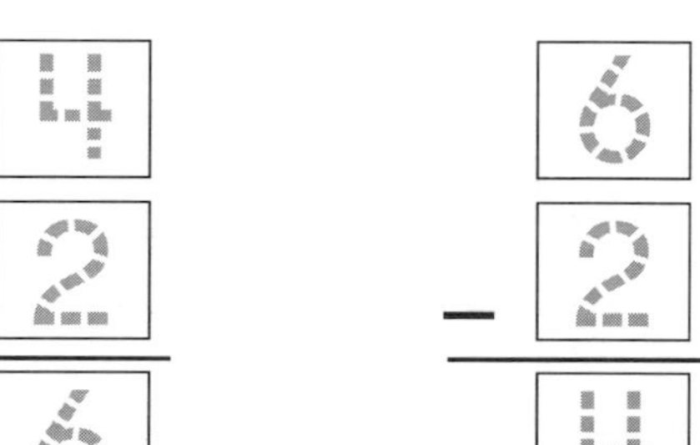

$$\begin{array}{r} 4 \\ +\ 2 \\ \hline 6 \end{array} \qquad \begin{array}{r} 6 \\ -\ 2 \\ \hline 4 \end{array}$$

2

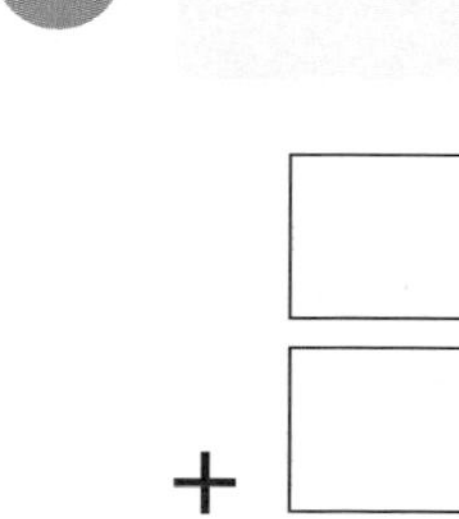

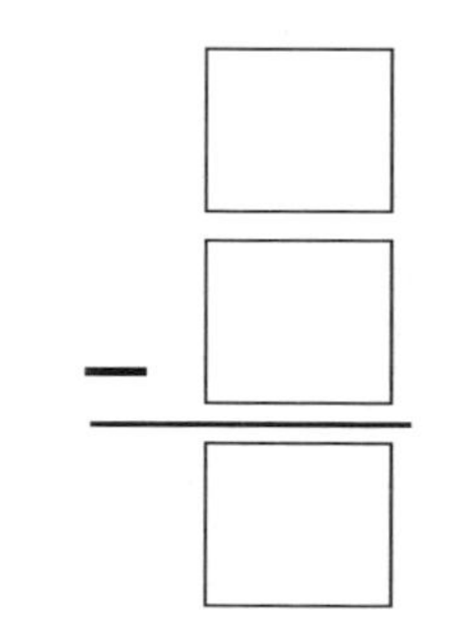

+ ☐ ☐ ☐   − ☐ ☐ ☐

3

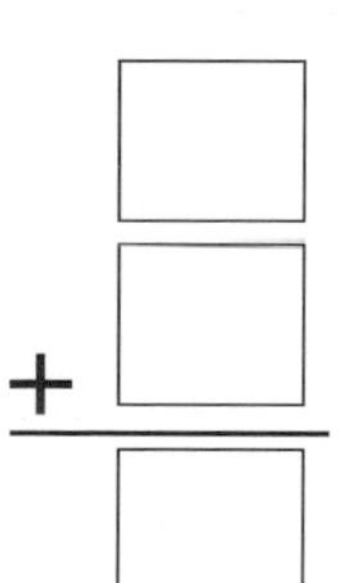

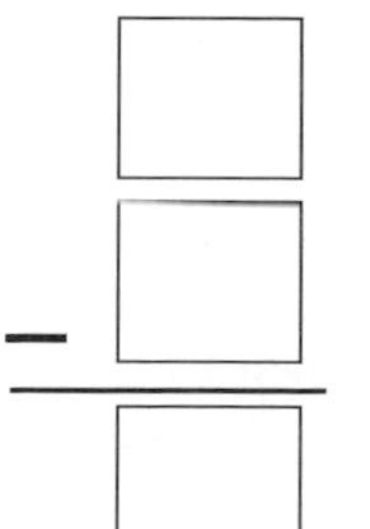

+ ☐ ☐ ☐   − ☐ ☐ ☐

4

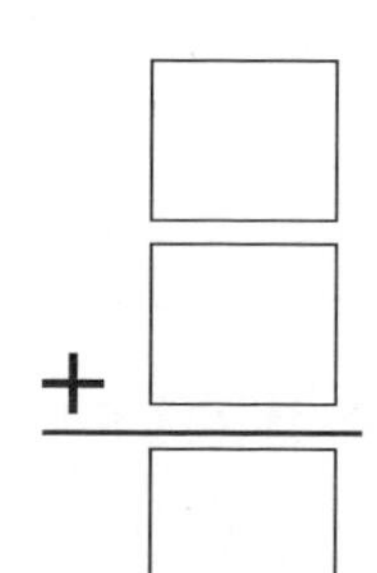

+ ☐ ☐ ☐   − ☐ ☐ ☐

Try These!

Use cubes if you want to.

Add or subtract.

1  

2	7
+ 5	− 5
7	2

2

6	6
+ 0	− 6

3

8	10	3	7	1	4
+ 2	− 2	+ 4	− 4	+ 3	− 3

4

5	6	7	9	6	8
+ 1	− 1	+ 2	− 2	+ 2	− 2

5

0	5	4	7	3	6
+ 5	− 5	+ 3	− 3	+ 3	− 3

6

3	10	8	9	5	10
+ 7	− 7	+ 1	− 1	+ 5	− 5

Draw a picture that shows addition and subtraction. Write the facts.

At Home

We learned how addition and subtraction can be related. Ask your child about the exercises on page 169.

Name

Problem - Solving Strategy

Choose the Operation

Read
Plan
Solve
Look Back

Read There were 2 clowns in the ring.
3 more clowns came in.
How many clowns are in the ring now?

What do you know?

What do you need to find out?

Plan Do you add or subtract?  $-$

Solve Try your plan.

$$\begin{array}{r} 2 \\ +\ 3 \\ \hline 5 \end{array}$$

What is the answer?

____ clowns

Look Back Does your answer make sense?
Explain.

Choose + or – . Solve.

1. There were 7 clowns playing.
2 clowns went home.
How many clowns are playing now?

$+$ 

____ clowns

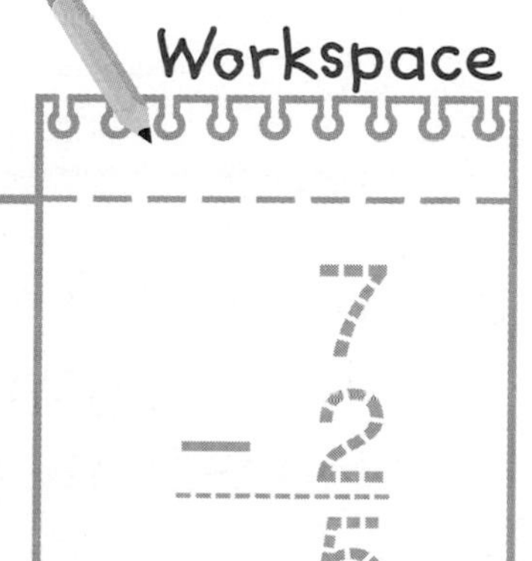

$$\begin{array}{r} 7 \\ -\ 2 \\ \hline 5 \end{array}$$

Try These!

Workspace

Choose + or –. Solve.

1. There are 3 dogs in one car.
There are 5 dogs in another car.
How many dogs are in the two cars?

+ –   ____ dogs

$$\begin{array}{r} 3 \\ +\ 5 \\ \hline 8 \end{array}$$

2. 9 cats wear hats.
6 of the cats take off their hats.
How many cats still wear hats?

+ –   ____ cats

3. There were 9 pigs in a pen.
2 pigs get away.
How many pigs are left?

+ –   ____ pigs

4. 8 goats dance in a circle.
1 more goat joins them.
How many goats are there now?

+ –   ____ goats

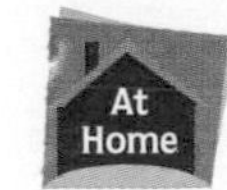

We are learning how to read and solve problems.
You may want to review those problems with your child.

Name

Use a Picture

Problem Solvers at Work

Read
Plan
Solve
Look Back

The picture shows what is for sale at a backyard circus.

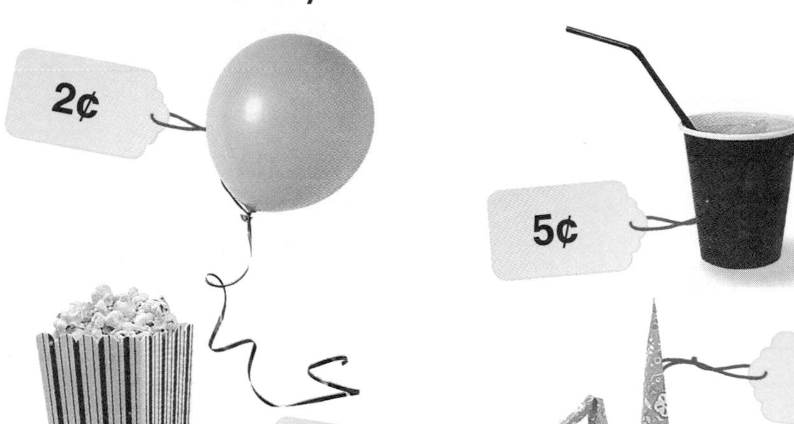

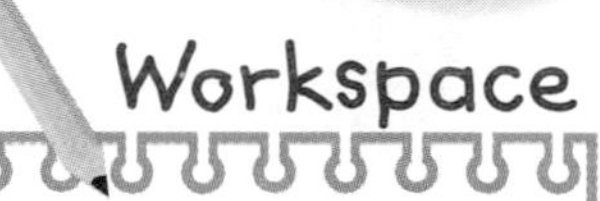

1. Jana had 10¢.
   She bought a [popcorn].
   How much money does she have left?

What is missing from the problem?
How can you find what you need?

Solve. What is the answer? 2¢

2. Rob bought a [crane]
   and a [cup].
   How much did he spend? ____

3. Katie had 7¢.
   She bought a [hat].
   How much does she have left? ____

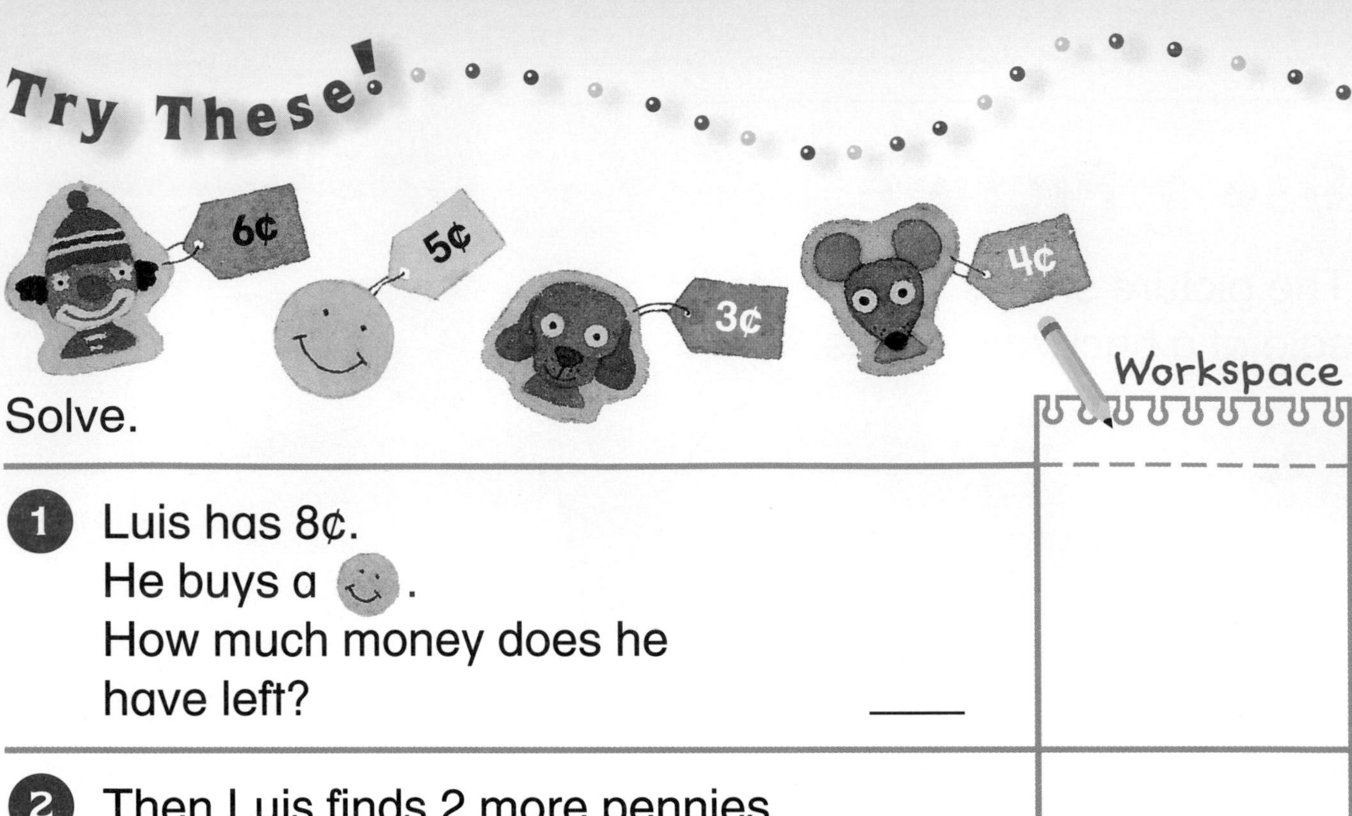

Solve.

1. Luis has 8¢.
He buys a .
How much money does he have left? ____

2. Then Luis finds 2 more pennies.
How much money does he have now? ____

How did you solve problem 2?

Neil wrote this problem.

Jennifer had 10¢. She bought a for 2¢. How much does she have left?

Neil Perrette
O'Rourke School
Mobile, Alabama

3. Solve Neil's problem. ____

How did you solve problem 3?

4. 

Write a problem.
Have a partner solve it.

Use your own paper.

Ask your child about the problem he or she wrote.

Name

Chapter Review

Add.

1 

  1
+ 6

2 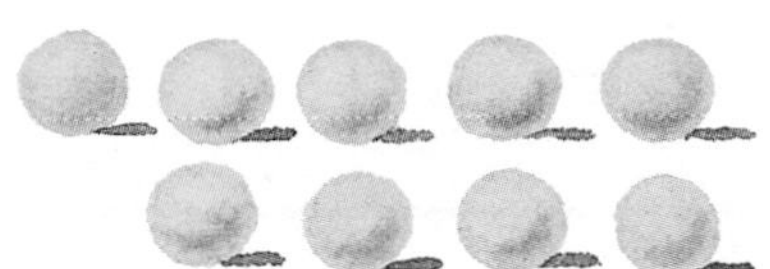

  5
+ 4

3
  3
+ 7

4
  9
+ 0

5
  6
+ 3

6
  2¢
+ 3¢
  ¢

7
  4¢
+ 4¢
  ¢

8
  2¢
+ 8¢
  ¢

Subtract.

9 

  8
− 4

10  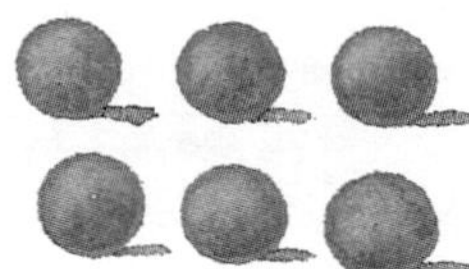

  6
− 0

11
  10
− 3

12
  7
− 5

13
  9
− 6

14
  5¢
− 1¢
  ¢

15
  10¢
− 6¢
  ¢

16
  8¢
− 3¢
  ¢

Choose + or –. Solve.

17 There are 6 cats playing.
3 more cats come to play.
How many cats are playing now?

\+ – ____ cats

18 There are 8 dogs playing.
5 dogs run home.
How many dogs are playing now?

\+ – ____ dogs

Solve.

19 Jill had 9¢.
She bought a [elephant].
How much money does she have left? ____

20 Carl bought a [cat] and a [clown].
How much money did he spend? ____

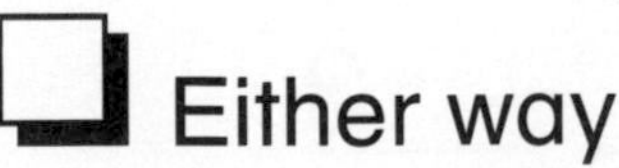

What Do You Think?

Which is a better way to subtract?
☑ Check one.

☐ $\begin{array}{r} 7 \\ -\ 2 \\ \hline \end{array}$ ☐ 7 – 2 = ____ ☐ Either way

Why? ______________________________

Show how you add and subtract money.

Name

Chapter Test

Add.

1. 

$$\begin{array}{r} 2 \\ +3 \\ \hline \end{array}$$

2. 

$$\begin{array}{r} 3 \\ +5 \\ \hline \end{array}$$

3. $\begin{array}{r} 9 \\ +1 \\ \hline \end{array}$ $\begin{array}{r} 8 \\ +0 \\ \hline \end{array}$

4. $\begin{array}{r} 1¢ \\ +5¢ \\ \hline \end{array}$ $\begin{array}{r} 4¢ \\ +3¢ \\ \hline \end{array}$

Subtract.

5. 

$$\begin{array}{r} 8 \\ -3 \\ \hline \end{array}$$

6. 

$$\begin{array}{r} 10 \\ -4 \\ \hline \end{array}$$

7. $\begin{array}{r} 7 \\ -2 \\ \hline \end{array}$ $\begin{array}{r} 8 \\ -0 \\ \hline \end{array}$

8. $\begin{array}{r} 6¢ \\ -3¢ \\ \hline \end{array}$ $\begin{array}{r} 9¢ \\ -5¢ \\ \hline \end{array}$

Choose + or –. Solve.

9. There are 6 clowns on a slide.
There are 4 clowns on a swing.
How many clowns is that in all?

+ –

____ clowns

Solve.

10. Rhonda has 8¢.
She spends 6¢.
How much money does she have left? ____

Performance Assessment

What Did You Learn?

You need 10 [bear counter icon].

Tell a circus story.
Use addition or subtraction.

Use [bear counter icon] to act it out.
Draw a picture of your problem.

Show how you solve your problem.

You may want to put this page in your portfolio.

Name

Addition and Subtraction

What patterns do you see?

Add 2.	
4	6
5	7
6	8

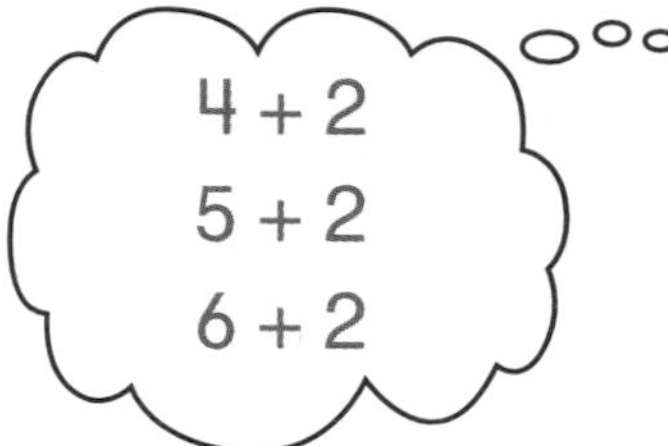

Complete the table.

Add 5.	
2	7
3	
4	

Subtract 3.	
5	
6	
7	

Add 0.	
7	
8	
9	

Make your own tables.

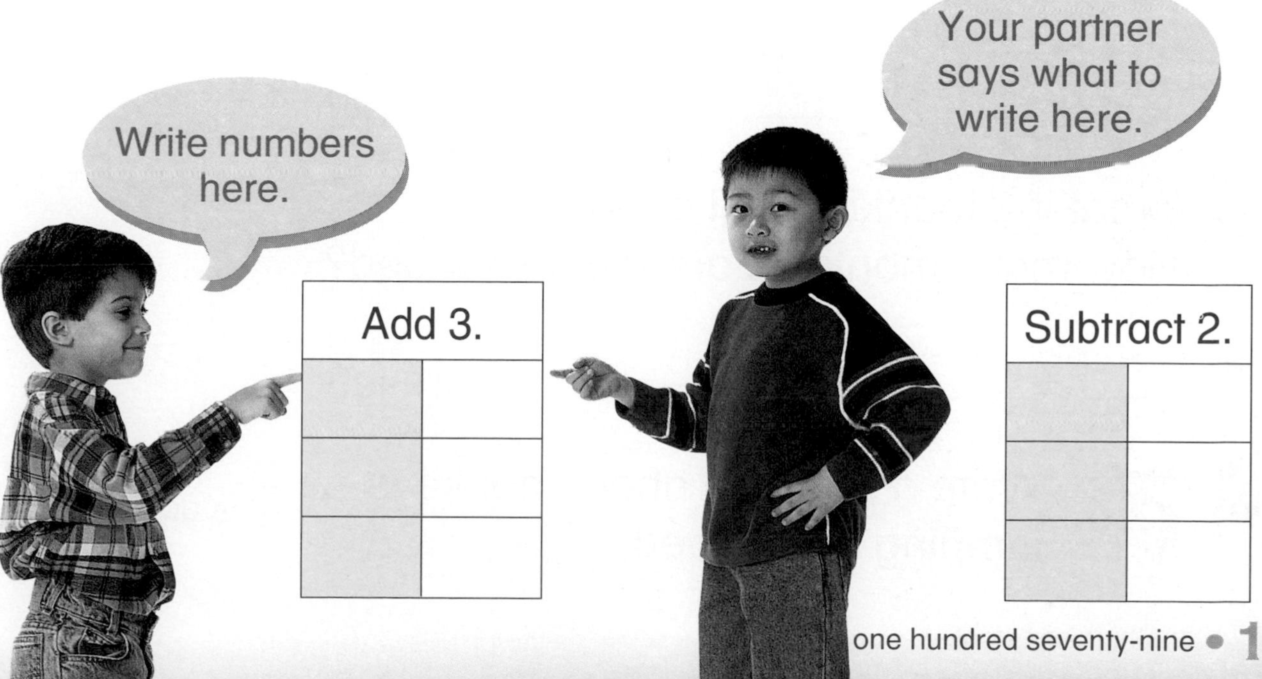

Add 3.	

Subtract 2.	

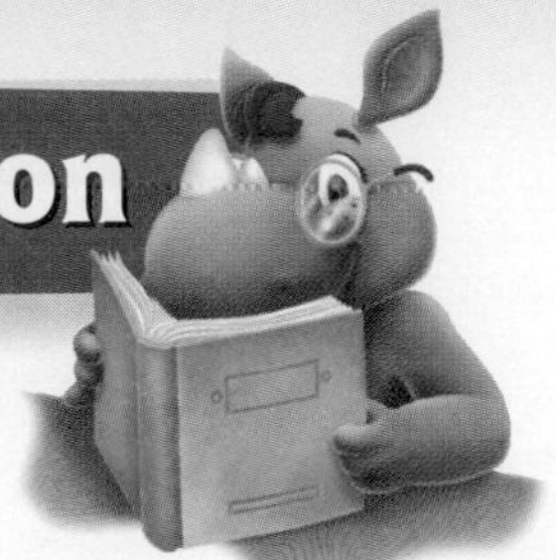

Subtraction Song

Ten Little Monkeys

B♭ F7
Ten lit - tle mon - keys jump - ing on the bed, One fell off and

B♭
bumped his___ head. Ma - ma called the Doc - tor and the

F7 B♭
Doc - tor___ said, "No more mon - key bus - iness, jump - ing on the bed!"

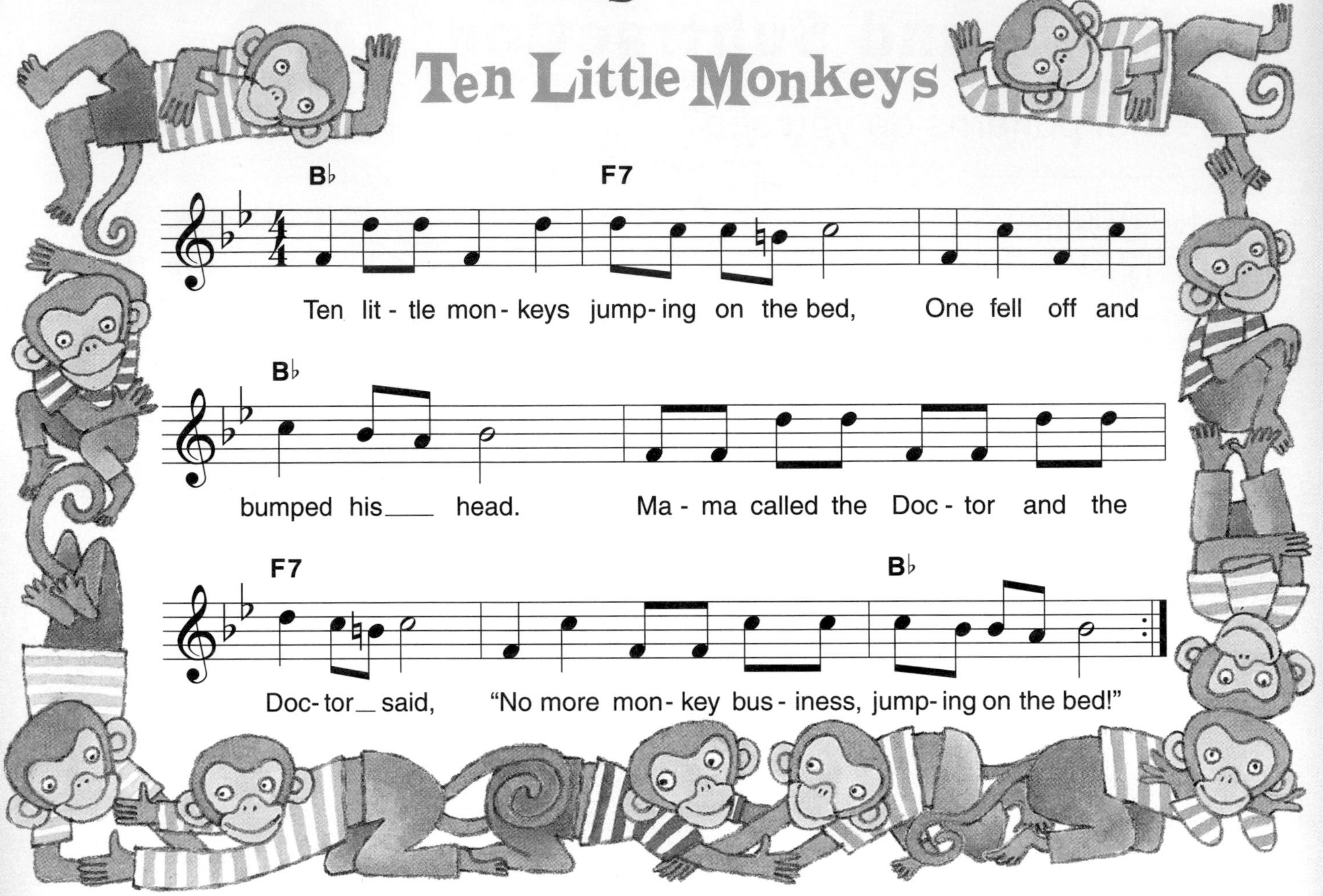

Sing the song.

1. How many monkeys are left on the bed?

   10 – 1 = 9   9 are left.

2. What if 2 monkeys fell off the bed.
   How many monkeys are left on the bed?

   ____ – ____ = ____   ____ are left.

3. Write a problem about monkeys jumping off the bed.

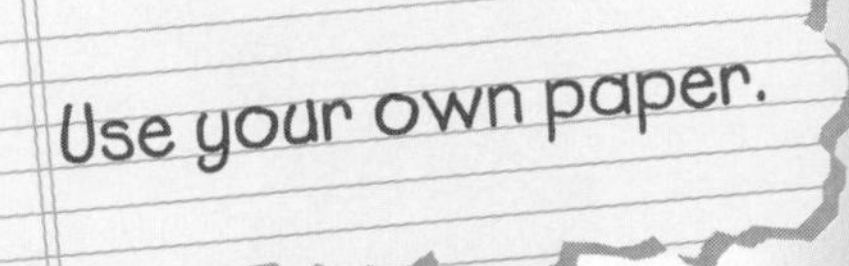

Home Connection

Chapter 5 Wrap-Up

Name ______________________________

Circus Sums!

PLAYERS 2

MATERIALS 2 coins

DIRECTIONS Drop 2 coins on the balloons. Add the 2 numbers. Find the sum below. Write the addition.

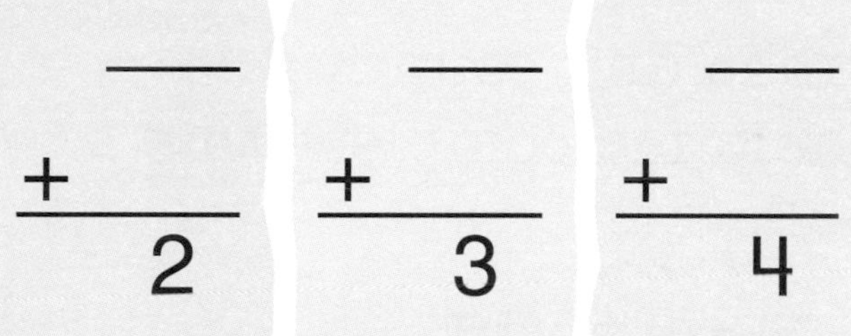

___ + ___ = 2	___ + ___ = 3	___ + ___ = 4
___ + ___ = 5	___ + ___ = 6	___ + ___ = 7
___ + ___ = 8	___ + ___ = 9	___ + ___ = 10

Play the game with your child to practice addition facts.

Dear Family,

Our new chapter in mathematics will be about numbers. We will explore different ways to count and to show numbers.

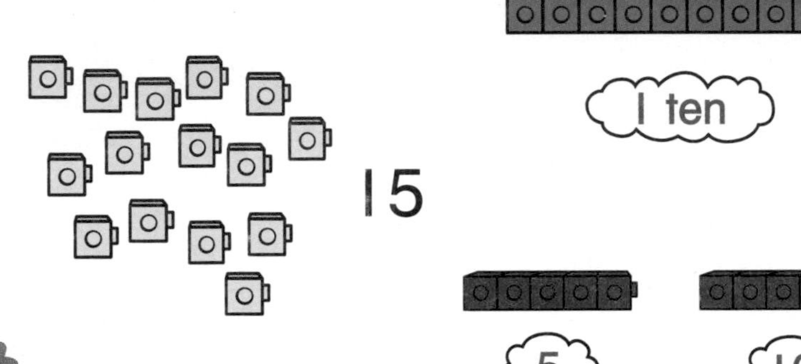

We will also be making graphs and counting people and things. Please help me complete this interview.

Your child,

____
Signature

Interview

How many people are in my family? ______
Whom do we count? (You may check more than one.)

- ❑ Parents
- ❑ Aunts/Uncles
- ❑ Grandparents
- ❑ Cousins
- ❑ Brothers/Sisters
- ❑ Friends
- ❑ Other ______________________

Our family is ❑ small. ❑ big. ❑ huge.

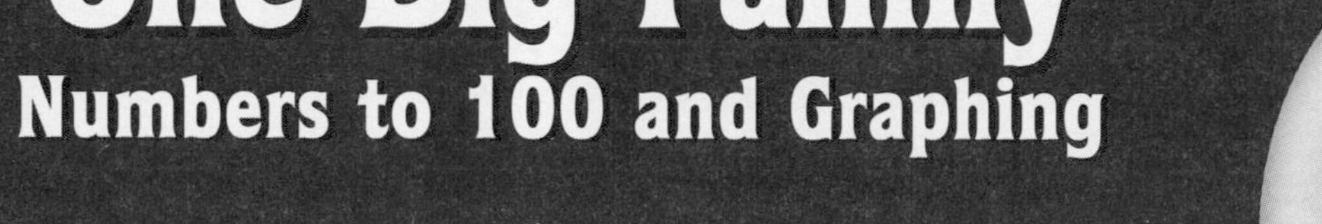

One Big Family

Numbers to 100 and Graphing

CHAPTER 6

Listen to the story *One Hundred Is a Family*.

Tell about one of the families in the story.

Name ______________________________

What Do You Know?

Listen to the problem.

How many?

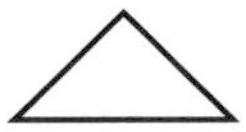

△ Guess ____ Count ____

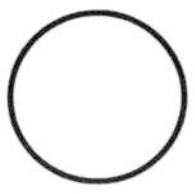

○ Guess ____ Count ____

□ Guess ____ Count ____

Write about the shapes.
Which color has the most shapes?
Which color has the fewest shapes?

Name

Count to 20

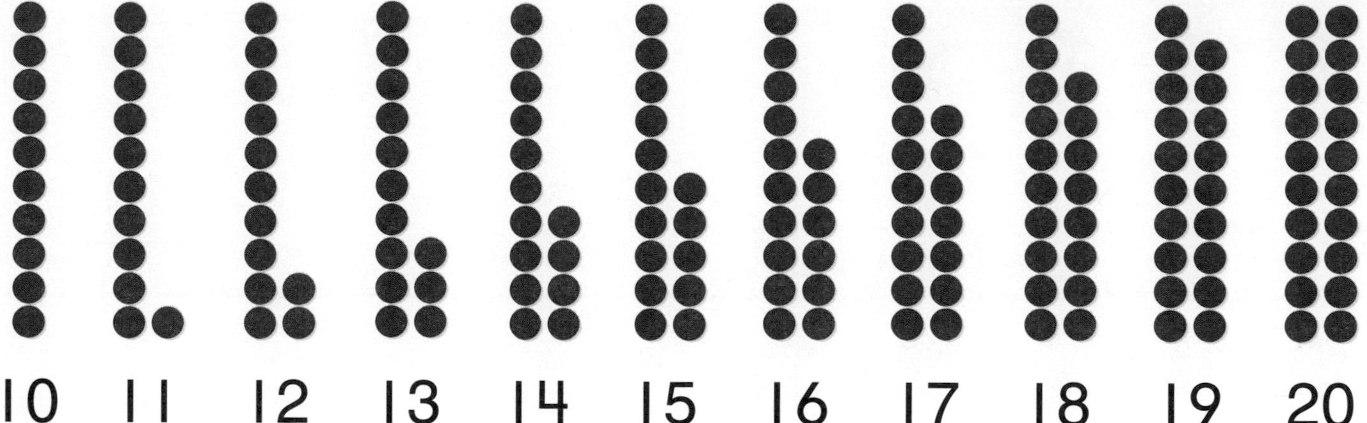

Talk about the numbers.
Tell what pattern you see.

Working Together

You need 20 ●.

Take turns.

- You show some ●.
- Your partner counts.
- Draw and write to show the number.

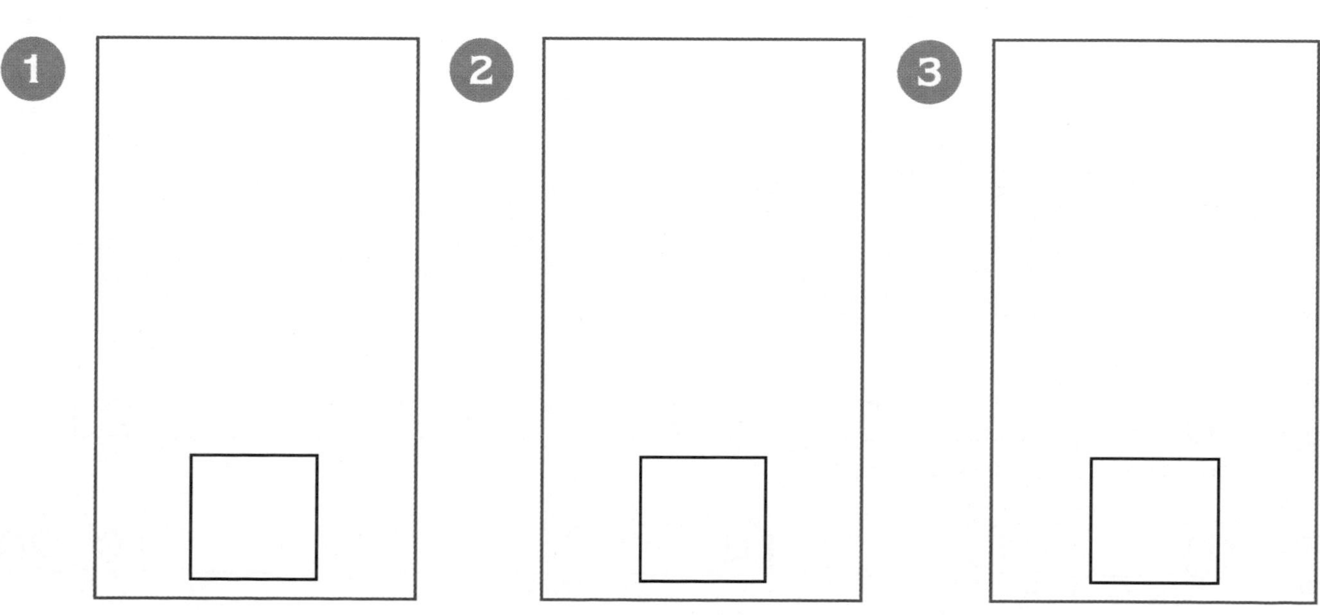

Try These!

Count. Draw 1 more. Write the number.

1 

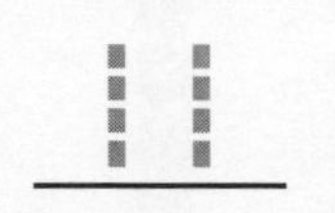

2 

____

3 

____

4 

____

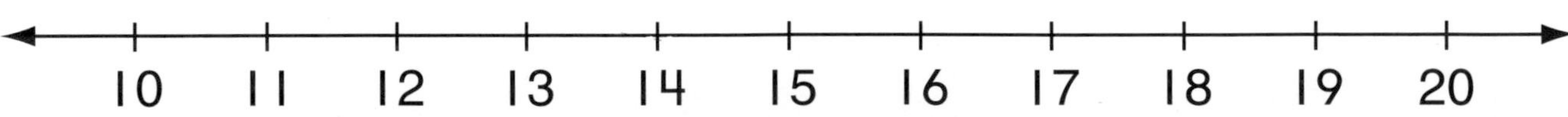

Write the missing numbers.

5 10, 11, ____, 13, ____, 15, ____, 17, 18, ____, 20

6 10, ____, 12, ____, 14, ____, ____, ____, ____, 19, 20

At Home Practice counting to 20 with your child.

Name

Working Together

You need 20 and a .

Take turns.

- Show 10 .
- Your partner adds more .
- Draw and write to show the numbers.

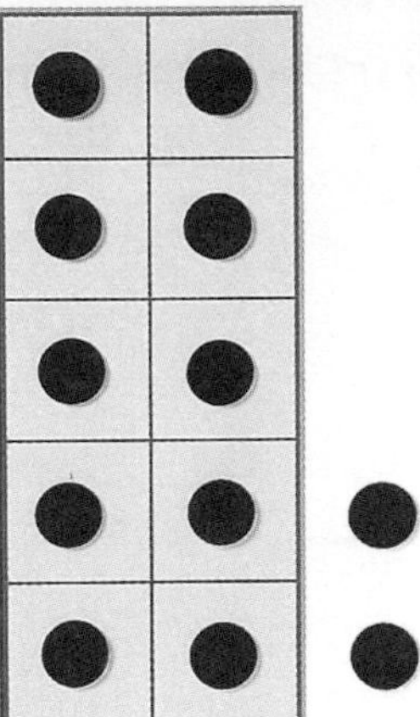

1

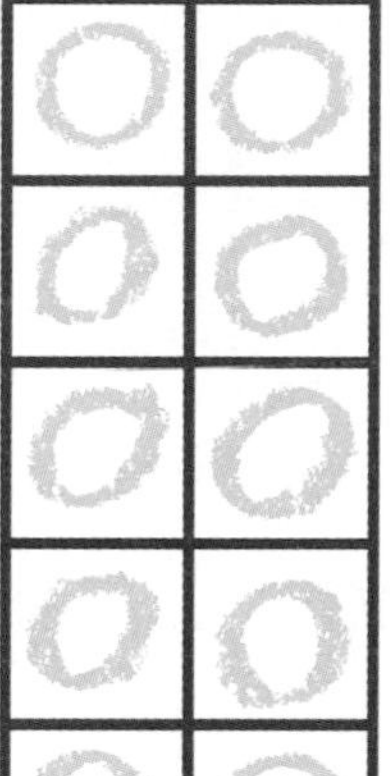

12

10 and 2 more

2

____

10 and ____ more

3

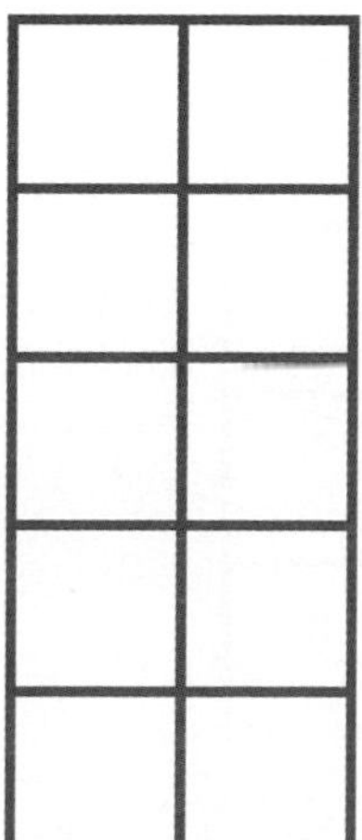

____

10 and ____ more

4

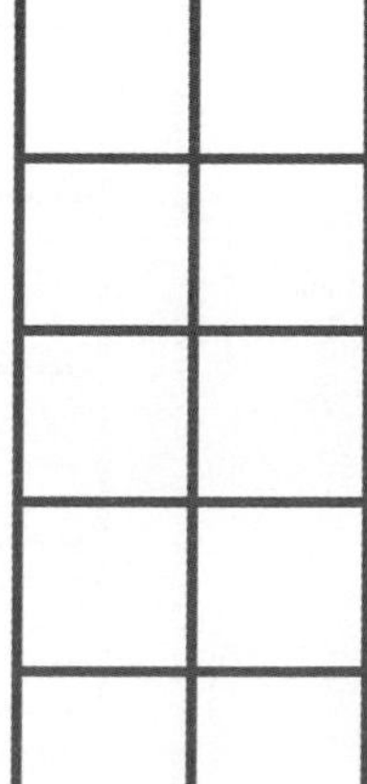

____

10 and ____ more

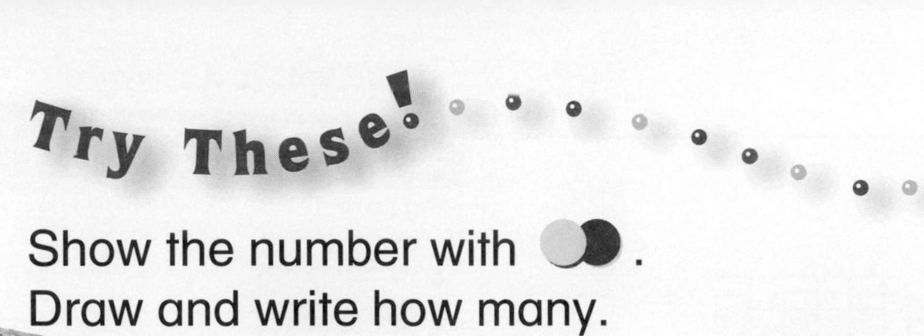

Show the number with ●●.
Draw and write how many.

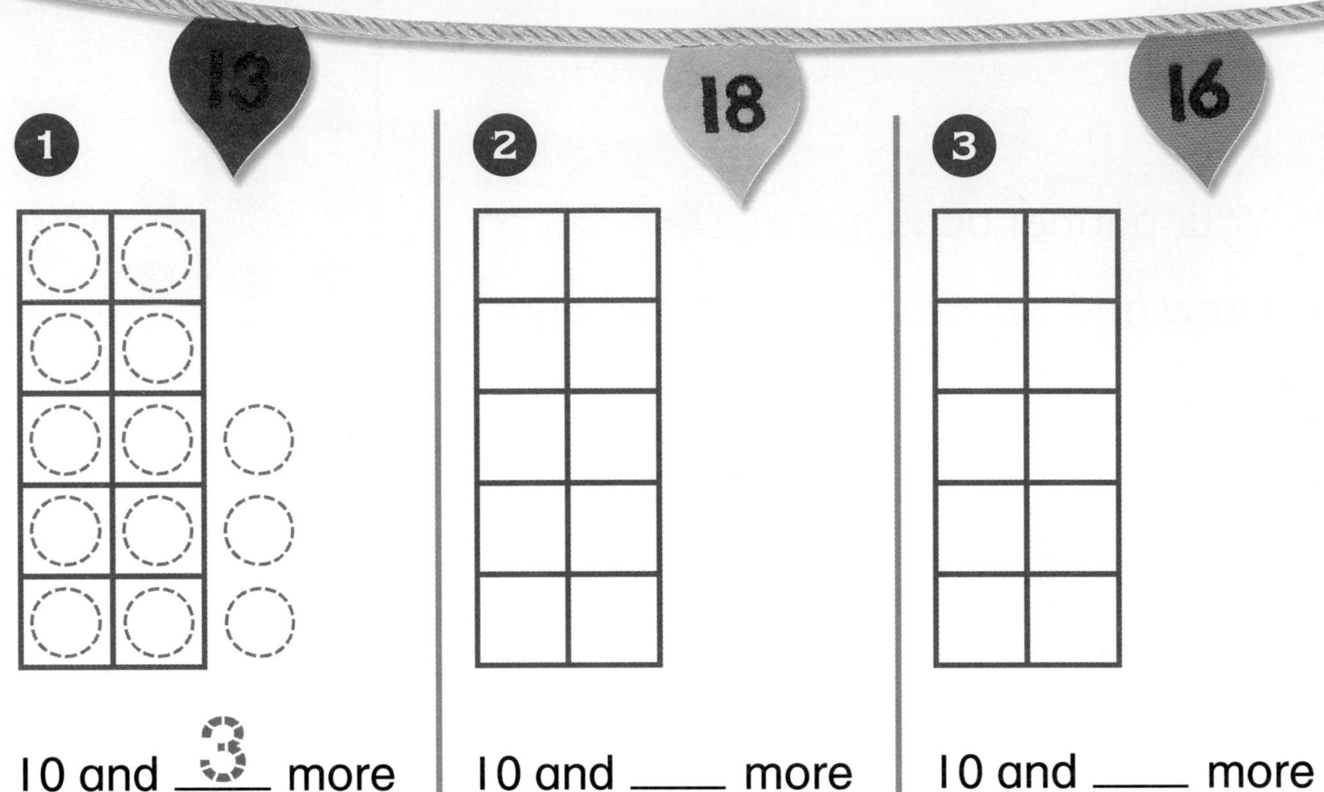

10 and 3 more | 10 and ____ more | 10 and ____ more

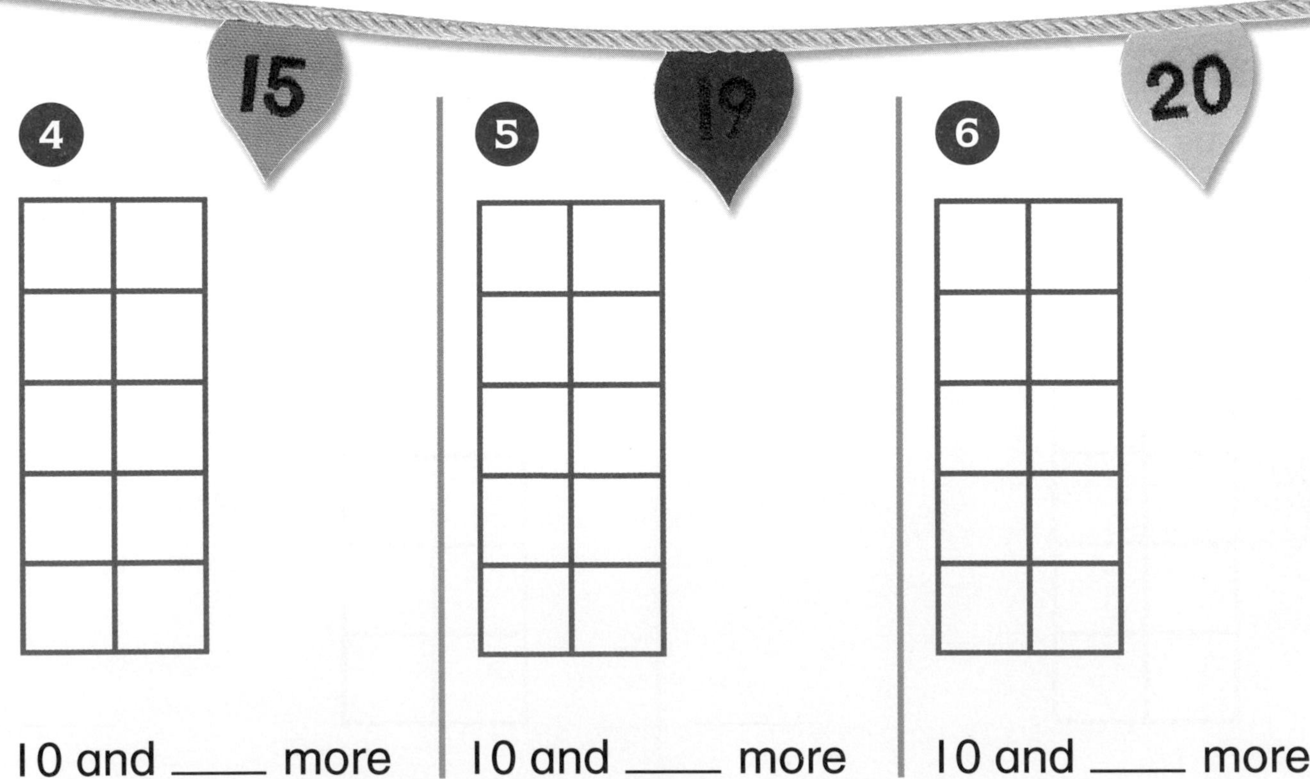

10 and ____ more | 10 and ____ more | 10 and ____ more

Write about the numbers between 10 and 20.

Have your child use pennies to show you how to make a *group of 10* and some *more*.

Name

Explore Activity

Count to 50

1	2	3	4	5	6	7	8	9	10
11	12	13	14	15	16	17	18	19	20
21	22	23	24	25	26	27	28	29	30
31	32	33	34	35	36	37	38	39	40
41	42	43	44	45	46	47	48	49	50

50 apples

Tell what patterns you see.

Working Together

You need 50 counters.

Take turns.

- Show some counters.
- Your partner counts.
- Draw and write the number.

1 ______

2 ______

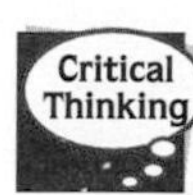

How many groups of 10 in 25?

Try These!

Count. Write the number.

1 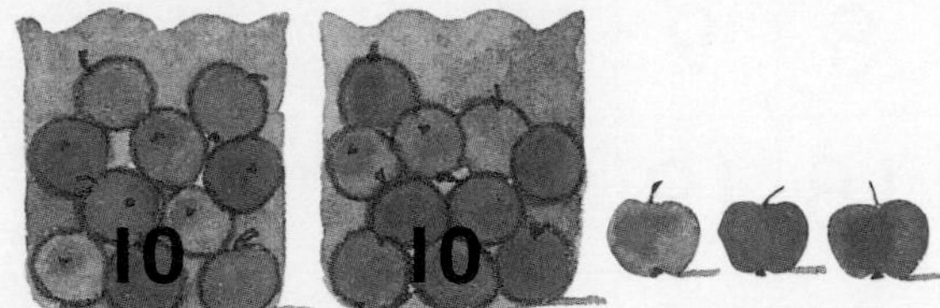

23

---

2 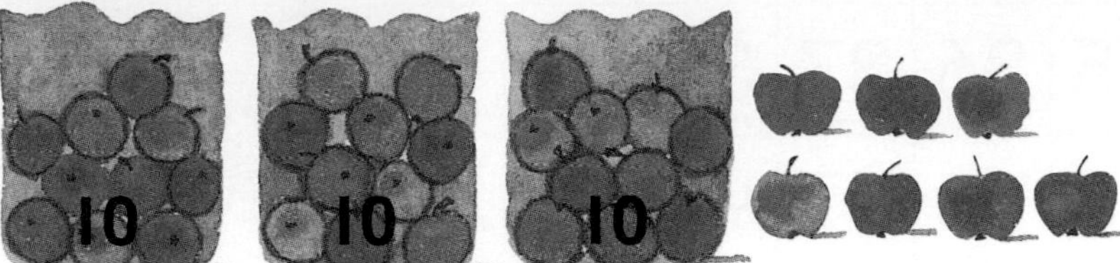

____

---

3 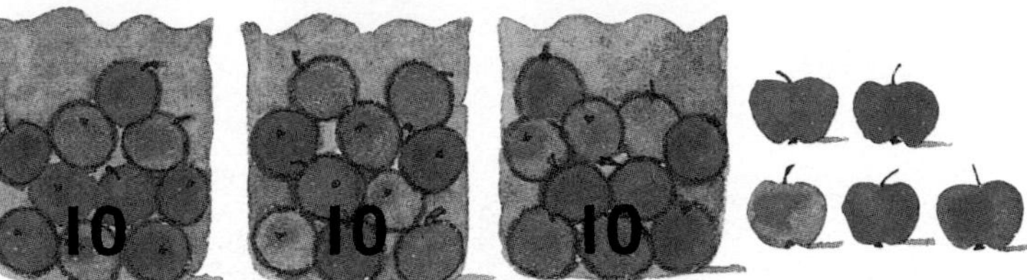

____

---

4 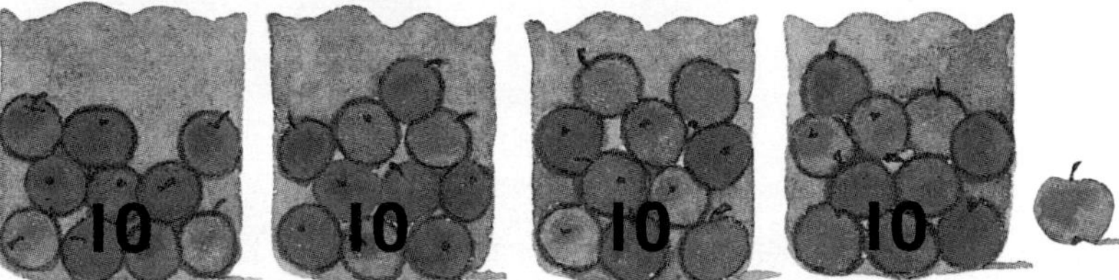

____

---

5 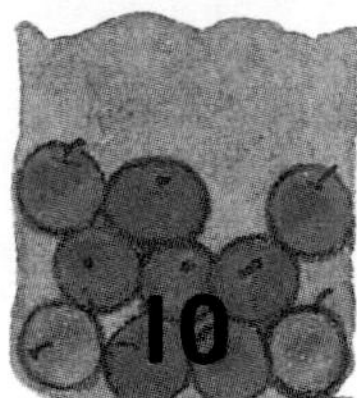

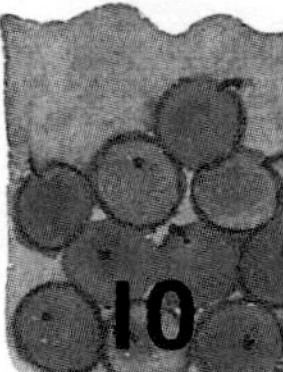

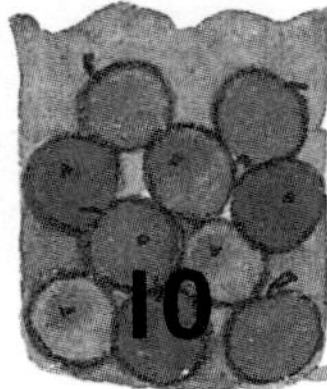

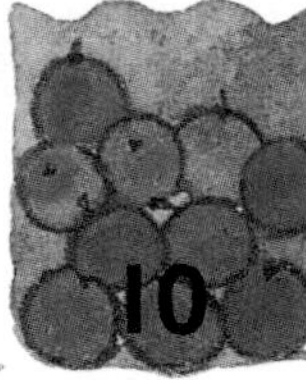

____

Mixed Review

Add.

6 4 + 1 = ____ 5 + 3 = ____ 3 + 2 = ____

7 6 + 3 = ____ 7 + 2 = ____ 9 + 1 = ____

At Home Practice counting to 50 with your child.

Name ____________________

Working Together

Your group needs 50 .

- You each take a handful of .
- Count how many in all.
- Make groups of ten.
- Count again.
- Write how many **tens and ones.**

35

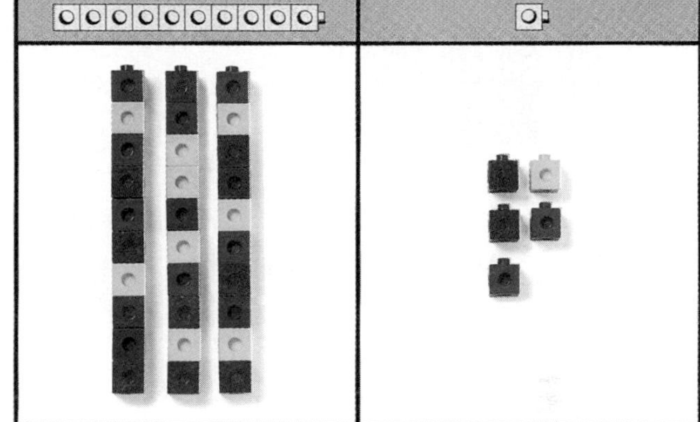

3 tens 5 ones

1 ______ ______ tens ______ ones

2 ______ ______ tens ______ ones

3 ______ ______ tens ______ ones

4 ______ ______ tens ______ ones

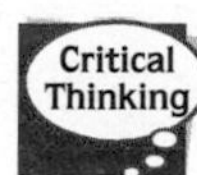

What if you have 4 tens and 0 ones. How many cubes do you have?

Try These!

Use cubes if you want to.

Count tens and ones.
Write the number.

1. 2 tens 4 ones 24

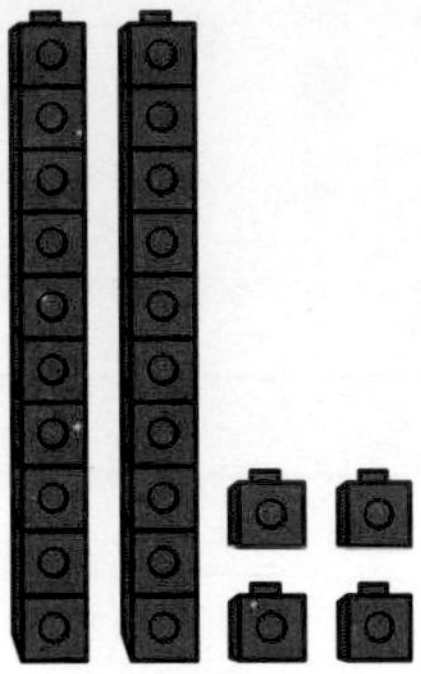

2. ____ tens ____ ones ____

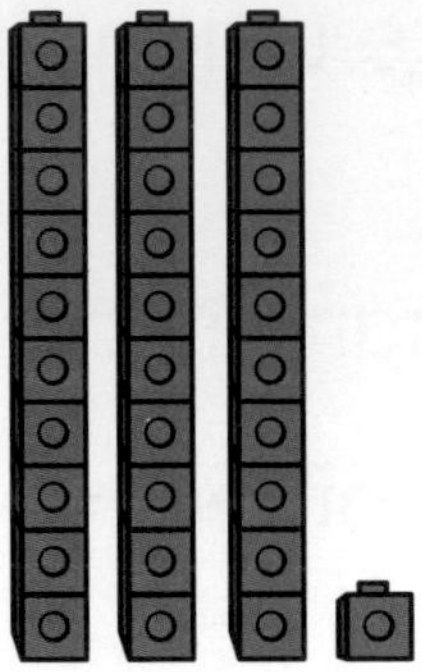

3. ____ tens ____ ones ____

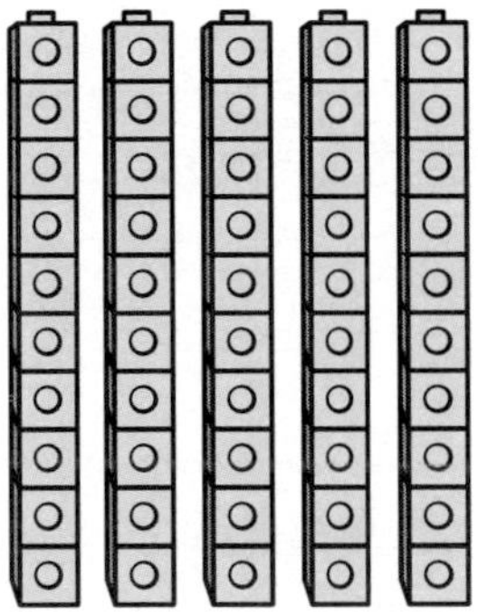

4. ____ tens ____ ones ____

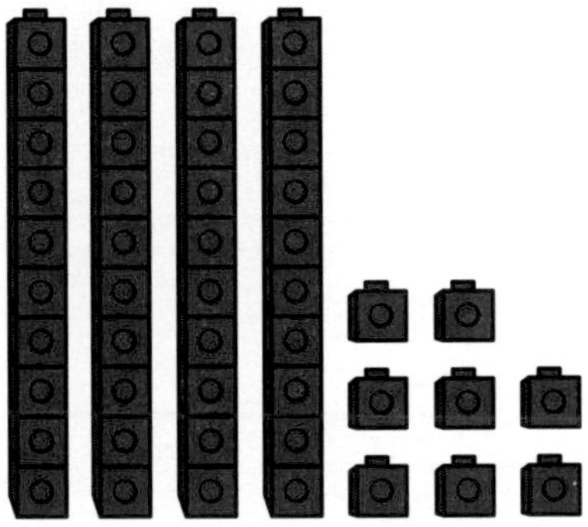

5. ____ tens ____ ones ____

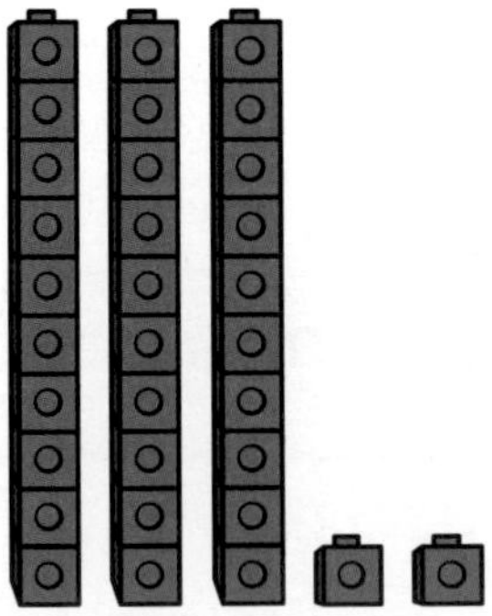

6. ____ tens ____ ones ____

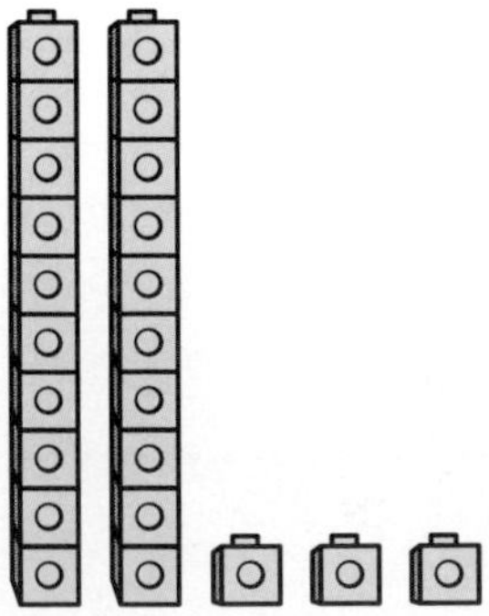

Tell a partner how you count.

At Home: Have your child count sets of fewer than 50 objects.

Name

Problem - Solving Strategy

Use Estimation

Read | Plan | Solve | Look Back

Read About how many children are in the picture?

Plan You can **estimate** about how many.

Solve Ring your estimate. about 20 about 40

Look Back Does your answer make sense? How can you check?

Estimate to solve.

1. About how many people are in the picture?

   about 20 about 40

Are there more people in the big picture or the little picture?

Estimate to solve.

1. About how many people?

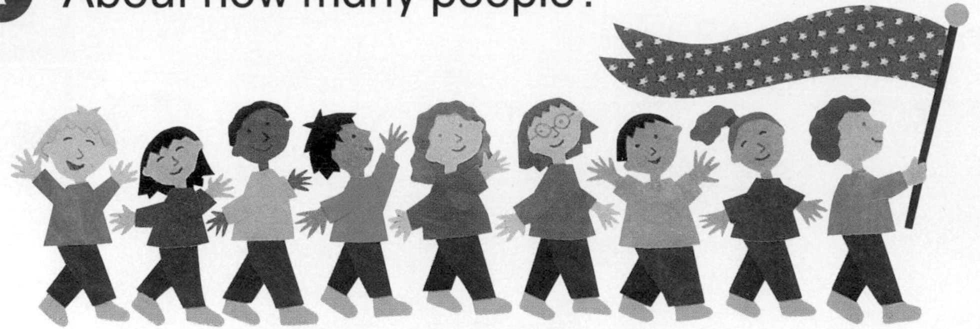

about 10

about 20

2. About how many people?

about 20

about 40

3. About how many people?

about 10

about 30

4. About how many children?

about 20

about 40

At Home: Show your child a handful of small objects. Ask about how many objects you have. Then count.

Name ______________________

Count to 100

51	52	53	54	55	56	57	58	59	60
61	62	63	64	65	66	67	68	69	70
71	72	73	74	75	76	77	78	79	80
81	82	83	84	85	86	87	88	89	90
91	92	93	94	95	96	97	98	99	100

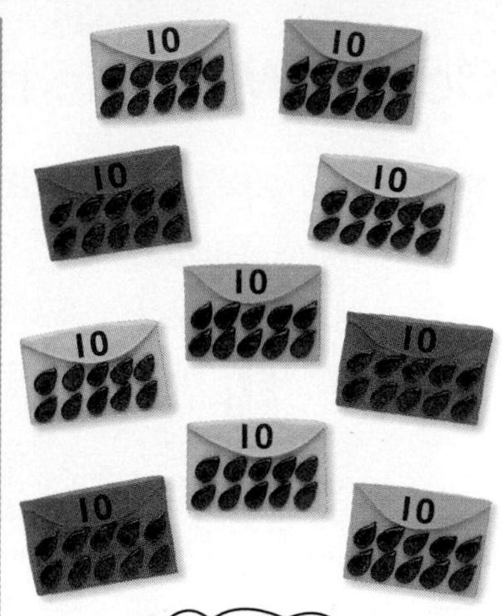

Tell what patterns you see.

Working Together

Your group needs 100 counters.

- Each of you take a big handful of counters.
- Count how many in all.
- Draw and write the number.

1 

______

2 

______

Try These!

Count. Write the number.

1. 10 10 10 10 10 10   61

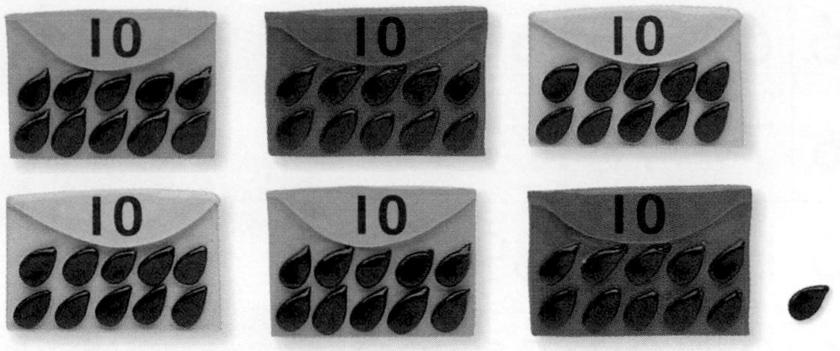

2. 10 10 10 10 10 10 10 10   ____

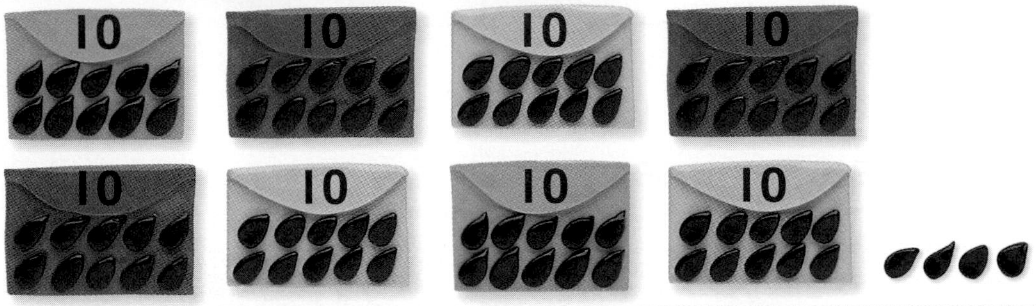

3. 10 10 10 10 10 10 10 10 10   ____

4. 10 10 10 10 10 10 10   ____

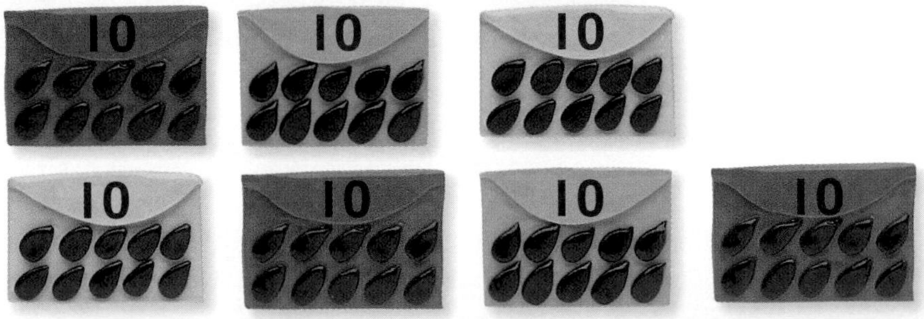

5. 10 10 10 10 10 10   ____

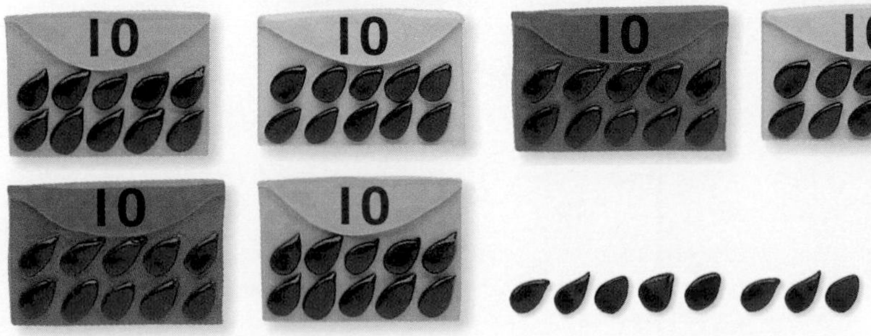

Tell a partner how you counted.

At Home Practice counting to 100 with your child.

Name ____________________

Working Together

Your group needs 100 ▢.

- ▶ Each of you take a big handful of ▢.
- ▶ Count how many in all.
- ▶ Make groups of ten.
- ▶ Count again.
- ▶ Write how many.

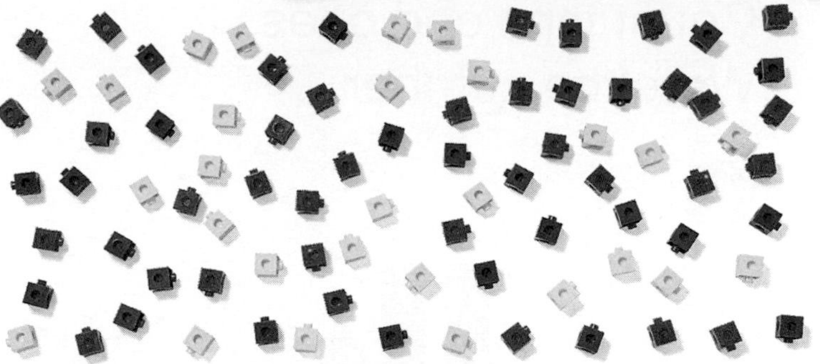

86

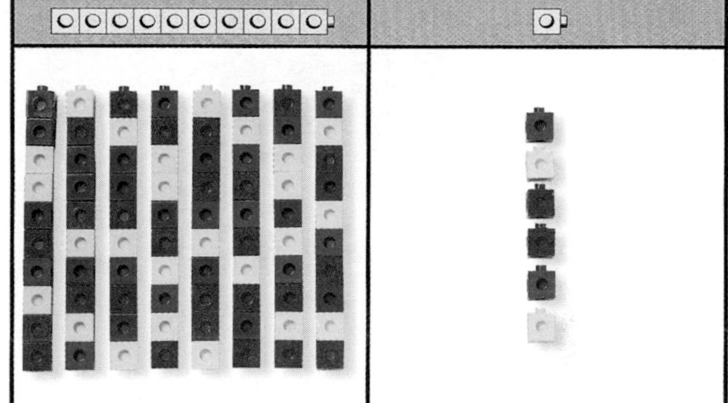

8 tens 6 ones

1. ______ ▢

   ______ tens ______ ones

2. ______ ▢

   ______ tens ______ ones

3. ______ ▢

   ______ tens ______ ones

4. ______ ▢

   ______ tens ______ ones

5. ______ ▢

   ______ tens ______ ones

6. ______ ▢

   ______ tens ______ ones

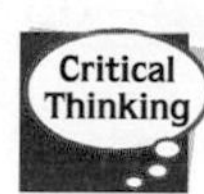

How can you show tens and ones with ◐?

Try These!

Count tens and ones.
Write the number.

1

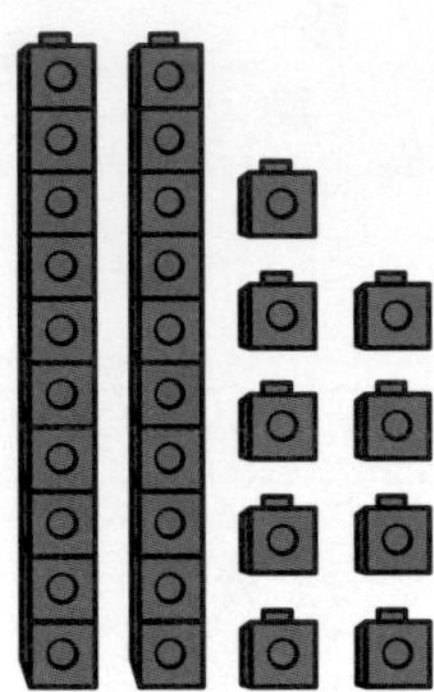

2 tens 9 ones 29

2

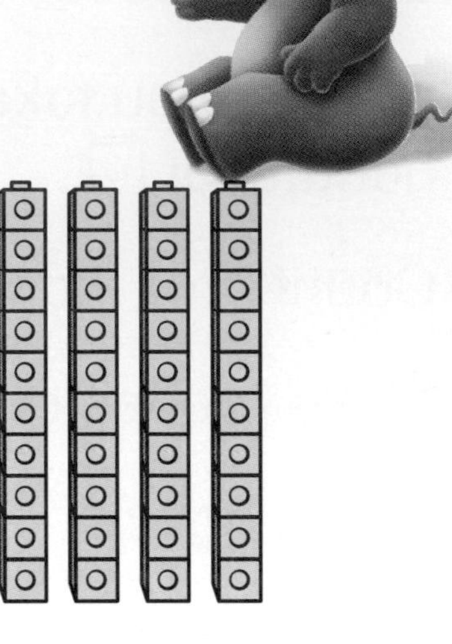

____ tens ____ ones ____

3

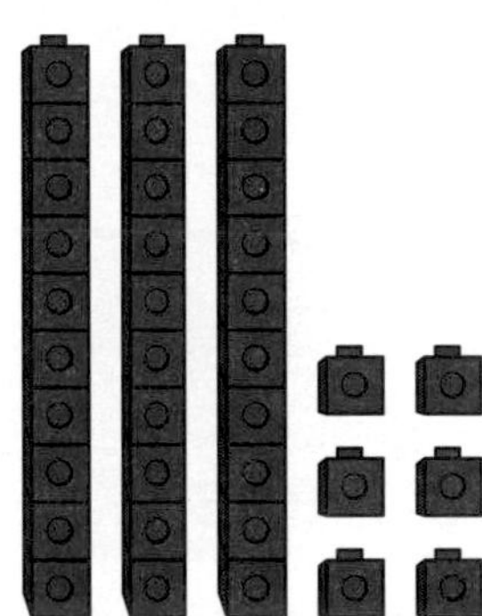

____ tens ____ ones ____

4

____ tens ____ ones ____

5

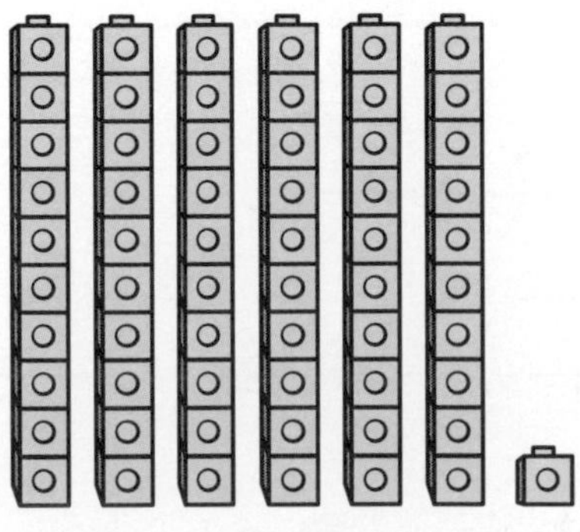

____ tens ____ ones ____

6

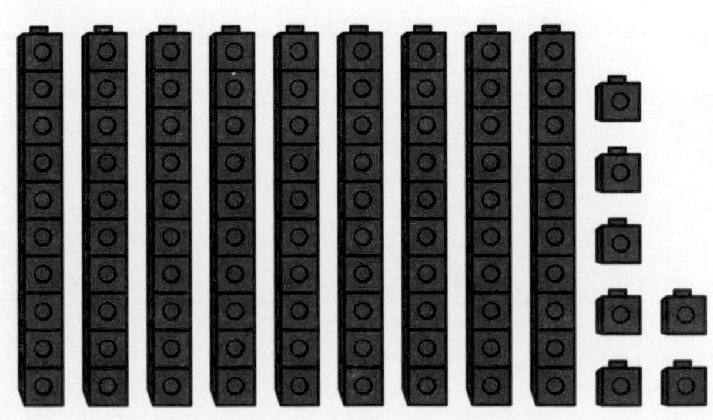

____ tens ____ ones ____

At Home

Have your child count sets of fewer than 100 items.

Name ______________________________

Midchapter Review

Write the number.

1  ____

2 ____

3 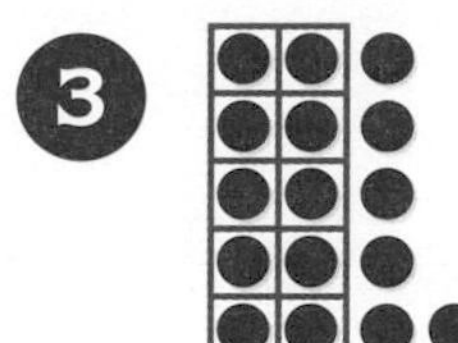 ____

4 ____

5 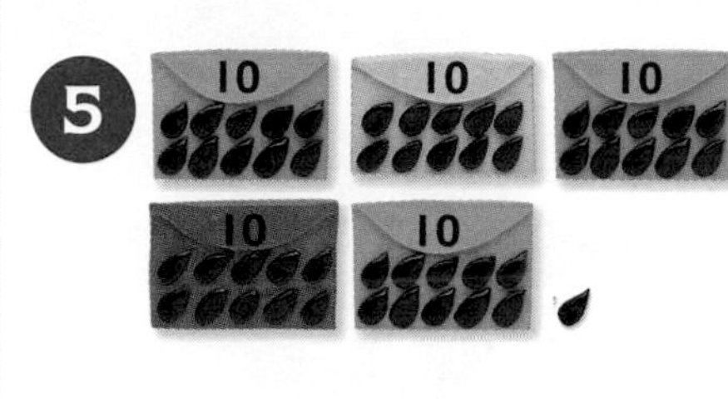 ____

6 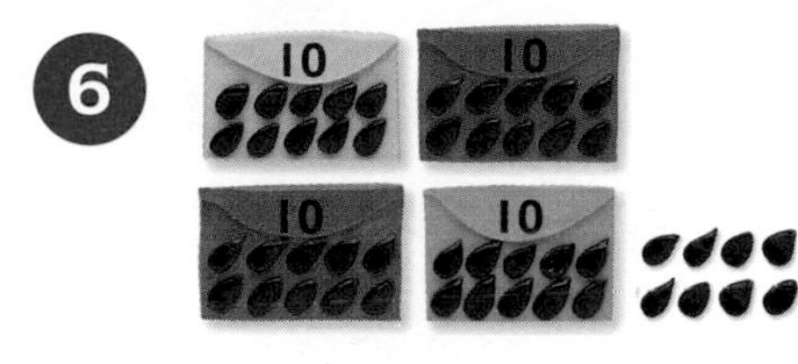 ____

Count tens and ones. Write the number.

7 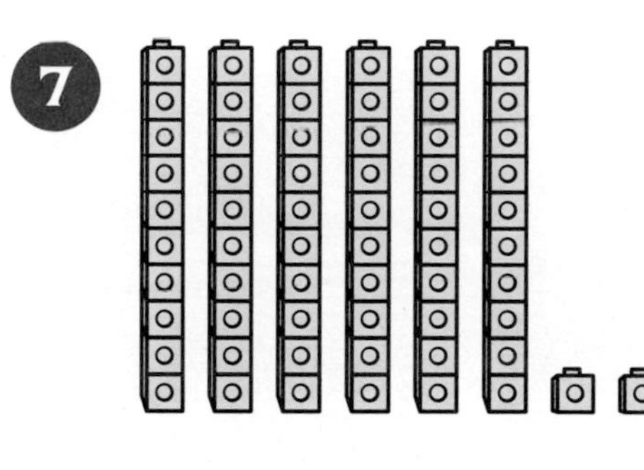

____ tens ____ ones ____

8 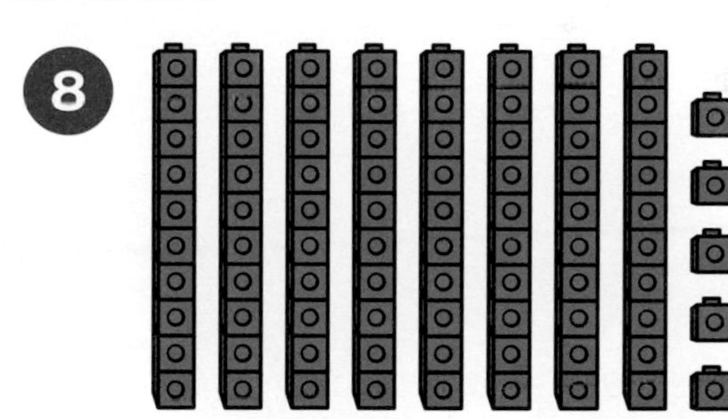

____ tens ____ ones ____

9 Estimate to solve. About how many?

about 10 about 20

10 How did you count to answer exercise 8?

____

____

Tell how you estimate about how many.

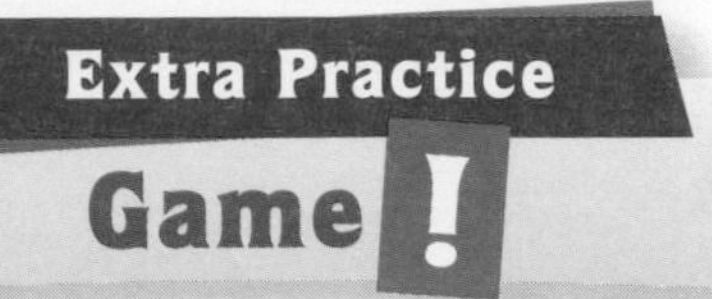

Around the Neighborhood

You need a [spinner] and a [crayon].

Take turns.

- Spin.
- Find the number.
- Color the tens and ones.
- Play until you color all the spaces.

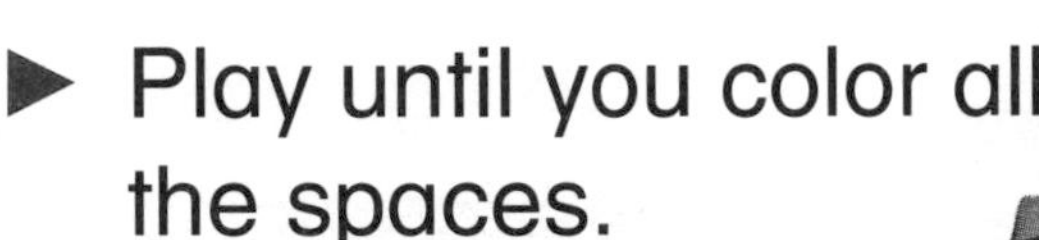

Real-Life Investigation

Applying Counting

Name

Container Collections

Tell what you know about 100.
Is 100 a lot? Is 100 a little?

Working Together

Work in small groups.

- Talk about what you want to count.
- Choose an object.
- Find different ways to count 100 objects.

Decision Making

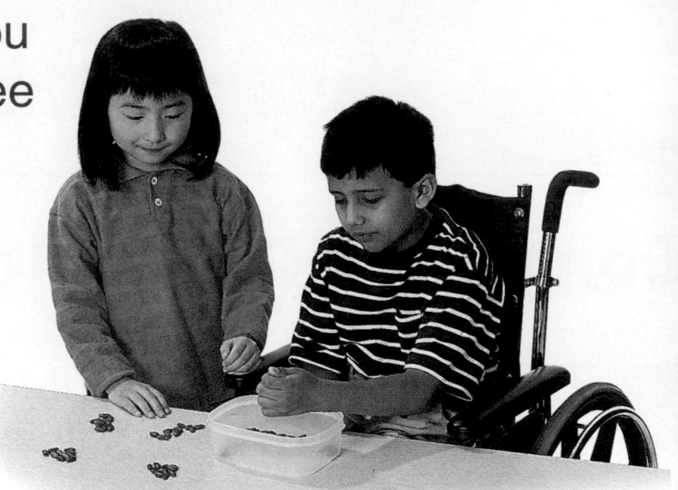

1. Choose a container that you think will hold 100. Then see if it does.
2. How many objects did the container hold?

____

Write a report.

3. Tell what you collected. Tell how you counted.
4. Describe how your collection fit in the container you chose.

More to Investigate

PREDICT Can your collection fit in a smaller container?

EXPLORE Choose a smaller container. Then try it.

FIND How did your collection fit in the container you chose?

Name ____________________

Order to 100

Count.
Write the numbers in **order.**

1	2	3							10
11				15			18		
	22		24					29	
		33			36				40
	42			45				49	
51					56		58		
			64			67			
		73		75				79	
			84		86		88		
		93				97			100

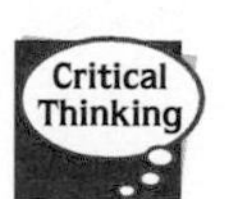

What patterns do you see?

Try These!

Count.
Write the numbers in order.

1. 11, 12, ___, ___, 15, 16, ___, ___, ___
2. 33, 34, ___, ___, ___, ___, 39, ___, ___
3. 51, ___, ___, 54, ___, ___, ___, ___, 59
4. 65, 66, ___, ___, ___, ___, 71, ___, ___
5. 79, ___, ___, ___, 83, ___, ___, ___, 87
6. 92, ___, ___, ___, ___, 97, ___, ___, ___

More to Explore Calculator

Press [2] [3] [+] [1]. Cover the number.
Press [=] three times.
What number do you think is hidden? ___
Check your answer by looking.
Do the same steps. Start with other numbers.

Ask your child to count on from numbers such as 11, 32, 69, and 90.

Name ______________________

Before, After, Between

38 is **just before** 39.

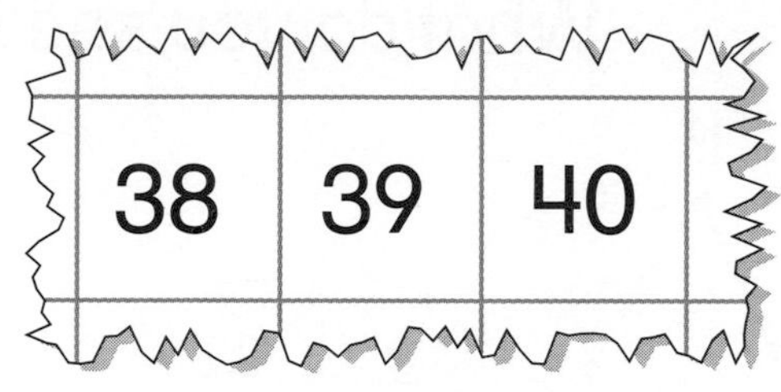

40 is **just after** 39.

39 is **between** 38 and 40.

Write the number that comes just before.

1	41	42		57		34
2		20		61		75

Write the number that comes just after.

3	89		14		97	
4	50		29		22	

Write the number that comes between.

5	71		73	48		50
6	98		100	69		71

Try These!

Count.
Connect the dots. What do you see? ________________

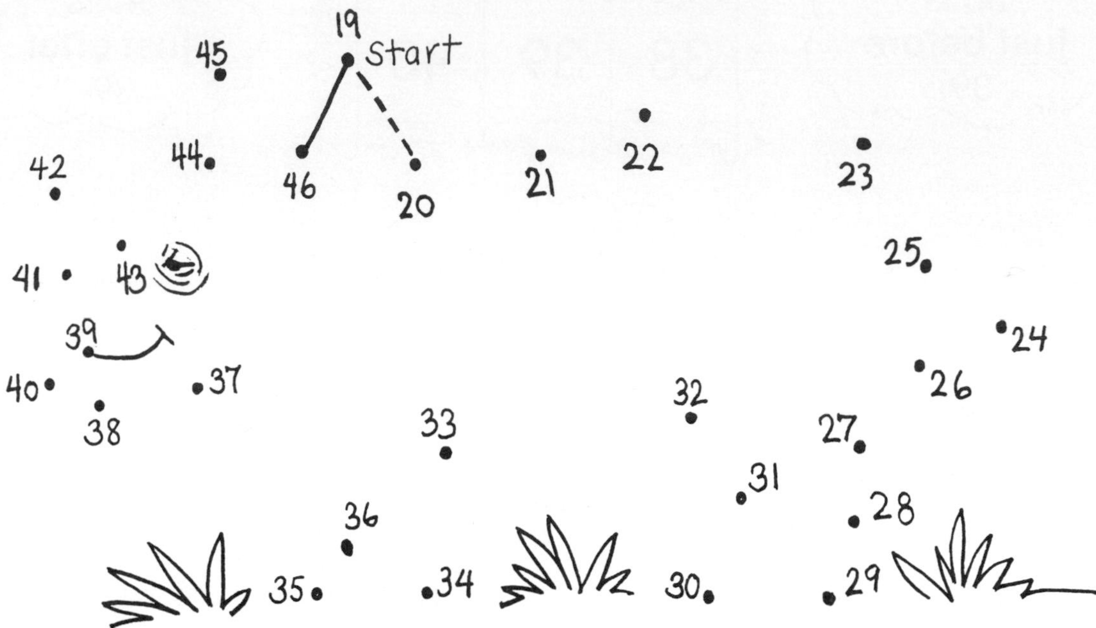

Cultural Connection

Roman Numerals

I	II	III	IV	V	VI	VII	VIII	IX	X
1	2	3	4	5	6	7	8	9	10

Write the Roman numeral that comes just after.

III IV VI ___ II ___

IX ___ VIII ___ V ___

At Home: Pick a number from 10 to 99. Ask your child what number comes just before and just after the number you pick.

Name ______________________

Skip-Count

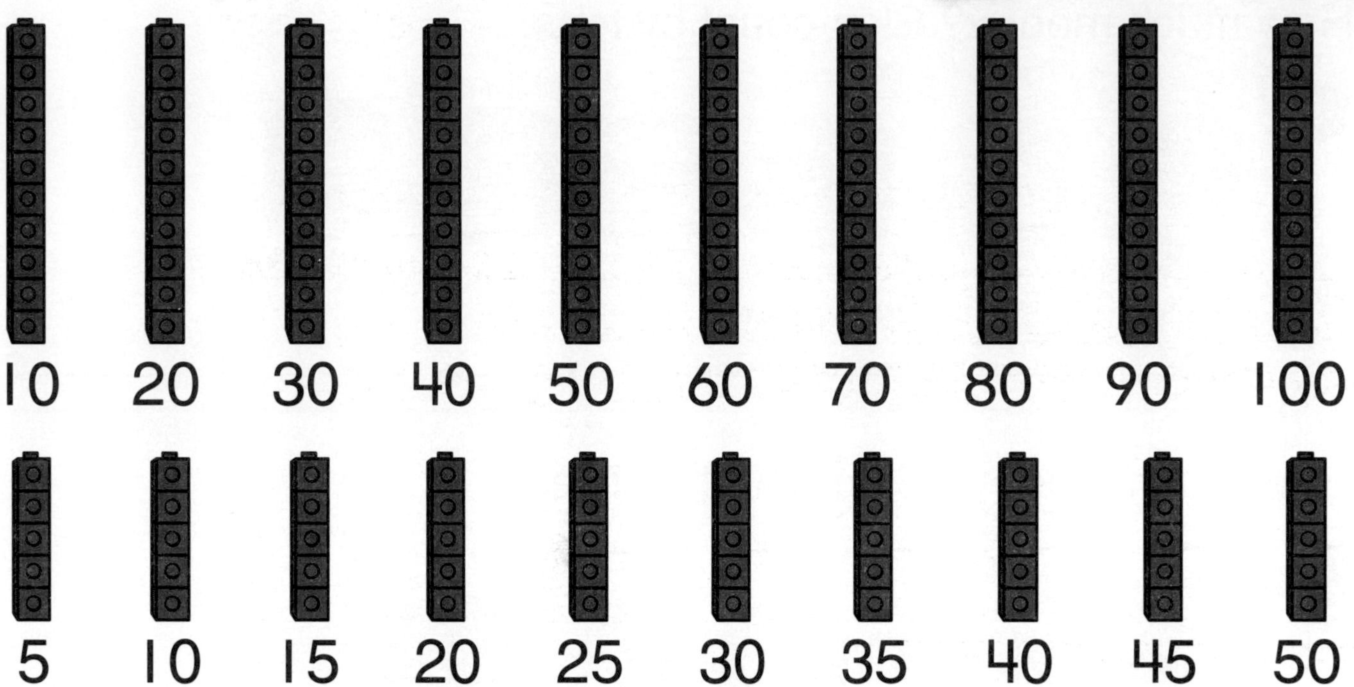

How many? Skip-count by tens.

1

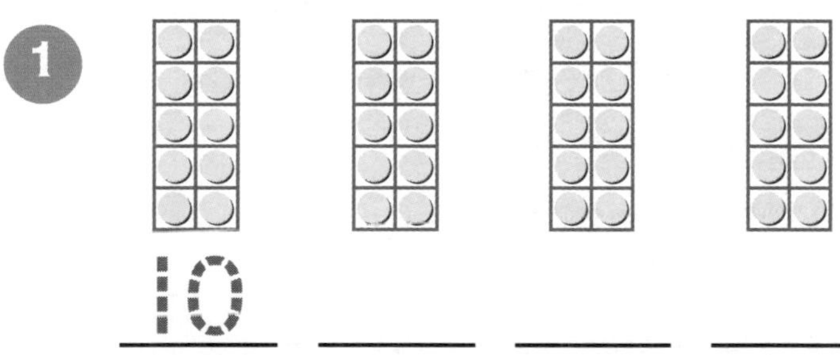

10 ______ ______ ______ ______ in all

2

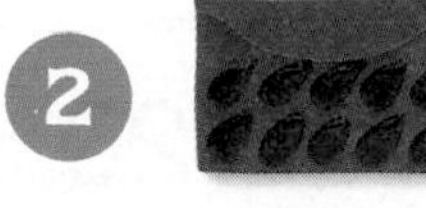 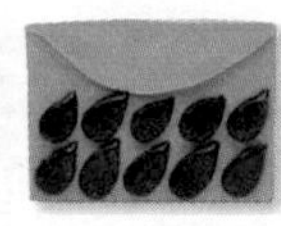 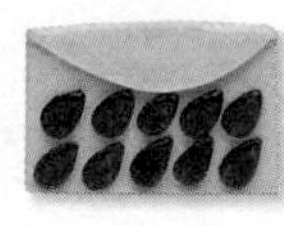 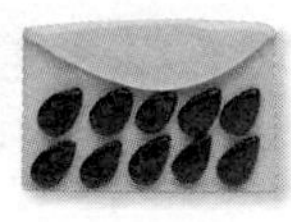 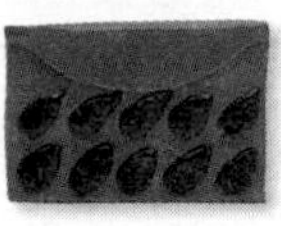 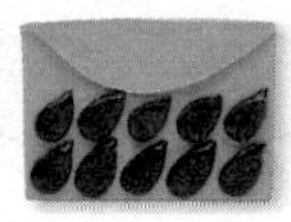

______ in all

How many? Skip-count by fives.

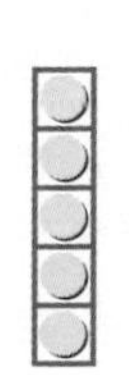 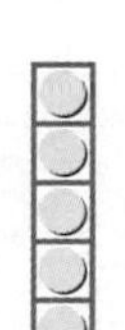 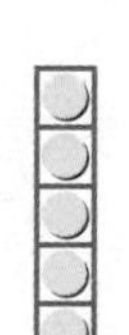 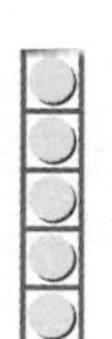

5 ______ ______ ______ ______ in all

  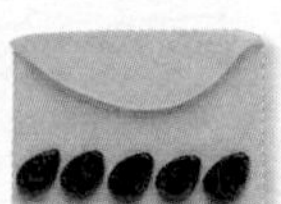   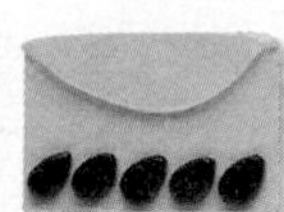

______ in all

Try These!

How much money? Skip-count by tens.

1

10 ____ ____ ____ ____ ____ ____ ____¢

How much money? Skip-count by fives.

2

5 ____ ____ ____ ____ ____ ____¢

Skip-count by tens. Color the boxes yellow.
Skip-count by fives. Color the boxes red.

3

1	2	3	4	5	6	7	8	9	10
11	12	13	14	15	16	17	18	19	20
21	22	23	24	25	26	27	28	29	30
31	32	33	34	35	36	37	38	39	40
41	42	43	44	45	46	47	48	49	50

Tell a partner about what happened when you colored the chart.

At Home

Help your child practice skip-counting by fives.

Name ______________________

More Skip-Counting

How many children?

2 4 6 8 10  in all

---

Skip-count by twos.

1 How many shoes?

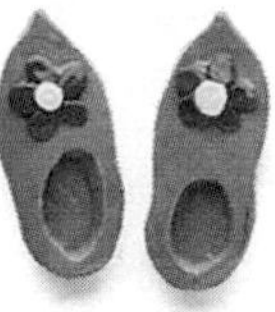

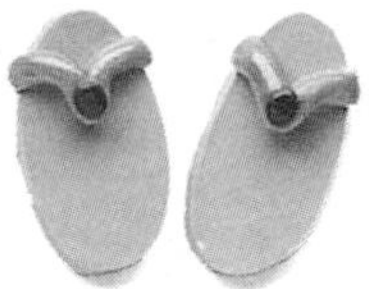

2 ____ ____ ____ ____ in all

2 How many mittens?

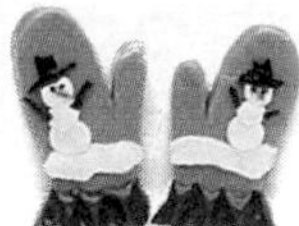
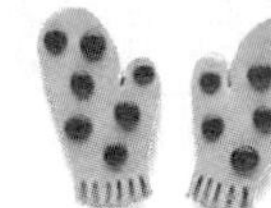

2 ____ ____ ____ ____ ____ ____ in all

3 How many boots?

2 ____ ____ ____ ____ ____ in all

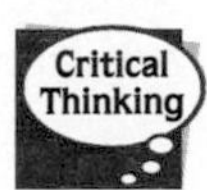

How could you count sets of triplets?

Try These!

Skip-count by twos. How much money?

1. 2 ___ ___ ___¢

2. 2 ___ ___ ___ ___ ___¢

Skip-count by twos. Color the boxes blue.

3.

1	2	3	4	5	6	7	8	9	10
11	12	13	14	15	16	17	18	19	20
21	22	23	24	25	26	27	28	29	30
31	32	33	34	35	36	37	38	39	40
41	42	43	44	45	46	47	48	49	50

More to Explore Calculator

Press ON/C 0 + 2.
Press = 8 times.
Write each number you see.

2 ___ ___ ___ ___ ___ ___ ___

At Home Help your child practice skip-counting by twos.

Name ____________________

Working Together

Your group needs 50 and 50 .

Take turns.

- ▶ Pick up a handful of .
- ▶ Pick up a handful of .
- ▶ Complete the chart.

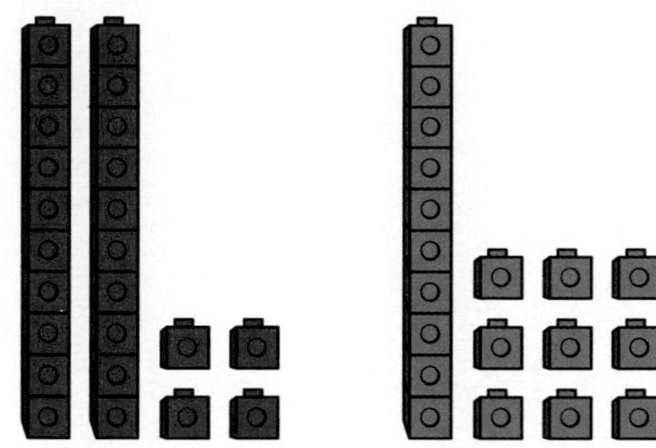

24 **is greater than** 19.

	Estimate which is more. Ring.	Count how many.	Write the greater number.
1		____ ____	____
2		____ ____	____
3		____ ____	____
4		____ ____	____
5		____ ____	____

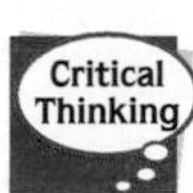

How can you find the number that is less?

Use cubes if you want to.

Ring the number that is less.

1 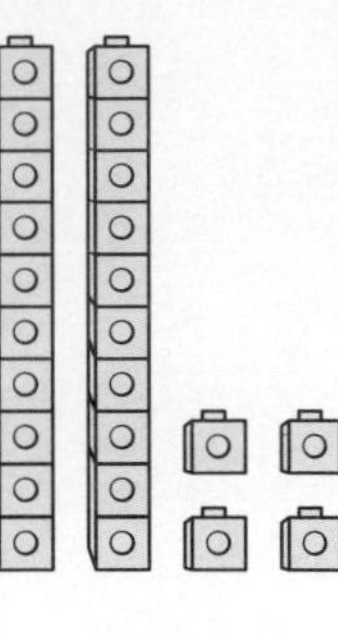
24

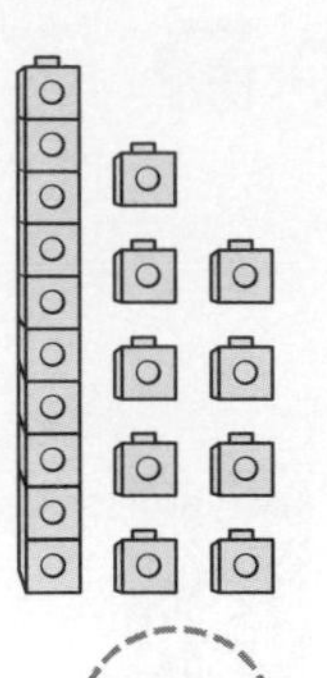
19

19 **is less than** 24.

2 16 12 | 17 20 | 31 29

3 27 24 | 15 19 | 34 43

Ring the number that is greater.

4 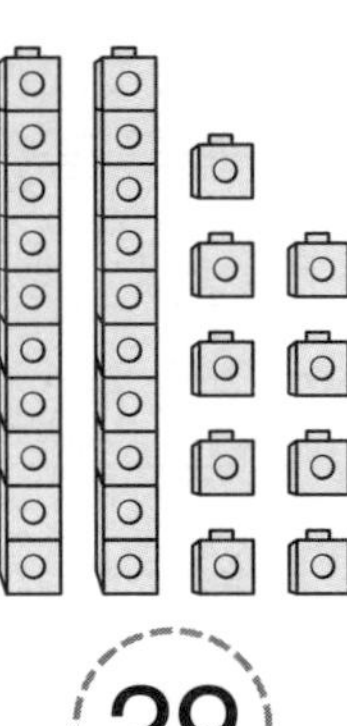
29

25

29 **is greater than** 25.

5 32 35 | 20 24 | 28 18

6 17 22 | 35 23 | 29 31

At Home

Ask your child to tell you if 25 is *less than* or *greater than* 52.

Name

Ordinal Numbers

first	second	third	fourth	fifth	sixth	seventh	eighth	ninth	tenth
1st	2nd	3rd	4th	5th	6th	7th	8th	9th	10th

Match.

1

first third fourth sixth

2

second third fifth seventh

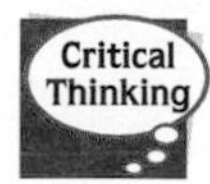

How do you know who is first in line?

Try These!

Start at the left. Color.

1 second (red) fourth (yellow) eighth (blue)

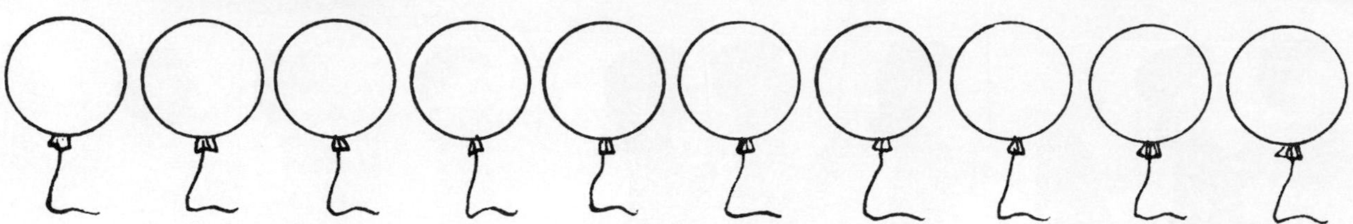

2 third (blue) sixth (red) ninth (yellow)

3 fifth (yellow) seventh (blue) tenth (red)

Mixed Review

Add or subtract.

4 $\begin{array}{r} 7 \\ +3 \\ \hline \end{array}$ $\begin{array}{r} 4 \\ +2 \\ \hline \end{array}$ $\begin{array}{r} 5 \\ +0 \\ \hline \end{array}$ $\begin{array}{r} 1 \\ +8 \\ \hline \end{array}$ $\begin{array}{r} 4 \\ +4 \\ \hline \end{array}$ $\begin{array}{r} 9 \\ +1 \\ \hline \end{array}$

5 $\begin{array}{r} 10 \\ -\ 2 \\ \hline \end{array}$ $\begin{array}{r} 8 \\ -4 \\ \hline \end{array}$ $\begin{array}{r} 6 \\ -6 \\ \hline \end{array}$ $\begin{array}{r} 7 \\ -4 \\ \hline \end{array}$ $\begin{array}{r} 9 \\ -1 \\ \hline \end{array}$ $\begin{array}{r} 5 \\ -0 \\ \hline \end{array}$

At Home: Line up some objects. Ask your child which is *first*, *second*, and so on.

Name

Working Together

You need ▲, ■, and ▰.

Make a **picture graph.**
Draw to show each block.

PATTERN BLOCKS		
green	orange	blue

Each picture stands for 1 block.

1. Write how many.

2. Which is more?

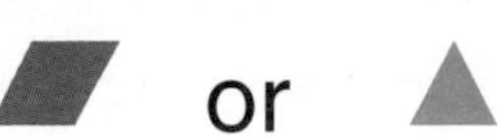

3. Which is fewer?

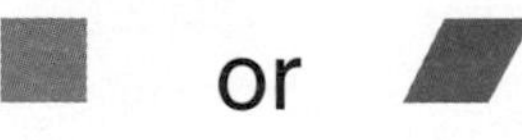

■ or ▲

Try These!

Tell a partner what this picture graph shows.

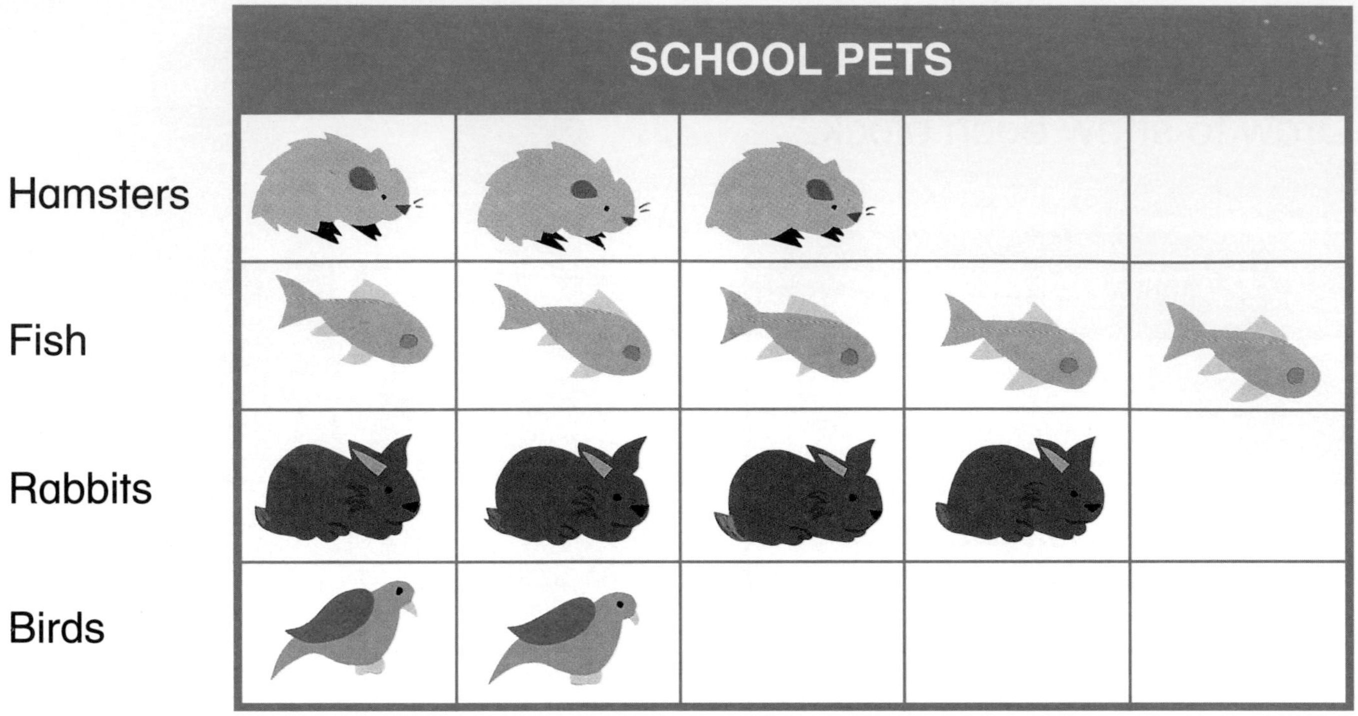

SCHOOL PETS					
Hamsters					
Fish					
Rabbits					
Birds					

Each picture stands for 1 pet.

Write how many.

1 ____ hamsters

2 ____ fish

3 ____ rabbits

4 ____ birds

Which is more?

Which is fewer?

At Home Have your child tell you about the picture graph.

Name

Bar Graphs

Working Together

You need , , , and .

Make a **bar graph.**
Color 1 box for each counter.

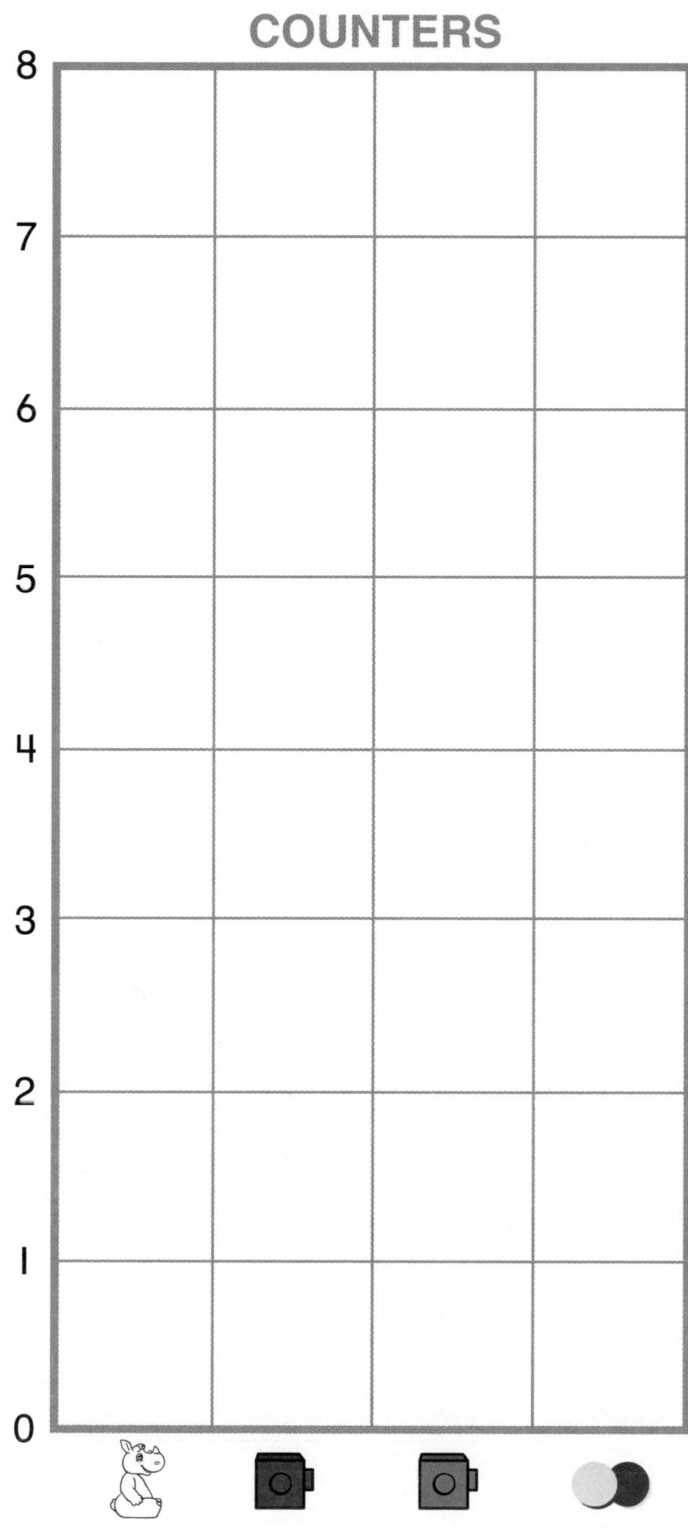

1 Write how many.

 ____  ____

 ____  ____

2 Which is fewer?

 or 

or

or

3 Which is more?

 or 

 or 

 or 

Try These!

Tell a partner what the tally marks show.

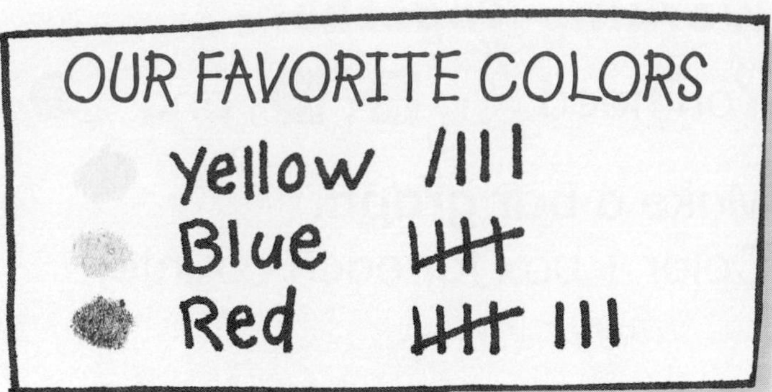

Use the tally marks to finish the graph.

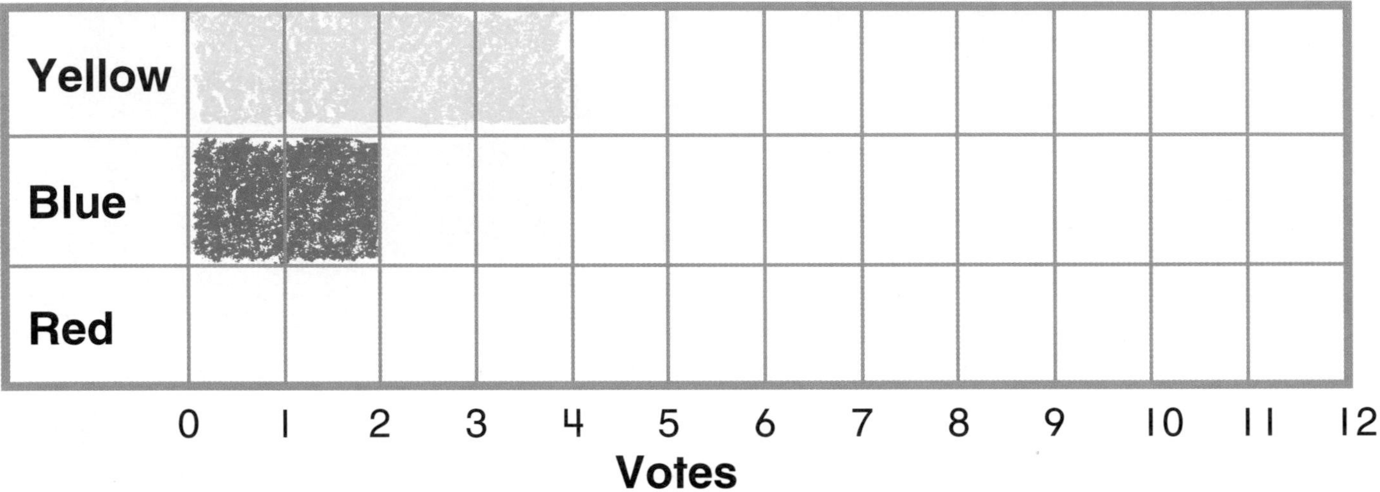

1. How many votes for blue? ____

2. Are there more votes for yellow or blue? __________

   How many more? ____

3. How many votes for red? ____

4. Which color got the most votes? __________

   How do you know? ______________________________

5. Which color would you vote for? __________

   Add your vote to the graph.

Ask your child about the graph. Add your vote to the graph.

Name ______________________

Problem Solvers at Work

Read
Plan
Solve
Look Back

Use a Graph

Nicole made a graph about some of her family.

1. Does Nicole have more aunts or uncles? ______________

   How many more? _____

2. What does Nicole have the most of? ______________

   How many does she have? _____

3. How many aunts and uncles does Nicole have in all? _____

4. Write a question about Nicole's graph.

   ____

How many relatives did Nicole count?

Try These!

Fred asked his family how many books they read. Then he made a graph.

BOOKS WE READ IN JANUARY

Mom

Dad

Lori

Fred (Me)

0 1 2 3 4 5 6 7 8 9 10

1 How many books did Lori and Fred read in all? ____ books

2 Did they read more books than their mom? ________

How many more? ________ more

Write and Share

Tearna wrote this problem.

Who read more books than Mom?

Tearna Powell
Elephant's Fork School
Suffolk, Virginia

3 Solve Tearna's problem. ________________

How did you solve Tearna's problem?

Write a problem.
Have a partner solve it.

Use your own paper.

Ask your child about the problem he or she wrote.

Name

Chapter Review

Write the number.

1 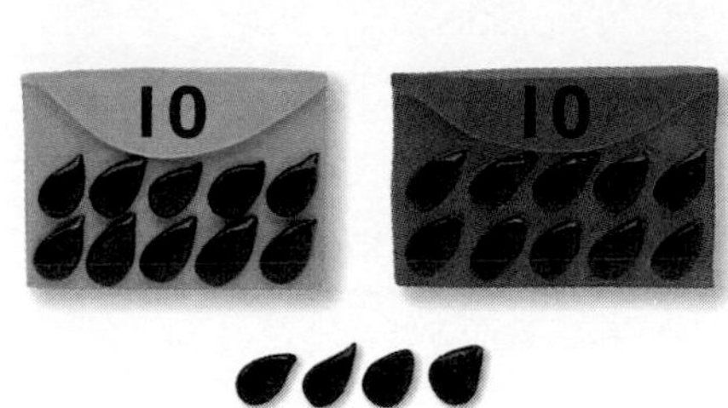

____

2 

____

3 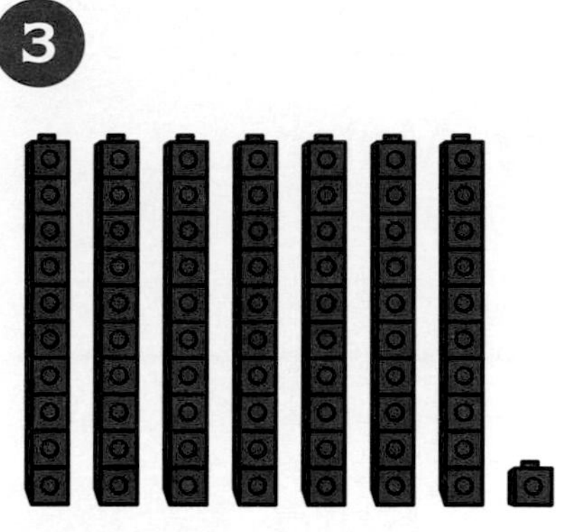

____

Ring the number that is greater.

4 78 85

5 21 12

6 31 29

Ring the number that is less.

7 13 31

8 87 79

9 15 25

Write the numbers in order.

10 22, 23, ____, ____, ____, 27, ____

11 47, 48, ____, ____, ____, ____, ____

Estimate to solve.

12 About how many?

about 10 about 20

13 About how many?

about 20 about 50

Skip-count.

14. 2, 4, ___, ___, ___, ___

15. 5, 10, ___, ___, ___, ___

16. 10, 20, ___, ___, ___, ___

17. Match.

third fifth seventh

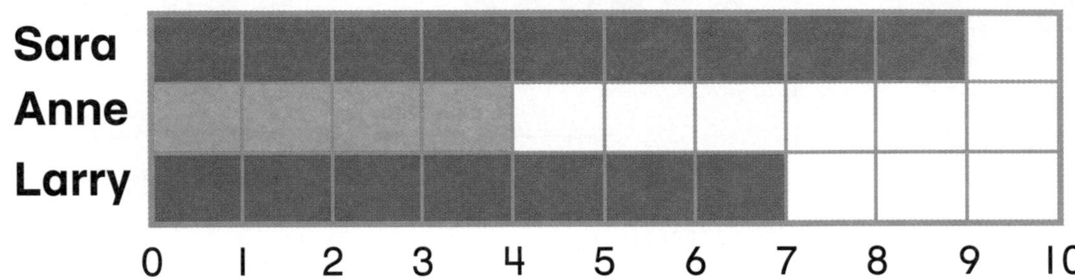

18. Who read the fewest books? ________________

19. How many books did Larry read? ________________

20. Who read the most books? ________________

What Do You Think?

How do you like to count?

☑ Check one.

☐ By ones ☐ By tens ☐ By fives ☐ By twos

Why? ________________________________

Show what you know about 100.

Name

Chapter Test

1. Write the number.

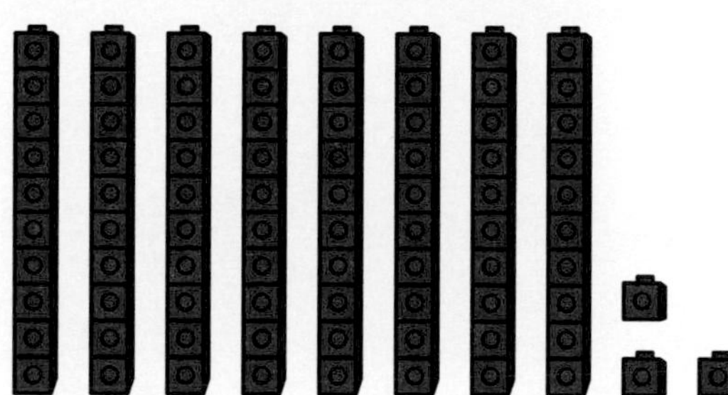

___

2. Ring the number that is greater.

58   39

3. Write the numbers in order.

68, 69, ___, ___, ___, 73, ___

Skip-count.

4. 2, 4, 6, 8, 10, ___, ___, ___

5. 5, 10, 15, ___, ___, ___, ___

6. 10, 20, 30, ___, ___, ___, ___

7. Match.

second   fourth   eighth

8. How many cousins does Lani have? ______

9. Who has the fewest cousins? ______

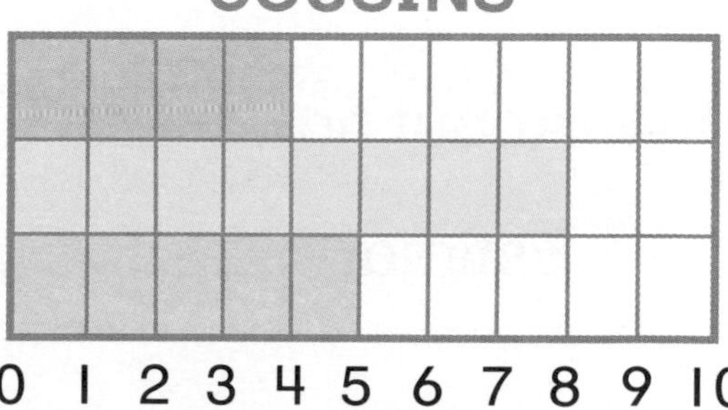

Estimate to solve.

10. About how many fish?

about 30   **about 50**

Performance Assessment

What Did You Learn?

You need 30 [cube], 30 [cube], and 30 [cube].

Take a big handful of each color [cube].

Count how many of each color.
Write the number.

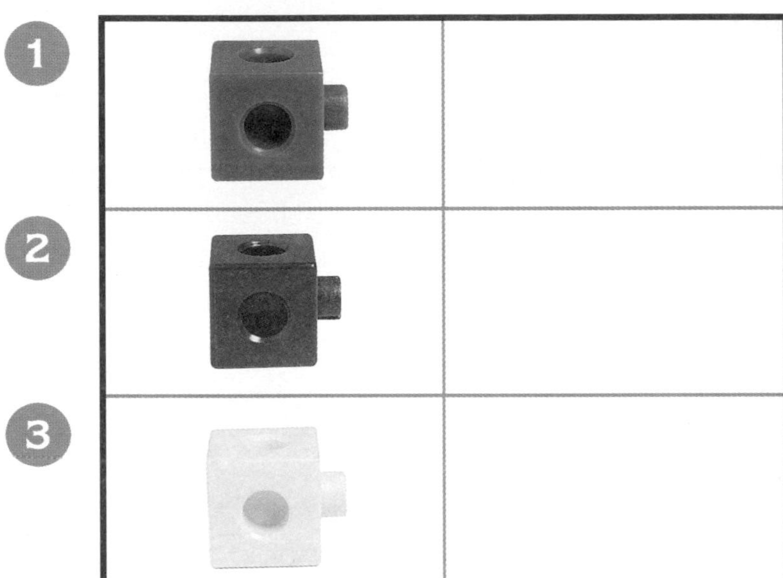

1	[cube]	
2	[cube]	
3	[cube]	

4. Do you have more [cube] or [cube]? ________

5. Do you have fewer [cube] or [cube]? ________

6. About how many [cube] do you have in all?

Estimate. ________ Count how many. ________

You may want to put this page in your portfolio.

Math Connection

Calculator

Name

Skip-Count

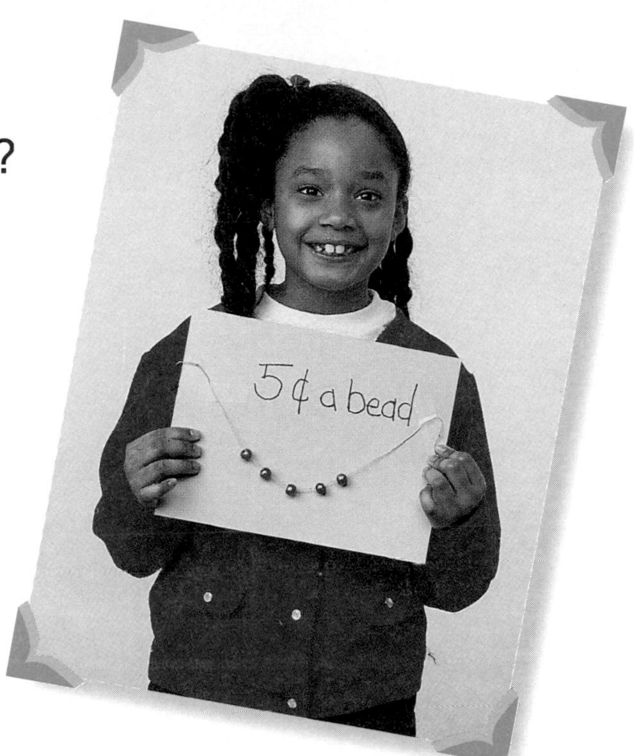

How much does the necklace cost?

You can skip-count by fives to find out.

Press ON/C + 5.

How many beads? 5

Press = 5 times.

The necklace costs 25 ¢.

Which keys would you press if each bead cost 10¢?

Find the cost of each necklace.

1 

7 beads ____ ¢

2 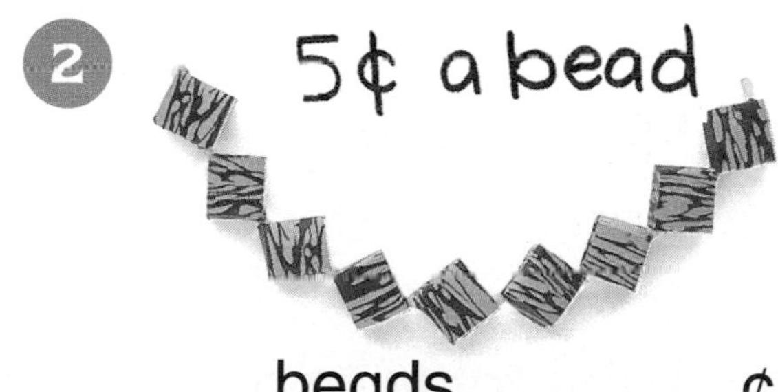

____ beads ____ ¢

3 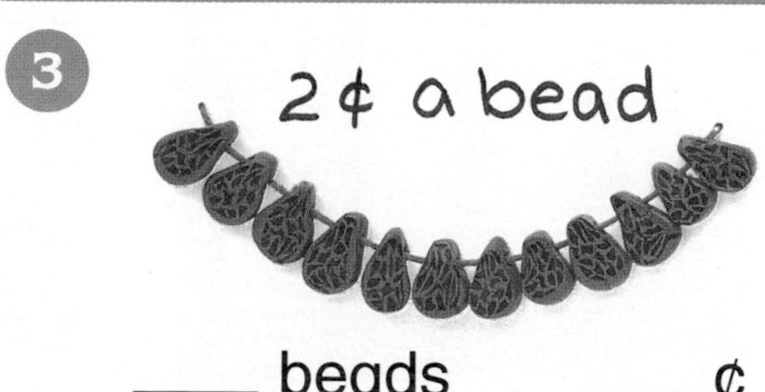

____ beads ____ ¢

4 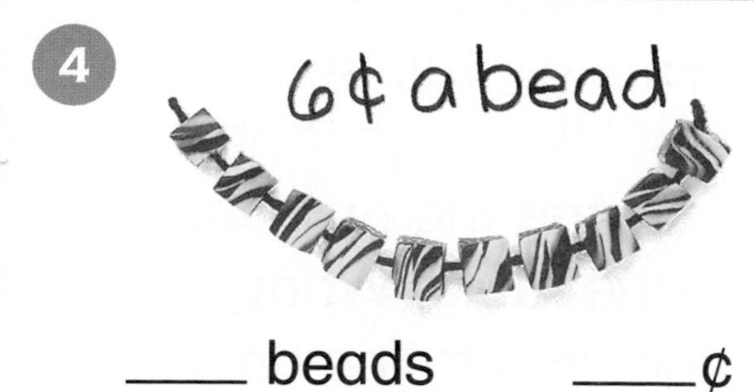

____ beads ____ ¢

Technology Connection

Computer

Use a Graph

Are there more toy vans or police cars? How do you know?

Vehicles

Vehicles	
Vans	19
Police Cars	22
Trucks	18
Race cars	20
Sports Cars	21

1. Which number of vehicles is the least? ______

2. Which number is the greatest? ______

At the Computer

3. Put the numbers in the table in order.

4. Link the table to a bar graph. What do you see?

5. Change the numbers in the table. What happens to the graph?

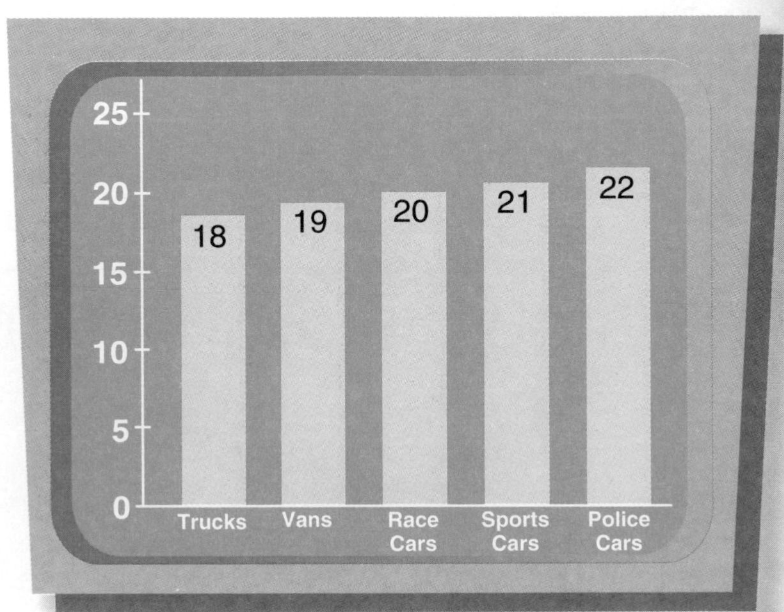

Name

Cumulative Review

Choose the letter of the correct answer.

$4 + 2 = \underline{\ ?\ }$

ⓐ 4
ⓑ 5
ⓒ 6
ⓓ 7

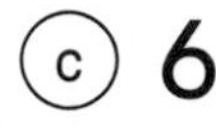

2 $9 + 1 = \underline{\ ?\ }$

ⓐ 4
ⓑ 5
ⓒ 6
ⓓ 10

3 $4 + 5 = \underline{\ ?\ }$

ⓐ 4
ⓑ 8
ⓒ 9
ⓓ 10

4

$$\begin{array}{r} 6¢ \\ +\ 3¢ \\ \hline \end{array}$$

ⓐ 6¢
ⓑ 7¢
ⓒ 8¢
ⓓ 9¢

5

$$\begin{array}{r} 3 \\ +\ 7 \\ \hline \end{array}$$

ⓐ 4
ⓑ 7
ⓒ 9
ⓓ 10

6

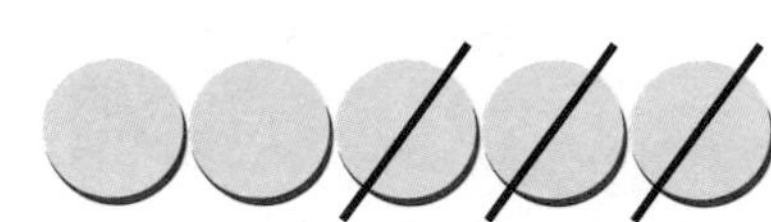

$5 - 3 = \underline{\ ?\ }$

ⓐ 1
ⓑ 2
ⓒ 3
ⓓ 4

7 $7 - 2 = \underline{\ ?\ }$

ⓐ 2
ⓑ 3
ⓒ 4
ⓓ 5

8 $9 - 4 = \underline{\ ?\ }$

ⓐ 4
ⓑ 5
ⓒ 6
ⓓ 9

9

$$\begin{array}{r} 10¢ \\ -\ \ 6¢ \\ \hline \end{array}$$

ⓐ 3¢
ⓑ 4¢
ⓒ 6¢
ⓓ 8¢

10 8 pigs in a pen.
2 pigs get away.
How many pigs are left?

ⓐ 5
ⓑ 6
ⓒ 7
ⓓ 8

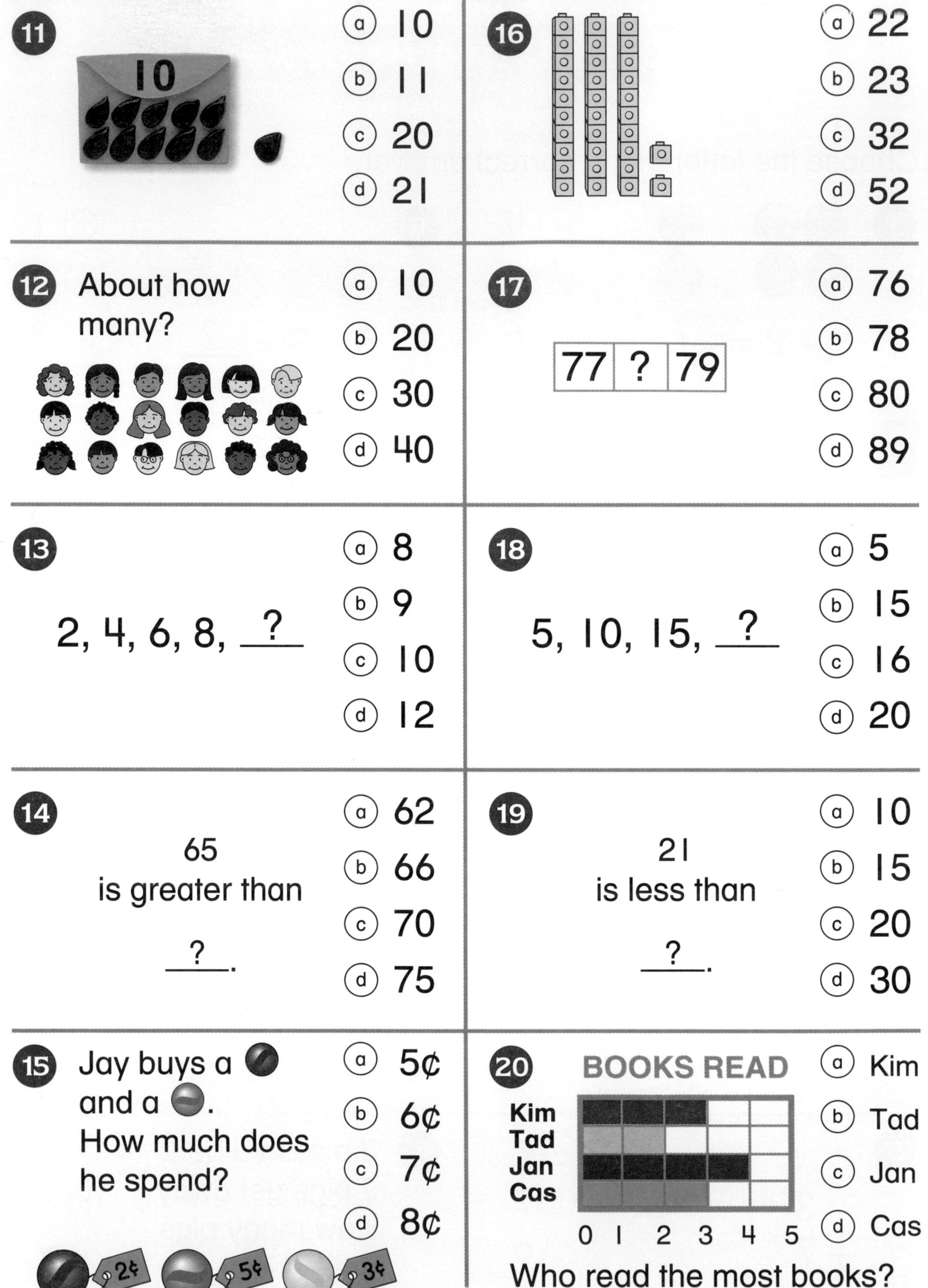

11

Ⓐ 10
Ⓑ 11
Ⓒ 20
Ⓓ 21

16

Ⓐ 22
Ⓑ 23
Ⓒ 32
Ⓓ 52

12 About how many?

Ⓐ 10
Ⓑ 20
Ⓒ 30
Ⓓ 40

17 77 | ? | 79

Ⓐ 76
Ⓑ 78
Ⓒ 80
Ⓓ 89

13 2, 4, 6, 8, ___?___

Ⓐ 8
Ⓑ 9
Ⓒ 10
Ⓓ 12

18 5, 10, 15, ___?___

Ⓐ 5
Ⓑ 15
Ⓒ 16
Ⓓ 20

14 65 is greater than ___?___.

Ⓐ 62
Ⓑ 66
Ⓒ 70
Ⓓ 75

19 21 is less than ___?___.

Ⓐ 10
Ⓑ 15
Ⓒ 20
Ⓓ 30

15 Jay buys a (marble) and a (marble). How much does he spend?

Ⓐ 5¢
Ⓑ 6¢
Ⓒ 7¢
Ⓓ 8¢

2¢ 5¢ 3¢

20 BOOKS READ

Kim
Tad
Jan
Cas

0 1 2 3 4 5

Who read the most books?

Ⓐ Kim
Ⓑ Tad
Ⓒ Jan
Ⓓ Cas

Home Connection

Chapter 6 Wrap-Up

Name

Every Penny Counts

MATERIALS 100 pennies, paper and pencil

DIRECTIONS Take turns. Find different ways to group 100 pennies in order to make it easy to count them. Keep a record of the ways you group.

How many ways did you group pennies? Which grouping made counting the easiest?

As you engage in this activity with your child, let your child make the grouping decisions. He or she will probably make groups, or stacks, of 2, 5, or 10. You may also choose to make groups of 20 or 25. Then discuss and have your child answer the two questions.

Dear Family,

Our new chapter in mathematics is about shapes and parts of shapes.

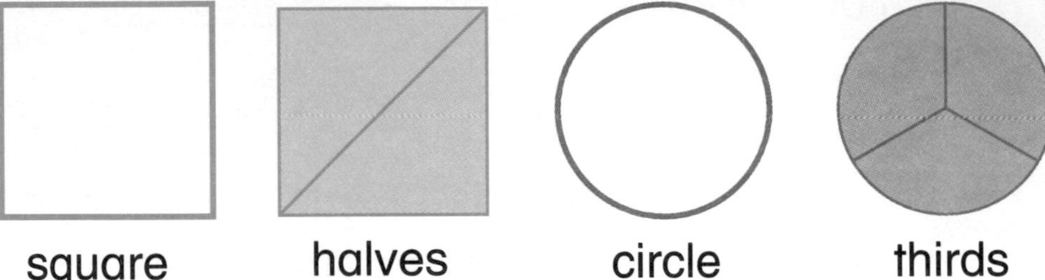

We will also be looking for shapes in the world around us, especially how shapes are used in kites. Please help me complete this interview.

Your child,

____

Signature

Interview

Did you ever fly a kite? ____________________

What shape was it? ____________________

Did you ever make a kite? ____________________

What did you use to make it? ____________________

____

High-Flying Kites

Geometry and Fractions

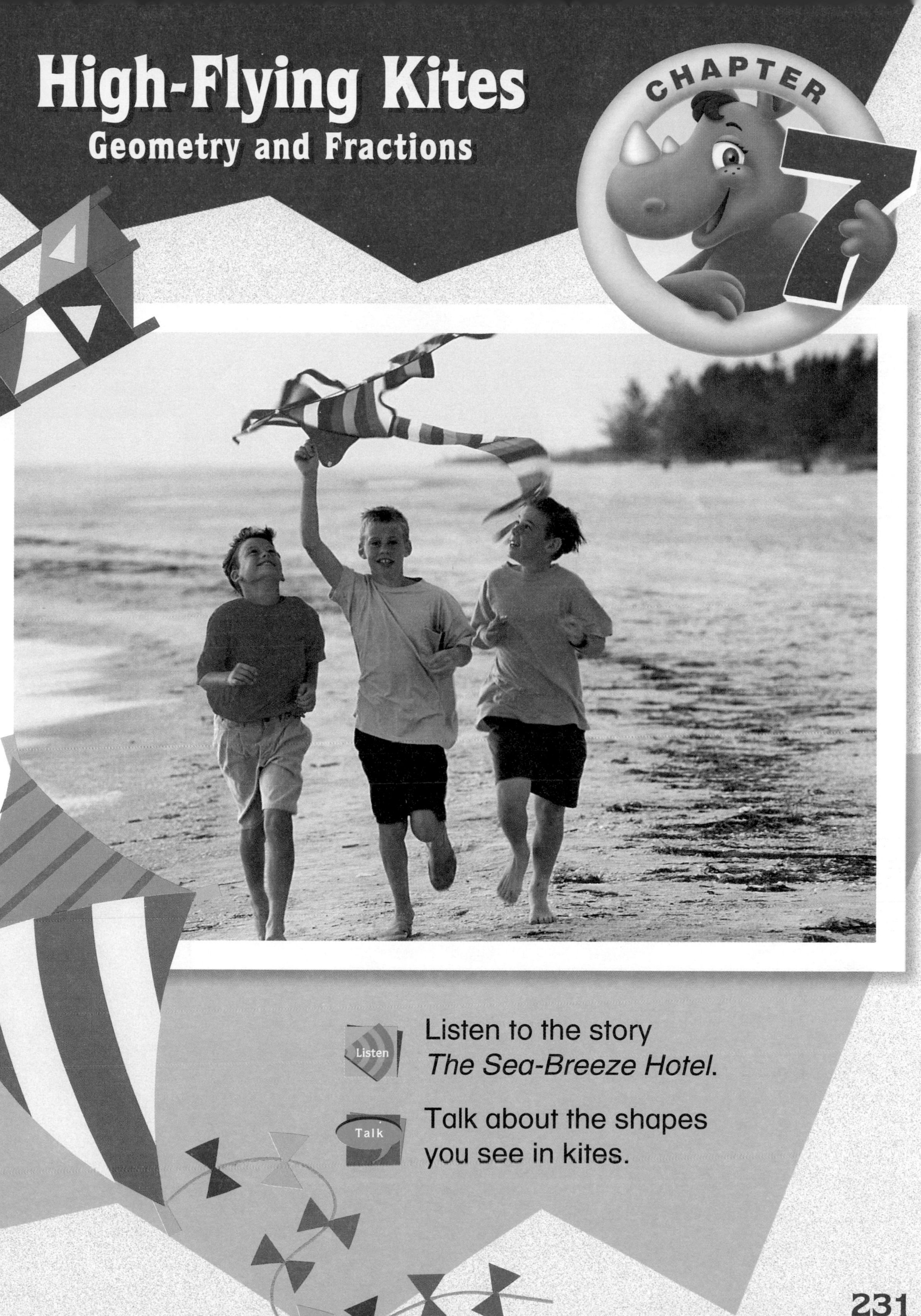

Listen to the story *The Sea-Breeze Hotel*.

Talk about the shapes you see in kites.

Name

What Do You Know?

Use a yellow to color shapes with 4 sides.
Use a red to color shapes with 3 sides.

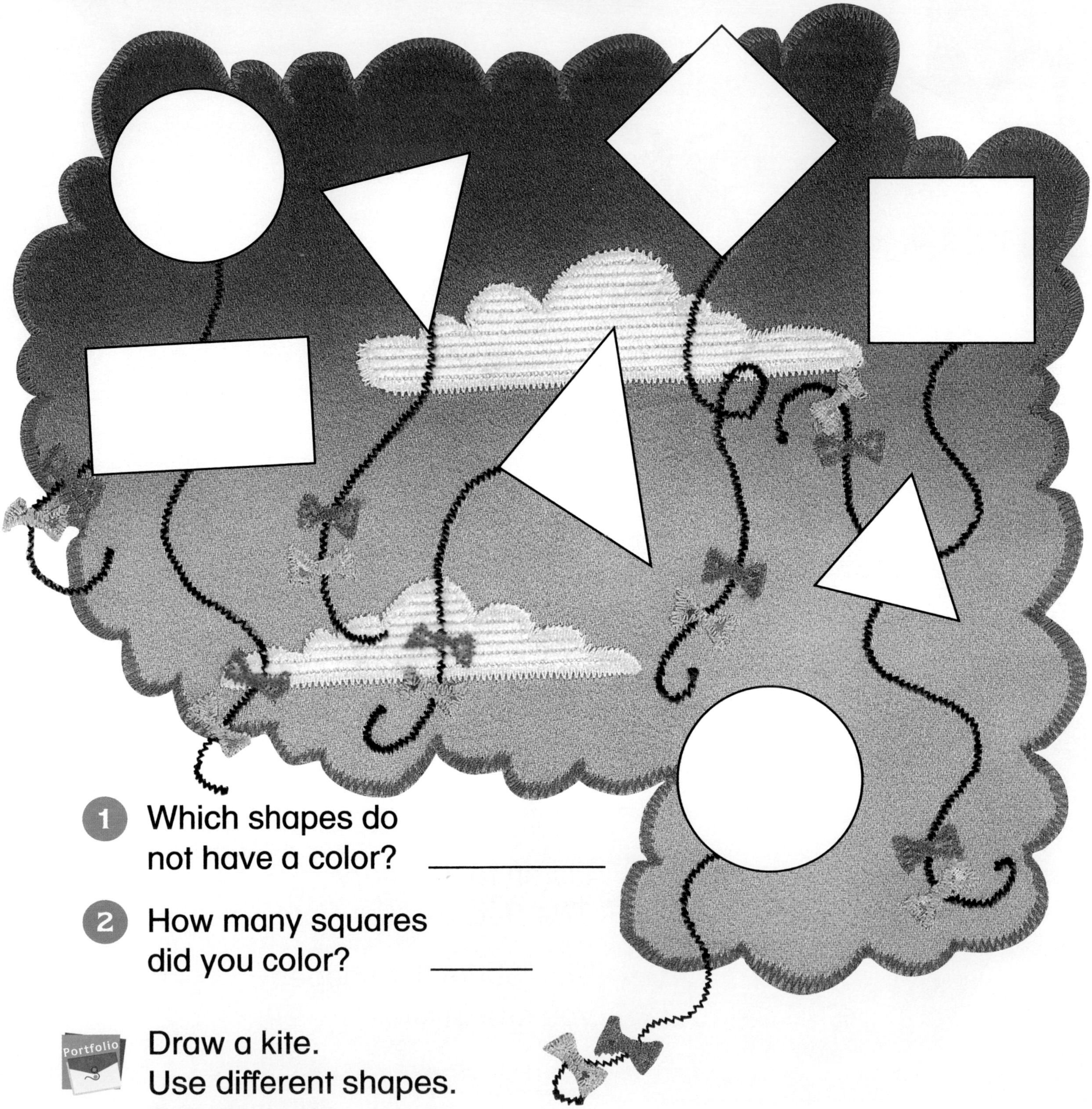

1. Which shapes do not have a color? ________

2. How many squares did you color? ______

Portfolio

Draw a kite.
Use different shapes.
Tell about the shapes.

Name

Explore Activity

3-Dimensional Shapes

cube

cone

cylinder

sphere

rectangular prism

Working Together

Use solid shapes like these to build something.

Talk Which shapes did you use?
What makes a shape good for building?

What can each shape do?
☑ Check.

	cube	cone	cylinder	sphere	rectangular prism
Stack					
Roll					

Why can some shapes stack *and* roll?

Try These!

Show what the shapes do.

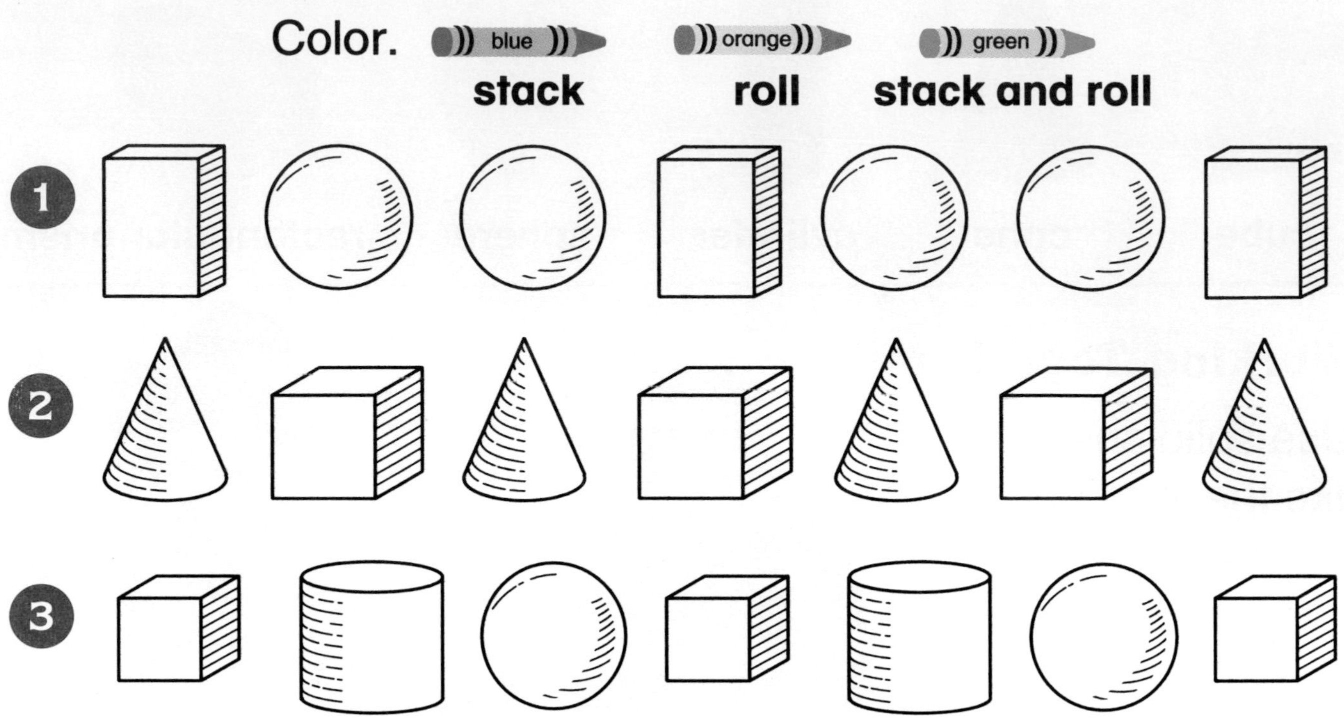

Talk Tell a partner what patterns you see.

More to Explore Spatial Sense

How many?

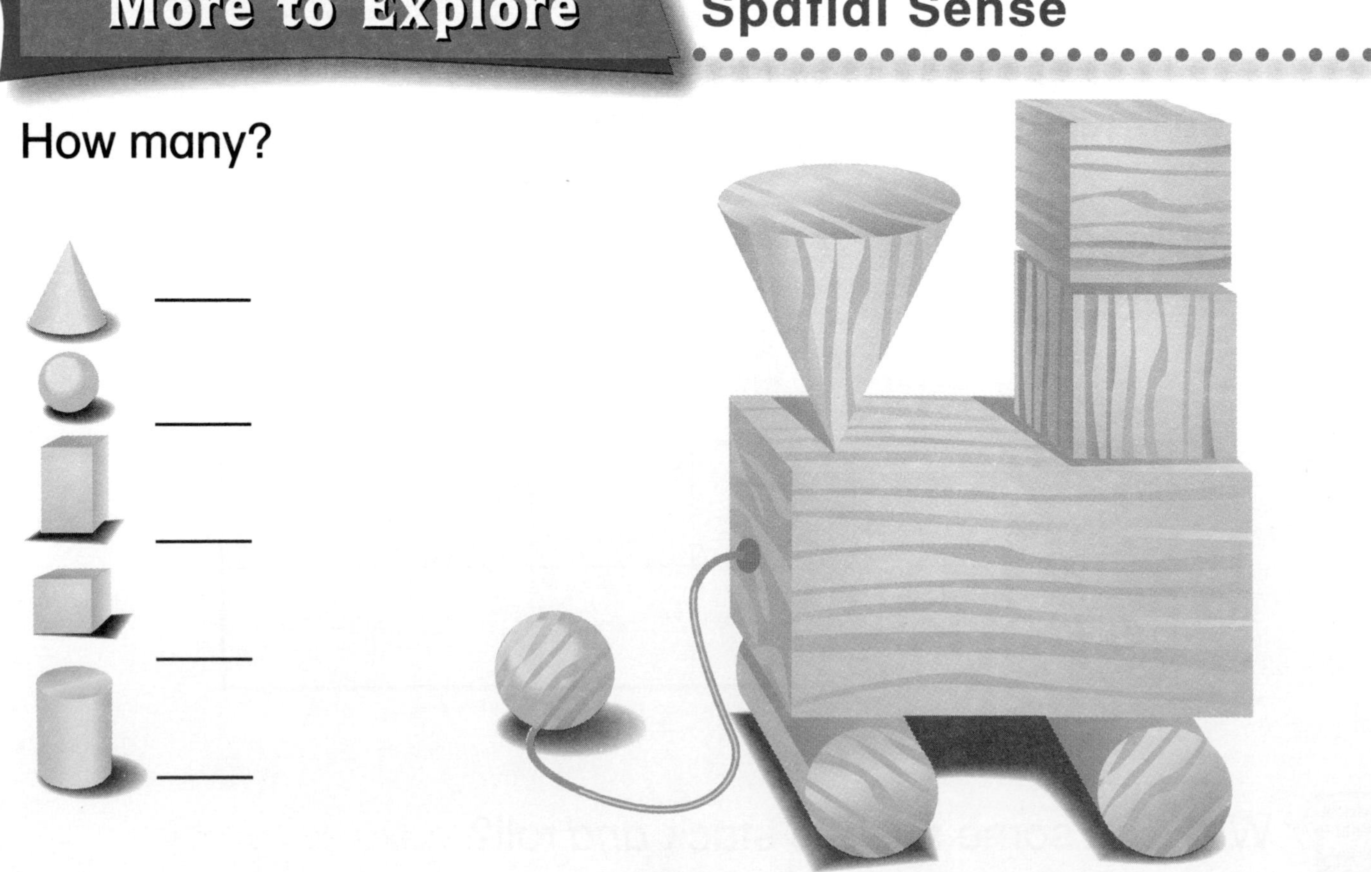

At Home Ask your child to describe each pictured shape.

Name

Make Shapes

Working Together

You and your partner need solid shapes.

Take turns.

- ▶ Place a solid shape on paper.
- ▶ Trace around the edges.
- ▶ Ring the shape you see.

	Object	Shape
1		
2		
3		
4		
5		

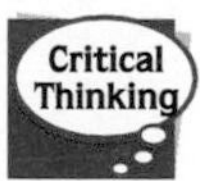

How many shapes can you trace from a cereal box?

Try These!

Color objects that make each shape.

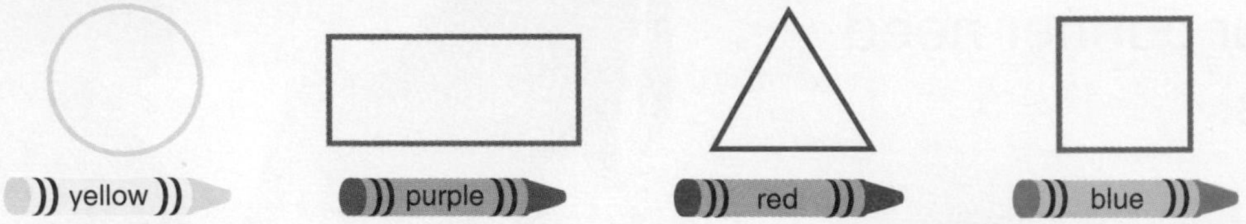

yellow — purple — red — blue

Popcorn

SOUP

More to Explore — Spatial Sense

These are open figures. These are closed figures.

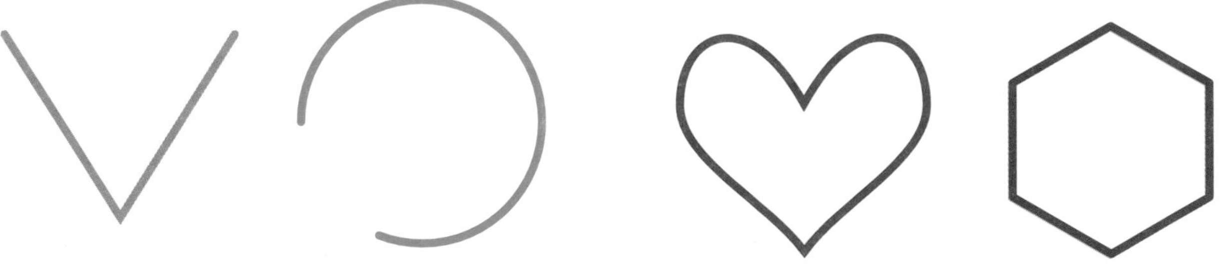

Color inside the closed figures.

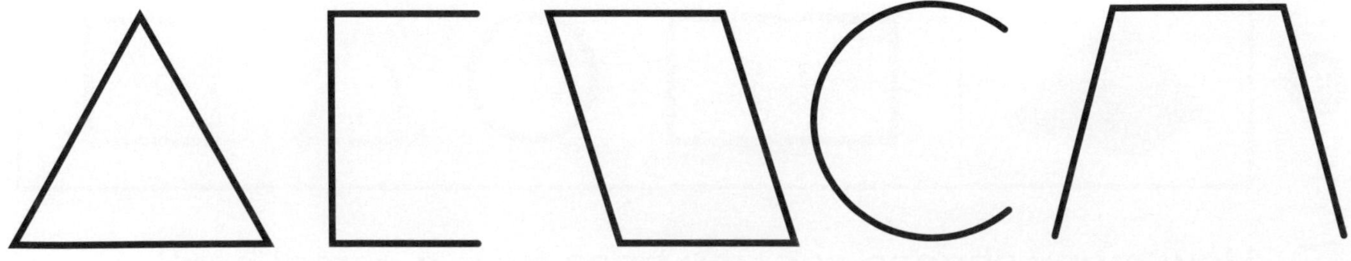

At Home: Ask your child to talk about the shapes found in your kitchen.

Name ______________________________

Explore Activity

2-Dimensional Shapes

circle

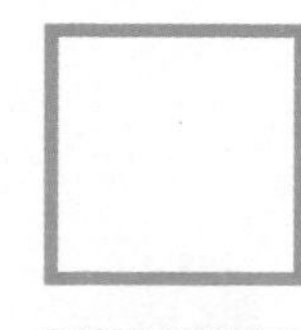

square

triangle

rectangle

Working Together

You and your partner need ○, □, △, ▭.

Take turns.

- Choose a shape.
- Say how many sides.
- Your partner says how many corners.

Complete the chart together.

	Shape	How many sides?	How many corners?
1	△	___	___
2	▭	___	___
3	□	___	___
4	○	___	___

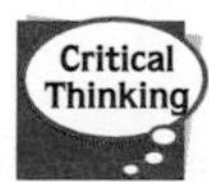

What if a shape has 5 sides. How many corners does it have?

Try These!

Trace the sides with a green crayon.
Circle the corners.

1
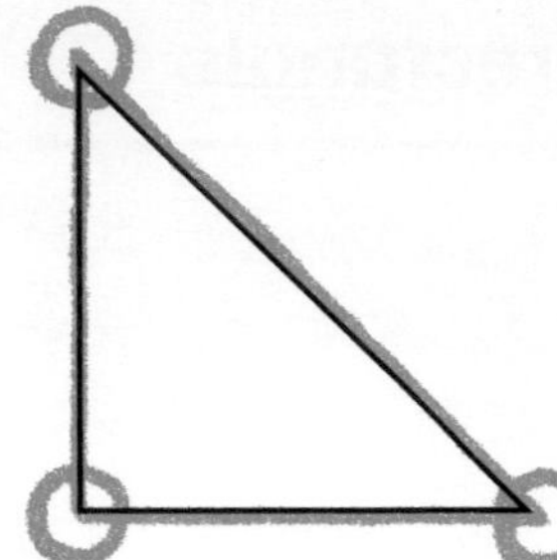

2
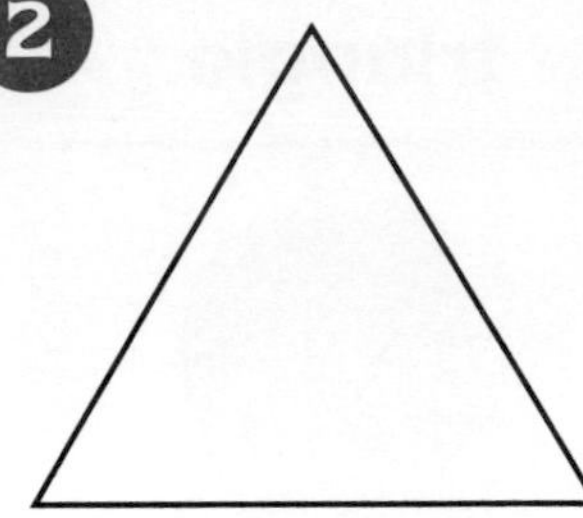

3
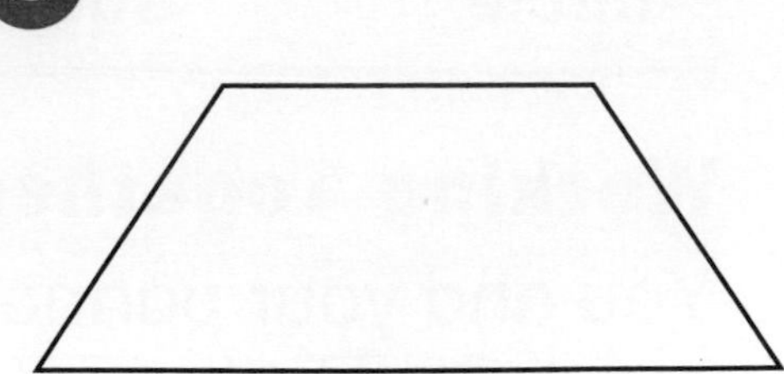

4

5
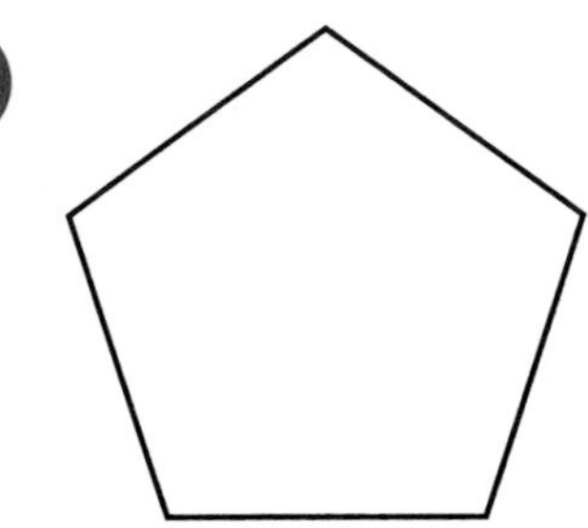

6
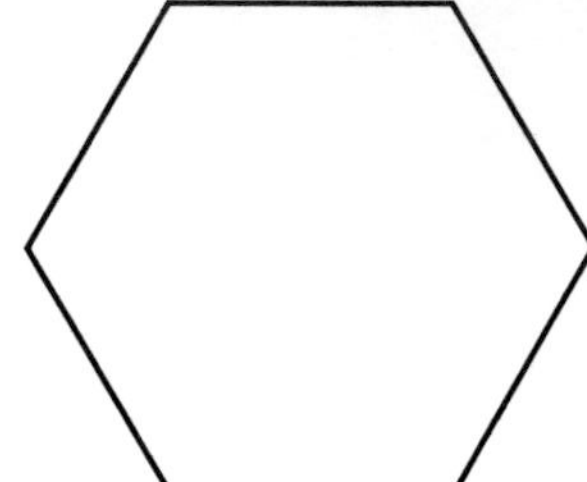

Count sides. Count corners.
Complete.

Look for a pattern.

7

Sides	3	4	5	6
Corners	3	___	___	___

Mixed Review

8 Add.

$$\begin{array}{r} 4 \\ +5 \\ \hline \end{array} \quad \begin{array}{r} 6 \\ +2 \\ \hline \end{array} \quad \begin{array}{r} 2 \\ +4 \\ \hline \end{array} \quad \begin{array}{r} 7 \\ +3 \\ \hline \end{array} \quad \begin{array}{r} 1 \\ +3 \\ \hline \end{array} \quad \begin{array}{r} 5 \\ +3 \\ \hline \end{array}$$

At Home: Have your child trace around boxes and count how many sides and corners there are.

Name

Use a Physical Model

You need ▨.

Read Josh used 3 **tangram** triangles. How did he make his kite?

Plan You can use a model to solve.

Solve Try different triangles.

Right.

Draw lines on the kite to show the answer.

Look Back Does your answer make sense? Explain.

Solve.

1. Lois used these pieces to make a kite.

Show how she did it.

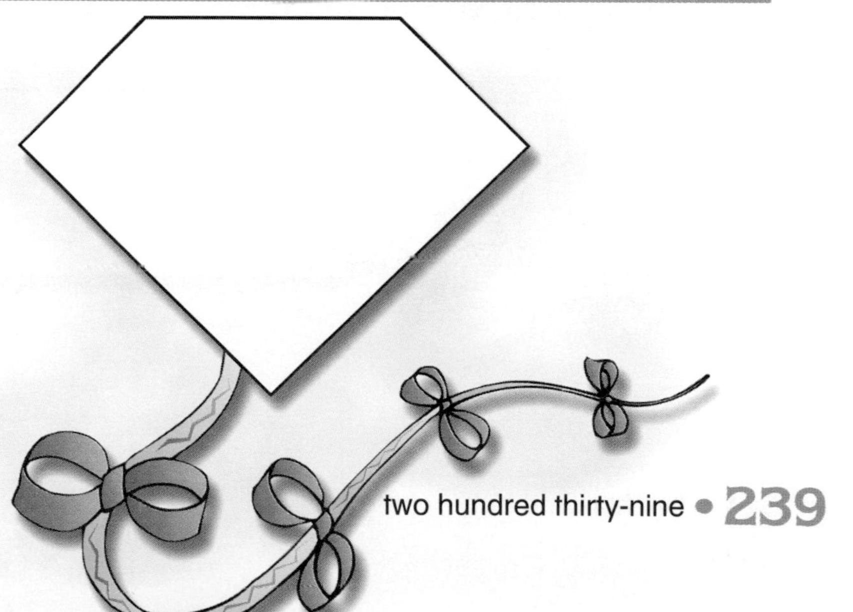

Use [tangram] to solve.
Draw lines to show your answer.

1. Sally made this kite.
Show how she did it.

2. Tim made this kite.
Show how he did it.

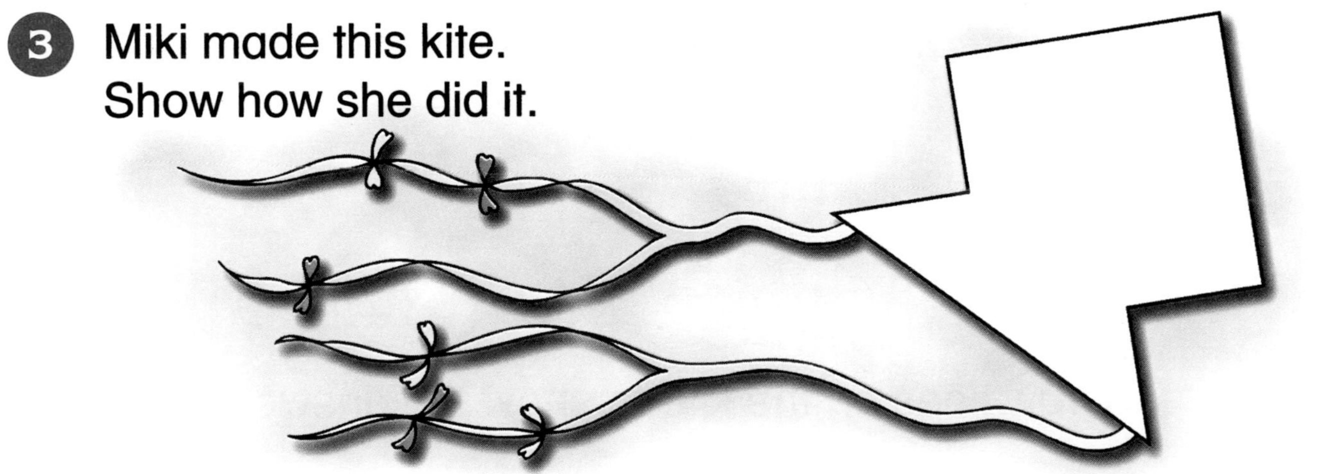

3. Miki made this kite.
Show how she did it.

4. Carl made this turtle kite.
Show how he did it.

At Home Ask your child to explain how to solve these problems.

Name

Midchapter Review

Match.

  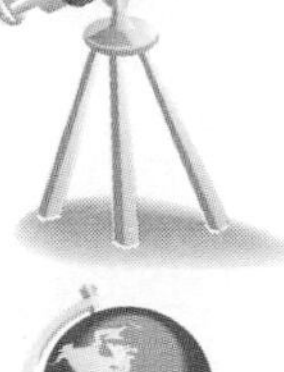

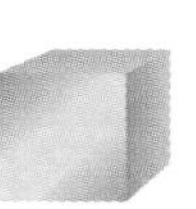

Complete.

4 A ○ is a  ____________.

5 A ▭ has ____ sides.

6 A △ has ____ sides.

7 A □ has ____ corners.

Ring the shape made by the solid shape.

8     

9    

Use a model.
Draw lines to show your answer.

10 Elly made this kite.
Show how she did it.

Draw some shapes. Tell what you know about the shapes.

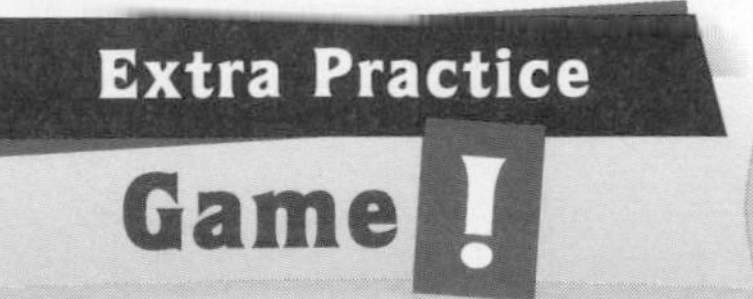

Fly a Kite!

You and your partner need 2 and a .

Take turns.

- ► Spin for a shape.
- ► Move your to the first kite with that shape.

The first player to reach the **Park** wins.

Do any kites have more than one shape?

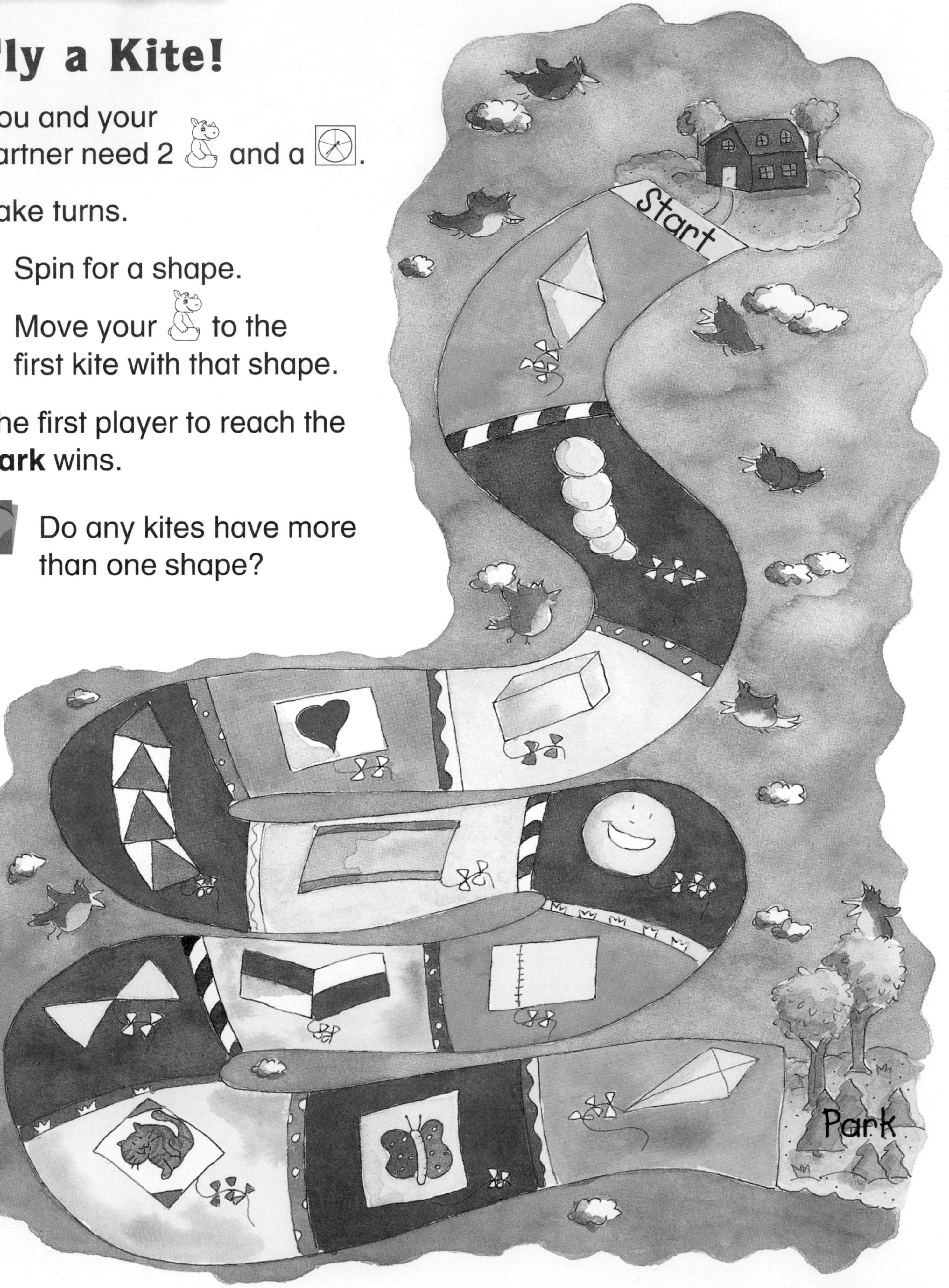

Start

Park

Name

Making a Kite

Listen to
The Sea-Breeze Hotel.

Tell what you know about kites.

Cultural Note
In China, a kite is a symbol of good luck.

Working Together

You and your partner will make a kite.

You need paper, tape, sticks, string, and a tail.

Decision Making

1. Look at the kites you made.
   Which kite do you like best? ______________________

   ____.

2. If you made another kite,
   would you choose another shape? ________________.

   Why? ______________________________________

Write a report

3. Draw your kite.
   Tell how you decided
   on a shape.

4. Tell how you made
   your kite.

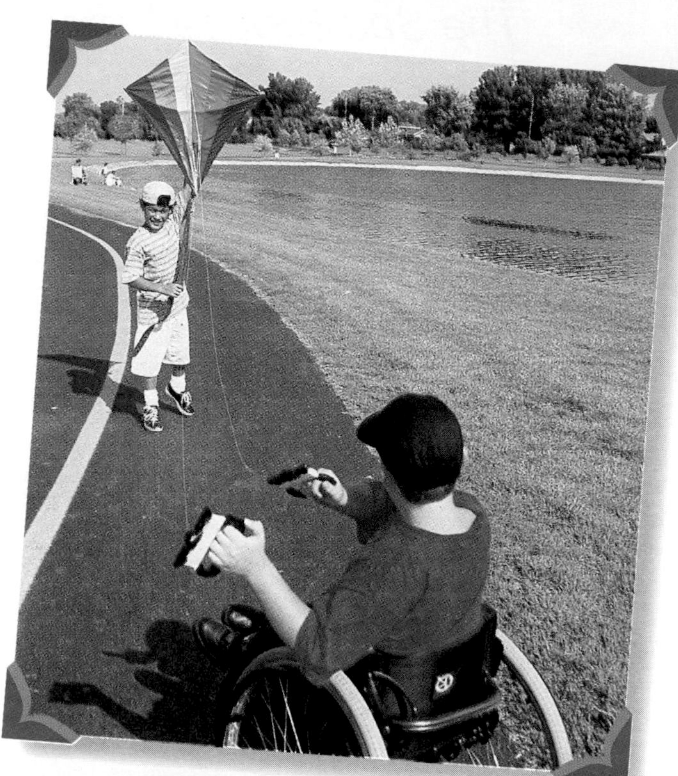

More to Investigate

Have a kite-flying day.

PREDICT Which kites will fly?

EXPLORE Try it. Stand with the wind at your back.

FIND Talk about the kites that fly. What is alike about them? What is different?

Name ___

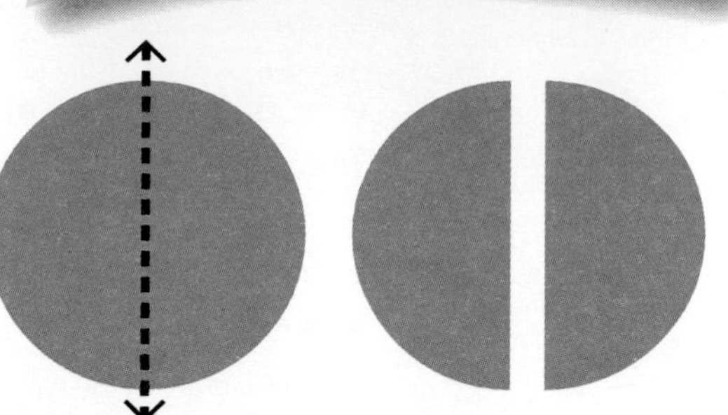

You need 1 ○, 2 □, 2 △.

Fold a ○ to make 2 parts that match.

Cut on the fold.

Both parts are the same size and shape.

Parts that match are **equal parts.**

Working Together

- Fold a □ into 2 equal parts.
- Fold a □ another way to make 2 equal parts.
- Draw a line to show each fold.

Tell about the equal parts you made.

- Fold a △ into 2 equal parts.
- Fold a △ into 2 parts that are not equal.
- Ring the △ that shows equal parts.

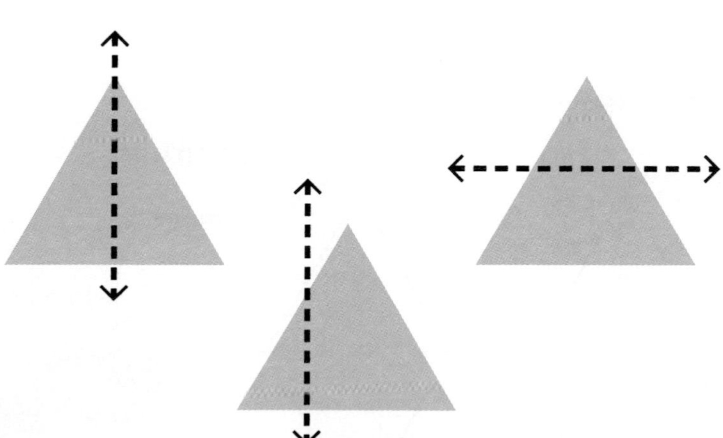

What does *equal parts* mean?

Try These!

Draw a line to show 2 equal parts.

1

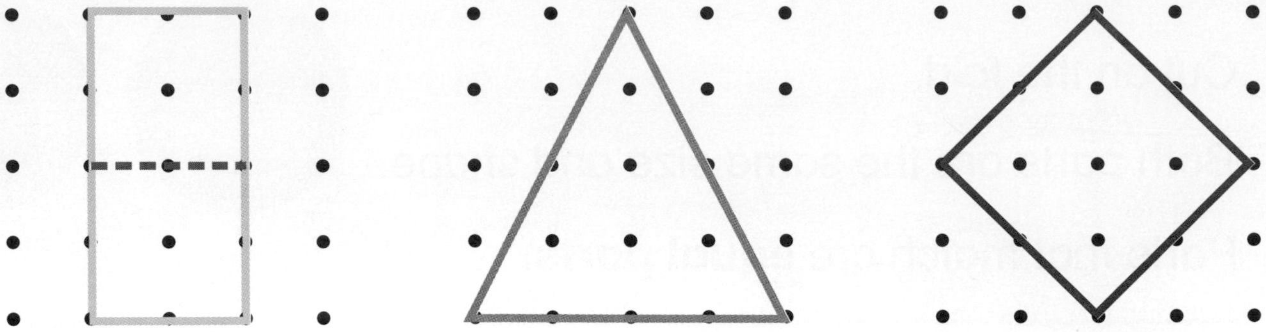

2

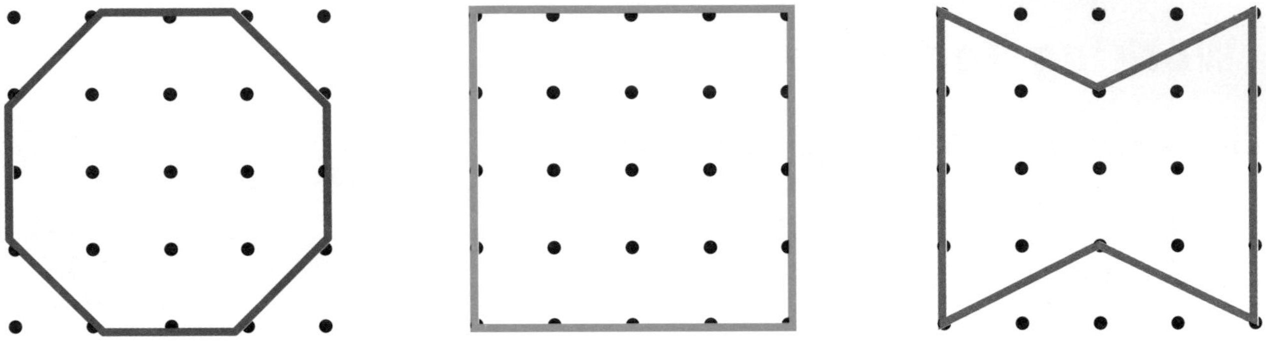

3

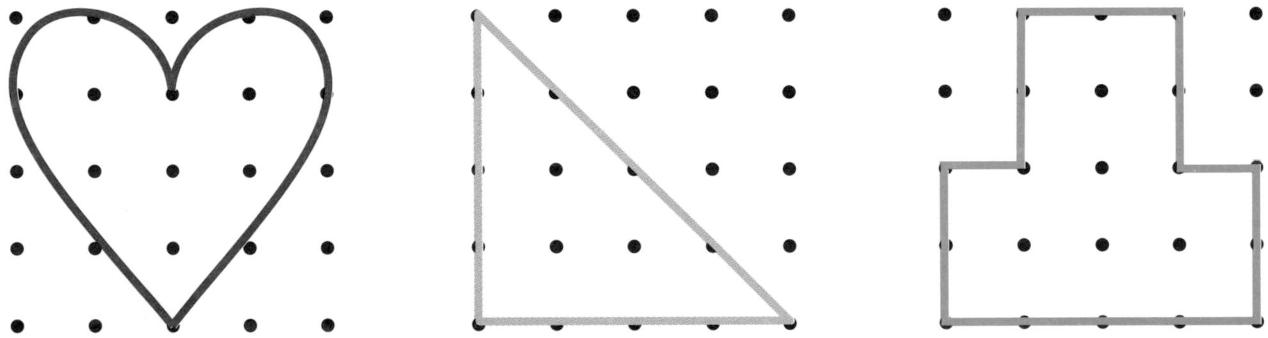

More to Explore

Spatial Sense

Color the shapes with equal parts.

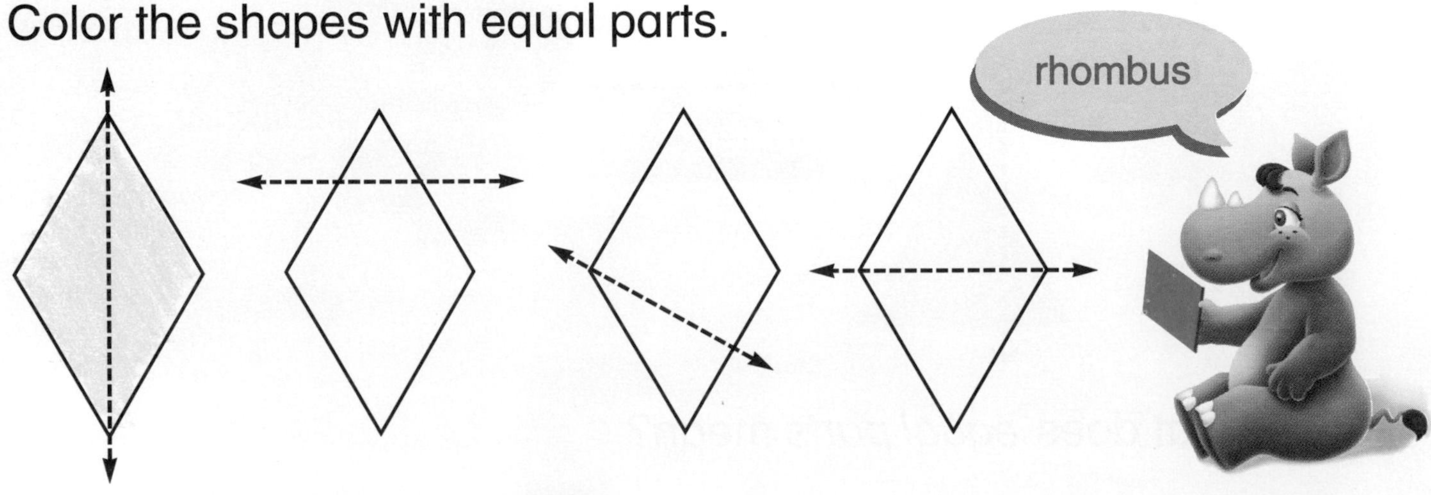

We explored identifying shapes with 2 equal parts. Ask your child to tell you about the shapes on this page.

Name

Working Together

You need paper shapes.

▶ Fold a ○ into 2 equal parts.

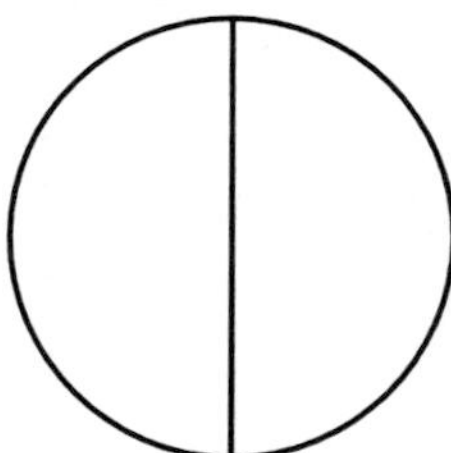

▶ Color 1 part blue.

1 of 2 equal parts

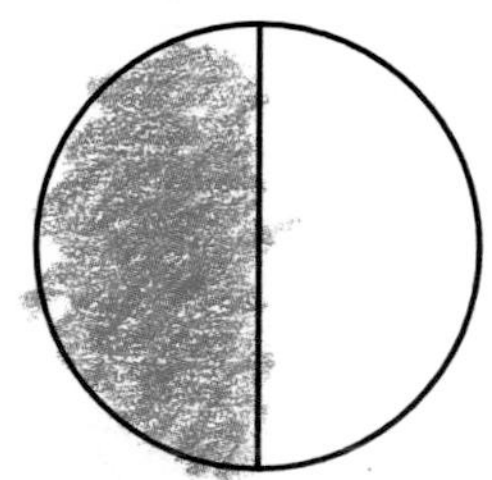

$\frac{1}{2}$

One half is blue.

▶ Fold other shapes.

▶ Make 2 equal parts.

▶ Color $\frac{1}{2}$.

Show how you made 2 equal parts.
Color $\frac{1}{2}$.

1 

2 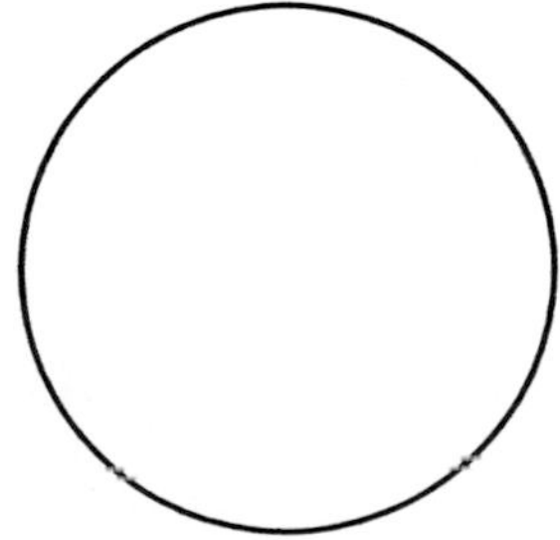

3 

How many halves make a whole?
What is each half called?

Try These!

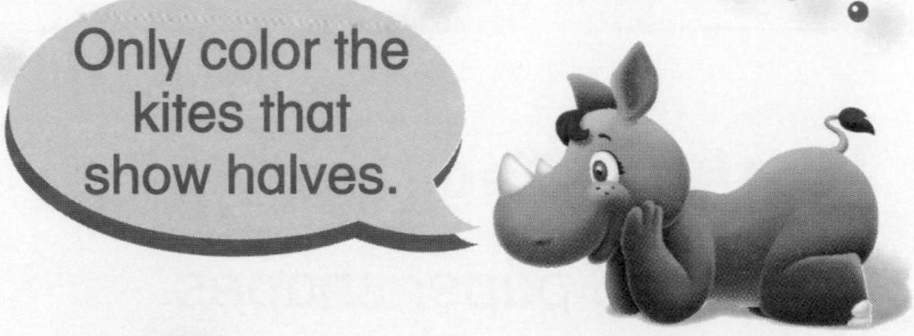

Only color the kites that show halves.

Color $\frac{1}{2}$.

1

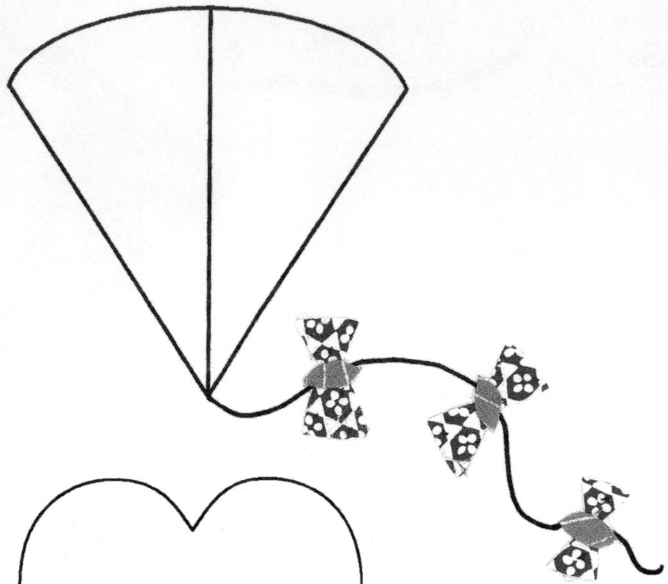

2

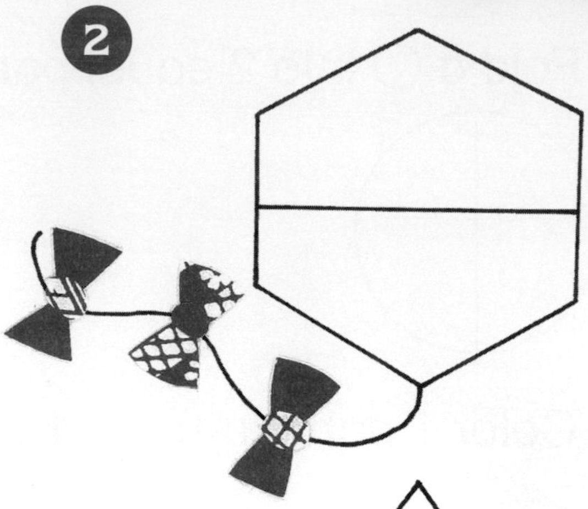

3

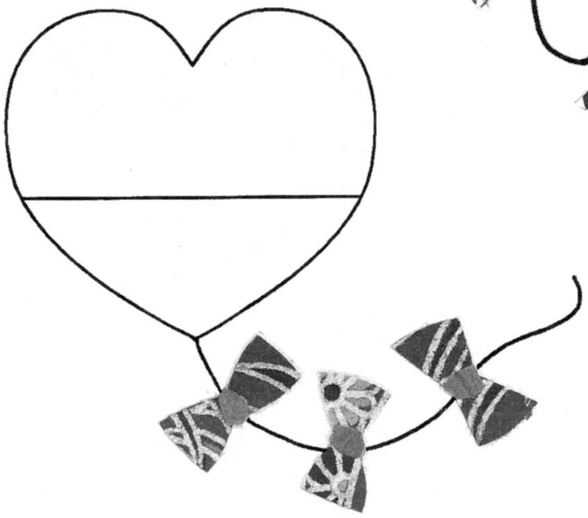

4

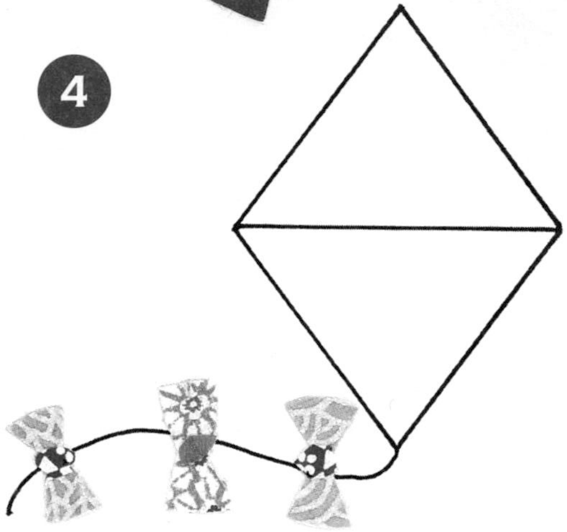

5

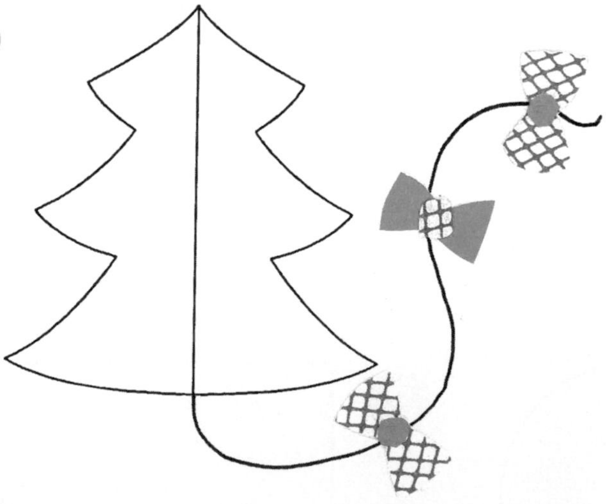

6

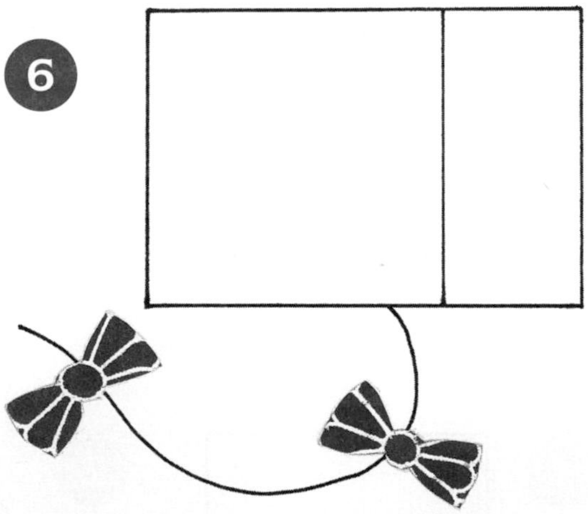

Tell a partner why you did not color some shapes.

Draw a kite. Color $\frac{1}{2}$.

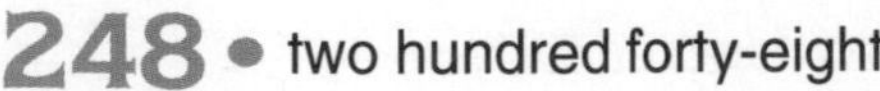

We learned about halves and one half. Ask your child to tell you about the pictures on this page.

Name

Fourths

Working Together

You need paper shapes.

▶ Fold a ○ into 4 equal parts.

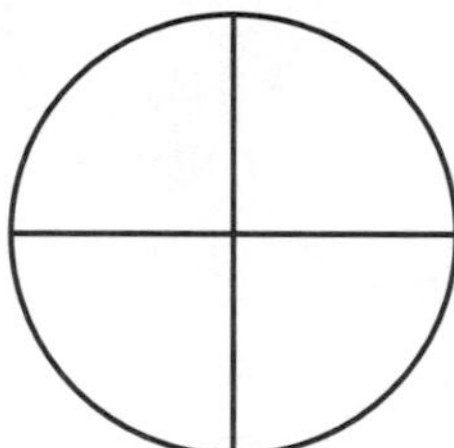

▶ Color 1 part blue.   1 of 4 equal parts

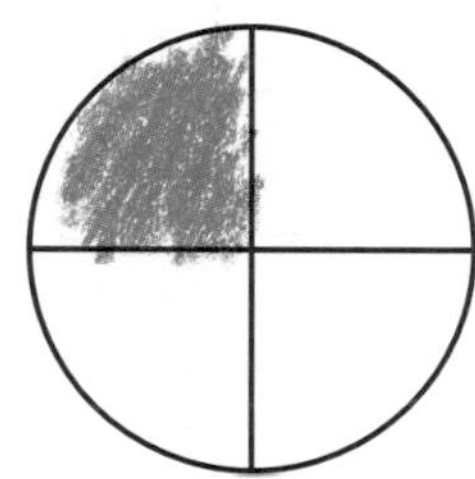

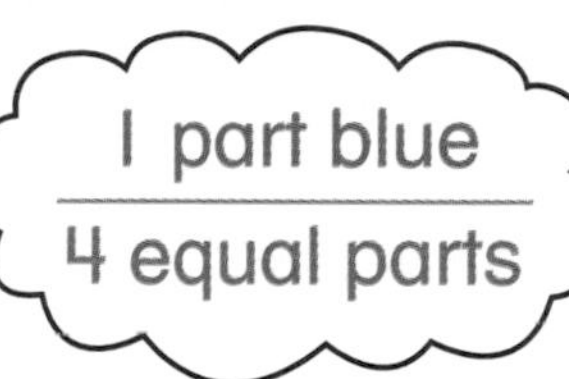

$\frac{1}{4}$

One fourth is blue.

▶ Fold other shapes.

▶ Make 4 equal parts.

▶ Color $\frac{1}{4}$.

Show how you made 4 equal parts.
Color $\frac{1}{4}$.

 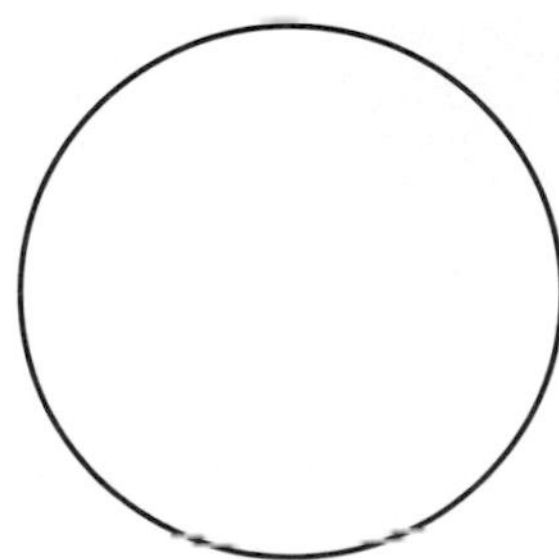

Critical Thinking How many fourths make a whole?
What is each fourth called?

Try These!

Only color the kites that show fourths.

Color $\frac{1}{4}$.

1

2

3

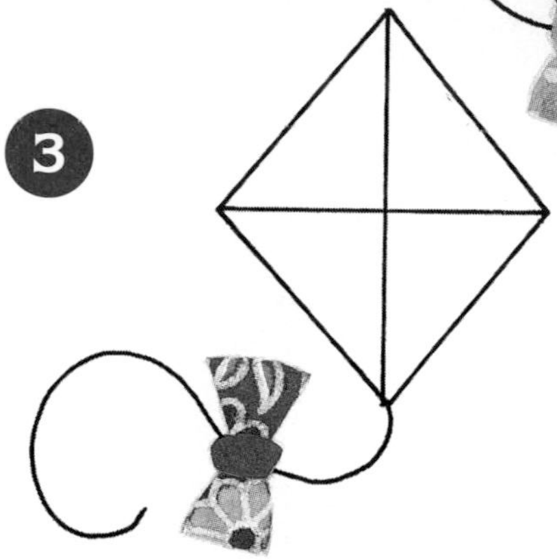

4

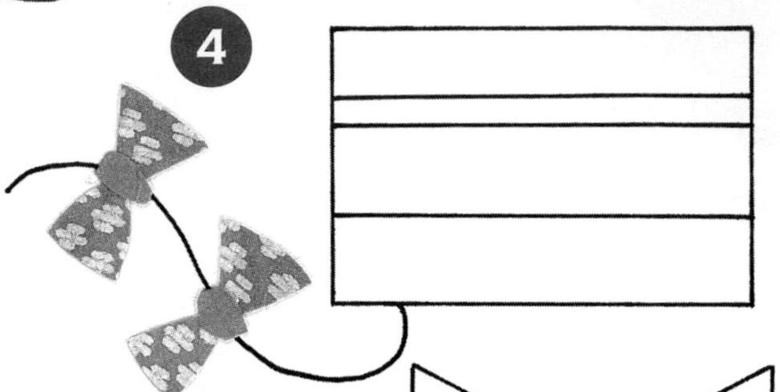

5

6

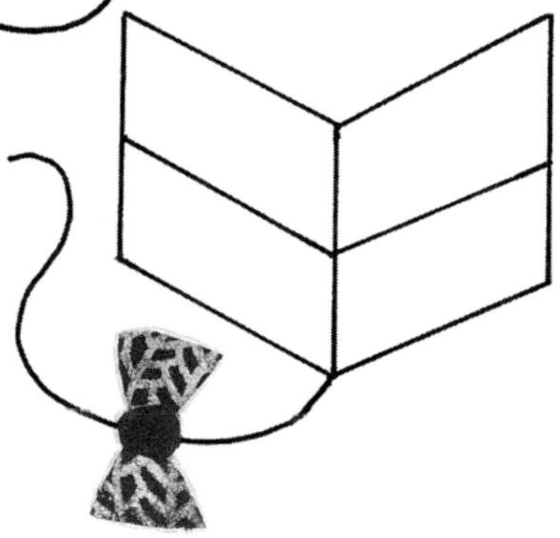

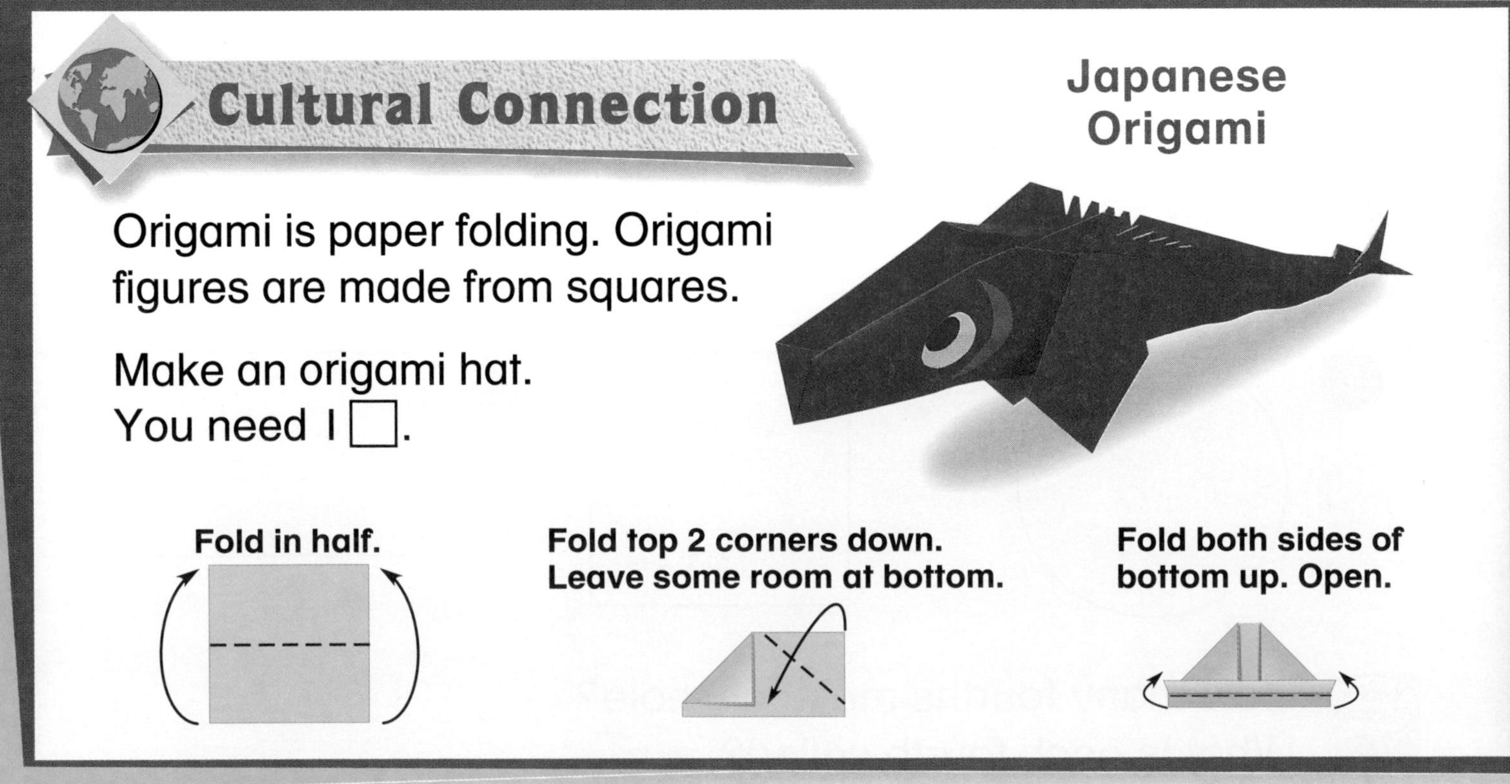

Cultural Connection

Japanese Origami

Origami is paper folding. Origami figures are made from squares.

Make an origami hat.
You need 1 □.

Fold in half.

Fold top 2 corners down. Leave some room at bottom.

Fold both sides of bottom up. Open.

At Home

We learned about fourths and one fourth. Have your child show how to fold a sheet of paper into fourths.

Name

Thirds

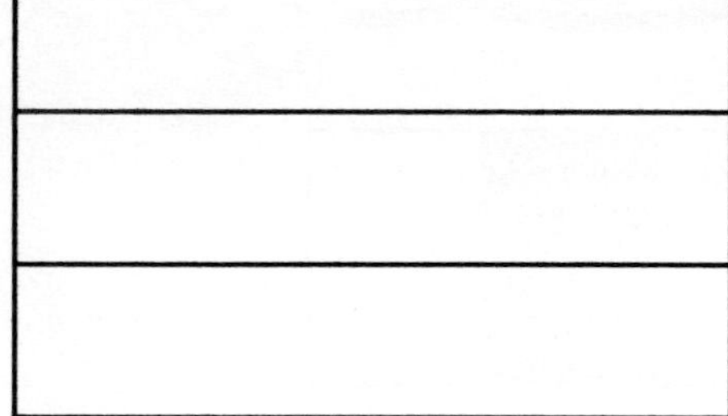

thirds

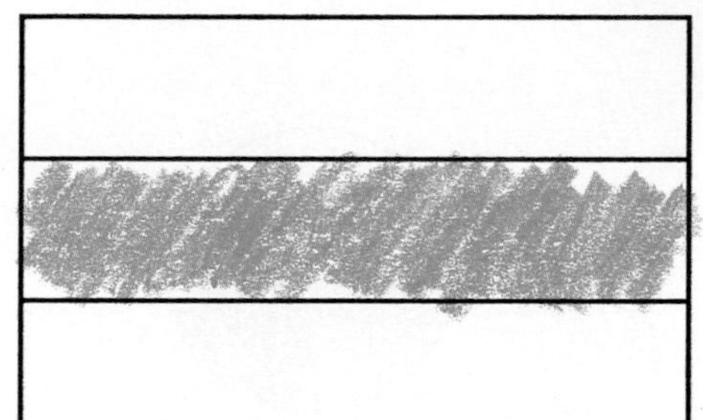

One third is green.

3 equal parts

1 of 3 equal parts

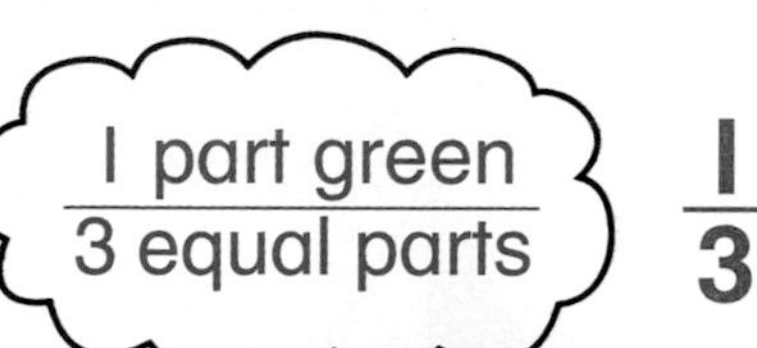

$\frac{1}{3}$

Working Together

You need paper shapes.

- Fold a ▭ into thirds.
  Fold another ▭ in half.
- Cut on the folds.
- Look at $\frac{1}{3}$ and $\frac{1}{2}$.

- Fold other shapes.
- Make 3 equal parts.
- Color $\frac{1}{3}$.

Show how you made 3 equal parts. Color $\frac{1}{3}$.

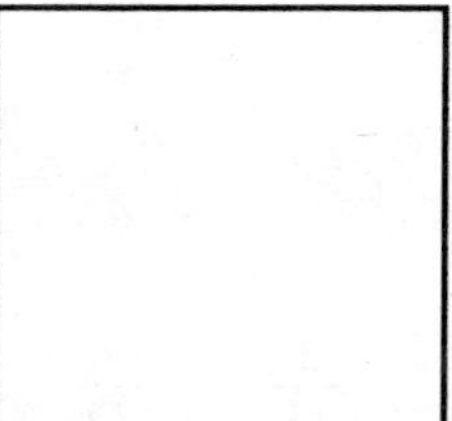

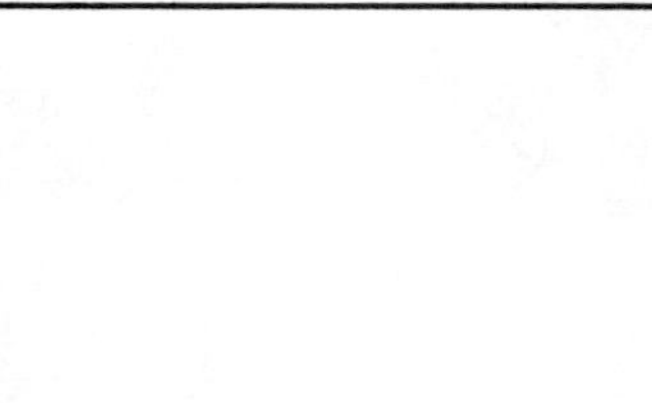

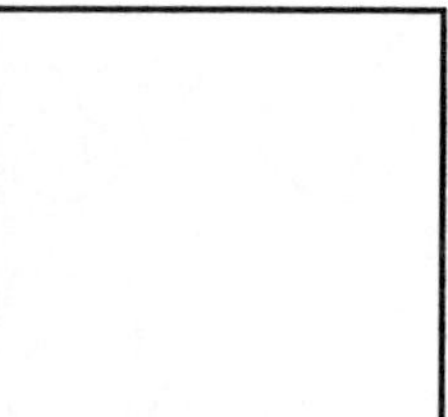

Try These!

$\frac{1}{2}$, $\frac{1}{4}$, and $\frac{1}{3}$ are **fractions.**

Ring the fraction.

1 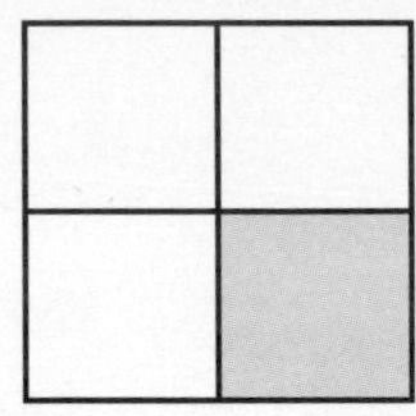  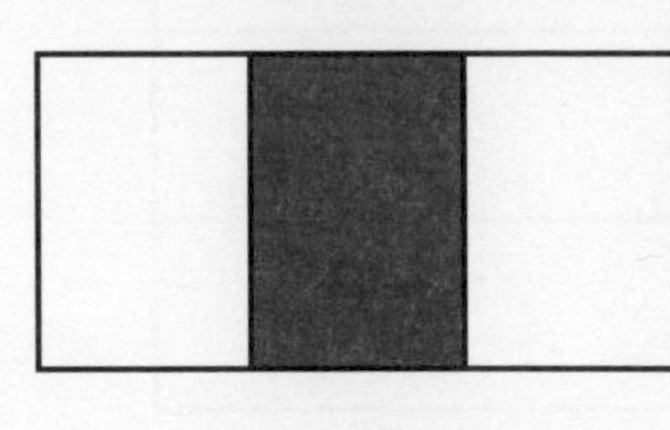

$\frac{1}{4}$ $\frac{1}{3}$ $\frac{1}{2}$ $\frac{1}{4}$ $\frac{1}{3}$ $\frac{1}{2}$ $\frac{1}{4}$ $\frac{1}{3}$ $\frac{1}{2}$

2 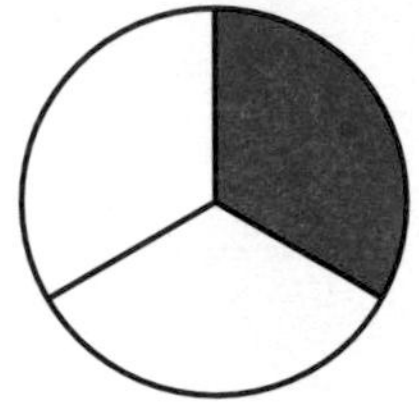 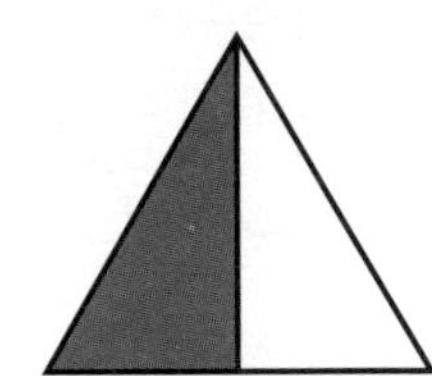 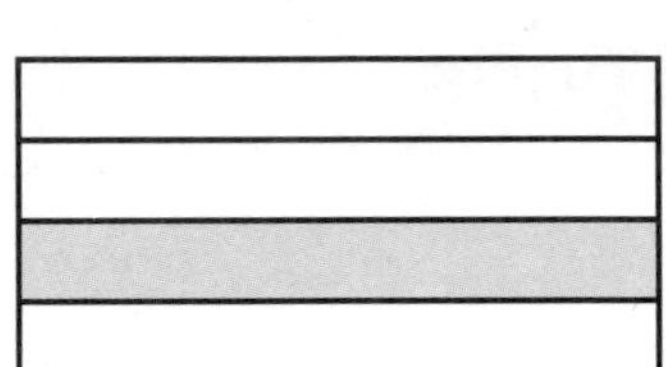

$\frac{1}{4}$ $\frac{1}{3}$ $\frac{1}{2}$ $\frac{1}{4}$ $\frac{1}{3}$ $\frac{1}{2}$ $\frac{1}{4}$ $\frac{1}{3}$ $\frac{1}{2}$

More to Explore Number Sense

$\frac{1}{3}$ of the kites are green.

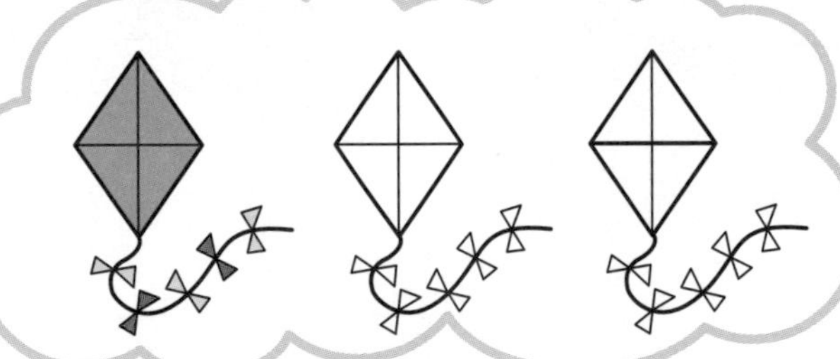

$\frac{\text{1 green kite}}{\text{3 kites in all}}$

Ring the fraction.

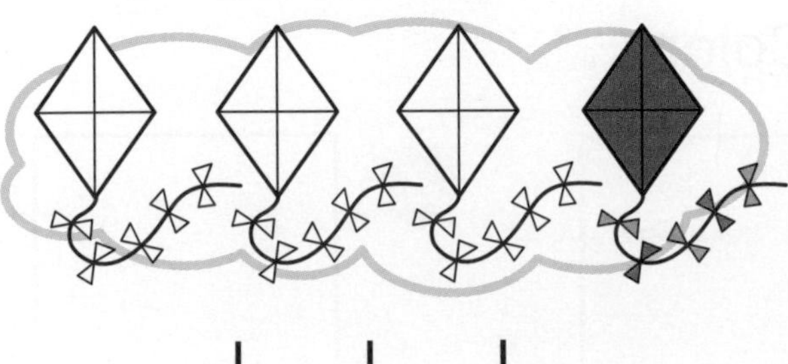 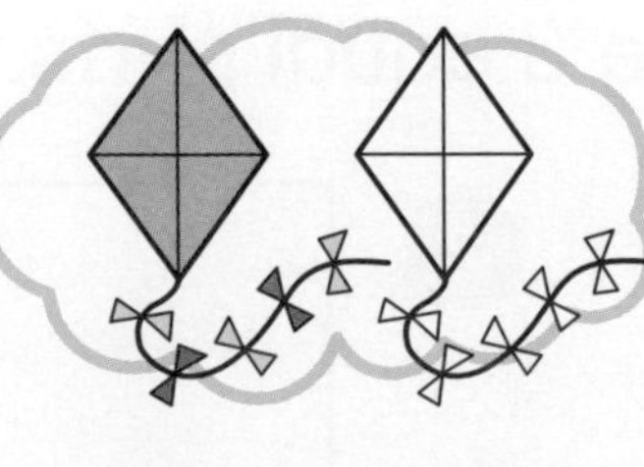 

$\frac{1}{4}$ $\frac{1}{3}$ $\frac{1}{2}$ $\frac{1}{4}$ $\frac{1}{3}$ $\frac{1}{2}$ $\frac{1}{4}$ $\frac{1}{3}$ $\frac{1}{2}$

Have your child tell you about the fractions on this page.

Name ______

Draw a Picture

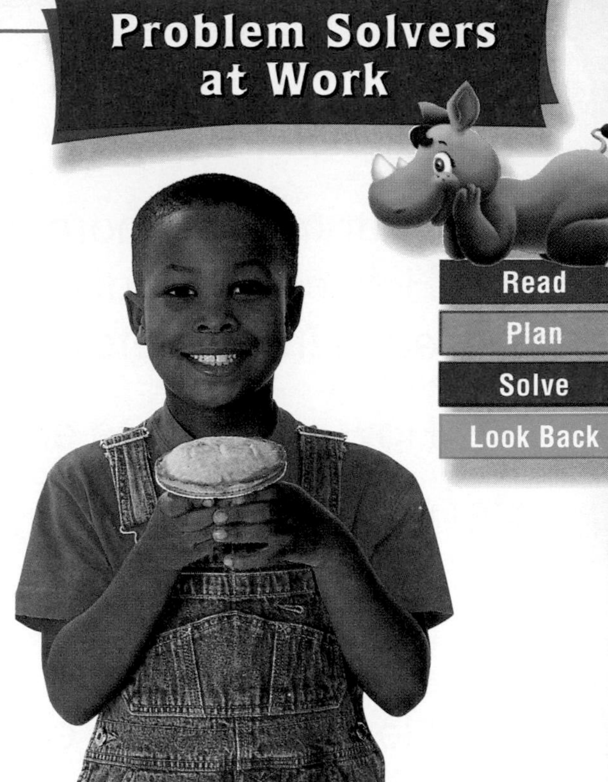

Meg and Jon share a pie.
How can they **divide** the pie so that each child gets an equal part?

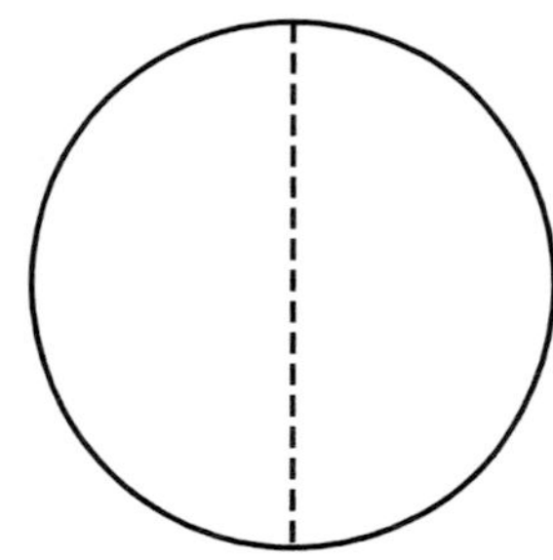

How much does each child get? $\frac{1}{2}$

Draw a picture to solve.

1. Two children share a sandwich.
How can they cut the sandwich so that each child gets an equal part?

How much does each child get? ____

---

2. Mike shares a cracker with May.
How can they divide the cracker so that each child gets an equal part?

How much does each child get? ____

---

3. Nina shares a pizza with 3 friends.
How can they cut the pizza so that each child gets an equal part?

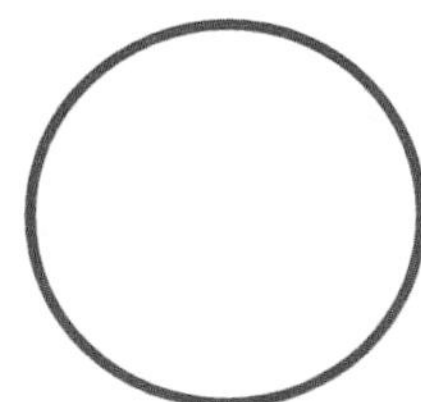

How much does each child get? ____

Try These!

Draw a picture to solve.

1. Four friends share a snack bar. How can they divide the bar so that each friend gets an equal part?

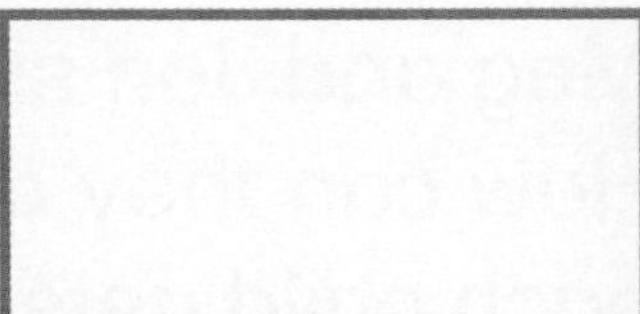

   How much does each friend get? ____

2. What if only 3 friends share the bar? How can they divide the bar so that each friend gets an equal part?

   How much does each friend get? ____

Would you like to have a part of the snack bar in problem 1 or in 2? Why?

Write and Share

Randy Hall
Mandarin Oaks School
Jacksonville, Florida

Randy wrote this problem.

Randy and Casey share a mango. How can they cut the mango so that each child gets an equal part?

3. Solve Randy's problem. How much does each child get? ____

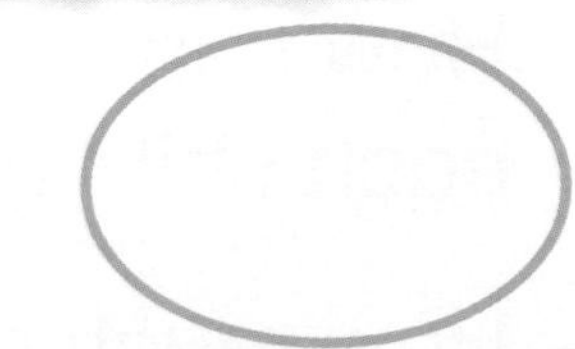

4. 

   Write a problem about sharing. Have a partner solve it.

   Use your own paper.

At Home: We drew pictures to solve problems. Ask your child how he or she solved Randy's problem.

Name

Chapter Review

Draw lines to match.

Ring the shape made by the object.

  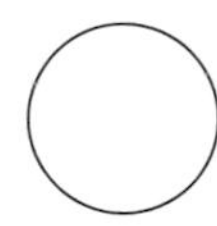 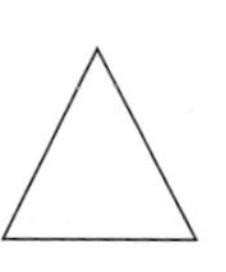 

 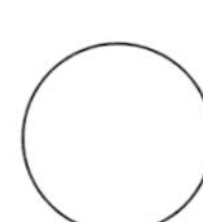 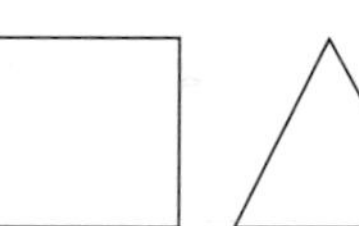

 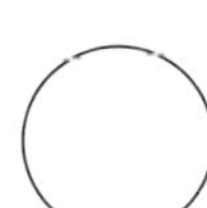  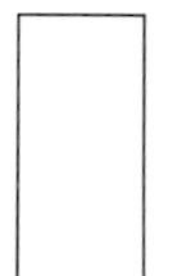

   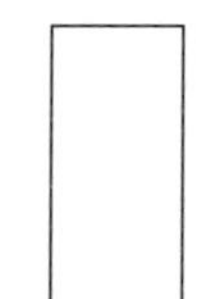

Complete.

9 A △ has ____ corners.

10 A □ has ____ sides.

Does the shape have equal parts?

11 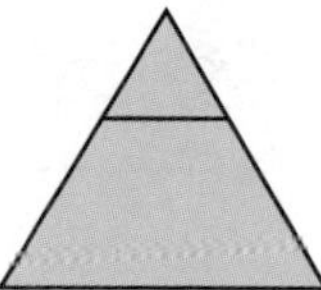

yes no

12 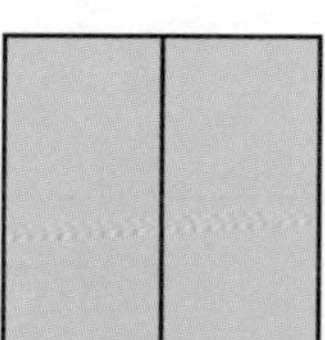

yes no

13 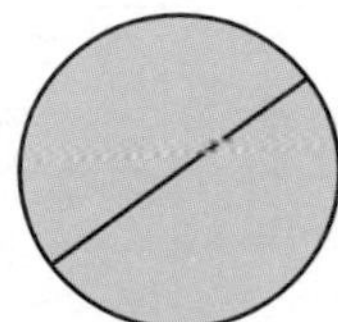

yes no

Color to show the fraction.

14 $\frac{1}{3}$

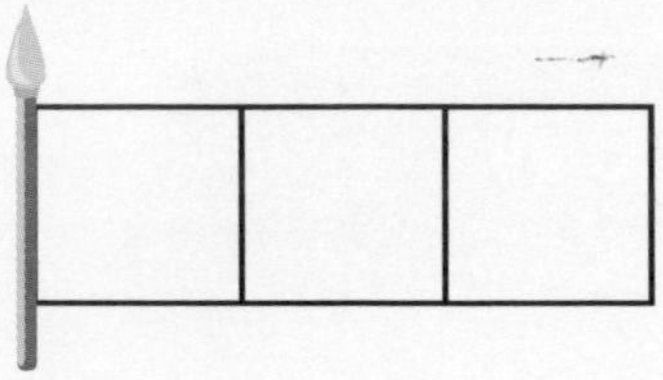

15 $\frac{1}{4}$

Ring the fraction.

16

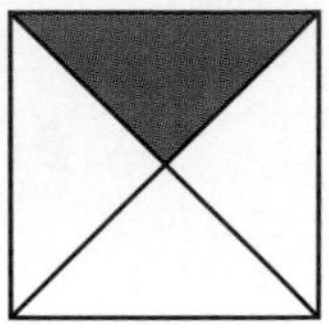

$\frac{1}{2}$ $\frac{1}{3}$ $\frac{1}{4}$

17

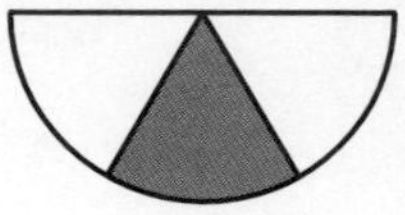

$\frac{1}{2}$ $\frac{1}{3}$ $\frac{1}{4}$

18

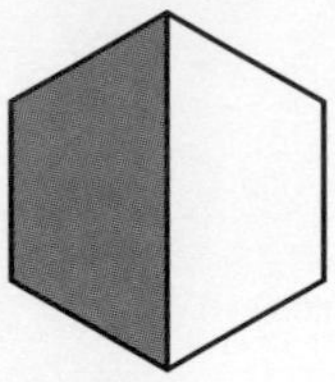

$\frac{1}{2}$ $\frac{1}{3}$ $\frac{1}{4}$

Use a  to solve.
Draw lines to show your answer.

19 Sue made this kite.
Show how she did it.

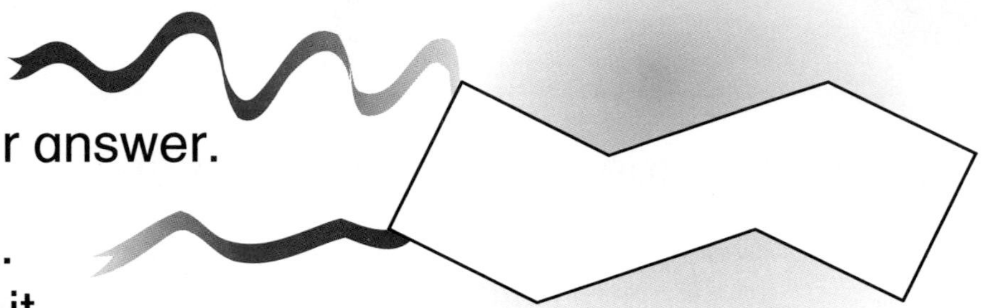

Draw a picture to solve.

20 Four children share a cake.
How can they cut it so that each child gets an equal part?

What Do You Think?

How do you think about one third?
✔ Check one.

☐ 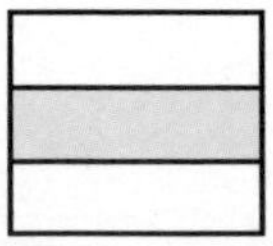 ☐ $\frac{1}{3}$ ☐ One third

Why? ______________________________

Journal

Draw a picture to show one fourth.

Name

Chapter Test

Draw lines to match.

1  

2 

Complete.

3 A  has ____ sides.

4 A  has ____ corners.

Does the shape have equal parts?

5 

yes no

6 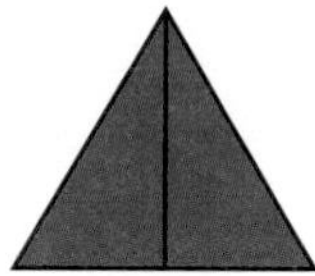

yes no

Ring the fraction.

7 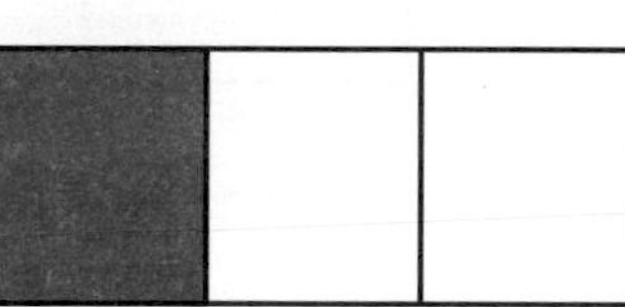

$\frac{1}{2}$ $\frac{1}{3}$ $\frac{1}{4}$

8 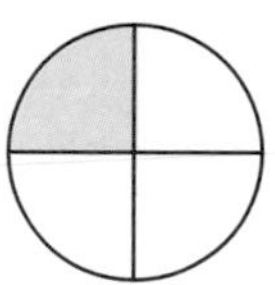

$\frac{1}{2}$ $\frac{1}{3}$ $\frac{1}{4}$

9 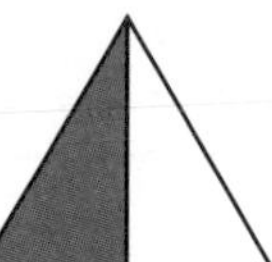

$\frac{1}{2}$ $\frac{1}{3}$ $\frac{1}{4}$

Use  to solve.
Draw lines to show your answer.

10 Thom made this kite.
Show how he did it.

Performance Assessment

What Did You Learn?

Draw lines in each shape.
Color to show the fraction.

1. $\frac{1}{2}$

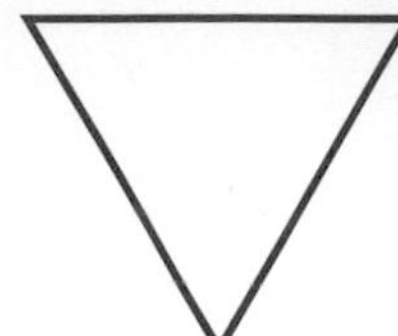 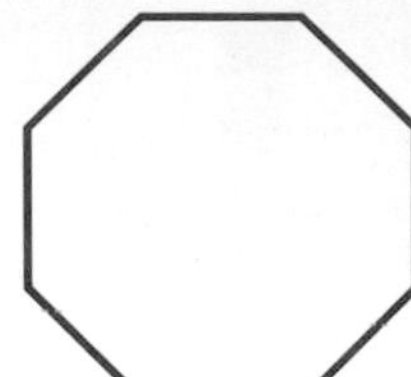 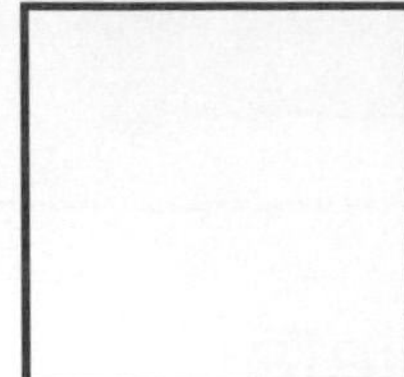

2. $\frac{1}{4}$

 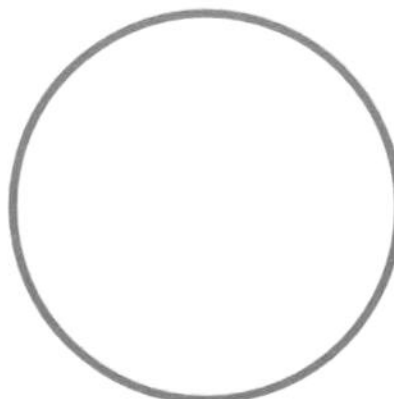 

3. $\frac{1}{3}$

4. Write what you know about this shape.

____

____

Portfolio You may want to put this page in your portfolio.

Name

Likely/Unlikely

Mark an X if the picture shows what is **unlikely.**
Mark an O if the picture shows what is **likely.**

1

2

Technology Connection

Computer

Shapes and Fractions

How many small squares were used to make the larger square?

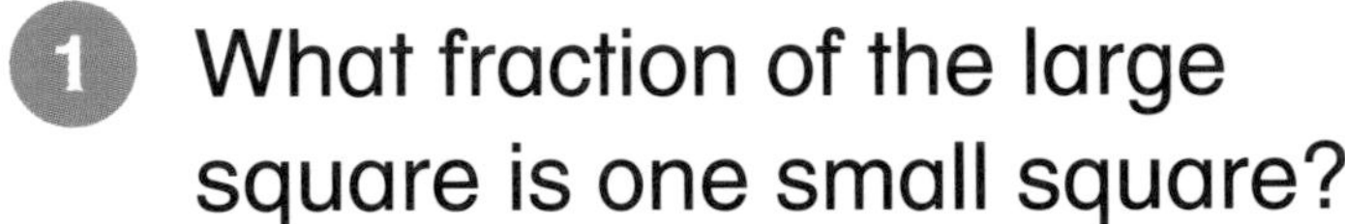

1. What fraction of the large square is one small square?

____

At the Computer

2. Draw a triangle like the one shown. Makes copies of it to build the larger triangle.

3. What fraction of the large triangle is one small triangle?

____

4. This triangle is $\frac{1}{2}$ of another triangle. Draw that triangle.

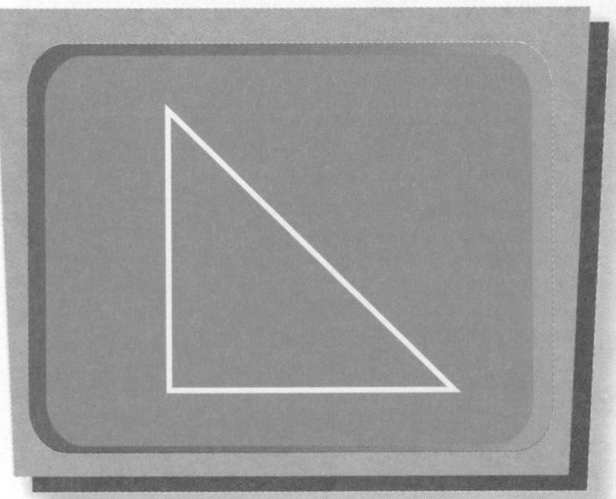

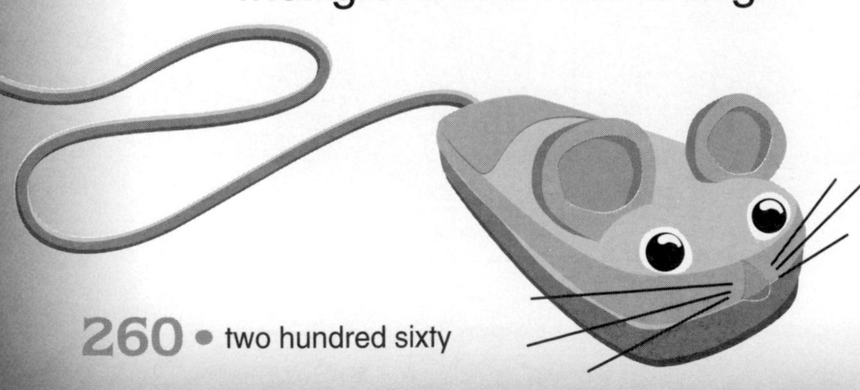

Home Connection

Chapter 7 Wrap-Up

Name ____________________

Shape Riddles

PLAYERS 2 or more

MATERIALS different-shape toys or other objects

DIRECTIONS Place all of the objects on the table. The first player describes one of the objects. The other player guesses what it is and names the geometric shape.

Play this game with your child. It will help your child become more familiar with 3-dimensional shape names.

At Home

Dear Family,

We are beginning a new chapter in mathematics. We will be learning about money and will be counting pennies, nickels, dimes, and quarters.

We will also be talking about stores and how money is used. Please help me complete this interview.

Your child,

____
Signature

Interview

Where do we shop?

- ❑ Supermarket
- ❑ Clothes store
- ❑ Bakery
- ❑ Hardware store
- ❑ Other _______________

How do I help when we go to the store?

____

____

Our Store

Money

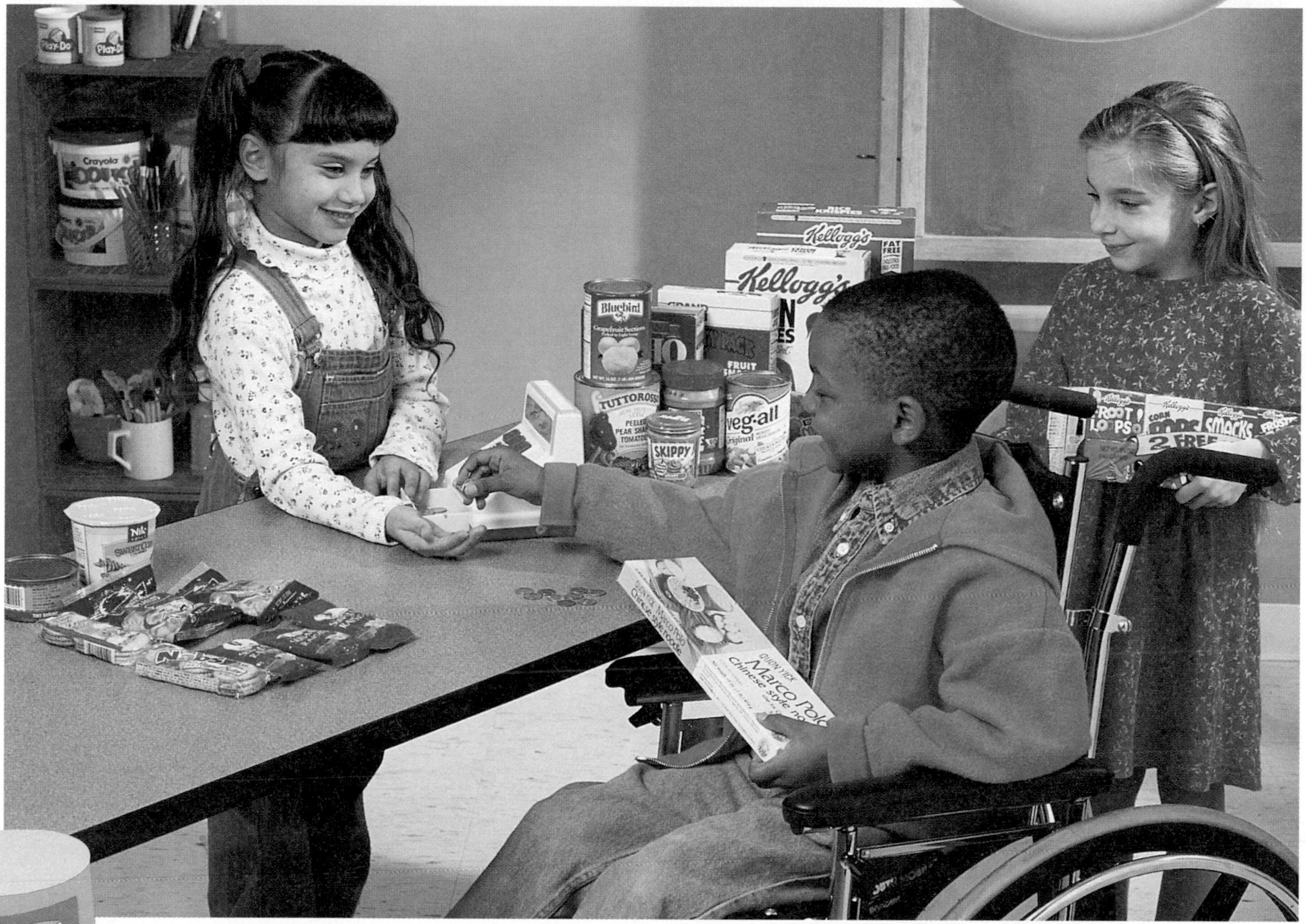

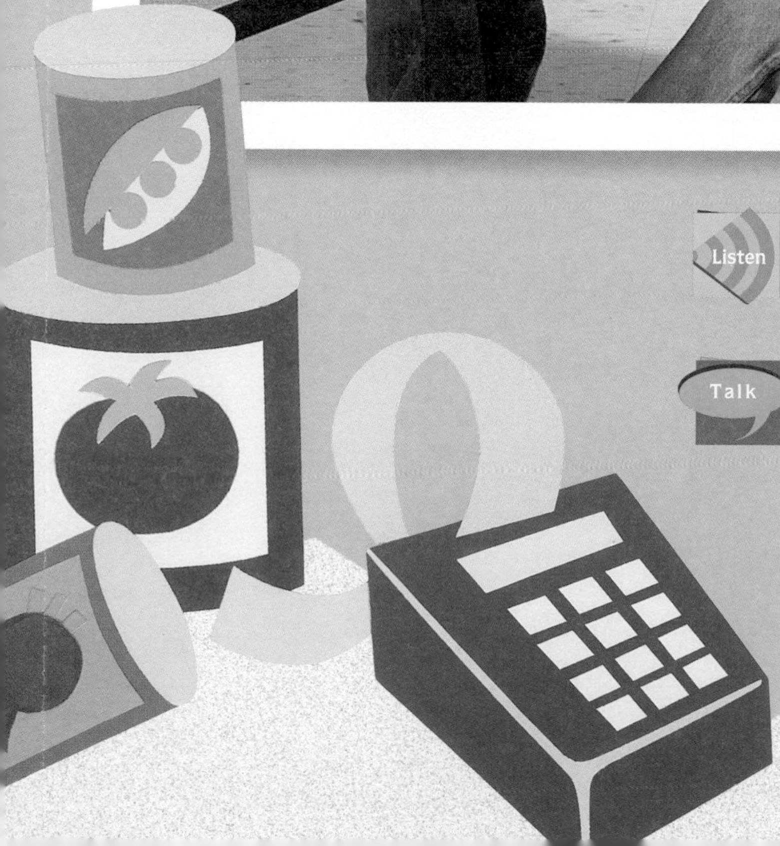

Listen to the story *General Store.*

Talk about how people use money at a store.

Name

What Do You Know?

Jill saves pennies.

The table shows how many pennies Jill saved in one week.

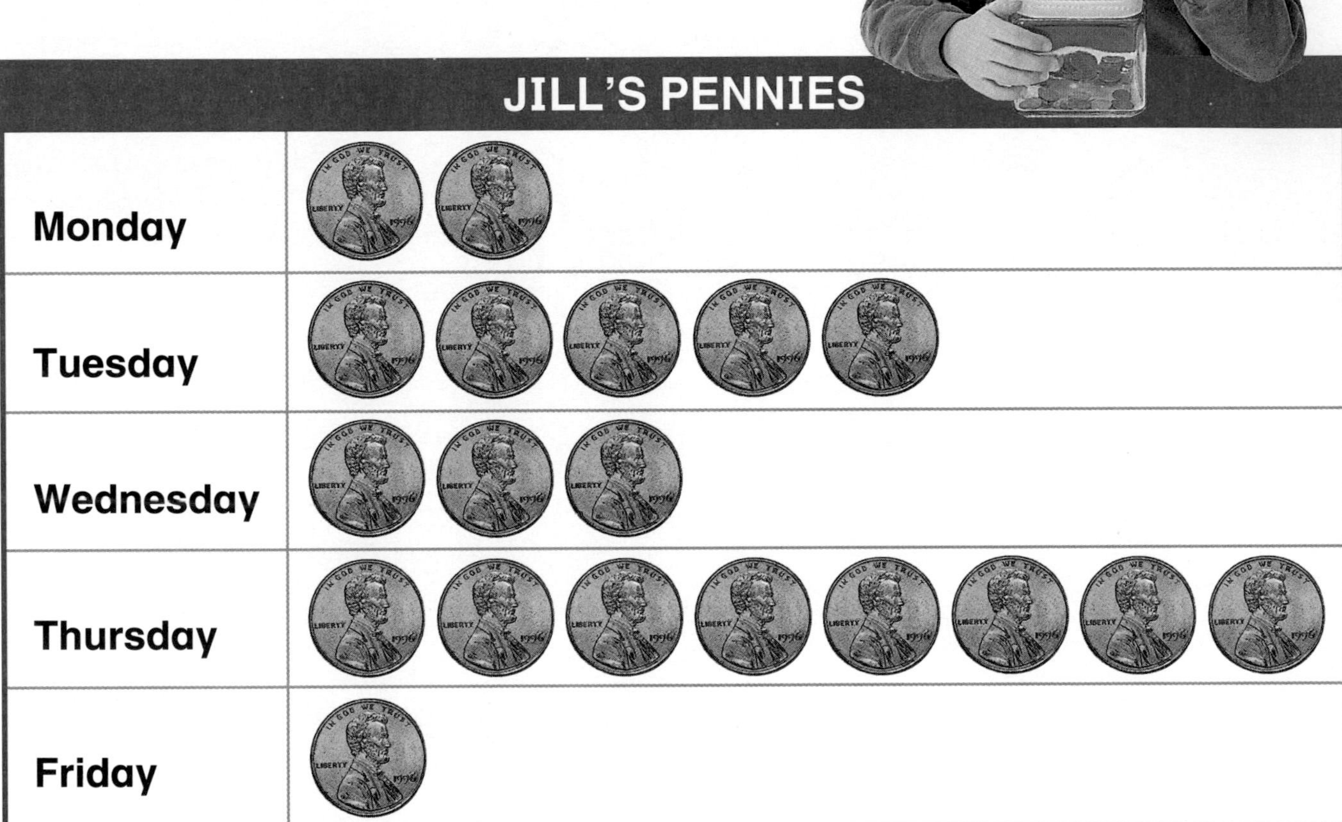

JILL'S PENNIES	
Monday	
Tuesday	
Wednesday	
Thursday	
Friday	

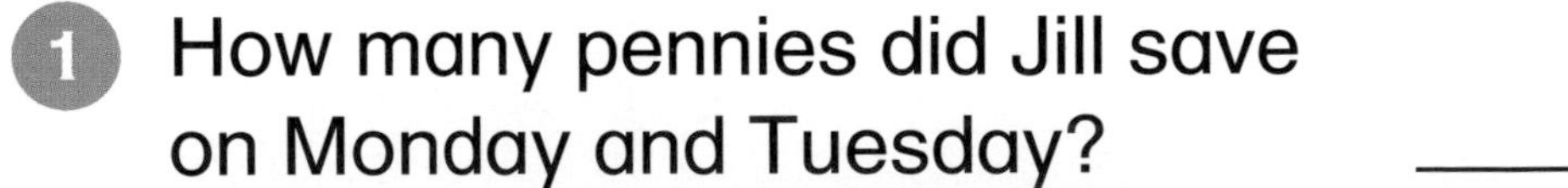

1. How many pennies did Jill save on Monday and Tuesday? ____

   How many cents is that? ____¢

2. How many cents for the two days with the most pennies? ____¢

Write a story about the pennies Jill saved.

Name ______________________

Pennies and Nickels

I penny
I cent
I¢

5 pennies
5 cents
5¢

I nickel
5 cents
5¢

Count by fives.
Then count on by ones.
Write how much money.

1 5¢ 10¢ 15¢ 16¢ 17¢

17¢

2

____ ¢

3

____ ¢

4

____ ¢

Why can you count by fives to count nickels?

Try These!

Write the ¢.

Count.
Write how much money.

      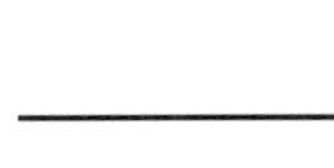

Mixed Review

Write how many.

 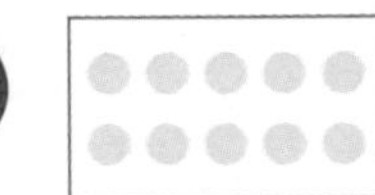  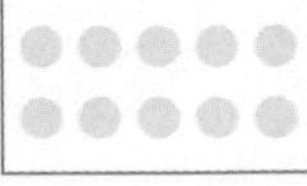

  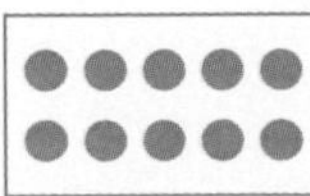 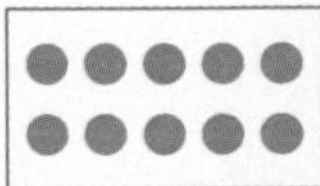 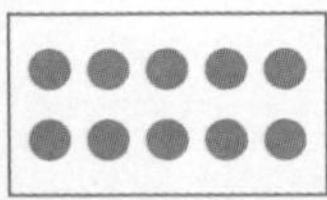 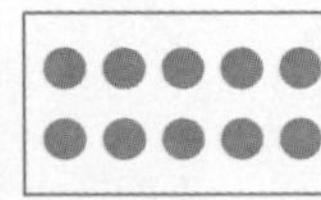 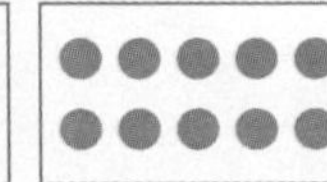

 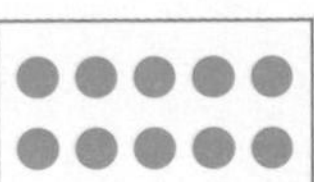    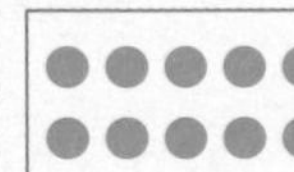

We counted pennies and nickels. Have your child count 5 nickels to find how many cents.

Name

Pennies and Dimes

10¢

10¢

1 dime
10 cents
10¢

Talk Why is trading 10 pennies for 1 dime fair?

Count by tens.
Then count on by ones.
Write how much money.

1     

10¢ 20¢ 30¢ 31¢  32¢

 32¢

2      ______

3       ______

4     ______

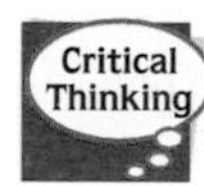

Critical Thinking How is counting dimes different from counting pennies?

Try These!

Count. Write how much money.

1 10¢ 20¢ 30¢ 40¢ 41¢ — 41¢

2 ______

3 ______

4 ______

5     ______

More to Explore — Number Sense

Find the pattern. Complete.

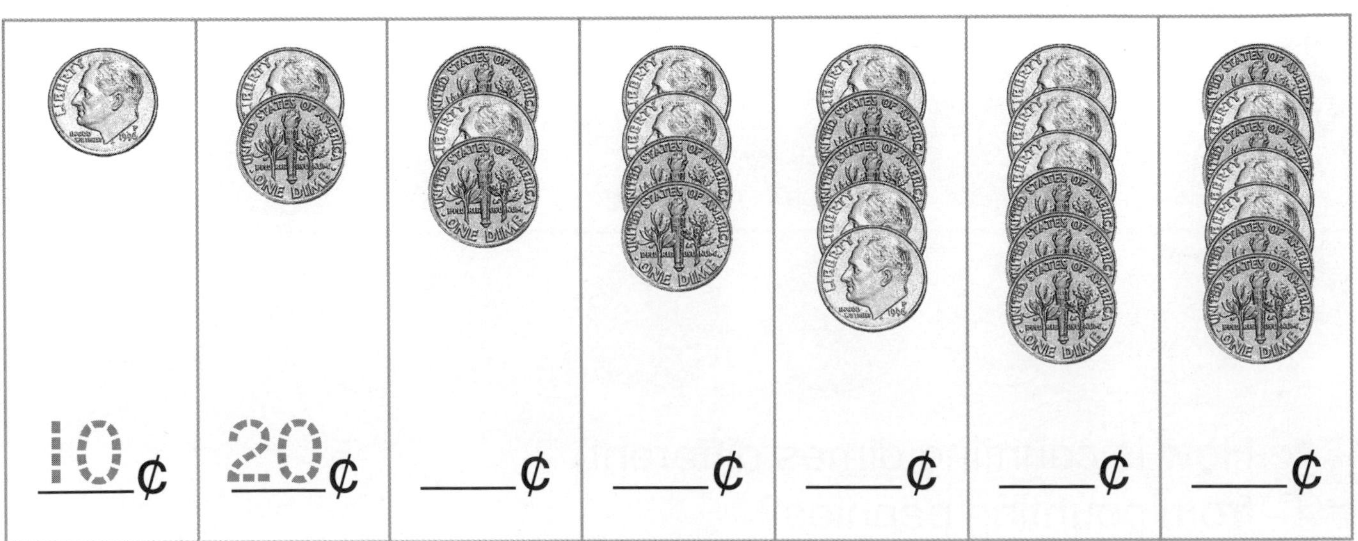

10 ¢	20 ¢	____ ¢	____ ¢	____ ¢	____ ¢	____ ¢

At Home: Have your child show you how to count a set of dimes and pennies.

Name ____________________

Working Together

You and your partner need 9 dimes, 9 nickels, and 9 pennies.

Write a **price** for each toy.

Take turns.

- Pretend to buy a toy.
- Show the price with coins.
- Your partner checks.
- Show how many of each coin you use.

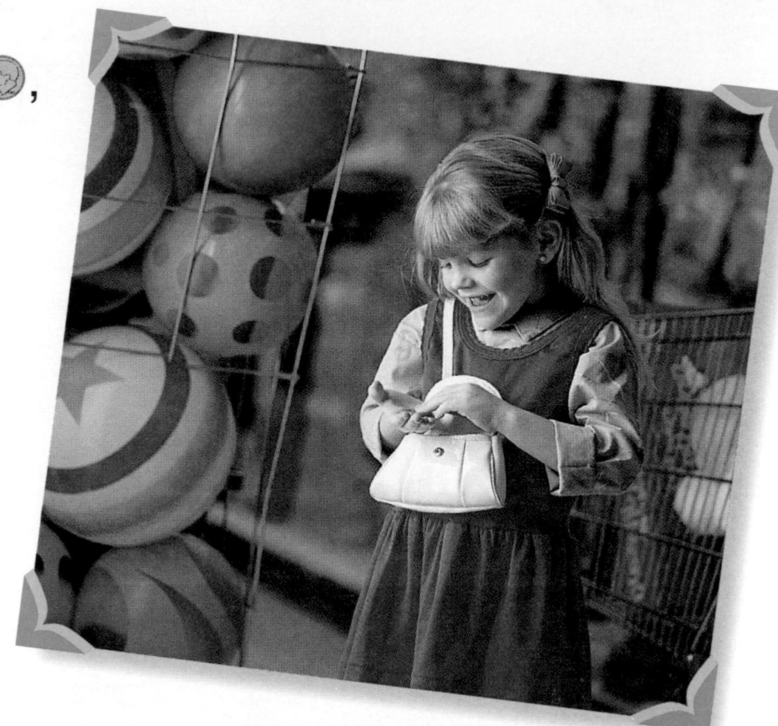

Toy	Dime	Nickel	Penny
Ball 27¢	◯ ◯	◯	◯ ◯
Doll ___¢			
Boat ___¢			
Spider ___¢			
Dog ___¢			

Count the coins.
Match each set to a price.

Pet Food Prices
32¢
36¢
18¢
23¢
28¢
41¢

Show how you count a set of dimes, nickels, and pennies.

Have your child show you how to count a set of dimes, nickels, and pennies.

Name

More Counting Money

Tad buys soap.
Mark the coins he needs.

Mark the coins each child needs.

1 Chris buys soap.

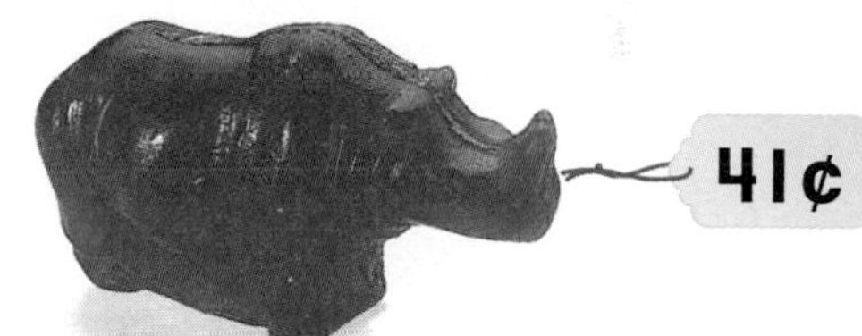

2 May buys a bag.

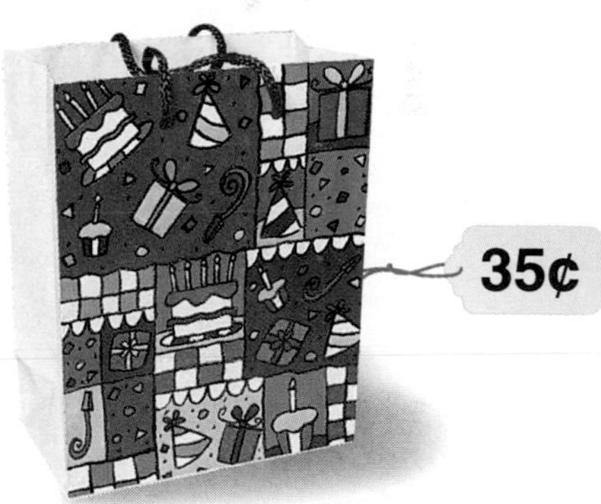

3 Ed buys a cup.

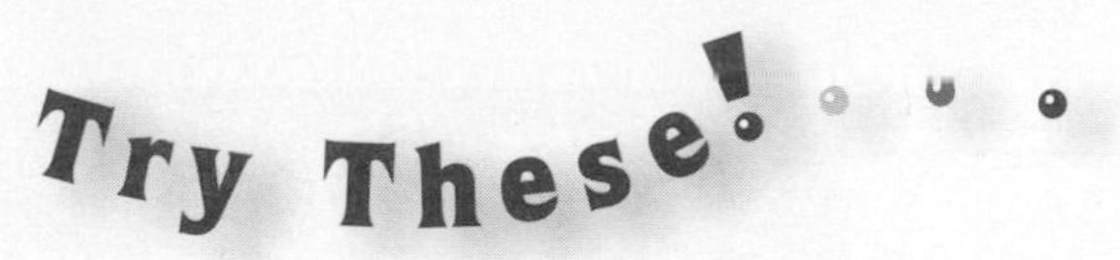

Mark the coins you need.

1

2

3

4

Mixed Review

5 Write the name of each shape.

circle	rectangle
triangle	square

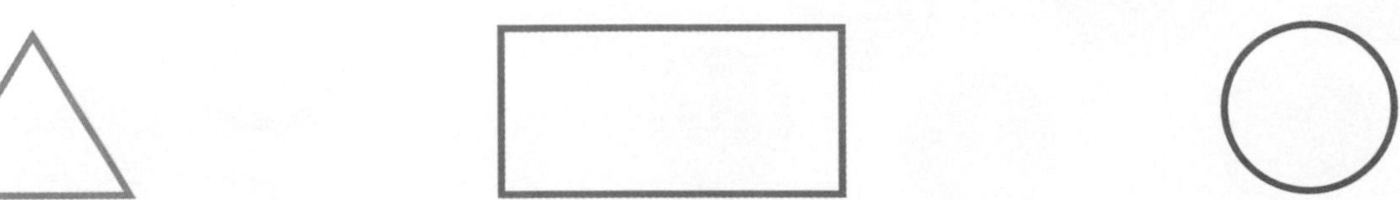

At Home — Ask your child which coins could be used to buy an item for 27¢.

Name

Problem-Solving Strategy

Read
Plan
Solve
Look Back

Guess and Test

Read Lin buys 2 cards.
She spends 9¢.
Which 2 cards does she buy?

Plan You can **guess and test** to solve.
Guess which 2 cards.
Test your guess by adding.

Solve
4¢ + 3¢ = 7¢ (No.)
3¢ + 5¢ = 8¢ (No.)
4¢ + 5¢ = 9¢ (Yes.)

Lin buys these cards.

Look Back Does the answer make sense? Explain.

Guess and test to solve.
Which 2 cards does Lin buy?

1. Lin spends 8¢.

2. Lin spends 6¢.

3. Lin spends 7¢.

Try These!

Guess and test to solve.
Which 2 items does each child buy?

1 Ana spends 10¢.

2 Sam spends 4¢.

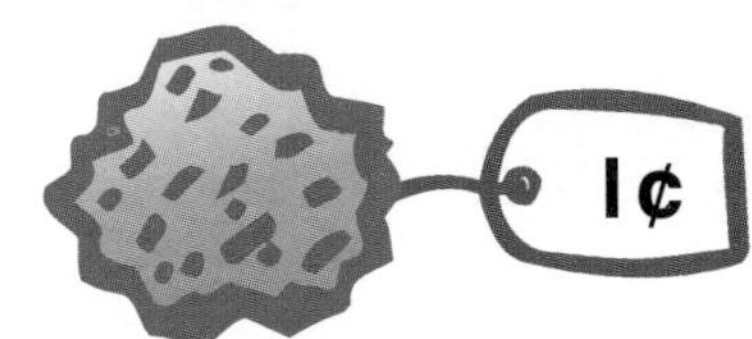

3 Tom spends 7¢.

4 Lily spends 8¢.

5 Dani spends 6¢.

6 

Write a guess-and-test problem.
Have a partner solve it.

Use your own paper.

We used the guess-and-test strategy to solve a problem.
Ask your child how to solve problem 5.

Name

Midchapter Review

Write how much money.

___

2

___

___

4

___

5

___

6

___

Mark the coins you need.

20¢

8

17¢

Solve.

9 Max spends 8¢.
Which 2 books does he buy?

10 How did you solve problem 9?

___

Show all the ways that you could have 20¢ in coins.

Extra Practice

Game!

Play and Pay

You and your partner need a [number cube] and 10 [pennies].

Each of you needs 5 [dimes], 5 [nickels], 10 [pennies], and 1 [game piece].

Take turns.

- Roll the [number cube] to move your [game piece].
- Use the **Bank** to take, pay, and trade money.
- Count how much money you have at **Stop.**

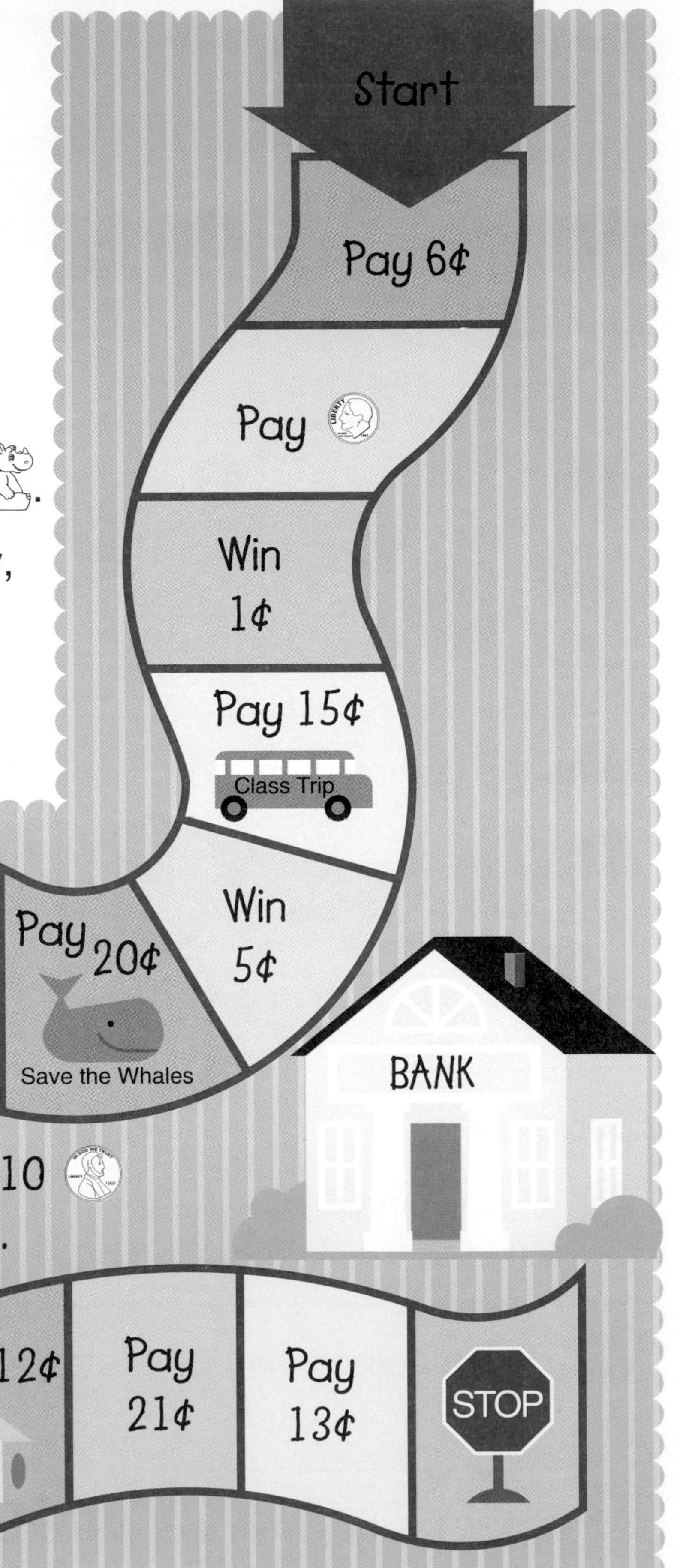

Real-Life Investigation
Applying Money

Name

100 Years Ago

Listen to *General Store.*

The story takes place 100 years ago. Many things cost pennies then.

Working Together

You need index cards, penny, nickel, and dime.

Make an Old Fashioned Store
1. choose items to sell.
2. Draw or paste pictures of items on cards.
3. Make up prices
4. What can you buy with 25¢?

Go Shopping!

5¢

2¢

2¢

Decision Making

1. Decide what to buy at the store. Take a card. Leave the correct amount of money.

2. Compare what you buy with your partner. Did you spend the same amount? ________

3. Did you buy the same things? ________

Write a report.

4. Tell about the store. What did you buy?

5. What do things cost now? Tell what you know.

More to Investigate

PREDICT What do you think things will cost 100 years from now?

EXPLORE How do stores decide on prices?

FIND Find today's price of three of the things you bought.

Name

I quarter
25 cents
25¢

Working Together

You and your partner need 2 dimes, 5 nickels, and 25 pennies.

- Find ways to show 25¢.
- Show as many different ways as you can.

	dime	nickel	penny
25¢	◯ ◯	◯	
25¢			
25¢			
25¢			

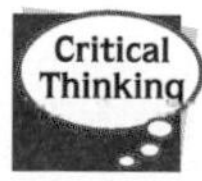

Did you and your class find all the ways to show 25¢?
How can you check?

Try These!

Count. Write how much money.

1    27¢

2     ______

3     ______

4   ______

5     ______

6     ______

Cultural Connection

Coins of the World

Somalia

 **10 senti**

Greece

 **2 drachma**

Brazil

 **5 cruzado**

Count by tens, fives, or twos.
Write how much money.

____ senti

      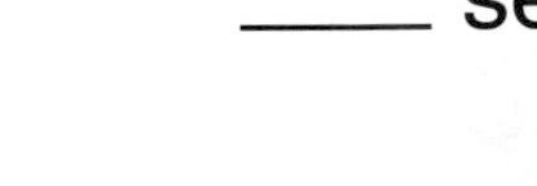

____ drachma

____ cruzado

At Home: Ask your child to show you two ways to make 25¢.

Name

Working Together

You and your partner need 4 quarters, 10 dimes, 10 nickels, 20 pennies.

Take turns.

- Show the **amount.**
- Your partner shows the amount a different way.
- Write how many of each coin.

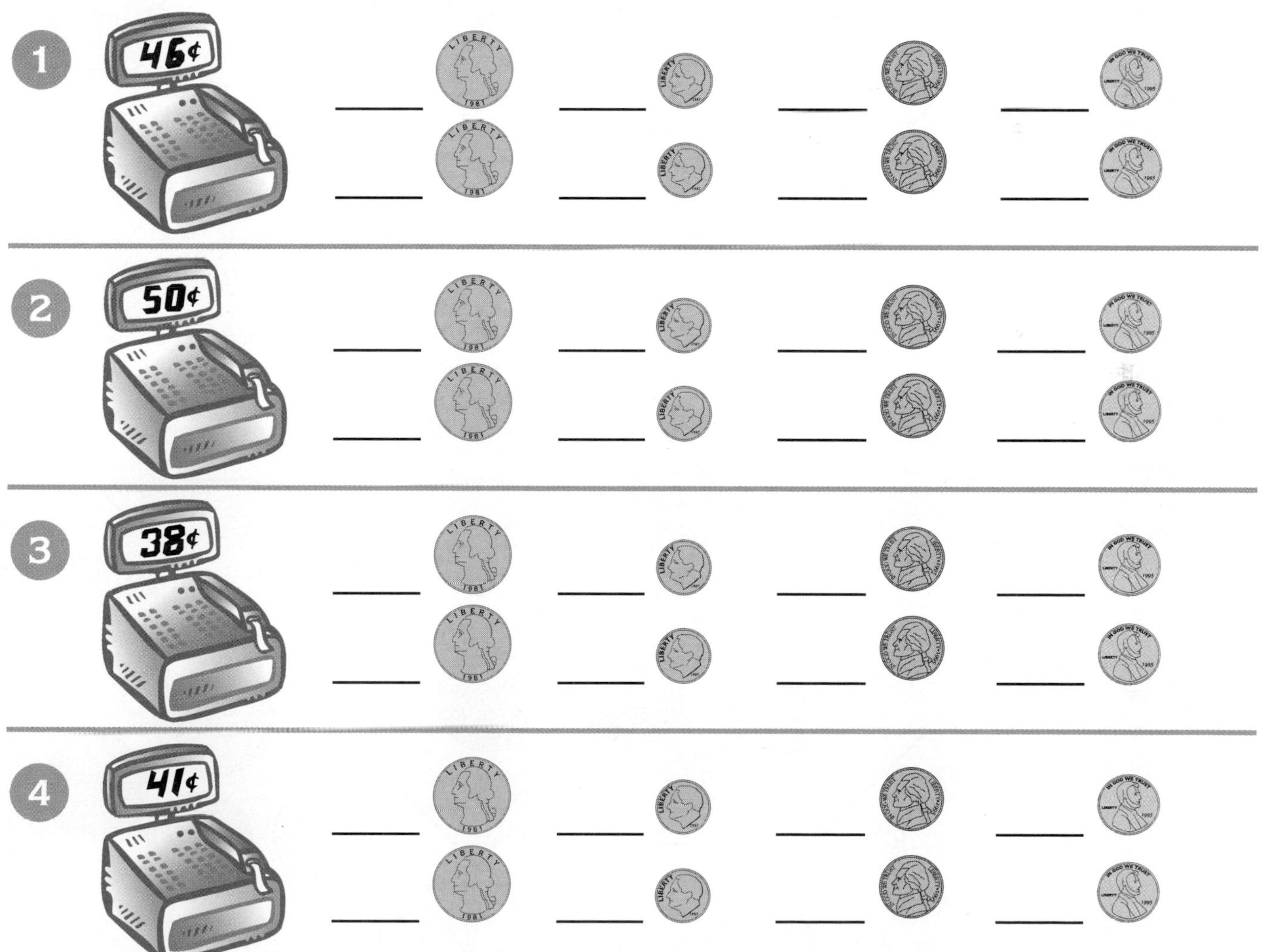

Tell your partner why you showed 41¢ the way you did.

Try These!

Count each set of coins. Write how much money. Color the shapes with the same amounts the same color.

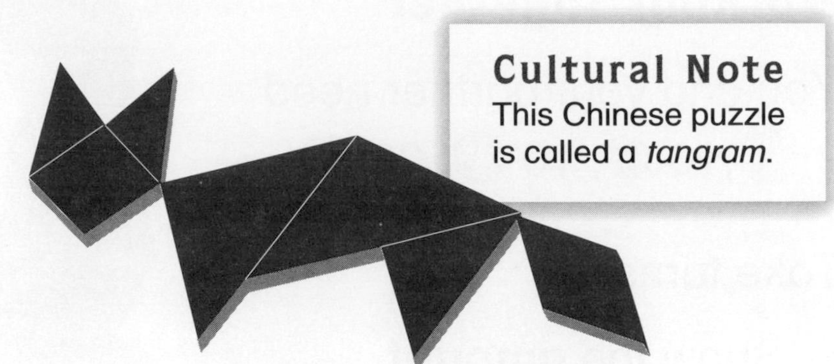

Cultural Note
This Chinese puzzle is called a *tangram*.

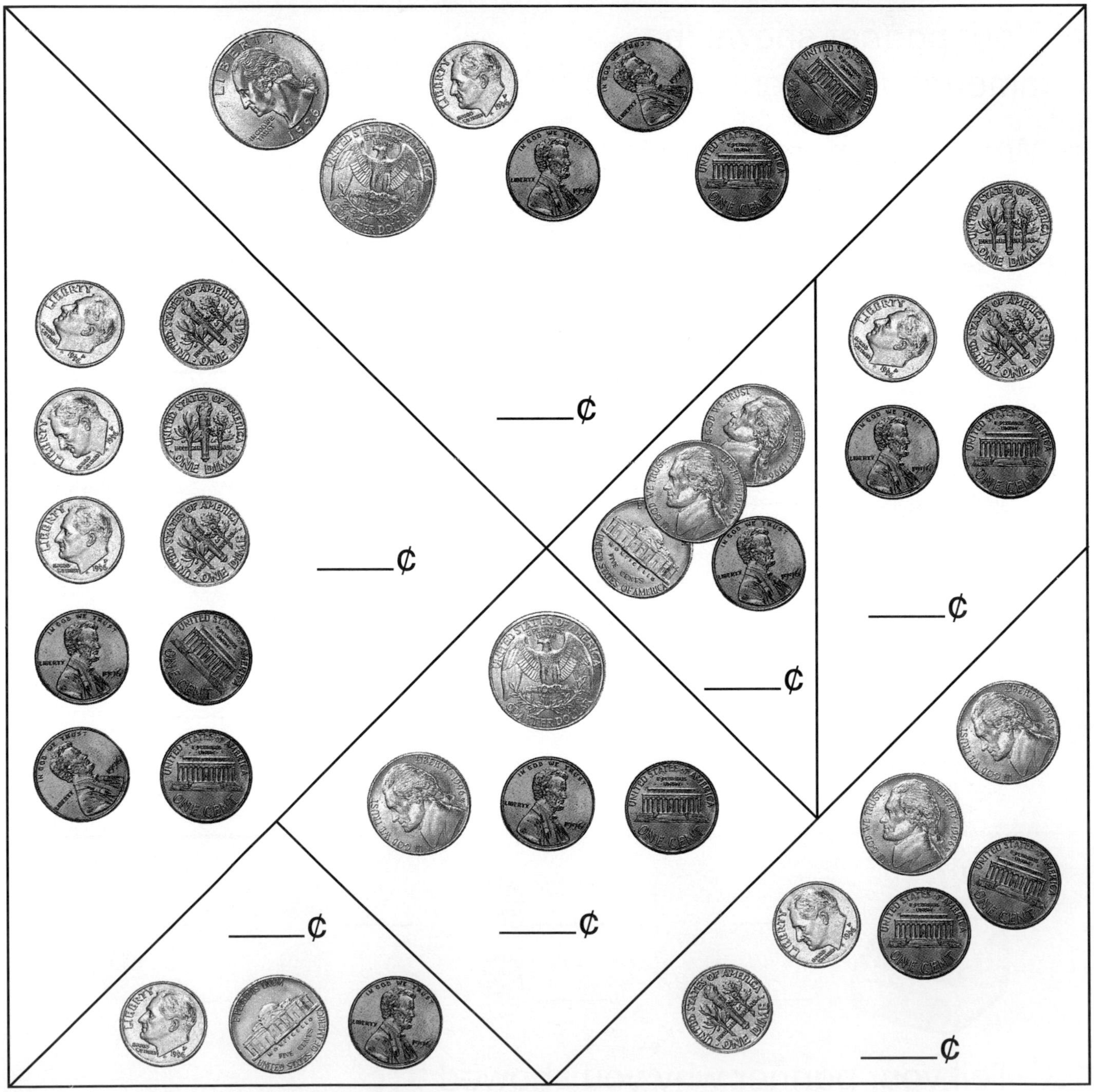

____¢

____¢

____¢

____¢

____¢

____¢

____¢

Tell a partner about any patterns you found.

Have your child show you two ways to make 31¢.

Name ______________________________

More Comparing Money

Who has more money?

Compare.

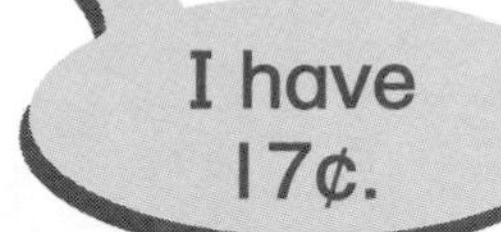

21¢ **is more than** 17¢.
Tom has more money.

17¢ **is less than** 21¢.
Maria has less money.

Who has **more** money?
Write how much. Compare.

1. Luis has     

   Sue has      Sue

---

2. Sari has     ______ Sari

   Kate has     ______ Kate

---

3. Joe has     ______ Joe

   Mark has    ______ Mark

Try These!

Which is **less** money?
Write how much. Compare.

1

16¢

25¢

2

_____

_____

3

_____

_____

4

_____

_____

More to Explore — Logical Reasoning

You can trade me for 25 pennies.
Who am I? Color me red.

I am not the biggest coin.
But I am worth more than a nickel!
Who am I? Color me black.

5 of me make a nickel.
10 of me make a dime.
Who am I? Color me green.

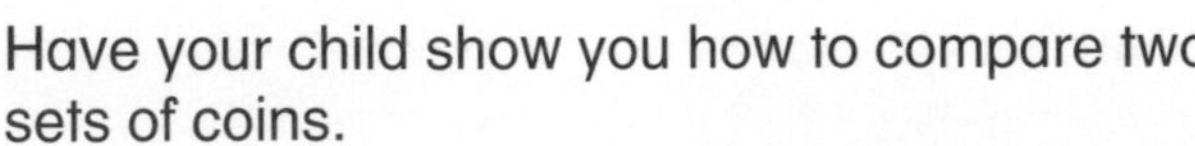

At Home: Have your child show you how to compare two sets of coins.

Name

Trade Up to Quarters

You and your partner need 20 , 4 , 4 , 8 , 2 , and 1 .

Take turns.

- Roll the to move your .
- Take money to match the amount on the space.
- Trade coins when you can.
- Play until each of you has 2 .

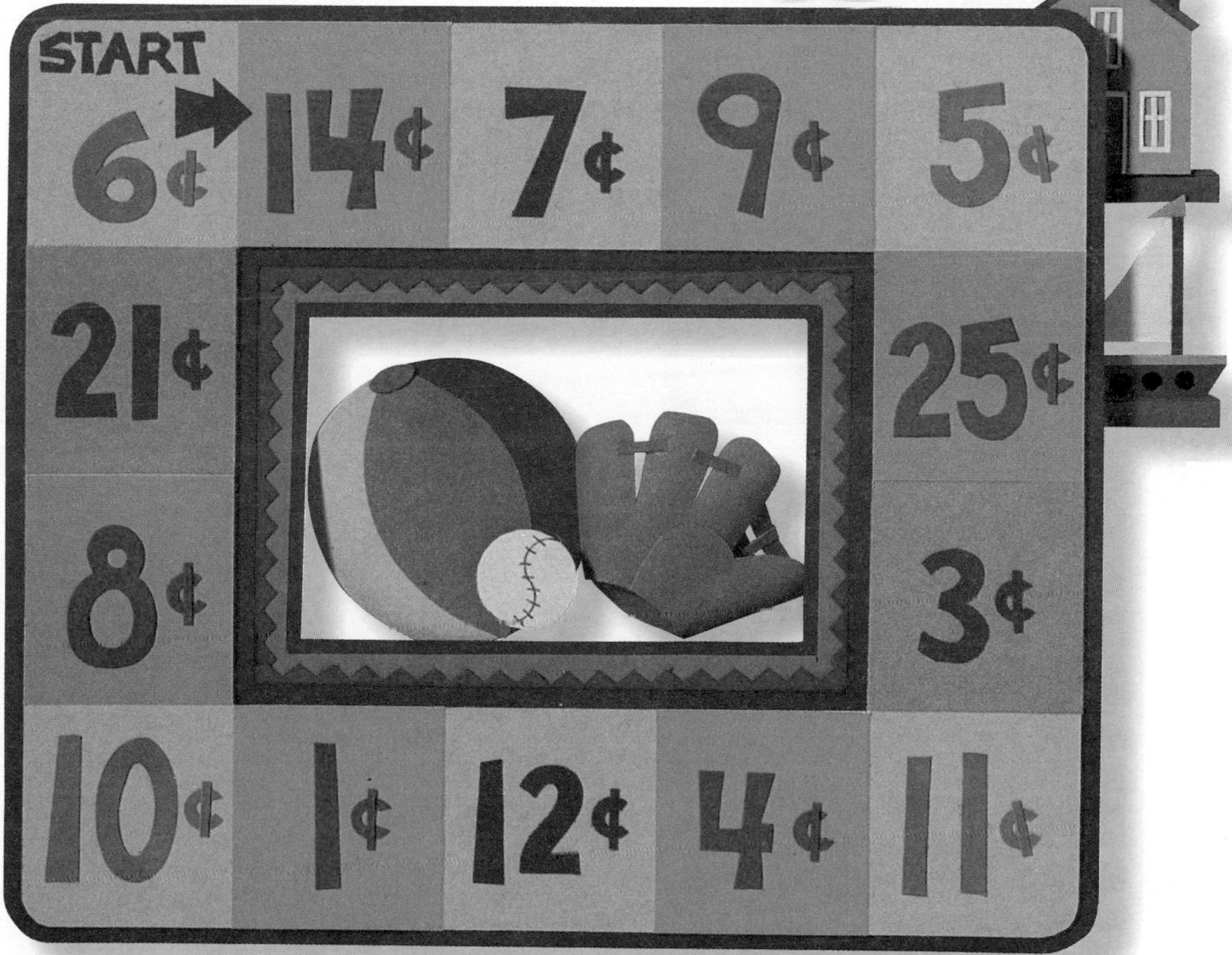

START
6¢ 14¢ 7¢ 9¢ 5¢
21¢ 25¢
8¢ 3¢
10¢ 1¢ 12¢ 4¢ 11¢

Which is **more** money?
Write how much. Compare.

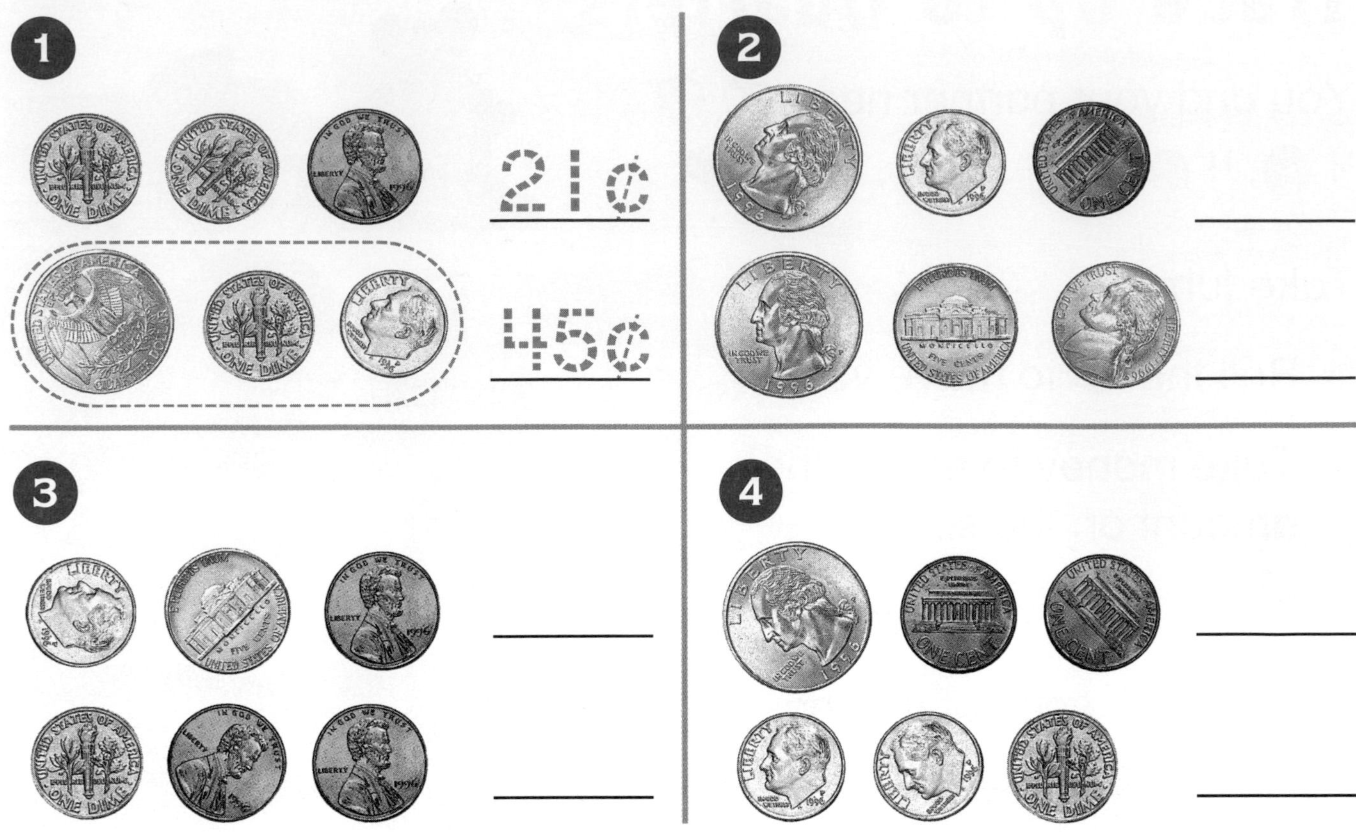

Match sets of coins that are the same amount.

Guess and test to solve.

7 Ann spends 9¢.
Which 2 fish does she buy?

Name

Problem Solvers at Work

Read
Plan
Solve
Look Back

Use Data from a Table

1 You have .

Do you have enough money to buy a notebook?

How can you use the table to solve the problem?

SCHOOL STORE

Item	Price
scissors	50¢
crayons	32¢
paste	18¢
notebook	45¢

What does the notebook cost? 45¢

How much money do you have? 32¢

Do you have enough money? yes no

Use the table to solve.

2 You have 32¢.
Do you have enough money to buy paste? yes no

3 You have 40¢.
Do you have enough money to buy scissors? yes no

Could you really buy scissors for 50¢? Explain.

Try These!

Use the table to solve.
Write *yes* or *no*.

1 You have [dime, nickel, nickel, nickel].
Do you have enough money to buy paint? ________

2 You have 29¢.
Can you buy glue? ________

3 You have 18¢.
Can you buy paint? ________

SCHOOL STORE	
Item	**Price**
paint	20¢
glue	25¢
chalk	35¢

Write and Share

Jessica wrote this problem.
You have 28¢. Can you buy the chalk?

Jessica Castillo
Ogden School
San Antonio, Texas

4 Solve Jessica's problem. ________
How did you solve Jessica's problem? ________

5 Write Use the table to write a problem.
Have a partner solve it.

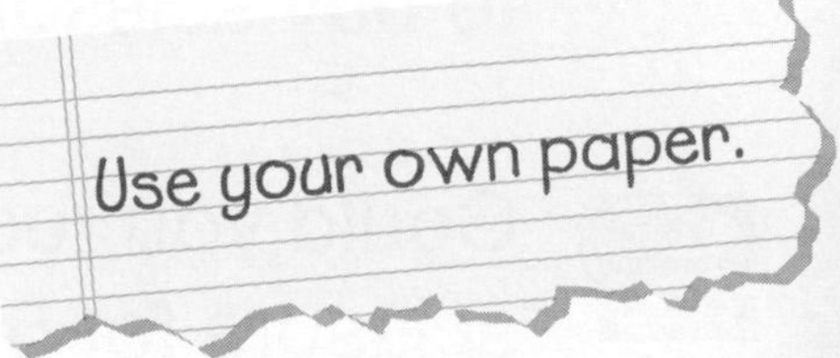

Try to solve your child's word problem.

Name

Chapter Review

Draw a line to match.

  **2**  **3**   

penny nickel quarter dime

Write how much money.

  ______

6  ______

7  ______

8    ______

9   ______

10    ______

11    ______

12  ______

13  ______

Mark the coins you need.

   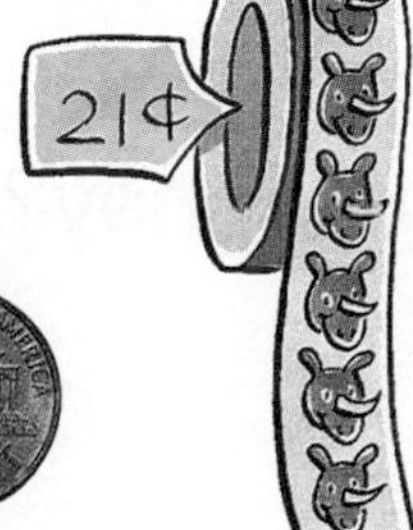

Guess and test to solve.

16 Mike spends 7¢.
Which 2 bags does he buy?

5¢ 4¢ 3¢

17 May spends 8¢.
Which 2 cards does she buy?

2¢ 4¢ 6¢

Use the table to solve.
Write **yes** or **no.**

Item	Price
ball	25¢
doll	34¢
car	39¢

18 You have 35¢.
Do you have enough money to buy a toy car? ______

19 You have 29¢.
Do you have enough money to buy a ball? ______

20 You have 34¢.
Can you buy a doll? ______

What Do You Think?

Which would you rather count?
☑ Check one.

☐ Nickels and pennies ☐ Dimes ☐ Pennies

Why? ________________________________

Journal What did you learn about money? Draw. Write.

Name

Chapter Test

Write how much money.

____

2

____

3

____

4

____

5

____

6

____

Mark the coins you need.

Guess and test to solve.

9 Lucy spends 9¢. Which 2 stickers does she buy?

10 Vince spends 10¢. Which 2 cards does he buy?

Performance Assessment

What Did You Learn?

You need 5 dimes, 5 nickels, and 5 pennies.
Choose 2 toys.

Write the price for each toy you choose.

Draw coins to show the price.

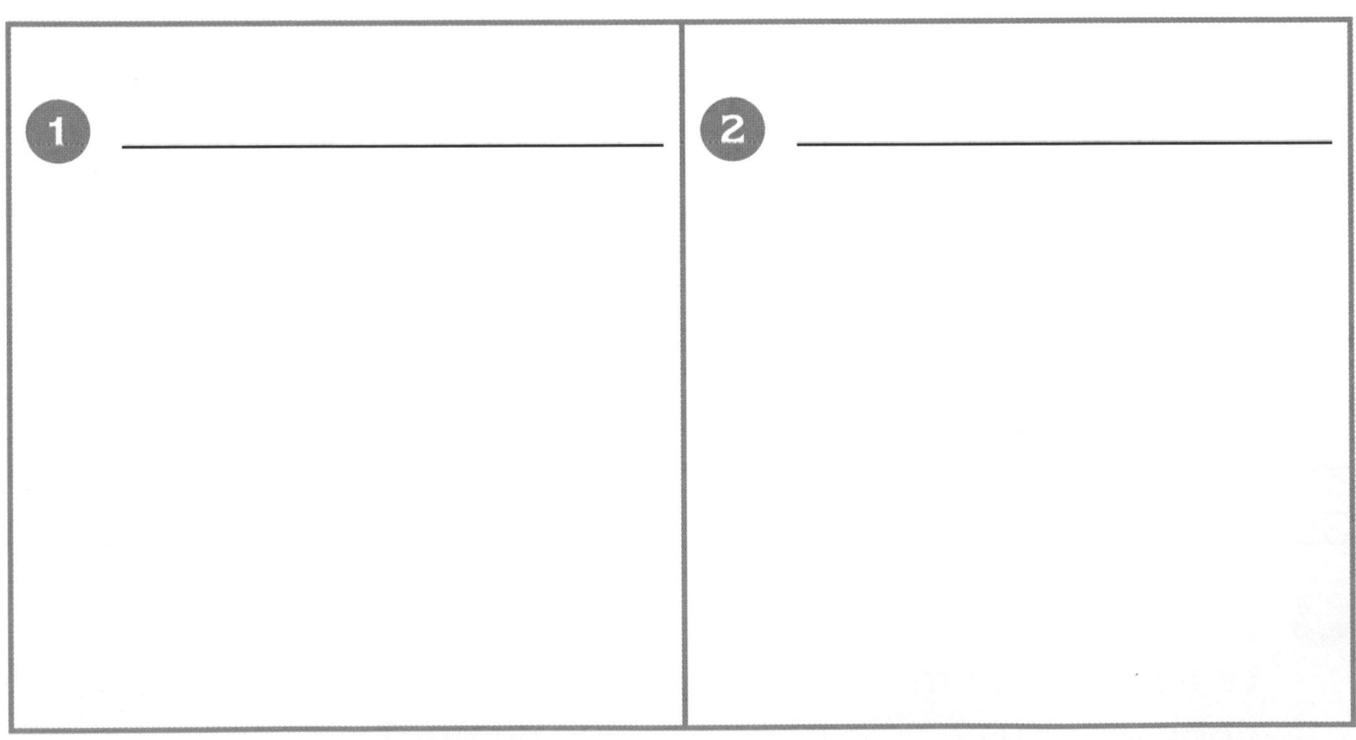

1 ______________________

2 ______________________

3 How much money do you have left? ________

You may want to put this page in your portfolio.

Math Connection

Place Value

Name

Penny Stacks

How can you trade stacks of 10 pennies for dimes?

Complete.

		How many? (dimes)	How many? (pennies)
	32¢	3	2

McGraw-Hill School Division

Curriculum Connection

Science

Healthful Snacks

What are some healthful snacks?

Make a sign for a new snack bar.

- Choose some healthful snacks.
- Write a price for each snack.

SNACK BAR			
Item	Price	Item	Price

Write a word problem about the snack-bar prices.

Have a partner solve it.

Name

Money Riddles!

PLAYERS 2

MATERIALS pennies, nickels, dimes, quarters, 2 cups

DIRECTIONS Hide some coins under a cup. (Count them first!) Make up a riddle about your coins. Have your partner guess which coins you have hidden.

Play this riddle game with your child. Play in turns and limit the number of coins to four or fewer. You may want to start with simple combinations.

At Home

Dear Family,

We are beginning a new chapter in mathematics. We will be learning about time and how to use clocks and calendars.

March						
Sun	Mon	Tue	Wed	Thu	Fri	Sat
1	2	3	4	5	6	7
8	9	10	11	12	13	14
15	16	17	18	19	20	21
22	23	24	25	26	27	28
29	30	31				

We will also be talking about games and other ways to have fun. Please help me complete this interview.

Your child,

____
Signature

Interview

What ways did you have fun when you were a child?

❑ Ball games
❑ Movies or TV
❑ Vacations
❑ Hobbies
❑ Other ______________________

What was your favorite way to have fun when you were my age?

____

Fun and Games

Time

Listen to the story *Clean Your Room, Harvey Moon.*

Tell about things you do to have fun.

Name

What Do You Know?

Draw lines to match.

1

first   second   last

2 How did you choose which came first, second, and last?

What do you do after school?
Write or draw a picture.
Tell the time.

Name ______________________________

Working Together

1 Which do you think takes **more** time?
☑ Check one.

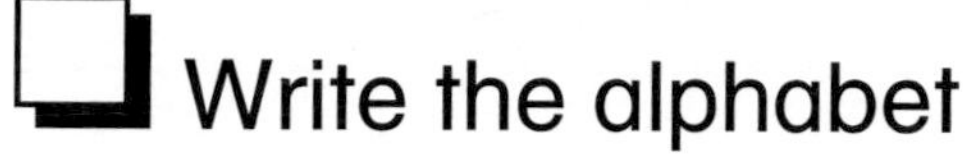

☐ Write the alphabet. ☐ Write the numbers 1 to 10.

► You and your partner try it.

► Your teacher will time you.

---

2 Which do you think takes **less** time?
☑ Check one.

☐ Connect 10 cubes. ☐ Write your first name.

► You and your partner try it.

► Your teacher will time you.

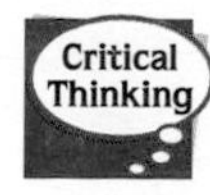

Why do some things take longer to do than others?

Try These!

Which takes **more** time to do?

Which takes **less** time to do?

3

Mixed Review

Write how much money.

_____¢

_____¢

Ask your child which takes more time to do—eating dinner or setting the table.

Name ______________________

Hour

This clock shows 7 o'clock.

minute hand

hour hand

Working Together

You and your partner need a .

Take turns.

▶ Show a time on the [clock].

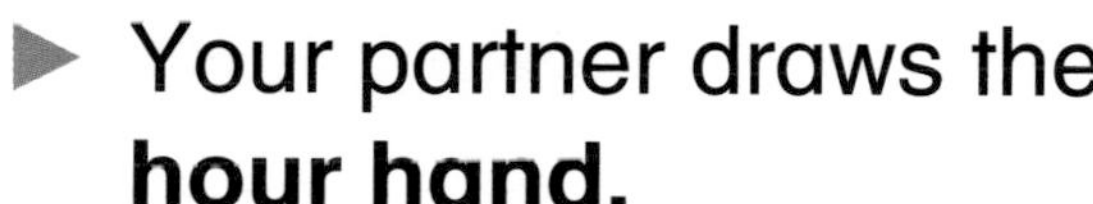

▶ Your partner draws the **hour hand.**

▶ Your partner writes the time.

1. 

3 o'clock

2. 

____ o'clock

3. 

____ o'clock

4. 

____ o'clock

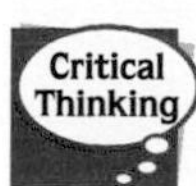

Where are the clock hands when the time is 12 o'clock?

Try These!

Show the time on a [clock]. Then write the time.

1 

7 o'clock

2 

____ o'clock

3 

____ o'clock

4 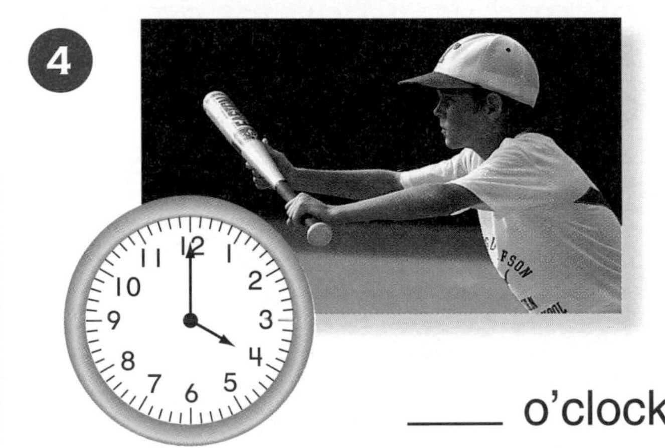

____ o'clock

5 

____ o'clock

6 

____ o'clock

We are learning to tell time to the hour. Set a watch or clock to the hour and ask your child what time it is.

Name ______________________

Time to the Hour

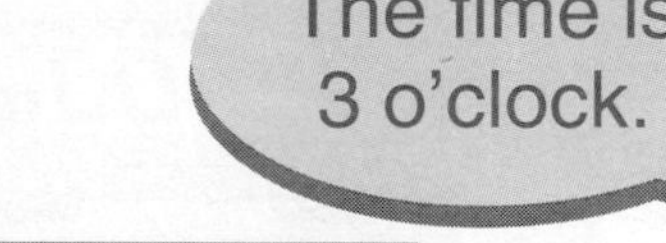

Both clocks show 3 o'clock.

Make the clocks match.
Draw the hour hand.

1

2

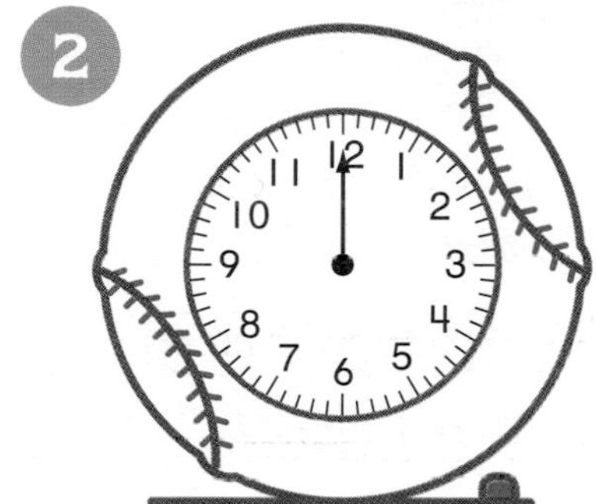

3

4

5

6

Try These!

Write the time.

What do you notice about the way you write the time?

More to Explore Number Sense

Draw the hour hand to show 1 hour later.

Ask your child to tell you the time on a digital clock when it shows time to the hour.

Name ____________________

Time Is Up!

You and your partner need

2 crayons, 1 number cube, 2 counters, and 1 clock.

Start

12 1 2 3 4 5 6 7 8 9 10 11

- Roll the number cube and move that many spaces.
- Show the time on the clock. Your partner checks.
- If you are correct, color the number on this clock.
- Play until all the numbers are colored in.

Show the time on each clock.

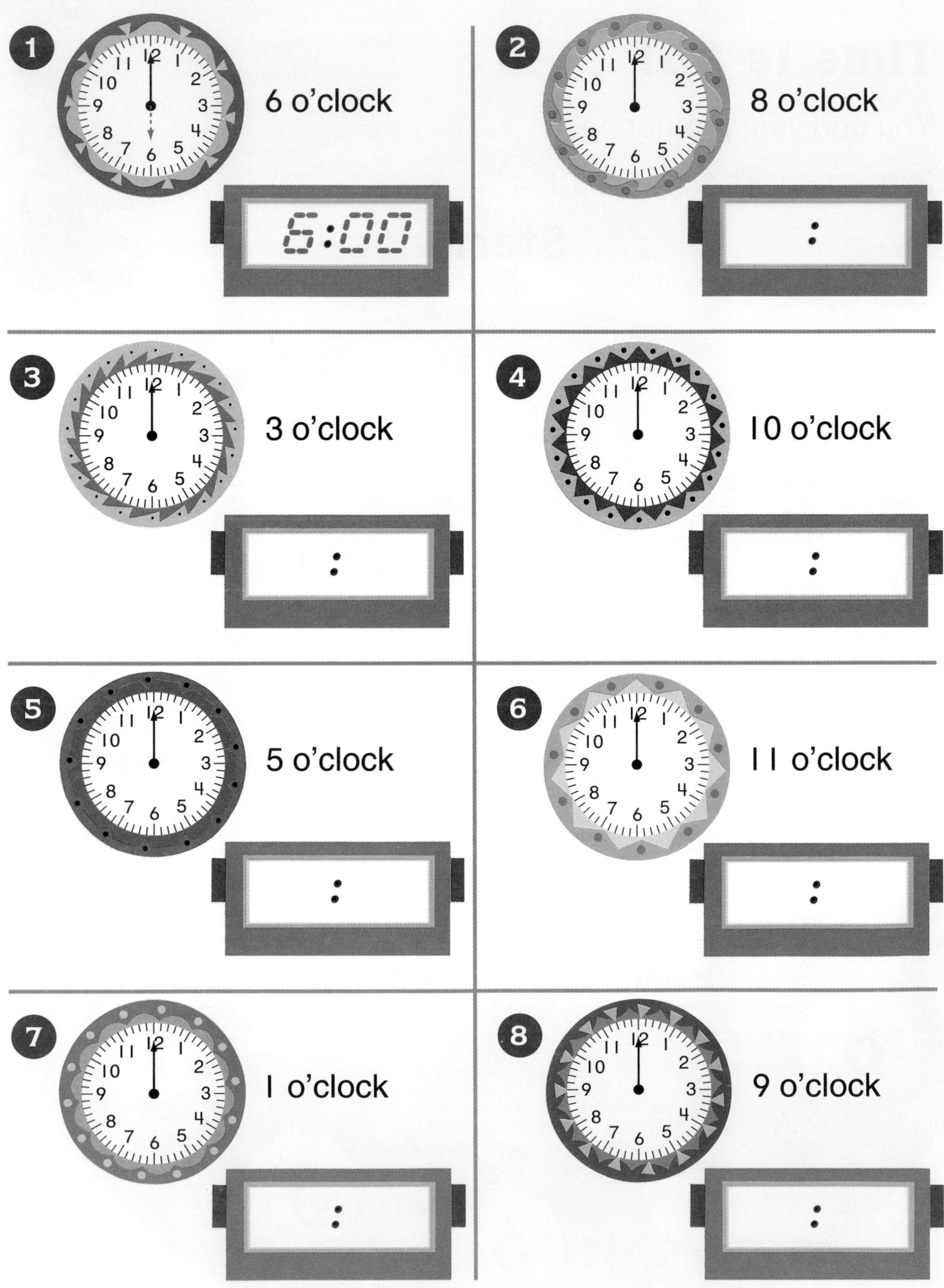

Name ________________________

Explore Activity
Half Hour

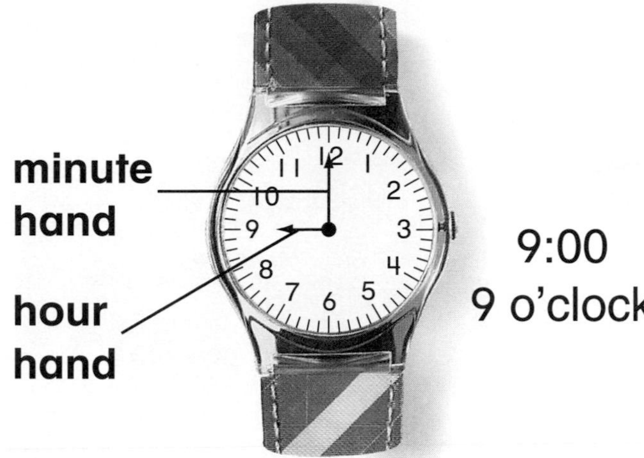

9:00
9 o'clock

9:30
nine-thirty
30 minutes
after 9 o'clock

Where is the hour hand at 9:00?
Where is the hour hand at 9:30?

Working Together

You and your partner need a 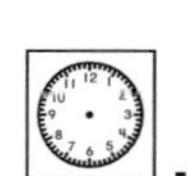.

Take turns.

- ▶ Show a time to the half hour on the clock.
- ▶ Your partner draws the hands.
- ▶ Your partner writes the time.

___ : ___

___ : ___

___ : ___

___ : ___

Try These!

Show the time on a [clock].
Then write the time.

1

7:30

2

___:___

3

___:___

4

___:___

5

___:___

6

___:___

Draw pictures of two things you do.
Write the time you do each thing.

Discuss with your child what time he or she does the activity shown in exercise 1.

Name

Time to the Half Hour

Both clocks show 30 minutes after 10 o'clock.

Match.

9 o'clock

1 [clock] — 5:30

2 [clock] — 1:30

3 [clock] — 3:30

4 [clock] — 8:30

McGraw-Hill School Division

Where do the hands of a clock point at 30 minutes after 4?

Try These!

Write the time.

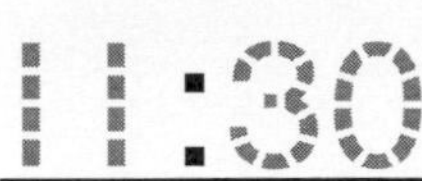

____ : ____

____ : ____

____ : ____

Cultural Connection

German and Swiss Clocks

Cuckoo clocks are made in Germany and Switzerland. A bird pops out and says "cuckoo" for each hour.

The bird says "cuckoo" 3 times at 3 o'clock.

Write how many times the bird will say "cuckoo."

____ times

____ times

Ask your child to write the time when a clock shows times to the hour or half hour.

Name

Midchapter Review

Show the time on each clock.

1 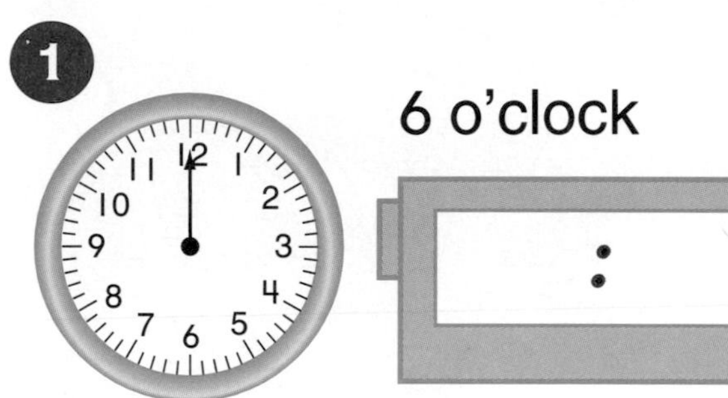

2 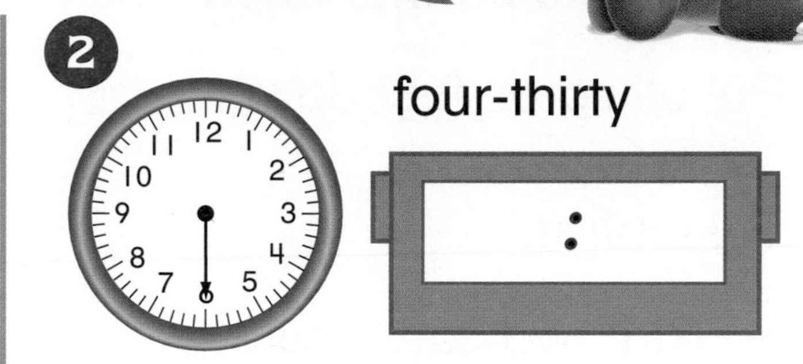

Write the time.

3 

____ o'clock

4 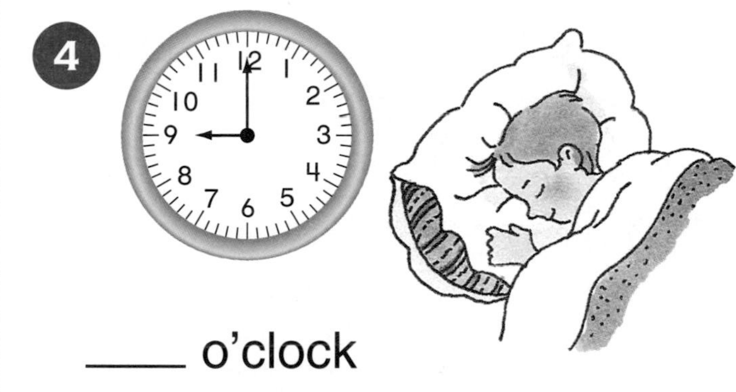

____ o'clock

5 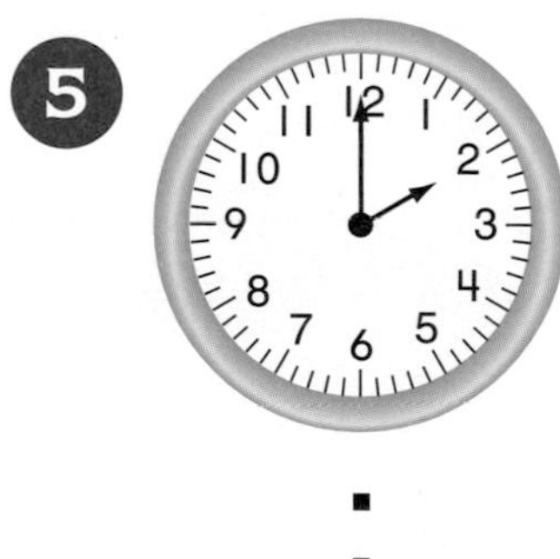

____:____

6 

____:____

7 

____:____

8 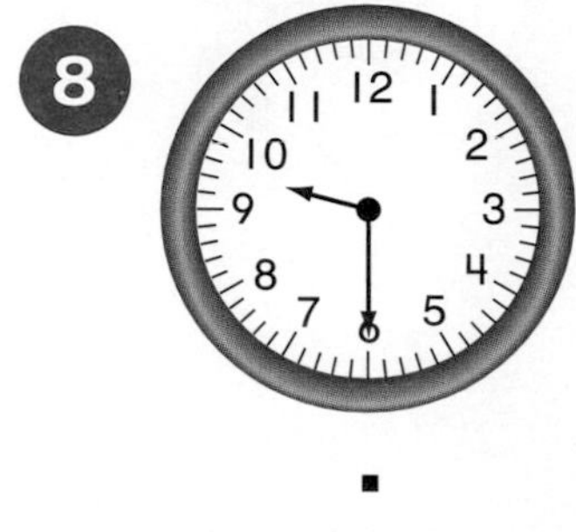

____:____

9 

____:____

10 

____:____

Write about the hands and numbers of a clock.

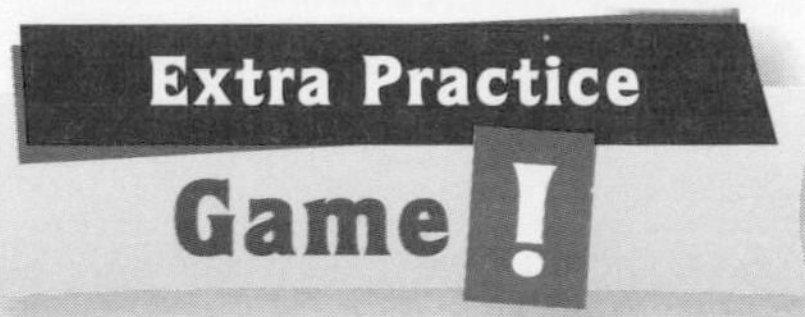

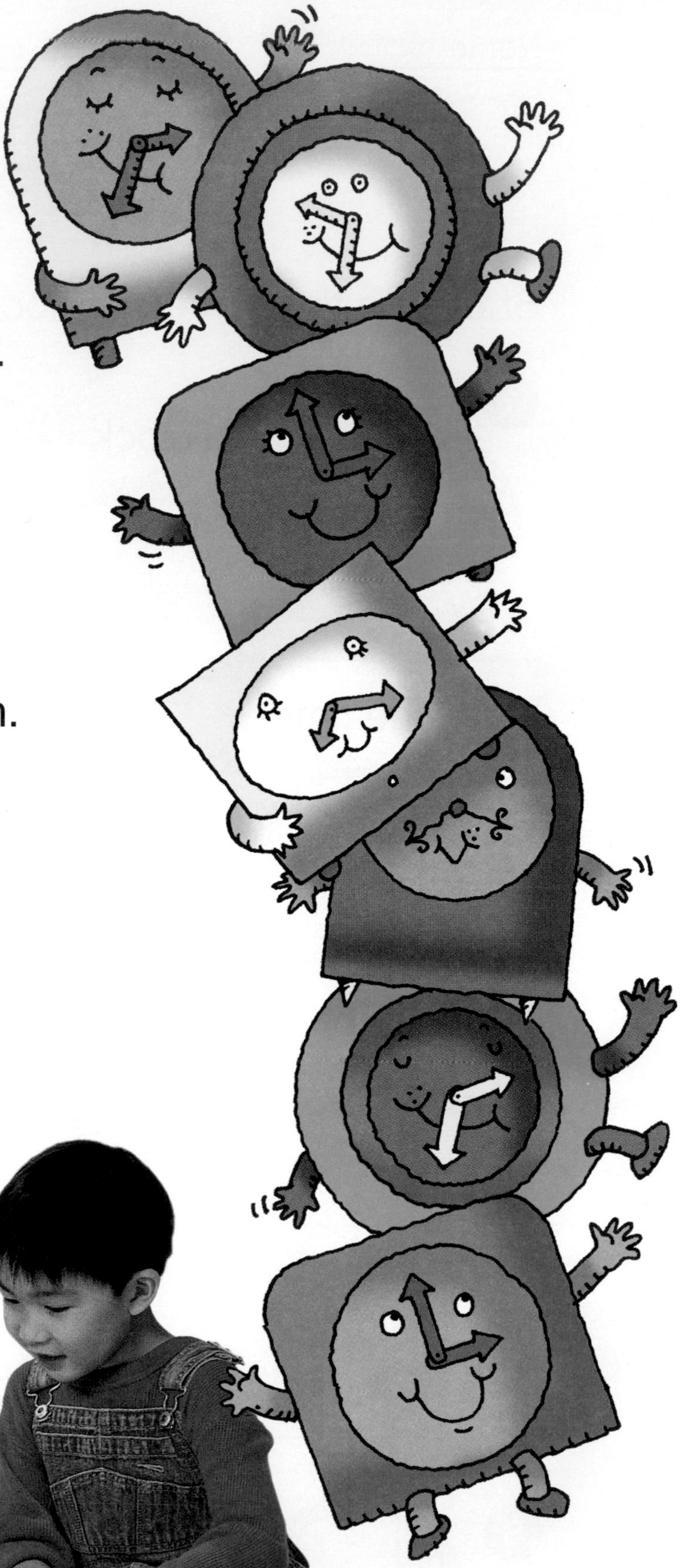

Time to Remember

You and a partner need clock cards.

Put all cards facedown.

Take turns.

- ▶ Turn two cards over.
- ▶ Keep the cards if the times match.
- ▶ Turn the cards over again if the times do not match.

The player with more cards wins.

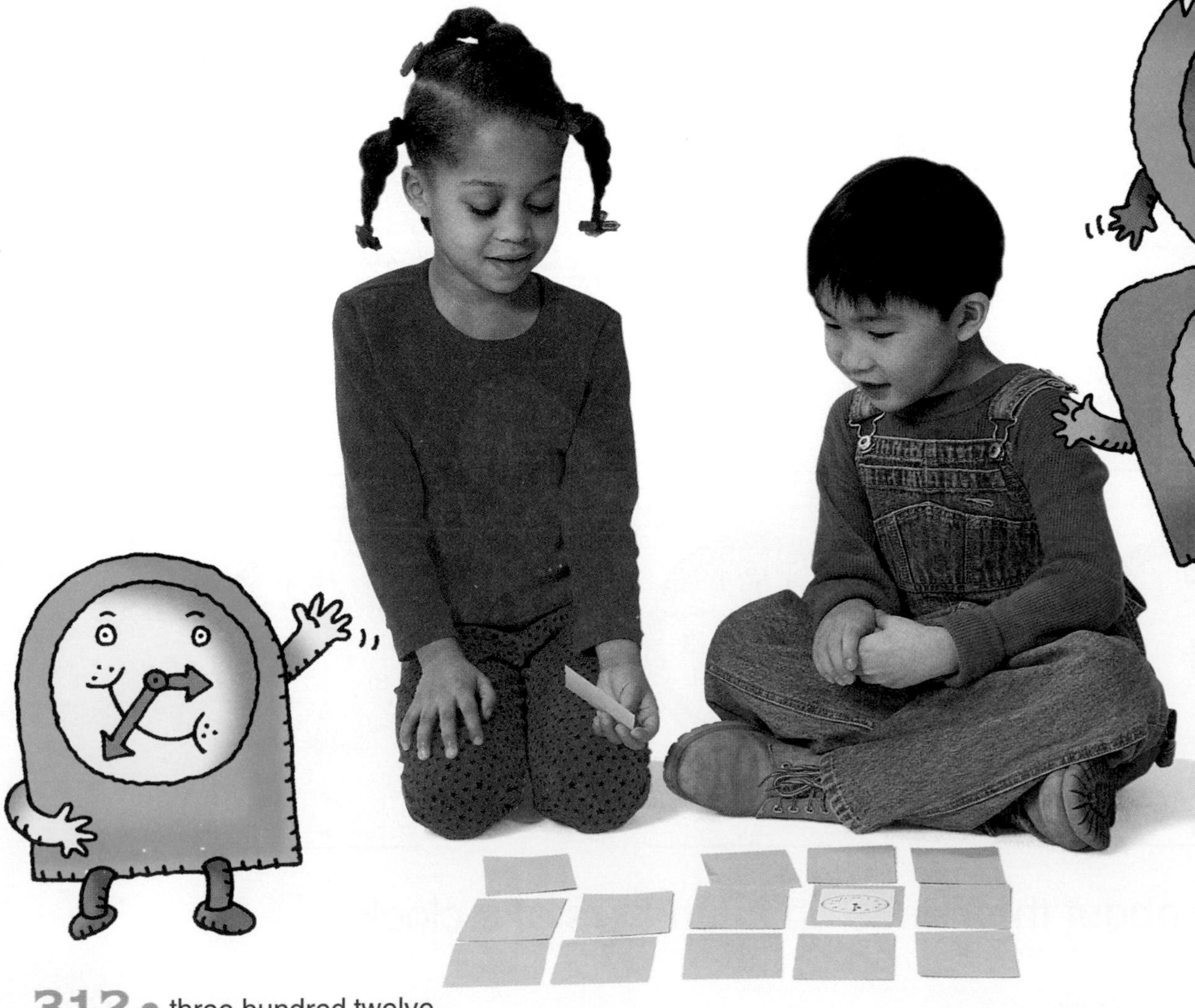

Real-Life Investigation
Applying Time

Name ______________________________

In a Minute

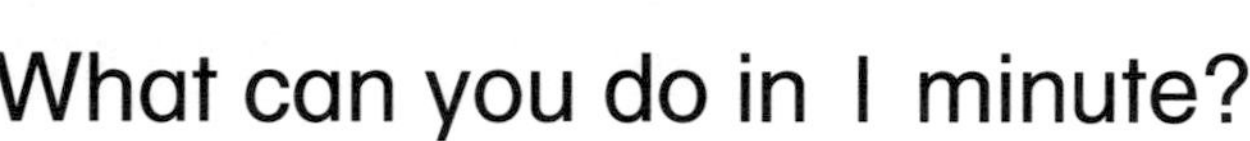

Talk What can you do in 1 minute?

Working Together

- Think of something you can do quickly.
- Estimate how many times you can do it in 1 minute.
- Try it. Your teacher will time you.
- Take turns counting how many. Record your work.

Decision Making

1. Decide on another thing to do for a minute. Try it. Count how many.

2. Make a graph. Show this count and your first count.

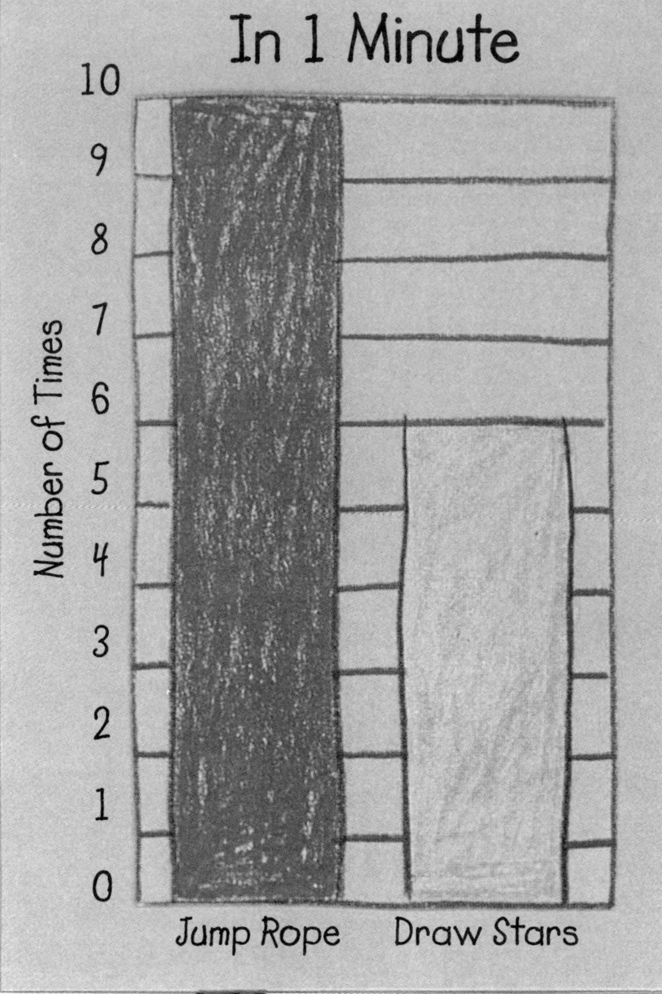

Write a report.

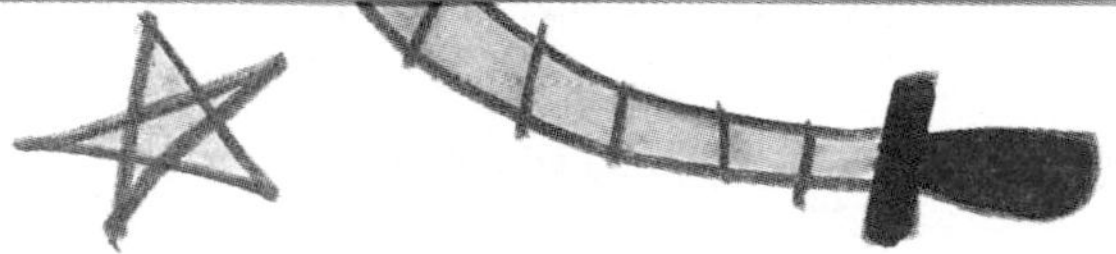

3. Write about what your graph shows.

4. Describe how long a minute is.

More to Investigate

PREDICT What can you do in 5 minutes?

EXPLORE Try it with a partner. Count how many.

FIND Find other things you can do in 5 minutes. Make a list.

Name

Make a List

Read Andy has these play clothes. How many different ways can he dress?

Plan You can **make a list.**

Read
Plan
Solve
Look Back

Solve Color.

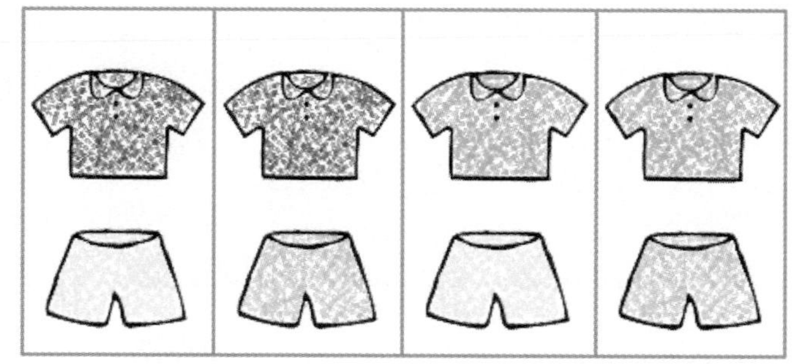

Andy can dress 4 different ways.

Look Back Have you answered the question? Explain.

Color to make a list.

1 Joy has these new clothes. How many different ways can she dress?

Joy can dress ____ different ways.

Try These!

Color to make a list.

1 Cindy has these shoes and socks. Show the different ways she can wear them.

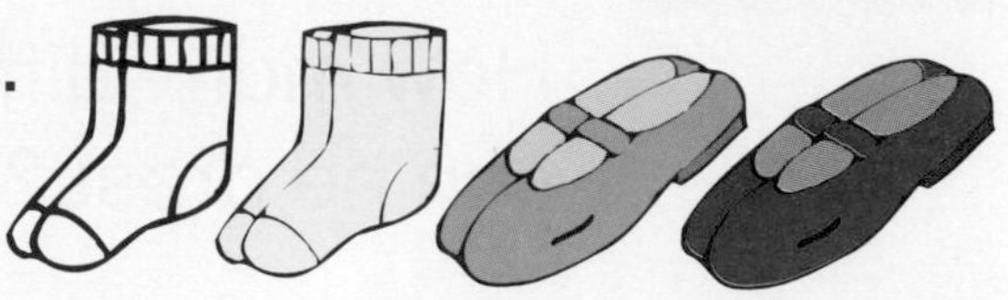

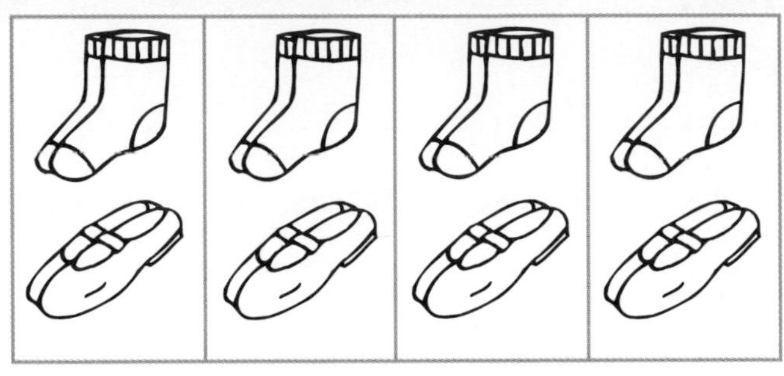

Tell about other ways to wear these shoes and socks.

2 Karl got these new clothes. Show the different ways he can wear them.

3 Lisa has these hats and mittens. Show the different ways she can wear them.

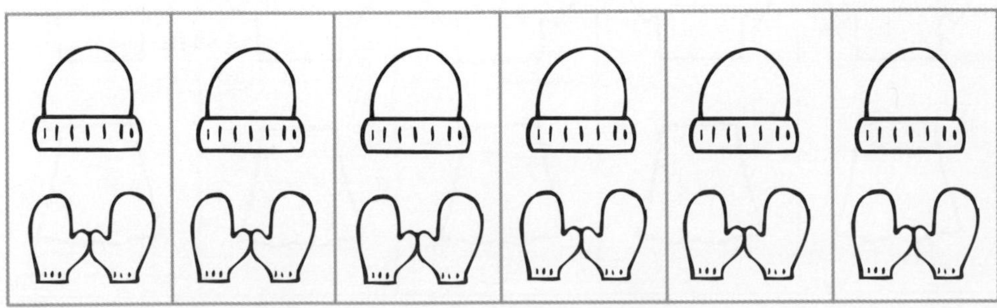

Show and tell about problem 3.

Have your child use clothing similar to the pictures above to find different combinations.

Name ______________________

Use a Calendar

Write the missing numbers.

January

Sunday	Monday	Tuesday	Wednesday	Thursday	Friday	Saturday
				1	2	3
4	5	6	7	8	9	10
11						
18						
					30	31

Talk: Which day of the week is your favorite? Why?

1. How many days are in a week? ____ days
2. How many days are in January? ____ days
3. What day comes after Monday? ______________
4. What day comes before Thursday? ______________
5. How many Saturdays do you see in this January? ____

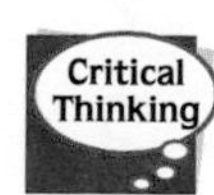

What patterns do you see on the calendar?

Try These!

Make a calendar for this month.

Month: ______________________

Sunday	Monday	Tuesday	Wednesday	Thursday	Friday	Saturday

Use the calendar to solve.

1. How many days are in this month? ____ days
2. What day of the week is **today**? ______________
3. What day of the week is **tomorrow**? ______________
4. What day of the week is the last day of the month? ______________

Mixed Review

Subtract.

5. $\begin{array}{r} 9 \\ -1 \\ \hline \end{array}$ $\begin{array}{r} 4 \\ -4 \\ \hline \end{array}$ $\begin{array}{r} 10 \\ -3 \\ \hline \end{array}$ $\begin{array}{r} 6 \\ -3 \\ \hline \end{array}$ $\begin{array}{r} 7 \\ -2 \\ \hline \end{array}$

At Home: We are learning to read a calendar. Ask your child what day of the week comes after Sunday.

Name

More About Calendars

June

Sunday	Monday	Tuesday	Wednesday	Thursday	Friday	Saturday
	1	2	3	4	5	6
7	8	9	10	11 Class field trip	12	13
14 Flag Day	15	16	17	18	19	20
21 Father's Day	22	23	24	25	26	27
28	29	30				

Use the calendar to solve.

1. What is the date of the class field trip?

   June 11 ________

2. What date is Flag Day?

   ____

3. What is the date of the last day of the month?

   ____

4. What date is Father's Day?

   ____

5. Summer vacation starts on June 25. What day of the week is that?

   ____

6. Jill's birthday is the second Tuesday of the month. What is the date of Jill's birthday?

   ____

Try These!

January

Sunday	Monday	Tuesday	Wednesday	Thursday	Friday	Saturday
				1 New Year's Day	2	3
4	5	6	7	8	9 School Play	10
11	12	13	14	15	16	17
18	19 Martin Luther King, Jr., Day	20	21	22	23	24
25	26	27	28	29	30	31

1. What is the date of the school play?

   January 9 ________________

2. What date is New Year's Day?

   ____

3. What is the date of the last Sunday of the month?

   ____

4. What is the date of Martin Luther King, Jr., Day?

   ____

More to Explore

Problem Solving

Dan is going to the circus the Sunday after the school play. What date is that?

____

What day of the week will February 1 be?

____

Use the calendar on this page. Ask your child the date of the last day of the month.

Name

Use Estimation

Problem Solvers at Work

Read
Plan
Solve
Look Back

1 About how long will the game take?

I minute

I hour

Why is I hour a good **estimate**?

Solve.

2 About how long will it take to eat?

I minute I hour

3 About how long will it take to read?

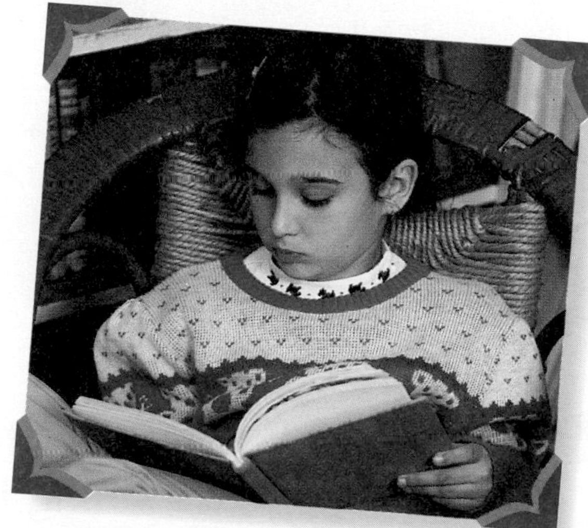

I minute I hour

Try These!

Solve.

1. About how long to watch a movie?

2 minutes

2 hours

2. About how long to brush your teeth?

3 minutes

3 hours

Write and Share

Josh wrote this problem.

About how long would it take to line up for a fire drill?

1 minute

1 hour

Josh Steen
West Lake School
Apex, North Carolina

3. Solve Josh's problem.

4. Write Draw or write a problem about something that takes 1 minute or 1 hour to do. Have a partner solve.

Talk with your child about how long it would take to do certain chores around the house.

Name

Chapter Review

Show the time on each clock.

1 

5 o'clock

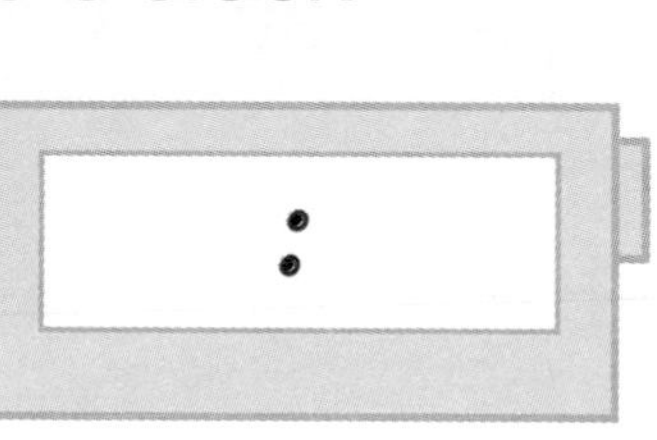

2 two-thirty

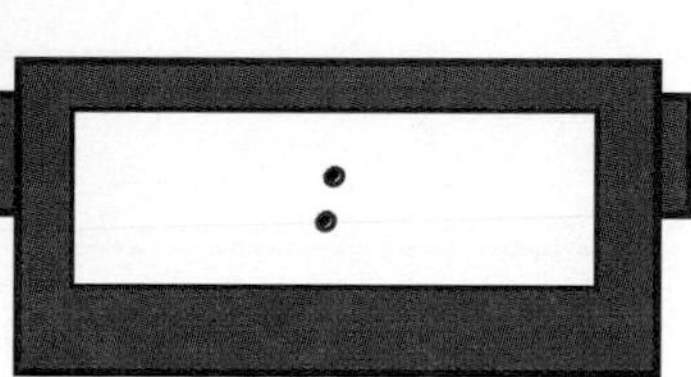

Write the time.

3 

____ : ____

4 

____ : ____

5 

____ : ____

6 

____ : ____

Solve.

7 About how long will it take?

3 minutes

3 hours

Use the calendar to solve.

✻ MARCH ✻						
Sun	Mon	Tue	Wed	Thu	Fri	Sat
1	2	3	4	5	6	7
8	9	10	11	12	13	14
15	16	17	18	19	20	21
22	23	24	25	26	27	28
29	30	31				

8. How many days in a week? ____ days

9. What day comes after Tuesday?

____

Color to show the different ways to wear the clothes.

10.

What Do You Think?

Which is better for telling time?

☑ Check one.

☐ ☐ 5:30 ☐

✻ MARCH ✻						
Sun	Mon	Tue	Wed	Thu	Fri	Sat
1	2	3	4	5	6	7
8	9	10	11	12	13	14
15	16	17	18	19	20	21
22	23	24	25	26	27	28
29	30	31				

Why? ______________________________

Write what you learned about time.

Name

Chapter Test

Show the time on each clock.

1  one-thirty 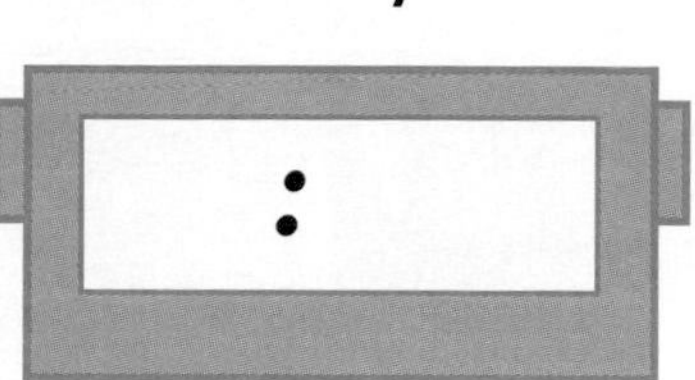

2 4 o'clock 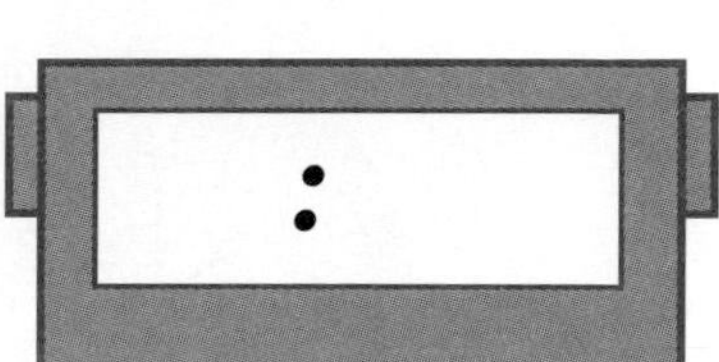

Write the time.

  ___:___

  ___:___

5  ___:___

6  ___:___

Use the calendar to solve.

7 How many days in October? ______________

8 What is the first Friday in October? ______________

9 What day comes after Thursday? ______________

October

Sun	Mon	Tue	Wed	Thu	Fri	Sat
				1	2	3
4	5	6	7	8	9	10
11	12	13	14	15	16	17
18	19	20	21	22	23	24
25	26	27	28	29	30	31

Color to show different ways to wear the clothes.

 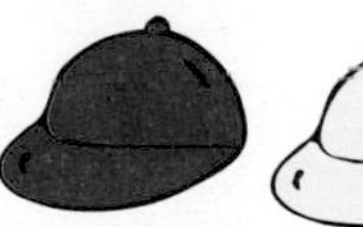 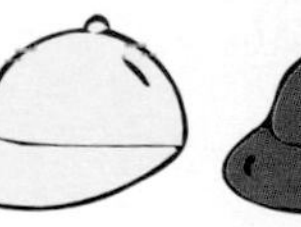  

Performance Assessment

What Did You Learn?

Draw lines to match.

Tell what happens first, second, third, last.

You may want to put this page in your portfolio.

Math Connection

Graphs

Name

Pictographs

Rosa asked some friends what time they eat dinner. Rosa made a chart.

Dinner hours	Tally
5:00	I
5:30	~~IIII~~ II
6:00	II
6:30	I

What does the chart show?

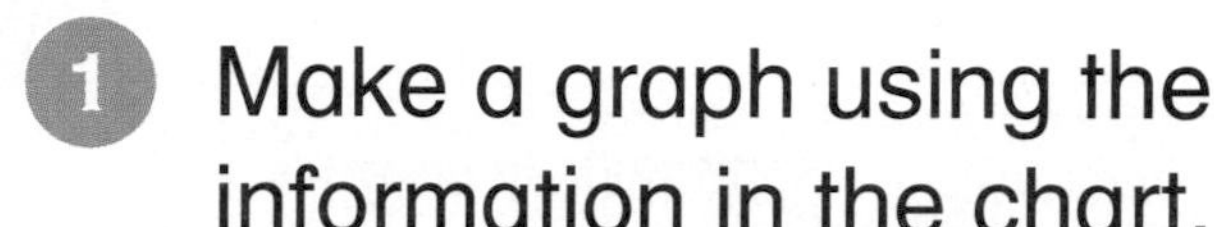

1 Make a graph using the information in the chart.

DINNER TIMES	
5:00	☺
5:30	
6:00	
6:30	

☺ stands for 1 friend.

2 How many friends did Rosa ask? ____

3 What time do most of Rosa's friends eat dinner? ___:___

4 Write a problem about the information in the graph. Have a partner solve it.

Technology Connection

Computer

Make Graphs

A computer helps you show information on a graph.

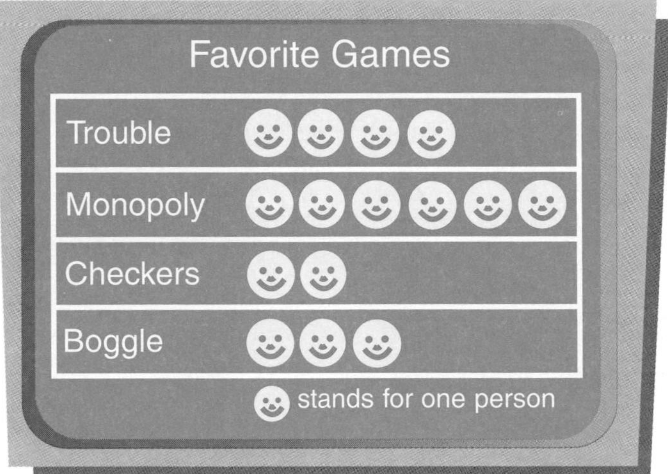

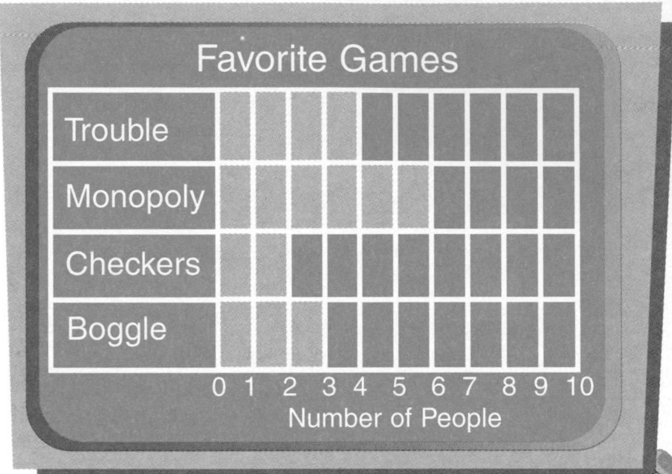

What do these graphs show?

Which graph do you think is better? Why?

At the Computer

1. Ask 10 people what game they like best. Put the information in a chart.
2. Use the chart to make a pictograph.
3. Then use the chart to make a bar graph.
4. Write about your graphs.

Name

Cumulative Review

Choose the letter of the correct answer.

$$\begin{array}{r} 7 \\ +\,2 \\ \hline \end{array}$$

(a) 3
(b) 5
(c) 9
(d) 10

2

$$\begin{array}{r} 8 \\ -\,3 \\ \hline \end{array}$$

(a) 5
(b) 6
(c) 10
(d) 11

3

10, 20, __?__, 40

(a) 21

(b) 25
(c) 30
(d) 50

4

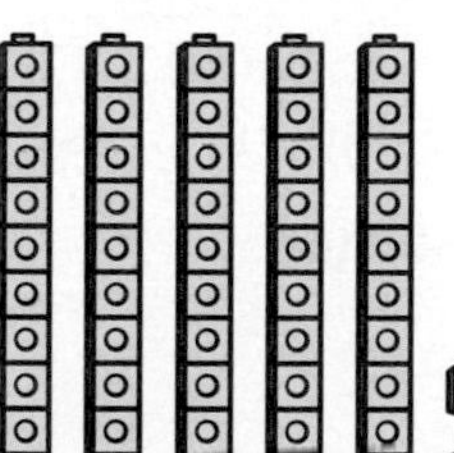

(a) 35

(b) 53
(c) 55
(d) 80

5

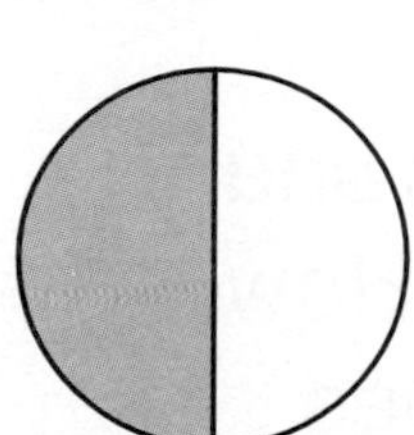

(a) $\frac{1}{5}$
(b) $\frac{1}{4}$
(c) $\frac{1}{3}$
(d) $\frac{1}{2}$

6

square

(a) 
(b) 
(c) 
(d) 

(a) 3¢
(b) 10¢
(c) 15¢
(d) 30¢

8

(a) 1¢
(b) 5¢
(c) 10¢
(d) 25¢

9

(a) 3:00
(b) 4:00
(c) 5:00
(d) 7:00

10

(a) 1:30
(b) 2:30
(c) 6:00
(d) 12:30

11 There are 3 dogs and 4 cats. How many animals in all?

ⓐ 1
ⓑ 6
ⓒ 7
ⓓ 8

12 Which number is just before?

	41

ⓐ 42
ⓑ 40
ⓒ 39
ⓓ 31

13 Lisa has 10¢. She spends 4¢. How much money does she have left?

ⓐ 3¢
ⓑ 4¢
ⓒ 5¢
ⓓ 6¢

BOOKS READ

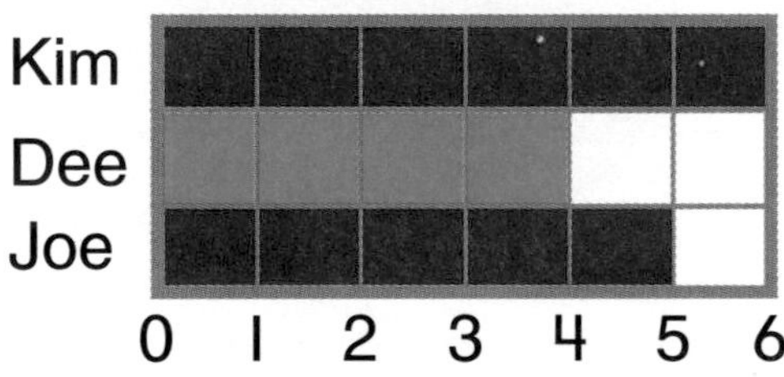

14 How many books did Joe read?

ⓐ 3
ⓑ 4
ⓒ 5
ⓓ 6

15 How many books did Kim read?

ⓐ 3
ⓑ 4
ⓒ 5
ⓓ 6

16 There are 8 pigs. 2 pigs run away. How many are left?

ⓐ 2
ⓑ 4
ⓒ 6
ⓓ 10

17 6 children are playing. Then 3 more children come. How many children in all?

ⓐ 9
ⓑ 6
ⓒ 5
ⓓ 3

18 José has 4¢. He finds 5¢. How much money does he have now?

ⓐ 1¢
ⓑ 5¢
ⓒ 9¢
ⓓ 10¢

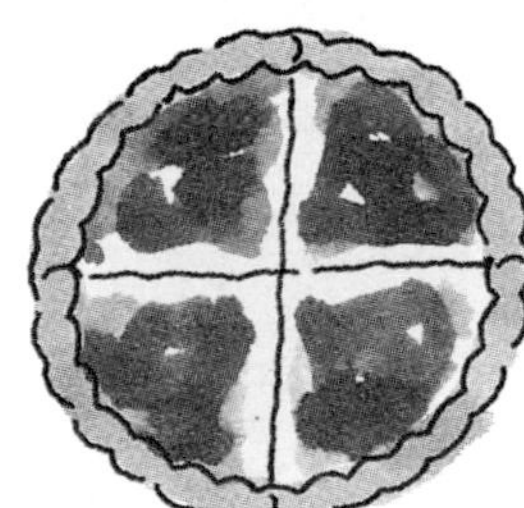

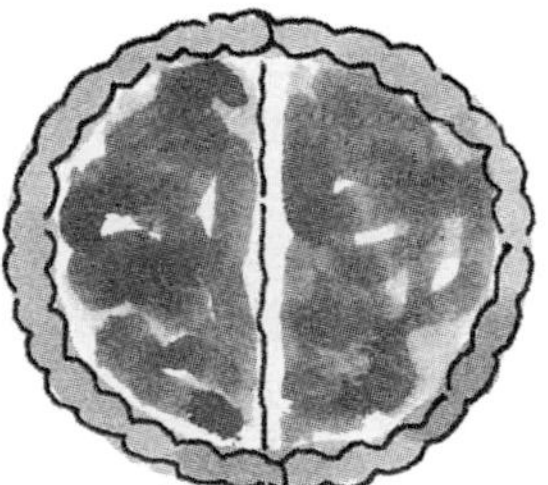

19 4 friends share a pizza. How much does each get?

ⓐ $\frac{1}{2}$
ⓑ $\frac{1}{3}$
ⓒ $\frac{1}{4}$
ⓓ $\frac{1}{5}$

20 2 friends share a pizza. How much does each get?

ⓐ $\frac{1}{2}$
ⓑ $\frac{1}{3}$
ⓒ $\frac{1}{4}$
ⓓ $\frac{1}{5}$

Name ___

Make a Water Clock

MATERIALS Small paper or plastic cup, masking tape, pin (for small hole), watch, small glass jar.

paper cup
tape scale
glass jar

DIRECTIONS Poke a small hole in the cup. Put the clock together (see picture). Fill the cup with water. Every 5 minutes, draw a line to show where the water is.

For how many minutes will your water clock run?

___ minutes

Which activity can you do before the water runs out?

☑ Check them.

- ☐ Read a book
- ☐ Clean your room
- ☐ Eat dinner

The duration of the clock will depend on the size of the container and the hole made in the bottom of the cup. A 6-ounce plastic yogurt cup pierced with a sewing needle and filled halfway with warm water will drip for about 30 minutes.

Dear Family,

We are beginning a new chapter in mathematics. We will be learning about strategies to help us add and subtract.

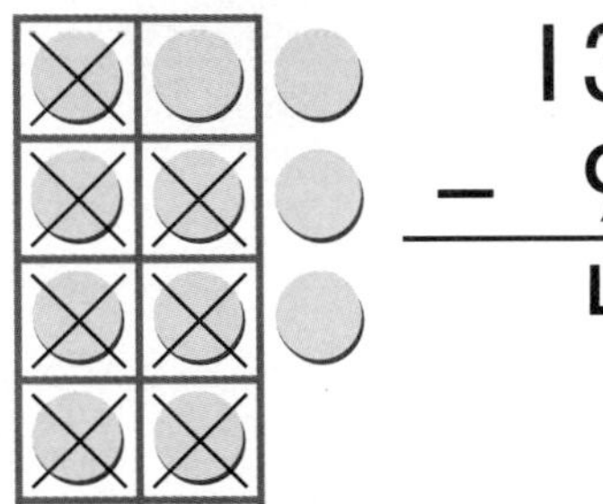

$$\begin{array}{r} 13 \\ -\ 9 \\ \hline 4 \end{array} \qquad \begin{array}{r} 6 \\ +\ 6 \\ \hline 12 \end{array} \qquad \begin{array}{r} 6 \\ +\ 7 \\ \hline 13 \end{array}$$

We will also be talking about different kinds of water, and animals and fish that live there. Please help me complete this interview.

Your child,

____
Signature

Interview

Which places do you like to visit?
(You may check more than one.)

- ❑ Pond
- ❑ Pool
- ❑ River
- ❑ Lake
- ❑ Ocean
- ❑ Other _______________

What is fun to do in or near the water?

____

Under the Water

Adding and Subtracting to 18

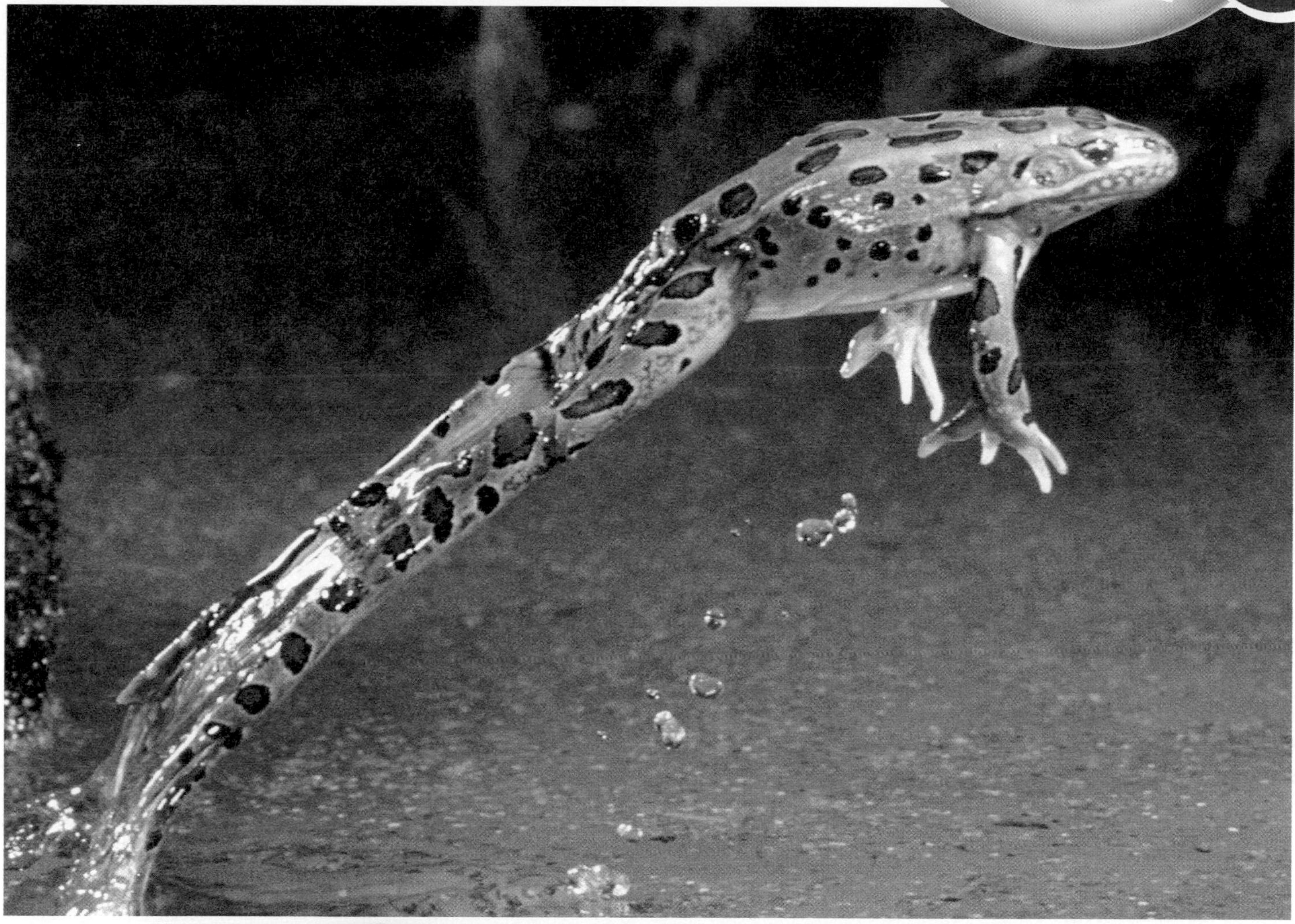

Listen to the story *Splash.*

Tell what you know about animals that live in or near water.

Name

What Do You Know?

Solve.

1. Sue caught 9 fish. She threw 6 fish back into the water. How many fish did Sue keep?

   ____ fish

Show or write about how you solved the problem.

2. Dan had 4 fish in his bowl. One morning there were 3 baby fish in the bowl. How many fish does Dan have now?

   ____ fish

Show or write about how you solved the problem.

Write a problem that uses addition or subtraction. Show how to solve it.

Name ______________________________

Doubles

$$\begin{array}{r} 7 \\ +\ 7 \\ \hline 14 \end{array} \qquad \begin{array}{r} 14 \\ -\ 7 \\ \hline 7 \end{array}$$

How can a doubles fact help you subtract?

Add or subtract.

$$\begin{array}{r} 2 \\ +\ 2 \\ \hline 4 \end{array} \qquad \begin{array}{r} 4 \\ -\ 2 \\ \hline 2 \end{array}$$

$$\begin{array}{r} 4 \\ +\ 4 \\ \hline \end{array} \qquad \begin{array}{r} 8 \\ -\ 4 \\ \hline \end{array}$$

$$\begin{array}{r} 3 \\ +\ 3 \\ \hline \end{array} \qquad \begin{array}{r} 6 \\ -\ 3 \\ \hline \end{array}$$

$$\begin{array}{r} 1 \\ +\ 1 \\ \hline \end{array} \qquad \begin{array}{r} 2 \\ -\ 1 \\ \hline \end{array}$$

Critical Thinking: How are doubles like halves?

Try These!

Add or subtract.

1

$$\begin{array}{r} 6 \\ +\ 6 \\ \hline 12 \end{array} \qquad \begin{array}{r} 12 \\ -\ 6 \\ \hline 6 \end{array}$$

2

$$\begin{array}{r} 5 \\ +\ 5 \\ \hline \end{array} \qquad \begin{array}{r} 10 \\ -\ 5 \\ \hline \end{array}$$

3

$$\begin{array}{r} 9 \\ +\ 9 \\ \hline \end{array} \quad \begin{array}{r} 3 \\ +\ 3 \\ \hline \end{array} \quad \begin{array}{r} 14¢ \\ -\ 7¢ \\ \hline \end{array} \quad \begin{array}{r} 1¢ \\ +\ 1¢ \\ \hline \end{array} \quad \begin{array}{r} 6 \\ -\ 3 \\ \hline \end{array} \quad \begin{array}{r} 8 \\ +\ 8 \\ \hline \end{array}$$

4

$$\begin{array}{r} 2¢ \\ +\ 2¢ \\ \hline \end{array} \quad \begin{array}{r} 8 \\ -\ 4 \\ \hline \end{array} \quad \begin{array}{r} 10 \\ -\ 5 \\ \hline \end{array} \quad \begin{array}{r} 18 \\ -\ 9 \\ \hline \end{array} \quad \begin{array}{r} 4 \\ +\ 4 \\ \hline \end{array} \quad \begin{array}{r} 7¢ \\ +\ 7¢ \\ \hline \end{array}$$

5

$$\begin{array}{r} 12 \\ -\ 6 \\ \hline \end{array} \quad \begin{array}{r} 2¢ \\ -\ 1¢ \\ \hline \end{array} \quad \begin{array}{r} 4¢ \\ -\ 2¢ \\ \hline \end{array} \quad \begin{array}{r} 5 \\ +\ 5 \\ \hline \end{array} \quad \begin{array}{r} 6 \\ +\ 6 \\ \hline \end{array} \quad \begin{array}{r} 16 \\ -\ 8 \\ \hline \end{array}$$

More to Explore — Algebra Sense

Complete.

$3 + \_\_\_ = 6$ $\quad$ $5 + \_\_\_ = 10$ $\quad$ $8 + \_\_\_ = 16$

Ask your child to tell you the addition doubles facts: 1 + 1, 2 + 2, 3 + 3, and so on.

Name ____________________

Doubles Plus One

5 + 5 = 10
5 + 6 is 1 more.
So 5 + 6 = 11.

$$\begin{array}{r} 5 \\ +\ 5 \\ \hline 10 \end{array} \qquad \begin{array}{r} 5 \\ +\ 6 \\ \hline 11 \end{array}$$

Add.

$$\begin{array}{r} 3 \\ +3 \\ \hline \end{array} \qquad \begin{array}{r} 3 \\ +4 \\ \hline \end{array}$$

2

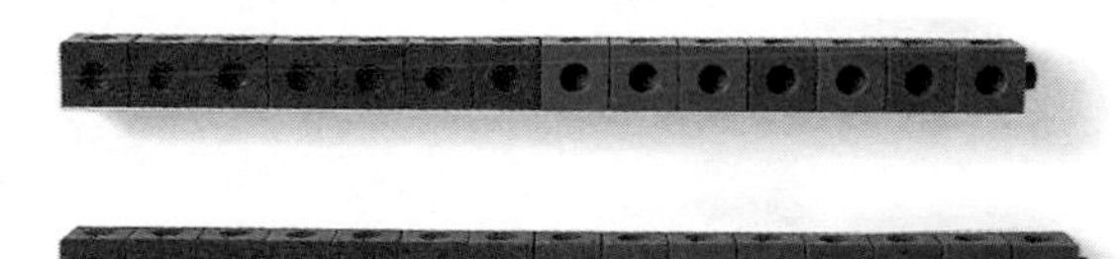

$$\begin{array}{r} 7 \\ +7 \\ \hline \end{array} \qquad \begin{array}{r} 7 \\ +8 \\ \hline \end{array}$$

3

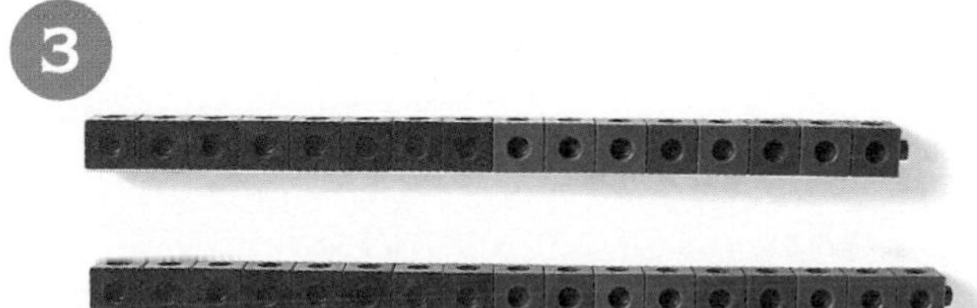

$$\begin{array}{r} 8 \\ +8 \\ \hline \end{array} \qquad \begin{array}{r} 9 \\ +8 \\ \hline \end{array}$$

$$\begin{array}{r} 6 \\ +6 \\ \hline \end{array} \qquad \begin{array}{r} 6 \\ +7 \\ \hline \end{array}$$

Critical Thinking How can you use 7 + 7 to find 6 + 7?

Try These!

Add.

1

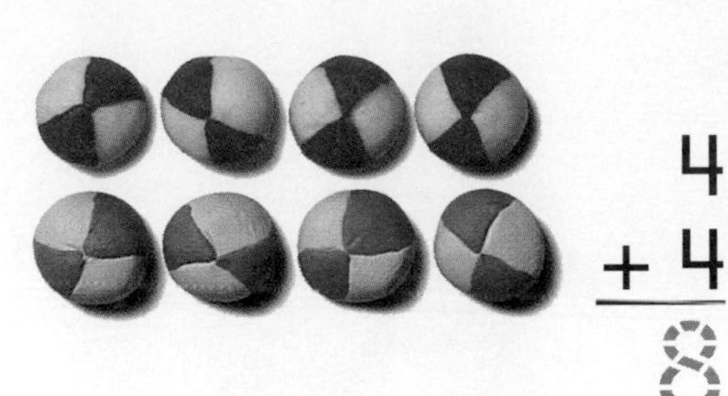

$$\begin{array}{r} 4 \\ +\ 4 \\ \hline 8 \end{array}$$

$$\begin{array}{r} 4 \\ +\ 5 \\ \hline 9 \end{array}$$

2

$$\begin{array}{r} 2 \\ +\ 2 \\ \hline \end{array}$$

$$\begin{array}{r} 2 \\ +\ 3 \\ \hline \end{array}$$

3

$$\begin{array}{r} 3 \\ +\ 3 \\ \hline \end{array} \qquad \begin{array}{r} 4 \\ +\ 3 \\ \hline \end{array}$$

4

$$\begin{array}{r} 7 \\ +\ 7 \\ \hline \end{array} \qquad \begin{array}{r} 7 \\ +\ 8 \\ \hline \end{array}$$

5

$$\begin{array}{r} 5 \\ +\ 5 \\ \hline \end{array} \qquad \begin{array}{r} 6 \\ +\ 5 \\ \hline \end{array}$$

6

$$\begin{array}{r} 6 \\ +\ 6 \\ \hline \end{array} \qquad \begin{array}{r} 3 \\ +\ 2 \\ \hline \end{array} \qquad \begin{array}{r} 8¢ \\ +\ 8¢ \\ \hline \end{array} \qquad \begin{array}{r} 1 \\ +\ 2 \\ \hline \end{array} \qquad \begin{array}{r} 4¢ \\ +\ 5¢ \\ \hline \end{array} \qquad \begin{array}{r} 9 \\ +\ 9 \\ \hline \end{array}$$

7

$$\begin{array}{r} 8 \\ +\ 9 \\ \hline \end{array} \qquad \begin{array}{r} 5¢ \\ +\ 4¢ \\ \hline \end{array} \qquad \begin{array}{r} 4¢ \\ +\ 4¢ \\ \hline \end{array} \qquad \begin{array}{r} 6 \\ +\ 7 \\ \hline \end{array} \qquad \begin{array}{r} 2 \\ +\ 1 \\ \hline \end{array} \qquad \begin{array}{r} 4¢ \\ +\ 3¢ \\ \hline \end{array}$$

Write all the doubles you know.
Tell how you use doubles.

At Home: Ask your child which double he or she can use to add 7 + 8.

Name

Working Together

You and your partner need 18 , a spinner, and a 10-frame.

Show 9. **Spin.** **Show.** **Add.**

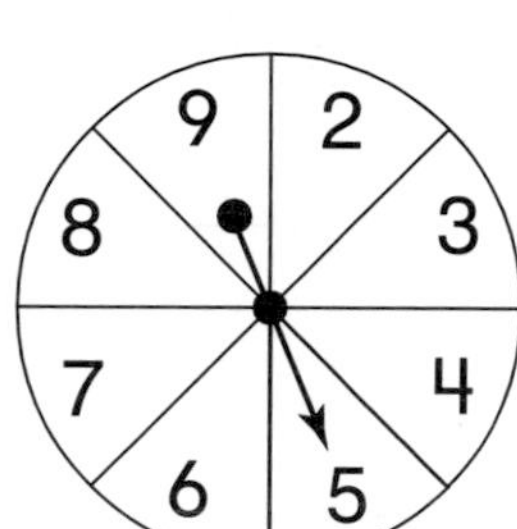

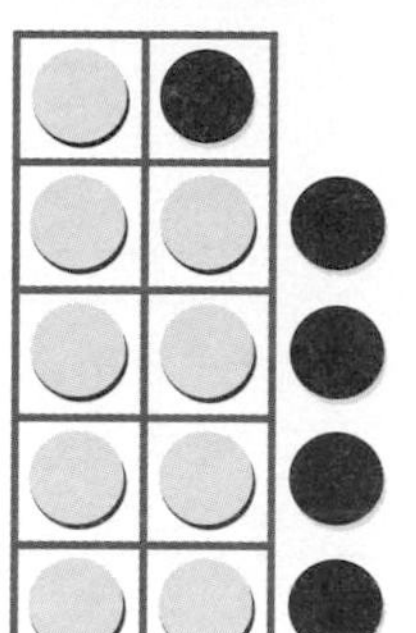

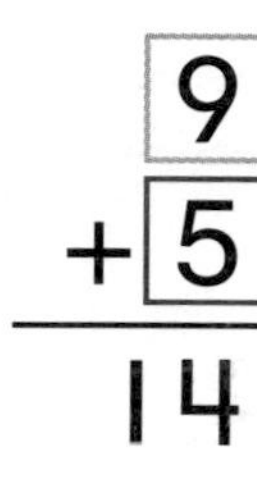

$$\begin{array}{r} 9 \\ +\ 5 \\ \hline 14 \end{array}$$

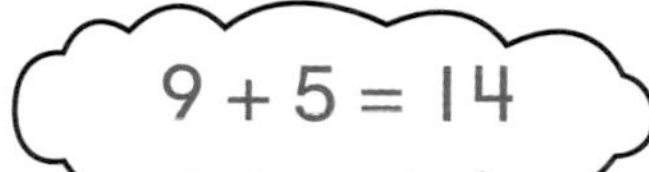

5

1.

9 + ☐   9 + ☐   9 + ☐

2.
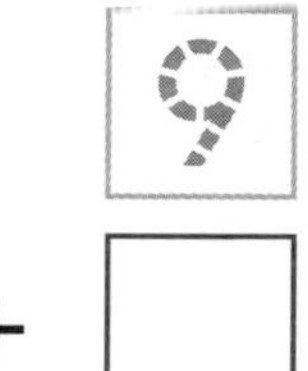

9 + ☐   9 + ☐   9 + ☐

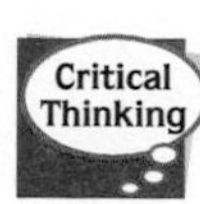

Critical Thinking: How does using a 10-frame help when adding 9?

Try These!

Draw the .
Write the sum.

1 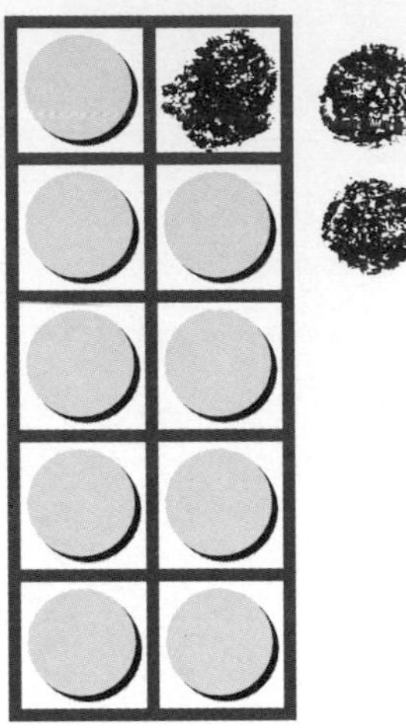

$$\begin{array}{r} 9 \\ +\ 3 \\ \hline 12 \end{array}$$

2 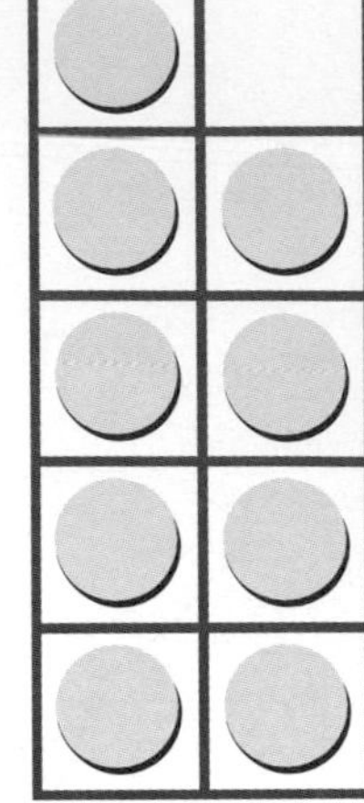

$$\begin{array}{r} 9 \\ +\ 6 \\ \hline \end{array}$$

3 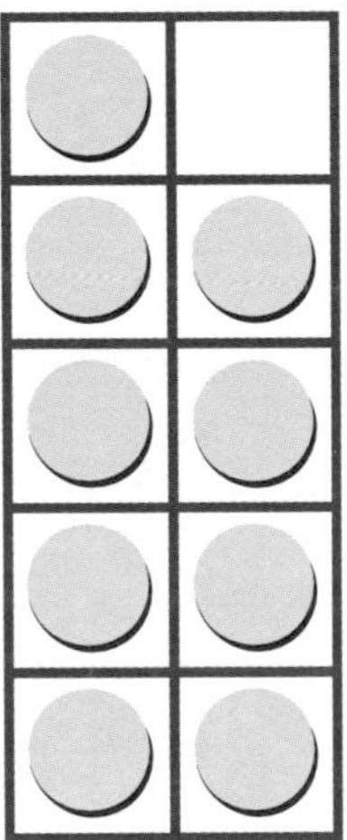

$$\begin{array}{r} 9 \\ +\ 4 \\ \hline \end{array}$$

4 

$$\begin{array}{r} 9 \\ +\ 8 \\ \hline \end{array}$$

5 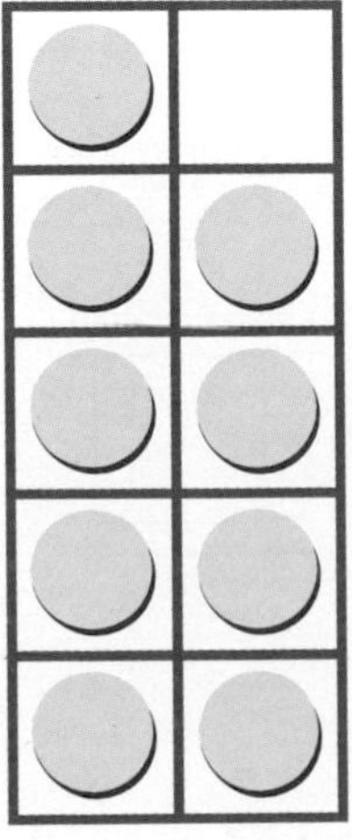

$$\begin{array}{r} 9 \\ +\ 2 \\ \hline \end{array}$$

6 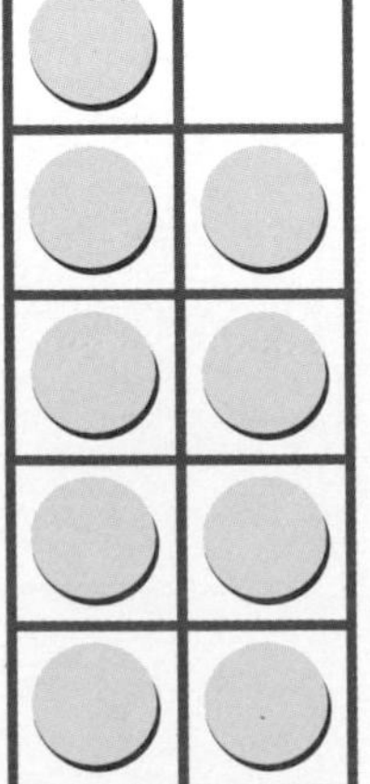

$$\begin{array}{r} 9 \\ +\ 7 \\ \hline \end{array}$$

At Home: Ask your child to explain how to add 9 on a 10-frame.

Name ______________________________

Add

Kim saw 9 sunfish in the pond.
Brian saw 8 goldfish in the pond.
How many fish did they see?

Which strategies can you use to add 9 + 8?

There are <u>17</u> fish in the pond.

Find the sum.

1

2	6	7	9	7¢	7
+ 9	+ 6	+ 8	+ 3	+ 7¢	+ 9

2

3	4	9¢	6	3	5
+ 8	+ 8	+ 9¢	+ 7	+ 9	+ 7

3

9	8	7	5	5¢	8
+ 5	+ 9	+ 4	+ 8	+ 6¢	+ 8

4

8	9	7	9¢	5	8
+ 6	+ 6	+ 6	+ 2¢	+ 9	+ 7

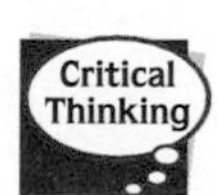

Why is it useful to know different strategies for addition?

Try These!

Add.

1.
```
  9
+ 3
 12
```

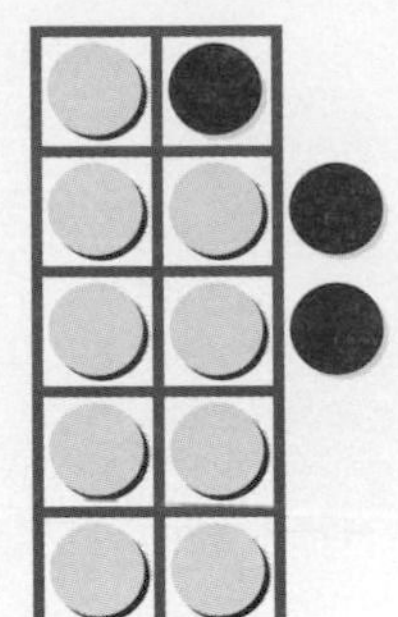

2.
```
  7
+ 8
 15
```

Doubles plus one
7 + 7 = 14
7 + 8 is one more.

3. $9 + 7$ $6 + 8$ $8 + 4$ $7 + 5$ 4¢ + 9¢ $9 + 7$

4. $6 + 5$ $8 + 5$ 6¢ + 9¢ $9 + 4$ $4 + 7$ 5¢ + 8¢

5. $5 + 9$ $8 + 3$ $9 + 8$ $6 + 7$ $5 + 6$ 8¢ + 7¢

Mixed Review

Write the number.

6. 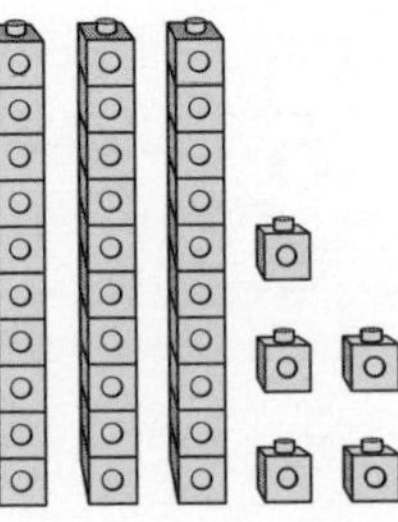 ____

7. 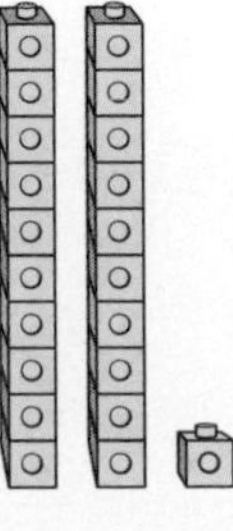 ____

8. 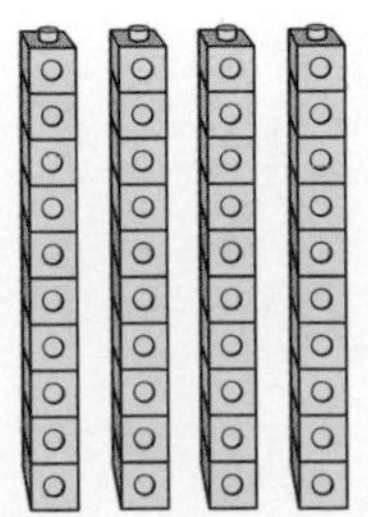 ____

At Home: We used strategies to add. Have your child explain how to add 6 + 7.

Name

Add Three Numbers

4 2 + 4 10 (8)	4 1 + 6 11 (10)

How can you use strategies to add three numbers?

Add.

1

3 4 + 4 (8) 11	9 2 + 1	2 3 + 7	7¢ 1¢ + 7¢	5 1 + 5	4 5 + 9

2

6¢ 1¢ + 3¢	5 6 + 2	9 3 + 3	6 4 + 4	2¢ 8¢ + 2¢	6 1 + 6

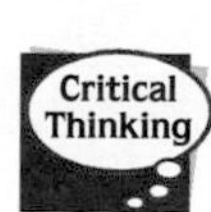

What are some strategies that you can use to add 3 + 3 + 7?

Try These!

Find the sum.

1

2	3	1	2	4¢	8
5	7	5	5	4¢	1
+ 3	+ 3	+ 5	+ 8	+ 4¢	+ 7
10					

2

1	2	5	3¢	5	7
2	2	4	4¢	4	0
+ 9	+ 6	+ 3	+ 7¢	+ 5	+ 4

Cultural Connection

Numbers can look the same all around the world. You can read numbers in Korea. But this is how you say the numbers.

1 yil	2 yee	3 sam	4 sa	5 oh	6 yuk	7 chil	8 par	9 goo
10 ship	11 ship yil	12 ship yee	13 ship sam	14 ship sa	15 ship oh	16 ship yuk	17 ship chil	18 ship par

At Home: Have your child add 4 pennies plus 5 pennies plus 3 pennies.

Name

Addition Fish

You need a 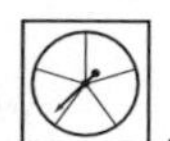.

Take turns.

► Spin. Write the number to add.

► Complete the table.

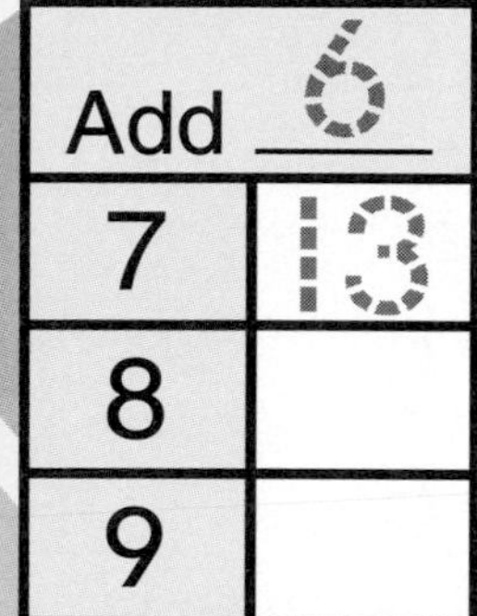

Add 6	
7	13
8	
9	

Tell a partner about the patterns that you see.

Add ___	
5	
6	
7	

Add ___	
3	
4	
5	

Add ___	
8	
7	
6	

Add ___	
9	
8	
7	

Cultural Note

People in Australia have laws to protect the fish and coral of the Great Barrier Reef.

Add.

1	5 + 9 14	4 + 8	7 + 6	9 + 3	8¢ + 3¢	8 + 9
2	7 + 7	5 + 6	4 + 9	5¢ + 7¢	8 + 5	7 + 9
3	9 + 6	8 + 8	9¢ + 8¢	6 + 7	6 + 8	8 + 7
4	2 4 + 8	5¢ 4¢ + 6¢	1 3 + 9	4 0 + 7	6 2 + 6	4 4 + 8

Solve.

Workspace

5 7 angelfish are eating.
8 more angelfish come to eat.
How many angelfish
are eating?

____ angelfish

6 3 lionfish swim into a cave.
8 butterfly fish join them.
How many fish are in
the cave?

____ fish

Name

Explore Activity

Subtract 9

Sue had 13 shells.
She gave away 9 shells.
How many shells does she have left?

Show 13. Subtract 9.

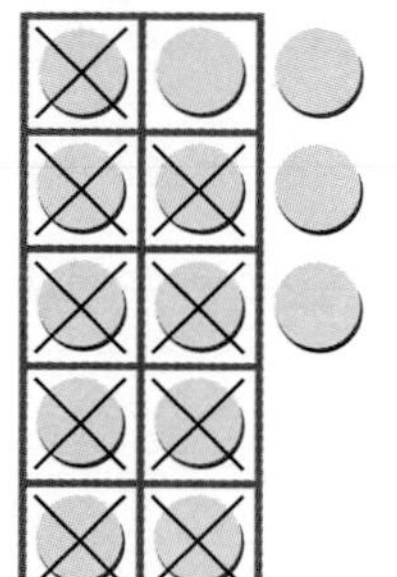

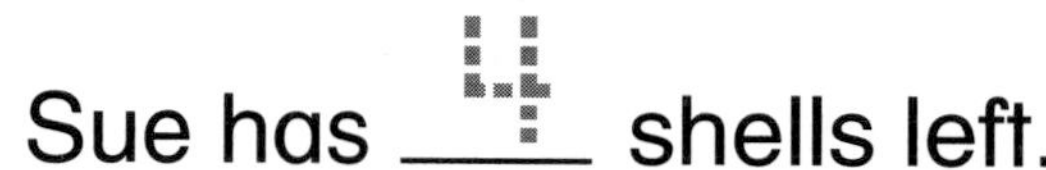

Sue has 4 shells left.

Working Together

You and your partner need a 10-frame, a spinner, and 18 counters.

- Spin to find how many shells.
- Show the number with counters and the 10-frame.
- Subtract 9.
- Write the subtraction.

1 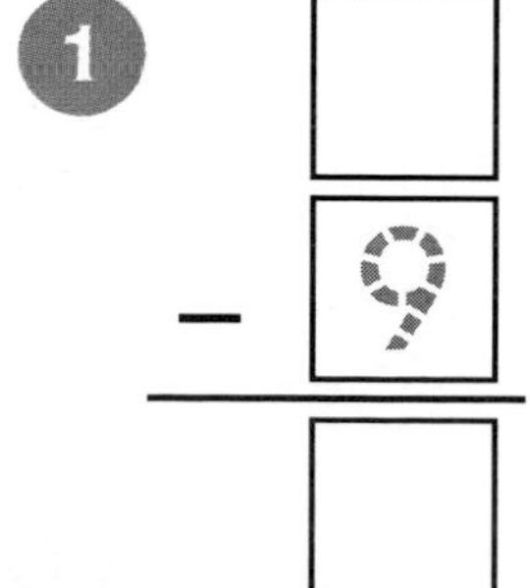

2 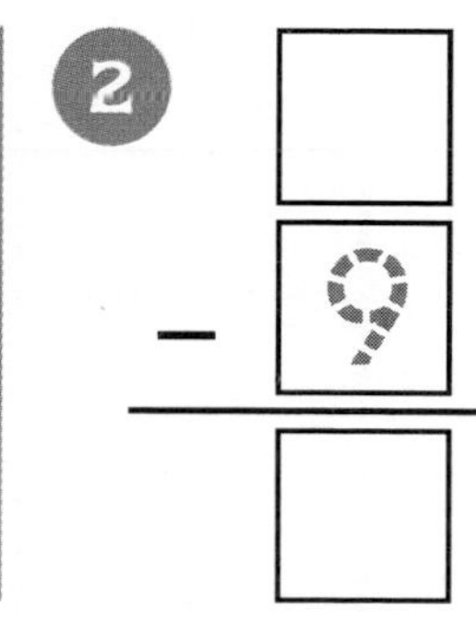

3 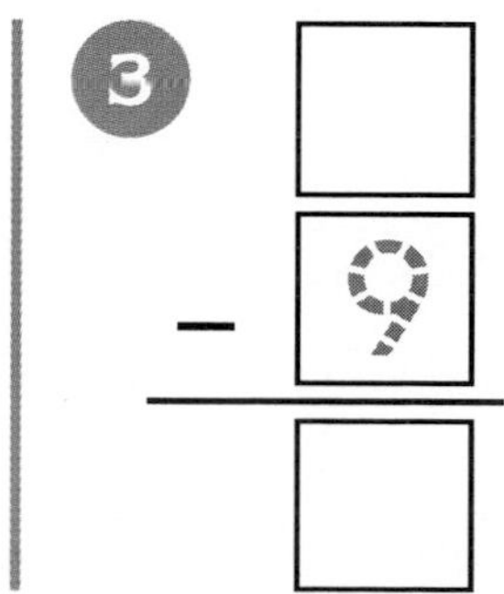

4 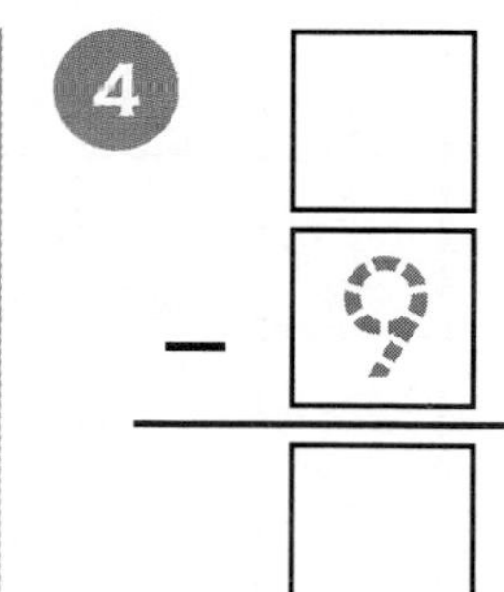

How does using a 10-frame help you subtract 9?

Try These!

Cross out 9.
Write how many are left.

1
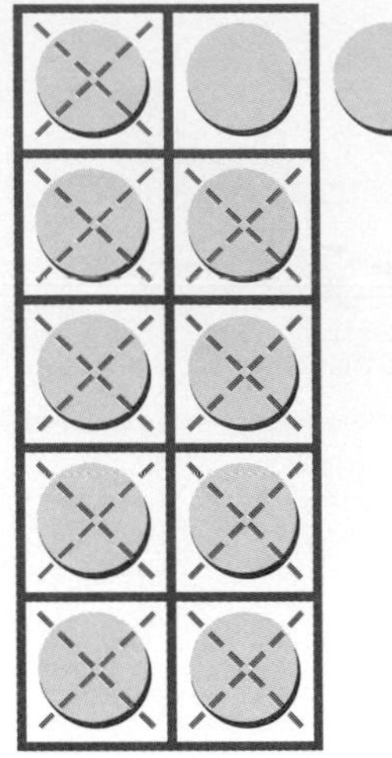

$$\begin{array}{r} 11 \\ -\ 9 \\ \hline 2 \end{array}$$

2
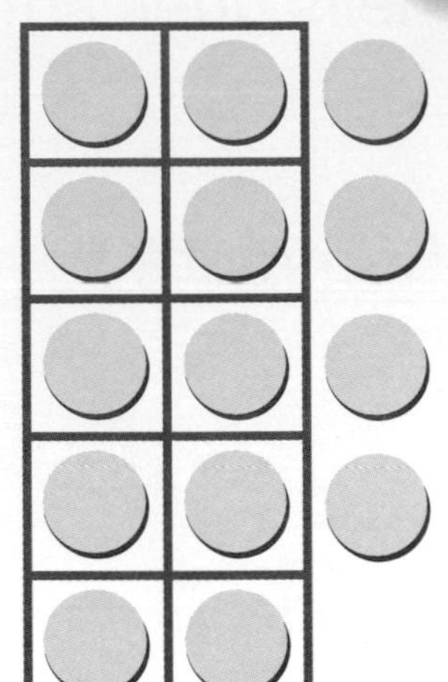

$$\begin{array}{r} 14 \\ -\ 9 \\ \hline \end{array}$$

3
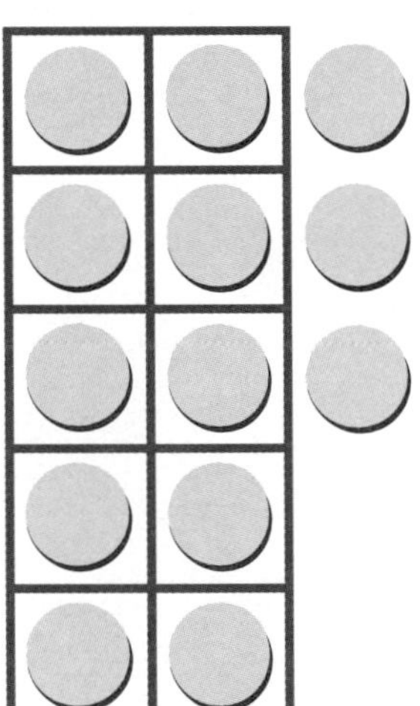

$$\begin{array}{r} 13 \\ -\ 9 \\ \hline \end{array}$$

4
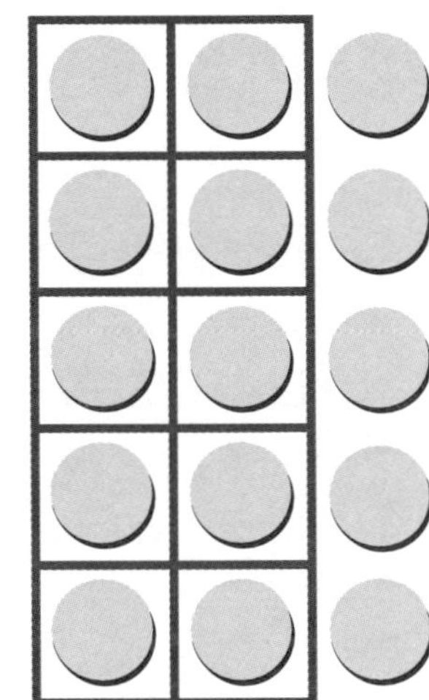

$$\begin{array}{r} 15 \\ -\ 9 \\ \hline \end{array}$$

5
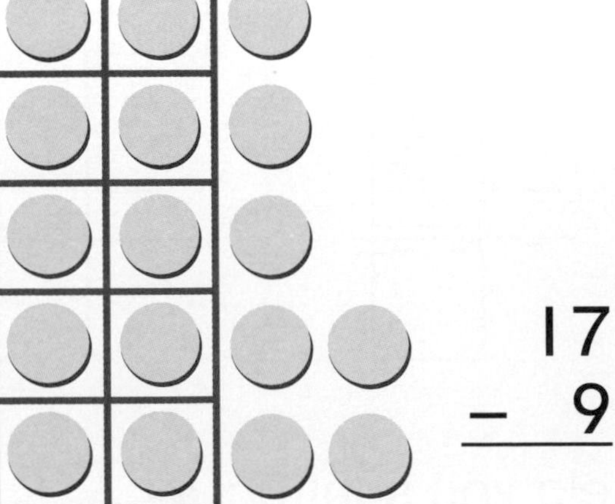

$$\begin{array}{r} 17 \\ -\ 9 \\ \hline \end{array}$$

6
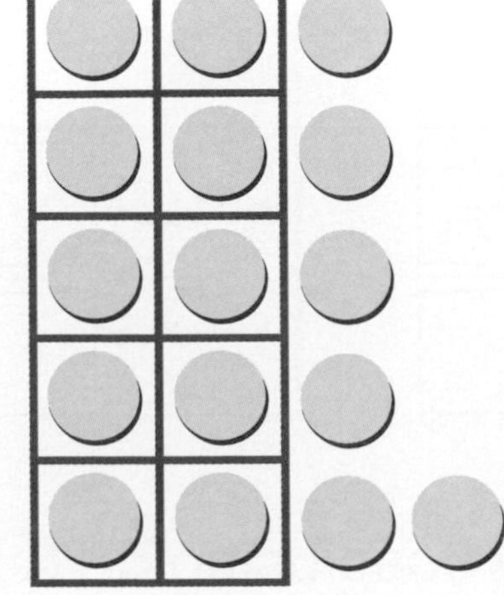

$$\begin{array}{r} 16 \\ -\ 9 \\ \hline \end{array}$$

At Home

We learned how to use a 10-frame to subtract.
Ask your child how to subtract 9.

Name ______________________________

Subtract

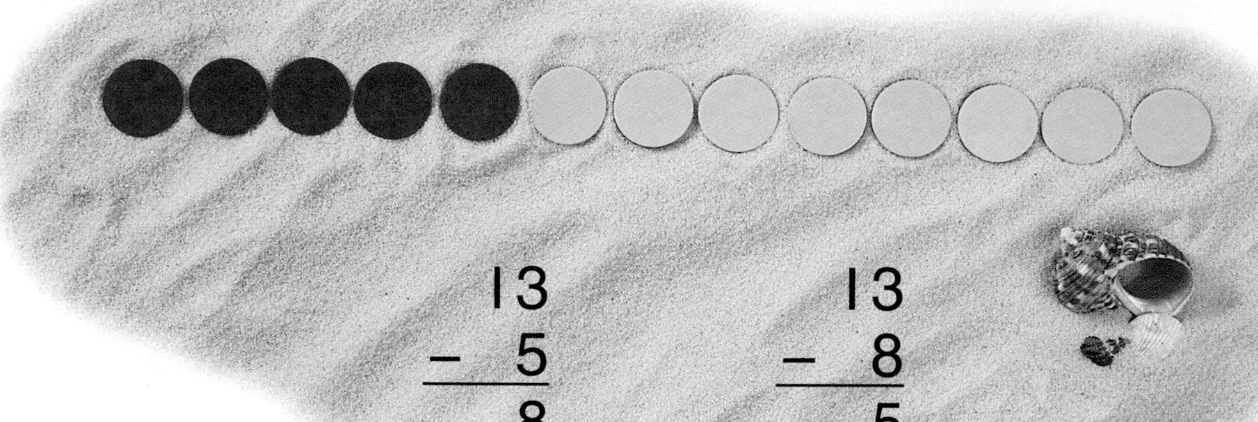

Why do you think these are called **related facts**?

Subtract.
Use if you want to.

1. $\begin{array}{r} 11 \\ -\ 4 \\ \hline 7 \end{array}$ $\begin{array}{r} 11 \\ -\ 7 \\ \hline 4 \end{array}$ $\begin{array}{r} 12 \\ -\ 5 \\ \hline \end{array}$ $\begin{array}{r} 12 \\ -\ 7 \\ \hline \end{array}$ $\begin{array}{r} 13 \\ -\ 4 \\ \hline \end{array}$ $\begin{array}{r} 13 \\ -\ 9 \\ \hline \end{array}$

2. $\begin{array}{r} 12 \\ -\ 3 \\ \hline \end{array}$ $\begin{array}{r} 12 \\ -\ 9 \\ \hline \end{array}$ $\begin{array}{r} 11 \\ -\ 8 \\ \hline \end{array}$ $\begin{array}{r} 11 \\ -\ 3 \\ \hline \end{array}$ $\begin{array}{r} 13 \\ -\ 6 \\ \hline \end{array}$ $\begin{array}{r} 13 \\ -\ 7 \\ \hline \end{array}$

3. $\begin{array}{r} 10 \\ -\ 4 \\ \hline \end{array}$ $\begin{array}{r} 10 \\ -\ 6 \\ \hline \end{array}$ $\begin{array}{r} 12 \\ -\ 8 \\ \hline \end{array}$ $\begin{array}{r} 12 \\ -\ 4 \\ \hline \end{array}$ $\begin{array}{r} 11 \\ -\ 9 \\ \hline \end{array}$ $\begin{array}{r} 11 \\ -\ 2 \\ \hline \end{array}$

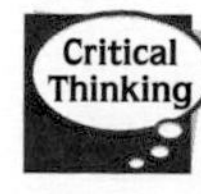

How do you use $11 - 5 = 6$ to help you subtract $11 - 6$?

Try These!

Subtract.

1

11	11
− 9	− 2
2	9

2

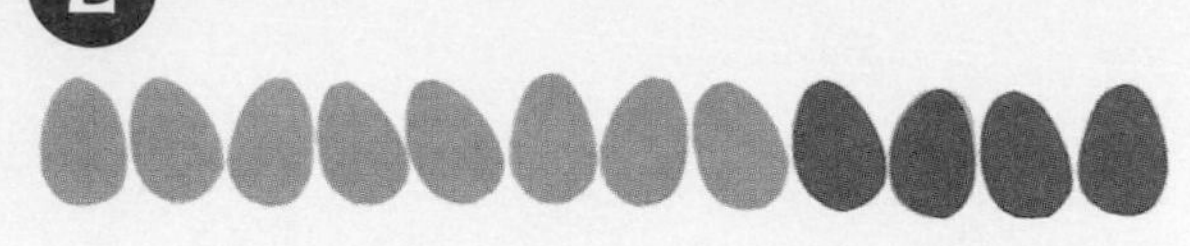

12	12
− 4	− 8

3

12	13	12¢	11	12	11¢
− 7	− 4	− 8¢	− 4	− 3	− 2¢

4

11	12	11¢	13¢	13¢	11
− 5	− 5	− 7¢	− 8¢	− 5¢	− 6

Solve.

Workspace

5 12 gulls were walking on the beach.
5 gulls flew away.
How many gulls are left on the beach? ____ gulls

6 11 puffins were on a rock.
2 dove into the water.
How many puffins are left on the rock? ____ puffins

At Home: We learned about related facts. Have your child find the related subtraction facts in exercise 4 above.

Name

More Subtracting

	15	15
	− 6	− 9
	9	6

Subtract.
Use counters if you want to.

1	17 − 8 = 9	17 − 9 = 8	14 − 6	14 − 8	15 − 7	15 − 8
2	14 − 5	14 − 9	16 − 7	16 − 9	13 − 4	13 − 9
3	11 − 3	11 − 8	13 − 8	13 − 5	15 − 9	15 − 6

Which subtraction facts do not have related subtraction facts? Why?

Try These!

Subtract.

1

14	14
− 6	− 8
8	6

2

13	13
− 7	− 6

3

16	17	16	14¢	15	18
− 7	− 8	− 9	− 8¢	− 7	− 9

4

15	17	14¢	14	16	14
− 8	− 9	− 6¢	− 9	− 8	− 5

Solve.

5 Kate has 14 shells.
8 of the shells are white.
How many shells are not white?

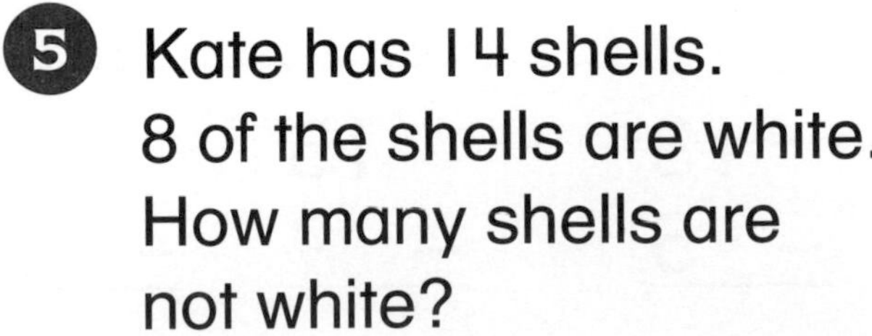

____ shells

6 Write a subtraction word problem. Have a partner solve it.

Use your own paper.

Ask your child how to solve problem 5 above.

Name

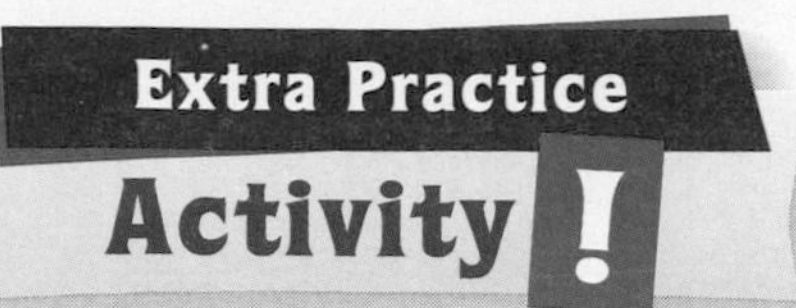

Ocean Colors

Subtract. Color to match differences.

5	6	7	8	9
yellow	red	orange	green	blue

$10 - 2$

$11 - 2$

$15 - 7$

$12 - 3$

$12 - 4$

$18 - 9$

$11 - 3$

$14 - 7 =$

$12 - 6 =$

$15 - 9 =$

$9 - 0$

$12 - 7$

$14 - 5 =$

$11 - 4 =$

$10 - 1 =$

$14 - 8$

$16 - 9 =$

$13 - 6$

$11 - 5$

$13 - 8$

$8 - 0$

$13 - 4$

$16 - 8$

$13 - 5$

$16 - 7$

$17 - 8$

$15 - 6$

$11 - 6 =$

$17 - 9$

$14 - 6$

$14 - 9 =$

$11 - 2$

Subtract.

1	11 − 4 7	12 − 5	18 − 9	15 − 7	
2	16 − 8	13 − 4	12¢ − 4¢	17 − 9	14 − 5
3	15 − 9	13 − 6	14 − 7	12 − 3	11¢ − 5¢
4	16 − 9	12 − 6	17 − 8	15¢ − 8¢	15 − 6
5	14 − 6	13¢ − 5¢	14 − 9	11 − 2	16 − 7

Solve.

Workspace

6 12 fish are in a cave.
3 swim away.
How many fish are left? ____ fish

7 13 sea turtles are on the beach.
5 walk into the water.
How many sea turtles
are left on the beach? ____ sea turtles

Name ______________________________

Midchapter Review

1 Find the sum and difference.

$$\begin{array}{r} 6 \\ +\ 6 \\ \hline \end{array} \qquad \begin{array}{r} 12 \\ -\ 6 \\ \hline \end{array}$$

2 Add.

$$\begin{array}{r} 7 \\ +\ 8 \\ \hline \end{array}$$

What doubles fact can help you do this addition? Why? ______________________________

____

3 $\begin{array}{r} 9 \\ +\ 7 \\ \hline \end{array}$ **4** $\begin{array}{r} 5 \\ +\ 8 \\ \hline \end{array}$ **5** $\begin{array}{r} 8¢ \\ +\ 6¢ \\ \hline \end{array}$ **6** $\begin{array}{r} 4 \\ 3 \\ +\ 4 \\ \hline \end{array}$

Subtract.

7 $\begin{array}{r} 12 \\ -\ 8 \\ \hline \end{array}$ **8** $\begin{array}{r} 15 \\ -\ 7 \\ \hline \end{array}$ **9** $\begin{array}{r} 11¢ \\ -\ 5¢ \\ \hline \end{array}$ **10** $\begin{array}{r} 17 \\ -\ 9 \\ \hline \end{array}$

Show how you use strategies to add and subtract.

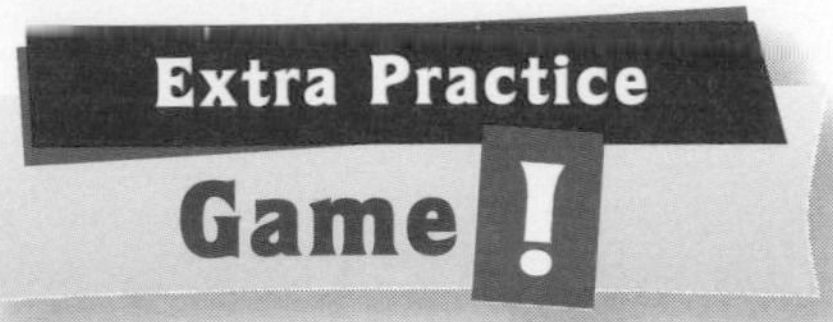

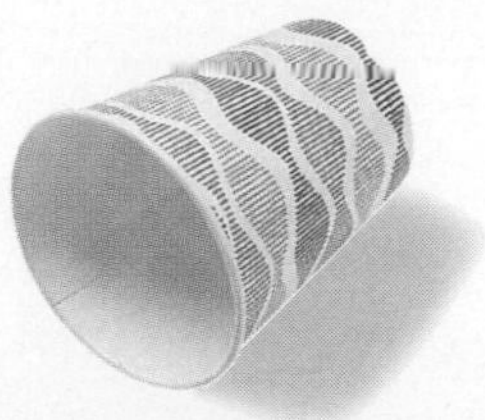

Fill the Fish Tank

You and your partner need 18 counters and a cup.

Take turns.

- ▶ Put some counters in the cup.
- ▶ Shake and spill.
- ▶ Write the addition and subtraction.
- ▶ Your partner finds the sum and the difference.

Play until you fill the fish tank.

+	−	+	−
+ ____	− ____	+ ____	− ____
+ ____	− ____	+ ____	− ____
+ ____	− ____	+ ____	− ____

Name

How Many Arms or Legs?

Listen to *Splash*.

How many legs does a turtle have?
How many legs do 2 turtles have?

Working Together

These animals have many arms.

- You and your partner choose ★ or octopus.
- Draw 3 of the animal you chose.
- Find the total number of arms.

Starfish

Octopus

Show your work here.

____ arms

Decision Making

1. Find how many legs for each number of turtles. Complete the table.

Number of Turtles	1	2	3	4	5
Number of Legs	4	8			

2. Choose another animal. Complete the table.

Number of ___________	1	2	3	4	5
Number of ___________					

Write a report.

3. Tell how you completed the tables.

4. Describe any patterns you see in the tables.

More to Investigate

PREDICT How many starfish are in a group with a total of 20 arms?

EXPLORE Try it. Use counters, draw pictures, or make a table.

FIND Find how many starfish are in the group.

Name

Problem-Solving Strategy

Choose the Operation

Read | Plan | Solve | Look Back

Read Meg has 8 goldfish. Alex has 5 goldfish. How many more goldfish does Meg have than Alex?

What do you know?

What do you need to find out?

Plan Do you add or subtract to compare? add 

Solve

What is the answer? ____ goldfish

Look Back Does your answer make sense? Why?

Choose **add** or **subtract.** Solve.

Workspace

1. There are 3 goldfish in a bowl. There are 9 snails in the bowl. How many more snails than goldfish are in the bowl?

add subtract ____ snails

Try These!

Workspace

Choose **add** or **subtract.** Solve.

1. Lee buys a shell for 7¢.
Then she buys a rock for 5¢.
How much money does Lee spend?

add subtract ____¢

2. There are 13 fish in a tank.
9 are goldfish and the rest are angelfish.
How many angelfish are in the tank?

add subtract ____ angelfish

3. Vic buys 12 fish. Joe buys 6 fish.
How many more fish does
Vic buy than Joe?

add subtract ____ fish

4. The store has 8 large fish tanks
and 6 small fish tanks.
How many fish tanks are in the store?

add subtract ____ fish tanks

At Home: Ask your child to explain how to solve these problems.

Name ____________________

Add and Subtract

$$\begin{array}{r} 8 \\ +\ 7 \\ \hline 15 \end{array} \qquad \begin{array}{r} 15 \\ -\ 7 \\ \hline 8 \end{array}$$

How are these facts the same?
How are these facts different?

Find the sum and difference.

1 

$$\begin{array}{r} 4 \\ +\ 9 \\ \hline 13 \end{array} \qquad \begin{array}{r} 13 \\ -\ 9 \\ \hline 4 \end{array}$$

2  

$$\begin{array}{r} 7 \\ +\ 5 \\ \hline \end{array} \qquad \begin{array}{r} 12 \\ -\ 7 \\ \hline \end{array}$$

3  

$$\begin{array}{r} 8 \\ +\ 6 \\ \hline \end{array} \qquad \begin{array}{r} 14 \\ -\ 6 \\ \hline \end{array}$$

4  

$$\begin{array}{r} 8 \\ +\ 3 \\ \hline \end{array} \qquad \begin{array}{r} 11 \\ -\ 3 \\ \hline \end{array}$$

5  

$$\begin{array}{r} 9 \\ +\ 7 \\ \hline \end{array} \qquad \begin{array}{r} 16 \\ -\ 7 \\ \hline \end{array}$$

6    

$$\begin{array}{r} 8 \\ +\ 9 \\ \hline \end{array} \qquad \begin{array}{r} 17 \\ -\ 8 \\ \hline \end{array}$$

Try These!

Add or subtract. Use 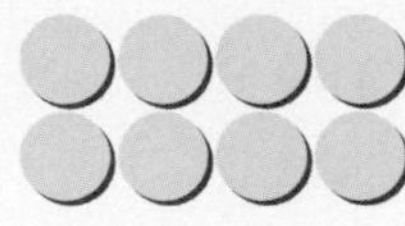 if you want to.

1 

```
  4      12
+ 8    -  8
 12       4
```

2 

```
  7      11
+ 4    -  4
```

3

```
  8     13      9     15     3¢     11¢
+ 5   -  5    + 6   -  6   + 8¢   -  8¢
```

4

```
  5     14     9¢     16¢     3     12
+ 9   -  9   + 7¢   -  7¢   + 9   -  9
```

5

```
  9     18      6     11     7¢     13¢
+ 9   -  9    + 5   -  5   + 6¢   -  6¢
```

Mixed Review

Write the time.

6 

___:___

7 

___:___

8 

___:___

Ask your child to write a subtraction fact related to 3 + 7 = 10.

Name ______________________

Fact Families

5 + 7 = 12 12 − 7 = 5

7 + 5 = 12 12 − 5 = 7

Why do you think this is called a **fact family**?

Complete the fact family.

1

2 + 9 = 11

9 + 2 = 11

11 − 9 = 2

11 − 2 = 9

2

7 + 8 = ___

8 + 7 = ___

15 − 8 = ___

15 − 7 = ___

3

5 + 8 = ___

8 + 5 = ___

13 − 8 = ___

13 − 5 = ___

4
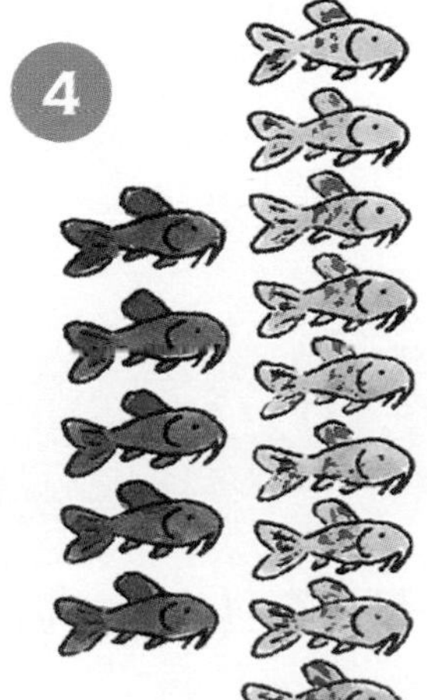

5 + 9 = ___

9 + ___ = 14

14 − 9 = ___

14 − ___ = 9

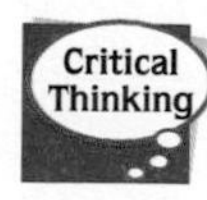

How many facts are in the 7 + 7 = 14 family? Why?

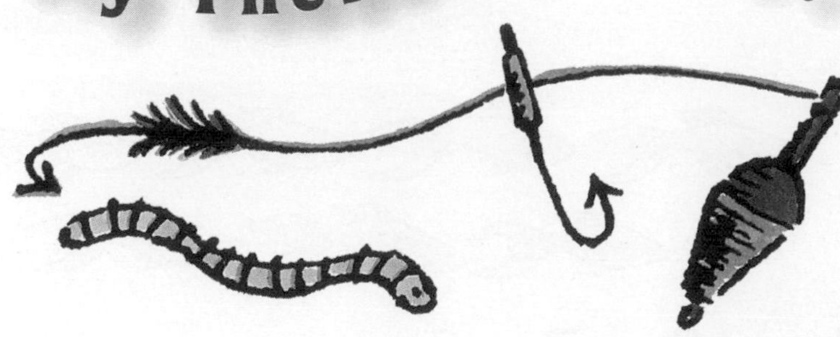

Complete the fact family.

1. $6 + 8 = 14$

   $8 + 6 = 14$

   $14 - 8 = 6$

   $14 - 6 = 8$

2. $7 + 9 = \_\_\_$

   $9 + \_\_\_ = 16$

   $16 - 9 = \_\_\_$

   $16 - 7 = \_\_\_$

3. $4 + 8 = \_\_\_$

   $\_\_\_ + 4 = 12$

   $12 - \_\_\_ = 4$

   $12 - 4 = \_\_\_$

4. $8 + 9 = \_\_\_$

   $9 + \_\_\_ = 17$

   $17 - 9 = \_\_\_$

   $17 - \_\_\_ = 9$

More to Explore Number Sense

Use the numbers 4, 7, 11 to write a fact family.

$\_\_\_ + \_\_\_ = \_\_\_$ $\_\_\_ - \_\_\_ = \_\_\_$

$\_\_\_ + \_\_\_ = \_\_\_$ $\_\_\_ - \_\_\_ = \_\_\_$

At Home: Ask your child to complete the fact family for $11 - 3 = 8$.

Name ____________________

Choose a Strategy

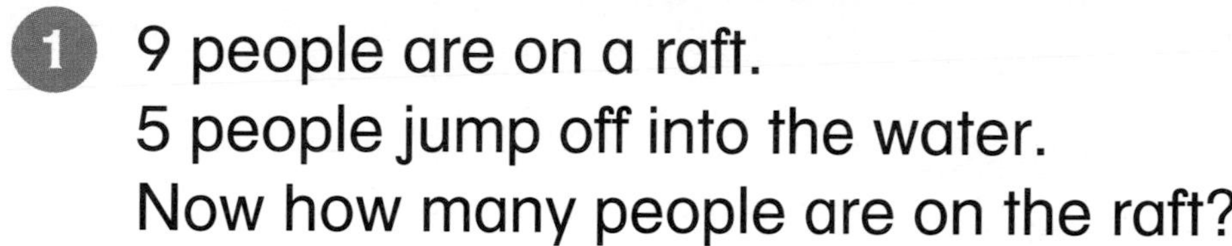

Solve.

1. 9 people are on a raft.
5 people jump off into the water.
Now how many people are on the raft?

____ people

2. 9 people are on a raft.
5 more people get on the raft.
Now how many people are on the raft?

____ people

Why would you subtract to solve problem 1 and add to solve problem 2?

3. Kyle has these clothes.
How many ways can he dress?
Color to show the different ways.

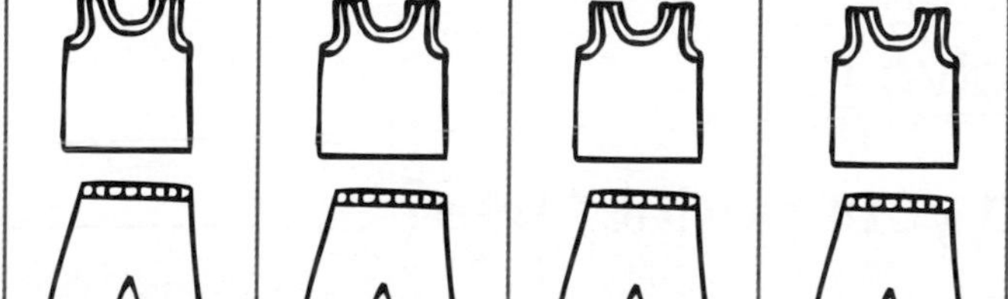

Kyle can dress

in ____ ways.

McGraw-Hill School Division

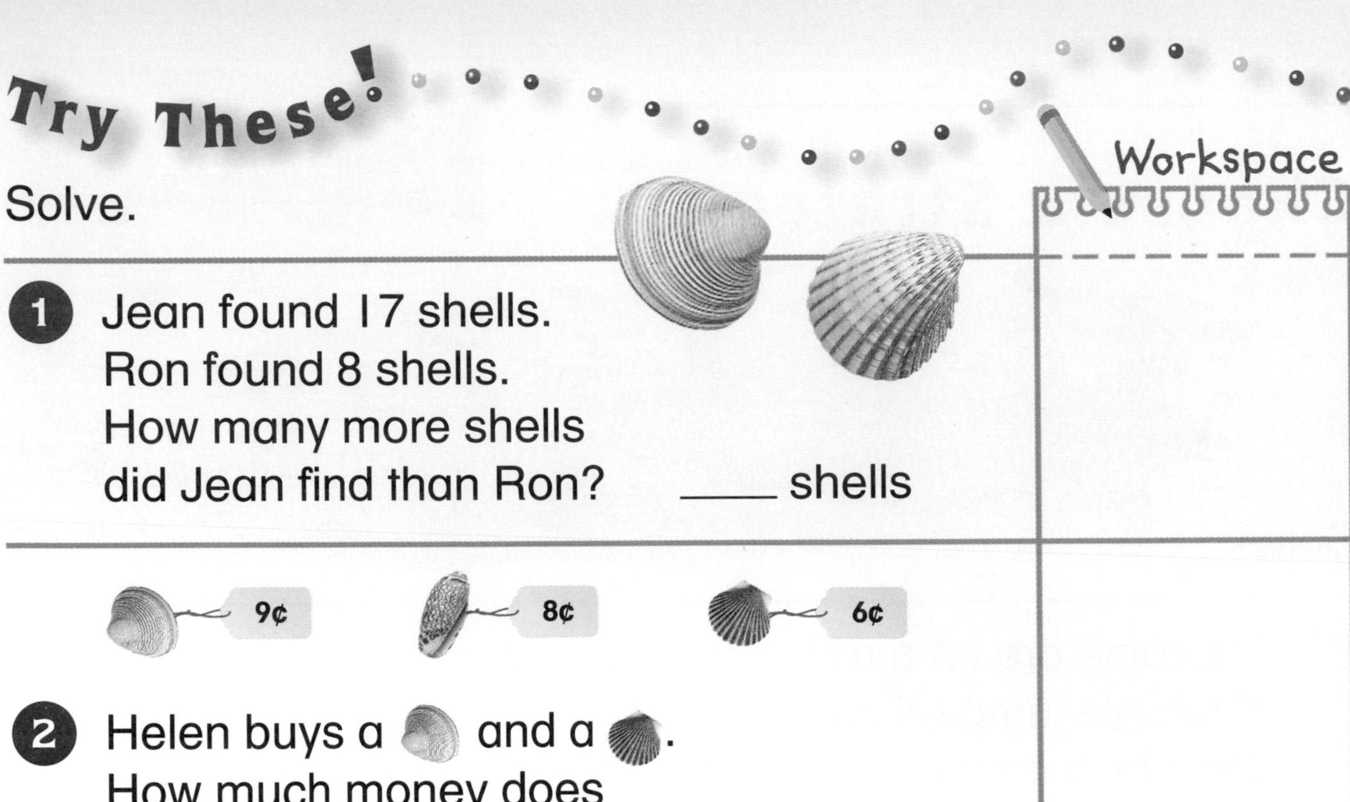

Try These!

Solve.

1. Jean found 17 shells.
Ron found 8 shells.
How many more shells
did Jean find than Ron? ____ shells

2. Helen buys a [shell] and a [shell].
How much money does
she spend? ____ ¢

Write and Share

STUDENT TO STUDENT

Bobby wrote this problem.

Ten people were having pizza and two joined in. Now how many people are there?

Bobby Wiggins
Mandarin Oaks School
Jacksonville, Florida

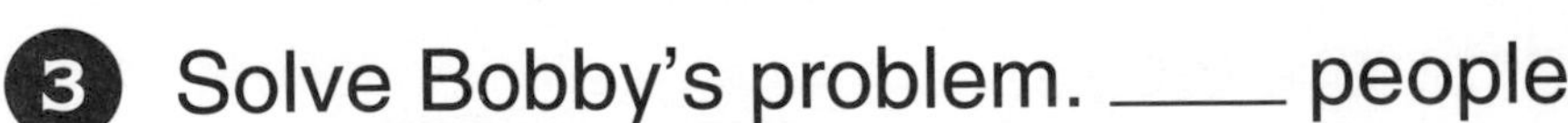

3. Solve Bobby's problem. ____ people

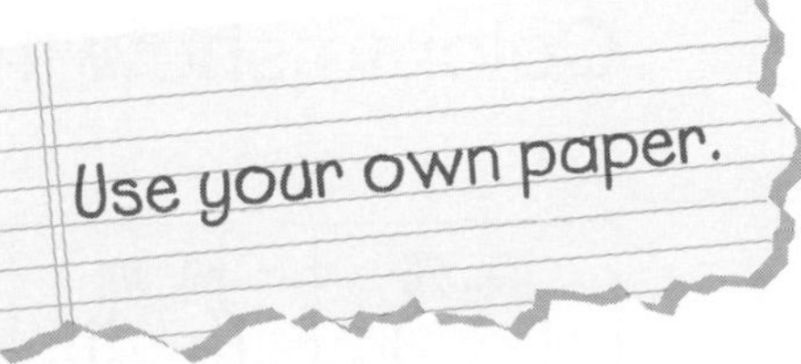

4. Write a word problem.
Have a partner solve it.

What strategy did your partner use? ______________

What strategy would you use? ______________

Have your child tell how to solve problem 2 above.

Name

Chapter Review

Find the sum or difference.

1. $\begin{array}{r} 7 \\ +\ 7 \\ \hline \end{array}$

2. $\begin{array}{r} 14 \\ -\ \ 7 \\ \hline \end{array}$

3. $\begin{array}{r} 8 \\ +\ 8 \\ \hline \end{array}$

4. $\begin{array}{r} 8 \\ +\ 9 \\ \hline \end{array}$

5. $\begin{array}{r} 11 \\ -\ \ 4 \\ \hline \end{array}$

6. $\begin{array}{r} 11 \\ -\ \ 7 \\ \hline \end{array}$

Complete the fact family.

7. 

7 + 8 = ____

8 + 7 = ____

15 − 8 = ____

15 − 7 = ____

Add.

8. $\begin{array}{r} 3 \\ +\ 8 \\ \hline \end{array}$

9. $\begin{array}{r} 9 \\ +\ 5 \\ \hline \end{array}$

10. $\begin{array}{r} 8 \\ +\ 5 \\ \hline \end{array}$

11. $\begin{array}{r} 9¢ \\ +\ 7¢ \\ \hline \end{array}$

12. $\begin{array}{r} 3 \\ 7 \\ +\ 3 \\ \hline \end{array}$

Subtract.

13. $\begin{array}{r} 12 \\ -\ \ 6 \\ \hline \end{array}$

14. $\begin{array}{r} 16 \\ -\ \ 9 \\ \hline \end{array}$

15. $\begin{array}{r} 15 \\ -\ \ 6 \\ \hline \end{array}$

16. $\begin{array}{r} 13 \\ -\ \ 9 \\ \hline \end{array}$

17. $\begin{array}{r} 11¢ \\ -\ \ 5¢ \\ \hline \end{array}$

Workspace

Solve.

18 There are 17 fish in a cave.
8 fish swim away.
How many fish are left in the cave?

____ fish

Choose **add** or **subtract.** Solve.

19 Ben had 12 fish. He gave 8 fish to Kim. Now how many fish does Ben have?

add subtract

____ fish

20 Eric has 5 brown shells and 9 white shells. How many shells does Eric have in all?

add subtract

____ shells

What Do You Think?

Which strategy do you like to use?
☑ Check one.

☐ Adding 9 ☐ Subtracting 9 ☐ Fact families

Why? ______________________

Journal

Tell what you learned about adding and subtracting.

Name ______________________________

Chapter Test

Find the sum and difference.

1

$$\begin{array}{r} 5 \\ +5 \\ \hline \end{array} \qquad \begin{array}{r} 10 \\ -5 \\ \hline \end{array}$$

2

$$\begin{array}{r} 9 \\ +9 \\ \hline \end{array} \qquad \begin{array}{r} 18 \\ -9 \\ \hline \end{array}$$

Complete the fact family.

3

$7 + 6 =$ ___

$6 + 7 =$ ___

$13 - 7 =$ ___

$13 - 6 =$ ___

4

$8 + 3 =$ ___

$3 + 8 =$ ___

$11 - 8 =$ ___

$11 - 3 =$ ___

Add.

5

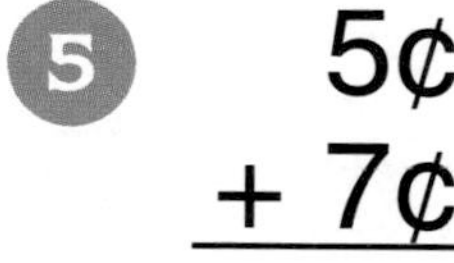

$$\begin{array}{r} 5¢ \\ +7¢ \\ \hline \end{array}$$

6

$$\begin{array}{r} 9 \\ +6 \\ \hline \end{array}$$

Subtract.

7

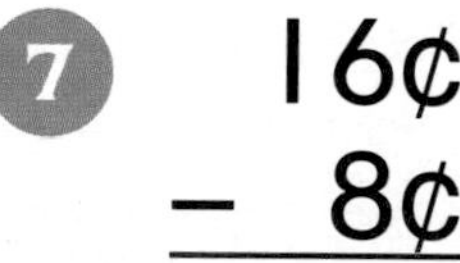

$$\begin{array}{r} 16¢ \\ -8¢ \\ \hline \end{array}$$

8

$$\begin{array}{r} 17 \\ -9 \\ \hline \end{array}$$

Choose *add* or *subtract*. Solve.

9 Lucas has 9 fish. He catches 5 more. How many fish does Lucas have now?

add subtract

___ fish

10 Lily sees 12 pink fish and 8 red fish. How many more pink fish than red fish does Lily see?

add subtract

___ pink fish

Performance Assessment

What Did You Learn?

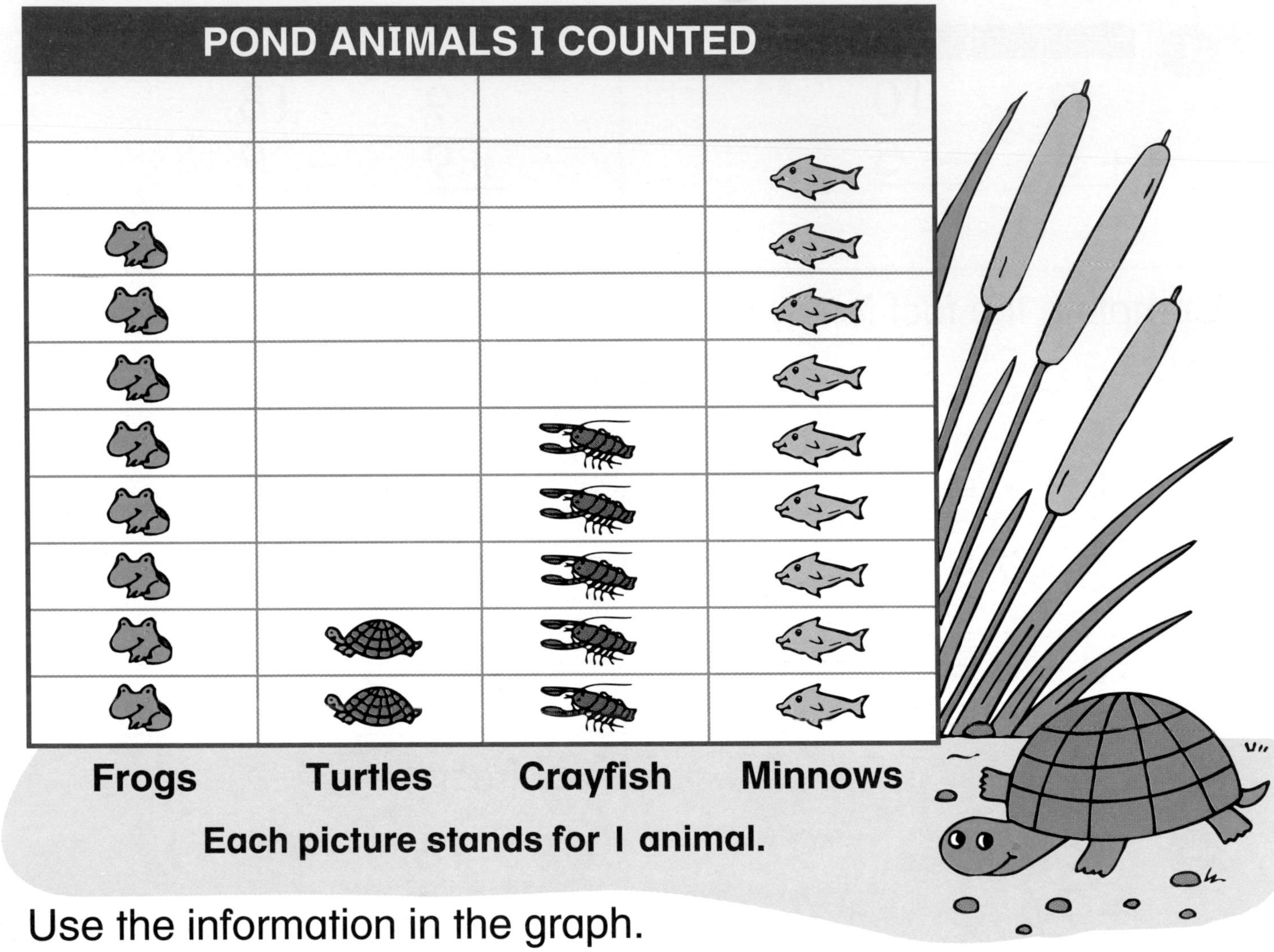

POND ANIMALS I COUNTED

Frogs **Turtles** **Crayfish** **Minnows**

Each picture stands for 1 animal.

Use the information in the graph.

1. Make up a problem that uses addition.
   Solve it.

   ____

2. Make up a problem that uses subtraction.
   Solve it.

   ____

You may want to put this page in your portfolio.

Math Connection

Calculator

Name ___________________

Add and Subtract

You can use a calculator to help solve problems.

Bob has 8 books about fish.
His sister Lee has 6 books about fish.
How many books about fish do they have altogether? ____ books

Press  ON/C. Press 8 + 6 =.
Write the sum as the answer to the problem.

Bob has 8 books about fish.
His sister Lee has 6 books about fish.
How many more fish books does Bob have than Lee? ____ books

Press   ON/C. Press 8 − 6 =.
Write the difference as the answer to the problem.

Write your own word problems.
Use a calculator to solve.

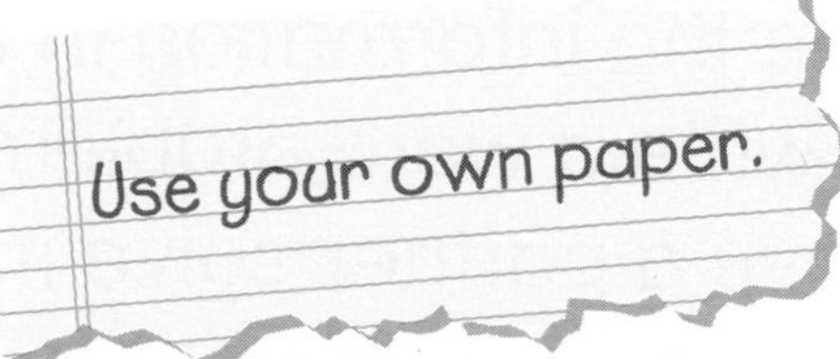

Curriculum Connection

Science

Beachcombing

Lisa and her family went to the beach.
This is what they found.

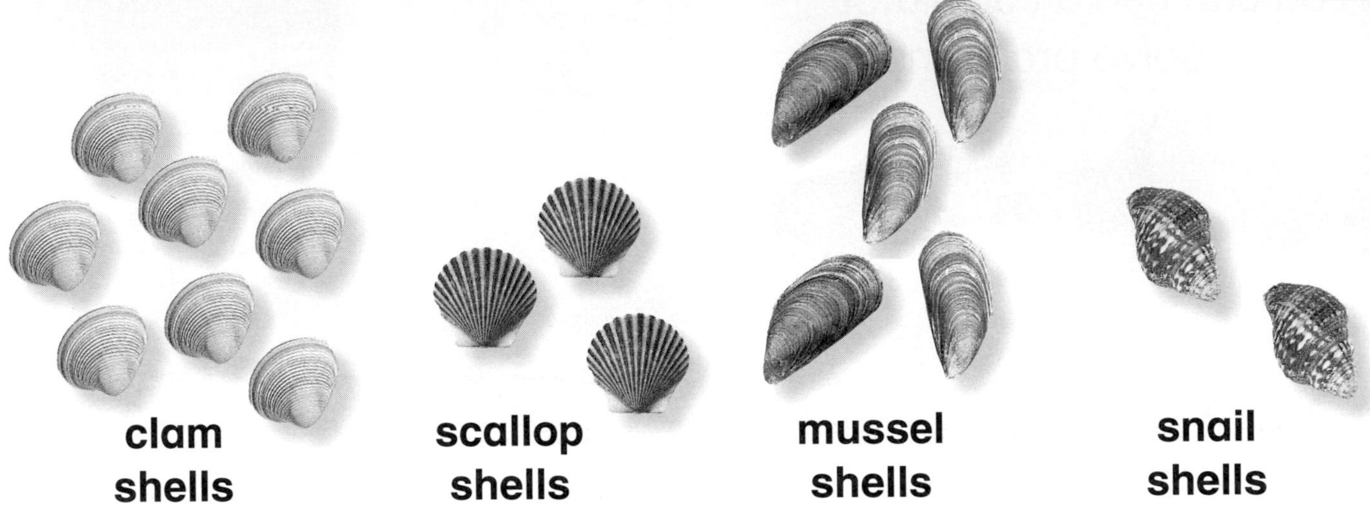

Use this information to complete the graph.

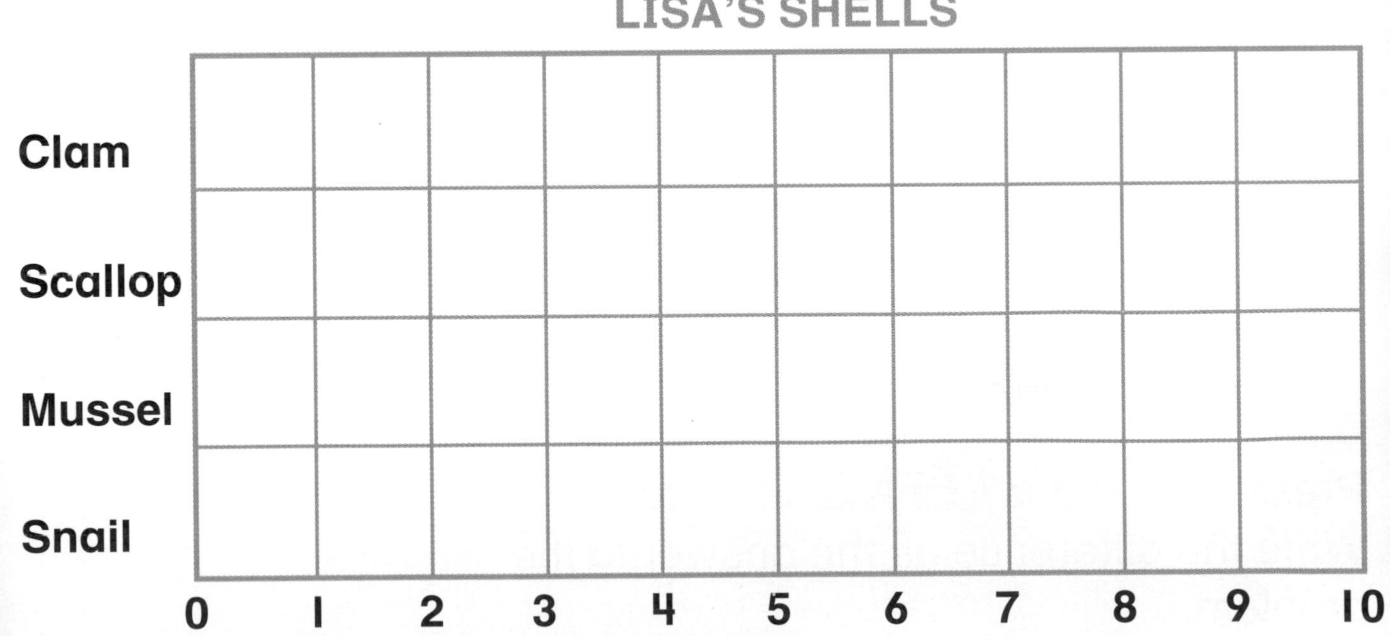

Use the information in the graph
to write a word problem.
Have a partner solve it.

Name ___

Hidden Pennies

PLAYERS 2

MATERIALS 18 pennies, 2 cups, pencil and paper

DIRECTIONS Put 18 pennies in the middle of the table.
Each player takes some pennies and puts them in a cup.

Use the pennies in your cup and the pennies left on the table to find out how many pennies your partner has.

Score 2 points for a correct answer.
Continue playing until you have 18 points altogether.

Play this game with your child to practice addition and to help him or her develop number sense.

Dear Family,

We are beginning a new chapter in mathematics. We will be learning about measurement. Some of the measurement tools that we will use are rulers, cups, and thermometers.

We will also be talking about dinosaurs. Please help me complete this interview.

Your child,

____
Signature

Interview

Which measuring tools do you use?
(You may check more than one.)

- ☐ Measuring spoons and cups
- ☐ Ruler
- ☐ Measuring tape
- ☐ Scale
- ☐ Thermometer
- ☐ Other ______________________

____

Dinosaurs and Me

Exploring Measurement

CHAPTER 11

Listen to the story *The Dinosaur Who Lived in My Backyard.*

Tell what you know about dinosaurs.

Name

What Do You Know?

1 Draw a line around the dinosaur that is longer.

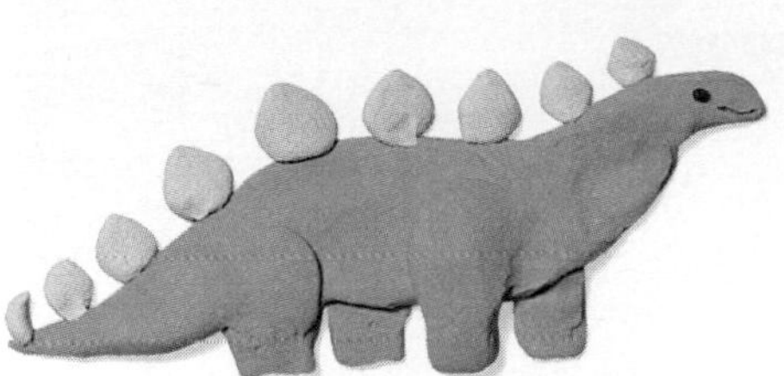

2 Draw a line around the dinosaur that is shortest.

3 Mark the object that is heavier.

4 Mark the object that is lighter.

How do you know which object is heavier?

Draw a picture that is longer than your pencil. Tell how you know the picture is longer.

Name

Explore Activity

Length

Working Together

You and your partners need 10 .

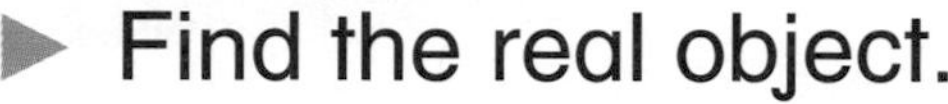

- Find the real object.
- **Measure** with .
- Write how **long** it is.

1

about ____ 

2

about ____ 

3

about ____ 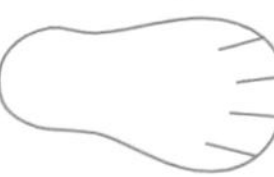

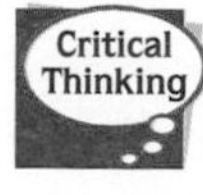

Does it make a difference if you use the footprints like this: ? Explain.

Try These!

Use your [footprint].

Find the real object.
Measure how long it is.

about ____ [footprints]

about ____ [footprints]

Do you need more dinosaur footprints or more of your footprints to measure the chalkboard?

We are learning how to measure length. Ask your child to show you how to measure an object using a footprint.

Name ______________________________

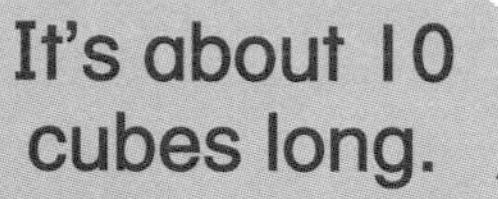

Working Together

You and your partner need 20 cubes.

- Find the real object.
- Estimate how many cubes long it is.
- Measure how long it is.

How can you use cubes to measure?

1. 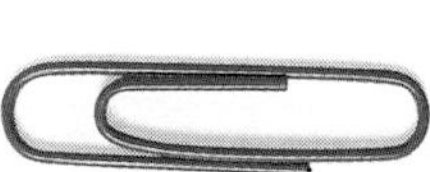

   estimate about ____ cubes

   measure about ____ cubes

2. 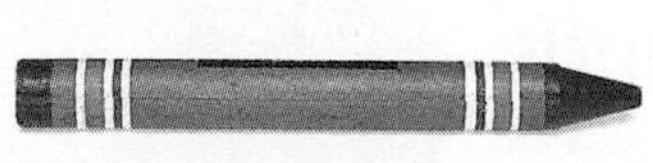

   estimate about ____ cubes

   measure about ____ cubes

estimate about ____ cubes

measure about ____ cubes

Try These!

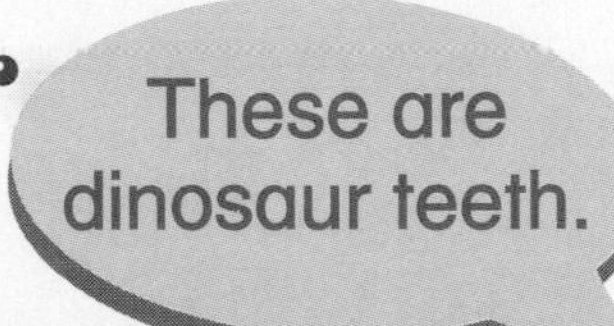

Use .

Estimate how long. Then measure.

1 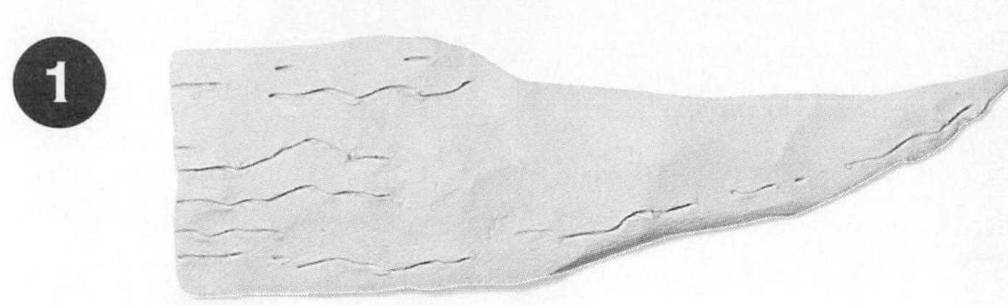

estimate about ____

measure about ____

2 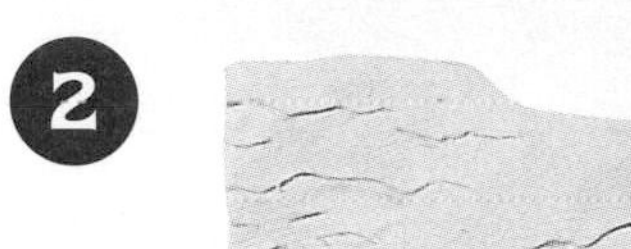

estimate about ____

measure about ____

3 

estimate about ____

measure about ____

4  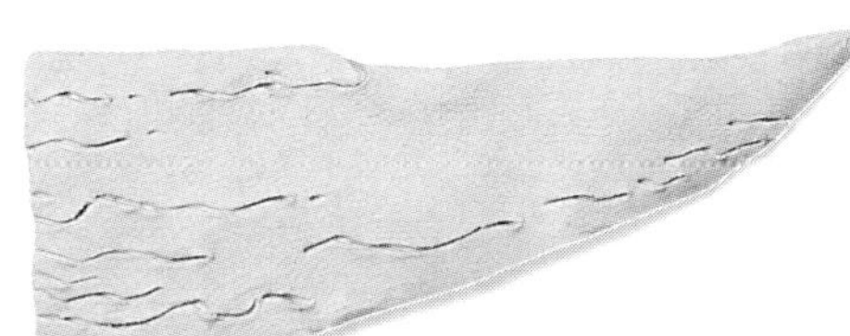

estimate about ____

measure about ____

Cultural Connection

England

People measure the height of a horse in hands.

Use your hands. Find the real object.
Measure the height.

 about ____ hands  about ____ hands

Name ______________________

Inch

You need a [inch ruler].

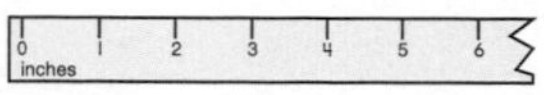

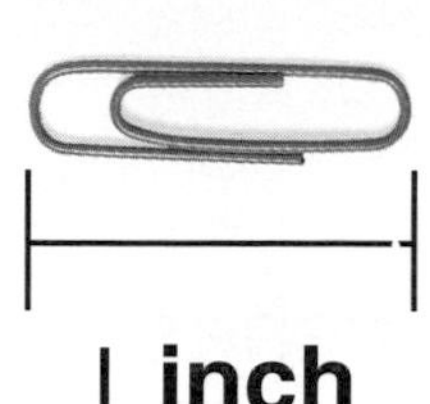

I **inch**

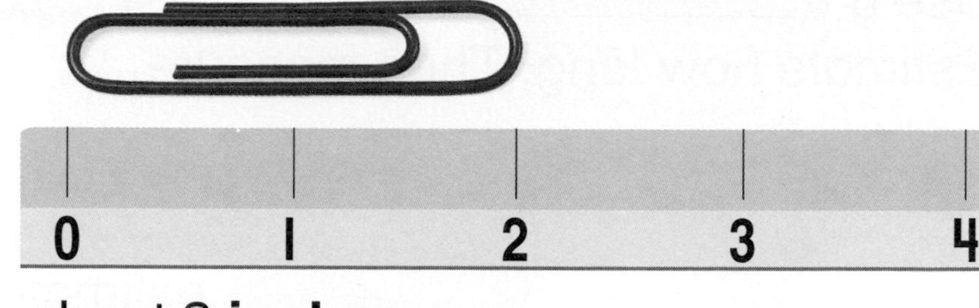

about 2 **inches**

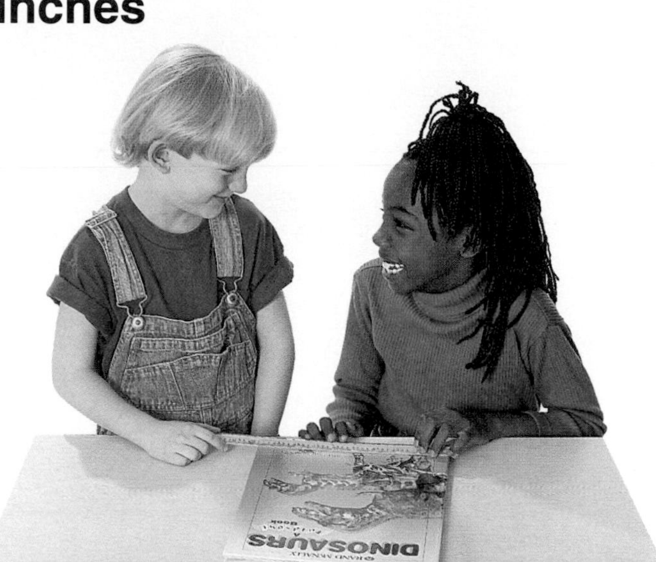

- Find the real object.
- Estimate how many inches long it is.
- Then measure.

	Estimate	Measure
	about ____ inches	about ____ inches
	about ____ inches	about ____ inches
	about ____ inches	about ____ inches
	about ____ inches	about ____ inches

Which objects are longer than your hand? Which objects are shorter?

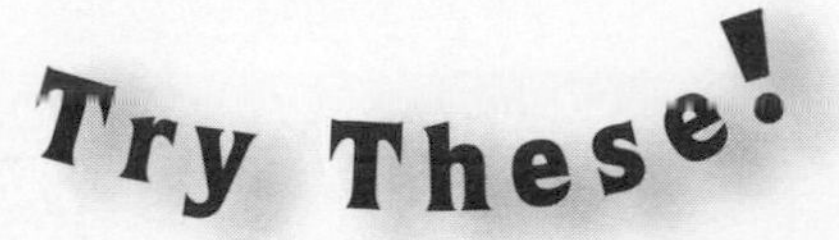

Use a [ruler].
Estimate how long. Then measure.

estimate about ____ inches

measure about 3 inches

estimate about ____ inches

measure about ____ inches

estimate about ____ inches

measure about ____ inches

estimate about ____ inches

measure about ____ inches

Mixed Review

Add or subtract.

5.

8	11	16	9	6	17
+ 6	− 5	− 8	+ 8	+ 7	− 9

At Home: Ask your child to use a ruler and show you how to measure for exercises 1 to 4 above.

Name

Foot

Working Together

You and your partner need a [ruler].

- Find things that look about I **foot** long.
- Measure each object.
- Draw or write to show things that are about I foot long.

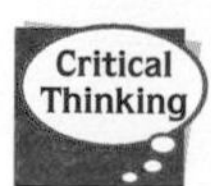

What did you find that is more than I foot long? What is less than I foot?

Try These!

Use a ruler.
Find the real object.
Estimate how long and record.
Measure and record.

		Estimate	Measure
1	pencil	less than 1 foot more than 1 foot	less than 1 foot more than 1 foot
2	book	less than 1 foot more than 1 foot	less than 1 foot more than 1 foot
3	cabinet	less than 1 foot more than 1 foot	less than 1 foot more than 1 foot
4	computer	less than 1 foot more than 1 foot	less than 1 foot more than 1 foot
5	shoe	less than 1 foot more than 1 foot	less than 1 foot more than 1 foot

Show and write about how you measure things.

Ask your child to show you an object that is more than 1 foot long and an object that is less than 1 foot long.

Name ____________________

Centimeter

You need a .

I **centimeter**
I **cm**

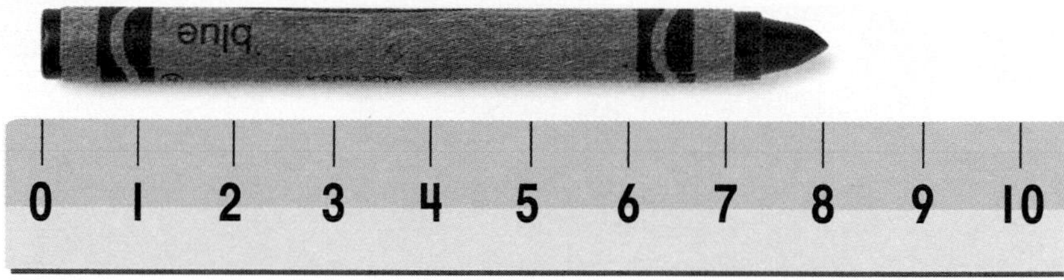

The crayon is about 8 **centimeters** long.

- Find the real object.
- Estimate how many centimeters long it is.
- Then measure.

	Estimate	Measure
	about ____ cm	about ____ cm
	about ____ cm	about ____ cm
	about ____ cm	about ____ cm
	about ____ cm	about ____ cm

Try These!

Use a 0 1 2 3 4 5 6 7 8 9 10 11 12 13 14 15 16 centimeters.

Estimate how long. Then measure.

1. 

estimate about ____ cm

measure about 7 cm

2. 

estimate about ____ cm

measure about ____ cm

3. 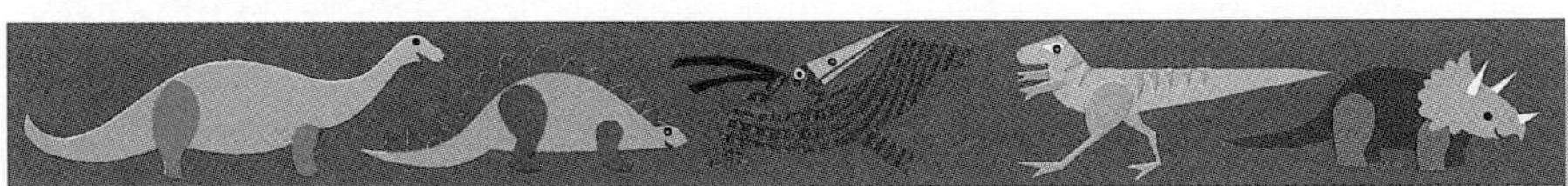

estimate about ____ cm

measure about ____ cm

4. 

estimate about ____ cm

measure about ____ cm

Mixed Review

5. Write the time.

___:___

___:___

___:___

___:___

At Home: Ask your child to use a centimeter ruler and show you how to measure some objects.

Name ______________________

Draw a Picture

Problem-Solving Strategy

Read · Plan · Solve · Look Back

You need a centimeter ruler.

Read Annie builds a fence around her toy dinosaur. It is 4 cm on one side. It is 7 cm on another side. How many centimeters around is the fence?

Plan You can **draw a picture** to solve.

Solve Draw the two missing sides. Measure each side and add the measures.

4 + 7 + 4 + 7 = 22  22 cm around

Look Back How can you check the answer?

Draw a picture to solve.

1. 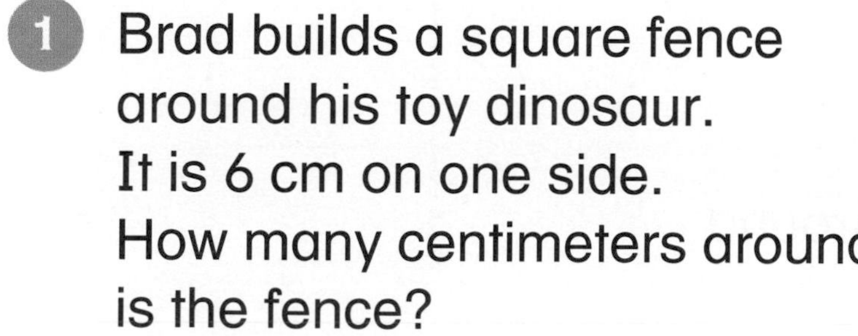
Brad builds a square fence around his toy dinosaur. It is 6 cm on one side. How many centimeters around is the fence?

___ + ___ + ___ + ___ = ___ ___ cm around

Try These!

Draw a picture to solve.

1. Luke draws a rectangle around a picture. It is 6 cm on one side. It is 3 cm on another side. How many centimeters around is the rectangle?

____ + ____ + ____ + ____ = ____ ____ cm around

2. Tess draws a triangle around a picture. One side is 5 cm. Another side is 6 cm. How many centimeters around is the triangle?

____ + ____ + ____ = ____ ____ cm around

3. Lee draws a shape with 4 sides. Two sides are 5 cm long. One side is 3 cm long. How many centimeters around is the shape?

____ + ____ + ____ + ____ = ____ ____ cm around

At Home: Ask your child to show you how to draw a picture to solve a problem.

Name

Midchapter Review

Measure how long.

Use [cube].

1. 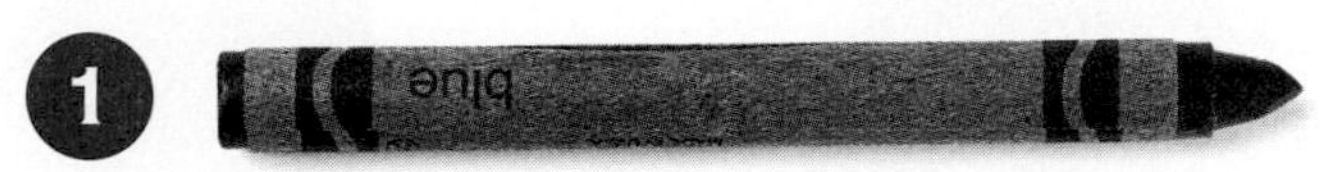

about ____ [cube]

Use a [inch ruler].

2. 

about ____ inches

Use a [centimeter ruler].

3. 

about ____ cm

Estimate how long.

4. 

less than 1 foot

more than 1 foot

Draw a picture to solve.

5. Emily builds a square fence.
It is 3 cm on one side.
How many centimeters around is the fence?

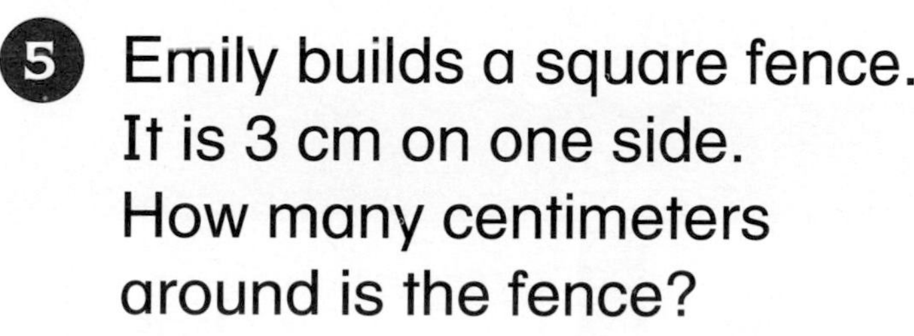

____ + ____ + ____ + ____ = ____

____ cm around

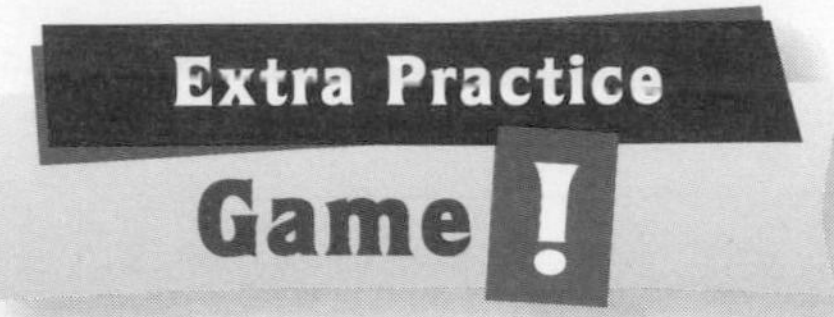

Draw Straws

You and your partner need straws, a , and a box.

Take turns.

- ▶ Put your straws in a box.
- ▶ Close your eyes. Take 1 straw.
- ▶ Measure how long. Write.
- ▶ Compare with your partner.
- ▶ Color the dinosaur if your straw is longer.

Play 3 times.

Play again. Take 1 straw.
Color the dinosaur if your straw is shorter.

Real-Life Investigation
Applying Measurement

Name

Last of the Dinosaurs

The largest living lizard is called a *komodo dragon.*

Komodo dragons are about 6 feet long and weigh about 60 pounds.

Komodo dragons live on the island of Komodo and other small islands in Indonesia.

Working Together

Your group will show how long a komodo dragon is.

You need yarn.

- Choose a starting point.
- Hold the yarn at the starting point.
- Use a ruler to measure 6 feet.
- Stretch the yarn to show the length.
- Cut the yarn at 6 feet.

Decision Making

1. How can you find out how many children long a komodo dragon is?

Write a report.

2. Tell how you found out how many children long a komodo dragon is.

3. Does a komodo dragon weigh more than you or less than you? Explain how you know.

More to Investigate

PREDICT A scelidosaurus was 12 feet long. About how many children long is that?

EXPLORE Try different ways to find out.

FIND Read a book about dinosaurs. How big was the biggest dinosaur?

Name

Explore Activity

Pound

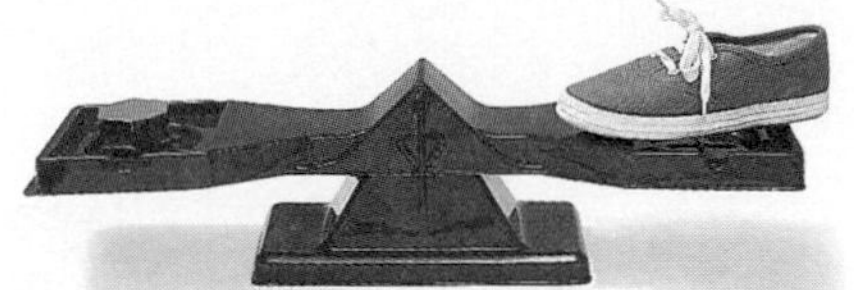
1 pound

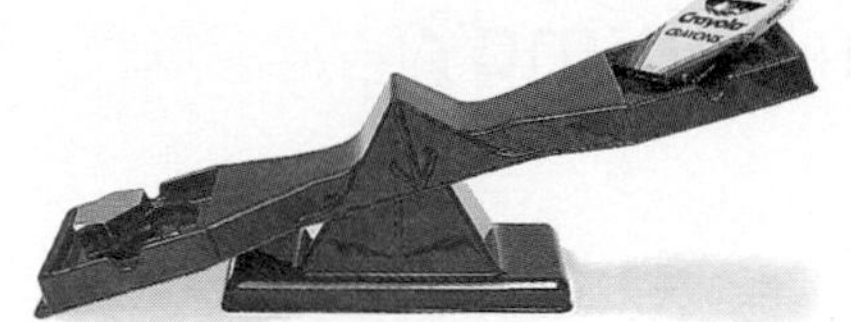

less than 1 pound

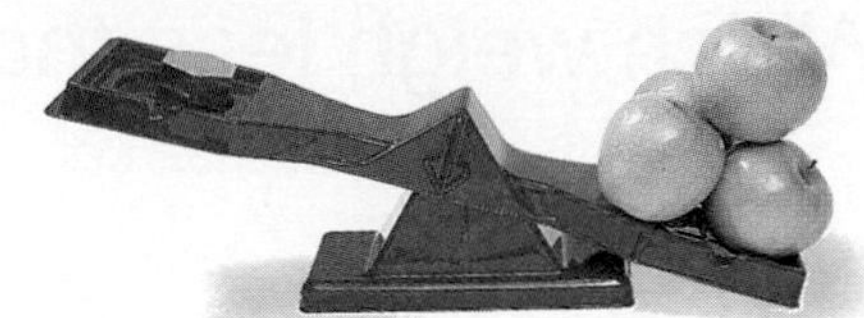
more than 1 pound

Working Together

You and your partners need a 1-pound weight and a balance.

Take turns.

- Hold the real object and the 1-pound weight.
- Estimate. Choose *more than 1 pound* or *less than 1 pound.*
- Measure and record.

	Estimate	Measure
stapler	less than 1 pound more than 1 pound	less than 1 pound more than 1 pound
ruler	less than 1 pound more than 1 pound	less than 1 pound more than 1 pound
Math book	less than 1 pound more than 1 pound	less than 1 pound more than 1 pound

Try These!

Estimate.

Which weigh less than 1 pound?

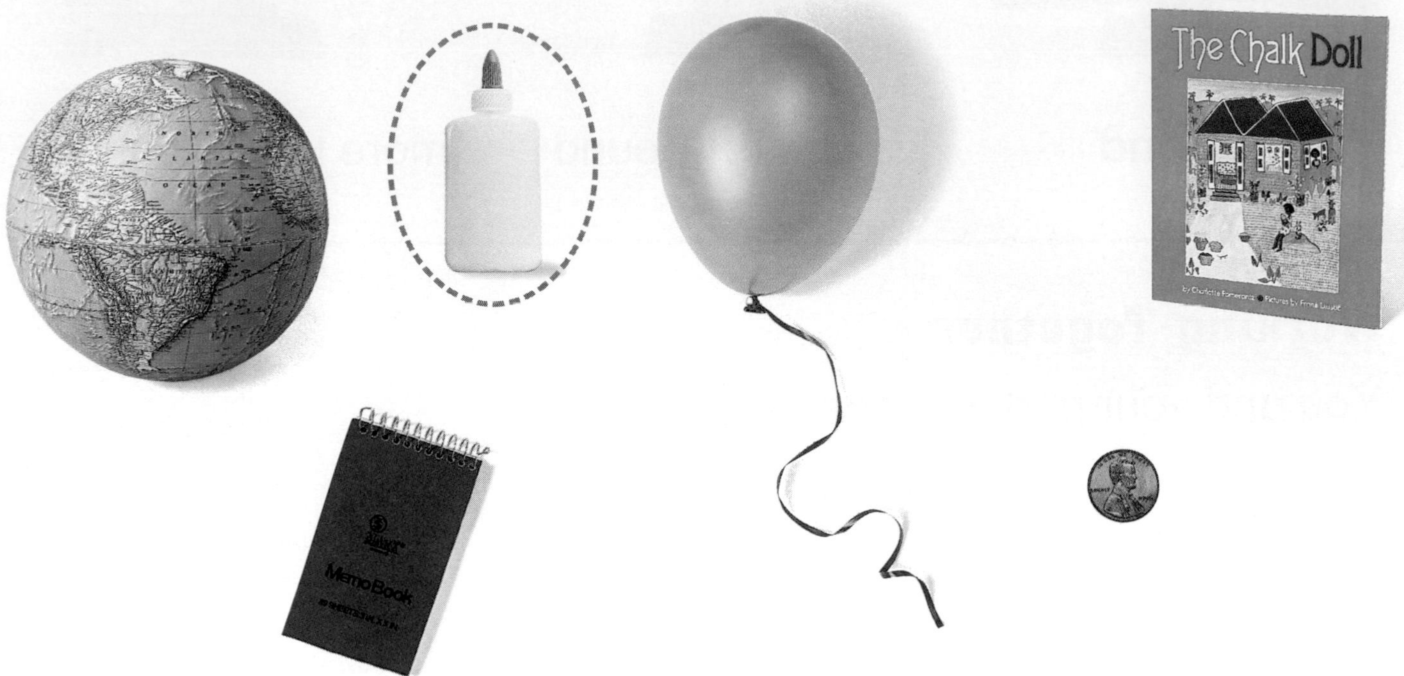

Which weigh more than 1 pound?

There are two objects.
Each weighs about 1 pound.
Draw how the balance will look.

Have your child hold two objects and tell which is heavier.

Name ___

Cup

I **cup**

Do you drink about a cup of milk or juice at lunch?

Working Together

You and your partner need a [measuring cup] and containers.

- ▶ Estimate how much a container will hold.
- ▶ Then measure.
- ▶ Draw or write.

Holds less than a cup	Holds about I cup	Holds more than I cup
spoon		

Does a cup hold more water or more juice?

Try These!

Estimate.

Color red if it holds less than 1 cup.

Color yellow if it holds more than 1 cup.

Color purple if it holds about 1 cup.

More to Explore — Measurement Sense

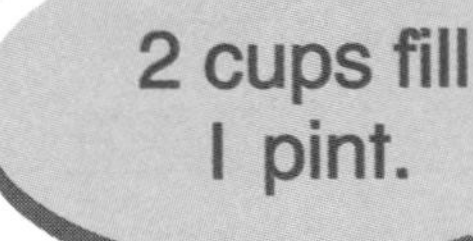

Color to show the cups you can fill.

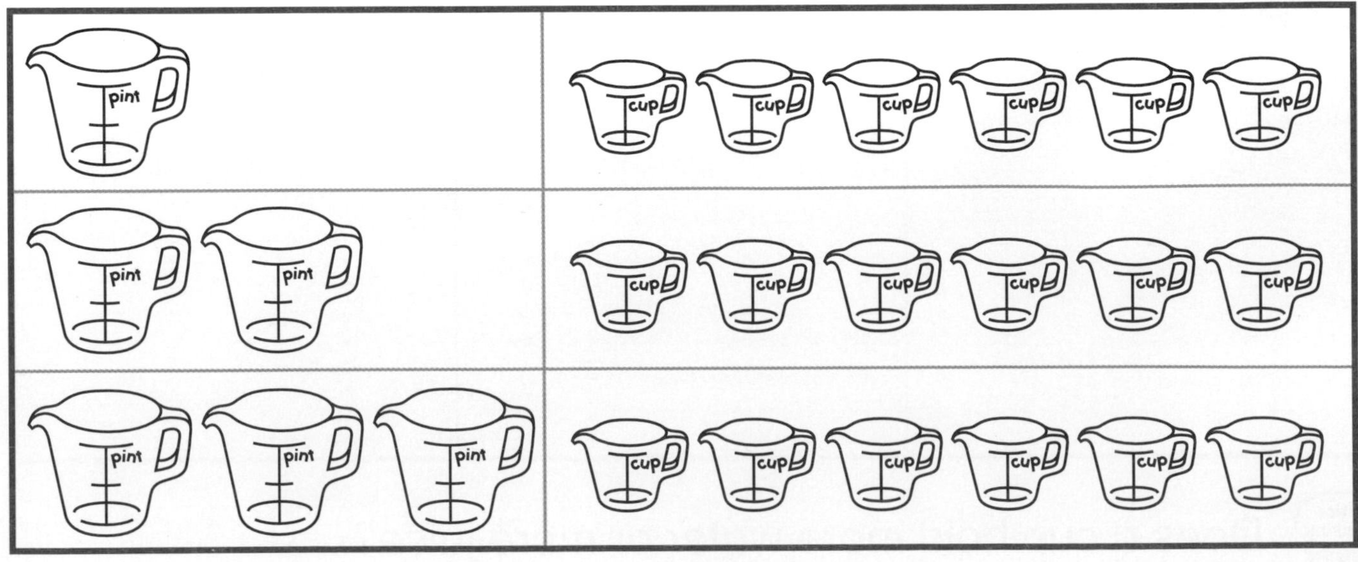

At Home: Ask your child to find a container that holds about 1 cup.

Name

Temperature

A **thermometer** measures **temperature.** Temperature is measured in **degrees.** The sign for degrees is °.

The thermometer shows 80°F.

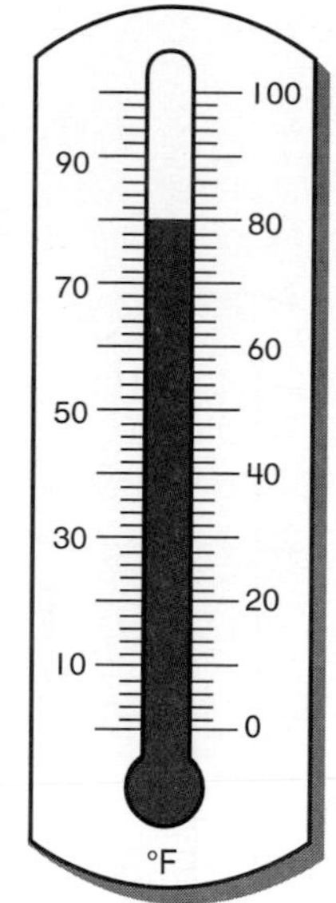

Is 80°F hot or cold? How do you know?

Write the temperature.

1

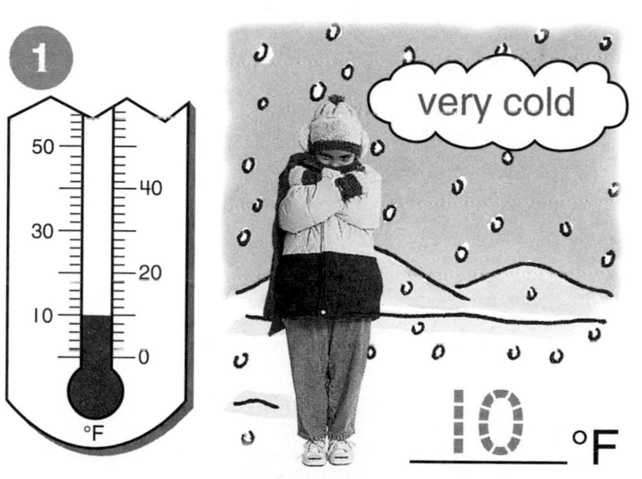

10 °F

2

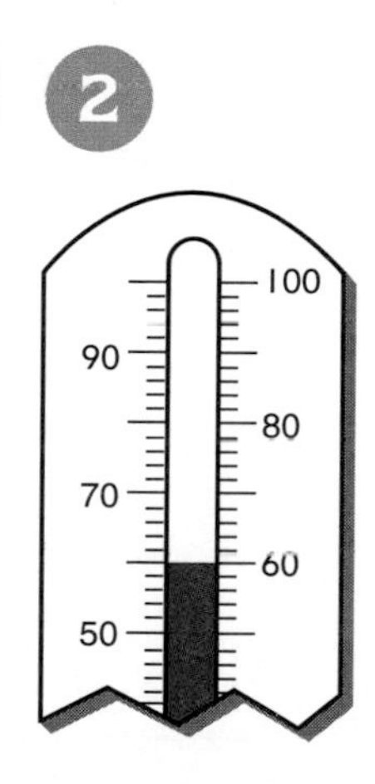

_____ °F

3

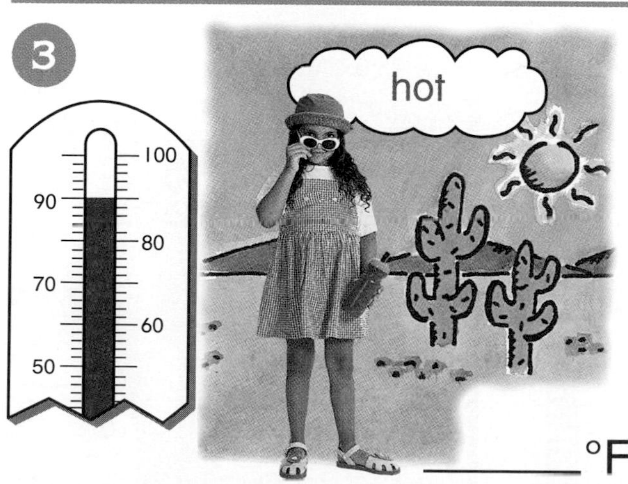

_____ °F

4

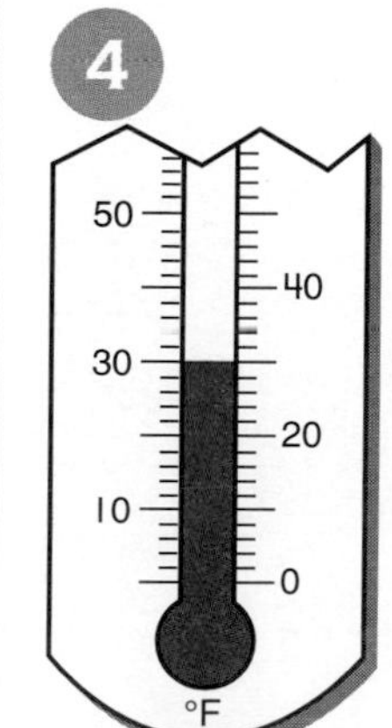

_____ °F

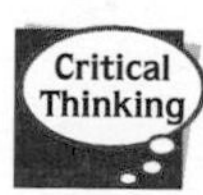

How can you find out what the temperature is today? Is it hot or cold?

Try These!

Color the thermometer.
Show the temperature.

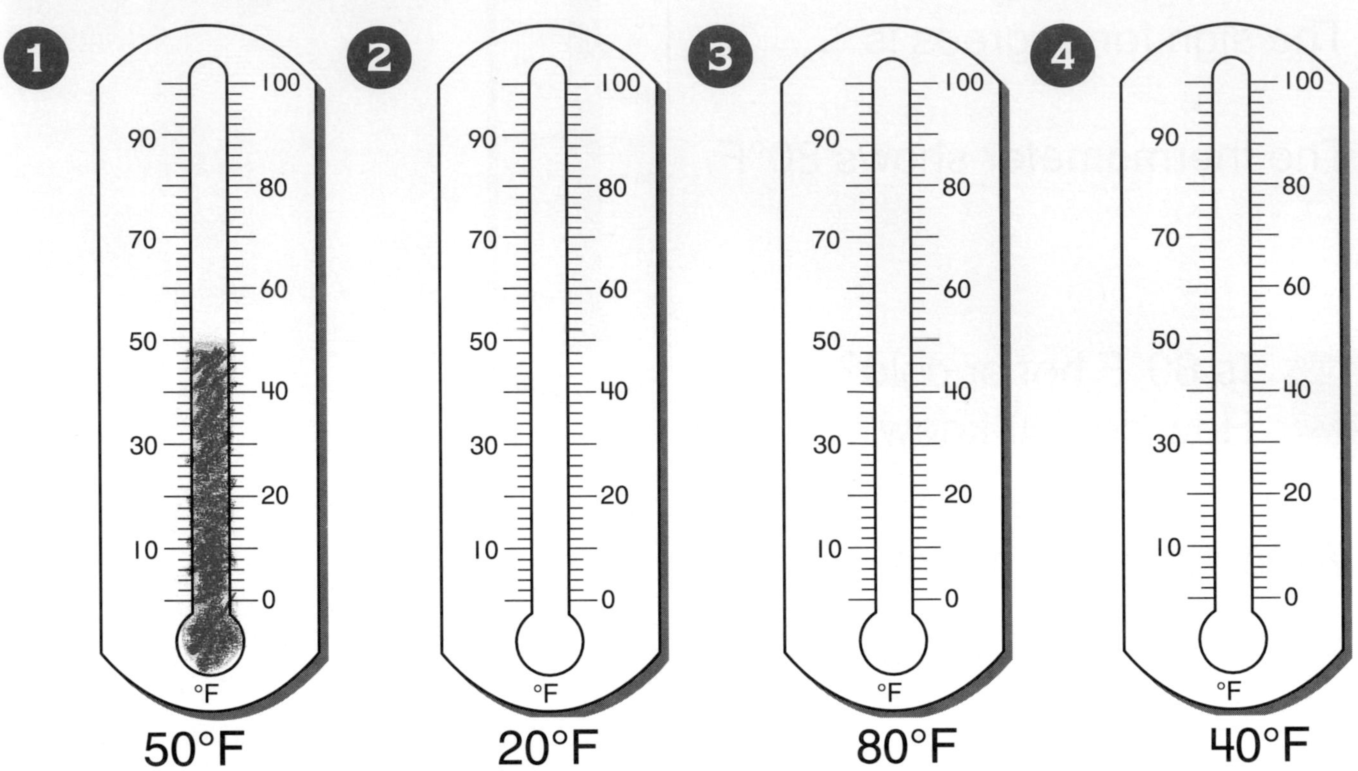

1. 50°F
2. 20°F
3. 80°F
4. 40°F

More to Explore Measurement

Temperature can be measured another way.
Write the temperature.

_______ °C

_______ °C

Ask your child to show you how to read the temperature on the thermometers above.

Name

Problem Solvers at Work

Read
Plan
Solve
Look Back

Choose Reasonable Answers

Yoon drinks a glass of water.
About how much does she drink?

1 cup 10 cups

Which answer makes sense?

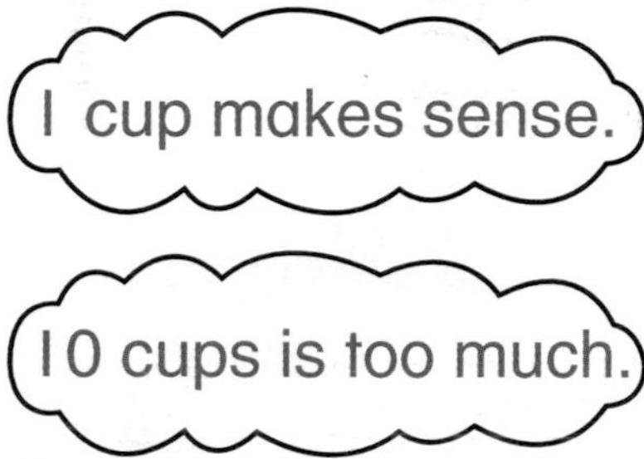

Yoon drinks about 1 cup of water.

Choose the answer that makes sense.

1. Amy wants a jump rope.
About how long should the rope be?

4 pounds  4 feet

2. Luis weighs his backpack.
About how much does the backpack weigh?

more than 1 pound more than 1 foot

3. Dana makes a string bracelet.
About how long is the bracelet?

7 feet 7 inches

Try These!

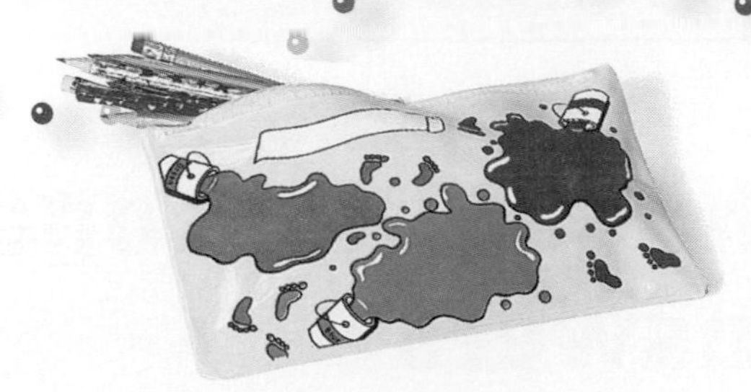

1. Célene measures her pencil.
   About how long is her pencil?

   5 centimeters   15 centimeters   5 degrees F

2. Wayne eats a box of popcorn.
   About how much does the popcorn weigh?

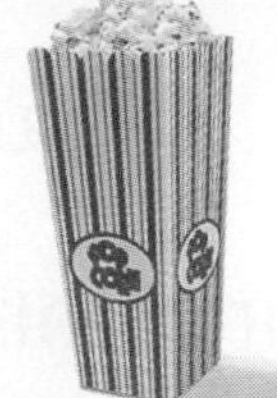

   more than 1 pound   less than 1 pound   less than 1 cup

Write and Share

Somephone wrote this problem.

Somephone wants to buy a bike. About how much does it cost?

50 dollars   50 cents

Somephone Sonenarong
Luis Muñoz Marin School
Bridgeport, Connecticut

3. Solve Somephone's problem.

4. Write your own problem.
   Write three answers.
   Ask a partner to solve the problem.

Did your partner choose the correct answer? ____________

Why didn't the other answers make sense? ____________

Ask your child to show you how to solve problem 4 above.

Name ______________________________

Chapter Review

1 Use a inch ruler. Measure how long.

about ____ inches

2 Use a centimeter ruler. Measure how long.

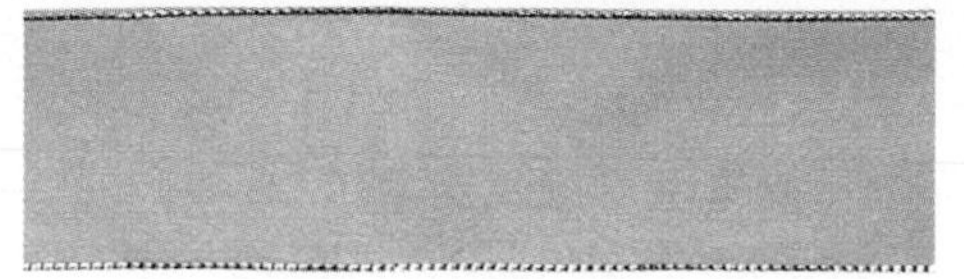

about ____ cm

Estimate. About how much does it weigh?

3 

less than 1 pound | more than 1 pound

4 

less than 1 pound | more than 1 pound

Estimate. About how much does it hold?

5 

less than 1 cup | more than 1 cup

6 

less than 1 cup | more than 1 cup

Write the temperature.

7 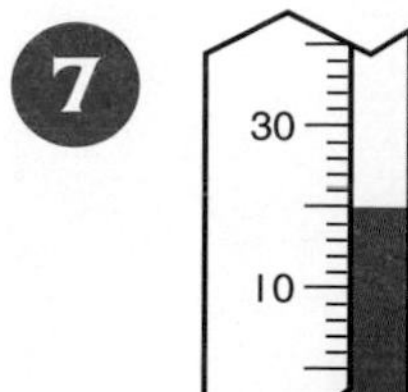
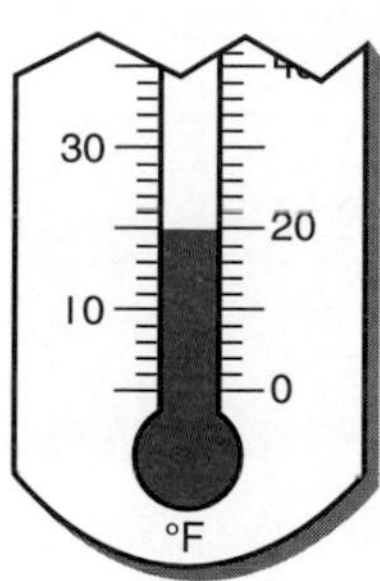

______ °F

8 
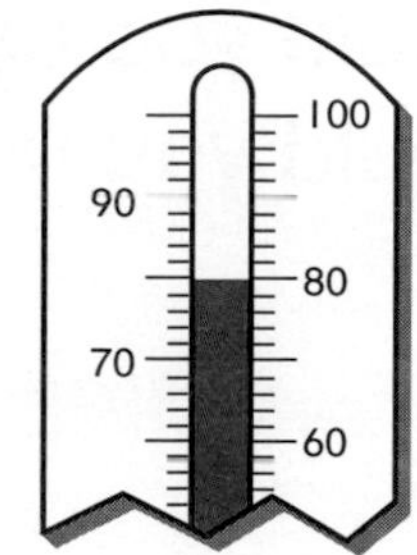

______ °F

Draw a picture to solve.
Use a 0 1 2 3 4 5 6 7 8 9 10 11 12 13 14 15 16 centimeters.

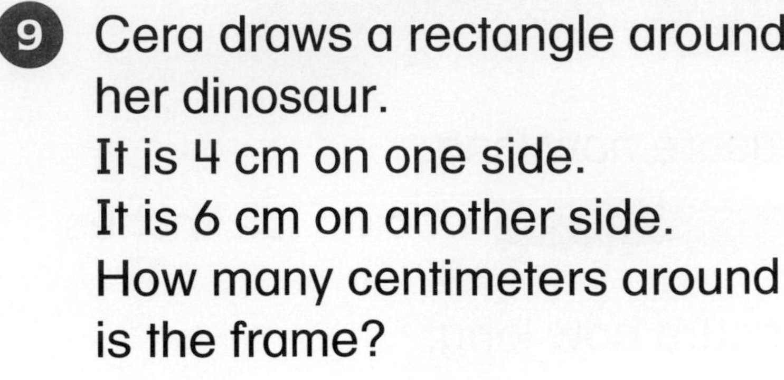

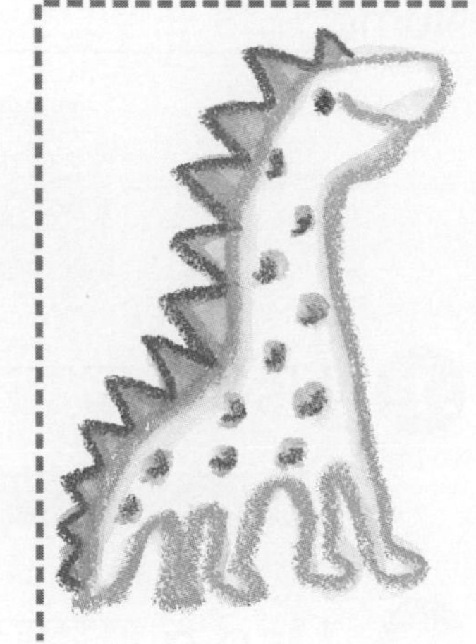

9 Cera draws a rectangle around her dinosaur.
It is 4 cm on one side.
It is 6 cm on another side.
How many centimeters around is the frame?

____ + ____ + ____ + ____ = ____ 　　 ____ cm around

---

10 Amy draws a square.
It is 3 cm on one side.
How many centimeters around is the square?

____ + ____ + ____ + ____ = ____ 　　 ____ cm around

What Do You Think?

Which tool do you like to use to measure?
☑ Check one.

   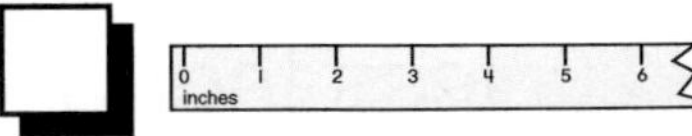

Why? ____

When would you use inches to measure?
When would you use feet?

Name

Chapter Test

1 Use a [inch ruler]. Measure how long.

about ____ inches

Use a [centimeter ruler]. Measure how long.

about ____ cm

Estimate. About how much does it weigh?

less than 1 pound   more than 1 pound

Estimate. About how much does it hold?

less than 1 cup   more than 1 cup

Write the temperature.

4

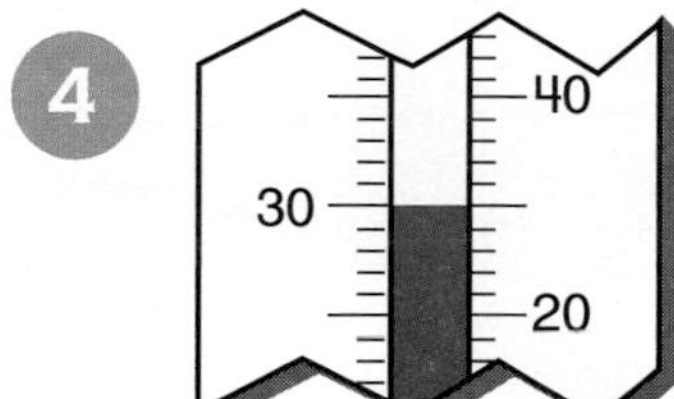

____ °F

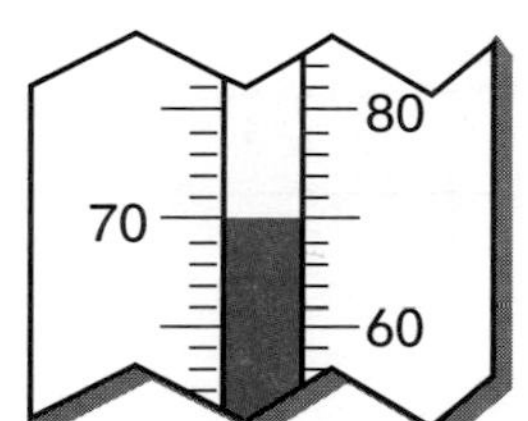

____ °F

Solve.

5 Tim draws a triangle.
One side is 4 cm.
Another side is 3 cm.
How many centimeters around
is the triangle?

____ + ____ + ____ = ____

____ cm around

Performance Assessment

What Did You Learn?

Work with a partner.

- Choose an object to measure.
- Write about the object you chose.

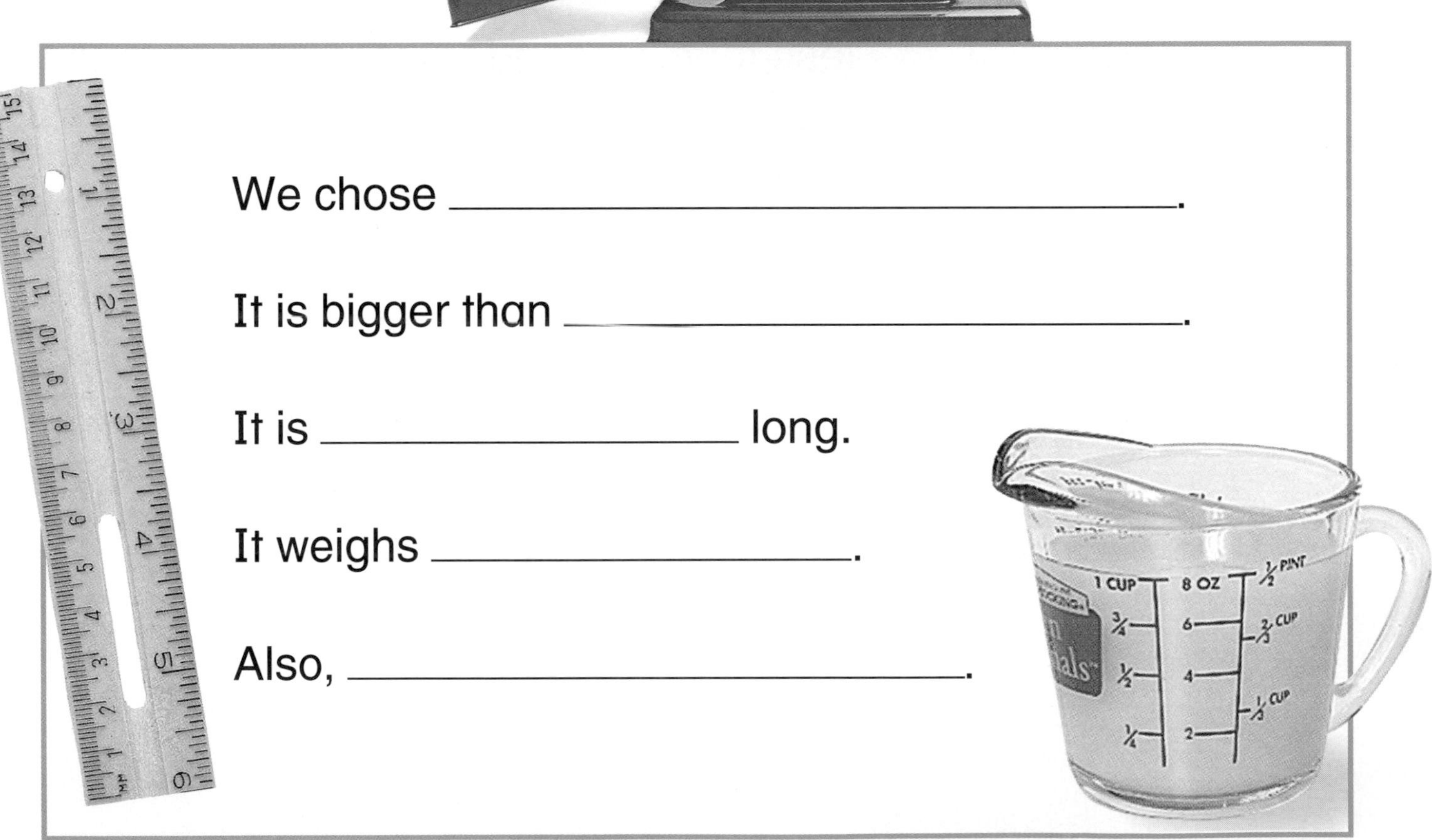

We chose ______________________.

It is bigger than ______________________.

It is ______________ long.

It weighs ______________.

Also, ______________________.

What did you use to measure the object?
Why?
What are some other ways you could measure the object?

You may want to put this page in your portfolio.

Math Connection

Algebra

Name

Coordinate Graphs

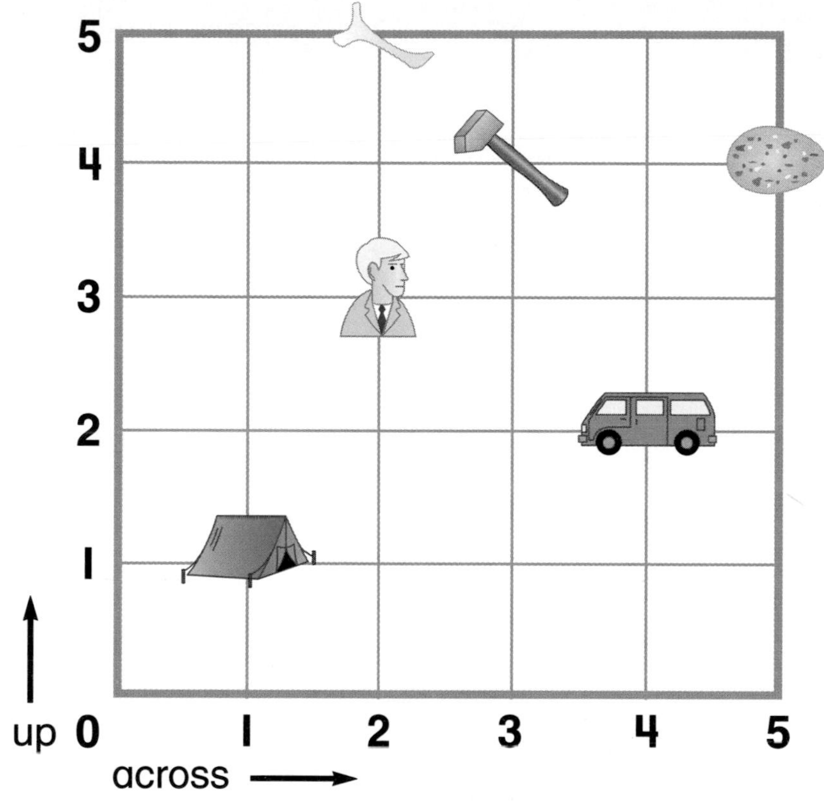

Visit the dinosaur dig.

Start at 0.
Go across 3. Go up 4.

You found the .

Complete.
Show what you find.

Across	Up	
4	2	
2	5	
1	1	
5	4	
2	3	

Curriculum Connection

Social Studies

Distance

Use a [inch ruler].
Measure each path.
Add to find how far.

1 From **A** to **C** ______ inches

2 From **C** to **E** ______ inches

3 From **B** to **D** ______ inches

4 From **D** to **F** ______ inches

Home Connection

Chapter 11 Wrap-Up

Name ____________________

How Many Cups?

MATERIALS I cup measure, a variety of containers, index cards, pencil

DIRECTIONS Put containers of different sizes on the table. Estimate how many cups each container will hold. Write your estimate on a card.

Then measure and record the number of cups each container holds.

How close are your estimates?

This activity will help your child develop an understanding of capacity.

Dear Family,

This is the last chapter in our mathematics book. We will be learning more about mental math and how to use what we know to add and subtract greater numbers.

20 + 30   36 + 20   60 – 10   54 – 30

We will also be talking about music and musical shows. Please help me complete this interview.

Your child,

____
Signature

Interview

How do you enjoy music?
(You may check more than one.)

- ❑ Going to musicals or concerts
- ❑ Playing an instrument
- ❑ Listening to CDs or tapes
- ❑ Dancing
- ❑ Other _______________________

We like music: ❑ a little. ❑ a lot.

Music
Exploring 2-Digit Addition and Subtraction

Listen to the story *Zin! Zin! Zin! a Violin*.

Tell about music that you enjoy.

Name ______________________________

What Do You Know?

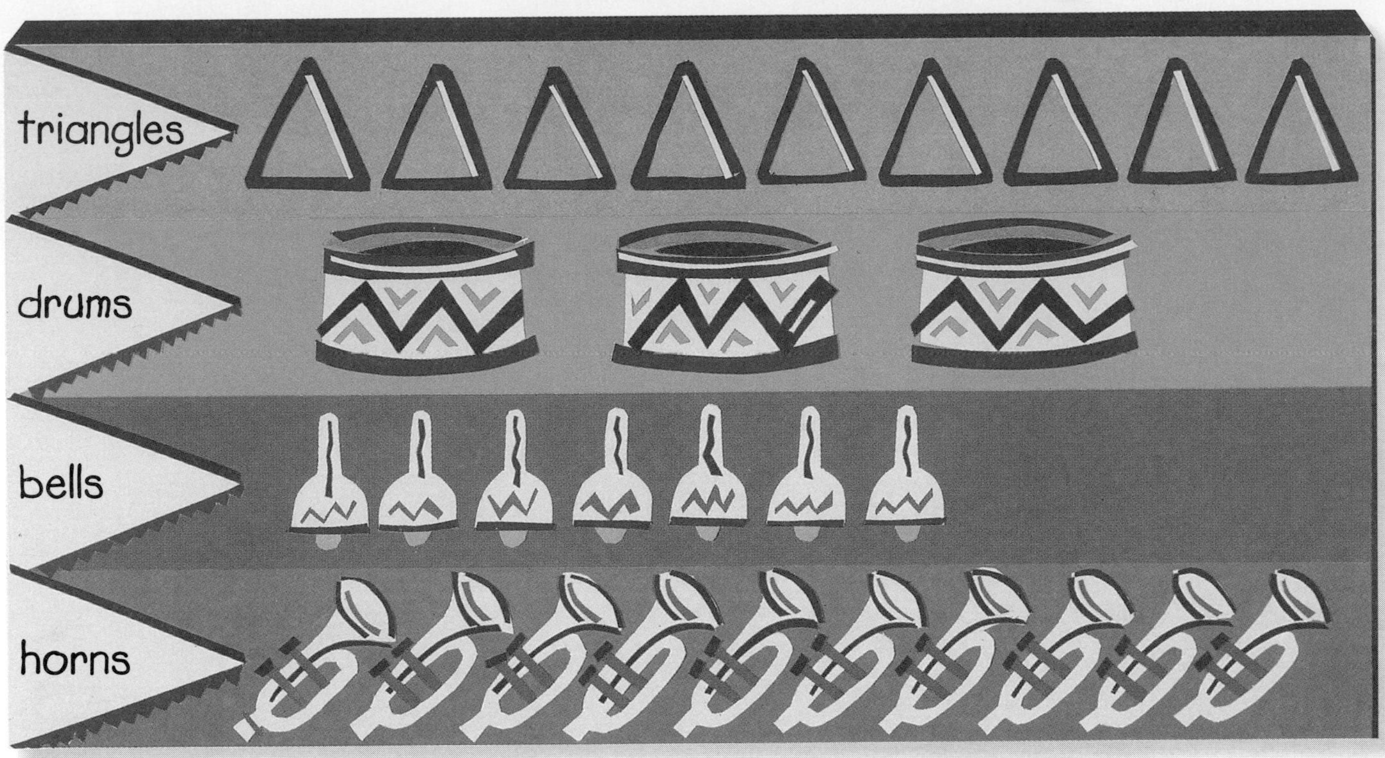

Solve. Show your work.

1. How many drums and bells? ______________________

2. 12 children want to play triangles.
   How many more triangles are needed?

   ____

Complete the problem. Then solve.

3. How many ______________

   and ______________? ______________________

Use the picture.
Find how many of each instrument.
Write pairs of numbers that are easy to add or subtract.

Name

Explore Activity

Count On to Add

Working Together

You and your partner need a spinner.

Take turns.

- Spin. Write the number.
- Count on to add.
- Write the total.

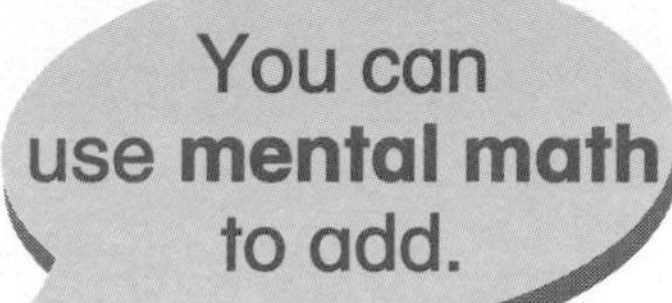

	Starting number	Count on.	Total
1	38	+ 3	41
2	26	+	
3	47	+	
4	53	+	
5	19	+	
6	35	+	
7	74	+	

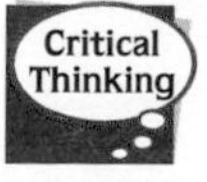

Look at the starting numbers.
What is the greatest total you could get?
What is the smallest total you could get?

Try These!

Use mental math.

Count on to add.

1. 59 + 2 = 61
2. 89 + 1 = ___
3. 45 + 3 = ___
4. 94 + 2 = ___
5. 39 + 2 = ___
6. 28 + 3 = ___
7. 17 + 2 = ___
8. 70 + 1 = ___
9. 67 + 3 = ___
10. 35 + 2 = ___
11. 29 + 1 = ___
12. 56 + 3 = ___

More to Explore — Algebra Sense

Think about how you count on.
Find the missing number.

48 + 2 = 50   37 + ___ = 38

63 + ___ = 64   25 + ___ = 27

31 + ___ = 34   72 + ___ = 75

80 + ___ = 82   90 + ___ = 92

We counted on to add 1, 2, and 3. Ask your child how to add 25 + 2 using mental math.

Name ____________________

Add Facts and Tens

You can use facts to help you add tens.

4 + 2 = 6

40 + 20 = 60

How are 4 + 2 and 40 + 20 the same? How are they different?

Add.

1. 3 + 5 = 8 30 + 50 = 80

2. 6 + 1 = ___ 60 + 10 = ___

3. 7 + 2 = ___ 70 + 20 = ___

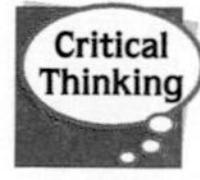

What addition fact helps you add 20 + 30? Why?

Try These!

Use cubes if you want to.

Add.

1. 4 + 4 = 8 2 + 6 = ___ 1 + 5 = ___

   40 + 40 = 80 20 + 60 = ___ 10 + 50 = ___

2. 5 + 4 = ___ 8 + 1 = ___ 4 + 2 = ___

   50 + 40 = ___ 80 + 10 = ___ 40 + 20 = ___

3. 17 + 1 = ___ 66 + 2 = ___ 71 + 3 = ___
4. 40 + 2 = ___ 83 + 1 = ___ 18 + 2 = ___
5. 29 + 3 = ___ 38 + 3 = ___ 59 + 2 = ___

Mixed Review

Skip-count by tens.

6. 10, 20, 30, ___, ___, ___, ___

7. 30, 40, 50, ___, ___, ___, ___
8. 23, 33, 43, ___, ___, ___, ___

9. 8, 18, 28, ___, ___, ___, ___

At Home: We used addition facts to help add tens. Ask your child how to add 50 + 30.

Name ______________________

Count On by Tens

32 children sing in the show.
20 children dance in the show.
How many children is that in all?

You can **count on by tens** to add.

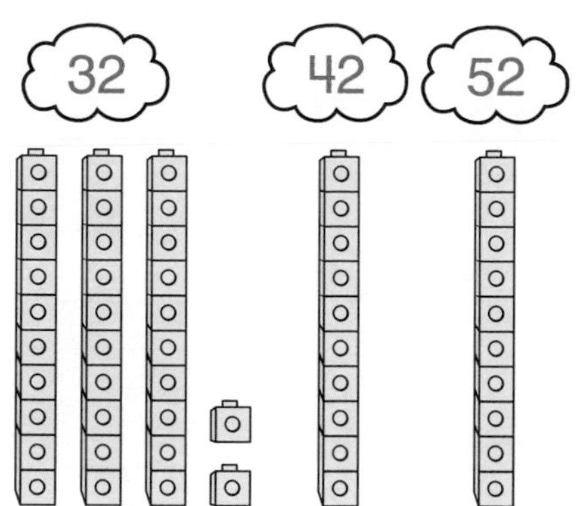

32 + 20 = 52   52 children are in the show.

Count on by tens to add.

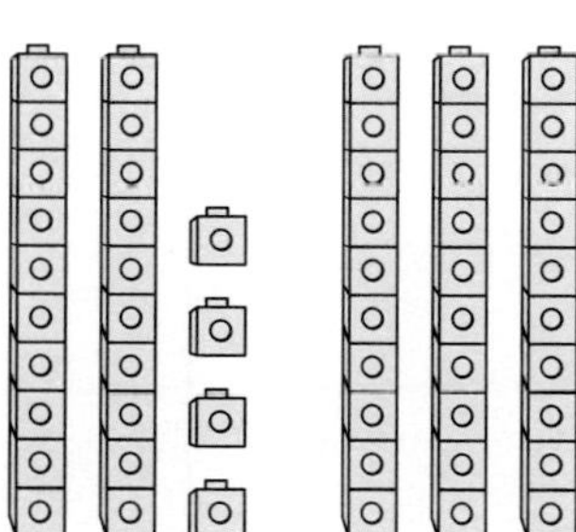

24 + 30 = 54

33 + 10 = ____

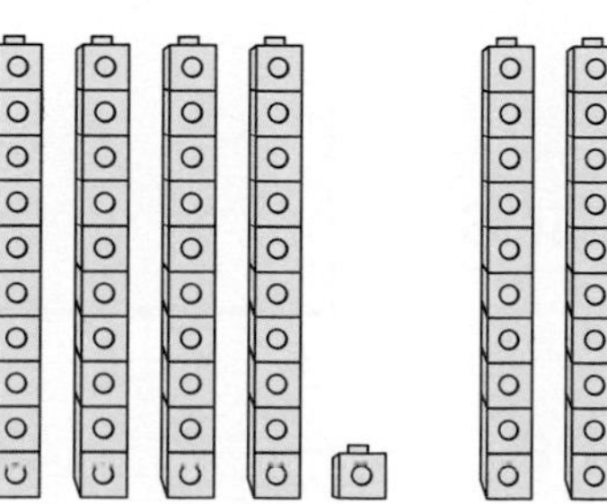

41 + 20 = ____

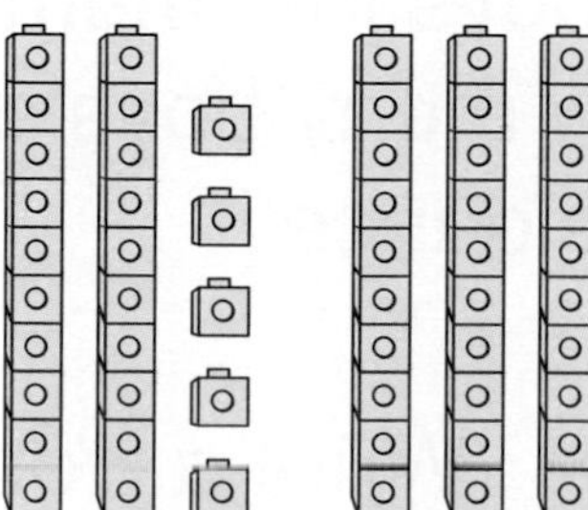

25 + 30 = ____

Try These!

Use cubes or a hundred chart.
Count on by tens to add.

1. 22 + 30 = 52
2. 41 + 20 = ___
3. 63 + 20 = ___
4. 56 + 30 = ___
5. 72 + 20 = ___
6. 15 + 30 = ___
7. 45 + 30 = ___
8. 34 + 10 = ___
9. 18 + 10 = ___
10. 63 + 20 = ___

Solve.

11. 15 children play triangles.
20 children play bells.
How many children is that in all? ___ children

12. 32 girls dance.
30 boys join them.
How many boys and girls dance? ___ boys and girls

13. 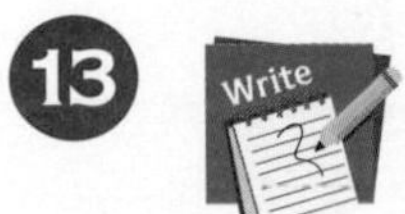

Write a word problem that can be solved by counting on by tens.
Have a partner solve it.
Check your partner's answer.

At Home: We counted on by tens to add. Ask your child to add 35 + 20.

Name ____________________

Working Together

You and your partner need 5 [10-cube trains], 18 [cubes], and a 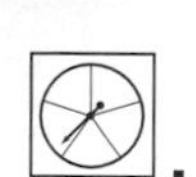.

Take turns.

- Show the number with cubes.
- Spin.
- Write the number. Show with cubes.
- Combine the cubes to add.
- Write the total.

	Show.		Spin and show.		Total
1	26	+	7	=	33
2	15	+	______	=	______
3	37	+	______	=	______
4	19	+	______	=	______
5	28	+	______	=	______
6	44	+	______	=	______

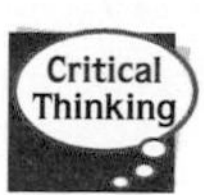

When did you make a 10-cube train?

Try These!

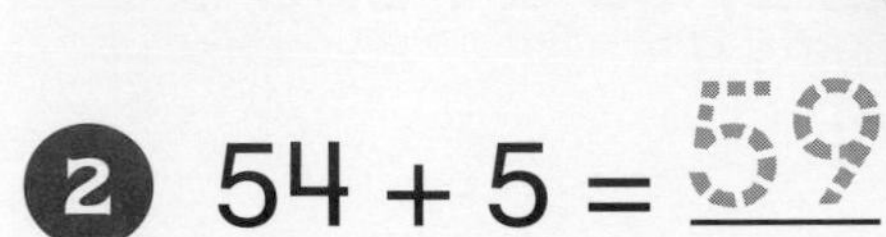

Add.
Use models.

1. 24 + 7 = 31
2. 54 + 5 = 59
3. 33 + 6 = ___
4. 32 + 9 = ___
5. 41 + 8 = ___
6. 26 + 4 = ___
7. 19 + 1 = ___
8. 53 + 4 = ___
9. 37 + 6 = ___
10. 42 + 7 = ___
11. 24 + 9 = ___
12. 14 + 5 = ___

Solve.

Workspace

13. Mai needs 17 blue hats and 5 red hats for the show. How many hats does she need?

___ hats

14. 12 children paint posters. 8 children make signs. How many children is that in all?

___ children

Show how you add 25 + 6.
Write or draw.

At Home: We added 2-digit and 1-digit numbers. Ask your child how to solve problems 13 and 14.

Name

More Addition

Working Together

You and your partner need 1 [ten-cube train] and 18 [cube].

- Choose a number from [dark note].
- Choose a number from [light note].
- Show them with cubes.
- Add. Write the addition sentence.

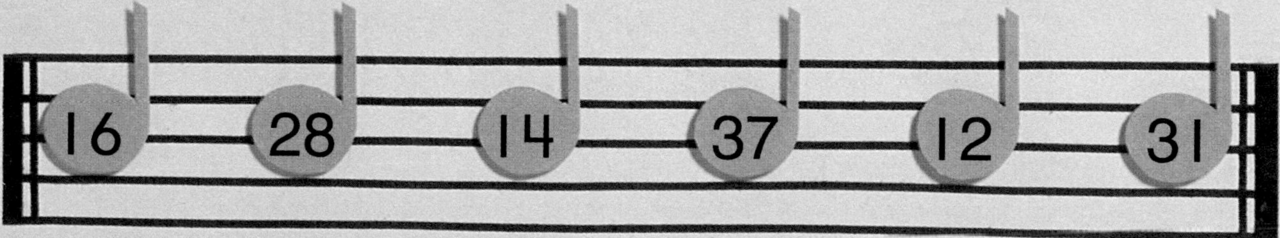

1. ___ + ___ = ___
2. ___ + ___ = ___
3. ___ + ___ = ___
4. ___ + ___ = ___
5. ___ + ___ = ___
6. ___ + ___ = ___

Try These!

Add. Use models to help.

1. 14 + 36 = 50
2. 24 + 15 = 39
3. 23 + 41 = ___
4. 17 + 12 = ___
5. 35 + 26 = ___
6. 52 + 25 = ___
7. 43 + 21 = ___
8. 29 + 11 = ___
9. 32 + 43 = ___
10. 19 + 32 = ___
11. 15 + 15 = ___
12. 28 + 14 = ___

More to Explore

Algebra Sense

This machine adds 3 to any number.

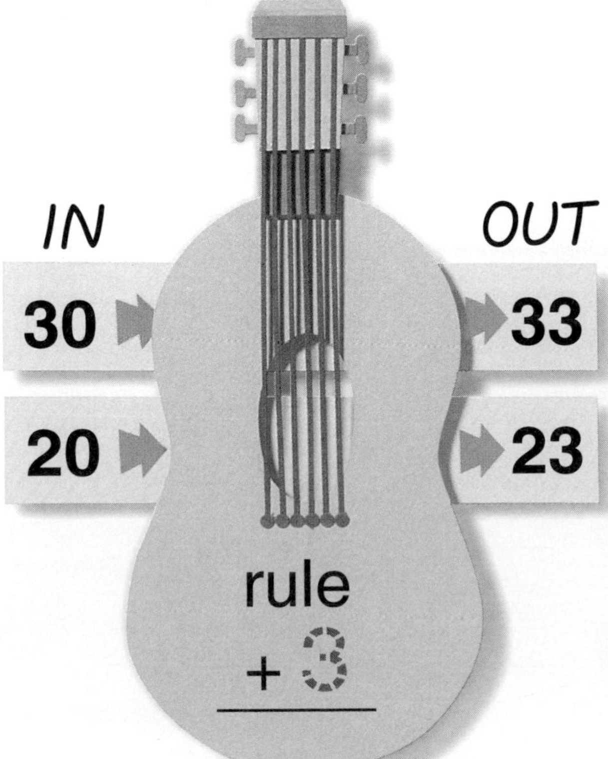

Find the rule for this machine.

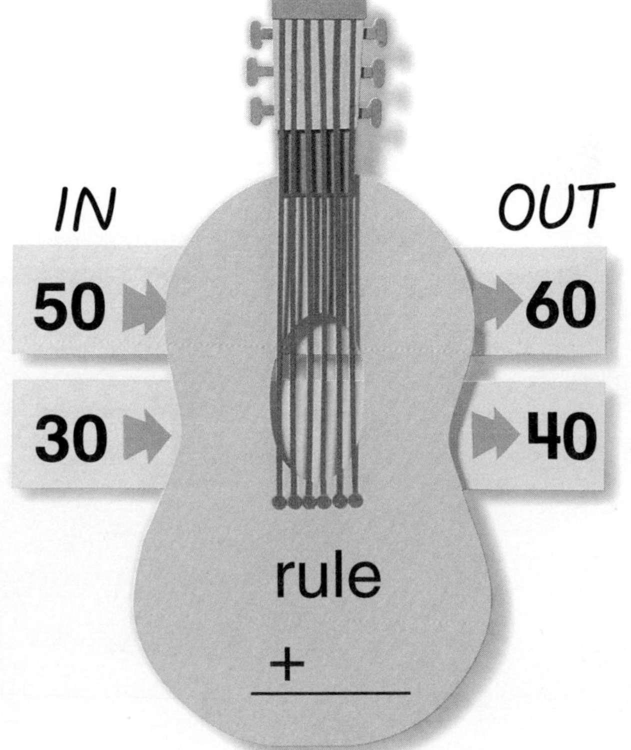

We explored adding two 2-digit numbers. Ask your child how to solve exercise 12.

Name

Use Estimation

Read Kevin helps make costumes.
He spends 43¢ for glitter.
He spends 21¢ for buttons.
About how much does he spend?

Plan You can **estimate** to find **about** how much.

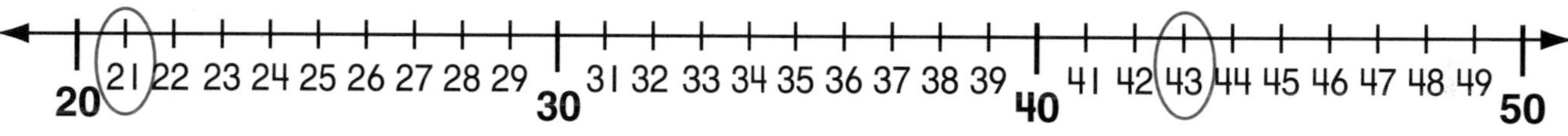

Solve Find 43 on the number line.
Find 21.
Look at the tens.

Is 43 nearer 40 or 50? 40

Is 21 nearer 20 or 30? 20

Add the tens.

40 + 20 = 60

Kevin spends **about** 60 ¢.

Did you answer the question? Explain.

Try These!

Use the number line to find the nearest ten.

Solve. Use estimation.

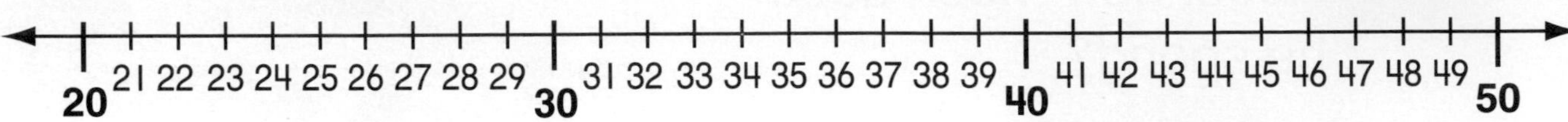

1. Steffi buys paint for 49¢.
   Al buys a brush for 22¢.
   About how much do they spend?

   50 + 20 = 70

about 70¢

2. Tom pays 47¢ for paper.
   He pays 41¢ for a marker.
   About how much does he pay in all?

about ____¢

3. Ling spends 28¢ for glue.
   He spends 47¢ for tape.
   About how much does he spend in all?

____ + ____ = ____

about ____¢

4. Carmen buys ribbon for 32¢
   and string for 43¢.
   About how much does she spend?

about ____¢

At Home

We estimated to solve problems. Ask your child to show you how to solve problem 2.

Name ______________________________

Midchapter Review

Do your best!

Add.

1. 24 + 2 = ___
2. 37 + 1 = ___
3. 29 + 10 = ___
4. 16 + 30 = ___
5. 5 + 4 = ___

   50 + 40 = ___
6. 2 + 6 = ___

   20 + 60 = ___
7. 22 + 7 = ___
8. 34 + 15 = ___

Solve. Use estimation.

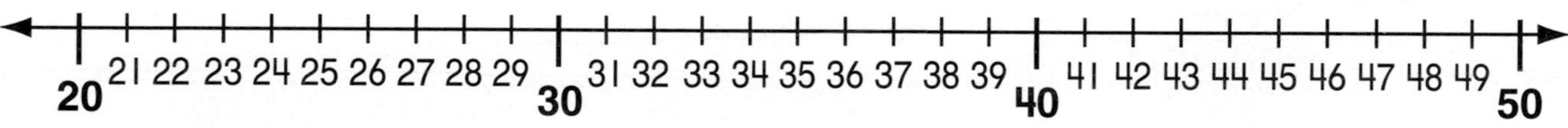

9. Ari buys a drum for 43¢ and a flute for 47¢. About how much does he spend?

___ + ___ = ___ about ___¢

10. How did you estimate to solve problem 9? ______________________

____

Tell how you would add 40 + 30.

Be Seated at the Show

You and your partner need and .

Take turns.

- ▶ Add. Write the sum on the seat.
- ▶ Your partner checks your answer.
- ▶ If correct, write your initials on the seat.

Play until all seats are taken.

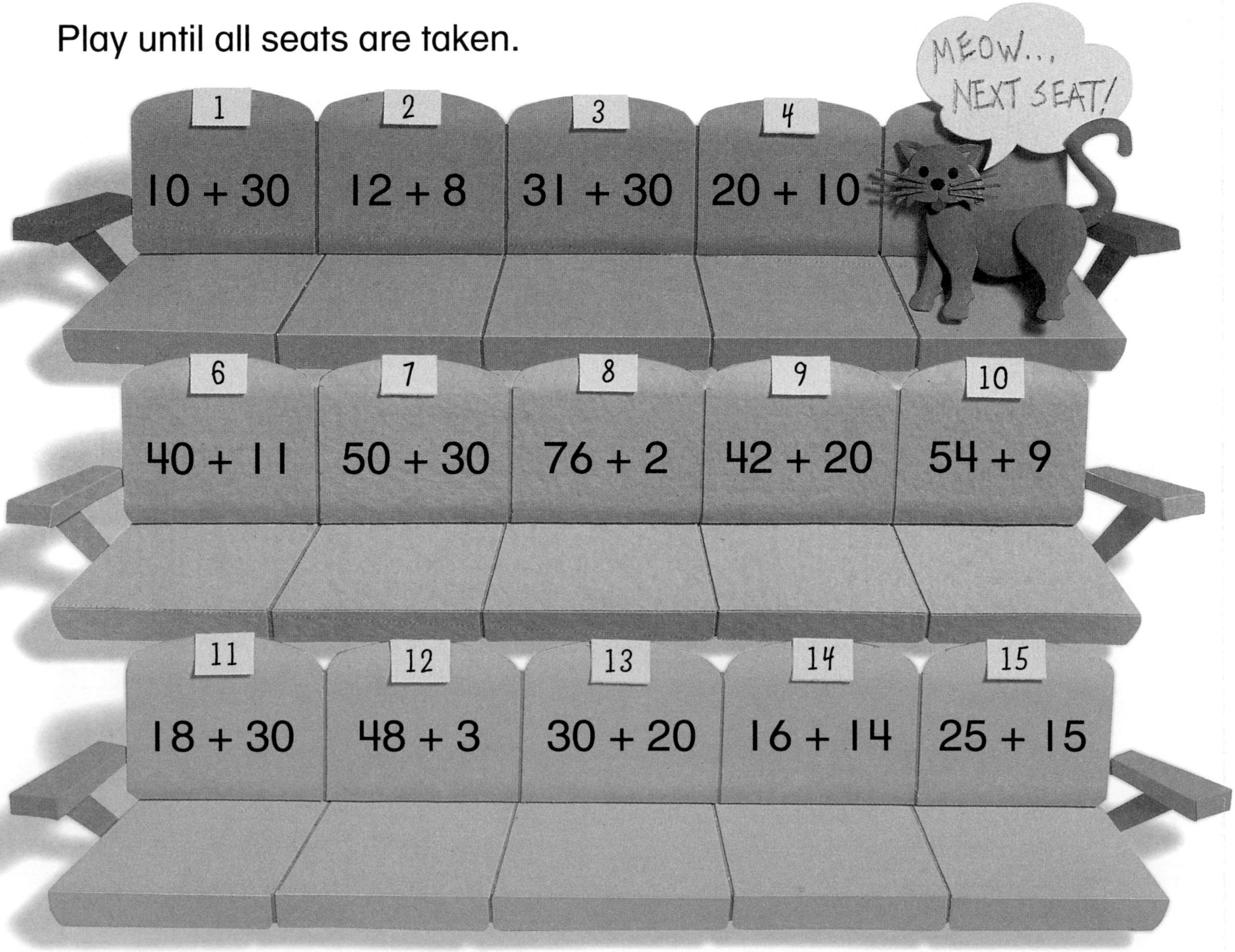

MEOW... NEXT SEAT!

1	2	3	4	
10 + 30	12 + 8	31 + 30	20 + 10	

6	7	8	9	10
40 + 11	50 + 30	76 + 2	42 + 20	54 + 9

11	12	13	14	15
18 + 30	48 + 3	30 + 20	16 + 14	25 + 15

Real-Life Investigation
Applying Addition

Name ______________________________

Class Trip

Listen to *Zin! Zin! Zin! a Violin.*

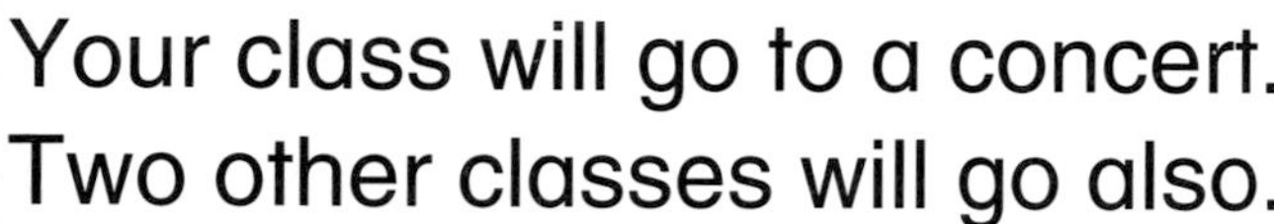

Your class will go to a concert.
Two other classes will go also.

Working Together

Find out how many children and teachers will go to the concert.

- ▶ Show how many children and teachers are in your class.
- ▶ Show how many children and teachers are in each of the other two classes.

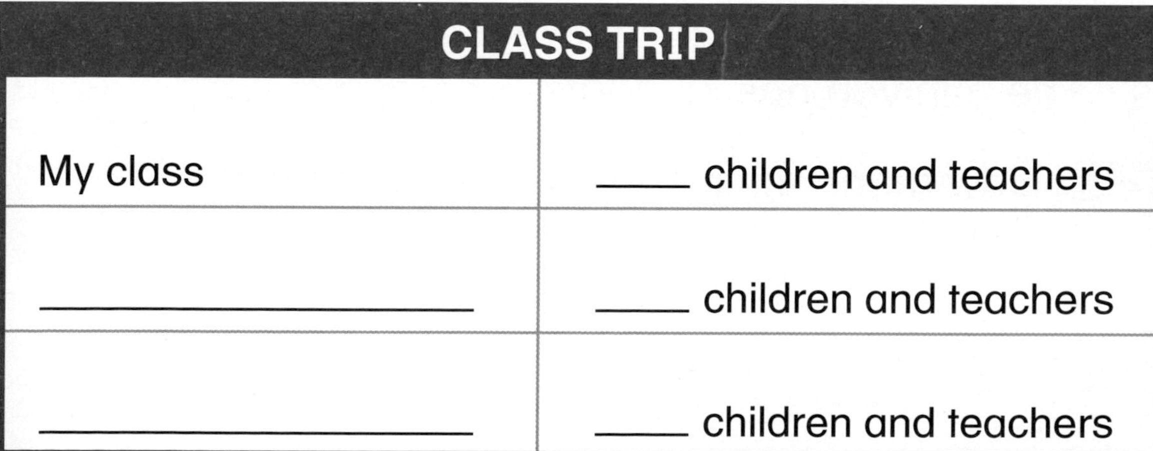

CLASS TRIP	
My class	____ children and teachers
__________________	____ children and teachers
__________________	____ children and teachers

▶ Find the total. ____ children and teachers

Decision Making

1. Use your data. Decide how many buses you need to seat all the children and teachers going on the trip.

   ____ buses

The school bus has 44 seats.

2. Will there be any empty seats? ____

   If so, how many? ____ seats

Write a report.

3. Tell how you added to find out how many children in all.

4. Tell how you decided how many buses you need.

More to Investigate

What if the children travel in minivans instead of buses? The minivan has 15 seats.

PREDICT How many minivans do you need for all 3 classes?

EXPLORE Try it. Use a calculator and your data.

FIND Find out how many minivans you need. Find out if there will be empty seats.

Name ________________________________

Explore Activity

Count Back to Subtract

Working Together

You and your partner need a hundred chart.

You can use mental math to subtract.

Take turns.

- Pick a number from the chart.
- Write that number under **Start.**
- Count back to subtract.
- Write the difference.

	Starting number	Count back.	Difference
1	24	−2	22
2		−3	
3		−1	
4		−2	
5		−3	
6		−3	
7		−1	

Look at the charts.
What is the greatest difference you could get?
What is the smallest difference you could get?

Try These!

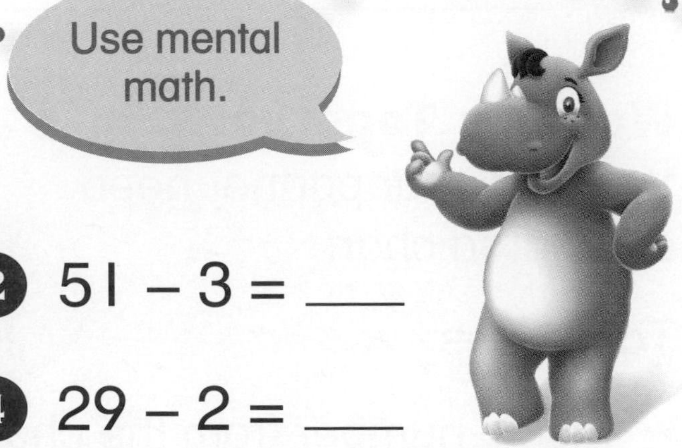

Use mental math.

Count back to subtract.

1. 41 − 2 = 39
2. 51 − 3 = ___
3. 63 − 3 = ___
4. 29 − 2 = ___
5. 70 − 1 = ___
6. 43 − 3 = ___
7. 15 − 2 = ___
8. 80 − 2 = ___
9. 92 − 1 = ___
10. 48 − 1 = ___
11. 37 − 3 = ___
12. 62 − 3 = ___

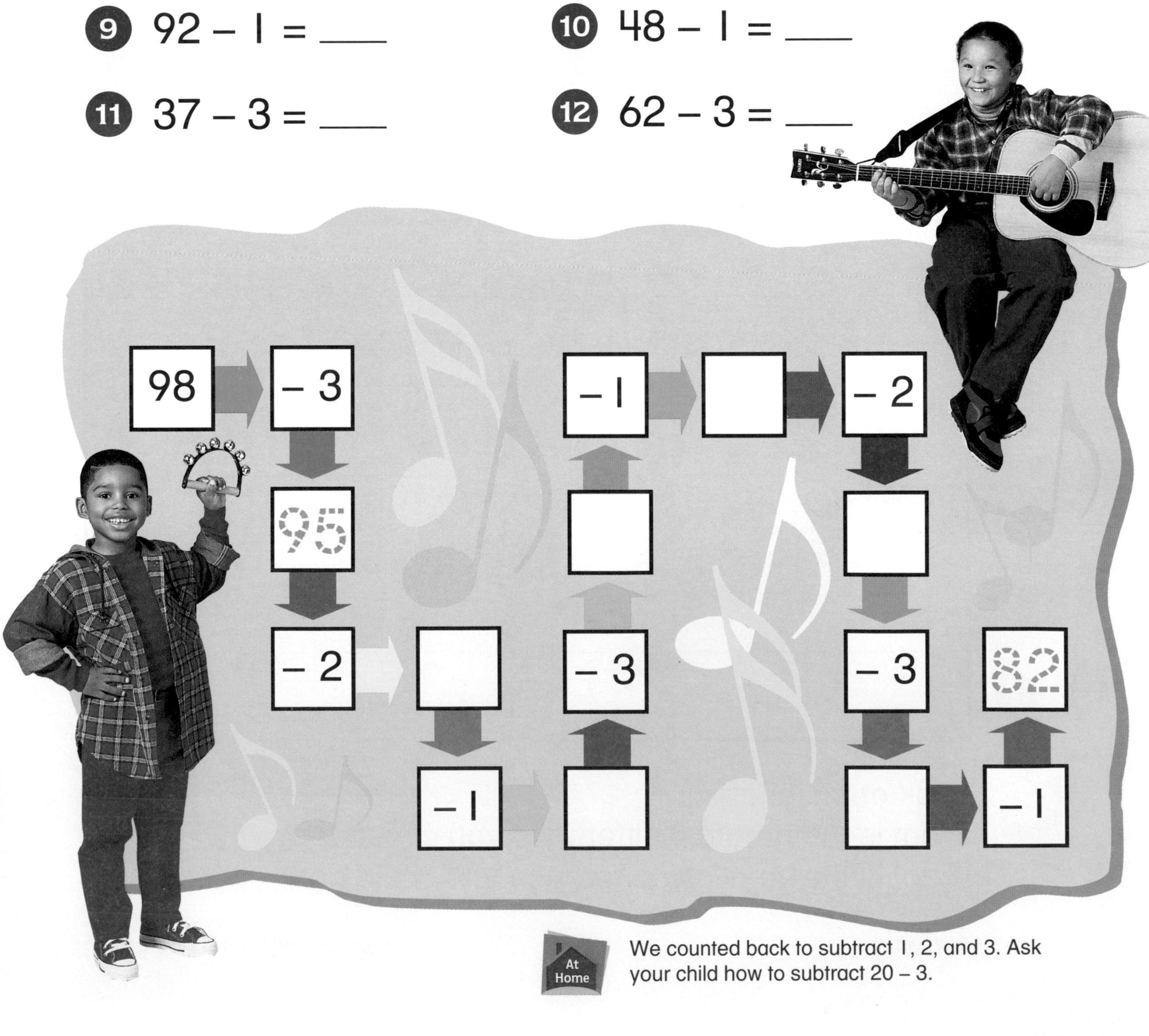

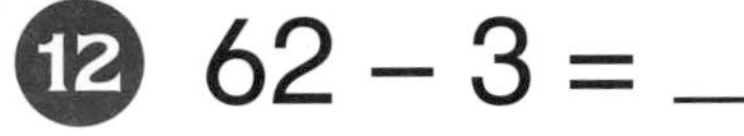

98 → − 3 → 95 → − 2 → ☐ → − 1 → ☐ → − 3 → ☐ → − 1 → ☐ → − 2 → ☐ → − 3 → ☐ → − 1 → 82

We counted back to subtract 1, 2, and 3. Ask your child how to subtract 20 − 3.

Name ______

Subtract Facts and Tens

You can use facts to help you subtract tens.

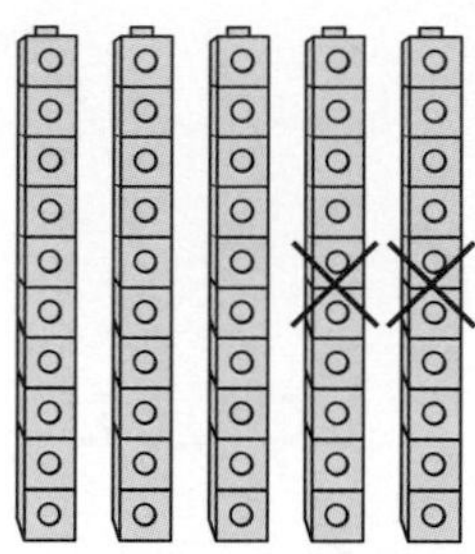

5 – 2 = 3   50 – 20 = 30

How are 5 – 2 and 50 – 20 the same?
How are they different?

Subtract.

1

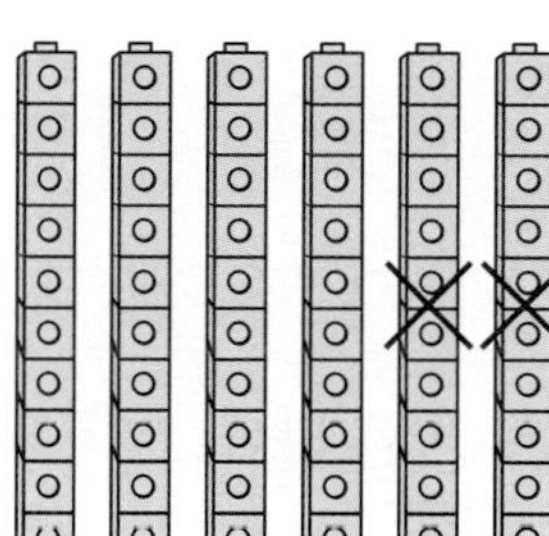

6 – 2 = 4   60 – 20 = 40

2

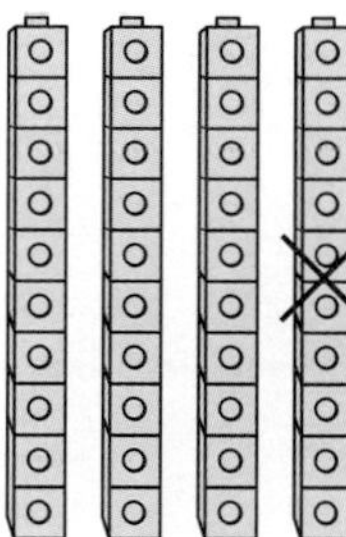

4 – 1 = ____   40 – 10 = ____

3

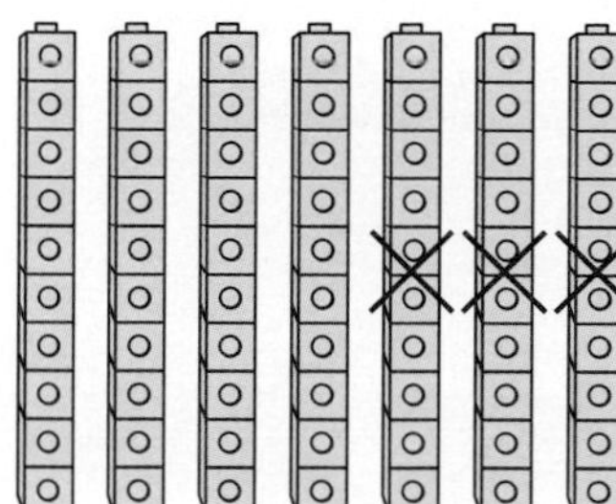

7 – 3 = ____   70 – 30 = ____

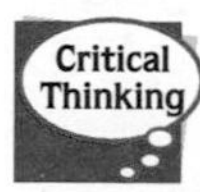

What subtraction fact helps you subtract 60 – 30? Why?

Try These!

Use cubes if you want to.

Subtract.

1. 3 − 1 = 2   9 − 4 = ___   5 − 3 = ___

   30 − 10 = 20   90 − 40 = ___   50 − 30 = ___

2. 8 − 6 = ___   6 − 1 = ___   7 − 4 = ___

   80 − 60 = ___   60 − 10 = ___   70 − 40 = ___

3. 90 − 2 = ___   64 − 2 = ___   17 − 3 = ___
4. 43 − 3 = ___   19 − 2 = ___   38 − 3 = ___
5. 22 − 3 = ___   59 − 1 = ___   61 − 2 = ___

Mixed Review

Use a centimeter ruler. Measure.

6. 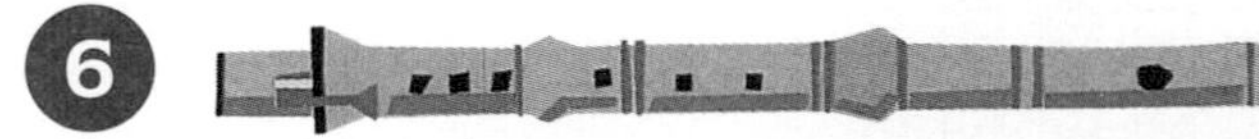 about ___ cm
7. 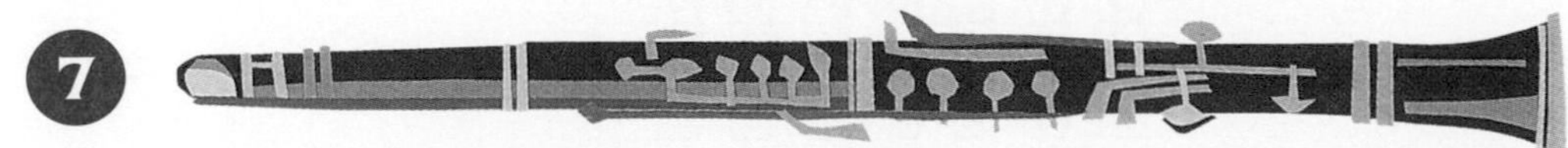 about ___ cm
8. 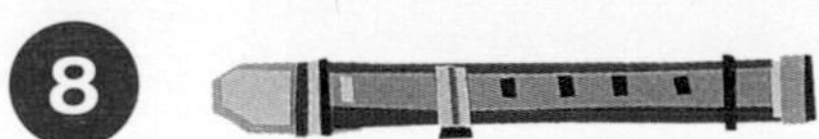 about ___ cm

At Home: We used subtraction facts to help subtract tens. Ask your child how to subtract 60 − 40.

Name ______________________________

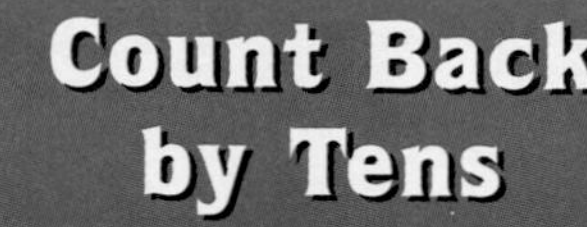

You can **count back by tens** to subtract.

42 – 20 = 22

Count back by tens to subtract.

51 – 30 = 21

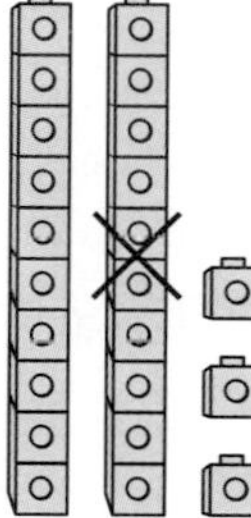

23 – 10 = 13

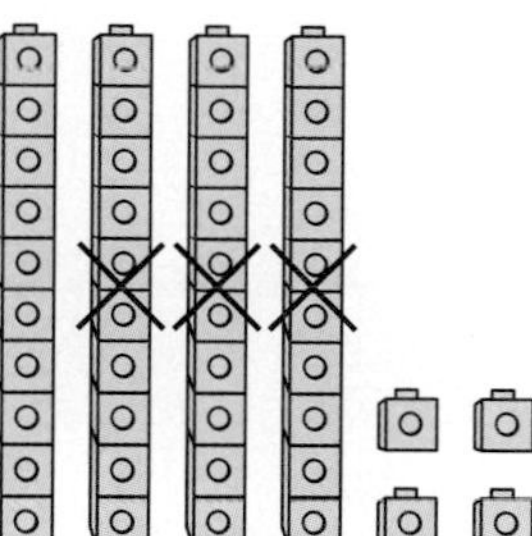

44 – 30 = ____

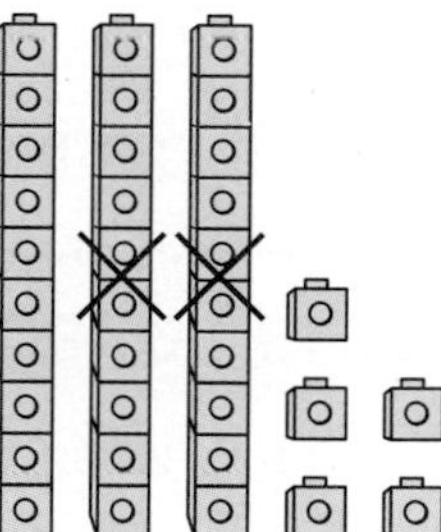

35 – 20 = ____

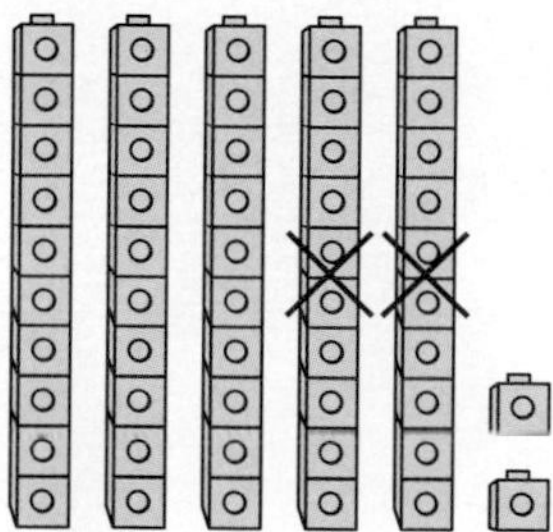

52 – 20 = ____

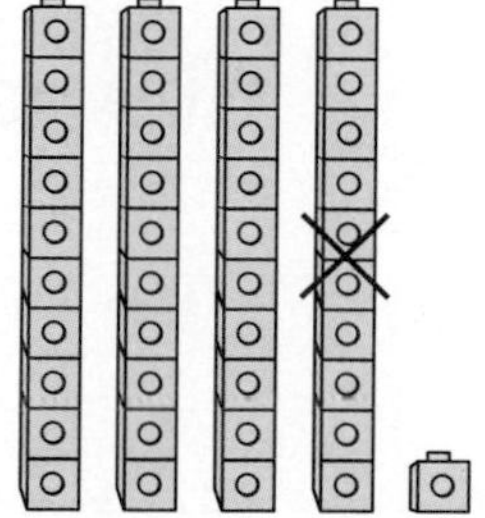

41 – 10 = ____

Try These!

Count back by tens to subtract.

1. 66 – 30 = 36
2. 29 – 20 = 9
3. 38 – 10 = ___
4. 71 – 30 = ___
5. 42 – 30 = ___
6. 57 – 20 = ___
7. 53 – 10 = ___
8. 49 – 20 = ___
9. 56 – 10 = ___
10. 45 – 30 = ___

Cultural Connection

Jamaica

In Jamaica, you can buy icicles!
What would you call an icicle?

Jamaican money is called Jamaican dollars.
Each child buys an icicle for J$20.
Find how much money each has left.

José had J$50. He has J$ 30 left.

Marie had J$51. She has J$_______ left.

Yvette had J$97. She has J$_______ left.

Philip had J$83. He has J$_______ left.

At Home: We counted back by tens to subtract. Ask your child to subtract 35 – 10.

Name ______________________

Explore Activity

2-Digit Subtraction

Working Together

You and your partner need

3 , 9, and a .

Take turns.

- Show the number with cubes.
- Spin. Write the number to subtract.
- Take away that number.
- Write the number that is left.

	Show.		Spin to subtract.		Number left
1	22	−	5	=	17
2	28	−	______	=	______
3	37	−	______	=	______
4	25	−	______	=	______
5	19	−	______	=	______
6	36	−	______	=	______

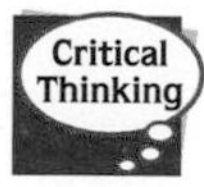

How did you use cubes to take away 5 from 22?

Try These!

Subtract.
Use models.

1. 34 − 6 = 28
2. 27 − 5 = 22
3. 26 − 4 = ____
4. 19 − 5 = ____
5. 31 − 6 = ____
6. 27 − 7 = ____
7. 29 − 3 = ____
8. 35 − 6 = ____
9. 30 − 5 = ____
10. 28 − 7 = ____
11. 39 − 9 = ____
12. 24 − 8 = ____

Solve.

Workspace

13. There are 21 bands on the field. 5 bands march away. How many bands are still on the field? ____ bands

14. 30 people watch the band. 8 of them go home. How many people now watch the band? ____ people

Show how you subtract 26 − 4.
Write or draw.

At Home: Ask your child to show how to solve problems 13 and 14.

Name ______________________

Working Together

You and your partner need 4 [ten-cube train] and 9 [cube].

Take turns.

- Show the number with cubes.
- Choose a number to take away.
- Write the number.
- Subtract using the cubes.
- Write the number that is left.

Show.		Take away.		Number left
36	−	18	=	18
29	−	____	=	____
34	−	____	=	____
45	−	____	=	____
26	−	____	=	____
47	−	____	=	____

Choose a number.
13
19
12
14
25
18

Try These!

Subtract. Use models to help.

1. 44 − 21 = 23
2. 33 − 16 = 17
3. 28 − 17 = ____
4. 42 − 12 = ____
5. 35 − 18 = ____
6. 26 − 23 = ____
7. 49 − 15 = ____
8. 22 − 19 = ____
9. 37 − 24 = ____
10. 41 − 13 = ____

More to Explore

Number Sense

Use a calculator.
Add.

3 + 3 = ____

3 + 3 + 3 = ____

3 + 3 + 3 + 3 = ____

3 + 3 + 3 + 3 + 3 = ____

4 + 4 = ____

4 + 4 + 4 = ____

4 + 4 + 4 + 4 = ____

4 + 4 + 4 + 4 + 4 = ____

What patterns do you see? ______________________

Ask your child how he or she solved exercise 3.

Name ______

Subtraction Race

You and your partner need a 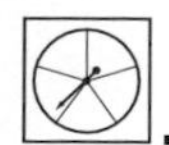.

Cultural Note

In Nigeria, people play the *kalungu*, or "talking drum." It sounds like people's voices.

Take turns.

- Spin. Write the number.
- Subtract the number from 50.
- Spin again.
- Subtract from the new number.
- Spin and subtract until both players reach **Score.**

The player with the lowest **Score** wins.

50 − ◯ (SPIN) = ☐ − ◯ (SPIN) = ☐ − ◯ (SPIN) = ☐ (SCORE)

50 − ◯ (SPIN) = ☐ − ◯ (SPIN) = ☐ − ◯ (SPIN) = ☐ (SCORE)

50 − ◯ (SPIN) = ☐ − ◯ (SPIN) = ☐ − ◯ (SPIN) = ☐ (SCORE)

50 − ◯ (SPIN) = ☐ − ◯ (SPIN) = ☐ − ◯ (SPIN) = ☐ (SCORE)

Add.

1. $42 + 3 =$ ____
2. $59 + 2 =$ ____
3. $31 + 20 =$ ____
4. $22 + 30 =$ ____
5. $20 + 60 =$ ____
6. $13 + 8 =$ ____
7. $14 + 12 =$ ____
8. $43 + 19 =$ ____

Subtract.

9. $43 - 2 =$ ____
10. $32 - 3 =$ ____
11. $50 - 20 =$ ____
12. $70 - 30 =$ ____
13. $45 - 20 =$ ____
14. $55 - 8 =$ ____
15. $36 - 14 =$ ____
16. $42 - 17 =$ ____

Solve.

	Workspace
17. The school has 12 large drums and 9 small drums. How many drums does the school have? ____ drums	
18. 25 children play the flute. 10 are boys, and the rest are girls. How many girls play the flute? ____ girls	

Name

Problem Solvers at Work

Read
Plan
Solve
Look Back

Choose the Method

The school band had 43 triangles.
They gave 20 triangles to another school.
How many triangles do they have left?

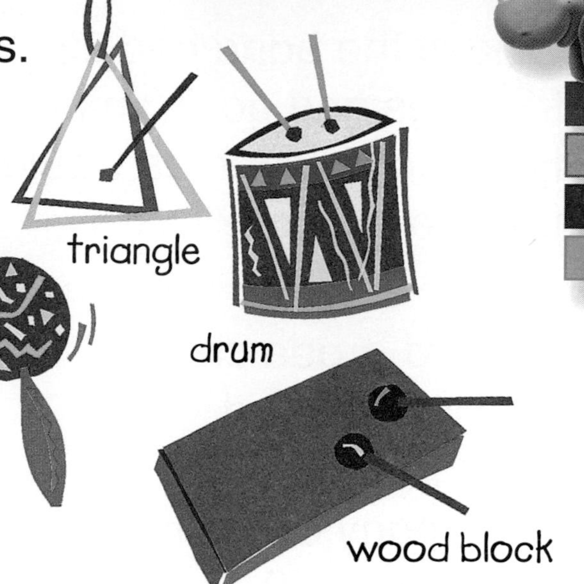

flute maracas

Solve.
Choose the best method for you.

1. How many triangles are left? ____ triangles

Which method did you choose?

---

2. 27 first-grade children play drums.
14 second-grade children play drums.
How many children play drums?

____ children

---

3. The band has 32 wood blocks and 30 flutes.
How many more wood blocks than flutes are there?

____ wood blocks

Try These!

Solve. Choose the best method for you.

1. What if the band had 23 triangles and got 10 more. How many triangles would they have in all? ____ triangles

2. 39 third-grade children play in the band. 7 of them play the flute. How many of them do not play the flute? ____ children

Write and Share

Staci-Ann wrote this problem.

There were 19 people playing the maracas. There were 12 people playing the drums. How many more people were playing the maracas?

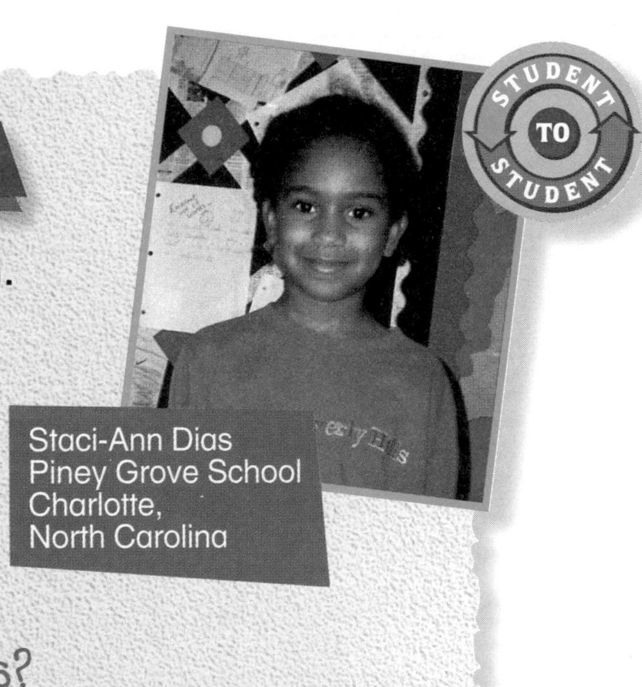

Staci-Ann Dias
Piney Grove School
Charlotte,
North Carolina

3. Solve Staci-Ann's problem. __________

4. Write an addition or subtraction word problem. Have a partner solve it.

Ask your child how to solve the problem he or she wrote.

Name ____________________

Chapter Review

Add.

1. 64 + 3 = ____
2. 39 + 2 = ____
3. 25 + 30 = ____
4. 38 + 20 = ____

---

5. 3 + 6 = ____

   30 + 60 = ____
6. 4 + 4 = ____

   40 + 40 = ____

---

7. 21 + 6 = ____
8. 17 + 5 = ____
9. 44 + 12 = ____
10. 35 + 14 = ____

Subtract.

11. 38 − 2 = ____
12. 22 − 3 = ____
13. 45 − 20 = ____
14. 59 − 10 = ____

---

15. 8 − 6 = ____

    80 − 60 = ____
16. 5 − 4 = ____

    50 − 40 = ____

---

17. 28 − 6 = ____
18. 30 − 5 = ____
19. 48 − 15 = ____
20. 26 − 24 = ____

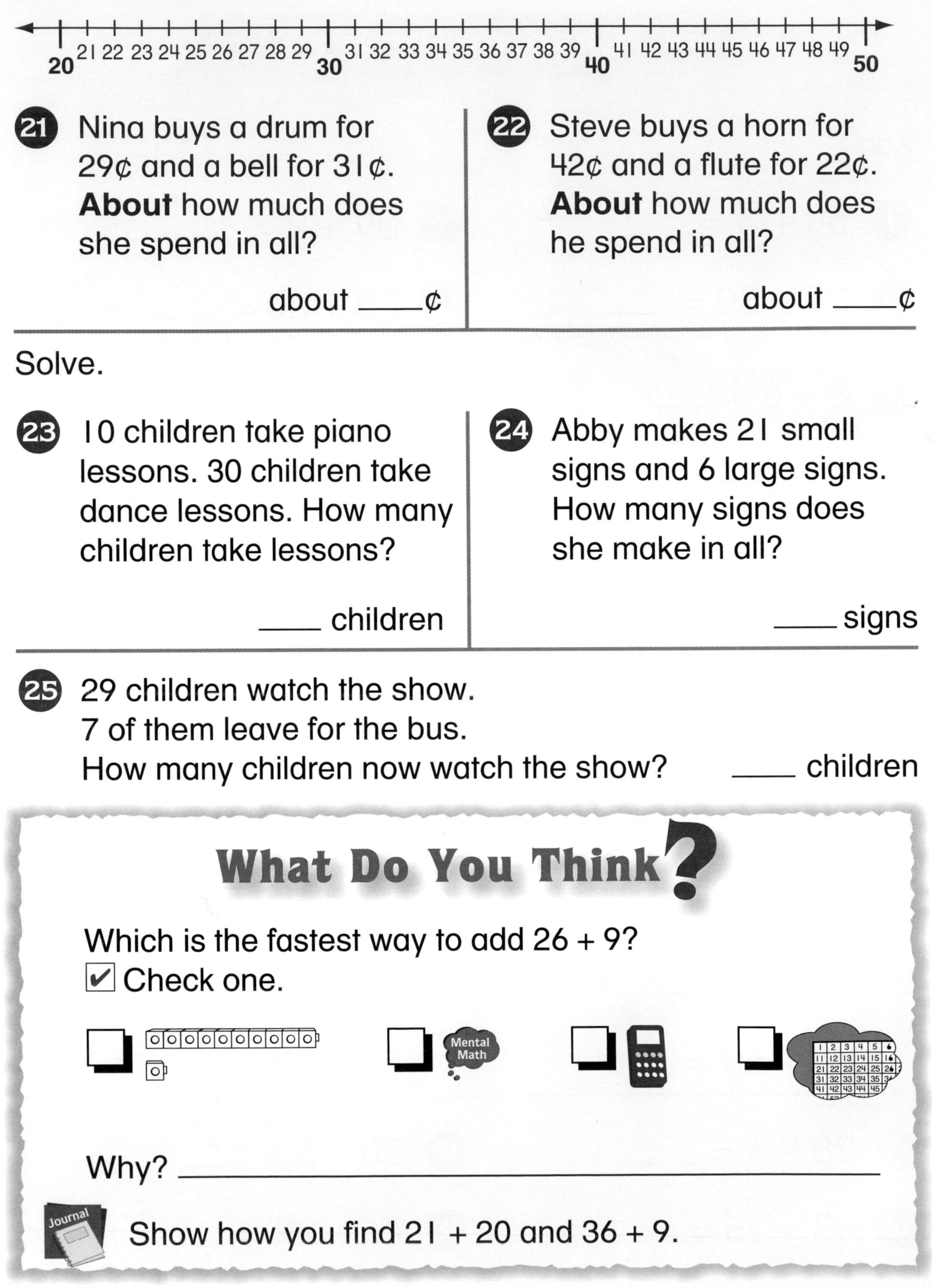

Solve. Use estimation.

20 21 22 23 24 25 26 27 28 29 30 31 32 33 34 35 36 37 38 39 40 41 42 43 44 45 46 47 48 49 50

21 Nina buys a drum for 29¢ and a bell for 31¢. **About** how much does she spend in all?

about ____¢

22 Steve buys a horn for 42¢ and a flute for 22¢. **About** how much does he spend in all?

about ____¢

Solve.

23 10 children take piano lessons. 30 children take dance lessons. How many children take lessons?

____ children

24 Abby makes 21 small signs and 6 large signs. How many signs does she make in all?

____ signs

25 29 children watch the show.
7 of them leave for the bus.
How many children now watch the show? ____ children

What Do You Think?

Which is the fastest way to add 26 + 9?

☑ Check one.

☐ ☐ Mental Math ☐ ☐

Why? ________________________________

Journal Show how you find 21 + 20 and 36 + 9.

Name

Chapter Test

Add.

1. 4 + 5 = ___
   40 + 50 = ___

2. 2 + 6 = ___
   20 + 60 = ___

3. 75 + 2 = ___

4. 18 + 30 = ___

Subtract.

5. 9 − 4 = ___
   90 − 40 = ___

6. 7 − 3 = ___
   70 − 30 = ___

7. 83 − 2 = ___

8. 32 − 10 = ___

Solve.

9. 20 children take tap lessons.
   40 children take ballet lessons.
   How many children take lessons? ___ children

Solve. Use estimation.

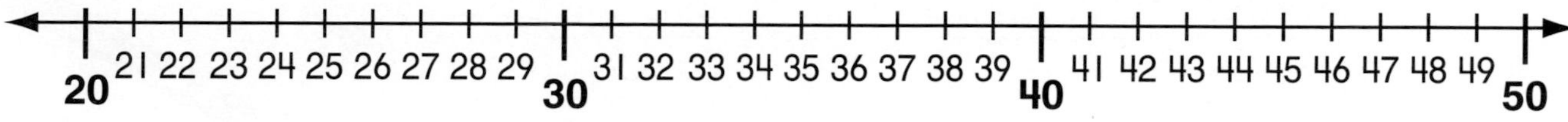

10. 32 children are in the big band.
    21 children are in the jazz band.
    About how many children are in both bands? about ___ children

Performance Assessment

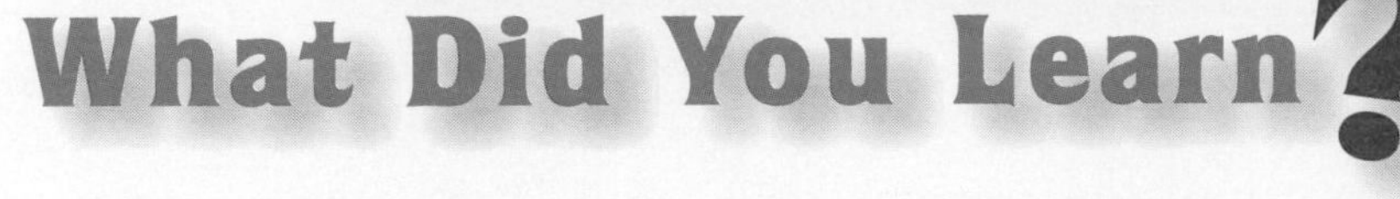

You and your partner need a .

Take turns.

- Toss the .
- Write the number.
- Add. Subtract.

65 + ___ = ___	41 + ___ = ___
30 + ___ = ___	22 + ___ = ___

Tell how you added.

50 – ___ = ___	93 – ___ = ___
86 – ___ = ___	70 – ___ = ___

Tell how you subtracted.

You may want to put this page in your portfolio.

Name ______________________________

Add and Subtract

Press [+] to add.
Press [−] to subtract.

Find 46 − 15.

Press [ON/C].

Press      .

Write what the display shows. 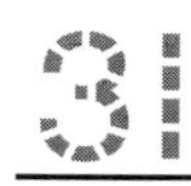

Use the calculator to add or subtract.
Write each key you press.
Write the answer.

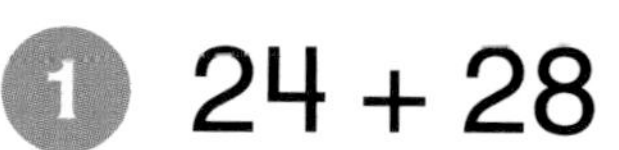
1. 24 + 28 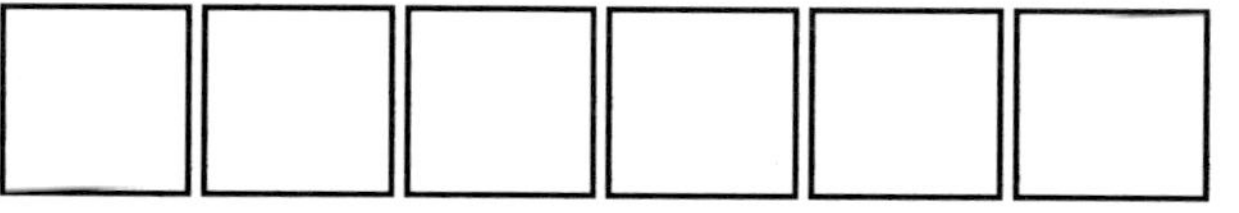 ____

2. 52 − 19 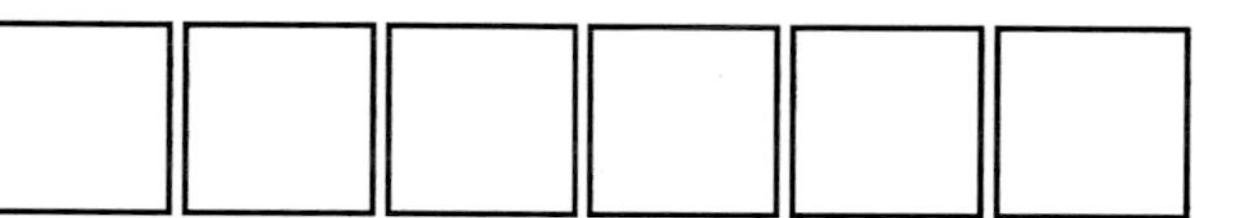 ____

3. 46 + 35 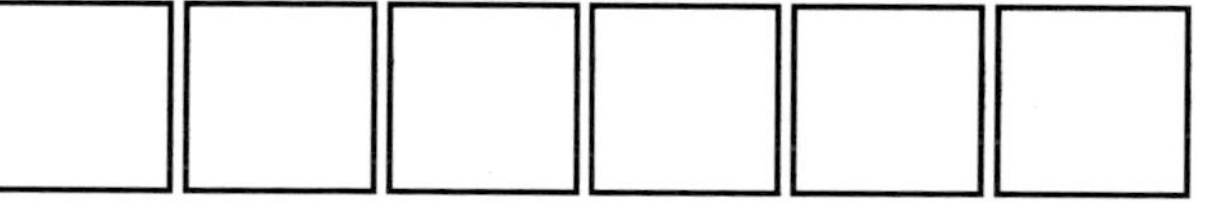 ____

4. 65 − 26 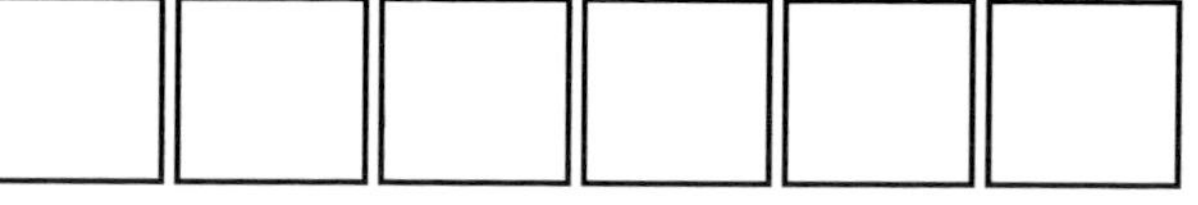 ____

5. 48 + 49 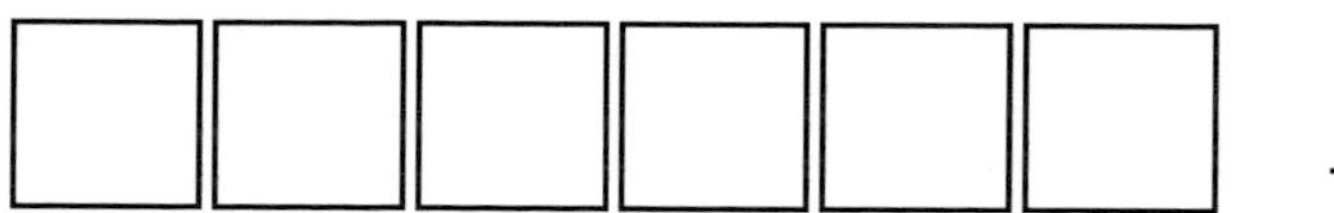 ____

Technology Connection

Computer

Tens and Ones

Tapes come 10 to a box.

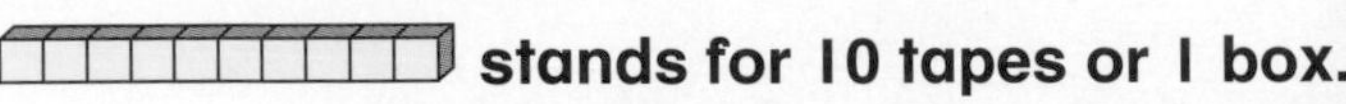
stands for 10 tapes or 1 box.

stands for 1 tape.

Mr. Neil buys 35 tapes for his class. Mrs. Lee buys 27 tapes for her class. How many tapes do they buy in all?

You can use tens and ones models to add. A computer can help you.

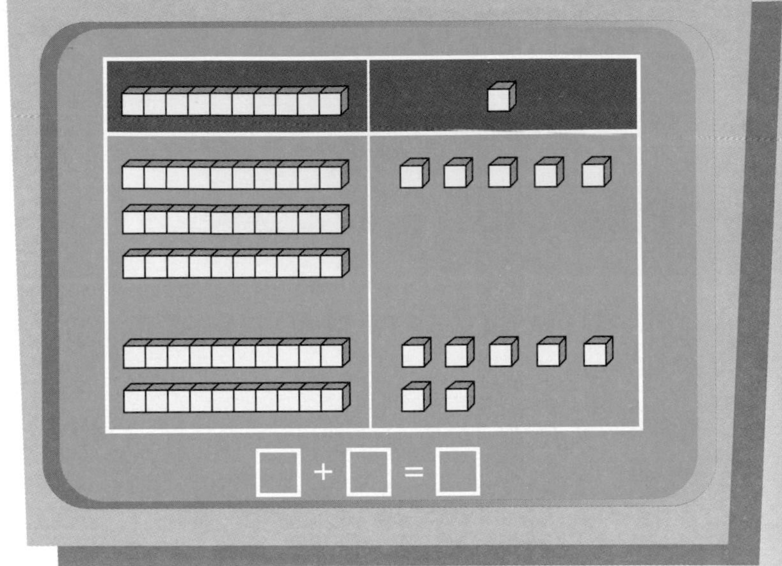

What numbers are on the mat?

____

At the Computer

1. Show the models. Combine them.
   How many tapes do they buy in all? ____ tapes

Use models to solve.

2. Sam buys 43 tapes.
   Tia buys 36 tapes.
   How many tapes do they buy in all?

   ____ tapes

3. Sam buys 51 tapes.
   Tia buys 29 tapes.
   How many tapes do they buy in all?

   ____ tapes

Name

Cumulative Review

Choose the letter of the correct answer.

1

$$\begin{array}{r} 3 \\ +\,7 \\ \hline \end{array}$$

ⓐ 4
ⓑ 7
ⓒ 10
ⓓ 12

2

$$\begin{array}{r} 9¢ \\ -\,2¢ \\ \hline \end{array}$$

ⓐ 6¢
ⓑ 7¢
ⓒ 9¢
ⓓ 11¢

3

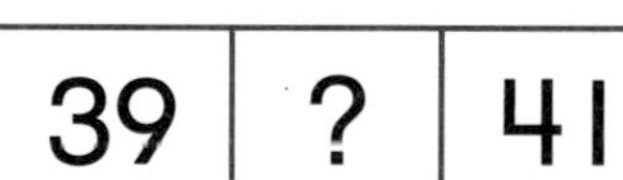

39	?	41

ⓐ 38
ⓑ 40
ⓒ 49
ⓓ 50

4

triangle

ⓐ 
ⓑ
ⓒ 
ⓓ

5

ⓐ 16¢
ⓑ 27¢
ⓒ 36¢
ⓓ 45¢

6

ⓐ 12:30
ⓑ 1:30
ⓒ 6:00
ⓓ 2:30

7

$$\begin{array}{r} 17 \\ -\;\;9 \\ \hline \end{array}$$

ⓐ 6
ⓑ 7
ⓒ 8
ⓓ 9

8

$29 + 3 =$ ___?___

ⓐ 21
ⓑ 30
ⓒ 31
ⓓ 32

9

$74 + 20 =$ ___?___

ⓐ 76
ⓑ 84
ⓒ 90
ⓓ 94

10

$38 - 2 =$ ___?___

ⓐ 18
ⓑ 36
ⓒ 37
ⓓ 38

11

Ⓐ 40°F
Ⓑ 30°F
Ⓒ 20°F
Ⓓ 10°F

12

Ⓐ 34
Ⓑ 29
Ⓒ 24
Ⓓ 19

13 9 goldfish and 7 sunfish are in the pond. How many fish in all?

Ⓐ 15
Ⓑ 16
Ⓒ 17
Ⓓ 18

14 14 gulls are on the beach. 6 gulls fly away. How many gulls are now on the beach?

Ⓐ 6
Ⓑ 7
Ⓒ 8
Ⓓ 9

15 Tim pays 29¢ for a hat and 43¢ for a horn. **About** how much does he spend in all?

Ⓐ 40¢
Ⓑ 50¢
Ⓒ 60¢
Ⓓ 70¢

16 3 friends share. How much does each person get?

Ⓐ $\frac{1}{2}$
Ⓑ $\frac{1}{3}$
Ⓒ $\frac{1}{4}$
Ⓓ $\frac{1}{5}$

17 4 friends share. How much does each person get?

Ⓐ $\frac{1}{2}$
Ⓑ $\frac{1}{3}$
Ⓒ $\frac{1}{4}$
Ⓓ $\frac{1}{5}$

18 There are 37 horns and 10 bells. How many horns and bells in all?

Ⓐ 27
Ⓑ 37
Ⓒ 47
Ⓓ 49

19 25 children are onstage. 10 children are dancing. How many are not dancing?

Ⓐ 18
Ⓑ 15
Ⓒ 20
Ⓓ 25

20 Lyn buys a bell for 22¢ and a mask for 39¢. **About** how much does she spend in all?

Ⓐ 40¢
Ⓑ 50¢
Ⓒ 60¢
Ⓓ 70¢

Home Connection

Chapter 12 Wrap-Up

Name ______________________________

PLAYERS 2 or more

MATERIALS index cards, pencil

DIRECTIONS Write these numbers on separate cards. Put cards for 10, 20, and 30 in one pile. Put cards for 40, 50, and 60 in another pile.

Take turns.

- ▶ Pick a card from each pile. Add the 2 numbers.
- ▶ Score 1 point for each correct sum. Return the cards to the piles.
- ▶ Play until each player has 5 points.

Play again.

- ▶ This time subtract the lesser number from the greater number.

Make 3 cards with each number. Make 2 sets of cards if there are more than 2 players. As you play this game with your child, have your child discuss what strategies he or she uses to find the answer.

Picture Glossary

add

$$\begin{array}{r} 4 \\ +\ 2 \\ \hline 6 \end{array}$$

addition sentence

2 + 1 = 3

after 43 44

↑ just after 43

before 42 43

↑ just before 43

between

42 43 44

↑ between 42 and 44

calendar

September

Sun.	Mon.	Tues.	Wed.	Thurs.	Fri.	Sat.
					1	2
3	4	5	6	7	8	9
10	11	12	13	14	15	16
17	18	19	20	21	22	23
24	25	26	27	28	29	30

centimeter

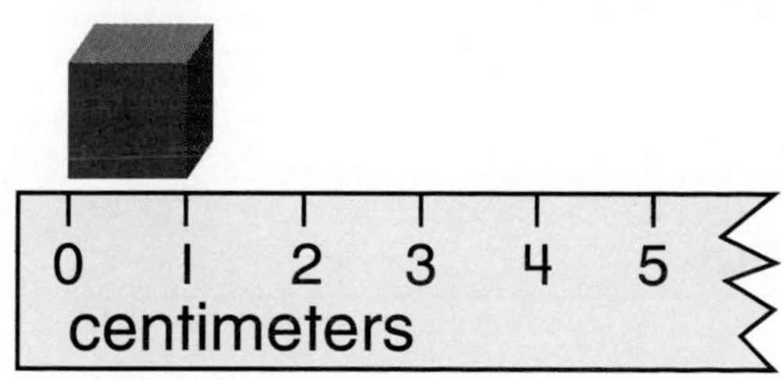

circle

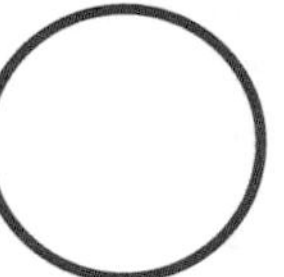

cone

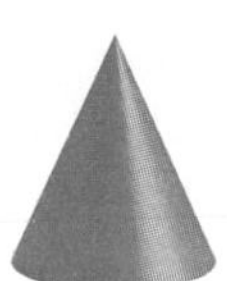

count back

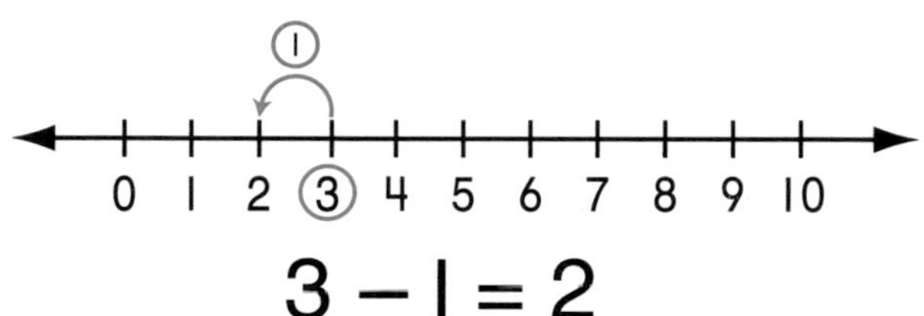

3 − 1 = 2

count on

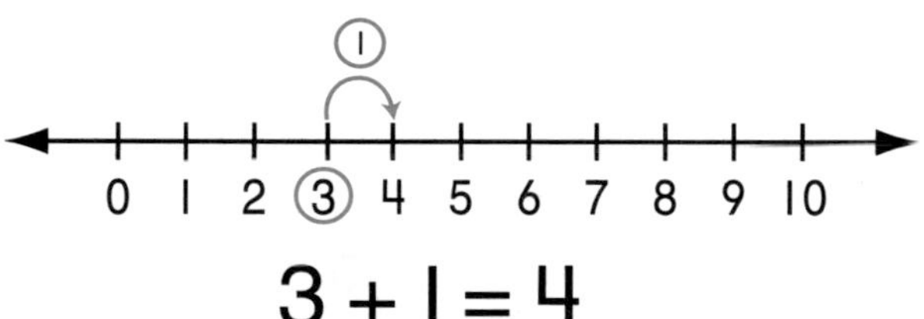

3 + 1 = 4

cube

cup

cylinder

difference

7 − 6 = 1 ← difference

dime

10¢

double

$$\begin{array}{r} 1 \\ +\,1 \\ \hline 2 \end{array} \qquad \begin{array}{r} 2 \\ +\,2 \\ \hline 4 \end{array} \qquad \begin{array}{r} 2 \\ -\,1 \\ \hline 1 \end{array} \qquad \begin{array}{r} 4 \\ -\,2 \\ \hline 2 \end{array}$$

equal parts

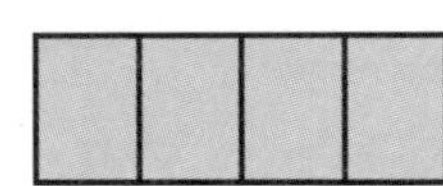

estimate

about 10

fact family

5 + 3 = 8   8 – 3 = 5

3 + 5 = 8   8 – 5 = 3

foot

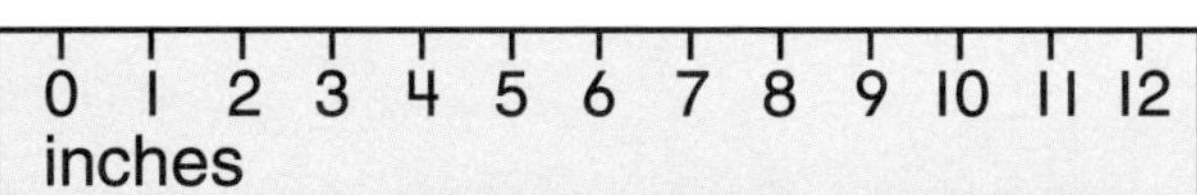

12 inches equal 1 foot.

fourths

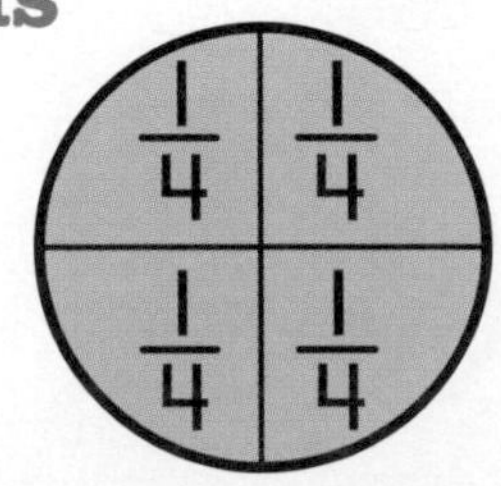

4 equal parts

fraction

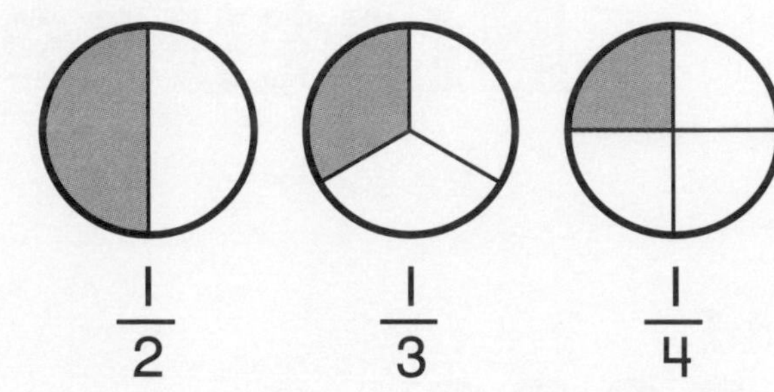

graph

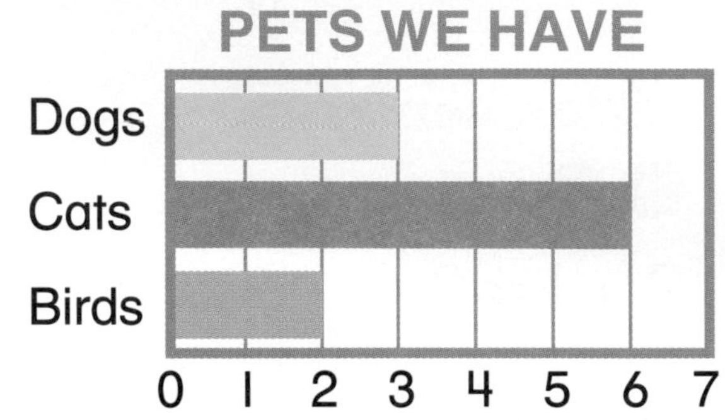

halves

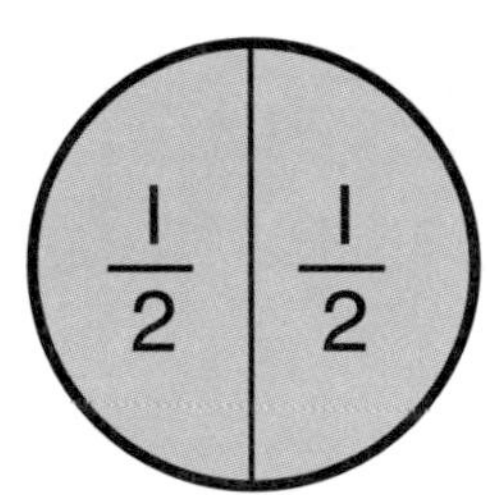

2 equal parts

hour hand

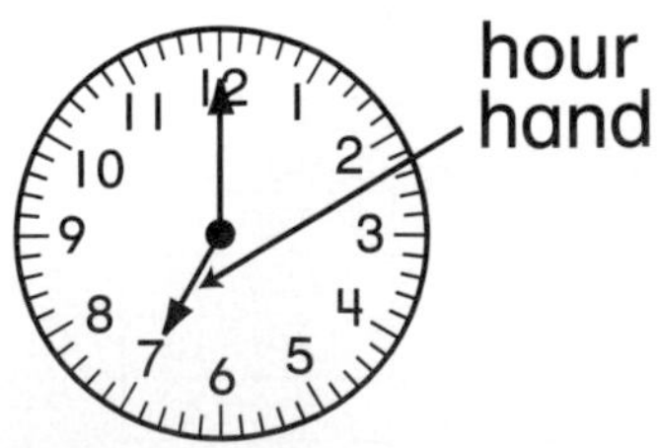

inch

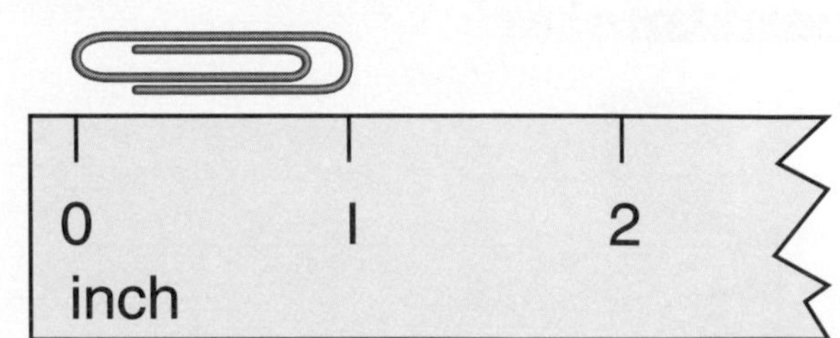

is greater than

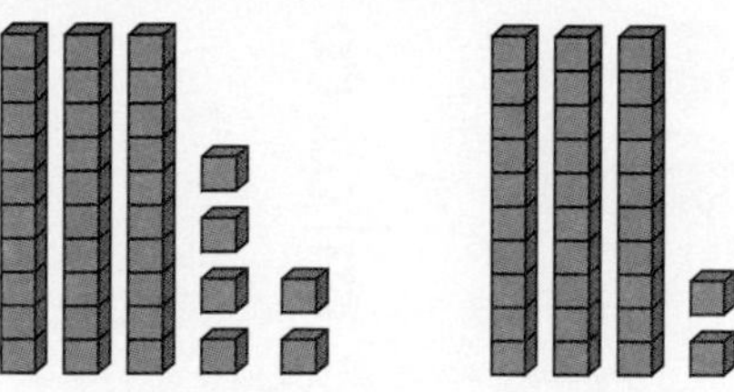

$36 > 32$

↑ is greater than

is less than

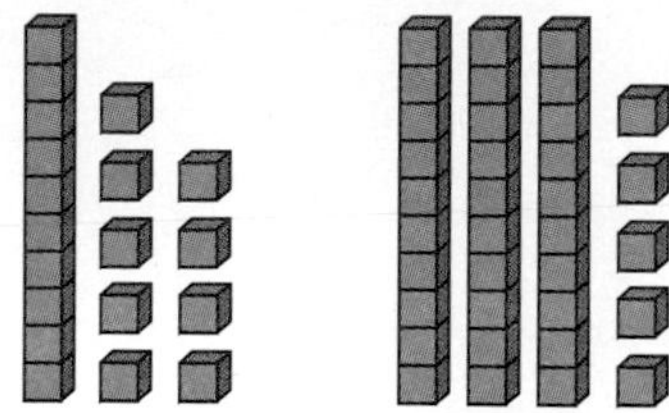

$19 < 35$

↑ is less than

mental math

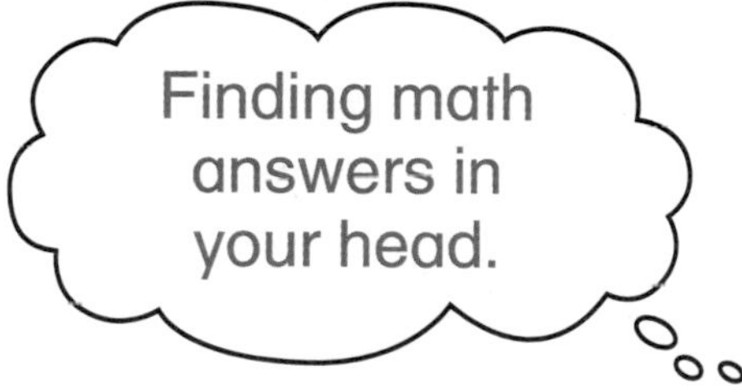

minute hand

nickel

5¢

number line

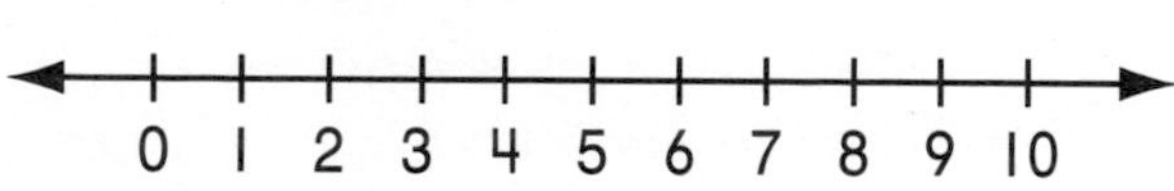

one half

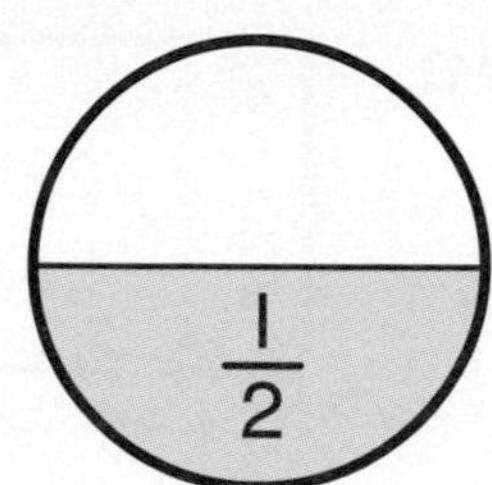

ones

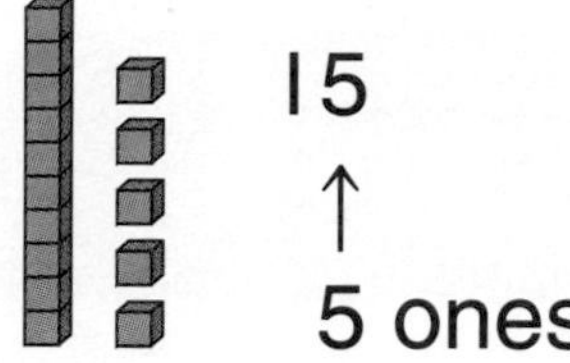

15

↑

5 ones

order

0, 1, 2, 3, 4, 5, 6, 7, 8, 9, 10

These numbers are in order.

part-part-total

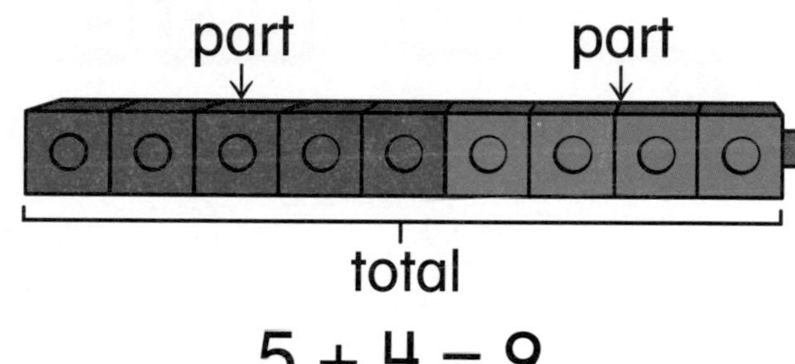

$5 + 4 = 9$

pattern

penny

1¢

pound

quarter

25¢

rectangle

rectangular prism

related facts

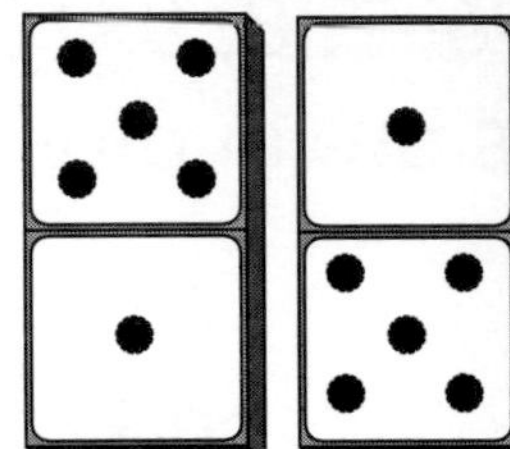

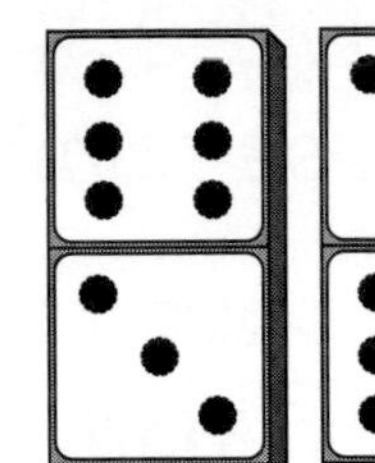

$$\begin{array}{r} 5 \\ +\ 1 \\ \hline 6 \end{array} \quad \begin{array}{r} 1 \\ +\ 5 \\ \hline 6 \end{array} \qquad \begin{array}{r} 9 \\ -\ 6 \\ \hline 3 \end{array} \quad \begin{array}{r} 9 \\ -\ 3 \\ \hline 6 \end{array}$$

skip-count

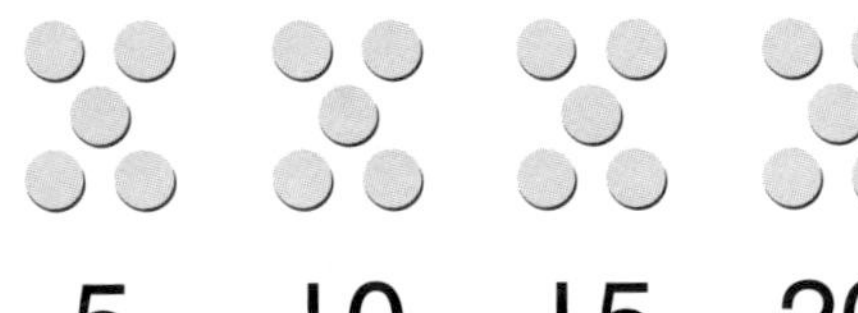

5 10 15 20

sphere

square

subtract

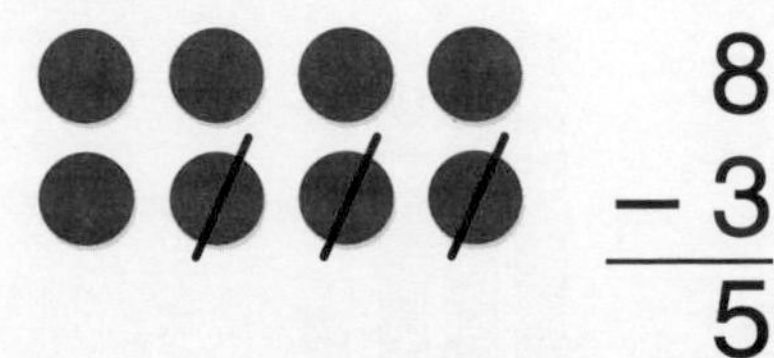

$$\begin{array}{r} 8 \\ -\ 3 \\ \hline 5 \end{array}$$

subtraction sentence

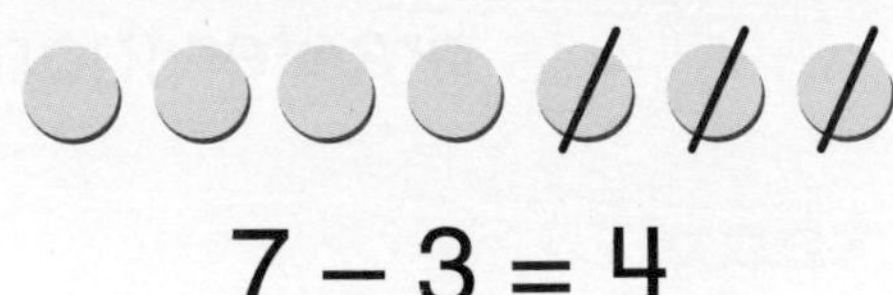

$7 - 3 = 4$

sum

$4 + 5 = 9 \leftarrow$ sum

tens

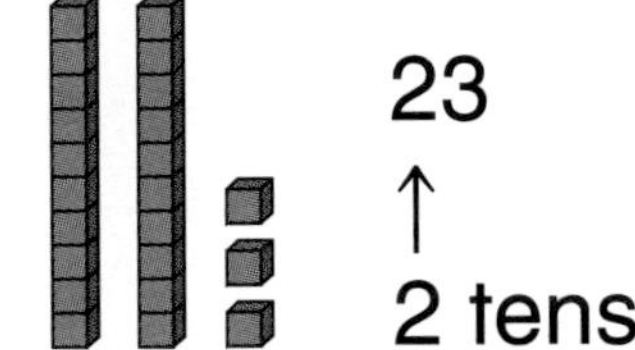

23
↑
2 tens

thirds

$\frac{1}{3}$ $\frac{1}{3}$ $\frac{1}{3}$

3 equal parts

triangle